Samuel Johnson

Selected Poetry and Prose

Samuel Johnson

Selected Poetry and Prose

EDITED WITH
AN INTRODUCTION
AND NOTES BY
FRANK BRADY
AND
W. K. WIMSATT

University of California Press
Berkeley
Los Angeles
London

University of California Press
Berkeley and Los Angeles, California

University of California Press, Ltd.
London, England

ISBN 0-520-03552-6 (alk. paper)

Library of Congress Catalog Card Number: 74-27285

Printed in the United States of America

11 10 09 08 07 06 05
14 13 12 11 10 9 8 7

The paper used in this publication meets the minimum requirements of ANSI/NISO Z39.48-1992 (R 1997) (*Permanence of Paper*). ♾

F. A. P.
MAGISTRO JOHNSONIANISSIMO
JOHNSONIANA HAEC PULCHRA
DEDICAVERUNT
DISCIPULI DUO

Contents

SELECTIONS FROM *THE RAMBLER*

CONTENTS

LIVES OF THE POETS

Preface

THE AIMS of this anthology are to provide an informative Introduction to the life and mind of Samuel Johnson, and a representative, amply annotated selection of his best work, which will illustrate Johnson's greatness as a biographer, critic, and moralist. Mr. Wimsatt wrote the Introduction; Mr. Brady, with Mr. Wimsatt's help, is responsible for the text and annotation.

The texts are taken from the following sources:

Letters—from sources as indicated.

London—Dodsley's *Collection,* 1748.

Prologue to Garrick's "Lethe"—the Folger manuscript. Reprinted by kind permission of the Folger Shakespeare Library, Washington, D.C.

Prologue Spoken at the Opening of the Theater in Drury Lane, 1747—first edition, 1747.

The Vanity of Human Wishes—Dodsley's *Collection,* 1755.

A New Prologue Spoken at the Representation of "Comus"—first edition, 1750.

Prologue to "The Good-Natured Man"—first edition of the play, 1768.

A Short Song of Congratulation—the Huntington manuscript. Reprinted by kind permission of the Henry E. Huntington Library and Art Gallery.

On the Death of Dr. Robert Levett—*Gentleman's Magazine,* August 1783.

Some variants are admitted into the texts of these poems.

Rasselas—second edition, 1759.

Ramblers—fourth edition, 1756. Titles of the essays (listed separately above, p. viii) from the first collected edition, 1752.

Idlers—and titles of the essays (listed above, p. ix) from the first collected edition, 1761, except no. 22 from the *Universal Chronicle,* 1758.

Preface to the "Dictionary"—fourth folio edition, 1773, with some substantive variants from the second folio edition, 1755, and a few phrases restored from the first folio edition, 1755. We wish to acknowledge a debt to Professor W. R. Keast's articles on the text of the *Preface.*

Preface to Shakespeare—first edition, 1765, of Johnson's edition of Shakespeare, the text being reprinted from W. K. Wimsatt's collection, *Samuel Johnson and Shakespeare,* 1960, by kind permission of Hill and Wang, Inc.

Life of Savage—second edition, 1748, with a few clear inadvertencies corrected. Except where indicated, Johnson's footnotes have been omitted. We wish to acknowledge a debt to Professor Clarence Tracy's definitive edition of this *Life.*

Other selections from the *Lives of the Poets*—last edition revised by Johnson, 1783, with various corrections. We wish to acknowledge a debt to the editions of the *Lives* by G. B. Hill, 1905, and J. P. Hardy, 1971.

Spelling and capitalization have been modernized and Americanized throughout, except when changes in spelling might affect pronunciation. Punctuation has been modernized to a lesser degree. We take pleasure in thanking Cynthia Brodhead and John P. Crigler for various kinds of help with text and annotation; Andrew Rosenheim, research helper on a Yale College bursary appointment; and also Jerome W. Hogan, Danny W. Jennings, Peter M. Jucovy, Silvine S. Marbury, Patricia H. Owen, Edward A. Weller, and Charles Whitney, research assistants at the Graduate School of the City University of New York, for similar help. Herman W. Liebert kindly lent a copy of the second edition of *Rasselas.* James L. Clifford and Joyce Hemlow generously answered questions.

F. B.
W. K. W.

New York and New Haven
November 1, 1975

Introduction

Samuel Johnson (1709–1784)

A Calendar Of His Career

1709–27
Lichfield

MICHAEL JOHNSON, a bookseller and stationer at Lichfield, in Staffordshire, having late in life married Sarah Ford, a lady of somewhat better origins but smaller learning than he, they became on 18 September 1709 the parents of a first child, baptized on the same day Samuel. A younger brother, Nathaniel, would die in his twenty-fifth year. Samuel Johnson, despite handicaps of physical constitution and of temperament and the narrow circumstances of his family, lived to become "the illustrious character . . . whose various excellence" the biographer James Boswell would record for posterity.

A large body, an active mind, and a species of mad melancholy were features which the son might be said to have "inherited" from his father. As a boy he was precocious, bad-tempered, scrofulous, near-sighted, almost blind in his left eye, and deaf in his left ear. He was taken by his mother to London to be "touched" for the "King's Evil" by Queen Anne. He studied English at elementary schools in Lichfield and Latin and Greek at the Free Grammar School. He dominated his fellow students. He was ambitious but indolent. He was "well-whipped" for idleness and misdemeanor by the headmaster John Hunter, in consequence of which, he said later, he learned much Latin. At the age of sixteen (1725–26), on a prolonged visit with a learned but worldly, rakish clerical cousin, Cornelius Ford, who lived near Stourbridge, in Worcestershire, he gained a fascinating vision of a world of wit and letters that lay in the direction of Cambridge and London. He spent a few months at a school in Stourbridge as a scholar and assistant. He came back to Lichfield and, stranded at his father's home and shop, idled through two more years of intense (if desultory) reading in the classics.

1728–31
Oxford
Lichfield

TAKING ADVANTAGE of a legacy of forty pounds received by his wife on the death of a cousin, Johnson's father took him to Oxford and entered him as a Commoner at Pembroke College on 31 October 1728. He spent a year there, reading in his fashion ("solidly" in Greek—Homer and Euripides—but hardly ever anything to the end). He exhibited a degree of unconcern for the usual relation between student and tutors. ("Sir, you have sconced me twopence for non-attendance at a lecture not worth a penny.") He made a Latin verse translation of Pope's sacred eclogue *Messiah,* winning thereby great applause, which echoed even outside the university. He was miserably poor and fiercely independent. Under an exterior of gaiety and frolic he concealed a bitter and savage hypochondria, which he himself looked upon as verging on madness. When he had been about nine years old, perhaps in response to the too insistent catechizing of a zealous mother, he had fallen into an "inattention" to religion. Now he read the book of the year (1729) in practical morality, William Law's *Serious Call to a Devout and Holy Life,* and found Law "quite an overmatch" for his indifference.

Johnson's father was a man of considerable eminence, a force for literary education in his community; he was a magistrate; he was a vendor of books on market days in the neighboring towns of Uttoxeter, Ashby-de-la-Zouch, and Birmingham. Nevertheless, he was now close to bankruptcy. On 12 December 1729 Samuel Johnson, oppressed by debts and suffering the onset of a severe melancholy, left the University (never to return as a student). He went home to a life centered once more at his father's shop. He enjoyed a fairly wide acquaintance among the gentry of the neighborhood; he wrote complimentary poems, in Popean couplets, for young ladies. One cultivated older friend who had always done much to brighten his life was Gilbert Walmesley, registrar of the ecclesiastical court of the diocese, who occupied on lease the bishop's palace in the Cathedral Close. In December 1731 Johnson's father died.

1733
Birmingham

DURING a prolonged residence in Birmingham, Johnson, lying in bed, dictated to his old friend Edmund Hector, a schoolfellow at Lichfield, an abridged English translation of a French version of the 17th-century Portuguese Jesuit Father Jerome Lobo's *Voyage to Abyssinia.* In the hands of another friend, Thomas Warren, bookseller in Birmingham (who gave Johnson five guineas), this became his first published book. It was dated 1735, with "London" on the title page.

1735
Birmingham

JOHNSON'S BIRMINGHAM connections brought him next a wife. She was Elizabeth Porter, a lady nearly twice his age, recently the widow of a Birmingham woollen draper. She and Johnson rode horseback to church in Derby on the morning of their wedding (with his mother's consent), 9 July 1735. For a few months in 1732 Johnson had been employed as an "usher" (or under-master) in a grammar school at Market Bosworth, leading a life of "complicated misery." And now he took a large part of his wife's dowry, which amounted apparently to about six hundred pounds, and invested it in setting up an academy of his own. "At Edial, near Lichfield, in Staffordshire, young gentlemen are boarded and taught the Latin and Greek languages, by SAMUEL JOHNSON." He never had many pupils, perhaps no more than three. One of these was David Garrick, who in later years as the illustrious actor-manager of the Drury Lane Theater would tell how the boys peeped through the keyhole of the bedchamber at the master's "tumultuous and awkward fondness" for his Tetty. She was "flaring and fantastic" in dress and manners, fat and bosomy, with cheeks puffy and florid from paint and the liberal use of liqueurs. When Johnson courted Mrs. Porter, he himself was lean and lank, an "immense structure of bones . . . hideously striking to the eye"; the scars of scrofula were deeply visible; he wore his own hair, "straight and stiff, and separated behind." He was given to "convulsive starts and odd gesticulations." In later life, his eyes are described as a light gray—wild, piercing, and fierce.

1737
London
The Strand

ON 2 March of this year Johnson turned his back on the school and with his pupil David Garrick, now companion at arms, set out for London (perhaps on horseback)—having between them, as they would much later say in jest, "twopence halfpenny" and "three halfpence." Johnson had also in his pocket an unfinished tragedy entitled *Irene.* (At Lichfield, only a day or two—perhaps only a few hours—after Johnson's departure, his brother Nathaniel died—and a few days later, Garrick's father.) Johnson took lodgings in Exeter Street, near the Strand and, maintaining himself frugally somehow, began the adventure of the metropolis. During the summer he returned to Lichfield and finished his tragedy, and in the autumn he brought back his wife to London.

1738
London

JOHNSON NOW FOUND his first secure literary connection through an approach to the progressive publisher Edward Cave, who in 1731 had, under the pen name Sylvanus Urban, founded the first English monthly magazine, the *Gentleman's.* Cave carried on business in an old gatehouse, once part of the priory of the Knights Hospitalers, St. John's Gate, Clerkenwell. In later life, Johnson would recollect that he first beheld this structure with "reverence." While still in the Midlands, he had sent Cave a letter somewhat bluntly proposing to "improve" the *Magazine's* "poetical article" or, more broadly even, its "literary article." On arrival in London he had written to Cave again, offering to prepare an English translation of Father Paul Sarpi's *History of the Council of Trent.* Now he addressed Cave yet again in a highly complimentary Latin ode of six Alcaic strophes, published in the March issue of the *Magazine.*

> URBANE, nullis fesse laboribus,
> URBANE, nullis victe calumniis,
> Cui fronte sertum in eruditâ
> Perpetuò viret et virebit. . . .[1]

This year Cave printed and Robert Dodsley published an anonymous folio, Johnson's first English masterpiece, his couplet satire *London, A Poem, in Imitation of the Third Satire of Juvenal.* London!

> Here malice, rapine, accident, conspire,
> And now a rabble rages, now a fire;
> Their ambush here relentless ruffians lay,
> And here the fell attorney prowls for prey;
> Here falling houses thunder on your head,
> And here a female atheist talks you dead.

The poem appeared on 12 May, at the same time as the first *Dialogue* of Alexander Pope's *Epilogue* to his Horatian *Satires.* When Pope was told that the author of the new poem was some obscure person named Johnson, he remarked, "He will soon be *déterré* [unearthed]."

1739–40
London
Ashbourne
Lichfield

LIKE POPE'S *Epilogue, London* was an anti-administration poem. A year later, or in April and May of 1739, Johnson, experimenting in a vein of Swiftian ironic prose, published two anonymous pamphlet attacks on the administration, *Marmor Norfolciense: or an Essay on an Ancient Prophetical Inscription, in Monkish Rhyme, Lately Discovered near Lynn in Norfolk* (Houghton in Norfolk was the seat of the Prime Minister, Sir Robert Walpole), and *A Complete Vindication of the Licensers of the Stage, from the Malicious and Scandalous Aspersions of Mr. Brooke, Author of "Gustavus Vasa"* (an assault upon the licensers for their suppression of that politically tendentious tragedy).

The editorial work which Johnson was doing for Cave did not bring him much money. He and his wife Tetty were miserably poor. In the late summer of 1739 he made a trip into Leicestershire in a vain quest for employment as a schoolmaster. The absence lengthened into an autumn vacation among well-to-do friends in the neighborhood of Ashbourne, in Derbyshire, and a winter stay at Lichfield, during which

1. "By no labors wearied, by no slanders daunted, Urban, upon whose learned brow the garland is and ever will be green. . . ."

he mortgaged the family home, a big house which his father had built in the market place. All this while, Tetty remained behind in London under circumstances which are not clear. Johnson's return to London in the spring was the end of an era. It would be more than twenty years before he visited his birthplace again. He would never again see his mother.

1740–43
London

ONE KIND of job for *The Gentleman's Magazine* was the compilation of biographical essays: on the learned Dutch physician (chemist, anatomist, and botanist) Herman Boerhaave, serially during 1739; on the Commonwealth national hero Admiral Robert Blake, in June, 1740; on the Elizabethan seadog Sir Francis Drake and the German philological boy wonder John Philip Barretier, both serially during 1740–1741. . . . Another feature was a department of illegal, semifictitious and thinly disguised reports on the proceedings of the Houses of Parliament, under the title "Debates in the Senate of Magna Lilliputia." During the years 1740–44 Johnson produced, on very slender evidence, sometimes hardly more than the names of the speakers and their topics, a series of Debates which were translated all over the Continent as the veritable words of English statesmen. At about the time when he fully realized the extent of this "propagation of falsehood," he dropped the job abruptly. After his death the debates would appear in a two-volume supplement to his own collected *Works.* Two of the speeches, meanwhile, had found their way into the *Miscellaneous Works* of Lord Chesterfield. Another, according to anecdote, Johnson once heard praised as an extraordinarily fine speech by the elder Pitt, upon which he broke in: "That speech I wrote in a garret in Exeter Street."

A bookseller, Thomas Osborne, in Gray's Inn, purchased the great library collected by the friend of Pope and Swift, Robert Harley, first Earl of Oxford, and his son Edward, the second Earl. Johnson wrote, and *The Gentleman's Magazine* for December 1742 published, "Proposals for Printing, by Subscription, the Two First Volumes of *Bibliotheca Harleiana.*" In 1743–44 appeared four large octavo volumes, for which Johnson and another hack writer William Oldys had listed the books and written numerous descriptive notes in English and Latin. Johnson apparently dipped into the books, and hence moved slowly. Osborne, according to the anecdote, complained, and Johnson knocked him down with a folio. An old school friend of Johnson's, Dr. Robert James, wrote a *Medicinal Dictionary,* published by Osborne in installments beginning in 1742 and collected in three large folio volumes (1743–45). Here was another occasion for Johnson to write biographies (at least half a dozen, of physicians, surgeons, and kindred scientists), as well as *Proposals* and the Dedication, and probably other things, in the hinterland of the vast work, which scholars have not yet identified.

1744
London

IN FEBRUARY of this year Johnson published his second book in prose, a work of moral analysis, a lay sermon, and an act of piety to the memory of a departed poet friend—*An Account of the Life of Mr. Richard Savage, Son of the Earl Rivers.* In Johnson's satire *London* (May 1738), an "injured" idealist named Thales inveighs against the corrupt city just before taking ship at Greenwich for exile in Wales. It must have seemed to Johnson almost as if poetry had predicted life when a year later, in July 1739, he himself, with tears in his eyes, said farewell to his friend Savage as he left on a similar journey, from which he never returned, dying in a debtor's prison at Bristol in the summer of 1743. In 1727 Savage had killed a man in a tavern brawl; he had been condemned and had been saved only by a royal pardon. He and Johnson roamed the streets of London for whole nights together in poverty and in sympathy, lying down to sleep (as Johnson narrates at least of Savage) on bulkheads along the Thames, or among the warm ashes outside a glass furnace. The *poet* Savage was a bitter social satirist (*The Bastard,* 1728) and a plaintive romantic visionary (*The Wanderer,* 1729); the *man* was a dissipated slave to his passions (as Johnson put it), an inveterate cultivator of alienation, a resolute failure, a derelict champion of "liberty"—either a cruelly disowned bastard child of nobility or a lifelong impostor (perhaps an unwitting one?). He was older than Johnson by about a dozen years. He made a profound impression on a spirit in some respects closely kindred.

1746
London
Holborn

JOHNSON'S CAREER as a literary scholar is marked by three prolonged major undertakings—one lexicographical (his *English Dictionary,* 1755), one editorial (his *Shakespeare,* 1765), and one biographical (his *Prefaces* to the *English Poets,* 1779–1781). The first of these was set up on 18 June of this year, when a consortium of London booksellers entered into a contract with him for the production of a *Dictionary of the English Language.* Johnson's price was 1,575 pounds. An early draft of a *Plan* for this *Dictionary* is dated 30 April in the same year.

1747
London
Holborn

ADDING an introductory bid for favor addressed to the influential statesman, accomplished orator and arbiter of taste, "the Right Honorable Philip Dormer, Earl of Chesterfield, one of his Majesty's Principal Secretaries of State," Johnson completed the *Plan* and published it in 1747. The

Dictionary was to be written on historical principles—definitions by Johnson, illustrations from all the great English prose and verse writers, and many of the less great, from the time of Spenser, Sidney, and Shakespeare. Johnson's enormous capacity as a reader, his vast memory, his habit of rapid, decisive judgment, and his strength of resolution were the capital investments of the enterprise. He set up shop, with six amanuenses, in an "upper room" in Holborn, and later at No. 17, Gough Square, Fleet Street.

In the same year he wrote a *Prologue,* spoken in September by his former pupil David Garrick, who had been improving his opportunities in a stage career and was now joint owner and manager of the Drury Lane Theater; he was inaugurating his reign by a production of *The Merchant of Venice.* The *Prologue* is a progress piece, in reverse, reciting the decline of the English stage since Shakespeare, centering a new hope in his name, and in effect proclaiming a great program for Shakespeare promotion. Johnson and Garrick, in their different ways, would do more during the next twenty-five years to further such a program than any other two men in England.

> 'Tis yours this night to bid the reign commence
> Of rescued Nature and reviving Sense.

1749
London
Gough Square

ALONG THE WAY of the *Dictionary* work ("beating the track of the alphabet with sluggish resolution"), his energies escaped too in other directions. On 9 January of this year he published a second Juvenalian poem, a somberly stoical "Imitation" of the tenth Satire, entitled *The Vanity of Human Wishes.* It was the first of his works to bear his name on the title page.

> There mark what ills the scholar's life assail,
> Toil, envy, want, the garret, and the jail.

The ills that assailed the scholar-poet were an immediate and inner experience of a state that Johnson the philosopher confronted resolutely as a human invariable. There were no bright consolations. At the other end of a scale of power and ambition, for instance, was the military conqueror, the modern Hannibal, subject of a biography by Voltaire, Charles XII of Sweden.

> His fall was destined to a barren strand,
> A petty fortress, and a dubious hand;
> He left the name, at which the world grew pale,
> To point a moral, or adorn a tale.

The stoically Christian conclusion of Johnson's pageant of woes is not in Juvenal; it is a special earning of Johnson's peculiar genius.

Must helpless man, in ignorance sedate,
Roll darkling down the torrent of his fate?

Still raise for good the supplicating voice,
But leave to heaven the measure and the choice,
Safe in His power, whose eyes discern afar
The secret ambush of a specious prayer.

On 6 February Garrick brought out the Turkish tragedy in blank verse, *Irene,* completed by Johnson at Lichfield so long ago. It was acted nine times, the profits for the author, along with the copyright when Dodsley published it, amounting to nearly 300 pounds. (At the time of his first negotiations with Cave in 1738, Johnson had been observed wearing a "loose horseman's coat" and a "great bushy uncombed wig." Now, for the first night of the play, he went out of character long enough to appear in a side box sporting a scarlet waistcoat with gold lace and a gold-laced hat.) In later years he would hear the play read aloud and remark: "Sir, I thought it had been better."

1750–52
London
Gough Square

GIVEN THE VOGUE established in the last generation by Addison and Steele, it was almost inevitable that a writer of Johnson's fertility and his constant social and moral concern should turn at some time to the periodical essay. The single-handed lexicographer took up the twice-weekly burden on Tuesday 20 March 1750. When he laid it down, with a 208th folio *Rambler* on Saturday 14 March 1752, he had accumulated a gargantuan anthology of solemn, sometimes somber, moral reflection, shrewdly cynical yet compassionate psychological analysis, judiciously blended hard-edged rationalism and emotive freedom in literary criticism, miscellaneous label-name character sketches, a few allegories, and a number of Oriental fables—the whole composed in a grandly (at moments pompously) Latinate, studiously balanced and antithetic style, creating an image and a name for himself that would prove persistently adhesive. His working habit in this enterprise was dilatory, distracted, and astonishingly rapid. He would send part of an essay to the press and write the rest while the first part was printing. Sometimes the printer's boy would come to a house where a party was going on and wait while Johnson "wrote off a paper . . . in a room full of company."

Three days after the last *Rambler,* Johnson's wife died. When he had walked the streets at night or had lain on bulkheads with Savage, where had Tetty been? The record does not say clearly. At one period, late in 1748, she was lodged for her health in a small house outside the city, at Hampstead. There Johnson had written *The Vanity of Human Wishes.* She was given to tippling and to lying in bed alone, for the purpose of reading romances. She had survived fifteen years of what must have been for her a cruel transplantation to Johnson's Fleet-Street London. He wrote a sermon for her funeral. For the rest of his life he recurred to her memory in prayers and tearful meditations.

1753
London
Gough Square

ON 3 April Johnson recorded in his diary the beginning of the second volume of the *Dictionary*. During 1753 and 1754, a friend, John Hawkesworth, fellow journalist and a close imitator of Johnson's style, was, with the help of several others, getting out a periodical essay called *The Adventurer*. Johnson contributed twenty-nine Rambleresque numbers.

1754
London
Gough Square

AT ST. JOHN'S GATE, on 10 January, Edward Cave died. Johnson wrote his biography for the February issue of *The Gentleman's Magazine*. "One of the last acts of reason" which Cave had exerted was "fondly to press the hand" that now was writing this "little narrative."[2]

As the *Dictionary* began to inch within sight of its goal, what of Lord Chesterfield, the elegant patron to whom Johnson had hopefully addressed his *Plan* in 1747? Nothing but "neglect" and "cold indifference" had come from that quarter, until in November and December 1754 Chesterfield published two studiously complimentary (and patronizing) essays on the projected dictionary in a gentlemanly periodical, *The World*.

1755
London
Gough Square

THE GESTURE provoked the controlled fury of Johnson's celebrated *Letter to Chesterfield* (7 February 1755), a trumpet call in the progressive emancipation of the English man of letters from the auspices of the aristocracy. "Is not a patron, my Lord, one who looks with unconcern on a man struggling for life in the water, and, when he has reached ground, encumbers him with help? . . . I hope it is no very cynical asperity not to confess obligations where no benefit has been received, or to be unwilling that the public should consider me as owing that to a patron, which Providence has enabled me to do for myself."

Revising his Juvenalian satire *The Vanity of Human Wishes* for an appearance this year in a volume of Dodsley's *Collection of Poems*, Johnson made a pointed change in a couplet which we have quoted above under the year 1749:

2. Like Johnson, Cave was a large, strong man, of humble country origin. He came to London from Warwickshire and made his way as a printer, journalist, and publisher. Unlike Johnson, he was a slow thinker, though exact, cool, and tenacious.

There mark what ills the scholar's life assail,
Toil, envy, want, the *patron,* and the jail.

On 20 February Johnson received the honorary degree of M.A. from Oxford, in time to write the letters on the title page of the *Dictionary,* which was published in two folio volumes on 15 April. He was now "Dictionary Johnson." One of the last parts to be written was the Preface, a noble, if melancholy, testimony both to Johnson's devoted familiarity with the great writings of the modern English language and to his simultaneous sense of the transience both of the collective human life of language and literature and the individual life of the lexicographer. "I have protracted my work till most of those whom I wished to please have sunk into the grave, and success and miscarriage are empty sounds."

1756–57
London
Gough Square

AS FAR BACK as 1745 Johnson had issued "Proposals for a New Edition of Shakespeare" and at the same time a specimen book entitled *Miscellaneous Observations on the Tragedy of Macbeth.* There were copyright obstacles, and soon he and Cave dropped the idea. Now, a little more than a year after being quit of the *Dictionary,* or in June 1756, with the copyright claimant Jacob Tonson on his side, he issued a new set of "Proposals"—in effect a pregnant short essay on the responsibilities of a modern Shakespeare editor. This was not as big a job as the *Dictionary,* but he was to take a year longer in getting it done. Johnson, wrote one of his friends, "never thinks of working if he has a couple of guineas in his pocket."

It would seem that there were too many minor ways of working. One was the writing of miscellaneous articles and reviews. In *The Literary Magazine,* for instance, a short-lived journal which he superintended during 1756–57: his judicious estimate of his friend Joseph Warton's "pre-romantic" *Essay on the Genius and Writings of Pope,* and his passionately bitter dissection (in three numbers) of the "male blue-stocking" Soame Jenyns's deistic *Free Inquiry into the Nature and Origin of Evil.* Or the writing of dedications and prefaces. 1756 was a characteristic year: he supplied a dedication to the Earl of Rochford for the mathematician William Payne's *Introduction to the Game of Draughts,* a preface to the hack compiler Richard Rolt's *New Dictionary of Trade and Commerce,* and the preliminary address "To the Public" for *The Literary Magazine.* In 1757, his dedication to Viscount Charlemont of the novelist-scholar Mrs. Charlotte Ramsay Lennox's *Philander, a Dramatic Pastoral* was one of a half-dozen such favors for this lady in the course of ten years. A special gift upon which Johnson prided himself (a part of his great talent for universalizing) was the capacity to write a good dedication or preface for any sort of book whatever. Concerning Rolt's *Dictionary,* he would tell Boswell: "Sir, I never saw the man and never read the book. . . . I knew very well what such a Dictionary should be, and I wrote a Preface accordingly." "The business of a poet," he would write, asserting the universal in a more important context, "is to examine not the individual but the species; . . . he does not number the streaks of the tulip" (*Rasselas,* 1759, ch. X).

1758
London
Gough Square

ON 15 April appeared the first number of a new periodical essay by Johnson, *The Idler,* leading feature of a newly launched journal, *The Universal Chronicle.* It would be a weekly task for two years, until 5 April 1760, 104 numbers in all. The *Idlers* were shorter and lighter essays than the *Ramblers.* At the same time, the new image and the new name seem to be derived by the writer much more deliberately out of his own character and personal preoccupations. *The Idler* exhibits a high degree of thematic unity—a central tripartite conception of idleness as damnable inertia; idleness, in disguise, as hurry or busification; idleness as trifling—inevitable, condonable, even praiseworthy. The poet James Thomson's *Castle of Indolence* was not a more dreamy, ambivalent place than the world of Johnson's *Idler.* The character of Sober in No. 31, that serious trifler in chemical experiments, was of course Johnson himself, a confirmed addict in several sorts of empirical parlor games. "Perhaps he will read [this paper] and laugh, and light the fire in his furnace; but my hope is that he will quit his trifles, and betake himself to rational and useful diligence."

1759
London
Gough Square
and Staple Inn

IN LICHFIELD, on 20 or 21 January, Johnson's mother died, at the age of ninety. "Such is the course of nature," wrote the Idler in his essay for 27 January, "that whoever lives long must outlive those whom he loves and honors. . . . Happiness is not found in self-contemplation; it is perceived only when it is reflected from another." To pay the expenses of the funeral he wrote, during the evenings of about one week, a solemn, gravely comic, philosophical fable, concerning "the choice of life." When brought out on 19 April, it bore the title *The Prince of Abyssinia, A Tale. Rasselas* is a fiction much more notable for cogent aphoristic wisdom than for lively plot or characterization. "Human life," says the philosopher Imlac, "is everywhere a state in which much is to be endured, and little to be enjoyed." "Marriage," says the Princess Nekayah, "has many pains, but celibacy has no pleasures." The royal fugitives from boredom in this story—geographic explorers for the meaning of existence—having arrived at a "conclusion in which nothing is concluded," resolve to wait for the inundation of the Nile to subside and to return to their native land—as the protagonist of Voltaire's *Candide,* published not many weeks earlier, had decided: "Il faut cultiver notre jardin." Johnson's *Rasselas* has been translated into nearly all European and into some Eastern languages and from 1759 to the present day has been reprinted in English on an average of about once a year.

1762
London
Inner Temple

EARLY IN THIS YEAR Johnson was granted an annual pension of 300 pounds by the Crown. He entertained some scruples at first about accepting it. Embarrassing definitions of "pension" and "pensioner" stood in his *Dictionary.* "Pension: An allowance made to anyone without an equivalent. In English it is generally understood to mean pay given to a state hireling for treason to his country."

One of Johnson's most recent friends was an indigent Irish writer who, after varied wanderings on the Continent, had arrived in London in 1756. On a morning of 1762 Oliver Goldsmith was under arrest by his landlady for his rent. He sent a call for help to Johnson, who responded first with a guinea and, when he was dressed, followed in person, looked into a manuscript novel, *The Vicar of Wakefield,* which Goldsmith had "ready for the press," took it out, and sold it to a bookseller for sixty guineas.

Several times Johnson thought and hoped he would finish his big edition of Shakespeare within the next few months. The delays became something of a scandal—giving the satirist Charles Churchill a welcome occasion:

> He for subscribers baits his hook,
> And takes their cash, but where's the book?
> No matter where; wise fear, we know,
> Forbids the robbing of a foe,
> But what, to serve our private ends,
> Forbids the cheating of our friends?

1763
London
Inner Temple

ON MONDAY 16 May Johnson walked into a shop in Russell Street, Covent Garden, kept by an actor and bookseller, his friend Thomas Davies. Going on into a back parlor, he found Davies over teacups with a young man who was a stranger. Mr. Davies introduced Mr. James Boswell, who, "much agitated" on recollecting one of Johnson's well-known prejudices, said impulsively, "Don't tell where I come from." "From Scotland," cried Davies. "Mr. Johnson," said the young man, "I do indeed come from Scotland, but I cannot help it." "That, Sir," retorted Johnson, "I find, is what a very great many of your countrymen cannot help." It was the beginning of an immortal friendship. Some days later Boswell ventured the first of many visits to Johnson, in his chambers at No. 1, Inner Temple Lane. This young Scot was a student of law, an aspiring author, an adventurer for a year, at his father's expense, in the great city of London, and soon to set out for further legal studies in Holland and a Grand Tour of other parts of the Continent. He was dedicated to the pursuit of girls, to conversation with great men, and to keeping a faithful record of his daily adventures and emotions. He was, in short, a journalist, and an extraordinary one—a fact which would make him an extraordinary biographer. On 5 August he and Johnson set out by stage coach for the port of Harwich, where the next afternoon, on the beach, they "embraced and parted with tenderness."

1764
London
Inner Temple

IN HIS *Dictionary* days, about 1754, Johnson had met a gifted portrait (or "biographical") painter, Joshua Reynolds, recently returned from studies in Italy. In 1756 Reynolds had painted the first of a series of portraits of Johnson. He had contributed three essays about painting to the *Idler*. Now, early in 1764, Reynolds, sitting at Johnson's fireside, proposed the formation of a Club. Nothing could have been more agreeable. From the start Johnson was a dominant figure. They invited a few friends, including Oliver Goldsmith and Edmund Burke (a philosopher and political journalist who would begin a famous career in Parliament the following year). They gathered weekly at a tavern called the Turk's Head, in Soho, for supper, punch, and, above all, conversation. In 1756 Johnson had met Thomas Percy, a clergyman whose taste in poetry was to make him one of the century's most creative literary antiquarians. In 1768, Percy too was invited into the Club, and in that year also the manager of the Covent Garden Theater, George Colman. In 1773 Colman's rival David Garrick was elected, despite some earlier presumption on his part and a consequent flourish of resistance by Johnson. At later intervals the group would grow larger, but not less elite.

"As soon as I enter the door of a tavern," said Johnson in an utterance the more characteristic as it is undated, "I experience an oblivion of care and a freedom from solicitude: when I am seated, I find the master courteous, and the servants obsequious to my call; . . . wine[3] there exhilarates my spirits, and prompts me to free conversation and an interchange of discourse with those whom I most love: I dogmatize and am contradicted, and in this conflict of opinions and sentiments I find delight." He looked on a tavern chair as "the throne of human

3. Always an extremist, Johnson had to choose between drinking a lot and hardly drinking at all. He seems to have abstained from wine (and other liquors) for one long period, 1736–57, and for the most part from about 1765 to the end of his life.

felicity." He had always been a powerful (often a bullying and overbearing) debater, a ready source of *ex tempore* moral sagacity, a witty and magnetic table companion. The ingredients of the punch bowl over which there is some evidence that he presided at meetings of the Club seemed to him an apt emblem for the "qualities requisite to conversation":—lemon and sugar, spirit and water. "He only will please long, who, by tempering the acid of satire with the sugar of civility, and allaying the heat of wit with the frigidity of humble chat, can make the true punch of conversation" (*Idler* No. 34).

On Good Friday, 20 April 1764, Johnson entered in his journal of *Prayers and Meditations:* "I have made no reformation, I have lived totally useless, more sensual in thought and more addicted to wine and meat; grant me, O God, to amend my life for the sake of Jesus Christ. Amen. I hope to put my rooms in order. Disorder I have found one great cause of idleness. I fasted all day."

1765
London
Inner Temple
and
Johnson's Court

IN MID-JANUARY a friend, the dramatist Arthur Murphy, taking a providential initiative, brought Johnson to be introduced to an attractive recently married couple, a prosperous brewer, soon to be M.P. for Southwark, Henry Thrale, and a lively young Welsh lady, his wife (Hester Lynch Salusbury). They had a town house across the river in Southwark and a country house at Streatham, in Surrey. They were in need of a lion; Johnson was in need of a family and of a salon. For the rest of the winter Johnson had dinner with the Thrales every Thursday.

On 14 February appeared Johnson's dedication (to the Countess of Northumberland . . . Baroness Percy) of his friend Thomas Percy's three-volume *Reliques of Ancient English Poetry,* derived in part from a seventeenth-century folio manuscript rescued from the fireplace of a country house in Shropshire. This work rode high on the contemporary tide of polite interest in Britain's ancient songs and ballads. In a certain mood, Samuel Johnson was capable of mocking the simplicity of the old ballads.

I put my hat upon my head
And walked into the Strand,
And there I met another man,
Whose hat was in his hand.

On Easter Day of this year he entered in his *Prayers and Meditations:* "Since the last Easter I have reformed no evil habit, my time has been unprofitably spent, and seems as a dream that has left nothing behind. My memory grows confused, and I know not how the days pass over me. Good Lord deliver me."

On 23 July of this year Johnson received a surprise award of the degree LL.D. from Trinity College, Dublin. Some time in the summer or early autumn he moved his lodging to No. 7, Johnson's Court, Fleet Street. In October appeared the long-awaited edition of Shakespeare, eight volumes in octavo, with Johnson's weighty commentary throughout—building upon and in effect submerging earlier editions by the dramatist Nicholas Rowe (1709), the poet Alexander Pope (1725), the scholars Lewis Theobald (1734), Sir Thomas Hanmer (1743–44), and William Warburton (1747). Johnson's edition would be the object of corrections and amplifications by a succession of other editors: George Steevens (1773, 1778), Edmond Malone (1780), and Isaac Reed (1785). His incomparable *Preface* to the edition of 1765 comes echoing down the avenues of Shakespeare criticism:

> Nothing can please many, and please long, but just representations of general nature. . . . In the writings of other poets a character is too often an individual; in those of Shakespeare it is commonly a species. . . . This, therefore, is the praise of Shakespeare, that his drama is the mirror of life. . . . Shakespeare's plays are not . . . either tragedies or comedies, but compositions of a distinct kind; exhibiting the real state of sublunary nature, which partakes of good and evil, joy and sorrow, mingled with endless variety. . . . The necessity of observing the unities of time and place arises from the supposed necessity of making the drama credible. . . . He that can take the stage at one time for the palace of the Ptolemies may take it in half an hour for the promontory of Actium. . . . The delight of tragedy proceeds from our consciousness of fiction; if we thought murders and treasons real, they would please no more.

1766
London
Johnson's Court
Streatham

"NO MAN IS obliged to do as much as he can do," said Johnson one evening to Goldsmith and Boswell. "A man is to have part of his life to himself." Now had arrived the time when he would "fold his legs" and sit back to enjoy the "bread and tea of life." On this evening, however, he was unwell and would not go out with them to the Mitre tavern. He was suffering, these days, much mental torment. As the kindly lady Mrs. Henry Thrale would describe one moment in their growing relation: "In the year 1766 his health, which he had always complained of, grew so exceedingly bad, that he could not stir out of his room in the court he inhabited for many *weeks* together, I think months. . . . He often lamented to us the horrible condition of his mind, which he said was nearly distracted . . . he charged us to make him odd solemn promises of secrecy on so strange a subject. . . . I felt excessively affected with grief, and well remember my husband involuntarily lifted up one hand to shut his mouth, from provocation at hearing a man so wildly proclaim what he could at last persuade no one to believe; and what, if true, would have been so very unfit to reveal." The Thrales picked Johnson up and took him home with them. He spent three months that summer at Streatham. For nearly twenty years, or until within about two years of his death, we may conceive him as intermittently domesticated with them, or spending the middle days of many weeks at one or the other of their houses. There was hardly one of his pleasures which he could not enjoy at Streatham—"conversation, a good library, pretty women, late hours, careful cookery, fruit."

"He who does not mind his belly," Johnson had said to Boswell, "will hardly mind any thing else." And Boswell has given us this striking vignette of Johnson the eater: "When at table, he was totally absorbed in the business of the moment; his looks seemed riveted to his plate; nor would he, unless when in very high company, say one word, or even pay the least attention to what was said by others, till he had satisfied his appetite, which was so fierce, and indulged with such intenseness, that while in the act of eating, the veins of his forehead swelled, and generally a strong perspiration was visible."

1767–69
London
Johnson's Court
Travels

THERE WAS one pleasure which could not be experienced in one place. That was traveling—close to conversation and eating among Johnson's priorities. He was contemptuous of the dangers and inconveniences commonly considered incident to this activity. In spite of his vast bulk, he was a sturdy traveler, nimble and durable. He liked bowling rapidly along in a horse-drawn vehicle. We may picture him, during his late middle years (with the income from his pension in his pocket), as more or less constantly in motion, by stagecoach or post chaise—and often on visits to favorite places in his native Midlands. In 1767 he spent six months at Lichfield; in 1768 two months at Oxford; in 1769, after a trip to Oxford, Lichfield, and Ashbourne, five weeks with the Thrales at Brighton.

In February 1767 occurred a moment which was highly gratifying to Johnson's "monarchical" temper. He was reading by the fire one day (as he occasionally did) in the new royal library at Buckingham House, when his friend Dr. Barnard the librarian surprised him by bringing in through a private door—His Majesty King George III! Johnson conversed "with profound respect" but in his usual "firm manly manner, with a sonorous voice." The King showed himself extremely courteous and very well informed. He asked intelligent questions about the libraries at Oxford and Cambridge, about recent literary events and journals. He inquired if Johnson was "then writing anything." Johnson said "he thought he had already done his part as a writer." "I should have thought so too," said the King, "if you had not written so well." His

Majesty expressed a desire to have the "literary biography" of the country ably executed, and he proposed to Johnson to undertake it. Johnson "signified his readiness."

In 1769 Johnson was named Professor of Ancient Literature in the Royal Academy of Arts, founded the year before, with Reynolds as first president. In 1769 Reynolds received the honor of knighthood. In this year too Reynolds painted his third portrait of Johnson—semi-fictional, highly dramatic, gesticulatory. It was hung at the Royal Academy in the exhibition of 1770 and the same year was engraved by James Watson in a large mezzotint.

* * *

1766–69
James Boswell

IN FEBRUARY of 1766, James Boswell, coming home from Paris on learning of the death of his mother, had stopped a few weeks in London and had renewed his acquaintance with Johnson. In the same year he was admitted to the Faculty of Advocates at Edinburgh. In 1768 appeared his first widely popular book, *An Account of Corsica, the Journal of a Tour to that Island; and Memoirs of Pascal Paoli.* He saw Johnson at both Oxford and London on his spring jaunt this year. In 1769 he came south again in September and made his spectacular appearance as an armed Corsican chief at the masquerade held during the Shakespeare Jubilee put on by Garrick at Stratford-on-Avon. Thence to London again, and once more Johnson and Boswell made a short journey together to a solemn parting. On 10 November, Johnson came in from Streatham with his young friend and saw him into a post chaise for Scotland, where two weeks later, at her family home Lainshaw, in Ayrshire, Boswell married his cousin Margaret Montgomerie. There is a peculiar sense in which this train of events has a close bearing on the biography—and even on the life—of Samuel Johnson.

* * *

1772
London
Johnson's Court

AFTER TWO YEARS of a sober and busy life at Edinburgh as a married man and a practicing advocate, Boswell in the spring of 1772 returned for a two-month visit to London, during which he lived in almost daily conversation with Johnson and members of his circle. He was a faithful adept in the art of writing up his journals of such conversations. It was the first of his regular visits to the south, the beginning of a habit which, kept up most springs for the next twelve years, or to the year of Johnson's death, preserved, in a generous sampling of the total fact, an image of Johnson the man and conversationalist unmatched in biographical literature for its vivid detail and its persuasive authenticity.

1773
London
Scotland

THE VERY NEXT year was an exceptionally good one. Boswell arrived in London at the beginning of April, in time to participate in the vibration which followed Goldsmith's success with *She Stoops to Conquer.* At the end of April, after a campaign of "assiduously and earnestly" recommending himself, he was proposed by Johnson for membership in the Club. "As one black ball could exclude, I sat in . . . anxious suspense. . . . I hastened to the Turk's Head in Gerard Street, Soho, and was introduced to such a society as can seldom be found. . . . Upon my entrance, Johnson . . . placed himself behind a chair, on which he leant as on a desk or pulpit, and with humorous formality gave me a *charge,* pointing out the duties incumbent upon me as a good member of the Club."

During this London jaunt, Boswell kept up a train of persuasions which on 14 August of that year brought Johnson by post chaise to the door of Boyd's Inn in the Canongate, Edinburgh. Boswell had engineered a supreme test of Johnson's skill and power as a traveler. Setting out on 18 August, the two friends traveled by post chaise up the east coast of Scotland, by St. Andrews and Aberdeen, then along the north coast to Inverness, and thence by horseback to Glenelg and by boat to the Isle of Skye. For seven rainy weeks of September and October they moved about through the inner Hebrides—by horse, by "little" horse or island "sheltie," on foot in the roughest places, and in boats of various kinds and sizes. They talked and ate their way through the countryside (Boswell also danced, sang, and drank), entertained and attended on all sides by lairds and their ladies, their families, tenants, factors, and retainers, by innkeepers, by the clergy, by doctors and soldiers.

On the night spent at the farm of Kingsburgh in Skye, Johnson slept in the very bed in which Prince Charles Edward had lain when he was sheltered by Flora Macdonald after the '45. He wrote frequent journal-like letters to Mrs. Thrale. In a letter to Henry Thrale from Skye, he enclosed an ode addressed to the lady in Sapphic strophes.

Inter erroris salebrosa longi,
Inter ignotae strepitus loquelae,
Quot modis mecum, quid agat, requiro,
Thralia dulcis?[4]

They spent a comfortable week at the Castle of Dunvegan, seat of MacLeod of MacLeod, head of the clan—on a rocky site at the extreme northwest corner of Skye. Blown out of course by a storm on the way to Mull, they endured nine days of imprisonment by wind and waves on the outlying island of Coll.

4. "Through long rough wandering, and mid the noise of dialects unknown, I turn the inner question: what does she now, sweet Mistress Thrale?"

On the island of Iona (Icolmkill), after a voyage of forty miles by longboat and a night on hay in a barn, they stepped forth amid the ruins of the ancient monastery and cathedral church and among the tombs of forgotten Scottish, Irish and Norwegian kings. "We were now treading that illustrious Island," meditated Johnson later, "which was once the luminary of the Caledonian regions, whence savage clans and roving barbarians derived the benefits of knowledge, and the blessings of religion. . . ."

On 22 October they reached the mainland once more at Oban in Argyll. They stopped in Ayrshire for six days at Boswell's ancestral seat, Auchinleck. (Boswell's "respected friend" and his "honored father," fierce old Lord of the Scottish Courts of Session and Justiciary, only momentarily forgot themselves and collided in a contest of "intellectual gladiators.") The travelers got to Edinburgh on 9 November, and on 22 November, 100 days after Johnson's arrival in August, Boswell, having accompanied Johnson fifteen miles south to Blackshiels, put him into the fly for London and returned to Edinburgh for a year of melancholy application to business.

1774
London
Johnson's Court
Wales

ON 4 April Oliver Goldsmith (who had suffered for some years from a recurrent "inflammation in the bladder" and was tormented by worries over heavy debts) died in his chambers at Brick Court in the Middle Temple; he was buried close by, in the yard of the Temple Church. Two years later his friends of the Club would erect a monument to him in Westminster Abbey. "Nullum fere scribendi genus/Non tetigit," wrote Johnson for the inscription ("There was hardly any species of writing that he did not put his hand to"). "Nullum quod tetigit non ornavit." ("None that he touched did he fail to adorn.")

During the summer of 1774 the Thrales took Johnson on an extended tour of North Wales.

1775
London
Midland Travels
France

ON 18 January Johnson published *A Journey to the Western Islands of Scotland,* his report on the adventure of 1773, a narrative survey of Highland social and economic life which has retained its authority and interest to this day.

On 8 March he published *Taxation No Tyranny,* his loyal government response to the Boston Tea Party. This was the last in a series which included three earlier slashing political pamphlets: *The False Alarm* (1770), his censure of the turbulent career of an old friend of Boswell's, the four-times unseated M.P. for Middlesex, soon to be Lord Mayor of London—John Wilkes; *Thoughts on the Late Transactions Respecting Falk-*

land's Islands (1771), concerning the folly of risking war with Spain through jingo agitation over the possession of "a bleak and gloomy solitude"; and *The Patriot* (1774), "addressed to the electors of Great Britain," on the false patriotism of some who, in the cause of "freedom," bawled most loudly against the government. ("Patriotism," he would say angrily in 1775, "is the last refuge of a scoundrel.") Johnson had received his pension as an award for literary merit, without political strings, from the administration of Lord Bute. He wrote his pamphlets in support of the policies of two later administrations, those of the Duke of Grafton and Lord North. Although he undertook the work with some misgivings, he succeeded in writing with a degree of sarcasm and "sophistry" that dismayed even his most devoted admirer—James Boswell. Mrs. Thrale would later say (and the claim is plausible) that the world owes his political pamphlets and the later *Lives of the Poets* to the comfort and support which the raging nerves of the author had found in the bosom of her household.

On 30 March Johnson received the degree D.C.L. from Oxford University; he toured to Oxford, Lichfield, and Ashbourne during the summer, and with the Thrales to France in the autumn.

1776
London
Bolt Court

ON 16 March, Boswell, newly arrived in London, discovered that Johnson had moved to No. 8, Bolt Court, Fleet Street—the house which was to be his last.

1777
London
Bolt Court

ON 27 March Mrs. Thrale brought Dr. Johnson to the home of their friend the musician and historian Dr. Charles Burney in St. Martin's Street, Leicester Fields, and here Johnson was seen for the first time by another keen observer, Dr. Burney's daughter Fanny, not quite twenty-five years old, a busy diarist and a secret novelist. She wrote: "He . . . is tall and stout, but stoops terribly; he is almost bent double. His mouth is almost continually opening and shutting, as if he was chewing. He has a strange method of frequently twirling his fingers, and twisting his hands. His body is in continual agitation, *see-sawing* up and down; his feet are never a moment quiet; and in short, his whole person is in *perpetual motion.*"

Two days later, on Easter Eve, Johnson received at Bolt Court a delegation of London booksellers (Thomas Davies, William Strahan, and Thomas Cadell—representing about forty others) and, without much resistance, agreed to produce for the sum of 200 guineas a series of biographical and critical prefaces to accompany a set of "elegant and uniform" volumes of the English Poets. This was the third and last of the great tasks of his career as a literary scholar.

In September James Boswell came south to Ashbourne and spent a happy ten days, of nearly uninterrupted conversation, with Johnson at the mansion of a Lichfield and Oxford schoolfellow Dr. John Taylor, wealthy pluralist parson and justice of the peace. Johnson and Taylor were friends in virtue of long acquaintance and habit, rather than close affinity of spirit. They could live for weeks together and scarcely speak. Taylor's passion was farm and garden. He had a waterfall, a deer park, and prize cattle. Johnson wrote sermons for him. They would be published, with others, in two volumes (1788–89) as *Sermons on Different Subjects, Left for Publication by John Taylor, LL.D. Late Prebendary of Westminster.* In this year Johnson sat for his bust by the sculptor Joseph Nollekens.

1778
London
Bolt Court
Streatham

IN JANUARY appeared (without her name) Fanny Burney's novel of London manners *Evelina.* On the wave of its semianonymous success she was taken to Streatham to talk with Johnson and Mrs. Thrale and in August became almost a member of the household. "Johnson," she confided to her diary, "has more fun, and comical humor, and love of nonsense about him, than almost anybody I ever saw."

"Miss Burney," said Mrs. Thrale, "is fond of [the] *Vicar of Wakefield,* and so am I;—don't you like it, Sir?"

"No, Madam, it is very faulty; there is nothing of real life in it, and very little of nature. It is a mere fanciful performance."

He then seated himself upon a sofa, and calling to me, said, "Come,—Evelina,—come and sit by me."

I obeyed; and he took me almost in his arms—that is, one of his arms, for one would go three times, at least, round me,—and, half-laughing, half-serious, he charged me to "be a good girl!"

On Easter Day, 19 April, Johnson wrote a dedication to the King for a volume of *Seven Discourses Delivered in the Royal Academy by the President,* Sir Joshua Reynolds. It was published about 19 May. Reynolds' Presidential *Discourses* (continued until 1790) were an eloquent exposition of the neoclassical ideal in visual art, closely paralleling and complementing that of his friend Johnson for literature.

1779
London
Bolt Court
Streatham

ON 20 January Johnson's old pupil David Garrick died. He had retired from the stage in 1776. At his funeral, Samuel Johnson was seen "standing beside his grave, at the foot of Shakespeare's monument, and bathed in tears." Writing his *Preface,* about this time, for a very minor poet, the Oxonian Edmund Smith, Johnson found occasion to insert a tender allusion to some Lichfield friends of early days, among them David Garrick, whom he "hoped to have gratified" by the reminiscence. "But what are the hopes of man! I am disappointed by that stroke of death, which has eclipsed the gaiety of nations and impoverished the public stock of harmless pleasure."

Johnson had been working with unusual speed on the *Prefaces* to the *Poets.* Some of them grew to memoirs of considerable length. With Fanny Burney he had sat in the summer house at Streatham reading proof, near the peach trees. In spring of this year the booksellers brought out the fifty-six volumes of the *Works of the English Poets* and along with them, in four volumes, the first twenty-two of the *Prefaces.* These included the "Cowley," Johnson's favorite, with its analytic dissertation on the wit by joining of contraries, the *discordia concors,*[5] of the Metaphysical poets; the "Dryden," written with generous sweep and brilliant empathy; and the "Milton," energized by a strong oppugnancy between the author and that "acrimonious and surly republican" the subject.

1781
London
Bolt Court
Streatham

ON 4 April Henry Thrale died, the apoplectic victim of a voracious habit at table. Johnson was at his bedside in a house in Grosvenor Square, where he had been moved to be near his doctors. "I am afraid of thinking what I have lost," wrote Johnson to Mrs. Thrale. "I never had such a friend." He was one of the executors of the estate and for a time was busied with the sale of great resources—not of "a parcel of boilers and vats," but of "the potentiality of growing rich beyond the dreams of avarice."

Some time in March Johnson had finished his *Prefaces* to the *Poets*—writing in his "usual way, dilatorily and hastily, unwilling to work, and working with vigor and haste." In mid-May appeared, in six volumes, the last thirty Prefaces—including the "Addison," with its notable closing paragraphs in praise of the "middle style" in English prose ("familiar but not coarse . . . elegant but not ostentatious"); two vigorous exercises in antipathy, the "Swift" (critical of the satirist's hard, plain style and his misanthropy) and the "Gray" (severe upon the strutting *Odes,* cordial to the pensive *Elegy*); and the "Pope"! Johnson had saved the writing of *Pope* to the last—a climax of his lifelong dual interest in biography and in literary criticism, his masterpiece in the tripartite pattern he had adopted for all the major *Prefaces:* life narrative (informative and intimate), character portrait, and critique of poetry (logical,

5. "The most heterogeneous ideas . . . yoked by violence together."

unsparing). "After all this it is surely superfluous to answer the question that has once been asked, whether Pope was a poet? otherwise than by asking in return, if Pope be not a poet, where is poetry to be found?" Johnson's Pope established patterns for the writing of Pope's biography which persist to the present day. The *Prefaces* (or *Lives of the Poets*, as they soon came to be known) are a masterly retrospective survey by the last of the Augustan literary giants—tinged delicately here and there with feelings of satiric elegy in contemplation of the inevitably frustrated ambitions of the *genus irritabile vatum*,[6] yet a heroic celebration of a great literary era. They constituted the most handsomely developed example, at that date, of English literary biography.

Johnson stood upon a pinnacle both of achievement and of fame. He had for some years been a conspicuous public figure, not only as writer but as conversationalist and center of his large circle. He was an object of fascination to the London literary world. He had become also, to a degree, notorious, a target of constant satire. In June of this year he said to Boswell: "I wish that I had copies of all the pamphlets written against me, as it is said Pope had. Had I known that I should make so much noise in the world, I should have been at pains to collect them. I believe there is hardly a day in which there is not something about me in the newspapers." He spent the summer of 1781 once more at Streatham.

1782
London
Bolt Court
Streatham
Brighton

AT HIS VARIOUS homes in the city, Johnson had for many years sustained another household, a sort of hospital of dilapidated dependents. They had begun to gather around him after the death of his wife in 1752:—a presiding lady, the blind poetess Anna Williams; a sort of house physician, "an apothecary," Dr. Robert Levett; a friend, Mrs. Desmoulins, whom he had known as a girl in Lichfield; another woman, of uncertain origin and disagreeable character, Poll Carmichael; and apparently, from time to time, some others. The house contained also Johnson's black servant Francis Barber and his white wife. To this establishment Johnson was accustomed to return on weekends—sometimes, no doubt, to divine service at St. Clement's Church in the Strand and to Sunday dinner at his own house. Here on 17 January of this year, Dr. Levett died. Johnson was moved to the composition of some severely restrained yet "pathetic" (to the twentieth-century mind, perhaps *strangely* effective) elegiac stanzas.

His virtues walked their narrow round,
Nor made a pause, nor left a void;
And sure th' Eternal Master found
His single talent well employed.

6. "The testy race of poets" (Horace, *Epistles*, II.ii. 102).

Once more Johnson spent the summer at Streatham. Toward its end, Mrs. Thrale, hard put to meet expenses, decided she would have to leave Streatham Park and rent it. On 6 October, the day before departure, Johnson pronounced a prayer:

> Almighty God, Father of all mercy, help me, by Thy grace, that I may with humble and sincere thankfulness remember the comforts and conveniences which I have enjoyed at this place, and that I may resign them with holy submission. . . .

With Mrs. Thrale, her daughters, and Fanny Burney, he spent a dismal season of six weeks (unwanted in society, uninvited to parties) at Brighton.

1783
London
Bolt Court
Argyle Street

THE PHLEGMATIC GLUTTON Henry Thrale had been the steadying influence that made possible the relation between the spirited lady and the suffering sage. That relation was now rapidly deteriorating. In her *Anecdotes* published after the death of Johnson, she was to supply some convincing illustrations of what she called his "roughness," "harshness," "asperity," or "coarseness"—the savage polemic spirit which seems to have become the settled habit of his conversation in his later years. Sometimes he repented or regretted a rude outburst. (Here is one instance from Boswell: "'I'll make Goldsmith forgive me'; . . . then called to him in a loud voice: 'Dr. Goldsmith, something passed today where you and I dined. I ask your pardon.'") But in general his talk was "arrogant," and his silence "supercilious." Mrs. Thrale experienced "horror" or "disgust." ("'I would advise you, Sir,' said he with a cold sneer, 'never to relate this story again: you really can scarce imagine how *very poor* a figure you make in the telling of it.'")

And now, since the death of her husband, Mrs. Thrale had been cherishing—in secret from Johnson and against the active disapproval of her daughters and Fanny Burney—a new passion. She was deeply in love with an Italian music master, Gabriel Piozzi. Early in 1783 she had yielded in anguish to the voice of duty and had sent Piozzi away. She endured some bad months at her house in Argyle Street, where Johnson was again domesticated. And then, in April:

> I . . . found it convenient, for every reason . . . to retire to Bath, where I knew Mr. Johnson would not follow me, and where I could for that reason command some little portion of time for my own use; a thing impossible while I remained at Streatham or at London, as my hours, carriage, and servants had long been at his command, who would not rise in the morning till twelve o'clock perhaps, and oblige me to make breakfast for him till the bell rung for dinner.

At Bolt Court, during the early morning hours of 17 June Johnson suffered a stroke of palsy, which almost totally deprived him of the power of speech. To test whether or not he had lost any of the power of his mind, he composed a Latin prayer in two elegiac couplets.

He got rapidly better and went on a visit to a friend at Rochester, and then to another near Salisbury. There he received news that on 6 September at Bolt Court Mrs. Williams had died. Dr. Levett had been "eminently cheerful" on the night before his death. For some years now Mrs. Williams had been "much decayed" in body and temper, a source of little gratification. Her passing, however, left a sad blank. On 18 September Johnson returned to a "disconsolate house," a "solitude." He was threatened for a while with painful surgery. On 3 December he organized a reunion, at the Queen's Arms, in St. Paul's Churchyard, with three old friends who in 1749 had been members with him of a club in Ivy Lane. He started another club, to meet three evenings a week, not far from his house, at the Essex Head in Essex Street. But when he went to a meeting, he was seized with a violent attack of spasmodic asthma.

1784
London
Bolt Court
Midland Travels

ON 21 April Johnson wrote to Mrs. Thrale that he had just emerged after 129 days of confinement. He returned thanks to God in St. Clement's Church for his recovery. On 13 May he bragged about a solid week of dinner engagements. From 3 to 16 June he was away on a jaunt with Boswell to Oxford, staying at the house of Dr. William Adams, now Master of Pembroke College.

> DR. ADAMS. 'What do you mean by damned?' JOHNSON. (passionately and loudly) 'Sent to Hell, Sir, and punished everlastingly.'

On 30 June, Johnson, Reynolds, and Boswell having dined together, Boswell accompanied Johnson in Reynolds's coach to the entry of Bolt Court, declined coming in, from an apprehension that his "spirits would sink," and bade affectionate adieu in the coach. "Fare you well," called Johnson from the pavement, and without looking back, sprang away "with a kind of pathetic briskness," which impressed Boswell (at least in retrospect) with a foreboding of long separation.

On the same day Mrs. Thrale had sent Johnson and the other guardians of her daughters a circular letter announcing her engagement to Piozzi. In a covering letter to Johnson, she begged pardon for having concealed the connection from him—to spare them both "needless pain."

On 2 July Johnson replied: "If I interpret your letter right, you are ignominiously married. . . ."

And she on 4 July: ". . . Till you have changed your opinion of Mr. Piozzi, let us converse no more. God bless you."

And he on 8 July: "I wish that God may grant you every blessing . . . and whatever I can contribute to your happiness I am very ready to repay, for that kindness which soothed twenty years of a life radically wretched."

For four months, starting on 13 July, Johnson traveled and visited: —at Lichfield (his stepdaughter, Mrs. Lucy Porter), at Ashbourne (his old schoolfellow Dr. John Taylor), at Birmingham (another old schoolfellow, Edmund Hector, in 1733 the prompter of Lobo's *Abyssinia*), at Oxford (Dr. William Adams again).

"It might have been supposed," writes Boswell, that Johnson would have "chosen to remain in the comfortable house of his beloved wife's daughter, and end his life where he began it." But: "I will be conquered," said Johnson, "I will not capitulate." "The town is my element," he had written on 25 October to one of his London physicians, Dr. Richard Brocklesby. "I am not afraid either of a journey to London, or a residence in it." On 16 November he came home to his metropolis. During his last illness his house was crowded with an almost constant levee of doctors and friends. He busied himself with burning papers. "For many years," Arthur Murphy would recall, when Johnson had been not "disposed to enter into the conversation going forward, whoever sat near his chair might hear him repeating . . . 'Ay, but to die, and go we know not where; / To lie in cold obstruction and to rot. . . .'"[7] And now he complained one morning to Dr. Brocklesby, "I have been as a dying man all night," and then broke out, "Canst thou not minister to a mind diseased, / Pluck from the memory a rooted sorrow . . . ?" To which the Doctor replied, "Therein the patient / Must minister to himself,"[8] and Johnson expressed his assent. He was facing his end with a strenuously won religious composure. His clerical friends read the church service for him regularly. On Sunday 5 December he received the Holy Sacrament. From the day when the doctors admitted to him that the end was near, he refused any further physic or opiates. On the morning of Monday 13 December, hard pressed for breath, he seized a lancet and then a pair of scissors and gashed his legs deeply in an attempt to let out the dropsical fluid. He lost some blood and fell into a doze. At about a quarter past seven that evening, shortly after uttering the words "Jam moriturus,"[9] he died. On 20 December he was buried in Westminster Abbey.

* * *

In autumn 1785 Boswell published a first installment of his biography of Johnson, the *Journal of a Tour to the Hebrides with Samuel*

7. *Measure for Measure*, III. i. 118–19.
8. *Macbeth*, V. iii. 40–41, 45–46.
9. "I am now about to die."

Johnson, LL.D. About six months later (in March 1786) Mrs. Thrale-Piozzi published (from Italy) her rivalrous *Anecdotes of the Late Samuel Johnson, LL.D. during the Last Twenty Years of his Life;* and in 1788, her *Letters to and from the Late Samuel Johnson, LL.D.* A dour magistrate and historian of music, one of the survivors of the Ivy Lane Club, and one of Johnson's executors, Sir John Hawkins, completed the first book-length *Life* of Johnson, volume 1 of the first collected edition of his *Works,* published by the booksellers in 1787. James Boswell took his time with the main task. His *Life of Samuel Johnson, LL.D.* appeared in two volumes quarto on 16 May 1791, the twenty-eighth anniversary of his first meeting with Johnson. An immense magazine of biographical narrative, of "epistolary correspondence," of "conversations with many eminent persons," and of "various original pieces of Johnson's composition," Boswell's classic *Life* "exhibits," as the title page boasts, a comprehensive "view of literature and literary men in Great Britain" for the nearly half a century during which Johnson flourished.

Bibliographical Note

I.
Johnson's Career:
Sources and Guides to Sources

1. James Boswell. *Boswell's Life of Johnson.* Edited by G. B. Hill and L. F. Powell. Vols. 1–6. Oxford: Clarendon Press, 1934–1964.
2. James L. Clifford, ed. *Twentieth Century Interpretations of Boswell's Life of Johnson.* Englewood Cliffs, N.J.: Prentice-Hall, 1970.
3. James Boswell. *The Yale Editions of the Private Papers of James Boswell,* ed. F. A. Pottle et al. New York: McGraw-Hill, 1950–1970. In the trade edition: vols. [1], *Boswell's London Journal, 1762–1763,* 1950; [6], *Boswell in Search of a Wife, 1766–1769,* 1956; [7], *Boswell for the Defence, 1769–1774,* 1959; [8], *Boswell's Journal of a Tour to the Hebrides with Samuel Johnson, LL.D., 1773,* 1961; [9], *Boswell: The Ominous Years, 1774–1776,* 1963; [10], *Boswell in Extremes, 1776–1778,* 1970.
4. G. B. Hill, ed. *Johnsonian Miscellanies.* Vols. 1–2. Oxford at the Clarendon Press, 1897. Reprint, New York: Barnes & Noble, 1970. Contains Mrs. Thrale-Piozzi's *Anecdotes of the Late Samuel Johnson, LL.D.,* 1786; Johnson's *Prayers and Meditations* and *Annals* of his childhood; and a large collection of minor memorials. Mrs. Thrale-Piozzi's *Anecdotes* may be read conveniently also in an edition by S. C. Roberts, Cambridge, Engl.: Cambridge University Press, 1932. The main source of the *Anecdotes* has been edited by Katherine C. Balderston: *Thraliana, The Diary of Mrs. Hester Lynch Thrale (Later Mrs. Piozzi), 1776–1809,* vols. 1–2, Oxford: Clarendon Press, 1942. Johnson's *Diaries, Prayers, and Annals* are elaborately edited as vol. 1 of *The Yale Edition of the Works of Samuel Johnson,* by E. L. McAdam, Jr. with Donald and Mary Hyde. New Haven: Yale University Press, 1958; 2nd ed. rev. 1960.
5. Fanny Burney. *Dr. Johnson and Fanny Burney,* edited by C. B. Tinker, New York: Moffat, Yard, 1911.
6. John Hawkins. *The Life of Samuel Johnson, LL.D.* London: J. Buckland, 1787. Vol. 1 of Johnson's collected *Works* in eleven volumes. (In abridged form, edited by Bertram H. Davis. New York: Macmillan, 1961.)
7. Robert E. Kelley and O M Brack, Jr. *Samuel Johnson's Early Biographers.* Iowa City: University of Iowa Press, 1971.
8. James L. Clifford. *Young Sam Johnson.* New York: McGraw-Hill, 1955. (Deepened perspective on Johnson's earlier years, 1709–1749.)
9. *The Early Biographies of Samuel Johnson.* Edited by O M Brack, Jr. and Robert E. Kelley. Iowa City: University of Iowa Press, 1974.

Various books on Johnson's friends and memorialists can be consulted with profit. See especially: on Boswell, C. B. Tinker, 1922; F. A. Pottle, 1929 and 1966; Frank Brady, 1965; on Mrs. Thrale-Piozzi, J. L. Clifford, 1941; Mary Hyde, 1972; on Fanny Burney, Joyce Hemlow, 1958; on Sir

Joshua Reynolds, F. W. Hilles, 1936; on Sir John Hawkins, Bertram H. Davis, 1960 and 1973.

10. W. P. Courtney. *A Bibliography of Samuel Johnson.* Revised by David Nichol Smith. Oxford: Clarendon Press, 1915. "Supplement," by R. W. Chapman and Allen T. Hazen, *Proceedings of The Oxford Bibliographical Society,* V (1938), 119–66.
11. James L. Clifford and Donald J. Greene. *Samuel Johnson: A Survey and Bibliography of Critical Studies.* Minneapolis: University of Minnesota Press, 1970.
12. Allen T. Hazen. *Samuel Johnson's Prefaces and Dedications.* New Haven: Yale University Press, 1937.
13. Edward A. Bloom. *Samuel Johnson in Grub Street.* Providence: Brown University Press, 1957. (A valuable guide to Johnson's career in journalism.)

II.
Secondary Biographies, Literary Careers

1. J. W. Krutch. *Samuel Johnson.* New York: Henry Holt, 1944.
2. M. J. C. Hodgart. *Samuel Johnson and His Times.* London: B. T. Batsford, 1962.
3. Donald J. Greene. *Samuel Johnson.* New York: Twayne, 1970.
4. Paul Fussell. *Samuel Johnson and the Life of Writing.* New York: Harcourt Brace Jovanovich, 1971.
5. John Wain. *Samuel Johnson.* New York: Viking Press, 1975.

III.
Special Studies:
Johnson's Character, Mind, Interests

(A number of these works, and especially those marked with an asterisk, are closely relevant to section IV below.)

*1. W. B. C. Watkins. *Perilous Balance, The Tragic Genius of Swift, Johnson, and Sterne.* Princeton: Princeton University Press, 1939. Reprinted, Cambridge, Mass.: Walker-De Berry, 1960.
*2. Bertrand H. Bronson. *Johnson Agonistes and Other Essays.* Cambridge, Engl.: Cambridge University Press, 1946. Three essays, republished from *University of California Publications in English,* iii, no. 9 (1944). Republished, with a fourth essay, Berkeley and Los Angeles: University of California Press, 1965.
3. E. L. McAdam, Jr. *Dr. Johnson and the English Law.* Syracuse: Syracuse University Press, 1951.
*4. Walter Jackson Bate. *The Achievement of Samuel Johnson.* New York: Oxford University Press, 1955.
5. Donald J. Greene. *The Politics of Samuel Johnson.* New Haven: Yale University Press, 1960.
6. Robert B. Voitle, Jr. *Samuel Johnson the Moralist.* Cambridge, Mass.: Harvard University Press, 1961.
7. Maurice J. Quinlan. *Samuel Johnson: A Layman's Religion.* Madison: University of Wisconsin Press, 1964.

8. Paul K. Alkon. *Samuel Johnson and Moral Discipline.* Evanston: Northwestern University Press, 1967.
*9. Arieh Sachs. *Passionate Intelligence, Imagination and Reason in the Works of Samuel Johnson.* Baltimore: Johns Hopkins Press, 1967.
10. Chester F. Chapin. *The Religious Thought of Samuel Johnson.* Ann Arbor: University of Michigan Press, 1968.
11. Richard B. Schwartz. *Samuel Johnson and the New Science.* Madison: University of Wisconsin Press, 1971.

IV.

Editions, Philology, and Literary Criticism

1. *Johnson's Lives of the English Poets.* 3 vols. Edited by G. B. Hill. Oxford: Clarendon Press, 1905. Reprinted, New York: Octagon Press, 1967. (Heavily annotated, indexed.)
2. Walter Raleigh. *Six Essays on Johnson.* Oxford: Clarendon Press, 1910. Reprinted, New York: Russell and Russell, 1965. (Includes essays on Johnson's *Shakespeare* and on the *Lives of the Poets.*)
3. Joseph Epes Brown. *Critical Opinions of Samuel Johnson.* Princeton: Princeton University Press, 1926. Reprinted, New York: Russell and Russell, 1961. (A dictionary in two alphabets, one of topics, one of names and titles.)
4. W. B. C. Watkins. *Johnson and English Poetry Before 1660.* Princeton: Princeton University Press, 1936.
5. W. K. Wimsatt. *The Prose Style of Samuel Johnson.* New Haven: Yale University Press, 1941.
6. ———. *Philosophic Words, A Study of Style and Meaning in the "Rambler" and "Dictionary" of Samuel Johnson.* New Haven: Yale University Press, 1948. Reprinted, Hamden: Archon Books, 1968.
7. Jean H. Hagstrum. *Samuel Johnson's Literary Criticism.* Minneapolis: University of Minnesota Press, 1952.
8. Benjamin B. Hoover. *Samuel Johnson's Parliamentary Reporting.* Berkeley and Los Angeles: University of California Press, 1953.
9. James H. Sledd and Gwin J. Kolb, Jr. *Dr. Johnson's Dictionary: Essays in the Biography of a Book.* Chicago: University of Chicago Press, 1955.
10. *The Yale Edition of the Works of Samuel Johnson,* ed. Allan T. Hazen, John H. Middendorf, et al. New Haven: Yale University Press, 1958– . (Standard edition, ten volumes published to date.)
11. *Samuel Johnson: A Collection of Critical Essays.* Edited by Donald J. Greene. Englewood Cliffs: Prentice-Hall, 1965.
12. Lawrence Lipking. *The Ordering of the Arts in Eighteenth-Century England.* Princeton: Princeton University Press, 1970. (Includes a substantial chapter on Johnson's *Lives of the Poets.*)
13. James T. Boulton. *Johnson, The Critical Heritage.* London: Routledge and Kegan Paul, 1971. (Anthology of early critical opinion on Johnson.)
14. Carey McIntosh. *The Choice of Life: Samuel Johnson and the World of Fiction.* New Haven: Yale University Press, 1973.

Letters

To Elizabeth Johnson[1]

Lichfield, 31 January 1740

Dearest Tetty,

After hearing that you are in so much danger, as I apprehend from a hurt on a tendon, I shall be very uneasy till I know that you are recovered, and beg that you will omit nothing that can contribute to it, nor deny yourself anything that may make confinement less melancholy. You have already suffered more than I can bear to reflect upon, and I hope more than either of us shall suffer again. One part at least I have often flattered myself we shall avoid for the future, our troubles will surely never separate us more.[2] If M ⟨ ⟩ does not easily succeed in his endeavors, let him not ⟨? scruple⟩[3] to call in another surgeon to consult with him. Y⟨ou may⟩ have two or three visits from Ranby or Shipton, who is ⟨? said⟩ to be the best, for a guinea, which you need not fear to part with on so pressing an occasion, for I can send you twenty pounds more on Monday which I have received this night; I beg therefore that you will more regard my happiness than to expose yourself to any hazards. I still promise myself many happy years from your tenderness and affection, which I sometimes hope our misfortunes have not yet deprived me of. David wrote to me this day on the affair of *Irene*, who is at last become a kind of favorite among the players.[4] Mr Fleetwood promises to give a promise in writing that it shall be the first next season if it cannot be introduced now, and Chetwood the prompter is desirous of bargaining for the copy, and offers fifty guineas for the

1. Johnson's wife, a widow whom he had married in 1735. Text from a facsimile in G. B. Hill's edition of Johnson's *Letters* (1892).

2. Johnson and his wife were living in London, but he had gone on a leisurely trip, in part to apply for a schoolmaster's post in Leicestershire. He was now staying in his native town.

3. The conjectures adopted here and below are those of R. W. Chapman in his edition of Johnson's *Letters* (1952).

4. David Garrick was at the beginning of his career as the greatest of English actors. He was trying to help Johnson, his former schoolmaster, get his tragedy *Irene* produced.

right of printing after it shall be played. I hope it will at length reward me for my perplexities.[5]

Of the time which I have spent from thee, and of my dear Lucy[6] and other affairs, my heart will be at ease on Monday[7] to give thee a particular account, especially if a letter should inform me that thy leg is better, for I hope you do not think so unkindly of me as to imagine that I can be at rest while I believe my dear Tetty in pain.

Be assured, my dear girl, that I have seen nobody in these rambles upon which I have been forced, that has not contribute[d] to confirm my esteem and affection for thee, though that esteem and affection only contributed to increase my unhappiness when I reflected that the most amiable woman in the world was exposed by my means to miseries which I could not relieve.

I am, my charming love, yours,
Sam. Johnson

Lucy always sends her duty and my mother her service.

To Philip Dormer Stanhope, fourth Earl of Chesterfield[1]

London, 7 February 1755

My Lord:

I have been lately informed by the proprietor of *The World* that two papers,[2] in which my "Dictionary" is recommended to the public, were written by your Lordship. To be so distinguished is an honor which, being very little accustomed to favors from the great, I know not well how to receive, or in what terms to acknowledge.

When, upon some slight encouragement, I first visited your Lordship, I was overpowered like the rest of mankind by the enchantment of your address; and could not forbear to wish that I might boast myself *le vainqueur du vainqueur de la terre,*[3] that I might obtain that regard for which I saw the world contending; but I found my attendance so little encouraged that neither pride nor modesty would suffer me to continue it. When I had once addressed your Lordship in public,[4] I had

5. Charles Fleetwood, manager of Drury Lane Theater, failed to produce *Irene,* and it was not performed until 1749 after Garrick had become manager. Robert Dodsley paid £100 for publication rights.

6. Lucy Porter, Mrs. Porter's daughter by her first husband. She helped Johnson's mother in her bookshop.

7. Johnson is writing on a Thursday.

1. Text from R. W. Chapman's edition of Johnson's *Letters* (1952). Letters from this edition are reprinted by kind permission of the Oxford University Press, Oxford.

2. Nos. 100, 101 (both 1754).

3. "The conqueror of the conqueror of the earth," a line quoted in Boileau's *Art of Poetry,* iii. 272.

4. Johnson addressed his *Plan of a Dictionary of the English Language* (1747) to Chesterfield.

exhausted all the art of pleasing which a retired and uncourtly scholar can possess. I had done all that I could, and no man is well pleased to have his all neglected, be it ever so little.

Seven years, my Lord, have now passed since I waited in your outward rooms or was repulsed from your door; during which time I have been pushing on my work through difficulties of which it is useless to complain, and have brought it at last to the verge of publication without one act of assistance, one word of encouragement, or one smile of favor. Such treatment I did not expect, for I never had a patron before.

The shepherd in Virgil grew at last acquainted with Love, and found him a native of the rocks.[5] Is not a patron, my Lord, one who looks with unconcern on a man struggling for life in the water, and, when he has reached ground, encumbers him with help? The notice which you have been pleased to take of my labors, had it been early, had been kind; but it has been delayed till I am indifferent and cannot enjoy it, till I am solitary and cannot impart it,[6] till I am known and do not want it. I hope it is no very cynical asperity not to confess obligations where no benefit has been received, or to be unwilling that the public should consider me as owing that to a patron, which Providence has enabled me to do for myself.

Having carried on my work thus far with so little obligation to any favorer of learning, I shall not be disappointed though I should conclude it, if less be possible, with less; for I have been long wakened from that dream of hope in which I once boasted myself with so much exultation, my Lord,

your Lordship's most humble, most obedient servant,

Sam. Johnson

To Sarah Johnson[1]

London, 13 January 1759

Honored Madam,

The account which Miss[2] gives me of your health pierces my heart. God comfort and preserve you and save you, for the sake of Jesus Christ.

I would have Miss read to you from time to time the Passion of our Saviour, and sometimes the sentences in the Communion Service, beginning, "Come unto me all ye that travel and are heavy laden, and I will give you rest."[3]

5. *Eclogues*, viii. 43–45 (see p. 173).
6. Johnson's wife had died in 1752.
1. Johnson's mother. Text from the 1804 edition of Boswell's *Life of Johnson* (first edition 1791).
2. Lucy Porter.
3. Slightly altered from the *Book of Common Prayer*. "Travel" means "travail."

I have just now read a physical[4] book, which inclines me to think that a strong infusion of the bark[5] would do you good. Do, dear Mother, try it.

Pray send me your blessing, and forgive all that I have done amiss to you. And whatever you would have done, and what debts you would have paid first, or anything else that you would direct, let Miss put it down; I shall endeavor to obey you.

I have got twelve guineas to send you, but unhappily am at a loss how to send it tonight. If I cannot send it tonight, it will come by the next post.

Pray do not omit anything mentioned in this letter. God bless you for ever and ever.

I am your dutiful son,
Sam. Johnson

Pray acknowledge the receipt of this by return of the post without fail.[6]

To Giuseppe Baretti[1]

London, 21 December 1762

Sir:

You are not to suppose, with all your conviction of my idleness, that I have passed all this time without writing to my Baretti. I gave a letter to Mr. Beauclerk, who, in my opinion and in his own, was hastening to Naples for the recovery of his health; but he has stopped at Paris, and I know not when he will proceed. Langton is with him.

I will not trouble you with speculations about peace and war.[2] The good or ill success of battles and embassies extends itself to a very small part of domestic life: we all have good and evil which we feel more sensibly than our petty part of public miscarriage or prosperity. I am sorry for your disappointment, with which you seem more touched than I should expect a man of your resolution and experience to have been, did I not know that general truths are seldom applied to particular occasions; and that the fallacy of our self-love extends itself as wide as our interest or affections. Every man believes that mistresses are unfaithful, and patrons capricious; but he excepts his own mistress and his own patron. We have all learned that greatness is negligent and contemptuous, and that in Courts life is often languished away in ungrati-

4. Medical.

5. Quinine, used to reduce fever.

6. This sentence is an endorsement in another hand. Mrs. Johnson, aged 90, died a week later.

1. Baretti was a critic and scholar. This letter is addressed to him at Milan. Text from the *European Magazine* for March 1788.

2. The preliminaries of peace ending the Seven Years War had been signed by England and France on November 3.

fied expectation; but he that approaches greatness, or glitters in a Court, imagines that destiny has at last exempted him from the common lot.

Do not let such evils overwhelm you as thousands have suffered and thousands have surmounted; but turn your thoughts with vigor to some other plan of life, and keep always in your mind that, with due submission to Providence, a man of genius has been seldom ruined but by himself. Your patron's weakness or insensibility will finally do you little hurt, if he is not assisted by your own passions. Of your love I know not the propriety, nor can estimate the power; but in love, as in every other passion of which hope is the essence, we ought always to remember the uncertainty of events. There is indeed nothing that so much seduces reason from her vigilance as the thought of passing life with an amiable woman; and if all would happen that a lover fancies, I know not what other terrestrial happiness would deserve pursuit. But love and marriage are different states. Those who are to suffer the evils together,[3] and to suffer often for the sake of one another, soon lose that tenderness of look and that benevolence of mind which arose from the participation of unmingled pleasure and successive amusement. A woman we are sure will not be always fair; we are not sure she will always be virtuous; and man cannot retain through life that respect and assiduity by which he pleases for a day or for a month. I do not however pretend to have discovered that life has anything more to be desired than a prudent and virtuous marriage; therefore know not what counsel to give you.

If you can quit your imagination of love and greatness, and leave your hopes of preferment[4] and bridal raptures to try once more the fortune of literature and industry, the way through France is now open. We flatter ourselves that we shall cultivate with great diligence the arts of peace; and every man will be welcome among us who can teach us anything we do not know. For your part, you will find all your old friends willing to receive you.

Reynolds still continues to increase in reputation and in riches. Miss Williams, who very much loves you, goes on in the old way. Miss Cotterel is still with Mrs. Porter. Miss Charlotte is married to Dean Lewis, and has three children. Mr. Levett has married a streetwalker.[5] But the gazette[6] of my narration must now arrive to tell you that Bathurst went physician to the army, and died at the Havana.[7]

3. The text may be corrupt.

4. Advancement in position.

5. Anna Williams, a blind lady, and Robert Levett, who practiced medicine among the poor, lived with Johnson. The others mentioned were common friends of Johnson and Baretti.

6. Report of news, especially official announcements.

7. Dr. Richard Bathurst, one of Johnson's most dearly loved friends, died on the British expedition which captured Havana in August 1762.

I know not whether I have sent you word that Huggins and Richardson are both dead. When we see our enemies and friends gliding away from us,[8] let us not forget that we are subject to the general law of mortality, and shall soon be where our doom will be fixed forever.

I pray God to bless you, and am, Sir,
Your most affectionate, humble servant,
Sam. Johnson

Write soon.

To James Boswell[1]

London, 8 December 1763

Dear Sir,

You are not to think yourself forgotten, or criminally neglected, that you have had yet no letter from me. I love to see my friends, to hear from them, to talk to them, and to talk of them; but it is not without a considerable effort of resolution that I prevail upon myself to write. I would not, however, gratify my own indolence by the omission of any important duty, or any office of real kindness.

To tell you that I am or am not well, that I have or have not been in the country, that I drank your health in the room in which we sat last together, and that your acquaintance continue to speak of you with their former kindness, topics with which those letters are commonly filled which are written only for the sake of writing, I seldom shall think worth communicating; but if I can have it in my power to calm any harassing disquiet, to excite any virtuous desire, to rectify any important opinion, or fortify any generous resolution, you need not doubt but I shall at least wish to prefer the pleasure of gratifying a friend much less esteemed than yourself before the gloomy calm of idle vacancy. Whether I shall easily arrive at an exact punctuality of correspondence, I cannot tell. I shall, at present, expect that you will receive this in return for two which I have had from you. The first, indeed, gave me an account so hopeless of the state of your mind that it hardly admitted or deserved an answer; by the second I was much better pleased; and the pleasure will still be increased by such a narrative of the progress of your studies as may evince the continuance of an equal and rational application of your mind to some useful inquiry.

You will perhaps wish to ask what study I would recommend. I shall not speak of theology, because it ought not to be considered as a question whether you shall endeavor to know the will of God.

8. William Huggins, the translator of Ariosto, had quarreled with both Johnson and Baretti. Samuel Richardson, the famous novelist, had helped Johnson when he was under arrest for debt.

1. Boswell was in Utrecht studying law, and unhappy. Text from Boswell's *Life of Johnson* (1791).

I shall therefore consider only such studies as we are at liberty to pursue or to neglect; and of these I know not how you will make a better choice than by studying the civil law, as your father advises, and the ancient languages, as you had determined for yourself; at least resolve, while you remain in any settled residence, to spend a certain number of hours every day amongst your books. The dissipation of thought of which you complain is nothing more than the vacillation of a mind suspended between different motives, and changing its direction as any motive gains or loses strength. If you can but kindle in your mind any strong desire, if you can but keep predominant any wish for some particular excellence or attainment, the gusts of imagination will break away without any effect upon your conduct, and commonly without any traces left upon the memory.

There lurks, perhaps, in every human heart a desire of distinction which inclines every man first to hope, and then to believe, that Nature has given him something peculiar to himself. This vanity makes one mind nurse aversions and another actuate desires, till they rise by art much above their original state of power; and as affectation, in time, improves to habit, they at last tyrannize over him who at first encouraged them only for show. Every desire is a viper in the bosom, who while he was chill, was harmless but, when warmth gave him strength, exerted it in poison. You know a gentleman[2] who, when first he set his foot in the gay world, as he prepared himself to whirl in the vortex of pleasure, imagined a total indifference and universal negligence to be the most agreeable concomitants of youth, and the strongest indication of an airy temper and a quick apprehension. Vacant to[3] every object and sensible of every impulse, he thought that all appearance of diligence would deduct something from the reputation of genius; and hoped that he should appear to attain, amidst all the ease of carelessness and all the tumult of diversion, that knowledge and those accomplishments which mortals of the common fabric obtain only by mute abstraction[4] and solitary drudgery. He tried this scheme of life awhile, was made weary of it by his sense and his virtue; he then wished to return to his studies; and finding long habits of idleness and pleasure harder to be cured than he expected, still willing to retain his claim to some extraordinary prerogatives, resolved the common consequences of irregularity into an unalterable decree of destiny, and concluded that Nature had originally formed him incapable of rational employment.

Let all such fancies, illusive and destructive, be banished henceforward from your thoughts forever. Resolve, and keep your resolution; choose, and pursue your choice. If you spend this day in study, you will

2. Presumably Boswell himself.
3. Receptive to.
4. Silent withdrawal from the world (?).

find yourself still more able to study tomorrow; not that you are to expect that you shall at once obtain a complete victory. Depravity[5] is not very easily overcome. Resolution will sometimes relax and diligence will sometimes be interrupted; but let no accidental surprise or deviation, whether short or long, dispose you to despondency. Consider these failings as incident to all mankind. Begin again where you left off, and endeavor to avoid the seducements that prevailed over you before.

This, my dear Boswell, is advice which perhaps has been often given you, and given you without effect. But this advice, if you will not take from others, you must take from your own reflections, if you purpose to do the duties of the station to which the bounty of Providence has called you.

Let me have a long letter from you as soon as you can. I hope you continue your journal, and enrich it with many observations upon the country in which you reside. It will be a favor if you can get me any books in the Frisic language, and can inquire how the poor are maintained in the Seven Provinces.[6]

I am, dear Sir, your most affectionate servant,
Sam. Johnson

To Hester Lynch Thrale[1]

Skye, 6 September 1773

Dearest Madam,

I am now looking on the sea from a house of Sir Alexander Macdonald in the isle of Skye. Little did I once think of seeing this region of obscurity, and little did you once expect a salutation from this verge of European life. I have now the pleasure of going where nobody goes, and of seeing what nobody sees. Our design is to visit several of the smaller islands, and then pass over to the southwest of Scotland.

I returned from the sight of Bullers Buchan[2] to Lord Errol's[3] and having seen his library had for a time only to look upon the sea which rolled between us and Norway. Next morning, August 25, we[4] continued our journey through a country not uncultivated but so denuded of its woods that in all this journey I had not traveled an hundred yards between hedges or seen five trees fit for the carpenter. A few small plantations may be found but I believe scarcely any thirty years old at

5. A bad habit.
6. The Netherlands.
1. Text from R. W. Chapman's edition of Johnson's *Letters* (1952).
2. The Bullers (boilers) of Buchan is a huge rocky caldron surmounted by a narrow circular ridge far above it, around which Johnson and Boswell walked.
3. The Earl of Errol's mansion at Slains, near Aberdeen, is now a ruin.
4. Johnson, Boswell, and Boswell's servant Joseph Ritter.

least, as I do not forget to tell they are all posterior to the Union.[5] This day we dined with a country gentleman who has in his grounds the remains of a Druid's temple, which when it is complete is nothing more than a circle or double circle of stones placed at equal distances, with a flat stone, perhaps an altar, at a certain point, and a stone taller than the rest at the opposite point. The tall stone is erected, I think, at the south. Of this [*sic*] circles there are many in all the unfrequented parts of the Island.[6] The inhabitants of these parts respect them as memorials of the sepulture of some illustrious person. Here I saw a few trees. We lay at Banff.

August 26, we dined at Elgin where we saw the ruins of a noble cathedral. The chapter house is yet standing. A great part of Elgin is built with small piazzas to the lower story. We went on to Forres over the heath where Macbeth met the witches, but had no adventure.[7] Only in the way we saw for the first time some houses with fruit trees about them. The improvements of the Scotch are for immediate profit; they do not yet think it worth while to plant what will not produce something to be eaten or sold in a very little time. We rested at Forres.

A very great proportion of the people are barefoot, and if one may judge by the rest of the dress, to send out boys without shoes into the streets or ways.[8] There are however more beggars than I have ever seen in England; they beg, if not silently, yet very modestly.

Next day we came to Nairn, a miserable town, but a royal burgh, of which the chief annual magistrate is styled Lord Provost. In the neighborhood we saw the castle of the old Thane of Cawdor. There is one ancient tower with its battlements and winding stairs yet remaining; the rest of the house is, though not modern, of later erection.

On the 28, we went to Fort George, which is accounted the most regular fortification in the Island. The major of artillery walked with us round the walls, and showed us the principles upon which every part was constructed and the way in which it could be defended. We dined with the Governor Sir Eyre Coote, and his officers. It was a very pleasant and instructive day. But nothing puts my honored Mistress[9] out of my mind.

At night we came to Inverness, the last considerable town in the North, where we stayed all the next day for it was Sunday,[10] and saw the ruins of what is called Macbeth's Castle. It never was a large house, but

5. Of England and Scotland in 1707.
6. Of Great Britain.
7. Actually they crossed the heath where, according to tradition, Macbeth met the witches, the next day.
8. So in the original.
9. Johnson customarily called Mr. and Mrs. Thrale his "Master" and "Mistress."
10. It was considered irreligious to travel on Sunday.

was strongly situated.[11] From Inverness we were to travel on horseback.

August 30. We set out with four horses. We had two Highlanders to run by us, who were active, officious,[12] civil, and hardy. Our journey was for many miles along a military way made upon the bank of Lough Ness, a water about eighteen miles long, but not, I think, half a mile broad. Our horses were not bad, and the way was very pleasant. The rock out of which the road was cut was covered with birch trees, fern, and heath. The lake below was beating its bank by a gentle wind, and the rocks beyond the water on the right stood sometimes horrid and wild and sometimes opened into a kind of bay in which there was a spot of cultivated ground, yellow with corn.[13] In one part of the way we had trees on both sides, for perhaps half a mile. Such a length of shade perhaps Scotland cannot show in any other place.

You are not to suppose that here are to be any more towns or inns. We came to a cottage which they call the General's hut where we alighted to dine, and had eggs and bacon, and mutton, with wine, rum, and whisky. I had water.

At a bridge over the river which runs into the Ness, the rocks rise on three sides with a direction almost perpendicular to a great height; they are in part covered with trees, and exhibit a kind of dreadful magnificence, standing like the barriers of nature placed to keep different orders of being in perpetual separation. Near this bridge is the fall of Fiers, a famous cataract, of which by clambering over the rocks we obtained the view. The water was low, and therefore we had only the pleasure of knowing that rain would make it at once pleasing and formidable. There will then be a mighty flood foaming along a rocky channel frequently obstructed by protuberances, and exasperated by reverberation,[14] at last precipitated with a sudden descent, and lost in the depth of a gloomy chasm.

We came somewhat late to Fort Augustus where the Lieutenant Governor met us beyond the gates, and apologized that at that hour he could not by the rule of a garrison admit us otherwise than at a narrow door which only one can enter at a time. We were well entertained and well lodged, and next morning after having viewed the fort we pursued our journey.

Our way now lay over the mountains, which were ⟨to⟩ be passed not by climbing them directly but by traversing, so that as we went forward we saw our baggage following us below in a direction exactly contrary. There is in these ways much labor but little danger, and perhaps other places of which very terrific representations are made, are not in them-

11. It was a building of a later date than Macbeth's.
12. Eager to be helpful.
13. That is, grain.
14. The action of being driven back.

selves more formidable. These roads have all been made by hewing the rock away with pickaxes, or bursting them with gunpowder. The stones so separated are often piled loose as a wall by the wayside. We saw an inscription importing the year in which one of the regiments made two thousand yards of the road eastward.[15]

After tedious travel of some hours we came to what, I believe, we must call a village, a place where there were three huts built of turf, at one of which we were to have our dinner and our bed, for we could not reach any better place that night. This place is called Enock in Glenmorrison.[16] The house in which we lodged was distinguished by a chimney, the rest had only a hole for the smoke. Here we had eggs and mutton and a chicken and a sausage and rum. In the afternoon tea was made by a very decent girl in a printed linen. She engaged me so much that I made her a present of Cocker's *Arithmetic*.

I am, Madam, your most &c.,
Sam. Johnson

To James Macpherson[1]

London, 20 January 1775

Mr. James Macpherson—
I received your foolish and impudent note. Whatever insult is offered me I will do my best to repel, and what I cannot do for myself the law will do for me. I shall not desist from detecting what I think a cheat from any fear of the menaces of a ruffian.[2]

You want me to retract. What shall I retract? I thought your book an imposture from the beginning. I think it upon yet surer reasons an imposture still. For this opinion I give the public my reasons which I here dare you to refute.

But however I may despise you, I reverence truth and if you can prove the genuineness of the work I will confess it. Your rage I defy, your abilities since your Homer are not so formidable,[3] and what I have heard of your morals disposes me to pay regard not to what you shall say, but to what you can prove.

You may print this if you will.

Sam. Johnson

15. The military built roads after the Rebellion of 1715 to make the Highlands accessible to troops.
16. That is, Anoch in Glen Moriston.
1. Text from a facsimile in *The R. B. Adam Library*, vol. 1 (1929).
2. In his forthcoming *Journey to the Western Islands of Scotland* (1775), Johnson was to denounce Macpherson's "translations" of the poems of the third-century Gaelic bard Ossian as fabrications. Macpherson, hearing this, wrote him a threatening letter.
3. Macpherson's translation of the *Iliad* (1773) was badly received.

To Hester Lynch Thrale[1]

Lichfield, 27 October 1777

Dear Madam,

You talk of writing and writing, as if you had all the writing to yourself. If our correspondence were printed, I am sure posterity, for posterity is always the author's favorite, would say that I am a good writer too. *Anch'io sono pittore.*[2] To sit down so often with nothing to say, to say something so often, almost without consciousness of saying, and without any remembrance of having said, is a power of which I will not violate my modesty by boasting, but I do not believe that everybody has it.

Some when they write to their friends are all affection, some are wise and sententious, some strain their powers for efforts of gaiety, some write news, and some write secrets; but to make a letter without affection, without wisdom, without gaiety, without news, and without a secret, is, doubtless, the great epistolic art.

In a man's letters, you know, Madam, his soul lies naked, his letters are only the mirror of his breast; whatever passes within him is shown undisguised in its natural process; nothing is inverted, nothing distorted; you see systems in their elements; you discover actions in their motives.

Of this great truth, sounded by the knowing to the ignorant, and so echoed by the ignorant to the knowing, what evidence have you now before you. Is not my soul laid open in these veracious pages? Do not you see me reduced to my first principles? This is the pleasure of corresponding with a friend, where doubt and distrust have no place, and everything is said as it is thought. The original idea is laid down in its simple purity, and all the supervenient conceptions are spread over it *stratum super stratum*[3] as they happen to be formed. These are the letters by which souls are united, and by which minds naturally in unison move each other as they are moved themselves. I know, dearest Lady, that in the perusal of this, such is the consanguinity of our intellects, you will be touched as I am touched. I have indeed concealed nothing from you, nor do I expect ever to repent of having thus opened my heart.

I am, Madam, your most humble servant,
Sam. Johnson

1. Text from R. W. Chapman's edition of Johnson's *Letters* (1952).
2. "I too am a painter," a remark (perhaps incorrectly) attributed to Correggio upon seeing the work of Raphael.
3. Layer upon layer.

To Hester Lynch Thrale[1]

London, 19 June 1783

Dear Madam,

I am sitting down in no cheerful solitude to write a narrative which would once have affected you with tenderness and sorrow, but which you will perhaps pass over now with the careless glance of frigid indifference. For this diminution of regard, however, I know not whether I ought to blame you who may have reasons which I cannot know, and I do not blame myself who have for a great part of human life done you what good I could, and have never done you evil.

I had been disordered in the usual way, and had been relieved by the usual methods, by opium and cathartics, but had rather lessened my dose of opium.

On Monday the 16 I sat for my picture, and walked a considerable way with little inconvenience. In the afternoon and evening I felt myself light and easy, and began to plan schemes of life. Thus I went to bed, and in a short time waked and sat up as has been long my custom, when I felt a confusion and indistinctness in my head which lasted I suppose about half a minute; I was alarmed and prayed God, that however he might afflict my body, he would spare my understanding. This prayer, that I might try the integrity of my faculties, I made in Latin verse. The lines were not very good, but I knew them not to be very good; I made them easily, and concluded myself to be unimpaired in my faculties.

Soon after I perceived that I had suffered a paralytic stroke, and that my speech was taken from me. I had no pain, and so little dejection in this dreadful state that I wondered at my own apathy, and considered that perhaps death itself when it should come would excite less horror than seems now to attend it.

In order to rouse the vocal organs I took two drams. Wine has been celebrated for the production of eloquence. I put myself into violent motion, and I think repeated it. But all was vain. I then went to bed and, strange as it may seem, I think, slept. When I saw light, it was time to contrive what I should do. Though God stopped my speech he left me my hand; I enjoyed a mercy which was not granted to my dear friend Lawrence, who now perhaps overlooks me as I am writing, and rejoices that I have what he wanted.[2] My first note was necessarily to my servant, who came in talking and could not immediately comprehend why he should read what I put into his hands.

1. Text from R. W. Chapman's edition of Johnson's *Letters* (1952).

2. Dr. Thomas Lawrence, Johnson's longtime friend and physician, had died earlier in this month.

I then wrote a card to Mr. Allen,[3] that I might have a discreet friend at hand to act as occasion should require. In penning this note I had some difficulty, my hand, I knew not how nor why, made wrong letters. I then wrote to Dr. Taylor[4] to come to me and bring Dr. Heberden, and I sent to Dr. Brocklesby, who is my neighbor. My physicians are very friendly and very disinterested, and give me great hopes, but you may imagine my situation. I have so far recovered my vocal powers as to repeat the Lord's Prayer with no very imperfect articulation. My memory, I hope, yet remains as it was. But such an attack produces solicitude for the safety of every faculty.

How this will be received by you I know not. I hope you will sympathize with me; but perhaps

> My mistress gracious, mild, and good,
> Cries! "Is he dumb? 'Tis time he should."[5]

But can this be possible? I hope it cannot. I hope that what, when I could speak, I spoke of you, and to you, will be in a sober and serious hour remembered by you; and surely it cannot be remembered but with some degree of kindness. I have loved you with virtuous affection, I have honored you with sincere esteem. Let not all our endearment be forgotten, but let me have in this great distress your pity and your prayers. You see I yet turn to you with my complaints as a settled and unalienable friend; do not, do not drive me from you, for I have not deserved either neglect or hatred.

To the girls, who do not write often, for Susy has written only once, and Miss Thrale owes me a letter, I earnestly recommend, as their guardian and friend,[6] that they remember their Creator in the days of their youth.[7]

I suppose you may wish to know how my disease is treated by the physicians. They put a blister upon my back, and two from my ear to my throat, one on a side. The blister on the back has done little, and those on the throat have not risen. I bullied and bounced (it sticks to our last sand),[8] and compelled the apothecary to make his salve according to the *Edinburgh Dispensatory* that it might adhere better. I have two on now of my own prescription. They likewise give me salt of hartshorn, which I take with no great confidence, but am satisfied that what can be done is done for me.

3. Edmund Allen, printer and neighbor of Johnson.
4. The Rev. John Taylor, an old friend of Johnson.
5. Johnson writes in imitation of Jonathan Swift's *Verses on the Death of Dr. Swift,* ll. 181–82.
6. Since the death of Henry Thrale in 1781, Johnson had served as one of the guardians of the Thrales' children, including Susanna Arabella (b. 1770) and Hester Maria (b. 1764), who as the eldest daughter is called "Miss Thrale."
7. See Ecclesiastes 12:1.
8. Alexander Pope, *To Richard Temple, Viscount Cobham,* l.225.

O God, give me comfort and confidence in Thee, forgive my sins, and if it be Thy good pleasure relieve my diseases for Jesus Christ's sake. Amen.

I am almost ashamed of this querulous letter, but now it is written, let it go.

I am, Madam, your most humble servant,
Sam. Johnson

To Hester Lynch Thrale[1]

London, 2 July 1784

Madam,

If I interpret your letter right, you are ignominiously married; if it is yet undone, let us once talk together.[2] If you have abandoned your children and your religion, God forgive your wickedness; if you have forfeited your fame[3] and your country, may your folly do no further mischief.

If the last act is yet to do, I who have loved you, esteemed you, reverenced you, and served you, I who long thought you the first of human kind, entreat that before your fate is irrevocable I may once more see you. I was, I once was,

Madam, most truly yours,
Sam. Johnson

I will come down if you permit it.

To Hester Lynch Thrale[1]

London, 8 July 1784

Dear Madam,

What you have done, however I may lament it, I have no pretense to resent, as it has not been injurious to me. I therefore breathe out one sigh more of tenderness, perhaps useless but at least sincere.

I wish that God may grant you every blessing, that you may be happy in this world for its short continuance, and eternally happy in a better state; and whatever I can contribute to your happiness I am very ready to repay, for that kindness which soothed twenty years of a life radically[2] wretched.

1. Text from R. W. Chapman's edition of Johnson's *Letters* (1952).

2. On 30 June, Mrs. Thrale had written Johnson from Bath to tell him that she intended to marry Gabriel Piozzi, an Italian musician, who was regarded as much her social inferior. Piozzi was a Roman Catholic.

3. Reputation.

1. Text from R. W. Chapman's edition of Johnson's *Letters* (1952).

2. At root, basically.

Do not think slightly of the advice which I now presume to offer. Prevail upon Mr. Piozzi to settle in England. You may live here with more dignity than in Italy and with more security. Your rank will be higher, and your fortune more under your own eye. I desire not to detail all my reasons, but every argument of prudence and interest is for England, and only some phantoms of imagination seduce you to Italy.

I am afraid however that my counsel is vain, yet I have eased my heart by giving it.

When Queen Mary took the resolution of sheltering herself in England, the Archbishop of St. Andrew's, attempting to dissuade her, attended on her journey, and when they came to the irremeable[3] stream that separated the two kingdoms, walked by her side into the water, in the middle of which he seized her bridle, and with earnestness proportioned to her danger and his own affection pressed her to return. The Queen went forward.—If the parallel reaches thus far, may it go no further.[4] The tears stand in my eyes.

I am going into Derbyshire, and hope to be followed by your good wishes, for I am, with great affection,

Your most humble servant,
Sam. Johnson

Any letters that come for me hither will be sent me.

3. Admitting of no return.
4. Mary Queen of Scots, fleeing her rebellious subjects, took refuge in England, where she was imprisoned and finally executed on charges of conspiracy against Queen Elizabeth.

Poems

London

A Poem in Imitation of the Third Satire of Juvenal

Quis ineptae
Tam patiens urbis, tam ferreus ut teneat se?
JUVENAL.[1]

Though grief and fondness in my breast rebel,
When injured Thales bids the town farewell,
Yet still my calmer thoughts his choice commend,
I praise the hermit, but regret the friend,
Resolved at length, from vice and London far,
To breathe in distant fields a purer air.
And, fixed on Cambria's solitary shore,
Give to St. David one true Briton more.[2]
  For who would leave, unbribed, Hibernia's land,
Or change the rocks of Scotland for the Strand?[3]
There none are swept by sudden fate away,
But all whom hunger spares, with age decay:
Here malice, rapine, accident, conspire,
And now a rabble rages, now a fire;
Their ambush here relentless ruffians lay,
And here the fell[4] attorney prowls for prey;
Here falling houses thunder on your head,
And here a female atheist talks you dead.
  While Thales waits the wherry[5] that contains
Of dissipated wealth the small remains,
On Thames's banks, in silent thought we stood,
Where Greenwich smiles upon the silver flood:

1. "Who can endure this monstrous city? Who is so iron-willed he can bear it?" (*Satires,* i. 30–31).
2. Cambria is an ancient name for Wales, and St. David the patron saint of the Welsh.
3. Street in the heart of London. 4. Cruel. 5. Narrow river vessel.

Struck with the seat that gave Eliza birth,[6]
We kneel, and kiss the consecrated earth;
In pleasing dreams the blissful age renew,
And call Britannia's glories back to view;
Behold her cross[7] triumphant on the main,
The guard of commerce, and the dread of Spain,
Ere masquerades debauched, excise[8] oppressed,
Or English honor grew a standing jest.[9]
   A transient calm the happy scenes bestow,
And for a moment lull the sense of woe.
At length awaking, with contemptuous frown,
Indignant Thales eyes the neighboring town.
   Since worth, he cries, in these degenerate days,
Wants even the cheap reward of empty praise;
In those cursed walls, devote[10] to vice and gain,
Since unrewarded science[11] toils in vain;
Since hope but soothes to double my distress,
And every moment leaves my little less;
While yet my steady steps no staff sustains,
And life still vigorous revels in my veins;
Grant me, kind heaven, to find some happier place,
Where honesty and sense are no disgrace;
Some pleasing bank where verdant osiers[12] play,
Some peaceful vale with nature's paintings gay;
Where once the harassed Briton found repose,
And safe in poverty defied his foes;[13]
Some secret cell, ye powers, indulgent give.
Let ——— live here, for ——— has learned to live.[14]
Here let those reign, whom pensions can incite
To vote a patriot black, a courtier white;[15]
Explain their country's dear-bought rights away,
And plead for pirates in the face of day;[16]

6. Queen Elizabeth I was born in Greenwich on the Thames, then an outlying village and now a district of London.

7. England's flag, the red cross of St. George.

8. A tax on commodities.

9. An allusion to the peaceful policies of the Prime Minister, Sir Robert Walpole. His opponents called them cowardly.

10. Devoted; doomed.

11. Learning.

12. Willows.

13. The ancient Britons retreated to Wales when the Saxons and other Germanic tribes invaded England.

14. "George" II (ruled 1727–60) seems a plausible suggestion to fill the blanks.

15. The "Patriots" were those who opposed Walpole and the Court party. Pension grants were a common means of influencing M.P.'s.

16. The Parliamentary Opposition denounced Walpole's policy of allowing the Spanish to stop and search all ships trading with their American colonies.

With slavish tenets taint our poisoned youth,
And lend a lie the confidence of truth.
  Let such raise palaces, and manors buy,
Collect a tax, or farm a lottery,[17]
With warbling eunuchs fill a licensed stage,[18]
And lull to servitude a thoughtless age.
  Heroes, proceed! what bounds your pride shall hold?
What check restrain your thirst of power and gold?
Behold rebellious virtue quite o'erthrown,
Behold our fame, our wealth, our lives your own.
  To such, a groaning nation's spoils are given,
When public crimes inflame the wrath of heaven:
But what, my friend, what hope remains for me,
Who start at theft, and blush at perjury?
Who scarce forbear, though Britain's Court he sing,
To pluck a titled poet's borrowed wing;
A statesman's logic unconvinced can hear,
And dare to slumber o'er the *Gazetteer;*[19]
Despise a fool in half his pension dressed,
And strive in vain to laugh at H——y's[20] jest.
  Others with softer smiles, and subtler art,
Can sap the principles, or taint the heart;
With more address[21] a lover's note convey,
Or bribe a virgin's innocence away.
Well may they rise, while I, whose rustic tongue
Ne'er knew to puzzle[22] right, or varnish wrong,
Spurned as a beggar, dreaded as a spy,
Live unregarded, unlamented die.
  For what but social guilt the friend endears?
Who shares Orgilio's crimes, his fortune shares.
But thou, should tempting villainy present
All Marlborough hoarded, or all Villiers spent,[23]
Turn from the glittering bribe thy scornful eye,

17. Tax collecting and "farming" a lottery (paying a fixed amount to the government to conduct a lottery and keeping the proceeds) were often highly profitable activities.

18. The Licensing Act of 1737 required approval by the Lord Chamberlain of all plays for which admission was charged. It was a way of censoring theatrical attacks on the Ministry. "Warbling eunuchs" refers to the *castrati* (male sopranos) who sang in Italian opera, then fashionable.

19. A newspaper subsidized by Walpole.

20. Perhaps the Rev. John "Orator" Henley, an eccentric preacher noted for his crude jests at the Opposition.

21. Skill.

22. Confuse.

23. The great general, John Churchill, first Duke of Marlborough (1650–1722), made an immense financial profit during his campaigns against the French in the War of the Spanish Succession (1702–11). George Villiers, second Duke of Buckingham (1628–87), was a notorious spendthrift.

Nor sell for gold, what gold could never buy,
The peaceful slumber, self-approving day,
Unsullied fame, and conscience ever gay.
The cheated nation's happy favorites, see!
Mark whom the great caress, who frown on me!
London! the needy villain's general home,
The common shore[24] of Paris and of Rome;
With eager thirst, by folly or by fate,
Sucks in the dregs of each corrupted state.
Forgive my transports on a theme like this,
I cannot bear a French metropolis.[25]
Illustrious Edward! from the realms of day,[26]
The land of heroes and of saints survey;
Nor hope the British lineaments to trace,
The rustic grandeur, or the surly grace,
But lost in thoughtless ease, and empty show,
Behold the warrior dwindled to a beau;[27]
Sense, freedom, piety, refined away,
Of France the mimic, and of Spain the prey.
All that at home no more can beg or steal,
Or like a gibbet better than a wheel;[28]
Hissed from the stage, or hooted from the court,
Their air, their dress, their politics import;
Obsequious, artful, voluble, and gay,
On Britain's fond[29] credulity they prey.
No gainful trade their industry can 'scape,
They sing, they dance, clean shoes, or cure a clap;
All sciences a fasting Monsieur knows,
And bid him go to hell, to hell he goes.
Ah! what avails it, that, from slavery far,
I drew the breath of life in English air;
Was early taught a Briton's right to prize,
And lisp the tale of Henry's victories;[30]
If the gulled conqueror receives the chain,
And flattery subdues when arms are vain?
Studious to please, and ready to submit,
The supple Gaul was born a parasite:
Still to his interest true, where'er he goes,

24. Sewer.

25. That is, a London whose customs imitate French ones.

26. From heaven. Edward III (1312–77) was famous for his victories over the French.

27. Dandy, fop.

28. Hanging and breaking on the wheel were the British and French methods of execution respectively.

29. Foolish.

30. The victories of Henry V (1387–1422) over the French.

Wit, bravery, worth, his lavish tongue bestows;
In every face a thousand graces shine,
From every tongue flows harmony divine.
These arts in vain our rugged natives try,
Strain out with faltering diffidence a lie,
And get a kick for awkward flattery.
Besides, with justice, this discerning age
Admires their wondrous talents for the stage:
Well may they venture on the mimic's art,
Who play from morn to night a borrowed part;
Practiced their master's notions to embrace,
Repeat his maxims, and reflect his face;
With every wild absurdity comply,
And view each object with another's eye;
To shake with laughter ere the jest they hear,
To pour at will the counterfeited tear,
And as their patron hints the cold or heat,
To shake in dog-days,[31] in December sweat.
How, when competitors like these contend,
Can surly virtue hope to fix a friend?
Slaves that with serious impudence beguile,
And lie without a blush, without a smile;
Exalt each trifle, every vice adore,
Your taste in snuff, your judgment in a whore;
Can Balbo's eloquence applaud, and swear
He gropes[32] his breeches with a monarch's air.
For arts like these preferred, admired, caressed,
They first invade your table, then your breast;
Explore your secrets with insidious art,
Watch the weak hour, and ransack all the heart;
Then soon your ill-placed confidence repay,
Commence your lords, and govern or betray.
By numbers here from shame or censure free,
All crimes are safe, but hated poverty.
This, only this, the rigid law pursues,
This, only this, provokes the snarling muse.[33]
The sober trader at a tattered cloak,
Wakes from his dream, and labors for a joke;
With brisker air the silken courtiers gaze,
And turn the varied taunt a thousand ways.
Of all the griefs that harass the distressed,

31. Late summer days when Sirius (the Dog Star) was prominent.
32. Grasps; handles. "Preferred," in the next line, means given public office or promotion.
33. The muse of satire.

Sure the most bitter is a scornful jest;
Fate never wounds more deep the generous heart
Than when a blockhead's insult points the dart.
Has heaven reserved, in pity to the poor,
No pathless waste, or undiscovered shore;
No secret island in the boundless main?
No peaceful desert yet unclaimed by Spain?
Quick let us rise, the happy seats explore,
And bear oppression's insolence no more.
This mournful truth is everywhere confessed,
SLOW RISES WORTH, BY POVERTY DEPRESSED:
But here more slow, where all are slaves to gold,
Where looks are merchandise, and smiles are sold;
Where won by bribes, by flatteries implored,
The groom retails the favors of his lord.
But hark! th' affrighted crowd's tumultuous cries
Roll through the streets, and thunder to the skies;
Raised from some pleasing dream of wealth and power,
Some pompous palace, or some blissful bower,
Aghast you start, and scarce with aching sight
Sustain th' approaching fire's tremendous light;
Swift from pursuing horrors take your way,
And leave your little ALL to flames a prey;
Then through the world a wretched vagrant roam,
For where can starving merit find a home?
In vain your mournful narrative disclose,
While all neglect, and most insult your woes.
Should heaven's just bolts Orgilio's wealth confound,[34]
And spread his flaming palace on the ground,
Swift o'er the land the dismal rumor flies,
And public mournings pacify the skies;
The laureate tribe in servile verse relate,
How virtue wars with persecuting fate;
With well-feigned gratitude the pensioned band
Refund the plunder of the beggared land.
See! while he builds, the gaudy vassals come,
And crowd with sudden wealth the rising dome;[35]
The price of boroughs and of souls restore,[36]
And raise his treasures higher than before.
Now blessed with all the baubles of the great,

34. Destroy. In a note Johnson reports that one of his contemporaries has remarked justly that the following description is true of ancient, but not of modern times.

35. Building.

36. Rich and powerful persons often "bought" and "sold" parliamentary boroughs. Also they often had the right to appoint clergymen to parishes.

The polished marble, and the shining plate,[37]
Orgilio sees the golden pile aspire,[38]
And hopes from angry heaven another fire.
  Couldst thou resign the park and play[39] content,
For the fair banks of Severn or of Trent;[40]
There might'st thou find some elegant retreat,
Some hireling senator's deserted seat;
And stretch thy prospects[41] o'er the smiling land,
For less than rent the dungeons[42] of the Strand;
There prune thy walks, support thy drooping flowers,
Direct thy rivulets, and twine thy bowers;
And, while thy grounds a cheap repast afford,
Despise the dainties of a venal lord:
There every bush with nature's music rings,
There every breeze bears health upon its wings;
On all thy hours security shall smile,
And bless thine evening walk and morning toil.[43]
  Prepare for death, if here at night you roam,
And sign your will before you sup from home.
Some fiery fop, with new commission vain,[44]
Who sleeps on brambles[45] till he kills his man;
Some frolic drunkard, reeling from a feast,
Provokes a broil, and stabs you for a jest.
Yet even these heroes, mischievously gay,
Lords of the street, and terrors of the way;
Flushed as they are with folly, youth, and wine,
Their prudent insults to the poor confine;
Afar they mark the flambeau's bright approach,[46]
And shun the shining train,[47] and golden coach.
  In vain, these dangers past, your doors you close,
And hope the balmy blessings of repose:
Cruel with guilt, and daring with despair,
The midnight murderer bursts the faithless bar;
Invades the sacred hour of silent rest,
And leaves, unseen, a dagger in your breast.

37. Vessels made of silver or gold, possibly plated ones.
38. Mount up.
39. Theater.
40. Rivers in the western and northern English countryside.
41. Views.
42. Basements.
43. "Oi" was usually pronounced "i," as in "line."
44. A newly commissioned army officer.
45. That is, sleeps uneasily.
46. The rich were lighted on their way home by servants or linkboys carrying torches (flambeaux).
47. Retinue.

Scarce can our fields, such crowds at Tyburn[48] die,
With hemp the gallows and the fleet supply.
Propose your schemes, ye Senatorian band,
Whose Ways and Means[49] support the sinking land;
Lest ropes be wanting in the tempting spring,
To rig another convoy for the k——g.[50]
A single jail, in Alfred's golden reign,[51]
Could half the nation's criminals contain;
Fair justice then, without constraint adored,
Held high the steady scale, but dropped the sword;
No spies were paid, no special juries[52] known,
Blessed age! but ah! how different from our own!
Much could I add,—but see the boat at hand,
The tide retiring, calls me from the land:
Farewell!—When youth, and health, and fortune spent,
Thou fly'st for refuge to the wilds of Kent;[53]
And tired like me with follies and with crimes,
In angry numbers[54] warn'st succeeding times;
Then shall thy friend, nor thou[55] refuse his aid,
Still foe to vice, forsake his Cambrian shade;
In virtue's cause once more exert his rage,[56]
Thy satire point,[57] and animate thy page.

Prologue to Garrick's *Lethe*[1]

Prodigious madness of the writing race!
Ardent of fame, yet fearless of disgrace.
Without a boding tear, or anxious sigh,
The bard obdurate sees his brother die.
Deaf to the critic, sullen to the friend,
Not one takes warning by another's end.

48. The customary place of execution in eighteenth-century London.

49. "A cant term in the House of Commons for methods of raising money" (Johnson's note).

50. George II, also Elector of Hanover (in Germany), visited it often.

51. Alfred the Great, King of the West Saxons (A.D. 849–899).

52. Juries selected from the prosperous, who tended to be repressive.

53. Perhaps meaning the Weald (sometimes spelled "Wild") of Kent, a large wooded area also covering part of Surrey and Sussex.

54. Verses.

55. If you do not.

56. Strong inspiration.

57. Sharpen.

1. *Lethe,* a comedy, was first produced in 1740, at the Drury Lane Theater. David Garrick (1717–79) had been Johnson's pupil. He became the greatest of all English actors.

Oft has our bard[2] in this disastrous year
Beheld the tragic heroes taught to fear.
Oft has he seen the poignant orange fly[3]
And heard th'ill-omened catcall's[4] direful cry.
Yet dares to venture on the dangerous stage
And weakly hopes to 'scape the critic's rage.
This night he hopes to show that farce may charm,
Though no lewd hint the mantling[5] virgin warm.
That useful truth with humor may unite,
That mirth may mend,[6] and innocence delight.

Prologue Spoken at the Opening of the Theater in Drury Lane, 1747[1]

When Learning's triumph o'er her barbarous foes
First reared the stage,[2] immortal Shakespeare rose;
Each change of many-colored life he drew,
Exhausted worlds, and then imagined new:
Existence saw him spurn her bounded reign,
And panting Time toiled after him in vain:
His powerful strokes presiding truth impressed,
And unresisted Passion stormed the breast.
Then Jonson came, instructed from the school,
To please in method, and invent by rule;
His studious patience, and laborious art,
By regular approach essayed the heart;[3]
Cold Approbation gave the lingering bays,[4]
For those who durst not censure, scarce could praise.
A mortal born he met the general doom,
But left, like Egypt's kings, a lasting tomb.
The wits of Charles[5] found easier ways to fame,

2. Garrick.
3. Oranges, sold in the theaters, sometimes turned into missiles.
4. A kind of whistle, used especially in the theater to express disapproval.
5. Blushing.
6. Amend.

1. The Drury Lane Theater was reopened in 1747 with David Garrick as joint manager.
2. At the Renaissance.
3. The plays of Ben Jonson (?1572–1637) were conventionally regarded as based on classical models and constructed by learning and art.
4. The laurel wreath symbolizing the poet, and in Jonson's case the Poet Laureate.
5. Dramatists of the Restoration period (1660–1700). Charles II ruled from 1660 to 1685.

Nor wished for Jonson's art, or Shakespeare's flame;
Themselves they studied, as they felt, they writ,
Intrigue was plot, obscenity was wit.
Vice always found a sympathetic friend;
They pleased their age, and did not aim to mend.[6]
Yet bards like these aspired to lasting praise,
And proudly hoped to pimp in future days.
Their cause was general, their supports were strong,
Their slaves were willing, and their reign was long;
Till Shame regained the post that Sense betrayed,
And Virtue called Oblivion to her aid.
  Then crushed by rules, and weakened as refined,
For years the power of Tragedy declined;
From bard to bard, the frigid caution crept,
Till Declamation roared, while Passion slept.[7]
Yet still did Virtue deign the stage to tread,
Philosophy remained, though Nature fled.
But forced at length her ancient reign to quit,
She saw great *Faustus* lay the ghost of wit:[8]
Exulting Folly hailed the joyful day,
And pantomime and song confirmed her sway.
But who the coming changes can presage,
And mark the future periods of the stage?—
Perhaps if skill could distant times explore,
New Behns, new D'Urfeys,[9] yet remain in store.
Perhaps, where Lear has raved, and Hamlet died,
On flying cars new sorcerers may ride.[10]
Perhaps, for who can guess th' effects of chance?
Here Hunt may box, or Mahomet may dance.[11]
  Hard is his lot that here by fortune placed
Must watch the wild vicissitudes of taste;
With every meteor of caprice must play,
And chase the new-blown bubbles of the day.
Ah! let not censure term our fate our choice,
The stage but echoes back the public voice.
The drama's laws the drama's patrons give,
For we that live to please, must please to live.

6. Amend, reform.

7. A reference to cold, classical tragedies, like Addison's *Cato* (1713).

8. Perhaps *Harlequin Doctor Faustus* (1723), one of many farces which emphasized spectacle rather than plot, character, thought, or language.

9. Aphra Behn (1640–89) and Tom D'Urfey (1653–1723) were minor dramatists who wrote ribald comedies and farces.

10. One of the spectacular effects characteristic of contemporary farce. "Cars" are chariots.

11. Edward Hunt was a boxer, Mahomet a rope dancer.

Then prompt no more the follies you decry,
As tyrants doom their tools of guilt to die,
'Tis yours this night to bid the reign commence
Of rescued Nature and reviving Sense;
To chase[12] the charms of sound, the pomp of show,
For useful mirth, and salutary woe;
Bid scenic Virtue form the rising age,
And Truth diffuse her radiance from the stage.

The Vanity of Human Wishes

The Tenth Satire of Juvenal Imitated

Let observation with extensive view,
Survey mankind, from China to Peru;
Remark each anxious toil, each eager strife,
And watch the busy scenes of crowded life;
Then say how hope and fear, desire and hate,
O'erspread with snares the clouded maze of fate,
Where wavering man, betrayed by venturous pride,
To tread the dreary paths without a guide,
As treacherous phantoms in the mist delude,
Shuns fancied ills, or chases airy[1] good;
How rarely reason guides the stubborn choice,
Rules the bold hand, or prompts the suppliant voice;
How nations sink, by darling schemes oppressed,
When vengeance listens to the fool's request.[2]
Fate wings with every wish th' afflictive dart,
Each gift of nature, and each grace of art,
With fatal heat impetuous courage glows,
With fatal sweetness elocution flows,
Impeachment stops the speaker's powerful breath,
And restless fire precipitates on[3] death.
But scarce observed, the knowing and the bold
Fall in the general massacre of gold;
Wide-wasting pest! that rages unconfined,
And crowds with crimes the records of mankind;
For gold his sword the hireling ruffian draws,
For gold the hireling judge distorts the laws;
Wealth heaped on wealth, nor truth nor safety buys,
The dangers gather as the treasures rise.

12. Chase away.
1. Imaginary.
2. Foolish wishes carry inherent destruction in their fulfillment.
3. Plunges into, or, hurls him upon.

Let history tell where rival kings command,
And dubious title shakes the madded land,
When statutes glean the refuse of the sword,[4]
How much more safe the vassal than the lord;
Low skulks the hind[5] beneath the rage of power,
And leaves the wealthy traitor in the Tower,[6]
Untouched his cottage, and his slumbers sound,
Though confiscation's vultures hover round.
The needy traveler, serene and gay,
Walks the wild heath, and sings his toil away.
Does envy seize thee? crush th' upbraiding joy,
Increase his riches and his peace destroy;
Now fears in dire vicissitude[7] invade,
The rustling brake[8] alarms, and quivering shade,
Nor light nor darkness bring his pain relief,
One shows the plunder, and one hides the thief.
Yet still one general cry the skies assails,
And gain and grandeur load the tainted gales;[9]
Few know the toiling statesman's fear or care,
Th' insidious rival and the gaping heir.
Once more, Democritus,[10] arise on earth,
With cheerful wisdom and instructive mirth,
See motley[11] life in modern trappings dressed,
And feed with varied fools th' eternal jest:
Thou who couldst laugh where want enchained caprice,
Toil crushed conceit, and man was of a piece;
Where wealth unloved without a mourner died,
And scarce a sycophant was fed by pride;
Where ne'er was known the form of mock debate,
Or seen a new-made mayor's unwieldy state;
Where change of favorites made no change of laws,
And senates heard before they judged a cause;
How wouldst thou shake at Britain's modish tribe,
Dart the quick taunt, and edge the piercing gibe!
Attentive truth and nature to descry,[12]

4. When laws confiscate or destroy whatever war has missed.
5. Farm laborer, rustic.
6. Persons accused of treason were often imprisoned in the Tower of London.
7. Alternation.
8. Bushes, thicket.
9. The air is tainted with the voice or breath of greed and ambition.
10. Greek philosopher (5th century B.C.), sometimes known as the "laughing philosopher."
11. Parti-colored clothes worn by a clown or fool.
12. Discern.

And pierce each scene with philosophic eye.
To thee were solemn toys or empty show,
The robes of pleasure and the veils of woe:
All aid the farce, and all thy mirth maintain,
Whose joys are causeless, or whose griefs are vain.
   Such was the scorn that filled the sage's mind,
Renewed at every glance on humankind;
How just that scorn ere yet thy voice declare,[13]
Search every state, and canvass[14] every prayer.
   Unnumbered suppliants crowd preferment's gate,[15]
Athirst for wealth, and burning to be great;
Delusive fortune hears th' incessant call,
They mount, they shine, evaporate, and fall.
On every stage the foes of peace attend,
Hate dogs their flight, and insult mocks their end.
Love ends with hope, the sinking statesman's door
Pours in the morning worshipper no more:
For growing names the weekly scribbler[16] lies,
To growing wealth the dedicator flies,
From every room descends the painted face,
That hung the bright palladium[17] of the place,
And smoked in kitchens, or in auctions sold,
To better features yields the frame of gold;
For now no more we trace in every line
Heroic worth, benevolence divine:
The form distorted justifies the fall,
And detestation rids th' indignant wall.
   But will not Britain hear the last appeal,
Sign her foes' doom, or guard her favorites' zeal?
Through freedom's sons no more remonstrance rings,
Degrading nobles and controlling kings;
Our supple tribes[18] repress their patriot[19] throats,
And ask no questions but the price of votes;
With weekly libels and septennial ale,[20]

13. Before you venture to say.

14. Scrutinize.

15. The entrance to preferment (government position or advance in rank.)

16. Hired journalist.

17. Guardian portrait. The Palladium was the statue of the goddess Pallas Athena, which safeguarded Troy.

18. Voters. In Rome, the tribe was a voting unit.

19. The Patriots originally were members of the Parliamentary Opposition, which had almost disappeared at this time.

20. A Parliamentary election had to be held within seven years of the previous one. It was common to bribe voters with food and drink, as well as money, during elections.

Their wish is full to riot and to rail.
  In full-blown dignity, see Wolsey[21] stand,
Law in his voice, and fortune in his hand:
To him the church, the realm, their powers consign,
Through him the rays of regal bounty shine,
Turned by his nod the stream of honor flows,[22]
His smile alone security bestows:
Still to new heights his restless wishes tower,
Claim leads to claim, and power advances power;
Till conquest unresisted ceased to please,
And rights submitted, left him none to seize.
At length his sovereign frowns—the train[23] of state
Mark the keen glance, and watch the sign to hate.
Where'er he turns he meets a stranger's eye,
His suppliants scorn him, and his followers fly;
At once is lost the pride of aweful state,
The golden canopy, the glittering plate,
The regal palace, the luxurious board,
The liveried army, and the menial lord.
With age, with cares, with maladies oppressed,
He seeks the refuge of monastic rest.
Grief aids disease, remembered folly stings,
And his last sighs reproach the faith of kings.[24]
  Speak thou, whose thoughts at humble peace repine,
Shall Wolsey's wealth, with Wolsey's end be thine?
Or liv'st thou now, with safer pride content,
The wisest justice on the banks of Trent?[25]
For why did Wolsey near the steeps[26] of fate,
On weak foundations raise th' enormous weight?
Why but to sink beneath misfortune's blow,
With louder ruin[27] to the gulfs below?
  What gave great Villiers to th' assassin's knife,
And fixed disease on Harley's closing life?

21. The career of Cardinal Wolsey (1475–1530) under Henry VIII was a model of the rise and fall of a great statesman.

22. The king is still called "the fount of honor," i.e. of peerages, etc.

23. Retinue.

24. In Shakespeare's and perhaps Fletcher's *Henry VIII,* Wolsey says,
"Had I but served my God with half the zeal
I served my king, he would not in mine age
Have left me naked to mine enemies" (III. ii. 455–57).

25. Justice of the Peace on the banks of the Trent river in northern England.

26. Precipices.

27. Literally, fall (Latin, *ruina*).

What murdered Wentworth, and what exiled Hyde,[28]
By kings protected, and to kings allied?
What but their wish indulged in courts to shine,
And power too great to keep, or to resign?
When first the college rolls receive his name,
The young enthusiast quits his ease for fame;
Through all his veins the fever of renown
Burns from the strong contagion of the gown;[29]
O'er Bodley's dome[30] his future labors spread,
And Bacon's mansion trembles o'er his head.[31]
Are these thy views? proceed, illustrious youth,
And virtue guard thee to the throne of Truth!
Yet should thy soul indulge the generous[32] heat,
Till captive Science[33] yields her last retreat;
Should Reason guide thee with her brightest ray,
And pour on misty Doubt resistless day;
Should no false Kindness lure to loose delight,
Nor Praise relax,[34] nor Difficulty fright;
Should tempting Novelty thy cell refrain,[35]
And Sloth effuse her opiate fumes in vain;
Should Beauty blunt on fops her fatal dart,
Nor claim the triumph of a lettered heart;
Should no disease thy torpid veins invade,
Nor Melancholy's phantoms haunt thy shade;[36]
Yet hope not life from grief or danger free,
Nor think the doom of man reversed for thee:

28. George Villiers, first Duke of Buckingham (1592–1628), was a favorite of James I. Responsible for repeated failures in military and foreign policy, he was stabbed fatally at Portsmouth by an army officer. Robert Harley, first Earl of Oxford (1661–1724), was a leading minister under Queen Anne (ruled 1702–14), and was disgraced under her successor, George I. Thomas Wentworth, first Earl of Strafford (1593–1641), chief adviser to Charles I, was executed at the instigation of the Parliamentary party. Edward Hyde, first Earl of Clarendon (1609–1674), Lord Chancellor under Charles II and father-in-law of the future James II, was impeached in 1667 by Parliament and fled to France.

29. Boswell noted the subdued allusion here to the fate of Hercules, who died when he put on a poisoned shirt.

30. The Bodleian Library, Oxford's main library. "Dome" means building.

31. "There is a tradition that the study of Friar Bacon, built on an arch over the bridge [Folly Bridge at Oxford, demolished in 1779], will fall, when a man greater than Bacon shall pass under it" (Johnson's note). Roger Bacon (? 1214–94) was a noted philosopher and scientist.

32. Noble, admirable.

33. Learning, knowledge.

34. Enfeeble.

35. Stay away from.

36. Obscurity, retirement.

Deign on the passing world to turn thine eyes,
And pause awhile from letters, to be wise;
There mark what ills the scholar's life assail,
Toil, envy, want, the patron, and the jail.
See nations slowly wise, and meanly just,
To buried merit raise the tardy bust.[37]
If dreams yet flatter, once again attend,
Hear Lydiat's life, and Galileo's end.[38]
  Nor deem, when learning her last prize bestows,
The glittering eminence exempt from foes;
See when the vulgar 'scape, despised or awed,
Rebellion's vengeful talons seize on Laud.[39]
From meaner minds, though smaller fines content,[40]
The plundered palace or sequestered rent;
Marked out by dangerous parts[41] he meets the shock,
And fatal Learning leads him to the block:
Around his tomb let Art and Genius weep,
But hear his death, ye blockheads, hear and sleep.
  The festal blazes, the triumphal show,
The ravished standard, and the captive foe,
The senate's thanks, the gazette's pompous tale,
With force resistless o'er the brave prevail.
Such bribes the rapid Greek[42] o'er Asia whirled,
For such the steady Romans shook the world;
For such in distant lands the Britons shine,
And stain with blood the Danube or the Rhine;[43]
This power has praise, that virtue scarce can warm,[44]
Till fame supplies the universal charm.
Yet reason frowns on war's unequal game,
Where wasted nations raise a single name,
And mortgaged states their grandsires' wreaths[45] regret,
From age to age in everlasting debt;
Wreaths which at last the dear-bought right convey

37. A conspicuous example was the bust of Milton, which was placed in Westminster Abbey in 1737, over sixty years after his death.

38. Thomas Lydiat (1572–1646), a distinguished mathematician, was imprisoned for debt. Galileo's brilliant discoveries in astronomy and physics made trouble for him with the Inquisition, and he spent the last years of his life in prescribed seclusion.

39. William Laud, Archbishop of Canterbury (1573–1645), was executed for treason by Parliament. He was noted for his claims in behalf of the Church of England, his persecution of the Dissenters, and his learning.

40. Less distinguished men escape with milder punishments.

41. Abilities.

42. Alexander the Great.

43. In the wars against France and other nations in the first half of the eighteenth century.

44. Praise has (as a rouser of men) a power that virtue lacks.

45. Of triumph.

To rust on medals, or on stones decay.
  On what foundation stands the warrior's pride,
How just his hopes let Swedish Charles[46] decide;
A frame of adamant, a soul of fire,
No dangers fright him, and no labors tire;
O'er love, o'er fear, extends his wide domain,
Unconquered lord of pleasure and of pain;
No joys to him pacific scepters yield,
War sounds the trump, he rushes to the field;
Behold surrounding kings their power combine,
And one capitulate, and one resign;[47]
Peace courts his hand, but spreads her charms in vain;
"Think nothing gained," he cries, "till nought remain,
"On Moscow's walls till Gothic[48] standards fly,
"And all be mine beneath the polar sky."
The march begins in military state,
And nations on his eye suspended wait;
Stern Famine guards the solitary coast,
And Winter barricades the realms of Frost;
He comes, not want and cold his course delay;—
Hide, blushing Glory, hide Pultowa's day:[49]
The vanquished hero leaves his broken bands,
And show his miseries in distant lands;
Condemned a needy supplicant to wait,
While ladies interpose, and slaves debate.[50]
But did not Chance at length her error mend?
Did no subverted[51] empire mark his end?
Did rival monarchs give the fatal wound?
Or hostile millions press him to the ground?
His fall was destined to a barren strand,
A petty fortress, and a dubious hand;[52]
He left the name, at which the world grew pale,
To point a moral, or adorn a tale.
  All times their scenes of pompous woes afford,

46. Charles XII of Sweden (1682–1718), known as the "Alexander of the North."

47. Frederick IV of Denmark "capitulated" (yielded on stipulated terms) in 1700. Augustus II of Poland was deposed in 1705 in favor of Charles's nominee, but regained the crown four years later.

48. Swedish. Sweden was considered the original land of the "Goths," a name used for all the Germanic nations.

49. Peter the Great of Russia defeated Charles at Pultowa (Poltava, in the Ukraine) in 1709. The winter of 1708–09 was remarkable for its coldness.

50. Charles took refuge in Turkey for a number of years. Voltaire's popular *History of Charles XII* (1731) supplies the details of Charles's stay there.

51. Overthrown.

52. Charles was killed at the siege of Fredericksten in Norway, probably by the enemy; contemporaries thought he had been shot by one of his own men.

From Persia's tyrant to Bavaria's lord.[53]
In gay hostility, and barbarous pride,
With half mankind embattled at his side,
Great Xerxes comes to seize the certain prey,
And starves exhausted regions in his way;
Attendant Flattery counts his myriads o'er,
Till counted myriads soothe his pride no more;
Fresh praise is tried till madness fires his mind,
The waves he lashes, and enchains the wind;
New powers are claimed, new powers are still bestowed,
Till rude resistance lops the spreading god;
The daring Greeks deride the martial show,
And heap their valleys with the gaudy foe;
Th' insulted sea with humbler thoughts he gains,
A single skiff to speed his flight remains;
Th' incumbered oar scarce leaves the dreaded coast
Through purple billows and a floating host.[54]
   The bold Bavarian in a luckless hour,
Tries the dread summits of Caesarean power,
With unexpected legions bursts away,
And sees defenseless realms receive his sway;
Short sway! fair Austria spreads her mournful charms,
The queen, the beauty, sets the world in arms;
From hill to hill the beacon's rousing blaze
Spreads wide the hope of plunder and of praise;
The fierce Croatian, and the wild Hussar,
And all the sons of ravage crowd the war;
The baffled prince in honor's flattering bloom
Of hasty greatness finds the fatal doom,
His foes' derision, and his subjects' blame,
And steals to death from anguish and from shame.[55]
   Enlarge my life with multitude of days,
In health, in sickness, thus the suppliant prays;
Hides from himself his state, and shuns to know,
That life protracted is protracted woe.
Time hovers o'er, impatient to destroy,

53. Xerxes (?519–465 B.C.) and Charles Albert, Elector of Bavaria (1697–1745).

54. Xerxes' invasion of Greece was decisively checked at the naval battle of Salamis (480 B.C.) and his army defeated at Platea in the following year. When his bridge of boats across the Hellespont broke down, he is supposed to have ordered chains thrown into the water and the waves whipped.

55. During the war of the Austrian Succession (1740–48) Charles Albert, Elector of Bavaria, was elected Holy Roman Emperor as Charles VII. His principal antagonist, Maria Theresa of Austria, roused her subjects, especially those she governed as Queen of Hungary—"Hussars" are Hungarian light cavalry—and after some initial successes Charles Albert lost his own Bavaria to Austrian troops. He spent the rest of his life mainly as a puppet ruler and refugee.

And shuts up all the passages of joy:
In vain their gifts the bounteous seasons pour,
The fruit autumnal, and the vernal flower,
With listless eyes the dotard views the store,[56]
He views, and wonders that they please no more;
Now pall the tasteless meats and joyless wines,
And Luxury[57] with sighs her slave resigns.
Approach, ye minstrels, try the soothing strain,
Diffuse the tuneful lenitives[58] of pain:
No sounds, alas, would touch th' impervious ear,
Though dancing mountains witnessed Orpheus near;[59]
Nor lute nor lyre his feeble powers attend,[60]
Nor sweeter music of a virtuous friend,
But everlasting dictates[61] crowd his tongue,
Perversely grave, or positively wrong.
The still returning tale, and lingering jest,
Perplex the fawning niece and pampered guest,
While growing hopes scarce awe the gathering sneer,
And scarce a legacy can bribe to hear;
The watchful guests still hint the last[62] offense,
The daughter's petulance, the son's expense,
Improve[63] his heady rage with treacherous skill,
And mold his passions till they make his will.
  Unnumbered maladies his joints invade,
Lay siege to life and press the dire blockade;
But unextinguished avarice still remains,
And dreaded losses aggravate his pains;
He turns, with anxious heart and crippled hands,
His bonds of debt, and mortgages of lands;
Or views his coffers with suspicious eyes,
Unlocks his gold, and counts it till he dies.
  But grant the virtues of a temperate prime,[64]
Bless with an age exempt from scorn or crime;
An age that melts with unperceived decay,
And glides in modest innocence away;
Whose peaceful day Benevolence endears,
Whose night congratulating Conscience cheers;

56. Stored-up belongings or wealth.
57. Addiction to pleasure.
58. Softeners.
59. The mythological Orpheus was supposed to move mountains by the power of his music.
60. Pay attention to.
61. Authoritarian pronouncements.
62. Latest.
63. Employ to advantage, increase.
64. Prime of life.

The general favorite as the general friend:
Such age there is, and who shall wish its end?
  Yet even on this her load Misfortune flings,
To press the weary minutes' flagging wings:
New sorrow rises as the day returns,
A sister sickens, or a daughter mourns.
Now kindred Merit fills the sable bier,
Now lacerated Friendship claims a tear.
Year chases year, decay pursues decay,
Still drops some joy from withering life away;
New forms arise, and different views engage,
Superfluous lags the veteran on the stage,
Till pitying Nature signs the last release,
And bids afflicted worth retire to peace.
  But few there are whom hours like these await,
Who set unclouded in the gulfs of fate.
From Lydia's monarch should the search descend,
By Solon cautioned to regard his end,[65]
In life's last scene what prodigies[66] surprise,
Fears of the brave, and follies of the wise?
From Marlborough's eyes the streams of dotage flow,
And Swift expires a driveler and a show.[67]
  The teeming mother, anxious for her race,
Begs for each birth the fortune of a face:
Yet Vane could tell what ills from beauty spring;
And Sedley cursed the form that pleased a king.[68]
Ye nymphs of rosy lips and radiant eyes,
Whom pleasure keeps too busy to be wise,
Whom joys with soft varieties invite,
By day the frolic, and the dance by night,
Who frown with vanity, who smile with art,
And ask the latest fashion of the heart,
What care, what rules your heedless charms shall save,
Each nymph your rival, and each youth your slave?

65. The Athenian, Solon, warned Croesus, the wealthy king of Lydia, that no man should think he had led a happy life until it ended. Croesus was later overthrown by Cyrus, king of the Persians.

66. Extraordinary or monstrous events.

67. The great Duke of Marlborough (see p. 49 n. 23) suffered two strokes in 1716 and was much enfeebled until his death in 1722. Swift was senile during his last few years; it is reported that his head was stripped of hair in an hour after his death by souvenir hunters who bribed his servants.

68. Anne Vane (1705–36), mistress of Frederick, Prince of Wales. Catherine Sedley (1657–1717), mistress of James, Duke of York (later James II). Though James made her Countess of Dorchester in 1686, she soon lost her influence with him.

Against your fame with fondness hate combines,
The rival batters, and the lover mines.
With distant voice neglected Virtue calls,
Less heard and less, the faint remonstrance falls;
Tired with contempt, she quits the slippery reign,
And Pride and Prudence take her seat in vain.
In crowd at once, where none the pass defend,
The harmless Freedom,[69] and the private Friend.
The guardians yield, by force superior plied;
By Interest,[70] Prudence; and by Flattery, Pride.
Now beauty falls betrayed, despised, distressed,
And hissing Infamy proclaims the rest.
  Where then shall hope and fear their objects find?
Must dull suspense corrupt the stagnant mind?
Must helpless man, in ignorance sedate,[71]
Roll darkling[72] down the torrent of his fate?
Must no dislike alarm, no wishes rise,
No cries attempt the mercies of the skies?
Inquirer, cease, petitions yet remain,
Which heaven may hear, nor deem religion vain.
Still raise for good the supplicating voice,
But leave to heaven the measure and the choice,
Safe in His power, whose eyes discern afar
The secret ambush of a specious prayer.
Implore His aid, in His decisions rest,
Secure whate'er He gives, He gives the best.
Yet when the sense of sacred presence fires,
And strong devotion to the skies aspires,
Pour forth thy fervors for a healthful mind,
Obedient passions, and a will resigned;
For love, which scarce collective man can fill;[73]
For patience sovereign o'er transmuted ill;[74]
For faith, that panting for a happier seat,
Counts death kind Nature's signal of retreat:
These goods for man the laws of heaven ordain,
These goods He grants, who grants the power to gain;
With these celestial wisdom calms the mind,
And makes the happiness she does not find.

69. Some deviation from strict virtue.
70. Self-interest.
71. Settled, complacent.
72. In the dark.
73. Love which knows a greater object than collective mankind—i.e. God(?).
74. Patience which can transform (or transcend) evils—i.e. make them bearable.

A New Prologue Spoken at the Representation of *Comus*[1]

Ye patriot crowds, who burn for England's fame,
Ye nymphs, whose bosoms beat at Milton's name,
Whose generous zeal, unbought by flattering rhymes,
Shames the mean pensions of Augustan times;[2]
Immortal patrons of succeeding days,
Attend this prelude of perpetual praise!
Let Wit, condemned the feeble war to wage
With close[3] malevolence, or public rage;
Let Study, worn with virtue's fruitless lore,[4]
Behold this theater, and grieve no more.
This night, distinguished by your smile, shall tell,
That never Briton can in vain excel;
The slighted arts futurity shall trust,
And rising ages hasten to be just.
At length our mighty bard's victorious lays[5]
Fill the loud voice of universal praise,
And baffled spite, with hopeless anguish dumb,
Yields to renown the centuries to come.
With ardent haste, each candidate of fame
Ambitious catches at his towering name:
He sees, and pitying sees, vain wealth bestow
Those pageant honors which he scorned below:
While crowds aloft the laureate bust behold,
Or trace his form on circulating gold,[6]
Unknown, unheeded, long his offspring lay,
And want hung threatening o'er her slow decay.
What though she shine with no Miltonian fire,
No favoring muse her morning dreams inspire;[7]
Yet softer claims the melting heart engage,
Her youth laborious, and her blameless age:

1. In 1750, Johnson discovered that Milton's one surviving grandchild, Elizabeth Foster, was struggling to make ends meet in a small grocery shop in London. He persuaded Garrick to stage a benefit performance of Milton's masque *Comus* for her and to speak this "Prologue," which Johnson wrote to introduce the performance.

2. Under the Emperor Augustus (63 B.C.–A.D. 14) the greatest poets, Horace and Virgil, paid in flattery for his patronage. British writers in the early eighteenth century often compared themselves to Roman ones.

3. Hidden.

4. Learning.

5. Songs.

6. A commemorative medal was engraved at the same time Milton's bust was placed in Westminster Abbey in 1737.

7. Milton composed many lines of poetry in his head during the night and early morning, before the arrival of the persons to whom he dictated his last great poems.

Hers the mild merits of domestic life,
The patient sufferer, and the faithful wife.
Thus graced with humble virtue's native charms
Her grandsire leaves her in Britannia's arms,
Secure with peace, with competence,[8] to dwell,
While tutelary[9] nations guard her cell.
Yours is the charge, ye fair, ye wise, ye brave!
'Tis yours to crown desert—beyond the grave!

Prologue to *The Good-Natured Man*[1]

Pressed by the load of life, the weary mind
Surveys the general toil of human kind;
With cool submission joins the laboring train,
And social sorrow loses half its pain:
Our anxious bard,[2] without complaint, may share
This bustling season's epidemic care,
Like Caesar's pilot, dignified by fate,
Tossed in one common storm with all the great;[3]
Distressed alike, the statesman and the wit,
When one a borough courts, and one the pit.[4]
The busy candidates for power and fame,
Have hopes, and fears, and wishes, just the same;
Disabled both to combat, or to fly,
Must hear all taunts, and hear without reply.
Unchecked on both, loud rabbles vent their rage,
As mongrels bay the lion in a cage.
Th' offended burgess[5] hoards his angry tale,
For that blest year when all that vote may rail;
Their schemes of spite the poet's foes dismiss,
Till that glad night when all that hate may hiss.
This day the powdered curls and golden coat,
Says swelling Crispin, begged a cobbler's vote.[6]

8. Enough money to live on.

9. Guardian.

1. Johnson wrote this "Prologue" to help promote Goldsmith's *The Good-Natured Man*, which was produced at Covent Garden Theater in January 1768.

2. Oliver Goldsmith (?1730–74).

3. Julius Caesar forced the pilot of a small boat to cross the Adriatic on a stormy night (Lucan, *Pharsalia*, v. 531–721).

4. A general election was about to be held. The theater "pit" corresponded to modern orchestra seats, though the pit was comparatively cheaper to sit in and its audience more vocal.

5. Voter in a borough (town).

6. The cobbler (his patron saint was Saint Crispin) boasts that the aristocrat had to beg for his vote.

This night our wit, the pert apprentice cries,
Lies at my feet, I hiss him, and he dies.
The great, 'tis true, can charm th' electing tribe;
The bard may supplicate, but cannot bribe.
Yet judged by those, whose voices ne'er were sold,
He feels no want of ill-persuading gold;
But confident of praise, if praise be due,
Trusts without fear, to merit, and to you.

A Short Song of Congratulation[1]

Long-expected one and twenty
  Lingering year at last is flown,
Pomp and pleasure, pride and plenty,
  Great Sir John, are all your own.

Loosened from the minor's tether,
  Free to mortgage or to sell,
Wild as wind, and light as feather,
  Bid the slaves of thrift farewell.

Call the Bettys, Kates, and Jennys,
  Every name that laughs at care,
Lavish of your grandsire's guineas,
  Show the spirit of an heir.

All that prey on vice and folly
  Joy to see their quarry fly,
Here the gamester[2] light and jolly,
  There the lender grave and sly.

Wealth, Sir John, was made to wander,
  Let it wander as it will;
See the jockey, see the pander,
  Bid them come, and take their fill.

When the bonny blade[3] carouses,
  Pockets full, and spirits high,

1. The poem celebrates the twenty-first birthday of Sir John Lade, nephew to Johnson's friends, the Thrales. Johnson enclosed it in a letter to Mrs. Thrale in 1780, asking her not to show it to anyone. It was only published after his death. The poem proved to be prophetic: Lade soon ran through the large fortune he inherited.
2. Gambler.
3. Cheerful man about town.

What are acres? What are houses?
  Only dirt, or wet or dry.

If the guardian or the mother
  Tell the woes of willful waste,
Scorn their counsel and their pother,[4]
  You can hang or drown at last.

On the Death of Dr. Robert Levett[1]

Condemned to hope's delusive mine,
  As on we toil from day to day,
By sudden blasts, or slow decline,
  Our social comforts drop away.

Well tried through many a varying year,
  See Levett to the grave descend;
Officious,[2] innocent, sincere,
  Of every friendless name the friend.

Yet still he fills affection's eye,
  Obscurely[3] wise, and coarsely kind;
Nor, lettered[4] arrogance, deny
  Thy praise to merit unrefined.

When fainting nature called for aid,
  And hovering death prepared the blow,
His vigorous remedy displayed
  The power of art without the show.

In misery's darkest caverns known,
  His useful care was ever nigh,
Where hopeless anguish poured his groan,
  And lonely want retired to die.

No summons mocked by chill delay,
  No petty gain disdained by pride,
The modest wants of every day
  The toil of every day supplied.

4. Fussing, noise.

1. Robert Levett was an obscure practitioner of medicine among the London poor. In his later years he became (1763) a member of Johnson's household, joining the group of friends already dependent on Johnson. He died in 1782, at the age of 76.

2. Quick to be helpful.

3. Without notice, quietly.

4. Educated.

His virtues walked their narrow round,
  Nor made a pause, nor left a void;
And sure th' Eternal Master found
  The single talent well employed.[5]

The busy day, the peaceful night,
  Unfelt, uncounted, glided by;
His frame was firm, his powers were bright,
  Though now his eightieth year was nigh.

Then with no throbbing fiery pain,
  No cold gradations of decay,
Death broke at once the vital chain,
  And freed his soul the nearest way.

5. Johnson alludes to the parable of the talents (Matthew 25: 14–30), in which Jesus commends those who use properly the abilities God has given them.

The History of Rasselas,

Prince of Abyssinia

I

Description of a Palace in a Valley

Ye who listen with credulity to the whispers of fancy, and pursue with eagerness the phantoms of hope; who expect that age will perform the promises of youth, and that the deficiencies of the present day will be supplied by the morrow; attend to the history of Rasselas[1] prince of Abyssinia.

Rasselas was the fourth son of the mighty emperor in whose dominions the Father of Waters[2] begins his course; whose bounty pours down the streams of plenty, and scatters over half the world the harvests of Egypt.

According to the custom which has descended from age to age among the monarchs of the torrid zone, Rasselas was confined in a private palace, with the other sons and daughters of Abyssinian royalty, till the order of succession should call him to the throne.

The place, which the wisdom or policy of antiquity had destined for the residence of the Abyssinian princes, was a spacious valley in the kingdom of Amhara, surrounded on every side by mountains, of which the summits overhang the middle part. The only passage by which it could be entered was a cavern that passed under a rock, of which it has long been disputed whether it was the work of nature or of human industry. The outlet of the cavern was concealed by a thick wood, and the mouth which opened into the valley was closed with gates of iron, forged by the artificers of ancient days, so massy that no man could, without the help of engines, open or shut them.

From the mountains on every side, rivulets descended that filled all

1. *Rasselas* is derived from *ras,* which means "chief" in Amharic. The word appears in Father Jerome Lobo's *Voyage to Abyssinia,* translated by Johnson in 1735.

2. The Nile.

the valley with verdure and fertility, and formed a lake in the middle inhabited by fish of every species, and frequented by every fowl whom nature has taught to dip the wing in water. This lake discharged its superfluities by a stream which entered a dark cleft of the mountain on the northern side, and fell with dreadful noise from precipice to precipice till it was heard no more.

The sides of the mountains were covered with trees, the banks of the brooks were diversified with flowers; every blast[3] shook spices from the rocks, and every month dropped fruits upon the ground. All animals that bite the grass, or browse the shrub, whether wild or tame, wandered in this extensive circuit, secured from beasts of prey by the mountains which confined them. On one part were flocks and herds feeding in the pastures, on another all the beasts of chase frisking in the lawns;[4] the sprightly kid was bounding on the rocks, the subtle[5] monkey frolicking in the trees, and the solemn elephant reposing in the shade. All the diversities of the world were brought together, the blessings of nature were collected, and its evils extracted and excluded.

The valley, wide and fruitful, supplied its inhabitants with the necessaries of life, and all delights and superfluities were added at the annual visit which the emperor paid his children, when the iron gate was opened to the sound of music; and during eight days every one that resided in the valley was required to propose whatever might contribute to make seclusion pleasant, to fill up the vacancies of attention, and lessen the tediousness of time. Every desire was immediately granted. All the artificers of pleasure were called to gladden the festivity; the musicians exerted the power of harmony, and the dancers showed their activity before the princes, in hope that they should pass their lives in this blissful captivity, to which these only were admitted whose performance was thought able to add novelty to luxury. Such was the appearance of security and delight which this retirement afforded that they to whom it was new always desired that it might be perpetual; and as those on whom the iron gate had once closed were never suffered to return, the effect of longer experience could not be known. Thus every year produced new schemes of delight, and new competitors for imprisonment.

The palace stood on an eminence raised about thirty paces above the surface of the lake. It was divided into many squares or courts, built with greater or less magnificence according to the rank of those for whom they were designed. The roofs were turned into arches of massy stone joined with a cement that grew harder by time, and the building stood from century to century, deriding the solstitial rains and equinoctial hurricanes, without need of reparation.

This house, which was so large as to be fully known to none but some

3. Gust of wind. 4. Meadows, glades. 5. Cunning.

ancient officers who successively inherited the secrets of the place, was built as if suspicion herself had dictated the plan. To every room there was an open and secret passage, every square had a communication with the rest, either from the upper stories by private galleries, or by subterranean passages from the lower apartments. Many of the columns had unsuspected cavities, in which a long race of monarchs had reposited their treasures. They then closed up the opening with marble, which was never to be removed but in the utmost exigencies of the kingdom; and recorded their accumulations in a book which was itself concealed in a tower not entered but by the emperor, attended by the prince who stood next in succession.

II

The Discontent of Rasselas in the Happy Valley

Here the sons and daughters of Abyssinia lived only to know the soft vicissitudes[6] of pleasure and repose, attended by all that were skillful to delight, and gratified with whatever the senses can enjoy. They wandered in gardens of fragrance, and slept in the fortresses of security. Every art was practiced to make them pleased with their own condition. The sages who instructed them told them of nothing but the miseries of public life, and described all beyond the mountains as regions of calamity, where discord was always raging, and where man preyed upon man.

To heighten their opinion of their own felicity, they were daily entertained with songs, the subject of which was the *happy valley*. Their appetites were excited by frequent enumerations of different enjoyments, and revelry and merriment was the business of every hour from the dawn of morning to the close of even.

These methods were generally successful; few of the princes had ever wished to enlarge their bounds, but passed their lives in full conviction that they had all within their reach that art or nature could bestow, and pitied those whom fate had excluded from this seat of tranquillity, as the sport of chance, and the slaves of misery.

Thus they rose in the morning and lay down at night, pleased with each other and with themselves, all but Rasselas, who, in the twenty-sixth year of his age, began to withdraw himself from their pastimes and assemblies, and to delight in solitary walks and silent meditation. He often sat before tables covered with luxury,[7] and forgot to taste the dainties that were placed before him: he rose abruptly in the midst of the song, and hastily retired beyond the sound of music. His attendants

6. Alternations. 7. Delicious food.

observed the change and endeavored to renew his love of pleasure: he neglected their officiousness, repulsed their invitations, and spent day after day on the banks of rivulets sheltered with trees, where he sometimes listened to the birds in the branches, sometimes observed the fish playing in the stream, and anon cast his eyes upon the pastures and mountains filled with animals, of which some were biting the herbage, and some sleeping among the bushes.

This singularity of his humor made him much observed. One of the sages, in whose conversation he had formerly delighted, followed him secretly, in hope of discovering the cause of his disquiet. Rasselas, who knew not that any one was near him, having for some time fixed his eyes upon the goats that were browsing among the rocks, began to compare their condition with his own.

"What," said he, "makes the difference between man and all the rest of the animal creation? Every beast that strays beside me has the same corporal necessities with myself; he is hungry and crops the grass, he is thirsty and drinks the stream, his thirst and hunger are appeased, he is satisfied and sleeps; he rises again and is hungry, he is again fed and is at rest. I am hungry and thirsty like him, but when thirst and hunger cease I am not at rest; I am, like him, pained with want, but am not, like him, satisfied with fullness. The intermediate hours are tedious and gloomy; I long again to be hungry that I may again quicken my attention. The birds peck the berries or the corn, and fly away to the groves where they sit in seeming happiness on the branches, and waste their lives in tuning one unvaried series of sounds. I likewise can call the lutanist and the singer, but the sounds that pleased me yesterday weary me today, and will grow yet more wearisome tomorrow. I can discover within me no power of perception which is not glutted with its proper[8] pleasure, yet I do not feel myself delighted. Man has surely some latent sense for which this place affords no gratification, or he has some desires distinct from sense which must be satisfied before he can be happy."

After this he lifted up his head and, seeing the moon rising, walked towards the palace. As he passed through the fields, and saw the animals around him, "Ye," said he, "are happy, and need not envy me that walk thus among you, burthened with myself; nor do I, ye gentle beings, envy your felicity; for it is not the felicity of man. I have many distresses from which ye are free; I fear pain when I do not feel it; I sometimes shrink at evils recollected, and sometimes start at evils anticipated: surely the equity of providence has balanced peculiar[9] sufferings with peculiar enjoyments."

With observations like these the prince amused himself as he returned, uttering them with a plaintive voice, yet with a look that discov-

8. Particular. 9. Particular.

ered[10] him to feel some complacence in his own perspicacity, and to receive some solace of the miseries of life from consciousness of the delicacy with which he felt, and the eloquence with which he bewailed them. He mingled cheerfully in the diversions of the evening, and all rejoiced to find that his heart was lightened.

III
The Wants of Him That Wants Nothing

On the next day his old instructor, imagining that he had now made himself acquainted with his disease of mind, was in hope of curing it by counsel, and officiously sought an opportunity of conference, which the prince, having long considered him as one whose intellects were exhausted, was not very willing to afford: "Why," said he, "does this man thus intrude upon me; shall I be never suffered to forget those lectures which pleased only while they were new, and to become new again must be forgotten?" He then walked into the wood, and composed himself to his usual meditations, when, before his thoughts had taken any settled form, he perceived his pursuer at his side, and was at first prompted by his impatience to go hastily away; but, being unwilling to offend a man whom he had once reverenced and still loved, he invited him to sit down with him on the bank.

The old man, thus encouraged, began to lament the change which had been lately observed in the prince, and to inquire why he so often retired from the pleasures of the palace, to loneliness and silence. "I fly from pleasure," said the prince, "because pleasure has ceased to please; I am lonely because I am miserable, and am unwilling to cloud with my presence the happiness of others." "You, sir," said the sage, "are the first who has complained of misery in the *happy valley*. I hope to convince you that your complaints have no real cause. You are here in full possession of all that the emperor of Abyssinia can bestow; here is neither labor to be endured nor danger to be dreaded, yet here is all that labor or danger can procure or purchase. Look round and tell me which of your wants is without supply: if you want nothing, how are you unhappy?"

"That I want nothing," said the prince, "or that I know not what I want, is the cause of my complaint; if I had any known want, I should have a certain wish; that wish would excite endeavor, and I should not then repine to see the sun move so slowly towards the western mountain, or lament when the day breaks and sleep will not longer hide me from myself. When I see the kids and the lambs chasing one another, I fancy that I should be happy if I had something to pursue.

10. Revealed.

But, possessing all that I can want, I find one day and one hour exactly like another, except that the latter is still more tedious than the former. Let your experience inform me how the day may now seem as short as in my childhood, while nature was yet fresh, and every moment showed me what I never had observed before. I have already enjoyed too much; give me something to desire."

The old man was surprised at this new species of affliction, and knew not what to reply, yet was unwilling to be silent. "Sir," said he, "if you had seen the miseries of the world, you would know how to value your present state." "Now," said the prince, "you have given me something to desire; I shall long to see the miseries of the world, since the sight of them is necessary to happiness."

IV

The Prince Continues to Grieve and Muse

At this time the sound of music proclaimed the hour of repast, and the conversation was concluded. The old man went away sufficiently discontented to find that his reasonings had produced the only conclusion which they were intended to prevent. But in the decline of life shame and grief are of short duration; whether it be that we bear easily what we have borne long, or that, finding ourselves in age less regarded, we less regard others; or that we look with slight regard upon afflictions, to which we know that the hand of death is about to put an end.

The prince, whose views were extended to a wider space, could not speedily quiet his emotions. He had been before terrified at the length of life which nature promised him, because he considered that in a long time much must be endured; he now rejoiced in his youth, because in many years much might be done.

This first beam of hope that had been ever darted into his mind rekindled youth in his cheeks, and doubled the luster of his eyes. He was fired with the desire of doing something, though he knew not yet with distinctness either end or means.

He was now no longer gloomy and unsocial; but, considering himself as master of a secret stock of happiness, which he could enjoy only by concealing it, he affected to be busy in all schemes of diversion, and endeavored to make others pleased with the state of which he himself was weary. But pleasures never can be so multiplied or continued as not to leave much of life unemployed; there were many hours, both of the night and day, which he could spend without suspicion in solitary thought. The load of life was much lightened: he went eagerly into the assemblies, because he supposed the frequency of his presence necessary to the success of his purposes; he retired gladly to privacy, because he had now a subject of thought.

His chief amusement was to picture to himself that world which he had never seen; to place himself in various conditions; to be entangled in imaginary difficulties, and to be engaged in wild adventures: but his benevolence always terminated his projects in the relief of distress, the detection of fraud, the defeat of oppression, and the diffusion of happiness.

Thus passed twenty months of the life of Rasselas. He busied himself so intensely in visionary bustle that he forgot his real solitude; and, amidst hourly preparations for the various incidents of human affairs, neglected to consider by what means he should mingle with mankind.

One day, as he was sitting on a bank, he feigned to himself an orphan virgin robbed of her little portion[11] by a treacherous lover, and crying after him for restitution and redress. So strongly was the image impressed upon his mind, that he started up in the maid's defense, and run[12] forward to seize the plunderer with all the eagerness of real pursuit. Fear naturally quickens the flight of guilt. Rasselas could not catch the fugitive with his utmost efforts; but, resolving to weary, by perseverance, him whom he could not surpass in speed, he pressed on till the foot of the mountain stopped his course.

Here he recollected himself, and smiled at his own useless impetuosity. Then raising his eyes to the mountain, "This," said he, "is the fatal obstacle that hinders at once the enjoyment of pleasure, and the exercise of virtue. How long is it that my hopes and wishes have flown beyond this boundary of my life, which yet I never have attempted to surmount!"

Struck with this reflection, he sat down to muse, and remembered that since he first resolved to escape from his confinement the sun had passed twice over him in his annual course. He now felt a degree of regret with which he had never been before acquainted. He considered how much might have been done in the time which had passed, and left nothing real behind it. He compared twenty months with the life of man. "In life," said he, "is not to be counted the ignorance of infancy, or imbecility[13] of age. We are long before we are able to think, and we soon cease from the power of acting. The true period of human existence may be reasonably estimated as forty years, of which I have mused away the four and twentieth part. What I have lost was certain, for I have certainly possessed it; but of twenty months to come who can assure me?"

The consciousness of his own folly pierced him deeply, and he was long before he could be reconciled to himself. "The rest of my time," said he, "has been lost by the crime or folly of my ancestors, and the absurd institutions of my country; I remember it with disgust, yet without remorse: but the months that have passed since new light darted

11. Inheritance; dowry. 12. Ran. 13. Physical or mental feebleness.

into my soul, since I formed a scheme of reasonable felicity, have been squandered by my own fault. I have lost that which can never be restored: I have seen the sun rise and set for twenty months, an idle gazer on the light of heaven: in this time the birds have left the nest of their mother, and committed themselves to the woods and to the skies: the kid has forsaken the teat, and learned by degrees to climb the rocks in quest of independent sustenance. I only have made no advances, but am still helpless and ignorant. The moon by more than twenty changes admonished me of the flux of life; the stream that rolled before my feet upbraided my inactivity. I sat feasting on intellectual luxury,[14] regardless alike of the examples of the earth and the instructions of the planets. Twenty months are passed, who shall restore them!"

These sorrowful meditations fastened upon his mind; he passed four months in resolving to lose no more time in idle resolves, and was awakened to more vigorous exertion by hearing a maid, who had broken a porcelain cup, remark that what cannot be repaired is not to be regretted.

This was obvious; and Rasselas reproached himself that he had not discovered it, having not known, or not considered, how many useful hints are obtained by chance, and how often the mind, hurried by her own ardor to distant views, neglects the truths that lie open before her. He, for a few hours, regretted his regret, and from that time bent his whole mind upon the means of escaping from the valley of happiness.

V
The Prince Meditates His Escape

He now found that it would be very difficult to effect that which it was very easy to suppose effected. When he looked round about him, he saw himself confined by the bars of nature which had never yet been broken, and by the gate, through which none that once had passed it were ever able to return. He was now impatient as an eagle in a grate.[15] He passed week after week in clambering the mountains to see if there was any aperture which the bushes might conceal, but found all the summits inaccessible by their prominence. The iron gate he despaired to open; for it was not only secured with all the power of art, but was always watched by successive sentinels, and was by its position exposed to the perpetual observation of all the inhabitants.

He then examined the cavern through which the waters of the lake were discharged; and, looking down at a time when the sun shone strongly upon its mouth, he discovered it to be full of broken rocks,

14. Self-indulgence. 15. Cage.

which, though they permitted the stream to flow through many narrow passages, would stop any body of solid bulk. He returned discouraged and dejected; but, having now known the blessing of hope, resolved never to despair.

In these fruitless searches he spent ten months. The time, however, passed cheerfully away: in the morning he rose with new hope, in the evening applauded his own diligence, and in the night slept sound after his fatigue. He met a thousand amusements which beguiled his labor, and diversified his thoughts. He discerned the various instincts of animals, and properties of plants, and found the place replete with wonders, of which he purposed to solace himself with the contemplation if he should never be able to accomplish his flight; rejoicing that his endeavors, though yet unsuccessful, had supplied him with a source of inexhaustible inquiry.

But his original curiosity was not yet abated; he resolved to obtain some knowledge of the ways of men. His wish still continued, but his hope grew less. He ceased to survey any longer the walls of his prison, and spared to search by new toils for interstices which he knew could not be found, yet determined to keep his design always in view and lay hold on any expedient that time should offer.

VI

A Dissertation on the Art of Flying

Among the artists[16] that had been allured into the happy valley, to labor for the accommodation and pleasure of its inhabitants, was a man eminent for his knowledge of the mechanic powers, who had contrived many engines both of use and recreation. By a wheel, which the stream turned, he forced the water into a tower, whence it was distributed to all the apartments of the palace. He erected a pavilion in the garden, around which he kept the air always cool by artificial showers. One of the groves, appropriated to the ladies, was ventilated by fans, to which the rivulet that run through it gave a constant motion; and instruments of soft music were placed at proper distances, of which some played by the impulse of the wind and some by the power of the stream.

This artist was sometimes visited by Rasselas, who was pleased with every kind of knowledge, imagining that the time would come when all his acquisitions should be of use to him in the open world. He came one day to amuse himself in his usual manner, and found the master busy in building a sailing chariot:[17] he saw that the design was practicable upon a level surface, and with expressions of great esteem solicited its com-

16. Engineers, in this case. 17. Land vehicle that moves by means of sails.

pletion. The workman was pleased to find himself so much regarded by the prince, and resolved to gain yet higher honors. "Sir," said he, "you have seen but a small part of what the mechanic sciences can perform. I have been long of opinion that, instead of the tardy conveyance of ships and chariots, man might use the swifter migration of wings; that the fields of air are open to knowledge, and that only ignorance and idleness need crawl upon the ground."

This hint rekindled the prince's desire of passing the mountains; having seen what the mechanist had already performed, he was willing to fancy that he could do more; yet resolved to inquire further before he suffered hope to afflict him by disappointment. "I am afraid," said he to the artist, "that your imagination prevails over your skill, and that you now tell me rather what you wish than what you know. Every animal has his element assigned him; the birds have the air, and man and beasts the earth." "So," replied the mechanist, "fishes have the water, in which yet beasts can swim by nature, and men by art. He that can swim needs not despair to fly: to swim is to fly in a grosser fluid, and to fly is to swim in a subtler. We are only to proportion our power of resistance to the different density of the matter through which we are to pass. You will be necessarily upborne by the air, if you can renew any impulse upon it faster than the air can recede from the pressure."

"But the exercise of swimming," said the prince, "is very laborious; the strongest limbs are soon wearied; I am afraid the act of flying will be yet more violent, and wings will be of no great use, unless we can fly further than we can swim."

"The labor of rising from the ground," said the artist, "will be great, as we see it in the heavier domestic fowls; but, as we mount higher, the earth's attraction, and the body's gravity, will be gradually diminished, till we shall arrive at a region where the man will float in the air without any tendency to fall: no care will then be necessary but to move forwards, which the gentlest impulse will effect. You, sir, whose curiosity is so extensive, will easily conceive with what pleasure a philosopher, furnished with wings and hovering in the sky, would see the earth and all its inhabitants rolling beneath him, and presenting to him successively, by its diurnal motion, all the countries within the same parallel. How must it amuse the pendent spectator to see the moving scene of land and ocean, cities, and deserts! To survey with equal security the marts of trade and the fields of battle; mountains infested by barbarians, and fruitful regions gladdened by plenty and lulled by peace! How easily shall we then trace the Nile through all his passage;[18] pass over to distant regions, and examine the face of nature from one extremity of the earth to the other!"

18. The sources of the Nile were then unknown.

"All this," said the prince, "is much to be desired, but I am afraid that no man will be able to breathe in these regions of speculation[19] and tranquillity. I have been told that respiration is difficult upon lofty mountains, yet from these precipices, though so high as to produce great tenuity[20] of the air, it is very easy to fall: therefore I suspect that from any height where life can be supported, there may be danger of too quick descent."

"Nothing," replied the artist, "will ever be attempted, if all possible objections must be first overcome. If you will favor my project I will try the first flight at my own hazard. I have considered the structure of all volant[21] animals, and find the folding continuity of the bat's wings most easily accommodated to the human form. Upon this model I shall begin my task tomorrow, and in a year expect to tower into the air beyond the malice or pursuit of man. But I will work only on this condition that the art shall not be divulged, and that you shall not require me to make wings for any but ourselves."

"Why," said Rasselas, "should you envy others so great an advantage? All skill ought to be exerted for universal good; every man has owed much to others, and ought to repay the kindness that he has received."

"If men were all virtuous," returned the artist, "I should with great alacrity teach them all to fly. But what would be the security of the good if the bad could at pleasure invade them from the sky? Against any army sailing through the clouds neither walls nor mountains nor seas could afford any security. A flight of northern savages might hover in the wind, and light at once with irresistible violence upon the capital of a fruitful region that was rolling under them. Even this valley, the retreat of princes, the abode of happiness, might be violated by the sudden descent of some of the naked nations that swarm on the coast of the southern sea."

The prince promised secrecy, and waited for the performance, not wholly hopeless of success. He visited the work from time to time, observed its progress, and remarked many ingenious contrivances to facilitate motion, and unite levity with strength. The artist was every day more certain that he should leave vultures and eagles behind him, and the contagion of his confidence seized upon the prince.

In a year the wings were finished, and, on a morning appointed, the maker appeared furnished for flight on a little promontory: he waved his pinions a while to gather air, then leaped from his stand, and in an instant dropped into the lake. His wings, which were of no use in the air, sustained him in the water, and the prince drew him to land, half dead with terror and vexation.

19. Theory. 20. Thinness. 21. Flying.

VII

The Prince Finds a Man of Learning

The prince was not much afflicted by this disaster, having suffered himself to hope for a happier event only because he had no other means of escape in view. He still persisted in his design to leave the happy valley by the first opportunity.

His imagination was now at a stand; he had no prospect of entering into the world; and, notwithstanding all his endeavors to support himself, discontent by degrees preyed upon him and he began again to lose his thoughts in sadness, when the rainy season, which in these countries is periodical, made it inconvenient to wander in the woods.

The rain continued longer and with more violence than had been ever known: the clouds broke on the surrounding mountains, and the torrents streamed into the plain on every side, till the cavern was too narrow to discharge the water. The lake overflowed its banks, and all the level of the valley was covered with the inundation. The eminence, on which the palace was built, and some other spots of rising ground, were all that the eye could now discover. The herds and flocks left the pastures, and both the wild beasts and the tame retreated to the mountains.

This inundation confined all the princes to domestic amusements, and the attention of Rasselas was particularly seized by a poem which Imlac rehearsed upon the various conditions of humanity. He commanded the poet to attend him in his apartment, and recite his verses a second time; then entering into familiar talk, he thought himself happy in having found a man who knew the world so well, and could so skillfully paint the scenes of life. He asked a thousand questions about things to which, though common to all other mortals, his confinement from childhood had kept him a stranger. The poet pitied his ignorance and loved his curiosity, and entertained him from day to day with novelty and instruction, so that the prince regretted the necessity of sleep, and longed till the morning should renew his pleasure.

As they were sitting together, the prince commanded Imlac to relate his history, and to tell by what accident he was forced, or by what motive induced, to close his life in the happy valley. As he was going to begin his narrative, Rasselas was called to a concert, and obliged to restrain his curiosity till the evening.

VIII

The History of Imlac

The close of the day is, in the regions of the torrid zone, the only season of diversion and entertainment, and it was therefore midnight before the music ceased, and the princesses retired. Rasselas then called for his companion and required him to begin the story of his life.

"Sir," said Imlac, "my history will not be long: the life that is devoted to knowledge passes silently away, and is very little diversified by events. To talk in public, to think in solitude, to read and to hear, to inquire and answer inquiries, is the business of a scholar. He wanders about the world without pomp or terror, and is neither known nor valued but by men like himself.

"I was born in the kingdom of Goiama, at no great distance from the fountain[22] of the Nile. My father was a wealthy merchant, who traded between the inland countries of Africk and the ports of the Red Sea. He was honest, frugal, and diligent, but of mean sentiments[23] and narrow comprehension: he desired only to be rich, and to conceal his riches lest he should be spoiled[24] by the governors of the province."

"Surely," said the prince, "my father must be negligent of his charge if any man in his dominions dares take that which belongs to another. Does he not know that kings are accountable for injustice permitted as well as done? If I were emperor, not the meanest[25] of my subjects should be oppressed with impunity. My blood boils when I am told that a merchant durst not enjoy his honest gains for fear of losing them by the rapacity of power. Name the governor who robbed the people, that I may declare his crimes to the emperor."

"Sir," said Imlac, "your ardor is the natural effect of virtue animated by youth: the time will come when you will acquit your father, and perhaps hear with less impatience of the governor. Oppression is, in the Abyssinian dominions, neither frequent nor tolerated; but no form of government has been yet discovered by which cruelty can be wholly prevented. Subordination[26] supposes power on one part and subjection on the other; and if power be in the hands of men it will sometimes be abused. The vigilance of the supreme magistrate may do much, but much will still remain undone. He can never know all the crimes that are committed, and can seldom punish all that he knows."

"This," said the prince, "I do not understand, but I had rather hear thee than dispute. Continue thy narration."

"My father," proceeded Imlac, "originally intended that I should have no other education than such as might qualify me for commerce; and discovering in me great strength of memory and quickness of apprehension often declared his hope that I should be some time the richest man in Abyssinia."

"Why," said the prince, "did thy father desire the increase of his wealth, when it was already greater than he durst discover or enjoy? I am unwilling to doubt thy veracity, yet inconsistencies cannot both be true."

22. Source. 23. Limited views or feelings. 24. Plundered. 25. Lowest. 26. Hierarchical government.

"Inconsistencies," answered Imlac, "cannot both be right, but, imputed to man, they may both be true. Yet diversity is not inconsistency. My father might expect a time of greater security. However, some desire is necessary to keep life in motion, and he whose real wants are supplied must admit those of fancy."

"This," said the prince, "I can in some measure conceive. I repent that I interrupted thee."

"With this hope," proceeded Imlac, "he sent me to school; but when I had once found the delight of knowledge, and felt the pleasure of intelligence and the pride of invention, I began silently to despise riches, and determined to disappoint the purpose of my father, whose grossness of conception raised my pity. I was twenty years old before his tenderness would expose me to the fatigue of travel, in which time I had been instructed, by successive masters, in all the literature[27] of my native country. As every hour taught me something new, I lived in a continual course of gratifications; but, as I advanced towards manhood, I lost much of the reverence with which I had been used to look on my instructors; because, when the lesson was ended, I did not find them wiser or better than common men.

"At length my father resolved to initiate me in commerce, and, opening one of his subterranean treasuries, counted out ten thousand pieces of gold. 'This, young man,' said he, 'is the stock with which you must negotiate.[28] I began with less than the fifth part, and you see how diligence and parsimony[29] have increased it. This is your own to waste or to improve. If you squander it by negligence or caprice, you must wait for my death before you will be rich: if, in four years, you double your stock, we will thenceforward let subordination cease, and live together as friends and partners; for he shall always be equal with me, who is equally skilled in the art of growing rich.'

"We laid our money upon camels, concealed in bales of cheap goods, and travelled to the shore of the Red Sea. When I cast my eye on the expanse of waters my heart bounded like that of a prisoner escaped. I felt an unextinguishable curiosity kindle in my mind, and resolved to snatch this opportunity of seeing the manners[30] of other nations, and of learning sciences[31] unknown in Abyssinia.

"I remembered that my father had obliged me to the improvement of my stock, not by a promise which I ought not to violate but by a penalty which I was at liberty to incur; and therefore determined to gratify my predominant desire, and by drinking at the fountains of knowledge to quench the thirst of curiosity.

"As I was supposed to trade without connection with my father, it was easy for me to become acquainted with the master of a ship and procure a passage to some other country. I had no motives of choice to regulate

27. Learning. 28. Start business. 29. Thrift.
30. Customary modes of behavior and action. 31. Fields of knowledge.

my voyage; it was sufficient for me that, wherever I wandered, I should see a country which I had not seen before. I therefore entered a ship bound for Surat,[32] having left a letter for my father declaring my intention.

IX
The History of Imlac Continued

"When I first entered upon the world of waters and lost sight of land, I looked round about me with pleasing terror, and thinking my soul enlarged by the boundless prospect imagined that I could gaze round for ever without satiety; but, in a short time, I grew weary of looking on barren uniformity, where I could only see again what I had already seen. I then descended into the ship, and doubted for a while whether all my future pleasures would not end like this in disgust and disappointment. Yet surely, said I, the ocean and the land are very different; the only variety of water is rest and motion, but the earth has mountains and valleys, deserts and cities: it is inhabited by men of different customs and contrary opinions; and I may hope to find variety in life, though I should miss it in nature.

"With this thought I quieted my mind; and amused myself during the voyage, sometimes by learning from the sailors the art of navigation, which I have never practiced, and sometimes by forming schemes for my conduct in different situations, in not one of which I have been ever placed.

"I was almost weary of my naval amusements when we landed safely at Surat. I secured my money, and purchasing some commodities for show joined myself to a caravan that was passing into the inland country. My companions, for some reason or other, conjecturing that I was rich, and, by my inquiries and admiration,[33] finding that I was ignorant, considered me as a novice whom they had a right to cheat, and who was to learn at the usual expense the art of fraud. They exposed me to the theft of servants and the exaction of officers, and saw me plundered upon false pretenses, without any advantage to themselves but that of rejoicing in the superiority of their own knowledge."

"Stop a moment," said the prince. "Is there such depravity in man as that he should injure another without benefit to himself? I can easily conceive that all are pleased with superiority; but your ignorance was merely accidental, which, being neither your crime nor your folly, could afford them no reason to applaud themselves; and the knowledge which they had, and which you wanted,[34] they might as effectually have shown by warning, as betraying you."

32. Indian port north of Bombay. 33. Naive astonishment. 34. Lacked.

"Pride," said Imlac, "is seldom delicate, it will please itself with very mean advantages; and envy feels not its own happiness but when it may be compared with the misery of others. They were my enemies because they grieved to think me rich, and my oppressors because they delighted to find me weak."

"Proceed," said the prince. "I doubt not of the facts which you relate, but imagine that you impute them to mistaken motives."

"In this company," said Imlac, "I arrived at Agra, the capital of Indostan, the city in which the great Mogul commonly resides. I applied myself to the language of the country, and in a few months was able to converse with the learned men; some of whom I found morose and reserved, and others easy and communicative; some were unwilling to teach another what they had with difficulty learned themselves; and some showed that the end of their studies was to gain the dignity of instructing.

"To the tutor of the young princes I recommended myself so much that I was presented to the emperor as a man of uncommon knowledge. The emperor asked me many questions concerning my country and my travels; and though I cannot now recollect anything that he uttered above the power of a common man, he dismissed me astonished at his wisdom and enamored of his goodness.

"My credit was now so high, that the merchants with whom I had travelled applied to me for recommendations to the ladies of the court. I was surprised at their confidence of solicitation, and gently reproached them with their practices on the road. They heard me with cold indifference and showed no tokens of shame or sorrow.

"They then urged their request with the offer of a bribe; but what I would not do for kindness I would not do for money; and refused them, not because they had injured me, but because I would not enable them to injure others; for I knew they would have made use of my credit to cheat those who should buy their wares.

"Having resided at Agra till there was no more to be learned, I traveled into Persia, where I saw many remains of ancient magnificence, and observed many new accommodations[35] of life. The Persians are a nation eminently social, and their assemblies afforded me daily opportunities of remarking characters and manners, and of tracing human nature through all its variations.

"From Persia I passed into Arabia, where I saw a nation at once pastoral and warlike; who live without any settled habitation; whose only wealth is their flocks and herds; and who have yet carried on, through all ages, an hereditary war with all mankind, though they neither covet nor envy their possessions.

35. Conveniences.

X

Imlac's History Continued. A Dissertation upon Poetry

"Wherever I went, I found that poetry was considered as the highest learning, and regarded with a veneration somewhat approaching to that which man would pay to the angelic nature. And it yet fills me with wonder, that, in almost all countries, the most ancient poets are considered as the best: whether it be that every other kind of knowledge is an acquisition gradually attained, and poetry is a gift conferred at once; or that the first poetry of every nation surprised them as a novelty, and retained the credit by consent which it received by accident at first: or whether, as the province of poetry is to describe nature and passion,[36] which are always the same, the first writers took possession of the most striking objects for description and the most probable occurrences for fiction, and left nothing to those that followed them but transcription of the same events and new combinations of the same images. Whatever be the reason, it is commonly observed that the early writers are in possession of nature, and their followers of art: that the first excel in strength and invention, and the latter in elegance and refinement.

"I was desirous to add my name to this illustrious fraternity. I read all the poets of Persia and Arabia, and was able to repeat by memory the volumes[37] that are suspended in the mosque of Mecca. But I soon found that no man was ever great by imitation. My desire of excellence impelled me to transfer my attention to nature and to life. Nature was to be my subject, and men to be my auditors: I could never describe what I had not seen: I could not hope to move those with delight or terror, whose interests and opinions I did not understand.

"Being now resolved to be a poet, I saw everything with a new purpose; my sphere of attention was suddenly magnified: no kind of knowledge was to be overlooked. I ranged mountains and deserts for images and resemblances, and pictured upon my mind every tree of the forest and flower of the valley. I observed with equal care the crags of the rock and the pinnacles of the palace. Sometimes I wandered along the mazes of the rivulet, and sometimes watched the changes of the summer clouds. To a poet nothing can be useless. Whatever is beautiful, and whatever is dreadful, must be familiar to his imagination: he must be conversant with all that is awfully[38] vast or elegantly little. The plants of the garden, the animals of the wood, the minerals of the earth, and meteors of the sky, must all concur to store his mind with inexhaustible variety: for every idea is useful for the enforcement or decoration of moral or religious truth; and he who knows most will

36. Feelings, emotions. 37. Prize-winning works. 38. Impressively.

have most power of diversifying his scenes, and of gratifying his reader with remote allusions and unexpected instruction.

"All the appearances of nature I was therefore careful to study, and every country which I have surveyed has contributed something to my poetical powers."

"In so wide a survey," said the prince, "you must surely have left much unobserved. I have lived, till now, within the circuit of these mountains, and yet cannot walk abroad without the sight of something which I had never beheld before, or never heeded."

"The business of a poet," said Imlac, "is to examine not the individual but the species; to remark general properties and large appearances: he does not number the streaks of the tulip, or describe the different shades in the verdure of the forest. He is to exhibit in his portraits of nature such prominent and striking features, as recall the original to every mind; and must neglect the minuter discriminations, which one may have remarked and another have neglected, for those characteristics which are alike obvious to vigilance and carelessness.

"But the knowledge of nature is only half the task of a poet; he must be acquainted likewise with all the modes of life. His character requires that he estimate the happiness and misery of every condition; observe the power of all the passions in all their combinations, and trace the changes of the human mind as they are modified by various institutions and accidental influences of climate or custom, from the sprightliness of infancy to the despondence of decrepitude. He must divest himself of the prejudices of his age or country; he must consider right and wrong in their abstracted and invariable state; he must disregard present laws and opinions,[39] and rise to general and transcendental truths, which will always be the same: he must therefore content himself with the slow progress of his name; contemn the applause of his own time, and commit his claims to the justice of posterity. He must write as the interpreter of nature, and the legislator of mankind, and consider himself as presiding over the thoughts and manners of future generations; as a being superior to time and place.

"His labor is not yet at an end: he must know many languages and many sciences; and, that his style may be worthy of his thoughts, must, by incessant practice, familiarize to himself every delicacy of speech and grace of harmony."

XI

Imlac's Narrative Continued. A Hint on Pilgrimage

Imlac now felt the enthusiastic fit[40] and was proceeding to aggrandize[41] his own profession, when the prince cried out, "Enough! Thou

39. Uninformed or unsupported views. 40. Extravagant, over-zealous mood.
41. Magnify.

hast convinced me, that no human being can ever be a poet. Proceed with thy narration."

"To be a poet," said Imlac, "is indeed very difficult." "So difficult," returned the prince, "that I will at present hear no more of his labors. Tell me whither you went when you had seen Persia."

"From Persia," said the poet, "I traveled through Syria, and for three years resided in Palestine, where I conversed with great numbers of the northern and western nations of Europe; the nations which are now in possession of all power and all knowledge; whose armies are irresistible and whose fleets command the remotest parts of the globe. When I compared these men with the natives of our own kingdom and those that surround us, they appeared almost another order of beings. In their countries it is difficult to wish for anything that may not be obtained: a thousand arts, of which we never heard, are continually laboring for their convenience and pleasure; and whatever their own climate has denied them is supplied by their commerce."

"By what means," said the prince, "are the Europeans thus powerful? or why, since they can easily visit Asia and Africa for trade or conquest, cannot the Asiatics and Africans invade their coasts, plant colonies in their ports, and give laws to their natural princes? The same wind that carries them back would bring us thither."

"They are more powerful, sir, than we," answered Imlac, "because they are wiser; knowledge will always predominate over ignorance, as man governs the other animals. But why their knowledge is more than ours, I know not what reason can be given, but the unsearchable will of the Supreme Being."

"When," said the prince with a sigh, "shall I be able to visit Palestine, and mingle with this mighty confluence of nations? Till that happy moment shall arrive, let me fill up the time with such representations as thou canst give me. I am not ignorant of the motive that assembles such numbers in that place, and cannot but consider it as the center of wisdom and piety, to which the best and wisest men of every land must be continually resorting."

"There are some nations," said Imlac, "that send few visitants[42] to Palestine; for many numerous and learned sects in Europe concur to censure pilgrimage as superstitious, or deride it as ridiculous."

"You know," said the prince, "how little my life has made me acquainted with diversity of opinions: it will be too long to hear the arguments on both sides; you, that have considered them, tell me the result."

"Pilgrimage," said Imlac, "like many other acts of piety, may be reasonable or superstitious, according to the principles upon which it is performed. Long journeys in search of truth are not commanded. Truth, such as is necessary to the regulation of life, is always found

42. Pilgrims.

where it is honestly sought. Change of place is no natural cause of the increase of piety, for it inevitably produces dissipation of mind.[43] Yet, since men go every day to view the fields where great actions have been performed, and return with stronger impressions of the event, curiosity of the same kind may naturally dispose us to view that country whence our religion had its beginning; and I believe no man surveys those awful scenes without some confirmation of holy resolutions. That the Supreme Being may be more easily propitiated in one place than in another is the dream of idle superstition; but that some places may operate upon our own minds in an uncommon manner is an opinion which hourly experience will justify. He who supposes that his vices may be more successfully combated in Palestine will, perhaps, find himself mistaken, yet he may go thither without folly: he who thinks they will be more freely pardoned dishonors at once his reason and religion."

"These," said the prince, "are European distinctions. I will consider them another time. What have you found to be the effect of knowledge? Are those nations happier than we?"

"There is so much infelicity," said the poet, "in the world, that scarce any man has leisure from his own distresses to estimate the comparative happiness of others. Knowledge is certainly one of the means of pleasure, as is confessed by the natural desire which every mind feels of increasing its ideas. Ignorance is mere privation, by which nothing can be produced: it is a vacuity in which the soul sits motionless and torpid for want of attraction; and, without knowing why, we always rejoice when we learn, and grieve when we forget. I am therefore inclined to conclude that, if nothing counteracts the natural consequence of learning, we grow more happy as our minds take a wider range.

"In enumerating the particular comforts of life we shall find many advantages on the side of the Europeans. They cure wounds and diseases with which we languish and perish. We suffer inclemencies of weather which they can obviate. They have engines for the despatch of many laborious works, which we must perform by manual industry. There is such communication between distant places that one friend can hardly be said to be absent from another. Their policy removes all public inconveniences: they have roads cut through their mountains and bridges laid upon their rivers. And, if we descend to the privacies of life, their habitations are more commodious, and their possessions are more secure."

"They are surely happy," said the prince, "who have all these conveniences, of which I envy none so much as the facility with which separated friends interchange their thoughts."

"The Europeans," answered Imlac, "are less unhappy than we, but

43. Scattering of attention.

they are not happy. Human life is everywhere a state in which much is to be endured, and little to be enjoyed."

XII
The Story of Imlac Continued

"I am not yet willing," said the prince, "to suppose that happiness is so parsimoniously distributed to mortals; nor can believe but that, if I had the choice of life, I should be able to fill every day with pleasure. I would injure no man, and should provoke no resentment: I would relieve every distress, and should enjoy the benedictions of gratitude. I would choose my friends among the wise, and my wife among the virtuous; and therefore should be in no danger from treachery or unkindness. My children should, by my care, be learned and pious, and would repay to my age what their childhood had received. What would dare to molest him who might call on every side to thousands enriched by his bounty or assisted by his power? And why should not life glide quietly away in the soft reciprocation of protection and reverence? All this may be done without the help of European refinements, which appear by their effects to be rather specious[44] than useful. Let us leave them and pursue our journey."

"From Palestine," said Imlac, "I passed through many regions of Asia; in the more civilized kingdoms as a trader, and among the barbarians of the mountains as a pilgrim. At last I began to long for my native country, that I might repose after my travels and fatigues in the places where I had spent my earliest years, and gladden my old companions with the recital of my adventures. Often did I figure[45] to myself those, with whom I had sported away the gay hours of dawning life, sitting round me in its evening, wondering at my tales and listening to my counsels.

"When this thought had taken possession of my mind, I considered every moment as wasted which did not bring me nearer to Abyssinia. I hastened into Egypt and, notwithstanding my impatience, was detained ten months in the contemplation of its ancient magnificence, and in inquiries after the remains of its ancient learning. I found in Cairo a mixture of all nations; some brought thither by the love of knowledge, some by the hope of gain, and many by the desire of living after their own manner without observation, and of lying hid in the obscurity of multitudes: for, in a city populous as Cairo, it is possible to obtain at the same time the gratifications of society and the secrecy of solitude.

"From Cairo I travelled to Suez, and embarked on the Red Sea, passing along the coast till I arrived at the port from which I had

44. Superficially pleasing. 45. Imagine.

departed twenty years before. Here I joined myself to a caravan and re-entered my native country.

"I now expected the caresses of my kinsmen and the congratulations of my friends, and was not without hope that my father, whatever value he had set upon riches, would own with gladness and pride a son who was able to add to the felicity and honor of the nation. But I was soon convinced that my thoughts were vain. My father had been dead fourteen years, having divided his wealth among my brothers, who were removed to some other provinces. Of my companions the greater part was in the grave, of the rest some could with difficulty remember me, and some considered me as one corrupted by foreign manners.

"A man used to vicissitudes is not easily dejected. I forgot, after a time, my disappointment, and endeavored to recommend myself to the nobles of the kingdom: they admitted me to their tables, heard my story, and dismissed me. I opened a school, and was prohibited to teach. I then resolved to sit down in the quiet of domestic life, and addressed a lady that was fond of my conversation,[46] but rejected my suit because my father was a merchant.

"Wearied at last with solicitation and repulses, I resolved to hide myself forever from the world, and depend no longer on the opinion or caprice of others. I waited for the time when the gate of the *happy valley* should open that I might bid farewell to hope and fear: the day came; my performance was distinguished with favor, and I resigned myself with joy to perpetual confinement."

"Hast thou here found happiness at last?" said Rasselas. "Tell me without reserve; art thou content with thy condition? or, dost thou wish to be again wandering and inquiring? All the inhabitants of this valley celebrate their lot, and, at the annual visit of the emperor, invite others to partake of their felicity."

"Great prince," said Imlac, "I shall speak the truth: I know not one of all your attendants who does not lament the hour when he entered this retreat. I am less unhappy than the rest, because I have a mind replete with images, which I can vary and combine at pleasure. I can amuse my solitude by the renovation of the knowledge which begins to fade from my memory, and by recollection of the accidents[47] of my past life. Yet all this ends in the sorrowful consideration that my acquirements are now useless, and that none of my pleasures can be again enjoyed. The rest, whose minds have no impression but of the present moment, are either corroded by malignant passions, or sit stupid in the gloom of perpetual vacancy."[48]

"What passions can infest those," said the prince, "who have no rivals? We are in a place where impotence precludes malice, and where all envy is repressed by community of enjoyments."

"There may be community," said Imlac, "of material possessions, but

46. Company. 47. Events. 48. Emptiness of thought.

there can never be community of love or of esteem. It must happen that one will please more than another; he that knows himself despised will always be envious; and still more envious and malevolent if he is condemned to live in the presence of those who despise him. The invitations, by which they allure others to a state which they feel to be wretched, proceed from the natural malignity of hopeless misery. They are weary of themselves and of each other, and expect to find relief in new companions. They envy the liberty which their folly has forfeited, and would gladly see all mankind imprisoned like themselves.

"From this crime, however, I am wholly free. No man can say that he is wretched by my persuasion. I look with pity on the crowds who are annually soliciting admission to captivity, and wish that it were lawful for me to warn them of their danger."

"My dear Imlac," said the prince, "I will open to thee my whole heart. I have long meditated an escape from the happy valley. I have examined the mountains on every side, but find myself insuperably barred: teach me the way to break my prison; thou shalt be the companion of my flight, the guide of my rambles, the partner of my fortune, and my sole director in the *choice of life*."

"Sir," answered the poet, "your escape will be difficult and, perhaps, you may soon repent your curiosity. The world, which you figure to yourself smooth and quiet as the lake in the valley, you will find a sea foaming with tempests and boiling with whirlpools: you will be sometimes overwhelmed by the waves of violence, and sometimes dashed against the rocks of treachery. Amidst wrongs and frauds, competitions and anxieties, you will wish a thousand times for these seats of quiet, and willingly quit hope to be free from fear."

"Do not seek to deter me from my purpose," said the prince, "I am impatient to see what thou hast seen; and, since thou art thyself weary of the valley, it is evident that thy former state was better than this. Whatever be the consequence of my experiment, I am resolved to judge with my own eyes of the various conditions of men, and then to make deliberately my *choice of life*."

"I am afraid," said Imlac, "you are hindered by stronger restraints than my persuasions; yet, if your determination is fixed, I do not counsel you to despair. Few things are impossible to diligence and skill."

XIII

Rasselas Discovers the Means of Escape

The prince now dismissed his favorite to rest, but the narrative of wonders and novelties filled his mind with perturbation. He revolved[49]

49. Thought over.

all that he had heard, and prepared innumerable questions for the morning.

Much of his uneasiness was now removed. He had a friend to whom he could impart his thoughts, and whose experience could assist him in his designs. His heart was no longer condemned to swell with silent vexation. He thought that even the *happy valley* might be endured with such a companion, and that, if they could range the world together, he should have nothing further to desire.

In a few days the water was discharged, and the ground dried. The prince and Imlac then walked out together to converse without the notice of the rest. The prince, whose thoughts were always on the wing, as he passed by the gate said, with a countenance of sorrow, "Why art thou so strong, and why is man so weak?"

"Man is not weak," answered his companion, "knowledge is more than equivalent to force. The master of mechanics laughs at strength. I can burst the gate, but cannot do it secretly. Some other expedient must be tried."

As they were walking on the side of the mountain, they observed that the conies, which the rain had driven from their burrows, had taken shelter among the bushes, and formed holes behind them, tending upwards in an oblique line. "It has been the opinion of antiquity," said Imlac, "that human reason borrowed many arts from the instinct of animals; let us, therefore, not think ourselves degraded by learning from the cony. We may escape by piercing the mountain in the same direction. We will begin where the summit hangs over the middle part, and labor upward till we shall issue out beyond the prominence."

The eyes of the prince, when he heard this proposal, sparkled with joy. The execution was easy, and the success certain.

No time was now lost. They hastened early in the morning to choose a place proper for their mine. They clambered with great fatigue among crags and brambles, and returned without having discovered any part that favored their design. The second and the third day were spent in the same manner, and with the same frustration. But, on the fourth, they found a small cavern concealed by a thicket, where they resolved to make their experiment.

Imlac procured instruments proper to hew stone and remove earth, and they fell to their work on the next day with more eagerness than vigor. They were presently exhausted by their efforts, and sat down to pant upon the grass. The prince, for a moment, appeared to be discouraged. "Sir," said his companion, "practice will enable us to continue our labor for a longer time; mark, however, how far we have advanced, and you will find that our toil will some time have an end. Great works are performed not by strength, but perseverance: yonder palace was raised by single stones, yet you see its height and spaciousness. He that shall walk with vigor three hours a day will pass in seven years a space equal to the circumference of the globe."

They returned to their work day after day, and, in a short time, found a fissure in the rock, which enabled them to pass far with very little obstruction. This Rasselas considered as a good omen. "Do not disturb your mind," said Imlac, "with other hopes or fears than reason may suggest: if you are pleased with prognostics of good, you will be terrified likewise with tokens of evil, and your whole life will be prey to superstition. Whatever facilitates our work is more than an omen, it is a cause of success. This is one of those pleasing surprises which often happen to active resolution. Many things difficult to design prove easy to performance."

XIV

Rasselas and Imlac Receive an Unexpected Visit

They had now wrought their way to the middle, and solaced their toil with the approach of liberty, when the prince, coming down to refresh himself with air, found his sister Nekayah standing before the mouth of the cavity. He started and stood confused, afraid to tell his design, and yet hopeless to conceal it. A few moments determined him to repose on her fidelity, and secure her secrecy by a declaration without reserve.

"Do not imagine," said the princess, "that I came hither as a spy: I had long observed from my window that you and Imlac directed your walk every day towards the same point, but I did not suppose you had any better reason for the preference than a cooler shade or more fragrant bank; nor followed you with any other design than to partake of your conversation. Since then not suspicion but fondness has detected you, let me not lose the advantage of my discovery. I am equally weary of confinement with yourself, and not less desirous of knowing what is done or suffered in the world. Permit me to fly with you from this tasteless tranquillity, which will yet grow more loathsome when you have left me. You may deny me to accompany you, but cannot hinder me from following."

The prince, who loved Nekayah above his other sisters, had no inclination to refuse her request, and grieved that he had lost an opportunity of showing his confidence by a voluntary communication. It was therefore agreed that she should leave the valley with them; and that, in the meantime, she should watch lest any other straggler should, by chance or curiosity, follow them to the mountain.

At length their labor was at an end; they saw light beyond the prominence and, issuing to the top of the mountain, beheld the Nile, yet a narrow current, wandering beneath them.

The prince looked round with rapture, anticipated all the pleasures of travel, and in thought was already transported beyond his father's dominions. Imlac, though very joyful at his escape, had less expectation of pleasure in the world, which he had before tried and of which he had been weary.

Rasselas was so much delighted with a wider horizon that he could not soon be persuaded to return into the valley. He informed his sister that the way was open, and that nothing now remained but to prepare for their departure.

XV

The Prince and Princess Leave the Valley, and See Many Wonders

The prince and princess had jewels sufficient to make them rich whenever they came into a place of commerce, which, by Imlac's direction, they hid in their clothes and, on the night of the next full moon, all left the valley. The princess was followed only by a single favorite, who did not know whither she was going.

They clambered through the cavity, and began to go down on the other side. The princess and her maid turned their eyes towards every part and, seeing nothing to bound their prospect, considered themselves as in danger of being lost in a dreary vacuity. They stopped and trembled. "I am almost afraid," said the princess, "to begin a journey of which I cannot perceive an end, and to venture into this immense plain where I may be approached on every side by men whom I never saw." The prince felt nearly the same emotions, though he thought it more manly to conceal them.

Imlac smiled at their terrors, and encouraged them to proceed; but the princess continued irresolute till she had been imperceptibly drawn forward too far to return.

In the morning they found some shepherds in the field, who set milk and fruits before them. The princess wondered that she did not see a palace ready for her reception, and a table spread with delicacies; but, being faint and hungry, she drank the milk and eat[50] the fruits, and thought them of a higher flavor than the products of the valley.

They traveled forward by easy journeys,[51] being all unaccustomed to toil or difficulty and knowing, that though they might be missed, they could not be pursued. In a few days they came into a more populous region, where Imlac was diverted with the admiration which his companions expressed at the diversity of manners, stations, and employments.

50. An old form of "ate," pronounced "et."

51. Distances covered in a day.

Their dress was such as might not bring upon them the suspicion of having anything to conceal, yet the prince, wherever he came, expected to be obeyed, and the princess was frighted, because those that came into her presence did not prostrate themselves before her. Imlac was forced to observe them with great vigilance, lest they should betray their rank by their unusual behavior, and detained them several weeks in the first village to accustom them to the sight of common mortals.

By degrees the royal wanderers were taught to understand that they had for a time laid aside their dignity, and were to expect only such regard as liberality and courtesy could procure. And Imlac, having by many admonitions prepared them to endure the tumults of a port and the ruggedness[52] of the commercial race, brought them down to the seacoast.

The prince and his sister, to whom everything was new, were gratified equally at all places, and therefore remained for some months at the port without any inclination to pass further. Imlac was content with their stay, because he did not think it safe to expose them, unpracticed in the world, to the hazards of a foreign country.

At last he began to fear lest they should be discovered, and proposed to fix a day for their departure. They had no pretensions to judge for themselves, and referred the whole scheme to his direction. He therefore took passage in a ship to Suez; and, when the time came, with great difficulty prevailed on the princess to enter the vessel. They had a quick and prosperous voyage, and from Suez travelled by land to Cairo.

XVI

They Enter Cairo, and Find Every Man Happy

As they approached the city, which filled the strangers with astonishment, "This," said Imlac to the prince, "is the place where travelers and merchants assemble from all the corners of the earth. You will here find men of every character and every occupation. Commerce is here honorable: I will act as a merchant, and you shall live as strangers who have no other end of travel than curiosity; it will soon be observed that we are rich; our reputation will procure us access to all whom we shall desire to know; you will see all the conditions of humanity, and enable yourself at leisure to make your *choice of life.*"

They now entered the town, stunned by the noise, and offended by the crowds. Instruction had not yet so prevailed over habit, but that they wondered to see themselves pass undistinguished along the street, and met by the lowest of the people without reverence or notice. The princess could not at first bear the thought of being leveled with the

52. Rough manners.

vulgar and, for some days, continued in her chamber, where she was served by her favorite Pekuah as in the palace of the valley.

Imlac, who understood traffic,[53] sold part of the jewels the next day, and hired a house, which he adorned with such magnificence that he was immediately considered as a merchant of great wealth. His politeness attracted many acquaintance, and his generosity made him courted by many dependents. His table was crowded by men of every nation, who all admired his knowledge, and solicited his favor. His companions, not being able to mix in the conversation, could make no discovery of their ignorance or surprise, and were gradually initiated in the world as they gained knowledge of the language.

The prince had, by frequent lectures,[54] been taught the use and nature of money; but the ladies could not, for a long time, comprehend what the merchants did with small pieces of gold and silver, or why things of so little use should be received as equivalent to the necessaries of life.

They studied the language two years, while Imlac was preparing to set before them the various ranks and conditions of mankind. He grew acquainted with all who had anything uncommon in their fortune[55] or conduct. He frequented the voluptuous and the frugal, the idle and the busy, the merchants and the men of learning.

The prince, being now able to converse with fluency, and having learned the caution necessary to be observed in his intercourse with strangers, began to accompany Imlac to places of resort, and to enter into all assemblies, that he might make his *choice of life*.

For some time he thought choice needless, because all appeared to him equally happy. Wherever he went he met gaiety and kindness, and heard the song of joy, or the laugh of carelessness. He began to believe that the world overflowed with universal plenty, and that nothing was withheld either from want or merit; that every hand showered liberality, and every heart melted with benevolence: "And who then," says he, "will be suffered to be wretched?"

Imlac permitted the pleasing delusion, and was unwilling to crush the hope of inexperience; till one day, having sat a while silent, "I know not," said the prince, "what can be the reason that I am more unhappy than any of our friends. I see them perpetually and unalterably cheerful, but feel my own mind restless and uneasy. I am unsatisfied with those pleasures which I seem most to court; I live in the crowds of jollity not so much to enjoy company as to shun myself, and am only loud and merry to conceal my sadness."

"Every man," said Imlac, "may, by examining his own mind, guess what passes in the minds of others: when you feel that your own gaiety is counterfeit, it may justly lead you to suspect that of your companions

53. Business. 54. Lessons. 55. Circumstances.

not to be sincere. Envy is commonly reciprocal. We are long before we are convinced that happiness is never to be found, and each believes it possessed by others, to keep alive the hope of obtaining it for himself. In the assembly, where you passed the last night, there appeared such sprightliness of air and volatility of fancy, as might have suited beings of an higher order, formed to inhabit serener regions inaccessible to care or sorrow: yet, believe me, prince, there was not one who did not dread the moment when solitude should deliver him to the tyranny of reflection."[56]

"This," said the prince, "may be true of others, since it is true of me; yet, whatever be the general infelicity of man, one condition is more happy than another, and wisdom surely directs us to take the least evil in the *choice of life.*"

"The causes of good and evil," answered Imlac, "are so various and uncertain, so often entangled with each other, so diversified by various relations, and so much subject to accidents which cannot be foreseen, that he who would fix his conditions upon incontestable reasons of preference, must live and die inquiring and deliberating."

"But surely," said Rasselas, "the wise men, to whom we listen with reverence and wonder, chose that mode of life for themselves which they thought most likely to make them happy."

"Very few," said the poet, "live by choice. Every man is placed in his present condition by causes which acted without his foresight, and with which he did not always willingly cooperate; and therefore you will rarely meet one who does not think the lot of his neighbor better than his own."

"I am pleased to think," said the prince, "that my birth has given me at least one advantage over others by enabling me to determine for myself. I have here the world before me; I will review it at leisure: surely happiness is somewhere to be found."

XVII
The Prince Associates with Young Men of Spirit and Gaiety

Rasselas rose next day, and resolved to begin his experiments upon life. "Youth," cried he, "is the time of gladness: I will join myself to the young men, whose only business is to gratify their desires, and whose time is all spent in a succession of enjoyments."

To such societies he was readily admitted, but a few days brought him back weary and disgusted. Their mirth was without images,[57] their laughter without motive; their pleasures were gross and sensual, in

56. Introspection. 57. Ideas.

which the mind had no part; their conduct was at once wild and mean; they laughed at order and at law, but the frown of power dejected, and the eye of wisdom abashed them.

The prince soon concluded that he should never be happy in a course of life of which he was ashamed. He thought it unsuitable to a reasonable being to act without a plan, and to be sad or cheerful only by chance. "Happiness," said he, "must be something solid and permanent, without fear and without uncertainty."

But his young companions had gained so much of his regard by their frankness and courtesy, that he could not leave them without warning and remonstrance. "My friends," said he, "I have seriously considered our manners and our prospects, and find that we have mistaken our own interest. The first years of man must make provision for the last. He that never thinks never can be wise. Perpetual levity must end in ignorance; and intemperance, though it may fire the spirits for an hour, will make life short or miserable. Let us consider that youth is of no long duration, and that in maturer age, when the enchantments of fancy shall cease and phantoms of delight dance no more about us, we shall have no comforts but the esteem of wise men, and the means of doing good. Let us, therefore, stop, while to stop is in our power: let us live as men who are sometime to grow old, and to whom it will be the most dreadful of all evils not to count their past years but by follies, and to be reminded of their former luxuriance of health only by the maladies which riot has produced."

They stared a while in silence one upon another and, at last, drove him away by a general chorus of continued laughter.

The consciousness that his sentiments were just, and his intentions kind, was scarcely sufficient to support him against the horror of derision. But he recovered his tranquillity, and pursued his search.

XVIII

The Prince Finds a Wise and Happy Man

As he was one day walking in the street, he saw a spacious building which all were, by the open doors, invited to enter: he followed the stream of people, and found it a hall or school of declamation, in which professors read lectures to their auditory. He fixed his eye upon a sage raised above the rest, who discoursed with great energy on the government of the passions. His look was venerable, his action graceful, his pronunciation clear, and his diction elegant. He showed, with great strength of sentiment, and variety of illustration, that human nature is degraded and debased, when the lower faculties predominate over the higher; that when fancy,[58] the parent of passion, usurps the dominion

58. Imagination, fantasy.

of the mind, nothing ensues but the natural effect of unlawful government, perturbation and confusion; that she betrays the fortresses of the intellect to rebels, and excites her children to sedition against reason, their lawful sovereign. He compared reason to the sun, of which the light is constant, uniform, and lasting; and fancy to a meteor, of bright but transitory luster, irregular in its motion, and delusive in its direction.

He then communicated the various precepts given from time to time for the conquest of passion, and displayed the happiness of those who had obtained the important victory, after which man is no longer the slave of fear nor the fool of hope; is no more emaciated by envy, inflamed by anger, emasculated by tenderness, or depressed by grief; but walks on calmly through the tumults or the privacies of life, as the sun pursues alike his course through the calm or the stormy sky.

He enumerated many examples of heroes immovable by pain or pleasure, who looked with indifference on those modes or accidents to which the vulgar[59] give the names of good and evil. He exhorted his hearers to lay aside their prejudices, and arm themselves against the shafts of malice or misfortune by invulnerable patience, concluding, that this state only was happiness, and that this happiness was in everyone's power.

Rasselas listened to him with the veneration due to the instructions of a superior being and, waiting for him at the door, humbly implored the liberty of visiting so great a master of true wisdom. The lecturer hesitated a moment, when Rasselas put a purse of gold into his hand, which he received with a mixture of joy and wonder.

"I have found," said the prince at his return to Imlac, "a man who can teach all that is necessary to be known, who, from the unshaken throne of rational fortitude, looks down on the scenes of life changing beneath him. He speaks, and attention watches his lips. He reasons, and conviction closes his periods.[60] This man shall be my future guide: I will learn his doctrines, and imitate his life."

"Be not too hasty," said Imlac, "to trust, or to admire, the teachers of morality: they discourse like angels, but they live like men."

Rasselas, who could not conceive how any man could reason so forcibly without feeling the cogency of his own arguments, paid his visit in a few days, and was denied admission. He had now learned the power of money, and made his way by a piece of gold to the inner apartment, where he found the philosopher in a room half darkened, with his eyes misty and his face pale. "Sir," said he, "you are come at a time when all human friendship is useless; what I suffer cannot be remedied, what I have lost cannot be supplied. My daughter, my only daughter, from whose tenderness I expected all the comforts of my age, died last night

59. Common people. 60. Sentences.

of a fever. My views, my purposes, my hopes are at an end: I am now a lonely being disunited from society."

"Sir," said the prince, "mortality is an event by which a wise man can never be surprised: we know that death is always near, and it should therefore always be expected." "Young man," answered the philosopher, "you speak like one that has never felt the pangs of separation." "Have you then forgot the precepts," said Rasselas, "which you so powerfully enforced? Has wisdom no strength to arm the heart against calamity? Consider, that external things are naturally variable, but truth and reason are always the same." "What comfort," said the mourner, "can truth and reason afford me? of what effect are they now, but to tell me that my daughter will not be restored?"

The prince, whose humanity would not suffer him to insult misery with reproof, went away convinced of the emptiness of rhetorical sound, and the inefficacy of polished periods and studied sentences.[61]

XIX
A Glimpse of Pastoral Life

He was still eager upon the same inquiry; and, having heard of a hermit that lived near the lowest cataract of the Nile, and filled the whole country with the fame of his sanctity, resolved to visit his retreat, and inquire whether that felicity, which public life could not afford, was to be found in solitude; and whether a man whose age and virtue made him venerable could teach any peculiar art of shunning evils or enduring them.

Imlac and the princess agreed to accompany him and, after the necessary preparations, they began their journey. Their way lay through fields, where shepherds tended their flocks, and the lambs were playing upon the pasture. "This," said the poet, "is the life which has been often celebrated for its innocence and quiet: let us pass the heat of the day among the shepherds' tents, and know whether all our searches are not to terminate in pastoral simplicity."

The proposal pleased them, and they induced the shepherds, by small presents and familiar questions, to tell their opinion of their own state: they were so rude[62] and ignorant, so little able to compare the good with the evil of the occupation, and so indistinct in their narratives and descriptions, that very little could be learned from them. But it was evident that their hearts were cankered with discontent; that they considered themselves as condemned to labor for the luxury of the rich, and looked up with stupid malevolence toward those that were placed above them.

61. Maxims. 62. Rustic.

The princess pronounced with vehemence that she would never suffer these envious savages to be her companions, and that she should not soon be desirous of seeing any more specimens of rustic happiness; but could not believe that all the accounts of primeval pleasures were fabulous, and was yet in doubt whether life had anything that could be justly preferred to the placid gratifications of fields and woods. She hoped that the time would come, when with a few virtuous and elegant companions she should gather flowers planted by her own hand, fondle the lambs of her own ewe, and listen, without care, among brooks and breezes, to one of her maidens reading in the shade.

XX
The Danger of Prosperity

On the next day they continued their journey, till the heat compelled them to look round for shelter. At a small distance they saw a thick wood, which they no sooner entered than they perceived that they were approaching the habitations of men. The shrubs were diligently cut away to open walks where the shades were darkest; the boughs of opposite trees were artificially[63] interwoven; seats of flowery turf were raised in vacant spaces, and a rivulet, that wantoned along the side of a winding path, had its banks sometimes opened into small basins and its stream sometimes obstructed by little mounds of stone heaped together to increase its murmurs.

They passed slowly through the wood, delighted with such unexpected accommodations,[64] and entertained each other with conjecturing what, or who, he could be that, in those rude and unfrequented regions, had leisure and art for such harmless luxury.

As they advanced, they heard the sound of music, and saw youths and virgins dancing in the grove; and, going still further, beheld a stately palace built upon a hill surrounded with woods. The laws of eastern hospitality allowed them to enter, and the master welcomed them like a man liberal and wealthy.

He was skillful enough in appearances soon to discern that they were no common guests, and spread his table with magnificence. The eloquence of Imlac caught his attention, and the lofty courtesy of the princess excited his respect. When they offered to depart he entreated their stay, and was the next day still more unwilling to dismiss them than before. They were easily persuaded to stop, and civility grew up in time to freedom and confidence.

The prince now saw all the domestics cheerful, and all the face of nature smiling round the place, and could not forbear to hope that he

63. Artfully. 64. Artful arrangements.

should find here what he was seeking; but when he was congratulating the master upon his possessions, he answered with a sigh, "My condition has indeed the appearance of happiness, but appearances are delusive. My prosperity puts my life in danger; the Bassa of Egypt is my enemy, incensed only by my wealth and popularity. I have been hitherto protected against him by the princes of the country; but, as the favor of the great is uncertain, I know not how soon my defenders may be persuaded to share the plunder with the Bassa. I have sent my treasures into a distant country, and upon the first alarm am prepared to follow them. Then will my enemies riot in my mansion, and enjoy the gardens which I have planted."

They all joined in lamenting his danger and deprecating his exile; and the princess was so much disturbed with the tumult of grief and indignation that she retired to her apartment. They continued with their kind inviter a few days longer, and then went forward to find the hermit.

XXI

The Happiness of Solitude. The Hermit's History

They came on the third day, by the direction of the peasants, to the hermit's cell: it was a cavern in the side of a mountain, overshadowed with palm trees; at such a distance from the cataract that nothing more was heard than a gentle uniform murmur, such as composed the mind to pensive meditation, especially when it was assisted by the wind whistling among the branches. The first rude essay[65] of nature had been so much improved by human labor that the cave contained several apartments, appropriated to different uses, and often afforded lodging to travelers whom darkness or tempests happened to overtake.

The hermit sat on a bench at the door to enjoy the coolness of the evening. On one side lay a book with pens and papers, on the other mechanical instruments of various kinds. As they approached him unregarded, the princess observed that he had not the countenance of a man that had found, or could teach, the way to happiness.

They saluted him with great respect, which he repaid like a man not unaccustomed to the forms of courts. "My children," said he, "if you have lost your way, you shall be willingly supplied with such conveniencies for the night as this cavern will afford. I have all that nature requires, and you will not expect delicacies in a hermit's cell."

They thanked him and, entering, were pleased with the neatness and regularity of the place. The hermit set flesh and wine before them, though he fed only upon fruits and water. His discourse was cheerful

65. Unskillful effort.

without levity, and pious without enthusiasm.[66] He soon gained the esteem of his guests, and the princess repented of her hasty censure.

At last Imlac began thus: "I do not now wonder that your reputation is so far extended; we have heard at Cairo of your wisdom, and came hither to implore your direction for this young man and maiden in the *choice of life.*"

"To him that lives well," answered the hermit, "every form of life is good; nor can I give any other rule for choice than to remove from all apparent evil."

"He will remove most certainly from evil," said the prince, "who shall devote himself to that solitude which you have recommended by your example."

"I have indeed lived fifteen years in solitude," said the hermit, "but have no desire that my example should gain any imitators. In my youth I professed arms, and was raised by degrees to the highest military rank. I have traversed wide countries at the head of my troops, and seen many battles and sieges. At last, being disgusted by the preferment[67] of a younger officer, and feeling that my vigor was beginning to decay, I resolved to close my life in peace, having found the world full of snares, discord, and misery. I had once escaped from the pursuit of the enemy by the shelter of this cavern, and therefore chose it for my final residence. I employed artificers to form it into chambers, and stored it with all that I was likely to want.

"For some time after my retreat, I rejoiced like a tempest-beaten sailor at his entrance into the harbor, being delighted with the sudden change of the noise and hurry of war to stillness and repose. When the pleasure of novelty went away, I employed my hours in examining the plants which grow in the valley, and the minerals which I collected from the rocks. But that inquiry is now grown tasteless and irksome. I have been for some time unsettled and distracted: my mind is disturbed with a thousand perplexities of doubt and vanities of imagination, which hourly prevail upon me, because I have no opportunities of relaxation or diversion. I am sometimes ashamed to think that I could not secure myself from vice but by retiring from the exercise of virtue, and begin to suspect that I was rather impelled by resentment, than led by devotion, into solitude. My fancy riots in scenes of folly, and I lament that I have lost so much and have gained so little. In solitude, if I escape the example of bad men, I want likewise the counsel and conversation of the good. I have been long comparing the evils with the advantages of society, and resolve to return into the world tomorrow. The life of a solitary man will be certainly miserable, but not certainly devout."

They heard his resolution with surprise but, after a short pause, offered to conduct him to Cairo. He dug up a considerable treasure

66. Extravagant emotion. 67. Preferential promotion.

which he had hid among the rocks, and accompanied them to the city, on which, as he approached it, he gazed with rapture.

XXII
The Happiness of a Life Led According to Nature

Rasselas went often to an assembly of learned men, who met at stated times to unbend their minds and compare their opinions. Their manners were somewhat coarse, but their conversation was instructive, and their disputations acute though sometimes too violent, and often continued till neither controvertist remembered upon what question they began. Some faults were almost general among them: every one was desirous to dictate to the rest, and every one was pleased to hear the genius[68] or knowledge of another depreciated.

In this assembly Rasselas was relating his interview with the hermit, and the wonder with which he heard him censure a course of life which he had so deliberately chosen and so laudably followed. The sentiments of the hearers were various. Some were of opinion that the folly of his choice had been[69] justly punished by condemnation to perpetual perseverance. One of the youngest among them, with great vehemence, pronounced him an hypocrite. Some talked of the right of society to the labor of individuals, and considered retirement as a desertion of duty. Others readily allowed that there was a time when the claims of the public were satisfied, and when a man might properly sequester himself to review his life and purify his heart.

One, who appeared more affected with the narrative than the rest, thought it likely, that the hermit would, in a few years, go back to his retreat and, perhaps, if shame did not restrain, or death intercept him, return once more from his retreat into the world: "For the hope of happiness," said he, "is so strongly impressed that the longest experience is not able to efface it. Of the present state, whatever it be, we feel, and are forced to confess, the misery, yet, when the same state is again at a distance, imagination paints it as desirable. But the time will surely come, when desire will be no longer our torment, and no man shall be wretched but by his own fault."

"This," said a philosopher, who had heard him with tokens of great impatience, "is the present condition of a wise man. The time is already come when none are wretched but by their own fault. Nothing is more idle than to inquire after happiness, which nature has kindly placed within our reach. The way to be happy is to live according to nature, in obedience to that universal and unalterable law with which every heart is originally impressed; which is not written on it by precept but en-

68. Mental abilities. 69. Would have been.

graven by destiny, not instilled by education but infused at our nativity. He that lives according to nature will suffer nothing from the delusions of hope or importunities of desire: he will receive and reject with equability of temper; and act or suffer as the reason of things shall alternately prescribe. Other men may amuse themselves with subtle definitions, or intricate ratiocination. Let them learn to be wise by easier means: let them observe the hind of the forest and the linnet of the grove: let them consider the life of animals, whose motions are regulated by instinct; they obey their guide and are happy. Let us therefore, at length, cease to dispute and learn to live; throw away the incumbrance of precepts, which they who utter them with so much pride and pomp do not understand, and carry with us this simple and intelligible maxim, that deviation from nature is deviation from happiness."

When he had spoken, he looked round him with a placid air, and enjoyed the consciousness of his own beneficence. "Sir," said the prince, with great modesty, "as I, like all the rest of mankind, am desirous of felicity, my closest attention has been fixed upon your discourse: I doubt not the truth of a position which a man so learned has so confidently advanced. Let me only know what it is to live according to nature."

"When I find young men so humble and so docile," said the philosopher, "I can deny them no information which my studies have enabled me to afford. To live according to nature is to act always with due regard to the fitness arising from the relations and qualities of causes and effects; to concur with the great and unchangeable scheme of universal felicity; to cooperate with the general disposition and tendency of the present system of things."

The prince soon found that this was one of the sages whom he should understand less as he heard him longer. He therefore bowed and was silent, and the philosopher, supposing him satisfied and the rest vanquished, rose up and departed with the air of a man that had cooperated with the present system.[70]

XXIII

The Prince and His Sister Divide between Them

Rasselas returned home full of reflections, doubtful how to direct his future steps. Of the way to happiness he found the learned and simple equally ignorant; but, as he was yet young, he flattered himself that he had time remaining for more experiments, and further inquiries. He communicated to Imlac his observations and his doubts, but was answered by him with new doubts, and remarks that gave him no

70. Existing nature of the world.

comfort. He therefore discoursed more frequently and freely with his sister, who had yet the same hope with himself, and always assisted him to give some reason why, though he had been hitherto frustrated, he might succeed at last.

"We have hitherto," said she, "known but little of the world: we have never yet been either great or mean. In our own country though we had royalty we had no power, and in this we have not yet seen the private recesses of domestic peace. Imlac favors not our search, lest we should in time find him mistaken. We will divide the task between us: you shall try what is to be found in the splendor of courts, and I will range the shades of humbler life. Perhaps command and authority may be the supreme blessings, as they afford most opportunities of doing good; or perhaps what this world can give may be found in the modest habitations of middle fortune: too low for great designs and too high for penury and distress."

XXIV

The Prince Examines the Happiness of High Stations

Rasselas applauded the design, and appeared next day with a splendid retinue at the court of the Bassa. He was soon distinguished for his magnificence, and admitted, as a prince whose curiosity had brought him from distant countries, to an intimacy with the great officers and frequent conversation with the Bassa himself.

He was at first inclined to believe that the man must be pleased with his own condition whom all approached with reverence and heard with obedience, and who had the power to extend his edicts to a whole kingdom. "There can be no pleasure," said he, "equal to that of feeling at once the joy of thousands all made happy by wise administration. Yet, since, by the law of subordination, this sublime delight can be in one nation but the lot of one, it is surely reasonable to think that there is some satisfaction more popular and accessible, and that millions can hardly be subjected to the will of a single man, only to fill his particular breast with incommunicable content."

These thoughts were often in his mind, and he found no solution of the difficulty. But as presents and civilities gained him more familiarity, he found that almost every man who stood high in employment hated all the rest and was hated by them, and that their lives were a continual succession of plots and detections, stratagems and escapes, faction and treachery. Many of those who surrounded the Bassa were sent only to watch and report his conduct; every tongue was muttering censure and every eye was searching for a fault.

At last the letters of revocation arrived, the Bassa was carried in chains to Constantinople, and his name was mentioned no more.

"What are we now to think of the prerogatives of power," said Rasselas to his sister; "is it without any efficacy to good? or is the subordinate degree only dangerous, and the supreme safe and glorious? Is the Sultan the only happy man in his dominions? or is the Sultan himself subject to the torments of suspicion, and the dread of enemies?"

In a short time the second Bassa was deposed. The Sultan, that had advanced him, was murdered by the Janissaries,[71] and his successor had other views and different favorites.

XXV

The Princess Pursues Her Inquiry with More Diligence Than Success

The princess, in the meantime, insinuated herself into many families; for there are few doors through which liberality, joined with good humor, cannot find its way. The daughters of many houses were airy[72] and cheerful, but Nekayah had been too long accustomed to the conversation of Imlac and her brother to be much pleased with childish levity and prattle which had no meaning. She found their thoughts narrow, their wishes low, and their merriment often artificial. Their pleasures, poor as they were, could not be preserved pure, but were embittered by petty competitions and worthless emulation. They were always jealous of the beauty of each other; of a quality to which solicitude can add nothing, and from which detraction can take nothing away. Many were in love with triflers like themselves, and many fancied that they were in love when in truth they were only idle. Their affection was seldom fixed on sense or virtue, and therefore seldom ended but in vexation. Their grief, however, like their joy, was transient; everything floated in their mind unconnected with the past or future, so that one desire easily gave way to another, as a second stone cast into the water effaces and confounds the circles of the first.

With these girls she played as with inoffensive animals, and found them proud of her countenance,[73] and weary of her company.

But her purpose was to examine more deeply, and her affability easily persuaded the hearts that were swelling with sorrow to discharge their secrets in her ear: and those whom hope flattered, or prosperity delighted, often courted her to partake their pleasures.

The princess and her brother commonly met in the evening in a private summer house on the bank of the Nile, and related to each other the occurrences of the day. As they were sitting together, the princess cast her eyes upon the river that flowed before her. "Answer," said she, "great Father of Waters, thou that rollest thy floods through

71. Elite Turkish guards. 72. Lively. 73. Favor.

eighty nations, to the invocations of the daughter of thy native king. Tell me if thou waterest, through all thy course, a single habitation from which thou dost not hear the murmurs of complaint?"

"You are then," said Rasselas, "not more successful in private houses than I have been in courts." "I have, since the last partition of our provinces,"[74] said the princess, "enabled myself to enter familiarly into many families[75] where there was the fairest show of prosperity and peace, and know not one house that is not haunted by some fury that destroys its quiet.

"I did not seek ease among the poor, because I concluded that there it could not be found. But I saw many poor whom I had supposed to live in affluence. Poverty has, in large cities, very different appearances: it is often concealed in splendor and often in extravagance. It is the care of a very great part of mankind to conceal their indigence from the rest: they support themselves by temporary expedients, and every day is lost in contriving for the morrow.

"This, however, was an evil which, though frequent, I saw with less pain because I could relieve it. Yet some have refused my bounties; more offended with my quickness to detect their wants, than pleased with my readiness to succor them: and others, whose exigencies compelled them to admit my kindness, have never been able to forgive their benefactress. Many, however, have been sincerely grateful without the ostentation of gratitude or the hope of other favors."

XXVI

The Princess Continues Her Remarks upon Private Life

Nekayah, perceiving her brother's attention fixed, proceeded in her narrative.

"In families where there is or is not poverty, there is commonly discord: if a kingdom be, as Imlac tells us, a great family, a family likewise is a little kingdom, torn with factions and exposed to revolutions. An unpracticed observer expects the love of parents and children to be constant and equal; but this kindness seldom continues beyond the years of infancy: in a short time the children become rivals to their parents. Benefits are allayed[76] by reproaches, and gratitude debased by envy.

"Parents and children seldom act in concert: each child endeavors to appropriate the esteem or fondness of the parents, and the parents, with yet less temptation, betray each other to their children; thus some place their confidence in the father and some in the mother, and, by degrees, the house is filled with artifices and feuds.

74. Business. 75. Households. 76. Alloyed.

"The opinions of children and parents, of the young and the old, are naturally opposite, by the contrary effects of hope and despondence, of expectation and experience, without crime or folly on either side. The colors of life in youth and age appear different, as the face of nature in spring and winter. And how can children credit the assertions of parents, which their own eyes show them to be false?

"Few parents act in such a manner as much to enforce their maxims by the credit of their lives. The old man trusts wholly to slow contrivance and gradual progression: the youth expects to force his way by genius,[77] vigor, and precipitance. The old man pays regard to riches, and the youth reverences virtue. The old man deifies prudence;[78] the youth commits himself to magnanimity and chance. The young man, who intends no ill, believes that none is intended, and therefore acts with openness and candor:[79] but his father, having suffered the injuries of fraud, is impelled to suspect, and too often allured to practice it. Age looks with anger on the temerity of youth, and youth with contempt on the scrupulosity of age. Thus parents and children, for the greatest part, live on to love less and less: and, if those whom nature has thus closely united are the torments of each other, where shall we look for tenderness and consolation?"

"Surely," said the prince, "you must have been unfortunate in your choice of acquaintance: I am unwilling to believe that the most tender of all relations is thus impeded in its effects by natural necessity."

"Domestic discord," answered she, "is not inevitably and fatally[80] necessary; but yet is not easily avoided. We seldom see that a whole family is virtuous: the good and evil cannot well agree; and the evil can yet less agree with one another: even the virtuous fall sometimes to variance, when their virtues are of different kinds and tending to extremes. In general, those parents have most reverence who most deserve it: for he that lives well cannot be despised.

"Many other evils infest private life. Some are the slaves of servants whom they have trusted with their affairs. Some are kept in continual anxiety to the caprice of rich relations, whom they cannot please and dare not offend. Some husbands are imperious, and some wives perverse: and, as it is always more easy to do evil than good, though the wisdom or virtue of one can very rarely make many happy, the folly or vice of one may often make many miserable."

"If such be the general effect of marriage," said the prince, "I shall, for the future, think it dangerous to connect my interest with that of another, lest I should be unhappy by my partner's fault."

"I have met," said the princess, "with many who live single for that reason; but I never found that their prudence ought to raise envy.

77. Natural ability. 78. Practical conduct in the world.
79. Here, generous belief in others. 80. Unavoidably, by decree of fate.

They dream away their time without friendship, without fondness, and are driven to rid themselves of the day, for which they have no use, by childish amusements or vicious delights. They act as beings under the constant sense of some known inferiority, that fills their minds with rancor and their tongues with censure. They are peevish at home, and malevolent abroad; and, as the outlaws of human nature, make it their business and their pleasure to disturb that society which debars them from its privileges. To live without feeling or exciting sympathy, to be fortunate without adding to the felicity of others, or afflicted without tasting the balm of pity, is a state more gloomy than solitude: it is not retreat but exclusion from mankind. Marriage has many pains, but celibacy has no pleasures."

"What then is to be done?" said Rasselas, "the more we inquire, the less we can resolve. Surely he is most likely to please himself that has no other inclination to regard."

XXVII

Disquisition upon Greatness

The conversation had a short pause. The prince, having considered his sister's observations, told her that she had surveyed life with prejudice, and supposed misery where she did not find it. "Your narrative," says he, "throws yet a darker gloom upon the prospects of futurity: the predictions of Imlac were but faint sketches of the evils painted by Nekayah. I have been lately convinced that quiet is not the daughter of grandeur or of power: that her presence is not to be bought by wealth nor enforced by conquest. It is evident that as any man acts in a wider compass, he must be more exposed to opposition from enmity or miscarriage from chance; whoever has many to please or to govern must use the ministry of many agents, some of whom will be wicked and some ignorant; by some he will be misled and by others betrayed. If he gratifies one he will offend another: those that are not favored will think themselves injured; and, since favors can be conferred but upon few, the greater number will be always discontented."

"The discontent," said the princess, "which is thus unreasonable, I hope that I shall always have spirit to despise, and you, power to repress."

"Discontent," answered Rasselas, "will not always be without reason under the most just or vigilant administration of public affairs. None, however attentive, can always discover that merit which indigence or faction may happen to obscure; and none, however powerful, can always reward it. Yet he that sees inferior desert advanced above him will naturally impute that preference to partiality or caprice; and, indeed, it can scarcely be hoped that any man, however magnanimous by nature or exalted by condition, will be able to persist forever in fixed and inexorable justice of distribution: he will sometimes indulge his own affections, and sometimes those of his favorites; he will permit some to please him who can never serve him; he will discover in those whom he loves qualities which in reality they do not possess; and to those, from whom he receives pleasure, he will in his turn endeavor to give it. Thus will recommendations sometimes prevail which were purchased by money, or by the more destructive bribery of flattery and servility.

"He that has much to do will do something wrong, and of that wrong must suffer the consequences; and, if it were possible that he should always act rightly, yet when such numbers are to judge of his conduct, the bad will censure and obstruct him by malevolence, and the good sometimes by mistake.

"The highest stations cannot therefore hope to be the abodes of happiness, which I would willingly believe to have fled from thrones and palaces to seats of humble privacy and placid obscurity. For what can hinder the satisfaction, or intercept the expectations, of him whose abilities are adequate to his employments, who sees with his own eyes the whole circuit of his influence, who chooses by his own knowledge all whom he trusts, and whom none are tempted to deceive by hope or fear? Surely he has nothing to do but to love and to be loved, to be virtuous and to be happy."

"Whether perfect happiness would be procured by perfect goodness," said Nekayah, "this world will never afford an opportunity of deciding. But this, at least, may be maintained, that we do not always find visible happiness in proportion to visible virtue. All natural and almost all political evils are incident alike to the bad and good: they are confounded in the misery of a famine, and not much distinguished in the fury of a faction; they sink together in a tempest, and are driven together from their country by invaders. All that virtue can afford is quietness of conscience, a steady prospect of a happier state; this may enable us to endure calamity with patience; but remember that patience must suppose pain."

XXVIII

Rasselas and Nekayah Continue Their Conversation

"Dear princess," said Rasselas, "you fall into the common errors of exaggeratory declamation by producing, in a familiar disquisition,[81] examples of national calamities and scenes of extensive misery which are found in books rather than in the world, and which, as they are horrid,[82] are ordained to be rare. Let us not imagine evils which we do

81. Discussion of domestic life. 82. Shocking, dreadful.

not feel, nor injure life by misrepresentations. I cannot bear that querulous eloquence which threatens every city with a siege like that of Jerusalem,[83] that makes famine attend on every flight of locusts, and suspends pestilence on the wing of every blast that issues from the south.

"On necessary and inevitable evils, which overwhelm kingdoms at once, all disputation is vain: when they happen they must be endured. But it is evident that these bursts of universal distress are more dreaded than felt: thousands and ten thousands flourish in youth and wither in age, without the knowledge of any other than domestic evils, and share the same pleasures and vexations whether their kings are mild or cruel, whether the armies of their country pursue their enemies, or retreat before them. While courts are disturbed with intestine competitions, and ambassadors are negotiating in foreign countries, the smith still plies his anvil, and the husbandman drives his plow forward; the necessaries of life are required and obtained, and the successive business of the seasons continues to make its wonted revolutions.

"Let us cease to consider what, perhaps, may never happen, and what, when it shall happen, will laugh at human speculation. We will not endeavor to modify the motions of the elements, or to fix the destiny of kingdoms. It is our business to consider what beings like us may perform, each laboring for his own happiness by promoting within his circle, however narrow, the happiness of others.

"Marriage is evidently the dictate of nature; men and women were made to be companions of each other, and therefore I cannot be persuaded but that marriage is one of the means of happiness."

"I know not," said the princess, "whether marriage be more than one of the innumerable modes of human misery. When I see and reckon the various forms of connubial infelicity, the unexpected causes of lasting discord, the diversities of temper, the oppositions of opinion, the rude collisions of contrary desire where both are urged by violent impulses, the obstinate contests of disagreeing virtues, where both are supported by consciousness of good intention, I am sometimes disposed to think with the severer casuists[84] of most nations that marriage is rather permitted than approved, and that none, but by the instigation of a passion too much indulged, entangle themselves with indissoluble compacts."

"You seem to forget," replied Rasselas, "that you have, even now, represented celibacy as less happy than marriage. Both conditions may be bad, but they cannot both be worst. Thus it happens when wrong opinions are entertained that they mutually destroy each other, and leave the mind open to truth."

83. Captured and destroyed by Titus (later Emperor) in 70 A.D.
84. Skilled reasoners on ethical problems.

"I did not expect," answered the princess, "to hear that imputed to falsehood which is the consequence only of frailty. To the mind, as to the eye, it is difficult to compare with exactness objects vast in their extent, and various in their parts. Where we see or conceive the whole at once we readily note the discriminations and decide the preference: but of two systems, of which neither can be surveyed by any human being in its full compass of magnitude and multiplicity of complication, where is the wonder that, judging of the whole by parts, I am alternately affected by one and the other as either presses on my memory or fancy? We differ from ourselves just as we differ from each other when we see only part of the question, as in the multifarious relations of politics and morality: but when we perceive the whole at once, as in numerical computations, all agree in one judgment and none ever varies his opinion."

"Let us not add," said the prince, "to the other evils of life the bitterness of controversy, nor endeavor to vie with each other in subtleties of argument. We are employed in a search, of which both are equally to enjoy the success, or suffer by the miscarriage. It is therefore fit that we assist each other. You surely conclude too hastily from the infelicity of marriage against its institution; will not the misery of life prove equally that life cannot be the gift of heaven? The world must be peopled by marriage, or peopled without it."

"How the world is to be peopled," returned Nekayah, "is not my care and needs not be yours. I see no danger that the present generation should omit to leave successors behind them: we are not now inquiring for the world but for ourselves."

XXIX
The Debate on Marriage Continued

"The good of the whole," says Rasselas, "is the same with the good of all its parts. If marriage be best for mankind it must be evidently best for individuals, or a permanent and necessary duty must be the cause of evil, and some must be inevitably sacrificed to the convenience of others. In the estimate which you have made of the two states, it appears that the incommodities of a single life are, in a great measure, necessary and certain, but those of the conjugal state accidental and avoidable.

"I cannot forbear to flatter myself that prudence and benevolence will make marriage happy. The general folly of mankind is the cause of general complaint. What can be expected but disappointment and repentance from a choice made in the immaturity of youth, in the ardor of desire, without judgment, without foresight, without inquiry after conformity of opinions, similarity of manners, rectitude of judgment, or purity of sentiment.

"Such is the common process of marriage. A youth and maiden meeting by chance, or brought together by artifice, exchange glances, reciprocate civilities, go home, and dream of one another. Having little to divert attention or diversify thought, they find themselves uneasy when they are apart, and therefore conclude that they shall be happy together. They marry, and discover what nothing but voluntary blindness had before concealed; they wear out life in altercations, and charge nature with cruelty.

"From those early marriages proceeds likewise the rivalry of parents and children: the son is eager to enjoy the world before the father is willing to forsake it, and there is hardly room at once for two generations. The daughter begins to bloom before the mother can be content to fade, and neither can forbear to wish for the absence of the other.

"Surely all these evils may be avoided by that deliberation and delay which prudence prescribes to irrevocable choice. In the variety and jollity of youthful pleasures life may be well enough supported without the help of a partner. Longer time will increase experience, and wider views will allow better opportunities of inquiry and selection: one advantage, at least, will be certain; the parents will be visibly older than their children."

"What reason cannot collect," said Nekayah, "and what experiment has not yet taught, can be known only from the report of others. I have been told that late marriages are not eminently happy. This is a question too important to be neglected, and I have often proposed it to those, whose accuracy of remark, and comprehensiveness of knowledge, made their suffrages[85] worthy of regard. They have generally determined that it is dangerous for a man and woman to suspend their fate upon each other, at a time when opinions are fixed and habits are established; when friendships have been contracted on both sides, when life has been planned into method, and the mind has long enjoyed the contemplation of its own prospects.

"It is scarcely possible that two traveling through the world under the conduct of chance should have been both directed to the same path, and it will not often happen that either will quit the track which custom has made pleasing. When the desultory levity of youth has settled into regularity, it is soon succeeded by pride ashamed to yield, or obstinacy delighting to contend. And even though mutual esteem produces mutual desire to please, time itself, as it modifies unchangeably the external mien, determines likewise the direction of the passions, and gives an inflexible rigidity to the manners. Long customs are not easily

85. Opinions.

broken: he that attempts to change the course of his own life very often labors in vain; and how shall we do that for others which we are seldom able to do for ourselves?"

"But surely," interposed the prince, "you suppose the chief motive of choice forgotten or neglected. Whenever I shall seek a wife, it shall be my first question whether she be willing to be led by reason?"

"Thus it is," said Nekayah, "that philosophers are deceived. There are a thousand familiar disputes which reason never can decide; questions that elude investigation and make logic ridiculous; cases where something must be done, and where little can be said. Consider the state of mankind, and inquire how few can be supposed to act upon any occasions, whether small or great, with all the reasons of action present to their minds. Wretched would be the pair above all names of wretchedness who should be doomed to adjust by reason every morning all the minute detail of a domestic day.

"Those who marry at an advanced age will probably escape the encroachments of their children; but, in diminution of this advantage, they will be likely to leave them, ignorant and helpless, to a guardian's mercy: or, if that should not happen, they must at least go out of the world before they see those whom they love best either wise or great.

"From their children, if they have less to fear, they have less also to hope, and they lose, without equivalent, the joys of early love, and the convenience of uniting with manners pliant, and minds susceptible of new impressions, which might wear away their dissimilitudes by long cohabitation, as soft bodies, by continual attrition, conform their surfaces to each other.

"I believe it will be found that those who marry late are best pleased with their children, and those who marry early with their partners."

"The union of these two affections," said Rasselas, "would produce all that could be wished. Perhaps there is a time when marriage might unite them, a time neither too early for the father, nor too late for the husband."

"Every hour," answered the princess, "confirms my prejudice in favor of the position so often uttered by the mouth of Imlac, 'That nature sets her gifts on the right hand and on the left.' Those conditions, which flatter hope and attract desire, are so constituted that, as we approach one, we recede from another. There are goods so opposed that we cannot seize both but, by too much prudence, may pass between them at too great a distance to reach either. This is often the fate of long consideration; he does nothing who endeavors to do more than is allowed to humanity. Flatter not yourself with contrarieties of pleasure. Of the blessings set before you make your choice, and be content. No man can taste the fruits of autumn while he is delighting his scent with the flowers of the spring: no man can, at the same time, fill his cup from the source and the mouth of the Nile."

XXX
Imlac Enters, and Changes the Conversation

Here Imlac entered, and interrupted them. "Imlac," said Rasselas, "I have been taking from the princess the dismal history of private life, and am almost discouraged from further search."

"It seems to me," said Imlac, "that while you are making the choice of life, you neglect to live. You wander about a single city which, however large and diversified, can now afford few novelties, and forget that you are in a country famous among the earliest monarchies for the power and wisdom of its inhabitants; a country where the sciences first dawned that illuminate the world, and beyond which the arts cannot be traced of civil society or domestic life.

"The old Egyptians have left behind them monuments of industry and power before which all European magnificence is confessed to fade away. The ruins of their architecture are the schools of modern builders, and from the wonders which time has spared we may conjecture, though uncertainly, what it has destroyed."

"My curiosity," said Rasselas, "does not very strongly lead me to survey piles of stone or mounds of earth; my business is with man. I came hither not to measure fragments of temples or trace choked aqueducts, but to look upon the various scenes of the present world."

"The things that are now before us," said the princess, "require attention, and deserve it. What have I to do with the heroes or the monuments of ancient times? with times which never can return, and heroes, whose form of life was different from all that the present condition of mankind requires or allows."

"To know anything," returned the poet, "we must know its effects; to see men we must see their works, that we may learn what reason has dictated or passion has incited, and find what are the most powerful motives of action. To judge rightly of the present we must oppose it to the past; for all judgment is comparative, and of the future nothing can be known. The truth is that no mind is much employed upon the present: recollection and anticipation fill up almost all our moments. Our passions are joy and grief, love and hatred, hope and fear. Of joy and grief the past is the object, and the future of hope and fear; even love and hatred respect the past, for the cause must have been before the effect.

"The present state of things is the consequence of the former, and it is natural to inquire what were the sources of the good that we enjoy or of the evil that we suffer. If we act only for ourselves, to neglect the study of history is not prudent: if we are entrusted with the care of others, it is not just. Ignorance, when it is voluntary, is criminal; and he may properly be charged with evil who refused to learn how he might prevent it.

"There is no part of history so generally useful as that which relates the progress of the human mind, the gradual improvement of reason, the successive advances of science, the vicissitudes of learning and ignorance which are the light and darkness of thinking beings, the extinction and resuscitation of arts, and all the revolutions of the intellectual world. If accounts of battles and invasions are peculiarly the business of princes, the useful or elegant arts are not to be neglected; those who have kingdoms to govern, have understandings to cultivate.

"Example is always more efficacious than precept. A soldier is formed in war, and a painter must copy pictures. In this, contemplative life has the advantage: great actions are seldom seen, but the labors of art are always at hand for those who desire to know what art has been able to perform.

"When the eye or the imagination is struck with any uncommon work the next transition of an active mind is to the means by which it was performed. Here begins the true use of such contemplation; we enlarge our comprehension by new ideas, and perhaps recover some art lost to mankind, or learn what is less perfectly known in our own country. At least we compare our own with former times, and either rejoice at our improvements or, what is the first motion towards good, discover our defects."

"I am willing," said the prince, "to see all that can deserve my search."

"And I," said the princess, "shall rejoice to learn something of the manners of antiquity."

"The most pompous[86] monument of Egyptian greatness, and one of the most bulky works of manual industry," said Imlac, "are the pyramids; fabrics raised before the time of history, and of which the earliest narratives afford us only uncertain traditions. Of these the greatest is still standing, very little injured by time."

"Let us visit them tomorrow," said Nekayah. "I have often heard of the pyramids, and shall not rest till I have seen them within and without with my own eyes."

XXXI
They Visit the Pyramids

The resolution being thus taken, they set out the next day. They laid tents upon their camels, being resolved to stay among the pyramids till their curiosity was fully satisfied. They traveled gently, turned aside to everything remarkable, stopped from time to time and conversed with the inhabitants, and observed the various appearances of towns, ruined and inhabited, of wild and cultivated nature.

86. Magnificent, impressive.

When they came to the great pyramid they were astonished at the extent of the base, and the height of the top. Imlac explained to them the principles upon which the pyramidal form was chosen for a fabric intended to coextend its duration with that of the world: he showed that its gradual diminution gave it such stability as defeated all the common attacks of the elements, and could scarcely be overthrown by earthquakes themselves, the least resistible of natural violence. A concussion that should shatter the pyramid would threaten the dissolution of the continent.

They measured all its dimensions, and pitched their tents at its foot. Next day they prepared to enter its interior apartments, and having hired the common guides climbed up to the first passage, when the favorite of the princess, looking into the cavity, stepped back and trembled. "Pekuah," said the princess, "of what art thou afraid?" "Of the narrow entrance," answered the lady, "and of the dreadful gloom. I dare not enter a place which must surely be inhabited by unquiet souls. The original possessors of these dreadful vaults will start up before us, and, perhaps, shut us in forever." She spoke, and threw her arms round the neck of her mistress.

"If all your fear be of apparitions," said the prince, "I will promise you safety: there is no danger from the dead; he that is once buried will be seen no more."

"That the dead are seen no more," said Imlac, "I will not undertake to maintain against the concurrent and unvaried testimony of all ages and of all nations. There is no people, rude or learned, among whom apparitions of the dead are not related and believed. This opinion, which perhaps prevails as far as human nature is diffused, could become universal only by its truth: those that never heard of one another would not have agreed in a tale which nothing but experience can make credible. That it is doubted by single cavilers can very little weaken the general evidence, and some who deny it with their tongues confess it by their fears.

"Yet I do not mean to add new terrors to those which have already seized upon Pekuah. There can be no reason why specters should haunt the pyramid more than other places, or why they should have power or will to hurt innocence and purity. Our entrance is no violation of their privileges; we can take nothing from them, how then can we offend them?"

"My dear Pekuah," said the princess, "I will always go before you, and Imlac shall follow you. Remember that you are the companion of the princess of Abyssinia."

"If the princess is pleased that her servant should die," returned the lady, "let her command some death less dreadful than enclosure in this horrid cavern. You know I dare not disobey you: I must go if you command me; but if I once enter, I never shall come back."

The princess saw that her fear was too strong for expostulation or reproof, and embracing her, told her that she should stay in the tent till their return. Pekuah was yet not satisfied, but entreated the princess not to pursue so dreadful a purpose as that of entering the recesses of the pyramid. "Though I cannot teach courage," said Nekayah, "I must not learn cowardice; nor leave at last undone what I came hither only to do."

XXXII
They Enter the Pyramid

Pekuah descended to the tents, and the rest entered the pyramid: they passed through the galleries, surveyed the vaults of marble, and examined the chest in which the body of the founder is supposed to have been reposited. They then sat down in one of the most spacious chambers to rest a while before they attempted to return.

"We have now," said Imlac, "gratified our minds with an exact view of the greatest work of man, except the wall of China.

"Of the wall it is very easy to assign the motives. It secured a wealthy and timorous nation from the incursions of barbarians, whose unskillfulness in arts made it easier for them to supply their wants by rapine than by industry, and who from time to time poured in upon the habitations of peaceful commerce, as vultures descend upon domestic fowl. Their celerity and fierceness made the wall necessary, and their ignorance made it efficacious.

"But for the pyramids no reason has ever been given adequate to the cost and labor of the work. The narrowness of the chambers proves that it could afford no retreat from enemies, and treasures might have been reposited at far less expense with equal security. It seems to have been erected only in compliance with that hunger of imagination which preys incessantly upon life, and must be always appeased by some employment. Those who have already all that they can enjoy, must enlarge their desires. He that has built for use, till use is supplied, must begin to build for vanity, and extend his plan to the utmost power of human performance, that he may not be soon reduced to form another wish.

"I consider this mighty structure as a monument of the insufficiency of human enjoyments. A king whose power is unlimited, and whose treasures surmount all real and imaginary wants, is compelled to solace, by the erection of a pyramid, the satiety of dominion and tastelessness of pleasures, and to amuse the tediousness of declining life by seeing thousands laboring without end, and one stone, for no purpose, laid upon another. Whoever thou art that, not content with a moderate condition, imaginest happiness in royal magnificence, and dreamest that command or riches can feed the appetite of novelty with perpetual gratifications, survey the pyramids and confess thy folly!"

XXXIII

The Princess Meets with an Unexpected Misfortune

They rose up, and returned through the cavity at which they had entered, and the princess prepared for her favorite a long narrative of dark labyrinths and costly rooms, and of the different impressions which the varieties of the way had made upon her. But, when they came to their train,[87] they found everyone silent and dejected: the men discovered shame and fear in their countenances, and the women were weeping in the tents.

What had happened they did not try to conjecture, but immediately inquired. "You had scarcely entered into the pyramid," said one of the attendants, "when a troop of Arabs rushed upon us: we were too few to resist them and too slow to escape. They were about to search the tents, set us on our camels, and drive us along before them, when the approach of some Turkish horsemen put them to flight; but they seized the lady Pekuah with her two maids, and carried them away: the Turks are now pursuing them by our instigation, but I fear they will not be able to overtake them."

The princess was overpowered with surprise and grief. Rasselas, in the first heat of his resentment, ordered his servants to follow him, and prepared to pursue the robbers with his saber in his hand. "Sir," said Imlac, "what can you hope from violence or valor? the Arabs are mounted on horses trained to battle and retreat; we have only beasts of burden. By leaving our present station we may lose the princess, but cannot hope to regain Pekuah."

In a short time the Turks returned, having not been able to reach the enemy. The princess burst out into new lamentations, and Rasselas could scarcely forbear to reproach them with cowardice; but Imlac was of opinion that the escape of the Arabs was no addition to their misfortune, for, perhaps, they would have killed their captives rather than have resigned[88] them.

XXXIV

They Return to Cairo without Pekuah

There was nothing to be hoped from longer stay. They returned to Cairo repenting of their curiosity, censuring the negligence of the

87. Attendants. 88. Surrendered.

government, lamenting their own rashness which had neglected to procure a guard, imagining many expedients by which the loss of Pekuah might have been prevented, and resolving to do something for her recovery, though none could find anything proper to be done.

Nekayah retired to her chamber, where her women attempted to comfort her by telling her that all had their troubles, and that lady Pekuah had enjoyed much happiness in the world for a long time, and might reasonably expect a change of fortune. They hoped that some good would befall her wheresoever she was, and that their mistress would find another friend who might supply her place.

The princess made them no answer, and they continued the form of condolence, not much grieved in their hearts that the favorite was lost.

Next day the prince presented to the Bassa a memorial[89] of the wrong which he had suffered, and a petition for redress. The Bassa threatened to punish the robbers, but did not attempt to catch them, nor, indeed, could any account or description be given by which he might direct the pursuit.

It soon appeared that nothing would be done by authority. Governors, being accustomed to hear of more crimes than they can punish and more wrongs than they can redress, set themselves at ease by indiscriminate negligence, and presently[90] forget the request when they lose sight of the petitioner.

Imlac then endeavored to gain some intelligence by private agents. He found many who pretended to an exact knowledge of all the haunts of the Arabs and to regular correspondence with their chiefs, and who readily undertook the recovery of Pekuah. Of these, some were furnished with money for their journey, and came back no more; some were liberally paid for accounts which a few days discovered to be false. But the princess would not suffer any means, however improbable, to be left untried. While she was doing something she kept her hope alive. As one expedient failed, another was suggested; when one messenger returned unsuccessful, another was despatched to a different quarter.

Two months had now passed, and of Pekuah nothing had been heard; the hopes which they had endeavored to raise in each other grew more languid, and the princess, when she saw nothing more to be tried, sunk down inconsolable in hopeless dejection. A thousand times she reproached herself with the easy compliance by which she permitted her favorite to stay behind her. "Had not my fondness," said she, "lessened my authority, Pekuah had not dared to talk of her terrors. She ought to have feared me more than specters. A severe look would have overpowered her; a peremptory command would have compelled obedience. Why did foolish indulgence prevail upon me? Why did I not speak and refuse to hear?"

89. Statement of facts. 90. Immediately.

"Great princess," said Imlac, "do not reproach yourself for your virtue, or consider that as blamable by which evil has accidentally been caused. Your tenderness for the timidity of Pekuah was generous and kind. When we act according to our duty, we commit the event to Him by whose laws our actions are governed, and who will suffer none to be finally punished for obedience. When in prospect of some good, whether natural or moral, we break the rules prescribed us, we withdraw from the direction of superior wisdom, and take all consequences upon ourselves. Man cannot so far know the connection of causes and events as that he may venture to do wrong in order to do right. When we pursue our end by lawful means, we may always console our miscarriage by the hope of future recompense. When we consult only our own policy, and attempt to find a nearer way to good by overleaping the settled boundaries of right and wrong, we cannot be happy even by success, because we cannot escape the consciousness of our fault; but if we miscarry, the disappointment is irremediably embittered. How comfortless is the sorrow of him who feels at once the pangs of guilt, and the vexation of calamity which guilt has brought upon him?

"Consider, princess, what would have been your condition, if the lady Pekuah had entreated to accompany you and, being compelled to stay in the tents, had been carried away; or how would you have borne the thought, if you had forced her into the pyramid, and she had died before you in agonies of terror."

"Had either happened," said Nekayah, "I could not have endured life till now: I should have been tortured to madness by the remembrance of such cruelty, or must have pined away in abhorrence of myself."

"This at least," said Imlac, "is the present reward of virtuous conduct, that no unlucky consequence can oblige us to repent it."

XXXV

The Princess Languishes for Want of Pekuah

Nekayah, being thus reconciled to herself, found that no evil is insupportable but that which is accompanied with consciousness of wrong. She was, from that time, delivered from the violence of tempestuous sorrow, and sunk into silent pensiveness and gloomy tranquillity. She sat from morning to evening recollecting all that had been done or said by her Pekuah, treasured up with care every trifle on which Pekuah had set an accidental value, and which might recall to mind any little incident or careless conversation. The sentiments of her whom she now expected to see no more were treasured in her memory as rules of life, and she deliberated to no other end than to conjecture on any occasion what would have been the opinion and counsel of Pekuah.

The women, by whom she was attended, knew nothing of her real condition, and therefore she could not talk to them but with caution and reserve. She began to remit her curiosity,[91] having no great care to collect notions which she had no convenience of uttering. Rasselas endeavored first to comfort and afterwards to divert her; he hired musicians, to whom she seemed to listen but did not hear them, and procured masters to instruct her in various arts, whose lectures, when they visited her again, were again to be repeated. She had lost her taste of pleasure and her ambition of excellence. And her mind, though forced into short excursions, always recurred to the image of her friend.

Imlac was every morning earnestly enjoined to renew his inquiries, and was asked every night whether he had yet heard of Pekuah, till not being able to return the princess the answer that she desired, he was less and less willing to come into her presence. She observed his backwardness, and commanded him to attend her. "You are not," said she, "to confound impatience with resentment, or to suppose that I charge you with negligence because I repine at your unsuccessfulness. I do not much wonder at your absence; I know that the unhappy are never pleasing, and that all naturally avoid the contagion of misery. To hear complaints is wearisome alike to the wretched and the happy; for who would cloud by adventitious grief the short gleams of gaiety which life allows us? or who that is struggling under his own evils will add to them the miseries of another?

"The time is at hand when none shall be disturbed any longer by the sighs of Nekayah: my search after happiness is now at an end. I am resolved to retire from the world with all its flatteries and deceits, and will hide myself in solitude, without any other care than to compose my thoughts and regulate my hours by a constant succession of innocent occupations, till, with a mind purified from all earthly desires, I shall enter into that state to which all are hastening, and in which I hope again to enjoy the friendship of Pekuah."

"Do not entangle your mind," said Imlac, "by irrevocable determinations, nor increase the burthen of life by a voluntary accumulation of misery: the weariness of retirement will continue or increase when the loss of Pekuah is forgotten. That you have been deprived of one pleasure is no very good reason for rejection of the rest."

"Since Pekuah was taken from me," said the princess, "I have no pleasure to reject or to retain. She that has no one to love or trust has little to hope. She wants the radical[92] principle of happiness. We may,

91. Allow her curiosity to subside. 92. Basic.

perhaps, allow that what satisfaction this world can afford, must arise from the conjunction of wealth, knowledge, and goodness: wealth is nothing but as it is bestowed, and knowledge nothing but as it is communicated: they must therefore be imparted to others, and to whom could I now delight to impart them? Goodness affords the only comfort which can be enjoyed without a partner, and goodness may be practiced in retirement."

"How far solitude may admit goodness or advance it, I shall not," replied Imlac, "dispute at present. Remember the confession of the pious hermit. You will wish to return into the world, when the image of your companion has left your thoughts." "That time," said Nekayah, "will never come. The generous frankness, the modest obsequiousness,[93] and the faithful secrecy of my dear Pekuah, will always be more missed as I shall live longer to see vice and folly."

"The state of a mind oppressed with a sudden calamity," said Imlac, "is like that of the fabulous inhabitants of the new-created earth, who, when the first night came upon them, supposed that day never would return. When the clouds of sorrow gather over us we see nothing beyond them, nor can imagine how they will be dispelled: yet a new day succeeded to the night, and sorrow is never long without a dawn of ease. But they who restrain themselves from receiving comfort do as the savages would have done, had they put out their eyes when it was dark. Our minds, like our bodies, are in continual flux; something is hourly lost and something acquired. To lose much at once is inconvenient to either, but while the vital powers remain uninjured, nature will find the means of reparation. Distance has the same effect on the mind as on the eye, and while we glide along the stream of time, whatever we leave behind us is always lessening and that which we approach increasing in magnitude. Do not suffer life to stagnate; it will grow muddy for want of motion: commit yourself again to the current of the world; Pekuah will vanish by degrees; you will meet in your way some other favorite, or learn to diffuse yourself[94] in general conversation."

"At least," said the prince, "do not despair before all remedies have been tried: the inquiry after the unfortunate lady is still continued, and shall be carried on with yet greater diligence on condition that you will promise to wait a year for the event, without any unalterable resolution."

Nekayah thought this a reasonable demand, and made the promise to her brother, who had been advised by Imlac to require it. Imlac had, indeed, no great hope of regaining Pekuah, but he supposed that if he could secure the interval of a year, the princess would be then in no danger of a cloister.

93. Eagerness to serve. 94. Extend your attention or interest.

XXXVI

Pekuah Is Still Remembered. The Progress of Sorrow

Nekayah, seeing that nothing was omitted for the recovery of her favorite, and having by her promise set her intention of retirement at a distance, began imperceptibly to return to common cares and common pleasures. She rejoiced without her own consent at the suspension of her sorrows, and sometimes caught herself with indignation in the act of turning away her mind from the remembrance of her, whom yet she resolved never to forget.

She then appointed a certain hour of the day for meditation on the merits and fondness of Pekuah, and for some weeks retired constantly at the time fixed, and returned with her eyes swollen and her countenance clouded. By degrees she grew less scrupulous, and suffered any important and pressing avocation to delay the tribute of daily tears. She then yielded to less occasions; sometimes forgot what she was indeed afraid to remember, and at last wholly released herself from the duty of periodical affliction.

Her real love of Pekuah was yet not diminished. A thousand occurrences brought her back to memory, and a thousand wants, which nothing but the confidence of friendship can supply, made her frequently regretted. She, therefore, solicited Imlac never to desist from inquiry, and to leave no art of intelligence untried that, at least, she might have the comfort of knowing that she did not suffer by negligence or sluggishness. "Yet what," said she, "is to be expected from our pursuit of happiness, when we find the state of life to be such, that happiness itself is the cause of misery? Why should we endeavor to attain that of which the possession cannot be secured? I shall henceforward fear to yield my heart to excellence however bright, or to fondness however tender, lest I should lose again what I have lost in Pekuah."

XXXVII

The Princess Hears News of Pekuah

In seven months, one of the messengers, who had been sent away upon the day when the promise was drawn from the princess, returned, after many unsuccessful rambles, from the borders of Nubia,[95] with an account that Pekuah was in the hands of an Arab chief, who possessed a castle or fortress on the extremity of Egypt. The Arab, whose revenue

95. A region now divided between Egypt and the Sudan.

was plunder, was willing to restore her with her two attendants for two hundred ounces of gold.

The price was no subject of debate. The princess was in ecstasies when she heard that her favorite was alive, and might so cheaply be ransomed. She could not think of delaying for a moment Pekuah's happiness or her own, but entreated her brother to send back the messenger with the sum required. Imlac, being consulted, was not very confident of the veracity of the relator, and was still more doubtful of the Arab's faith, who might, if he were too liberally trusted, detain at once the money and the captives. He thought it dangerous to put themselves in the power of the Arab by going into his district, and could not expect that the rover[96] would so much expose himself as to come into the lower country, where he might be seized by the forces of the Bassa.

It is difficult to negotiate where neither will trust. But Imlac, after some deliberation, directed the messenger to propose that Pekuah should be conducted by ten horsemen to the monastery of St. Anthony, which is situated in the deserts of Upper Egypt, where she should be met by the same number, and her ransom should be paid.

That no time might be lost, as they expected that the proposal would not be refused, they immediately began their journey to the monastery; and, when they arrived, Imlac went forward with the former messenger to the Arab's fortress. Rasselas was desirous to go with them, but neither his sister nor Imlac would consent. The Arab, according to the custom of his nation, observed the laws of hospitality with great exactness to those who put themselves into his power, and in a few days brought Pekuah with her maids by easy journeys to their place appointed, where receiving the stipulated price he restored her with great respect to liberty and her friends, and undertook to conduct them back towards Cairo beyond all danger of robbery or violence.

The princess and her favorite embraced each other with transport too violent to be expressed, and went out together to pour the tears of tenderness in secret, and exchange professions of kindness and gratitude. After a few hours they returned into the refectory of the convent, where, in the presence of the prior and his brethren, the prince required of Pekuah the history of her adventures.

XXXVIII

The Adventures of the Lady Pekuah

"At what time, and in what manner, I was forced away," said Pekuah, "your servants have told you. The suddenness of the event struck me

96. Robber.

with surprise, and I was at first rather stupified than agitated with any passion of either fear or sorrow. My confusion was increased by the speed and tumult of our flight while we were followed by the Turks, who, as it seemed, soon despaired to overtake us, or were afraid of those whom they made a show of menacing.

"When the Arabs saw themselves out of danger they slackened their course, and, as I was less harassed by external violence, I began to feel more uneasiness in my mind. After some time we stopped near a spring shaded with trees in a pleasant meadow, where we were set upon the ground and offered such refreshments as our masters were partaking. I was suffered to sit with my maids apart from the rest, and none attempted to comfort or insult us. Here I first began to feel the full weight of my misery. The girls sat weeping in silence, and from time to time looked on me for succor. I knew not to what condition we were doomed, nor could conjecture where would be the place of our captivity, or whence to draw any hope of deliverance. I was in the hands of robbers and savages, and had no reason to suppose that their pity was more than their justice, or that they would forbear the gratification of any ardor of desire or caprice of cruelty. I, however, kissed my maids, and endeavored to pacify them by remarking, that we were yet treated with decency, and that, since we were now carried beyond pursuit, there was no danger of violence to our lives.

"When we were to be set again on horseback, my maids clung round me and refused to be parted, but I commanded them not to irritate those who had us in their power. We traveled the remaining part of the day through an unfrequented and pathless country, and came by moonlight to the side of a hill where the rest of the troop was stationed. Their tents were pitched and their fires kindled, and our chief was welcomed as a man much beloved by his dependents.

"We were received into a large tent, where we found women who had attended their husbands in the expedition. They set before us the supper which they had provided, and I eat it rather to encourage my maids than to comply with any appetite of my own. When the meat was taken away they spread the carpets for repose. I was weary, and hoped to find in sleep that remission of distress which nature seldom denies. Ordering myself therefore to be undressed, I observed that the women looked very earnestly upon me, not expecting, I suppose, to see me so submissively attended. When my upper vest was taken off, they were apparently struck with the splendor of my clothes, and one of them timorously laid her hand upon the embroidery. She then went out and, in a short time, came back with another woman, who seemed to be of higher rank and greater authority. She did, at her entrance, the usual act of reverence, and, taking me by the hand, placed me in a smaller tent spread with finer carpets, where I spent the night quietly with my maids.

"In the morning as I was sitting on the grass, the chief of the troop came towards me. I rose up to receive him, and he bowed with great respect. "Illustrious lady," said he, "my fortune is better than I had presumed to hope; I am told by my women that I have a princess in my camp." "Sir," answered I, "your women have deceived themselves and you; I am not a princess, but an unhappy stranger who intended soon to have left this country, in which I am now to be imprisoned forever." "Whoever, or whencesoever, you are," returned the Arab, "your dress and that of your servants show your rank to be high and your wealth to be great. Why should you, who can so easily procure your ransom, think yourself in danger of perpetual captivity? The purpose of my incursions is to increase my riches, or more properly to gather tribute. The sons of Ishmael[97] are the natural and hereditary lords of this part of the continent, which is usurped by late invaders and low-born tyrants, from whom we are compelled to take by the sword what is denied to justice. The violence of war admits no distinction; the lance that is lifted at guilt and power will sometimes fall on innocence and gentleness."

"How little," said I, "did I expect that yesterday it should have fallen upon me."

"Misfortunes," answered the Arab, "should always be expected. If the eye of hostility could learn reverence or pity, excellence like yours had been exempt from injury. But the angels of affliction spread their toils alike for the virtuous and the wicked, for the mighty and the mean. Do not be disconsolate; I am not one of the lawless and cruel rovers of the desert; I know the rules of civil[98] life: I will fix your ransom, give a passport to your messenger, and perform my stipulation with nice[99] punctuality."

"You will easily believe that I was pleased with his courtesy; and finding that his predominant passion was desire of money, I began now to think my danger less, for I knew that no sum would be thought too great for the release of Pekuah. I told him that he should have no reason to charge me with ingratitude if I was used with kindness, and that any ransom, which could be expected for a maid of common rank, would be paid, but that he must not persist to rate me as a princess. He said, he would consider what he should demand, and then, smiling, bowed and retired.

"Soon after the women came about me, each contending to be more officious[1] than the other, and my maids themselves were served with reverence. We traveled onward by short journeys. On the fourth day the chief told me, that my ransom must be two hundred ounces of gold,

97. Ishmael, the son of Abraham and Hagar (Genesis 16:15), traditionally was considered the ancestor of the Arabs.

98. Civilized. 99. Exact, strict. 1. Helpful.

which I not only promised him, but told him that I would add fifty more if I and my maids were honorably treated.

"I never knew the power of gold before. From that time I was the leader of the troop. The march of every day was longer or shorter as I commanded, and the tents were pitched where I chose to rest. We now had camels and other conveniencies for travel, my own women were always at my side, and I amused myself with observing the manners of the vagrant[2] nations, and with viewing remains of ancient edifices with which these deserted countries appear to have been, in some distant age, lavishly embellished.

"The chief of the band was a man far from illiterate: he was able to travel by the stars or the compass, and had marked in his erratic[3] expeditions such places as are most worthy the notice of a passenger.[4] He observed to me that buildings are always best preserved in places little frequented and difficult of access: for, when once a country declines from its primitive splendor, the more inhabitants are left, the quicker ruin will be made. Walls supply stones more easily than quarries, and palaces and temples will be demolished to make stables of granite and cottages of porphyry.

XXXIX
The Adventures of Pekuah Continued

"We wandered about in this manner for some weeks whether, as our chief pretended, for my gratification, or, as I rather suspected, for some convenience of his own. I endeavored to appear contented where sullenness and resentment would have been of no use, and that endeavor conduced much to the calmness of my mind; but my heart was always with Nekayah, and the troubles of the night much overbalanced the amusements of the day. My women, who threw all their cares upon their mistress, set their minds at ease from the time when they saw me treated with respect, and gave themselves up to the incidental alleviations of our fatigue without solicitude or sorrow. I was pleased with their pleasure, and animated with their confidence. My condition had lost much of its terror, since I found that the Arab ranged the country merely to get riches. Avarice is an uniform and tractable vice: other intellectual distempers are different in different constitutions of mind; that which soothes the pride of one will offend the pride of another; but to the favor of the covetous there is a ready way, bring money and nothing is denied.

"At last we came to the dwelling of our chief, a strong and spacious house built with stone in an island of the Nile, which lies, as I was told,

2. Nomadic. 3. Wandering. 4. Traveler.

under the tropic.[5] "Lady," said the Arab, "you shall rest after your journey a few weeks in this place, where you are to consider yourself as sovereign. My occupation is war: I have therefore chosen this obscure residence, from which I can issue unexpected and to which I can retire unpursued. You may now repose in security: here are few pleasures, but here is no danger." He then led me into the inner apartments, and seating me on the richest couch, bowed to the ground. His women, who considered me as a rival, looked on me with malignity; but being soon informed that I was a great lady detained only for my ransom, they began to vie with each other in obsequiousness and reverence.

"Being again comforted with new assurances of speedy liberty, I was for some days diverted from impatience by the novelty of the place. The turrets overlooked the country to a great distance, and afforded a view of many windings of the stream. In the day I wandered from one place to another as the course of the sun varied the splendor of the prospect, and saw many things which I had never seen before. The crocodiles and river-horses[6] are common in this unpeopled region, and I often looked upon them with terror though I knew that they could not hurt me. For some time I expected to see mermaids and tritons,[7] which, as Imlac has told me, the European travelers have stationed in the Nile, but no such beings ever appeared, and the Arab, when I inquired after them, laughed at my credulity.

"At night the Arab always attended me to a tower set apart for celestial observations, where he endeavored to teach me the names and courses of the stars. I had no great inclination to this study, but an appearance of attention was necessary to please my instructor, who valued himself for his skill, and, in a little while, I found some employment requisite to beguile the tediousness of time, which was to be passed always amidst the same objects. I was weary of looking in the morning on things from which I had turned away weary in the evening: I therefore was at last willing to observe the stars rather than do nothing, but could not always compose my thoughts, and was very often thinking on Nekayah when others imagined me contemplating the sky. Soon after the Arab went upon another expedition, and then my only pleasure was to talk with my maids about the accident by which we were carried away, and the happiness that we should all enjoy at the end of our captivity."

"There were women in your Arab's fortress," said the princess, "why did you not make them your companions, enjoy their conversation, and partake their diversions? In a place where they found business or amusement, why should you alone sit corroded with idle melancholy? or why could not you bear for a few months that condition to which they were condemned for life?"

5. Boundary of the torrid zone. 6. Hippopotamuses.
7. Men with fish tails, often represented as carrying a shell as a trumpet.

"The diversions of the women," answered Pekuah, "were only childish play, by which the mind accustomed to stronger operations could not be kept busy. I could do all which they delighted in doing by powers merely sensitive,[8] while my intellectual faculties were flown to Cairo. They ran from room to room as a bird hops from wire to wire in his cage. They danced for the sake of motion, as lambs frisk in a meadow. One sometimes pretended to be hurt that the rest might be alarmed, or hid herself that another might seek her. Part of their time passed in watching the progress of light bodies that floated on the river, and part in marking the various forms into which clouds broke in the sky.

"Their business was only needlework, in which I and my maids sometimes helped them; but you know that the mind will easily straggle from the fingers, nor will you suspect that captivity and absence from Nekayah could receive solace from silken flowers.

"Nor was much satisfaction to be hoped from their conversation: for of what could they be expected to talk? They had seen nothing; for they had lived from early youth in that narrow spot: of what they had not seen they could have no knowledge, for they could not read. They had no ideas but of the few things that were within their view, and had hardly names for anything but their clothes and their food. As I bore a superior character, I was often called to terminate their quarrels, which I decided as equitably as I could. If it could have amused me to hear the complaints of each against the rest, I might have been often detained by long stories, but the motives of their animosity were so small that I could not listen without intercepting the tale."

"How," said Rasselas, "can the Arab, whom you represented as a man of more than common accomplishments, take any pleasure in his seraglio, when it is filled only with women like these? Are they exquisitely beautiful?"

"They do not," said Pekuah, "want[9] that unaffecting and ignoble beauty which may subsist without sprightliness or sublimity, without energy of thought or dignity of virtue. But to a man like the Arab such beauty was only a flower casually plucked and carelessly thrown away. Whatever pleasures he might find among them, they were not those of friendship or society. When they were playing about him he looked on them with inattentive superiority: when they vied for his regard he sometimes turned away disgusted. As they had no knowledge, their talk could take nothing from the tediousness of life: as they had no choice, their fondness, or appearance of fondness, excited in him neither pride nor gratitude; he was not exalted in his own esteem by the smiles of a woman who saw no other man, nor was much obliged[10] by that regard of which he could never know the sincerity, and which he might often perceive to be exerted not so much to delight him as to pain

8. Sensory. 9. Lack. 10. Gratified.

a rival. That which he gave, and they received, as love, was only a careless distribution of superfluous time, such love as man can bestow upon that which he despises, such as has neither hope nor fear, neither joy nor sorrow."

"You have reason, lady, to think yourself happy," said Imlac, "that you have been thus easily dismissed. How could a mind, hungry for knowledge, be willing, in an intellectual famine, to lose such a banquet as Pekuah's conversation?"

"I am inclined to believe," answered Pekuah, "that he was for some time in suspense; for, notwithstanding his promise, whenever I proposed to dispatch a messenger to Cairo, he found some excuse for delay. While I was detained in his house he made many incursions into the neighboring countries, and, perhaps, he would have refused to discharge me, had his plunder been equal to his wishes. He returned always courteous, related his adventures, delighted to hear my observations, and endeavored to advance my acquaintance with the stars. When I importuned him to send away my letters, he soothed me with professions of honor and sincerity; and, when I could be no longer decently denied, put his troop again in motion, and left me to govern in his absence. I was much afflicted by this studied procrastination, and was sometimes afraid that I should be forgotten; that you would leave Cairo, and I must end my days in an island of the Nile.

"I grew at last hopeless and dejected, and cared so little to entertain him that he for a while more frequently talked with my maids. That he should fall in love with them, or with me, might have been equally fatal, and I was not much pleased with the growing friendship. My anxiety was not long; for, as I recovered some degree of cheerfulness, he returned to me, and I could not forbear to despise my former uneasiness.

"He still delayed to send for my ransom, and would, perhaps, never have determined, had not your agent found his way to him. The gold which he would not fetch he could not reject when it was offered. He hastened to prepare for our journey hither, like a man delivered from the pain of an intestine[11] conflict. I took leave of my companions in the house, who dismissed me with cold indifference."

Nekayah, having heard her favorite's relation,[12] rose and embraced her, and Rasselas gave her an hundred ounces of gold, which she presented to the Arab for the fifty that were promised.

XL

The History of a Man of Learning

They returned to Cairo, and were so well pleased at finding themselves together that none of them went much abroad. The prince began

11. Inner. 12. Narrative.

to love learning, and one day declared to Imlac, that he intended to devote himself to science,[13] and pass the rest of his days in literary solitude.

"Before you make your final choice," answered Imlac, "you ought to examine its hazards, and converse with some of those who are grown old in the company of themselves. I have just left the observatory of one of the most learned astronomers in the world, who has spent forty years in unwearied attention to the motions and appearances of the celestial bodies, and has drawn out his soul in endless calculations. He admits a few friends once a month to hear his deductions and enjoy his discoveries. I was introduced as a man of knowledge worthy of his notice. Men of various ideas and fluent conversation are commonly welcome to those whose thoughts have been long fixed upon a single point, and who find the images[14] of other things stealing away. I delighted him with my remarks, he smiled at the narrative of my travels, and was glad to forget the constellations, and descend for a moment into the lower world.

"On the next day of vacation I renewed my visit, and was so fortunate as to please him again. He relaxed from that time the severity of his rule, and permitted me to enter at my own choice. I found him always busy, and always glad to be relieved. As each knew much which the other was desirous of learning, we exchanged our notions with great delight. I perceived that I had every day more of his confidence, and always found new cause of admiration in the profundity of his mind. His comprehension is vast, his memory capacious and retentive, his discourse is methodical, and his expression clear.

"His integrity and benevolence are equal to his learning. His deepest researches and most favorite studies are willingly interrupted for any opportunity of doing good by his counsel or his riches. To his closest[15] retreat, at his most busy moments, all are admitted that want his assistance: 'For though I exclude idleness and pleasure, I will never,' says he, 'bar my doors against charity. To man is permitted the contemplation of the skies, but the practice of virtue is commanded.'"

"Surely," said the princess, "this man is happy."

"I visited him," said Imlac, "with more and more frequency, and was every time more enamored of his conversation: he was sublime[16] without haughtiness, courteous without formality, and communicative without ostentation. I was at first, great princess, of your opinion, thought him the happiest of mankind, and often congratulated him on the blessing that he enjoyed. He seemed to hear nothing with indifference but the praises of his condition, to which he always returned a general answer, and diverted the conversation to some other topic.

"Amidst this willingness to be pleased, and labor to please, I had

13. Knowledge in general. 14. Ideas. 15. Most private.
16. Lofty, impressive in manner.

quickly reason to imagine that some painful sentiment pressed upon his mind. He often looked up earnestly towards the sun, and let his voice fall in the midst of his discourse. He would sometimes, when we were alone, gaze upon me in silence with the air of a man who longed to speak what he was yet resolved to suppress. He would often send for me with vehement injunctions of haste, though, when I came to him, he had nothing extraordinary to say. And sometimes, when I was leaving him, would call me back, pause a few moments and then dismiss me.

XLI

The Astronomer Discovers the Cause of His Uneasiness

"At last the time came when the secret burst his reserve. We were sitting together last night in the turret of his house, watching the emersion[17] of a satellite of Jupiter. A sudden tempest clouded the sky, and disappointed our observation. We sat a while silent in the dark, and then he addressed himself to me in these words: 'Imlac, I have long considered thy friendship as the greatest blessing of my life. Integrity without knowledge is weak and useless, and knowledge without integrity is dangerous and dreadful. I have found in thee all the qualities requisite for trust: benevolence, experience, and fortitude. I have long discharged an office which I must soon quit at the call of nature, and shall rejoice in the hour of imbecility[18] and pain to devolve it upon thee.'

"I thought myself honored by this testimony, and protested that whatever could conduce to his happiness would add likewise to mine.

"'Hear, Imlac, what thou wilt not without difficulty credit. I have possessed for five years the regulation of weather and the distribution of the seasons: the sun has listened to my dictates, and passed from tropic to tropic by my direction; the clouds, at my call, have poured their waters, and the Nile has overflowed at my command; I have restrained the rage of the Dog Star[19] and mitigated the fervors of the Crab.[20] The winds alone, of all the elemental powers, have hitherto refused my authority, and multitudes have perished by equinoctial tempests[21] which I found myself unable to prohibit or restrain. I have administered this great office with exact justice, and made to the different nations of the earth an impartial dividend of rain and sunshine.

17. Reappearance of a star after it has been eclipsed or obscured.

18. Feebleness.

19. Sirius, in the constellation Canis Major (Great Dog); its rise in late summer supposedly was conducive to insanity.

20. The constellation, Cancer, associated with the summer solstice and the approach of hot weather.

21. Storms are incorrectly supposed to be very common at the equinoxes.

What must have been the misery of half the globe if I had limited the clouds to particular regions, or confined the sun to either side of the equator?'

XLII
The Opinion of the Astronomer Is Explained and Justified

"I suppose he discovered in me, through the obscurity of the room, some tokens of amazement and doubt, for after a short pause he proceeded thus:

"'Not to be easily credited will neither surprise nor offend me; for I am probably the first of human beings to whom this trust has been imparted. Nor do I know whether to deem this distinction a reward or punishment; since I have possessed it I have been far less happy than before, and nothing but the consciousness of good intention could have enabled me to support the weariness of unremitted vigilance.'

"'How long, sir,' said I, 'has this great office been in your hands?'

"'About ten years ago,' said he, 'my daily observations of the changes of the sky led me to consider whether, if I had the power of the seasons, I could confer greater plenty upon the inhabitants of the earth. This contemplation fastened on my mind, and I sat days and nights in imaginary dominion, pouring upon this country and that the showers of fertility, and seconding every fall of rain with a due proportion of sunshine. I had yet only the will to do good, and did not imagine that I should ever have the power.

"'One day as I was looking on the fields withering with heat, I felt in my mind a sudden wish that I could send rain on the southern mountains and raise the Nile to an inundation. In the hurry of my imagination I commanded rain to fall, and, by comparing the time of my command, with that of the inundation, I found that the clouds had listened to my lips.'

"'Might not some other cause,' said I, 'produce this concurrence? the Nile does not always rise on the same day.'

"'Do not believe,' said he with impatience, 'that such objections could escape me: I reasoned long against my own conviction, and labored against truth with the utmost obstinacy. I sometimes suspected myself of madness, and should not have dared to impart this secret but to a man like you, capable of distinguishing the wonderful from the impossible, and the incredible from the false.'

"'Why, sir,' said I, 'do you call that incredible, which you know or think you know, to be true?'

"'Because,' said he, 'I cannot prove it by any external evidence; and I know too well the laws of demonstration to think that my conviction ought to influence another who cannot, like me, be conscious of its force. I, therefore, shall not attempt to gain credit by disputation. It is sufficient that I feel this power that I have long possessed, and every day exerted it. But the life of man is short, the infirmities of age increase upon me, and the time will soon come when the regulator of the year must mingle with the dust. The care of appointing a successor has long disturbed me; the night and the day have been spent in comparisons of all the characters which have come to my knowledge, and I have yet found none so worthy as thyself.

XLIII

The Astronomer Leaves Imlac His Directions

"'Hear therefore what I shall impart with attention, such as the welfare of a world requires. If the task of a king be considered as difficult, who has the care only of a few millions to whom he cannot do much good or harm, what must be the anxiety of him, on whom depend the action of the elements, and the great gifts of light and heat!—Hear me therefore with attention.

"'I have diligently considered the position of the earth and sun, and formed innumerable schemes in which I changed their situation. I have sometimes turned aside the axis of the earth, and sometimes varied the ecliptic of the sun: but I have found it impossible to make a disposition by which the world may be advantaged; what one region gains, another loses by any imaginable alteration, even without considering the distant parts of the solar system with which we are unacquainted. Do not, therefore, in thy administration of the year, indulge thy pride by innovation; do not please thyself with thinking that thou canst make thyself renowned to all future ages by disordering the seasons. The memory of mischief is no desirable fame. Much less will it become thee to let kindness or interest[22] prevail. Never rob other countries of rain to pour it on thine own. For us the Nile is sufficient.'

"I promised that when I possessed the power, I would use it with inflexible integrity, and he dismissed me, pressing my hand. 'My heart,' said he, 'will be now at rest, and my benevolence will no more destroy my quiet: I have found a man of wisdom and virtue to whom I can cheerfully bequeath the inheritance of the sun.'"

The prince heard this narration with very serious regard, but the princess smiled, and Pekuah convulsed herself with laughter. "Ladies," said Imlac, "to mock the heaviest of human afflictions is neither charitable nor wise. Few can attain this man's knowledge and few practice his virtues; but all may suffer his calamity. Of the uncertainties of our

22. Self-interest.

present state the most dreadful and alarming is the uncertain continuance of reason."

The princess was recollected,[23] and the favorite was abashed. Rasselas, more deeply affected, inquired of Imlac, whether he thought such maladies of the mind frequent, and how they were contracted.

XLIV
The Dangerous Prevalence[24] of Imagination

"Disorders of intellect," answered Imlac, "happen much more often than superficial observers will easily believe. Perhaps, if we speak with rigorous exactness, no human mind is in its right state. There is no man whose imagination does not sometimes predominate over his reason, who can regulate his attention wholly by his will, and whose ideas will come and go at his command. No man will be found in whose mind airy[25] notions do not sometimes tyrannize, and force him to hope or fear beyond the limits of sober probability. All power of fancy over reason is a degree of insanity; but while this power is such as we can control and repress, it is not visible to others nor considered as any depravation of the mental faculties; it is not pronounced madness but when it comes[26] ungovernable, and apparently[27] influences speech or action.

"To indulge the power of fiction, and send imagination out upon the wing, is often the sport of those who delight too much in silent speculation. When we are alone we are not always busy; the labor of excogitation is too violent to last long; the ardor of inquiry will sometimes give way to idleness or satiety. He who has nothing external that can divert him must find pleasure in his own thoughts, and must conceive himself what he is not; for who is pleased with what he is? He then expatiates[28] in boundless futurity, and culls from all imaginable conditions that which for the present moment he should most desire, amuses his desires with impossible enjoyments, and confers upon his pride unattainable dominion. The mind dances from scene to scene, unites all pleasures in all combinations, and riots in delights which nature and fortune, with all their bounty, cannot bestow.

"In time some particular train of ideas fixes the attention, all other intellectual gratifications are rejected, the mind, in weariness or leisure, recurs constantly to the favorite conception, and feasts on the luscious falsehood whenever she is offended with the bitterness of truth. By degrees the reign of fancy is confirmed; she grows first imperious and in time despotic. Then fictions begin to operate as realities, false opin-

23. Recalled to seriousness. 24. Domination. 25. Unreal.
26. Becomes. 27. Openly. 28. Wanders freely.

ions fasten upon the mind, and life passes in dreams of rapture or of anguish.

"This, sir, is one of the dangers of solitude, which the hermit has confessed not always to promote goodness, and the astronomer's misery has proved to be not always propitious to wisdom."

"I will no more," said the favorite, "imagine myself the queen of Abyssinia. I have often spent the hours which the princess gave to my own disposal in adjusting ceremonies and regulating the court; I have repressed the pride of the powerful and granted the petitions of the poor; I have built new palaces in more happy situations, planted groves upon the tops of mountains, and have exulted in the beneficence of royalty, till, when the princess entered, I had almost forgotten to bow down before her."

"And I," said the princess, "will not allow myself any more to play the shepherdess in my waking dreams. I have often soothed my thoughts with the quiet and innocence of pastoral employments, till I have in my chamber heard the winds whistle and the sheep bleat; sometimes freed the lamb entangled in the thicket, and sometimes with my crook[29] encountered the wolf. I have a dress like that of the village maids which I put on to help my imagination, and a pipe on which I play softly, and suppose myself followed by my flocks."

"I will confess," said the prince, "an indulgence of fantastic delight more dangerous than yours. I have frequently endeavored to image the possibility of a perfect government by which all wrong should be restrained, all vice reformed, and all the subjects preserved in tranquillity and innocence. This thought produced innumerable schemes of reformation, and dictated many useful regulations and salutary edicts. This has been the sport and sometimes the labor of my solitude; and I start when I think with how little anguish I once supposed the death of my father and my brothers."

"Such," says Imlac, "are the effects of visionary schemes: when we first form them we know them to be absurd, but familiarize them by degrees, and in time lose sight of their folly."

XLV

They Discourse with an Old Man

The evening was now far past, and they rose to return home. As they walked along the bank of the Nile, delighted with the beams of the moon quivering on the water, they saw at a small distance an old man whom the prince had often heard in the assembly of the sages. "Yonder," said he, "is one whose years have calmed his passions, but not

29. Staff.

clouded his reason: let us close the disquisitions of the night, by inquiring what are his sentiments of his own state, that we may know whether youth alone is to struggle with vexation, and whether any better hope remains for the latter part of life."

Here the sage approached and saluted[30] them. They invited him to join their walk, and prattled[31] awhile as acquaintance that had unexpectedly met one another. The old man was cheerful and talkative, and the way seemed short in his company. He was pleased to find himself not disregarded, accompanied them to their house and, at the prince's request, entered with them. They placed him in the seat of honor, and set wine and conserves before him.

"Sir," said the princess, "an evening walk must give to a man of learning, like you, pleasures which ignorance and youth can hardly conceive. You know the qualities and the causes of all that you behold, the laws by which the river flows, the periods in which the planets perform their revolutions. Every thing must supply you with contemplation, and renew the consciousness of your own dignity."[32]

"Lady," answered he, "let the gay and the vigorous expect pleasure in their excursions, it is enough that age can obtain ease. To me the world has lost its novelty: I look round, and see what I remember to have seen in happier days. I rest against a tree, and consider that in the same shade I once disputed upon the annual overflow of the Nile with a friend who is now silent in the grave. I cast my eyes upwards, fix them on the changing moon, and think with pain on the vicissitudes of life. I have ceased to take much delight in physical truth;[33] for what have I to do with those things which I am soon to leave?"

"You may at least recreate[34] yourself," said Imlac, "with the recollection of an honorable and useful life, and enjoy the praise which all agree to give you."

"Praise," said the sage with a sigh, "is to an old man an empty sound. I have neither mother to be delighted with the reputation of her son, nor wife to partake the honors of her husband. I have outlived my friends and my rivals. Nothing is now of much importance; for I cannot extend my interest beyond myself. Youth is delighted with applause, because it is considered as the earnest of some future good, and because the prospect of life is far extended: but to me, who am now declining to decrepitude, there is little to be feared from the malevolence of men, and yet less to be hoped from their affection or esteem. Something they may yet take away, but they can give me nothing. Riches would now be useless, and high employment would be pain. My retrospect of life recalls to my view many opportunities of good neglected, much time squandered upon trifles, and more lost in idleness and vacancy.[35] I

30. Greeted. 31. Chatted. 32. Worth (as a learned man).
33. Scientific knowledge. 34. Refresh. 35. Listlessness; inactivity.

leave many great designs unattempted, and many great attempts unfinished. My mind is burthened with no heavy crime, and therefore I compose myself to tranquillity; endeavor to abstract my thoughts from hopes and cares which, though reason knows them to be vain, still try to keep their old possession of the heart; expect with serene humility that hour which nature cannot long delay; and hope to possess in a better state that happiness which here I could not find, and that virtue which here I have not attained."

He rose and went away, leaving his audience not much elated with the hope of long life. The prince consoled himself with remarking that it was not reasonable to be disappointed by this account; for age had never been considered as the season of felicity, and if it was possible to be easy in decline and weakness, it was likely that the days of vigor and alacrity might be happy: that the noon of life might be bright, if the evening could be calm.

The princess suspected that age was querulous and malignant, and delighted to repress the expectations of those who had newly entered the world. She had seen the possessors of estates look with envy on their heirs, and known many who enjoy pleasure no longer than they can confine it to themselves.

Pekuah conjectured that the man was older than he appeared, and was willing to impute his complaints to delirious[36] dejection; or else supposed that he had been unfortunate, and was therefore discontented: "For nothing," said she, "is more common than to call our own condition, the condition of life."

Imlac, who had no desire to see them depressed, smiled at the comforts which they could so readily procure to themselves, and remembered, that at the same age, he was equally confident of unmingled prosperity, and equally fertile of consolatory expedients. He forbore to force upon them unwelcome knowledge, which time itself would too soon impress. The princess and her lady retired; the madness of the astronomer hung upon their minds, and they desired Imlac to enter upon his office,[37] and delay next morning the rising of the sun.

XLVI

The Princess and Pekuah Visit the Astronomer

The princess and Pekuah, having talked in private of Imlac's astronomer, thought his character at once so amiable and so strange that they could not be satisfied without a nearer knowledge, and Imlac was requested to find the means of bringing them together.

This was somewhat difficult; the philosopher had never received any

36. Crazed. 37. Take up his duties.

visits from women, though he lived in a city that had in it many Europeans who followed the manners of their own countries, and many from other parts of the world that lived there with European liberty. The ladies would not be refused, and several schemes were proposed for the accomplishment of their design. It was proposed to introduce them as strangers in distress, to whom the sage was always accessible; but, after some deliberation, it appeared, that by this artifice no acquaintance could be formed, for their conversation would be short, and they could not decently importune him often. "This," said Rasselas, "is true; but I have yet a stronger objection against the misrepresentation of your state. I have always considered it as treason against the great republic of human nature to make any man's virtues the means of deceiving him, whether on great or little occasions. All imposture weakens confidence and chills benevolence. When the sage finds that you are not what you seemed, he will feel the resentment natural to a man who, conscious of great abilities, discovers that he has been tricked by understandings meaner than[38] his own, and perhaps the distrust, which he can never afterwards wholly lay aside, may stop the voice of counsel and close the hand of charity; and where will you find the power of restoring his benefactions to mankind or his peace to himself?"

To this no reply was attempted, and Imlac began to hope that their curiosity would subside; but, next day, Pekuah told him she had now found an honest pretense for a visit to the astronomer, for she would solicit permission to continue under him the studies in which she had been initiated by the Arab, and the princess might go with her either as a fellow-student, or because a woman could not decently come alone. "I am afraid," said Imlac, "that he will be soon weary of your company: men advanced far in knowledge do not love to repeat the elements of their art, and I am not certain that even of the elements, as he will deliver them connected with inferences and mingled with reflections, you are a very capable auditress." "That," said Pekuah, "must be my care: I ask of you only to take me thither. My knowledge is perhaps more than you imagine it, and by concurring always with his opinions I shall make him think it greater than it is."

The astronomer, in pursuance of this resolution, was told that a foreign lady, traveling in search of knowledge, had heard of his reputation and was desirous to become his scholar. The uncommonness of the proposal raised at once his surprise and curiosity and when, after a short deliberation, he consented to admit her, he could not stay[39] without impatience till the next day.

The ladies dressed themselves magnificently, and were attended by Imlac to the astronomer, who was pleased to see himself approached

38. Inferior to. 39. Wait.

with respect by persons of so splendid an appearance. In the exchange of the first civilities he was timorous and bashful; but when the talk became regular, he recollected his powers, and justified the character which Imlac had given. Inquiring of Pekuah what could have turned her inclination towards astronomy, he received from her a history of her adventure at the pyramid, and of the time passed in the Arab's island. She told her tale with ease and elegance, and her conversation took possession of his heart. The discourse was then turned to astronomy: Pekuah displayed what she knew; he looked upon her as a prodigy of genius, and entreated her not to desist from a study which she had so happily begun.

They came again and again, and were every time more welcome than before. The sage endeavored to amuse them that they might prolong their visits, for he found his thoughts grow brighter in their company; the clouds of solicitude[40] vanished by degrees as he forced himself to entertain them, and he grieved when he was left at their departure to his old employment of regulating the seasons.

The princess and her favorite had now watched his lips for several months, and could not catch a single word from which they could judge whether he continued or not in the opinion of his preternatural commission. They often contrived to bring him to an open declaration, but he easily eluded all their attacks, and on which side soever they pressed him escaped from them to some other topic.

As their familiarity increased they invited him often to the house of Imlac, where they distinguished him by extraordinary respect. He began gradually to delight in sublunary pleasures. He came early and departed late; labored to recommend himself by assiduity and compliance; excited their curiosity after new arts that they might still want his assistance; and when they made any excursion of pleasure or inquiry entreated to attend them.

By long experience of his integrity and wisdom, the prince and his sister were convinced that he might be trusted without danger; and lest he should draw any false hopes from the civilities which he received, discovered to him their condition, with the motives of their journey, and required his opinion on the choice of life.

"Of the various conditions which the world spreads before you, which you shall prefer," said the sage, "I am not able to instruct you. I can only tell that I have chosen wrong. I have passed my time in study without experience; in the attainment of sciences which can, for the most part, be but remotely useful to mankind. I have purchased knowledge at the expense of all the common comforts of life: I have missed the endearing elegance of female friendship, and the happy commerce[41] of domestic tenderness. If I have obtained any prerogatives

40. Anxiety. 41. Relationships and activities.

above other students, they have been accompanied with fear, disquiet, and scrupulosity;[42] but even of these prerogatives, whatever they were, I have, since my thoughts have been diversified by more intercourse with the world, begun to question the reality. When I have been for a few days lost in pleasing dissipation, I am always tempted to think that my inquiries have ended in error, and that I have suffered much, and suffered it in vain."

Imlac was delighted to find that the sage's understanding was breaking through its mists, and resolved to detain him from the planets till he should forget his task of ruling them, and reason should recover its original influence.

From this time the astronomer was received into familiar friendship, and partook of all their projects and pleasures: his respect kept him attentive, and the activity of Rasselas did not leave much time unengaged. Something was always to be done; the day was spent in making observations which furnished talk for the evening, and the evening was closed with a scheme for the morrow.

The sage confessed to Imlac that since he had mingled in the gay tumults of life, and divided his hours by a succession of amusements, he found the conviction of his authority over the skies fade gradually from his mind, and began to trust less to an opinion which he never could prove to others, and which he now found subject to variation from causes in which reason had no part. "If I am accidentally left alone for a few hours," said he, "my inveterate persuasion rushes upon my soul, and my thoughts are chained down by some irresistible violence, but they are soon disentangled by the prince's conversation, and instantaneously released at the entrance of Pekuah. I am like a man habitually afraid of specters, who is set at ease by a lamp, and wonders at the dread which harassed him in the dark, yet, if his lamp be extinguished, feels again the terrors which he knows that when it is light he shall feel no more. But I am sometimes afraid lest I indulge my quiet by criminal negligence, and voluntarily forget the great charge with which I am entrusted. If I favor myself in a known error, or am determined by my own ease in a doubtful question of this importance, how dreadful is my crime!"

"No disease of the imagination," answered Imlac, "is so difficult of cure as that which is complicated with the dread of guilt: fancy and conscience then act interchangeably upon us, and so often shift their places that the illusions of one are not distinguished from the dictates of the other. If fancy presents images not moral or religious, the mind drives them away when they give it pain, but when melancholic notions take the form of duty, they lay hold on the faculties without opposition, because we are afraid to exclude or banish them. For this reason the

42. Too great concern with small matters of conscience.

superstitious are often melancholy, and the melancholy almost always superstitious.

"But do not let the suggestions of timidity overpower your better reason: the danger of neglect can be but as the probability of the obligation, which when you consider it with freedom, you find very little, and that little growing every day less. Open your heart to the influence of the light, which, from time to time, breaks in upon you: when scruples importune you which you in your lucid moments know to be vain, do not stand to parley, but fly to business or to Pekuah, and keep this thought always prevalent, that you are only one atom of the mass of humanity, and have neither such virtue nor vice as that you should be singled out for supernatural favors or afflictions."

XLVII

The Prince Enters and Brings a New Topic

"All this," said the astronomer, "I have often thought, but my reason has been so long subjugated by an uncontrollable and overwhelming idea that it durst not confide in its own decisions. I now see how fatally I betrayed my quiet, by suffering chimeras to prey upon me in secret; but melancholy shrinks from communication, and I never found a man before, to whom I could impart my troubles, though I had been certain of relief. I rejoice to find my own sentiments confirmed by yours, who are not easily deceived and can have no motive or purpose to deceive. I hope that time and variety will dissipate the gloom that has so long surrounded me, and the latter part of my days will be spent in peace."

"Your learning and virtue," said Imlac, "may justly give you hopes."

Rasselas then entered with the princess and Pekuah, and inquired whether they had contrived any new diversion for the next day. "Such," said Nekayah, "is the state of life that none are happy but by the anticipation of change: the change itself is nothing; when we have made it, the next wish is to change again. The world is not yet exhausted; let me see something tomorrow which I never saw before."

"Variety," said Rasselas, "is so necessary to content that even the happy valley disgusted me by the recurrence of its luxuries; yet I could not forbear to reproach myself with impatience when I saw the monks of St. Anthony support without complaint a life, not of uniform delight, but uniform hardship."

"Those men," answered Imlac, "are less wretched in their silent convent than the Abyssinian princes in their prison of pleasure. Whatever is done by the monks is incited by an adequate and reasonable motive. Their labor supplies them with necessaries; it therefore cannot be omitted, and is certainly rewarded. Their devotion prepares them for another state, and reminds them of its approach while it fits them for it.

Their time is regularly distributed; one duty succeeds another, so that they are not left open to the distraction of unguided choice nor lost in the shades of listless inactivity. There is a certain task to be performed at an appropriated[43] hour; and their toils are cheerful, because they consider them as acts of piety by which they are always advancing towards endless felicity."

"Do you think," said Nekayah, "that the monastic rule[44] is a more holy and less imperfect state than any other? May not he equally hope for future happiness who converses[45] openly with mankind, who succors the distressed by his charity, instructs the ignorant by his learning, and contributes by his industry to the general system of life; even though he should omit some of the mortifications[46] which are practiced in the cloister, and allow himself such harmless delights as his condition may place within his reach?"

"This," said Imlac, "is a question which has long divided the wise and perplexed the good. I am afraid to decide on either part. He that lives well in the world is better than he that lives well in a monastery. But perhaps everyone is not able to stem the temptations of public life; and, if he cannot conquer, he may properly retreat. Some have little power to do good and have likewise little strength to resist evil. Many are weary of their conflicts with adversity, and are willing to eject those passions which have long busied them in vain. And many are dismissed by age and diseases from the more laborious duties of society. In monasteries the weak and timorous may be happily sheltered, the weary may repose, and the penitent may meditate. Those retreats of prayer and contemplation have something so congenial to the mind of man that perhaps there is scarcely one that does not purpose to close his life in pious abstraction[47] with a few associates serious as himself."

"Such," said Pekuah, "has often been my wish, and I have heard the princess declare that she should not willingly die in a crowd."

"The liberty of using[48] harmless pleasures," proceeded Imlac, "will not be disputed; but it is still to be examined what pleasures are harmless. The evil of any pleasure that Nekayah can image is not in the act itself but in its consequences. Pleasure, in itself harmless, may become mischievous by endearing to us a state which we know to be transient and probatory,[49] and withdrawing our thoughts from that, of which every hour brings us nearer to the beginning, and of which no length of time will bring us to the end. Mortification is not virtuous in itself, nor has any other use but that it disengages us from the allurements of sense. In the state of future perfection to which we all aspire, there will be pleasure without danger and security without restraint."

The princess was silent and Rasselas, turning to the astronomer,

43. Fixed. 44. Government of a monastery by specific "rules."
45. Lives, has relations. 46. Exercises in self-denial. 47. Seclusion.
48. Enjoying. 49. Probationary.

asked him whether he could not delay her retreat by showing her something which she had not seen before.

"Your curiosity," said the sage, "has been so general, and your pursuit of knowledge so vigorous, that novelties are not now very easily to be found: but what you can no longer procure from the living may be given by the dead. Among the wonders of this country are the catacombs, or the ancient repositories in which the bodies of the earliest generations were lodged, and where, by the virtue of the gums which embalmed them, they yet remain without corruption."

"I know not," said Rasselas, "what pleasure the sight of the catacombs can afford; but, since nothing else is offered, I am resolved to view them, and shall place this with many other things which I have done because I would do something."

They hired a guard of horsemen, and the next day visited the catacombs. When they were about to descend into the sepulchral caves, "Pekuah," said the princess, "we are now again invading the habitations of the dead; I know that you will stay behind; let me find you safe when I return." "No, I will not be left," answered Pekuah, "I will go down between you and the prince."

They then all descended, and roved with wonder through the labyrinth of subterraneous passages where the bodies were laid in rows on either side.

XLVIII

Imlac Discourses on the Nature of the Soul

"What reason," said the prince, "can be given why the Egyptians should thus expensively preserve those carcasses which some nations consume with fire, others lay to mingle with the earth, and all agree to remove from their sight as soon as decent rites can be performed?"

"The original[50] of ancient customs," said Imlac, "is commonly unknown; for the practice often continues when the cause has ceased; and concerning superstitious ceremonies it is vain to conjecture; for what reason did not dictate reason cannot explain. I have long believed that the practice of embalming arose only from tenderness to the remains of relations or friends, and to this opinion I am more inclined because it seems impossible that this care should have been general: had all the dead been embalmed, their repositories must in time have been more spacious than the dwellings of the living. I suppose only the rich or honorable were secured from corruption, and the rest left to the course of nature.

50. Origin.

"But it is commonly supposed that the Egyptians believed the soul to live as long as the body continued undissolved, and therefore tried this method of eluding death."

"Could the wise Egyptians," said Nekayah, "think so grossly of the soul? If the soul could once survive its separation, what could it afterwards receive or suffer from the body?"

"The Egyptians would doubtless think erroneously," said the astronomer, "in the darkness of heathenism, and the first dawn of philosophy. The nature of the soul is still disputed amidst all our opportunities of clearer knowledge: some yet say that it may be material, who nevertheless believe it to be immortal."

"Some," answered Imlac, "have indeed said that the soul is material, but I can scarcely believe that any man has thought it who knew how to think; for all the conclusions of reason enforce the immateriality of mind, and all the notices of sense and investigations of science concur to prove the unconsciousness of matter.

"It was never supposed that cogitation is inherent in matter, or that every particle is a thinking being. Yet, if any part of matter be devoid of thought, what part can we suppose to think? Matter can differ from matter only in form, density, bulk, motion, and direction of motion: to which of these, however varied or combined, can consciousness be annexed? To be round or square, to be solid or fluid, to be great or little, to be moved slowly or swiftly one way or another, are modes of material existence, all equally alien from the nature of cogitation. If matter be once without thought, it can only be made to think by some new modification, but all the modifications which it can admit are equally unconnected with cogitative powers."

"But the materialists,"[51] said the astronomer, "urge that matter may have qualities with which we are unacquainted."

"He who will determine," returned Imlac, "against that which he knows, because there may be something which he knows not; he that can set hypothetical possibility against acknowledged certainty, is not to be admitted among reasonable beings. All that we know of matter is that matter is inert, senseless, and lifeless; and if this conviction cannot be opposed but by referring us to something that we know not, we have all the evidence that human intellect can admit. If that which is known may be overruled by that which is unknown, no being, not omniscient, can arrive at certainty."

"Yet let us not," said the astronomer, "too arrogantly limit the Creator's power."

"It is no limitation of omnipotence," replied the poet, "to suppose that one thing is not consistent with another, that the same proposition

51. Those who argue that only matter exists.

cannot be at once true and false, that the same number cannot be even and odd, that cogitation cannot be conferred on that which is created incapable of cogitation."

"I know not," said Nekayah, "any great use of this question. Does that immateriality which, in my opinion, you have sufficiently proved, necessarily include eternal duration?"

"Of immateriality," said Imlac, "our ideas are negative and therefore obscure. Immateriality seems to imply a natural power of perpetual duration as a consequence of exemption from all causes of decay: whatever perishes is destroyed by the solution of its contexture, and separation of its parts; nor can we conceive how that which has no parts, and therefore admits no solution,[52] can be naturally corrupted or impaired."

"I know not," said Rasselas, "how to conceive any thing without extension: what is extended must have parts, and you allow that whatever has parts may be destroyed."

"Consider your own conceptions," replied Imlac, "and the difficulty will be less. You will find substance without extension. An ideal form[53] is no less real than material bulk: yet an ideal form has no extension. It is no less certain, when you think on a pyramid, that your mind possesses the idea of a pyramid, than that the pyramid itself is standing. What space does the idea of a pyramid occupy more than the idea of a grain of corn? or how can either idea suffer laceration?[54] As is the effect such is the cause; as thought is, such is the power that thinks; a power impassive[55] and indiscerptible."[56]

"But the Being," said Nekayah, "whom I fear to name, the Being which made the soul can destroy it."

"He, surely, can destroy it," answered Imlac, "since, however unperishable, it receives from a superior nature its power of duration. That it will not perish by any inherent cause of decay, or principle of corruption, may be shown by philosophy; but philosophy can tell no more. That it will not be annihilated by Him that made it, we must humbly learn from higher authority."

The whole assembly stood awhile silent and collected.[57] "Let us return," said Rasselas, "from this scene of mortality. How gloomy would be these mansions of the dead to him who did not know that he shall never die; that what now acts shall continue its agency, and what now thinks shall think on for ever. Those that lie here stretched before us, the wise and the powerful of ancient times, warn us to remember the shortness of our present state: they were perhaps snatched away while they were busy, like us, in the choice of life."

52. Dissolution. 53. An idea. 54. Tearing into parts.
55. Not susceptible to injury. 56. Indivisible. 57. Thoughtful.

"To me," said the princess, "the choice of life is become less important; I hope hereafter to think only on the choice of eternity."

They then hastened out of the caverns and, under the protection of their guard, returned to Cairo.

XLIX

The Conclusion, in Which Nothing Is Concluded

It was now the time of the inundation of the Nile: a few days after their visit to the catacombs, the river began to rise.

They were confined to their house. The whole region being under water gave them no invitation to any excursions and, being well supplied with materials for talk, they diverted themselves with comparisons of the different forms of life which they had observed, and with various schemes of happiness which each of them had formed.

Pekuah was never so much charmed with any place as the convent of St. Anthony, where the Arab restored her to the princess, and wished only to fill it with pious maidens, and to be made prioress of the order: she was weary of expectation and disgust,[58] and would gladly be fixed in some unvariable state.

The princess thought that of all sublunary things knowledge was the best: she desired first to learn all sciences, and then purposed to found a college of learned women in which she would preside, that, by conversing with the old and educating the young, she might divide her time between the acquisition and communication of wisdom, and raise up for the next age models of prudence and patterns of piety.

The prince desired a little kingdom in which he might administer justice in his own person, and see all the parts of government with his own eyes; but he could never fix the limits of his dominion, and was always adding to the number of his subjects.

Imlac and the astronomer were contented to be driven along the stream of life without directing their course to any particular port.

Of these wishes that they had formed they well knew that none could be obtained. They deliberated awhile what was to be done and resolved, when the inundation should cease, to return to Abyssinia.

58. Repulsion.

Selections from *The Rambler*

No. 4.

Saturday, 31 March 1750.

And join both profit and delight in one.
HORACE, *ART OF POETRY*, L. 334, TRANS. CREECH.[1]

The works of fiction, with which the present generation seems more particularly delighted, are such as exhibit life in its true state, diversified only by accidents that daily happen in the world, and influenced by passions and qualities which are really to be found in conversing with mankind.

This kind of writing may be termed not improperly the comedy of romance, and is to be conducted nearly by the rules of comic poetry. Its province is to bring about natural events by easy means, and to keep up curiosity without the help of wonder: it is therefore precluded from the machines[2] and expedients of the heroic romance, and can neither employ giants to snatch away a lady from the nuptial rites, nor knights to bring her back from captivity; it can neither bewilder its personages in deserts, nor lodge them in imaginary castles.

I remember a remark made by Scaliger upon Pontanus,[3] that all his writings are filled with the same images; and that if you take from him his lilies and his roses, his satyrs and his dryads, he will have nothing left that can be called poetry. In like manner, almost all the fictions of the last age will vanish if you deprive them of a hermit and a wood, a battle and a shipwreck.

1. Johnson's original Latin or Greek mottoes are omitted, but the line numbers, not given by Johnson, are those of the originals, not the translations.

2. Supernatural interpositions or devices.

3. Julius Caesar Scaliger (1484–1558) was an influential Renaissance humanist. In his *Poetics* (1561), he commented on the work of the Italian poet Giovanni Pontano (1426–1503).

Why this wild strain of imagination found reception so long, in polite[4] and learned ages, it is not easy to conceive; but we cannot wonder that, while readers could be procured, the authors were willing to continue it: for when a man had by practice gained some fluency of language, he had no further care than to retire to his closet,[5] let loose his invention,[6] and heat his mind with incredibilities; a book was thus produced without fear of criticism, without the toil of study, without knowledge of nature, or acquaintance with life.

The task of our present writers is very different; it requires, together with that learning which is to be gained from books, that experience which can never be attained by solitary diligence, but must arise from general converse and accurate observation of the living world. Their performances have, as Horace expresses it, *plus oneris quantum veniae minus*, little indulgence, and therefore more difficulty.[7] They are engaged in portraits of which everyone knows the original, and can detect any deviation from exactness of resemblance. Other writings are safe except from the malice of learning, but these are in danger from every common reader; as the slipper ill executed was censured by a shoemaker who happened to stop in his way at the Venus of Apelles.[8]

But the fear of not being approved as just copiers of human manners[9] is not the most important concern that an author of this sort ought to have before him. These books are written chiefly to the young, the ignorant, and the idle, to whom they serve as lectures of conduct and introductions into life. They are the entertainment of minds unfurnished with ideas, and therefore easily susceptible of impressions; not fixed by principles, and therefore easily following the current of fancy; not informed by experience, and consequently open to every false suggestion and partial account.

That the highest degree of reverence should be paid to youth, and that nothing indecent should be suffered to approach their eyes or ears, are precepts extorted by sense and virtue from an ancient writer, by no means eminent for chastity of thought.[10] The same kind, though not the same degree of caution, is required in everything which is laid before them, to secure them from unjust prejudices, perverse opinions, and incongruous combinations of images.

In the romances formerly written, every transaction and sentiment was so remote from all that passes among men that the reader was in very little danger of making any applications to himself; the virtues and crimes were equally beyond his sphere of activity; and he amused himself with heroes and with traitors, deliverers and persecutors, as with beings of another species, whose actions were regulated upon motives

4. Civilized. 5. Study. 6. Imagination. 7. *Epistles*, II. i. 170.
8. The Greek painter Apelles was renowned for the verisimilitude of his works.
9. Customary modes of behavior.
10. Juvenal, *Satires*, xiv. 1–58.

of their own, and who had neither faults nor excellencies in common with himself.

But when an adventurer is leveled with the rest of the world, and acts in such scenes of the universal drama as may be the lot of any other man, young spectators fix their eyes upon him with closer attention, and hope by observing his behavior and success to regulate their own practices when they shall be engaged in the like part.

For this reason these familiar histories may perhaps be made of greater use than the solemnities of professed morality, and convey the knowledge of vice and virtue with more efficacy than axioms and definitions. But if the power of example is so great as to take possession of the memory by a kind of violence, and produce effects almost without the intervention of the will, care ought to be taken that, when the choice is unrestrained, the best examples only should be exhibited; and that which is likely to operate so strongly should not be mischievous or uncertain in its effects.

The chief advantage which these fictions have over real life is that their authors are at liberty, though not to invent, yet to select objects, and to cull from the mass of mankind those individuals upon which the attention ought most to be employed; as a diamond, though it cannot be made, may be polished by art, and placed in such a situation as to display that luster which before was buried among common stones.

It is justly considered as the greatest excellency of art to imitate nature; but it is necessary to distinguish those parts of nature which are most proper for imitation: greater care is still required in representing life, which is so often discolored by passion or deformed by wickedness. If the world be promiscuously[11] described, I cannot see of what use it can be to read the account, or why it may not be as safe to turn the eye immediately upon mankind, as upon a mirror which shows all that presents itself without discrimination.

It is therefore not a sufficient vindication of a character that it is drawn as it appears, for many characters ought never to be drawn; nor of a narrative that the train of events is agreeable to observation and experience, for that observation which is called knowledge of the world will be found much more frequently to make men cunning than good. The purpose of these writings is surely not only to show mankind, but to provide that they may be seen hereafter with less hazard; to teach the means of avoiding the snares which are laid by treachery for innocence, without infusing any wish for that superiority with which the betrayer flatters his vanity; to give the power of counteracting fraud without the temptation to practice it; to initiate youth by mock encounters in the art of necessary defense, and to increase prudence[12] without impairing virtue.

11. Indiscriminately.
12. The art of conduct in ordinary life.

Many writers, for the sake of following nature, so mingle good and bad qualities in their principal personages, that they are both equally conspicuous; and as we accompany them through their adventures with delight, and are led by degrees to interest ourselves in their favor, we lose the abhorrence of their faults, because they do not hinder our pleasure or, perhaps, regard them with some kindness for being united with so much merit.

There have been men indeed splendidly wicked, whose endowments threw a brightness on their crimes, and whom scarce any villainy made perfectly detestable, because they never could be wholly divested of their excellencies; but such have been in all ages the great corrupters of the world, and their resemblance ought no more to be preserved than the art of murdering without pain.

Some have advanced, without due attention to the consequences of this notion, that certain virtues have their correspondent faults, and therefore that to exhibit either apart is to deviate from probability. Thus men are observed by Swift to be "grateful in the same degree as they are resentful."[13] This principle, with others of the same kind, supposes man to act from a brute impulse, and pursue a certain degree of inclination without any choice of the object; for, otherwise, though it should be allowed that gratitude and resentment arise from the same constitution of the passions, it follows not that they will be equally indulged when reason is consulted; yet unless that consequence be admitted, this sagacious maxim becomes an empty sound, without any relation to practice or to life.

Nor is it evident, that even the first motions[14] to these effects are always in the same proportion. For pride, which produces quickness of resentment, will obstruct gratitude, by unwillingness to admit that inferiority which obligation implies; and it is very unlikely that he who cannot think he receives a favor will acknowledge or repay it.

It is of the utmost importance to mankind that positions of this tendency should be laid open and confuted; for while men consider good and evil as springing from the same root, they will spare the one for the sake of the other, and in judging, if not of others at least of themselves, will be apt to estimate their virtues by their vices. To this fatal error all those will contribute who confound the colors of right and wrong,[15] and instead of helping to settle their boundaries, mix them with so much art that no common mind is able to disunite them.

In narratives where historical veracity has no place, I cannot discover why there should not be exhibited the most perfect idea of virtue: of virtue not angelical, nor above probability, for what we cannot credit we shall never imitate, but the highest and purest that humanity can

13. Pope made this remark, in the Pope-Swift *Miscellanies*, vol. 2.
14. Impulses.
15. Confuse right and wrong; blur the distinction between them.

reach, which, exercised in such trials as the various revolutions of things shall bring upon it, may, by conquering some calamities and enduring others, teach us what we may hope, and what we can perform. Vice, for vice is necessary to be shown, should always disgust; nor should the graces of gaiety, or the dignity of courage, be so united with it as to reconcile it to the mind. Wherever it appears, it should raise hatred by the malignity of its practices, and contempt by the meanness of its stratagems; for while it is supported by either parts[16] or spirit, it will be seldom heartily abhorred. The Roman tyrant was content to be hated, if he was but feared;[17] and there are thousands of the readers of romances willing to be thought wicked, if they may be allowed to be wits. It is therefore to be steadily inculcated that virtue is the highest proof of understanding, and the only solid basis of greatness; and that vice is the natural consequence of narrow thoughts, that it begins in mistake, and ends in ignominy.

No. 8.
Saturday, 14 April 1750.

For he that but conceives a crime in thought,
Contracts the danger of an actual fault.
JUVENAL, *SATIRES*, XIII. 208–10, TRANS. CREECH.

If the most active and industrious of mankind was able, at the close of life, to recollect distinctly his past moments, and distribute them in a regular account according to the manner in which they have been spent, it is scarcely to be imagined how few would be marked out to the mind by any permanent or visible effects, how small a proportion his real action would bear to his seeming possibilities of action, how many chasms he would find of wide and continued vacuity, and how many interstitial spaces unfilled, even in the most tumultuous hurries of business, and the most eager vehemence of pursuit.

It is said by modern philosophers[1] that not only the great globes of matter are thinly scattered through the universe, but the hardest bodies are so porous that, if all matter were compressed to perfect solidity, it might be contained in a cube of a few feet. In like manner, if all the employment of life were crowded into the time which it really occupied, perhaps a few weeks, days, or hours, would be sufficient for its accomplishment, so far as the mind was engaged in the performance. For such is the inequality of our corporeal to our intellectual faculties that we contrive in minutes what we execute in years, and the

16. Natural abilities.
17. Caligula (Suetonius, *Lives of the Caesars*).
1. Scientists.

soul often stands an idle spectator of the labor of the hands and expedition of the feet.

For this reason, the ancient generals often found themselves at leisure to pursue the study of philosophy in the camp; and Lucan, with historical veracity, makes Caesar relate of himself, that he noted the revolutions of the stars in the midst of preparations for battle.

Media inter proelia semper
Sideribus, coelique plagis, superisque vacavi.

PHARSALIA, X.185–86.

Amid the storms of war, with curious eyes
I trace the planets and survey the skies.

That the soul always exerts her peculiar powers with greater or less force is very probable, though the common occasions of our present condition require but a small part of that incessant cogitation; and by the natural frame of our bodies, and general combination of the world, we are so frequently condemned to inactivity that as through all our time we are thinking, so for a great part of our time we can only think.

Lest a power so restless should be either unprofitably or hurtfully employed, and the superfluities of intellect run to waste, it is no vain speculation to consider how we may govern our thoughts, restrain them from irregular motions, or confine them from boundless dissipation.[2]

How the understanding is best conducted to the knowledge of science,[3] by what steps it is to be led forwards in its pursuit, how it is to be cured of its defects, and habituated to new studies, has been the inquiry of many acute and learned men, whose observations I shall not either adopt or censure; my purpose being to consider the moral discipline of the mind, and to promote the increase of virtue rather than of learning.

This inquiry seems to have been neglected for want of remembering that all action has its origin in the mind, and that therefore to suffer the thoughts to be vitiated, is to poison the fountains of morality: irregular desires will produce licentious practices; what men allow themselves to wish they will soon believe, and will be at last incited to execute what they please themselves with contriving.

For this reason the casuists of the Romish church, who gain, by confession, great opportunities of knowing human nature, have generally determined that what it is a crime to do, it is a crime to think. Since by revolving with pleasure, the facility, safety or advantage of a wicked deed, a man soon begins to find his constancy relax, and his detestation soften; the happiness of success glittering before him withdraws his attention from the atrociousness of the guilt, and acts are at

2. Distraction, lack of concentration.
3. Any field of study.

last confidently perpetrated, of which the first conception only crept into the mind, disguised in pleasing complications, and permitted rather than invited.

No man has ever been drawn to crimes, by love or jealousy, envy or hatred, but he can tell how easily he might at first have repelled the temptation, how readily his mind would have obeyed a call to any other object, and how weak his passion has been after some casual avocation,[4] till he has recalled it again to his heart and revived the viper by too warm a fondness.

Such, therefore, is the importance of keeping reason a constant guard over imagination that we have otherwise no security for our own virtue, but may corrupt our hearts in the most recluse solitude with more pernicious and tyrannical appetites and wishes than the commerce of the world will generally produce; for we are easily shocked by crimes which appear at once in their full magnitude, but the gradual growth of our own wickedness, endeared by interest, and palliated by all the artifices of self-deceit, gives us time to form distinctions in our own favor, and reason by degrees submits to absurdity, as the eye is in time accommodated to darkness.

In this disease of the soul, it is of the utmost importance to apply remedies at the beginning; and, therefore, I shall endeavor to show what thoughts are to be rejected or improved, as they regard the past, present, or future; in hopes that some may be awakened to caution and vigilance who, perhaps, indulge themselves in dangerous dreams, so much the more dangerous because being yet only dreams they are concluded innocent.

The recollection of the past is only useful by way of provision for the future; and therefore, in reviewing all occurrences that fall under a religious consideration, it is proper that a man stop at the first thoughts, to remark how he was led thither, and why he continues the reflection. If he is dwelling with delight upon a stratagem of successful fraud, a night of licentious riot, or an intrigue of guilty pleasure, let him summon off his imagination as from an unlawful pursuit, expel those passages from his remembrance, of which, though he cannot seriously approve them, the pleasure overpowers the guilt, and refer them to a future hour when they may be considered with greater safety. Such an hour will certainly come; for the impressions of past pleasure are always lessening, but the sense of guilt, which respects futurity, continues the same.

The serious and impartial retrospect of our conduct is indisputably necessary to the confirmation or recovery of virtue, and is therefore recommended under the name of self-examination by divines as the first act previous to repentance. It is, indeed, of so great use that with-

4. Interruption; call of business.

out it we should always be to begin life, be seduced for ever by the same allurements, and misled by the same fallacies. But in order that we may not lose the advantage of our experience, we must endeavor to see every thing in its proper form, and excite in ourselves those sentiments which the great author of nature has decreed the concomitants or followers of good or bad actions. . . .

> Let not sleep, says Pythagoras, fall upon thy eyes till thou hast thrice reviewed the transactions of the past day. Where have I turned aside from rectitude? What have I been doing? What have I left undone which I ought to have done? Begin thus from the first act and proceed; and in conclusion, at the ill which thou hast done be troubled, and rejoice for the good.[5]

Our thoughts on present things being determined by the objects before us fall not under those indulgences or excursions which I am now considering. But I cannot forbear, under this head, to caution pious and tender minds that are disturbed by the irruptions of wicked imaginations against too great dejection and too anxious alarms; for thoughts are only criminal when they are first chosen and then voluntarily continued.

> Evil into the mind of god or man
> May come and go, so unapproved, and leave
> No spot or stain behind.
>
> *PARADISE LOST*, V. 117–19.

In futurity chiefly are the snares lodged by which the imagination is entangled. Futurity is the proper abode of hope and fear, with all their train and progeny of subordinate apprehensions and desires. In futurity events and chances are yet floating at large without apparent connection with their causes, and we therefore easily indulge the liberty of gratifying ourselves with a pleasing choice. To pick and cull among possible advantages is, as the civil law terms it, *in vacuum venire,* to take what belongs to nobody; but it has this hazard in it that we shall be unwilling to quit what we have seized, though an owner should be found. It is easy to think on that which may be gained till at last we resolve to gain it, and to image the happiness of particular conditions till we can be easy in no other. We ought, at least, to let our desires fix upon nothing in another's power for the sake of our quiet, or in another's possession for the sake of our innocence. When a man finds himself led, though by a train of honest sentiments, to a wish for that to which he has no right, he should start back as from a pitfall covered with flowers. He that fancies he should benefit the public more in a great station than the man that fills it will in time imagine it an act of virtue to supplant him; and, as opposition readily kindles into hatred,

5. *Aurea Carmina (Golden Verses),* 11.40–44. Johnson's quotation of the Greek original is omitted.

his eagerness to do that good to which he is not called will betray him to crimes, which in his original scheme were never purposed.

He therefore that would govern his actions by the laws of virtue must regulate his thoughts by those of reason; he must keep guilt from the recesses of his heart, and remember that the pleasures of fancy and the emotions of desire are more dangerous as they are more hidden, since they escape the awe of observation, and operate equally in every situation without the concurrence of external opportunities.

No. 14.
Saturday, 5 May 1750.

Sure such a various creature ne'er was known.
HORACE, *SATIRES*, I.iii. 18–19, TRANS. FRANCIS.

Among the many inconsistencies which folly produces, or infirmity suffers in the human mind, there has often been observed a manifest and striking contrariety between the life of an author and his writings; and Milton, in a letter to a learned stranger, by whom he had been visited, with great reason congratulates himself upon the consciousness of being found equal to his own character, and having preserved in a private and familiar interview[1] that reputation which his works had procured him.[2]

Those whom the appearance of virtue, or the evidence of genius, have tempted to a nearer knowledge of the writer in whose performances they may be found, have indeed had frequent reason to repent their curiosity; the bubble that sparkled before them has become common water at the touch; the phantom of perfection has vanished when they wished to press it to their bosom. They have lost the pleasure of imagining how far humanity may be exalted and, perhaps, felt themselves less inclined to toil up the steeps of virtue, when they observe those who seem best able to point the way, loitering below, as either afraid of the labor or doubtful of the reward.

It has been long the custom of the oriental monarchs to hide themselves in gardens and palaces, to avoid the conversation of[3] mankind, and to be known to their subjects only by their edicts. The same policy is no less necessary to him that writes, than to him that governs; for men would not more patiently submit to be taught, than commanded, by one known to have the same follies and weaknesses with themselves. A sudden intruder into the closet of an author would perhaps feel equal indignation with the officer, who having long solicited admission into

1. Visit.
2. To Emeric Bigot, 24 March 1657.
3. Familiar relationships with.

the presence of Sardanapalus,[4] saw him not consulting upon laws, inquiring into grievances, or modeling armies, but employed in feminine amusements, and directing the ladies in their work.

It is not difficult to conceive, however, that for many reasons a man writes much better than he lives. For, without entering into refined speculations,[5] it may be shown much easier to design than to perform. A man proposes his schemes of life in a state of abstraction and disengagement, exempt from the enticements of hope, the solicitations of affection, the importunities of appetite, or the depressions of fear, and is in the same state with him that teaches upon land the art of navigation, to whom the sea is always smooth and the wind always prosperous.[6]

The mathematicians are well acquainted with the difference between pure science, which has to do only with ideas, and the application of its laws to the use of life, in which they are constrained to submit to the imperfection of matter and the influence of accidents.[7] Thus, in moral discussions it is to be remembered that many impediments obstruct our practice, which very easily give way to theory. The speculatist is only in danger of erroneous reasoning, but the man involved in life has his own passions and those of others to encounter, and is embarrassed with a thousand inconveniences, which confound him with variety of impulse, and either perplex or obstruct his way. He is forced to act without deliberation, and obliged to choose before he can examine; he is surprised by sudden alterations of the state of things, and changes his measures according to superficial appearances; he is led by others, either because he is indolent or because he is timorous; he is sometimes afraid to know what is right, and sometimes finds friends or enemies diligent to deceive him.

We are, therefore, not to wonder that most fail, amidst tumult and snares and danger, in the observance of those precepts, which they laid down in solitude, safety, and tranquillity, with a mind unbiased, and with liberty unobstructed. It is the condition of our present state to see more than we can attain, the exactest vigilance and caution can never maintain a single day of unmingled innocence, much less can the utmost efforts of incorporated mind[8] reach the summits of speculative virtue.

It is, however, necessary for the idea of perfection to be proposed, that we may have some object to which our endeavors are to be directed; and he that is most deficient in the duties of life makes some atonement for his faults if he warns others against his own failings, and

4. Ninth-century B.C. Assyrian ruler.
5. Theories.
6. Favorable.
7. Non-essentials.
8. Mind united with the body.

hinders, by the salubrity of his admonitions, the contagion of his example.

Nothing is more unjust, however common, than to charge with hypocrisy him that expresses zeal for those virtues, which he neglects to practice; since he may be sincerely convinced of the advantages of conquering his passions, without having yet obtained the victory, as a man may be confident of the advantages of a voyage or a journey, without having courage or industry to undertake it, and may honestly recommend to others those attempts which he neglects himself.

The interest which the corrupt part of mankind have in hardening themselves against every motive to amendment has disposed them to give to these contradictions, when they can be produced against the cause of virtue, that weight which they will not allow them in any other case. They see men act in opposition to their interest, without supposing that they do not know it; those who give way to the sudden violence of passion, and forsake the most important pursuits for petty pleasures, are not supposed to have changed their opinions or to approve their own conduct. In moral or religious questions alone, they determine the sentiments by the actions, and charge every man with endeavoring to impose upon the world, whose writings are not confirmed by his life. They never consider that they themselves neglect or practice something every day inconsistently with their own settled judgment, nor discover that the conduct of the advocates for virtue can little increase or lessen the obligations of their dictates; argument is to be invalidated only by argument, and is in itself of the same force whether or not it convinces him by whom it is proposed.

Yet since this prejudice, however unreasonable, is always likely to have some prevalence, it is the duty of every man to take care lest he should hinder the efficacy of his own instructions. When he desires to gain the belief of others, he should show that he believes himself; and when he teaches the fitness of virtue by his reasonings, he should by his example prove its possibility: thus much at least may be required of him, that he shall not act worse than others because he writes better, nor imagine that, by the merit of his genius, he may claim indulgence beyond mortals of the lower classes, and be excused for want of prudence or neglect of virtue.

Bacon, in his "History of the Winds,"[9] after having offered something to the imagination as desirable, often proposes lower advantages in its place to the reason as attainable. The same method may be sometimes pursued in moral endeavors, which this philosopher has observed in natural[10] inquiries; having first set positive and absolute excellence before us, we may be pardoned though we sink down to hum-

9. Included in the *Natural and Experimental History* (1622) of Francis Bacon.
10. Scientific.

bler virtue, trying, however, to keep our point always in view, and struggling not to lose ground though we cannot gain it.

It is recorded of Sir Matthew Hale that he, for a long time, concealed the consecration of himself to the stricter duties of religion, lest, by some flagitious[11] and shameful action, he should bring piety into disgrace.[12] For the same reason, it may be prudent for a writer, who apprehends that he shall not enforce his own maxims by his domestic character, to conceal his name that he may not injure them.

There are, indeed, a greater number whose curiosity to gain a more familiar knowledge of successful writers, is not so much prompted by an opinion of their power to improve as to delight, and who expect from them not arguments against vice, or dissertations on temperance or justice, but flights of wit, and sallies of pleasantry, or, at least, acute remarks, nice distinctions, justness of sentiment, and elegance of diction.

This expectation is, indeed, specious and probable, and yet such is the fate of all human hopes, that it is very often frustrated, and those who raise admiration by their books, disgust[13] by their company. A man of letters for the most part spends, in the privacies of study, that season of life in which the manners are to be softened into ease, and polished into elegance, and, when he has gained knowledge enough to be respected, has neglected the minuter acts by which he might have pleased. When he enters life, if his temper be soft and timorous, he is diffident and bashful from the knowledge of his defects; or if he was born with spirit and resolution, he is ferocious and arrogant from the consciousness of his merit: he is either dissipated[14] by the awe of company, and unable to recollect his reading and arrange his arguments; or he is hot and dogmatical, quick in opposition, and tenacious in defense, disabled by his own violence, and confused by his haste to triumph.

The graces of writing and conversation are of different kinds, and though he who excels in one might have been with opportunities and application equally successful in the other, yet as many please by extemporary talk, though utterly unacquainted with the more accurate method and more labored beauties which composition requires; so it is very possible that men, wholly accustomed to works of study, may be without that readiness of conception and affluence of language always necessary to colloquial[15] entertainment. They may want address[16] to watch the hints which conversation offers for the display of their particular attainments, or they may be so much unfurnished with matter on common subjects that discourse not professedly literary glides over

11. Scandalous.

12. Sir Matthew Hale (1609–76), Lord Chief Justice of the King's Bench, and author of religious works.

13. Displease. 14. Confused. 15. Conversational. 16. Skill.

them as heterogeneous bodies, without admitting their conceptions to mix in the circulation.

A transition from an author's books to his conversation is too often like an entrance into a large city, after a distant prospect. Remotely, we see nothing but spires of temples and turrets of palaces, and imagine it the residence of splendor, grandeur, and magnificence; but, when we have passed the gates, we find it perplexed with narrow passages, disgraced with despicable cottages, embarrassed with obstructions, and clouded with smoke.

No. 36.
Saturday, 21 July 1750.

Piping on their reeds, the shepherds go,
Nor fear an ambush, nor suspect a foe.
HOMER, *ILIAD*, XVIII. 525–26, TRANS. POPE.

There is scarcely any species of poetry that has allured more readers or excited more writers than the pastoral. It is generally pleasing because it entertains the mind with representations of scenes familiar to almost every imagination, and of which all can equally judge whether they are well described. It exhibits a life to which we have been always accustomed to associate peace and leisure and innocence: and therefore we readily set open the heart for the admission of its images, which contribute to drive away cares and perturbations, and suffer ourselves without resistance to be transported to Elysian regions,[1] where we are to meet with nothing but joy and plenty and contentment; where every gale whispers pleasure, and every shade promises repose.

It has been maintained by some who love to talk of what they do not know that pastoral is the most ancient poetry; and, indeed, since it is probable that poetry is nearly of the same antiquity with rational nature, and since the life of the first men was certainly rural, we may reasonably conjecture, that, as their ideas[2] would necessarily be borrowed from those objects with which they were acquainted, their composures,[3] being filled chiefly with such thoughts on the visible creation as must occur to the first observers, were pastoral hymns like those which Milton introduces the original pair singing, in the day of innocence, to the praise of their Maker.[4]

For the same reason that pastoral poetry was the first employment of the human imagination, it is generally the first literary amusement of our minds. We have seen fields and meadows and groves from the time

1. In Greek mythology, the abode of the blessed after death.
2. Images.
3. Compositions.
4. Adam and Eve in *Paradise Lost* (v. 153–208).

that our eyes opened upon life; and are pleased with birds and brooks and breezes, much earlier than we engage among the actions and passions of mankind. We are therefore delighted with rural pictures, because we know the original at an age when our curiosity can be very little awakened by descriptions of courts which we never beheld, or representations of passion which we never felt.

The satisfaction received from this kind of writing not only begins early, but lasts long; we do not, as we advance into the intellectual world, throw it away among other childish amusements and pastimes, but willingly return to it in any hour of indolence and relaxation. The images of true pastoral have always the power of exciting delight, because the works of nature, from which they are drawn, have always the same order and beauty, and continue to force themselves upon our thoughts, being at once obvious to the most careless regard, and more than adequate to the strongest reason and severest contemplation. Our inclination to stillness and tranquillity is seldom much lessened by long knowledge of the busy and tumultuary part of the world. In childhood we turn our thoughts to the country, as to the region of pleasure; we recur to it in old age as a port of rest, and perhaps with that secondary and adventitious[5] gladness, which every man feels on reviewing those places, or recollecting those occurrences, that contributed to his youthful enjoyments, and bring him back to the prime of life, when the world was gay with the bloom of novelty, when mirth wantoned[6] at his side, and hope sparkled before him.

The sense of this universal pleasure has invited "numbers without number"[7] to try their skill in pastoral performances, in which they have generally succeeded after the manner of other imitators, transmitting the same images in the same combination from one to another, till he that reads the title of a poem may guess at the whole series of the composition; nor will a man, after the perusal of thousands of these performances, find his knowledge enlarged with a single view of nature not produced before, or his imagination amused with any new application of those views to moral purposes.

The range of pastoral is indeed narrow, for though nature itself, philosophically considered, be inexhaustible, yet its general effects on the eye and on the ear are uniform, and incapable of much variety of description. Poetry cannot dwell upon the minuter distinctions by which one species differs from another, without departing from that simplicity of grandeur which fills the imagination; nor dissect the latent qualities of things, without losing its general power of gratifying every mind by recalling its conceptions. However, as each age makes some discoveries, and those discoveries are by degrees generally known, as

5. Accidental, not inherent.
6. Played gaily.
7. *Paradise Lost,* iii. 346.

new plants or modes of culture[8] are introduced, and by little and little become common, pastoral might receive, from time to time, small augmentations, and exhibits once in a century a scene somewhat varied.

But pastoral subjects have been often, like others, taken into the hands of those that were not qualified to adorn them, men to whom the face of nature was so little known, that they have drawn it only after their own imagination, and changed or distorted her features, that their portraits might appear something more than servile copies from their predecessors.

Not only the images of rural life, but the occasions on which they can be properly produced, are few and general. The state of a man confined to the employments and pleasures of the country, is so little diversified, and exposed to so few of those accidents which produce perplexities, terrors and surprises, in more complicated transactions, that he can be shown but seldom in such circumstances as attract curiosity. His ambition is without policy, and his love without intrigue. He has no complaints to make of his rival but that he is richer than himself; nor any disasters to lament, but a cruel mistress or a bad harvest.

The conviction of the necessity of some new source of pleasure induced Sannazarius to remove the scene from the fields to the sea, to substitute fishermen for shepherds, and derive his sentiments from the piscatory life;[9] for which he has been censured by succeeding critics, because the sea is an object of terror, and by no means proper to amuse the mind and lay the passions asleep. Against this objection he might be defended by the established maxim, that the poet has a right to select his images, and is no more obliged to show the sea in a storm, than the land under an inundation; but may display all the pleasures, and conceal the dangers of the water, as he may lay his shepherd under a shady beech, without giving him an ague, or letting a wild beast loose upon him.

There are however two defects in the piscatory eclogue, which perhaps cannot be supplied. The sea, though in hot countries it is considered by those who live, like Sannazarius, upon the coast, as a place of pleasure and diversion, has notwithstanding much less variety than the land, and therefore will be sooner exhausted by a descriptive writer. When he has once shown the sun rising or setting upon it, curled its waters with the vernal breeze, rolled the waves in gentle succession to the shore, and enumerated the fish sporting in the shallows, he has nothing remaining but what is common to all other poetry, the complaint of a nymph for a drowned lover, or the indignation of a fisher that his oysters are refused, and Mycon's accepted.

8. Cultivation.

9. Jacopo Sannazaro's poem *Arcadia* (1504) described an ideal pastoral landscape in Greece. His later poems were *Piscatory Eclogues,* which presented idealized fishermen rather than shepherds.

Another obstacle to the general reception of this kind of poetry is the ignorance of maritime pleasures, in which the greater part of mankind must always live. To all the inland inhabitants of every region, the sea is only known as an immense diffusion of waters, over which men pass from one country to another, and in which life is frequently lost. They have, therefore, no opportunity of tracing, in their own thoughts, the descriptions of winding shores and calm bays, nor can look on the poem in which they are mentioned, with other sensations, than on a sea chart, or the metrical geography of Dionysius.[10]

This defect Sannazarius was hindered from perceiving, by writing in a learned language[11] to readers generally acquainted with the works of nature; but if he had made his attempt in any vulgar tongue,[12] he would soon have discovered how vainly he had endeavored to make that loved which was not understood.

I am afraid it will not be found easy to improve the pastorals of antiquity, by any great additions or diversifications. Our descriptions may indeed differ from those of Virgil, as an English from an Italian summer, and, in some respects, as modern from ancient life; but as nature is in both countries nearly the same, and as poetry has to do rather with the passions of men, which are uniform, than their customs, which are changeable, the varieties, which time or place can furnish, will be inconsiderable: and I shall endeavor to show, in the next paper, how little the latter ages have contributed to the improvement of the rustic muse.

No. 37.
Tuesday, 24 July 1750.

Such strains I sing as once Amphion played,
When listening flocks the powerful call obeyed.
VIRGIL, *ECLOGUES*, II. 23–24, TRANS. ELPHINSTON.

In writing or judging of pastoral poetry, neither the authors nor critics of latter times seem to have paid sufficient regard to the originals left us by antiquity, but have entangled themselves with unnecessary difficulties, by advancing principles which, having no foundation in the nature of things, are wholly to be rejected from a species of composition in which, above all others, mere[1] nature is to be regarded.

It is, therefore, necessary to inquire after some more distinct and

10. Greek poet of the first century A.D., who wrote a poem entitled *A Description of the Inhabited World.* He is not to be confused with Dionysius of Halicarnassus, who is quoted in *Rambler*, no. 94.
11. Latin.
12. Modern language.
1. Pure, unmixed.

exact idea of this kind of writing. This may, I think, be easily found in the pastorals of Virgil, from whose opinion it will not appear very safe to depart if we consider that every advantage of nature, and of fortune, concurred to complete his productions; that he was born with great accuracy and severity of judgment, enlightened with all the learning of one of the brightest ages, and embellished with the elegance of the Roman court; that he employed his powers rather in improving, than inventing, and therefore must have endeavored to recompense the want of novelty by exactness; that taking Theocritus[2] for his original, he found pastoral far advanced towards perfection, and that having so great a rival, he must have proceeded with uncommon caution.

If we search the writings of Virgil for the true definition of a pastoral, it will be found "a poem in which any action or passion is represented by its effects upon a country life." Whatsoever therefore may, according to the common course of things, happen in the country, may afford a subject for a pastoral poet.

In this definition, it will immediately occur to those who are versed in the writings of the modern critics, that there is no mention of the Golden Age. I cannot indeed easily discover why it is thought necessary to refer descriptions of a rural state to remote times, nor can I perceive that any writer has consistently preserved the Arcadian[3] manners and sentiments. The only reason, that I have read, on which this rule has been founded is that, according to the customs of modern life, it is improbable that shepherds should be capable of harmonious numbers,[4] or delicate sentiments; and therefore the reader must exalt his ideas of the pastoral character by carrying his thoughts back to the age in which the care of herds and flocks was the employment of the wisest and greatest men.

These reasoners seem to have been led into their hypothesis by considering pastoral, not in general, as a representation of rural nature, and consequently as exhibiting the ideas and sentiments of those, whoever they are, to whom the country affords pleasure or employment, but simply as a dialogue, or narrative of men actually tending sheep, and busied in the lowest and most laborious offices;[5] from whence they very readily concluded, since characters must necessarily be preserved, that either the sentiments must sink to the level of the speakers, or the speakers must be raised to the height of the sentiments.

In consequence of these original errors, a thousand precepts have been given which have only contributed to perplex and to confound. Some have thought it necessary that the imaginary manners of the

2. The *Idylls* of the Greek poet Theocritus (third century B.C.) mark the beginning of pastoral poetry.

3. The inhabitants of Arcadia, a rural region of Greece, were thought to live the idyllic existence of the Golden Age.

4. Musical or smooth verses.

5. Employments.

Golden Age should be universally preserved, and have therefore believed, that nothing more could be admitted in pastoral, than lilies and roses, and rocks and streams, among which are heard the gentle whispers of chaste fondness, or the soft complaints of amorous impatience. In pastoral, as in other writings, chastity of sentiment ought doubtless to be observed, and purity of manners to be represented; not because the poet is confined to the images of the Golden Age, but because, having the subject in his own choice, he ought always to consult the interest of virtue.

These advocates for the Golden Age lay down other principles, not very consistent with their general plan; for they tell us that, to support the character of the shepherd, it is proper that all refinement should be avoided, and that some slight instances of ignorance should be interspersed. Thus the shepherd in Virgil is supposed to have forgot the name of Anaximander,[6] and in Pope the term "Zodiac" is too hard for a rustic apprehension.[7] But if we place our shepherds in their primitive condition, we may give them learning among their other qualifications; and if we suffer them to allude at all to things of later existence which, perhaps, cannot with any great propriety be allowed, there can be no danger of making them speak with too much accuracy, since they conversed with divinities, and transmitted to succeeding ages the arts of life.

Other writers, having the mean and despicable condition of a shepherd always before them, conceive it necessary to degrade the language of pastoral, by obsolete terms and words, which they very learnedly call Doric,[8] without reflecting, that they thus become authors of a mingled dialect, which no human being ever could have spoken, that they may as well refine the speech as the sentiments of their personages, and that none of the inconsistencies which they endeavor to avoid, is greater than that of joining elegance of thought with coarseness of diction. Spenser begins one of his pastorals with studied barbarity;

> Diggon Davie, I bid her good day:
> Or, Diggon her is, or I missay.
> *Dig.* Her was her while it was daylight,
> But now her is a most wretched wight.

[*SHEPHERD'S CALENDAR*, "SEPTEMBER," ll. 1–4.]

What will the reader imagine to be the subject on which speakers like these exercise their eloquence? Will he not be somewhat disappointed, when he finds them met together to condemn the corruptions of the

6. Johnson supposes that the name of the astronomer forgotten in Virgil's third *Eclogue* (l. 40) is Anaximander, a sixth-century B.C. Greek.
7. Pope, *Pastorals*, "Spring," ll. 39–40.
8. Rustic Greek dialect.

church of Rome? Surely, at the same time that a shepherd learns theology, he may gain some acquaintance with his native language.

Pastoral admits of all ranks of persons, because persons of all ranks inhabit the country. It excludes not, therefore, on account of the characters necessary to be introduced, any elevation or delicacy of sentiment; those ideas only are improper which, not owing their original to rural objects, are not pastoral. Such is the exclamation in Virgil.

Nunc scio quid sit Amor, duris in cautibus illum
Ismarus, aut Rhodope, aut extremi Garamantes,
Nec generis nostri puerum nec sanguinis, edunt.[9]

I know thee, love, in deserts thou wert bred,
And at the dugs of savage tigers fed:
Alien of birth, usurper of the plains.

DRYDEN.

which Pope endeavoring to copy, was carried to still greater impropriety.

I know thee, Love, wild as the raging main,
More fierce than tigers on the Libyan plain;
Thou wert from Etna's burning entrails torn,
Begot in tempests, and in thunders born![10]

["AUTUMN," ll.89–92.]

Sentiments like these, as they have no ground in nature, are indeed of little value in any poem, but in pastoral they are particularly liable to censure, because it wants that exaltation above common life, which in tragic or heroic writings often reconciles us to bold flights and daring figures.[11]

Pastoral being the "representation of an action or passion by its effects upon a country life," has nothing peculiar but its confinement to rural imagery, without which it ceases to be pastoral. This is its true characteristic, and this it cannot lose by any dignity of sentiment, or beauty of diction. The Pollio of Virgil,[12] with all its elevation, is a composition truly bucolic, though rejected by the critics; for all the images are either taken from the country, or from the religion of the age common to all parts of the empire.

The Silenus is indeed of a more disputable kind, because though the scene lies in the country, the song being religious and historical had been no less adapted to any other audience or place. Neither can it well be defended as a fiction, for the introduction of a god seems to imply

9. "Now I know what love is: it is brought forth in Ismarus, or in Rhodope, or in distant Garamant, in harsh, rocky regions; it is not of human race or blood" (*Eclogues,* viii. 43–45).

10. From Pope's *Pastorals.*

11. Images or metaphors.

12. The fourth *Eclogue,* often interpreted as foreshadowing the coming of Christ, since it celebrates a newborn child and the beginning of an age of peace.

the Golden Age, and yet he alludes to many subsequent transactions, and mentions Gallus, the poet's contemporary.[13]

It seems necessary to the perfection of this poem that the occasion which is supposed to produce it, be at least not inconsistent with a country life, or less likely to interest those who have retired into places of solitude and quiet than the more busy part of mankind. It is therefore improper to give the title of a pastoral to verses, in which the speakers, after the slight mention of their flocks, fall to complaints of errors in the church and corruptions in the government, or to lamentations of the death of some illustrious person, whom when once the poet has called a shepherd, he has no longer any labor upon his hands, but can make the clouds weep, and lilies wither, and the sheep hang their heads, without art or learning, genius or study.

It is part of Claudian's character of his rustic that he computes his time not by the succession of consuls, but of harvests.[14] Those who pass their days in retreats distant from the theaters of business, are always least likely to hurry[15] their imagination with public affairs.

The facility of treating actions or events in the pastoral style has incited many writers, from whom more judgment might have been expected, to put the sorrow or the joy which the occasion required into the mouth of Daphne or of Thyrsis,[16] and as one absurdity must naturally be expected to make way for another, they have written with an utter disregard both of life and nature, and filled their productions with mythological allusions, with incredible fictions, and with sentiments which neither passion nor reason could have dictated, since the change which religion has made in the whole system of the world.

No. 45.
Tuesday, 21 August 1750.

This is the chief felicity of life,
That concord smile on the connubial bed;
But now 'tis hatred all.
EURIPIDES, *MEDEA*, ll. 14–16 [TRANS. JOHNSON].

To the Rambler.

Sir,

Though in the dissertations which you have given us on marriage, very just cautions are laid down against the common causes of infelic-

13. In the sixth *Eclogue*, Silenus, a woodland god, sings of the creation of the world, recalls old myths of Greece, and greets Virgil's friend Gallus as a son of Apollo, the god of poetry.

14. Claudian, the last of the great Roman poets, described this rustic in *The Old Man of Verona*.

15. Agitate.

16. Names frequently used for characters in pastoral poetry.

ity,[1] and the necessity of having in that important choice the first regard to virtue is carefully inculcated; yet I cannot think the subject so much exhausted but that a little reflection would present to the mind many questions in the discussion of which great numbers are interested, and many precepts which deserve to be more particularly and forcibly impressed.

You seem like most of the writers that have gone before you to have allowed, as an uncontested principle, that "Marriage is generally unhappy"; but I know not whether a man who professes to think for himself and concludes from his own observations does not depart from his character when he follows the crowd thus implicitly, and receives maxims without recalling them to a new examination, especially when they comprise so wide a circuit of life and include such variety of circumstances. As I have an equal right with others to give my opinion of the objects about me, and a better title to determine concerning that state which I have tried than many who talk of it without experience, I am unwilling to be restrained by mere authority from advancing what I believe an accurate view of the world will confirm, that marriage is not commonly unhappy otherwise than as life is unhappy; and that most of those who complain of connubial miseries have as much satisfaction as their nature would have admitted or their conduct procured in any other condition.

It is indeed common to hear both sexes repine at their change, relate the happiness of their earlier years, blame the folly and rashness of their own choice, and warn those whom they see coming into the world against the same precipitance and infatuation. But it is to be remembered that the days which they do much wish to call back are the days not only of celibacy but of youth, the days of novelty and improvement, of ardor and of hope, of health and vigor of body, of gaiety and lightness of heart. It is not easy to surround life with any circumstances in which youth will not be delightful; and I am afraid that whether married or unmarried we shall find the vesture of terrestrial existence more heavy and cumbrous the longer it is worn.

That they censure themselves for the indiscretion of their choice is not a sufficient proof that they have chosen ill, since we see the same discontent at every other part of life which we cannot change. Converse with almost any man, grown old in a profession, and you will find him regretting that he did not enter into some different course to which he too late finds his genius better adapted, or in which he discovers that wealth and honor are more easily attained. "The merchant," says Horace, "envies the soldier, and the soldier recounts the felicity of the merchant; the lawyer when his clients harass him calls out for the quiet of the countryman; and the countryman, when business calls him to

1. Such as marrying in haste or for money (See *Ramblers*, nos. 18, 35, and 39).

town, proclaims that there is no happiness but amidst opulence and crowds."[2] Every man recounts the inconveniencies of his own station and thinks those of any other less because he has not felt them. Thus the married praise the ease and freedom of a single state, and the single fly to marriage from the weariness of solitude. From all our observations we may collect with certainty that misery is the lot of man, but cannot discover in what particular condition it will find most alleviations; or whether all external appendages[3] are not, as we use them, the causes either of good or ill.

Whoever feels great pain naturally hopes for ease from change of posture; he changes it and finds himself equally tormented: and of the same kind are the expedients by which we endeavor to obviate or elude those uneasinesses to which mortality will always be subject. It is not likely that the married state is eminently miserable, since we see such numbers whom the death of their partners has set free from it entering it again.

Wives and husbands are indeed incessantly complaining of each other; and there would be reason for imagining that almost every house was infested with perverseness or oppression beyond human sufferance, did we not know upon how small occasions some minds burst out into lamentations and reproaches, and how naturally every animal revenges his pain upon those who happen to be near without any nice[4] examination of its cause. We are always willing to fancy ourselves within a little of happiness and when, with repeated efforts, we cannot reach it, persuade ourselves that it is intercepted by an ill-paired mate, since if we could find any other obstacle it would be our own fault that it was not removed.

Anatomists have often remarked that though our diseases are sufficiently numerous and severe, yet when we inquire into the structure of the body, the tenderness of some parts, the minuteness of others, and the immense multiplicity of animal functions that must concur to the healthful and vigorous exercise of all our powers, there appears reason to wonder rather that we are preserved so long than that we perish so soon, and that our frame subsists for a single day or hour without disorder, rather than that it should be broken or obstructed by violence of accidents or length of time.

The same reflection arises in my mind upon observation of the manner in which marriage is frequently contracted. When I see the avaricious and crafty taking companions to their tables and their beds without any inquiry but after farms and money; or the giddy and thoughtless uniting themselves for life to those whom they have only seen by the

2. Johnson paraphrases the opening twelve lines of Horace, *Satire,* I. i.

3. Extrinsic circumstances.

4. Exact.

light of tapers at a ball; when parents make articles[5] for their children without inquiring after their consent; when some marry for heirs to disappoint their brothers, and others throw themselves into the arms of those whom they do not love because they have found themselves rejected where they were more solicitous to please; when some marry because their servants cheat them, some because they squander their own money, some because their houses are pestered with company, some because they will live like other people, and some only because they are sick of themselves, I am not so much inclined to wonder that marriage is sometimes unhappy as that it appears so little loaded with calamity; and cannot but conclude that society has something in itself eminently agreeable to human nature, when I find its pleasures so great that even the ill choice of a companion can hardly overbalance them.

By the ancient custom of the Muscovites the men and women never saw each other till they were joined beyond the power of parting. It may be suspected that by this method many unsuitable matches were produced and many tempers associated that were not qualified to give pleasure to each other. Yet perhaps among a people so little delicate, where the paucity of gratifications and the uniformity of life gave no opportunity for imagination to interpose its objections, there was not much danger of capricious dislike, and while they felt neither cold nor hunger they might live quietly together, without any thought of the defects of one another.

Amongst us, whom knowledge has made nice[6] and affluence wanton, there are, indeed, more cautions requisite to secure tranquillity; and yet if we observe the manner in which those converse who have singled out each other for marriage, we shall perhaps not think that the Russians lost much by their restraint. For the whole endeavor of both parties during the time of courtship is to hinder themselves from being known, and to disguise their natural temper and real desires, in hypocritical imitation, studied compliance, and continued affectation. From the time that their love is avowed, neither sees the other but in a mask, and the cheat is managed often on both sides with so much art and discovered afterwards with so much abruptness that each has reason to suspect that some transformation has happened on the wedding night, and that by a strange imposture one has been courted and another married.

I desire you, therefore, Mr. Rambler, to question all who shall hereafter come to you with matrimonial complaints, concerning their behavior in the time of courtship, and inform them that they are

5. Draw up marriage contracts.
6. Delicate.

neither to wonder nor repine when a contract begun with fraud has ended in disappointment.

I am, etc.

No. 54.
Saturday, 22 September 1750.

Day presses on the heels of day,
And moons increase to their decay;
But you, with thoughtless pride elate,
Unconscious of impending fate,
Command the pillared dome to rise,
When lo! thy tomb forgotten lies.

HORACE, *ODES*, II.xviii. 18–19, TRANS. FRANCIS.

To the Rambler.

Sir,

I have lately been called from a mingled life of business and amusement to attend the last hours of an old friend, an office which has filled me, if not with melancholy, at least with serious reflections, and turned my thoughts towards the contemplation of those subjects which, though of the utmost importance and of indubitable certainty, are generally secluded from our regard by the jollity of health, the hurry of employment, and even by the calmer diversions of study and speculation; or if they become accidental topics of conversation and argument yet rarely sink deep into the heart, but give occasion only to some subtilties of reasoning or elegancies of declamation, which are heard, applauded, and forgotten.

It is indeed not hard to conceive how a man accustomed to extend his views through a long concatenation of causes and effects, to trace things from their origin to their period, and compare means with ends, may discover the weakness of human schemes; detect the fallacies by which mortals are deluded; show the insufficiency of wealth, honors, and power to real happiness; and please himself and his auditors with learned lectures on the vanity of life.

But though the speculatist[1] may see and show the folly of terrestrial hopes, fears, and desires, every hour will give proofs that he never felt it. Trace him through the day or year and you will find him acting upon principles which he has in common with the illiterate and unenlightened, angry and pleased like the lowest of the vulgar, pursuing with the same ardor the same designs, grasping with all the eagerness of transport those riches which he knows he cannot keep, and swelling

1. Theorist.

with the applause which he has gained by proving that applause is of no value.

The only conviction that rushes upon the soul and takes away from our appetites and passions the power of resistance is to be found, where I have received it, at the bed of a dying friend. To enter this school of wisdom is not the peculiar privilege of geometricians;[2] the most sublime and important precepts require no uncommon opportunities nor laborious preparations; they are enforced without the aid of eloquence and understood without skill in analytic science. Every tongue can utter them and every understanding can conceive them. He that wishes in earnest to obtain just sentiments concerning his condition, and would be intimately acquainted with the world, may find instructions on every side. He that desires to enter behind the scene which every art has been employed to decorate and every passion labors to illuminate, and wishes to see life stripped of those ornaments which make it glitter on the stage, and exposed in its natural meanness, impotence, and nakedness, may find all the delusion laid open in the chamber of disease: he will there find vanity divested of her robes, power deprived of her scepter, and hypocrisy without her mask.

The friend whom I have lost was a man eminent for genius and, like others of the same class, sufficiently pleased with acceptance and applause. Being caressed by those who have preferments[3] and riches in their disposal, he considered himself as in the direct road of advancement, and had caught the flame of ambition by approaches to its object. But in the midst of his hopes, his projects, and his gaieties, he was seized by a lingering disease, which, from its first stage, he knew to be incurable. Here was an end of all his visions of greatness and happiness; from the first hour that his health declined, all his former pleasures grew tasteless. His friends expected to please him by those accounts of the growth of his reputation, which were formerly certain of being well received; but they soon found how little he was now affected by compliments, and how vainly they attempted by flattery to exhilarate the languor of weakness, and relieve the solicitude of approaching death. Whoever would know how much piety and virtue surpass all external goods might here have seen them weighed against each other, where all that gives motion to the active and elevation to the eminent, all that sparkles in the eye of hope and pants in the bosom of suspicion, at once became dust in the balance, without weight and without regard. Riches, authority, and praise lose all their influence when they are considered as riches which tomorrow shall be bestowed upon another, authority which shall this night expire forever, and praise which, how-

2. Johnson is alluding to the inscription over Plato's door: "Let no one without geometry enter" (W. J. Bate).
3. Positions of honor or profit.

ever merited or however sincere, shall after a few moments be heard no more.

In those hours of seriousness and wisdom, nothing appeared to raise his spirits, or gladden his heart, but the recollection of acts of goodness, nor to excite his attention but some opportunity for the exercise of the duties of religion. Every thing that terminated on this side of the grave was received with coldness and indifference, and regarded rather in consequence of the habit of valuing it, than from any opinion that it deserved value; it had little more prevalence over his mind than a bubble that was now broken, a dream from which he was awake. His whole powers were engrossed by the consideration of another state, and all conversation was tedious that had not some tendency to disengage him from human affairs and open his prospects into futurity.

It is now past, we have closed his eyes, and heard him breathe the groan of expiration. At the sight of this last conflict, I felt a sensation never known to me before: a confusion of passions, an awful stillness of sorrow, a gloomy terror without a name. The thoughts that entered my soul were too strong to be diverted and too piercing to be endured; but such violence cannot be lasting, the storm subsided in a short time, I wept, retired, and grew calm.

I have from that time frequently revolved in my mind the effects which the observation of death produces in those who are not wholly without the power and use of reflection; for by far the greater part it is wholly unregarded; their friends and their enemies sink into the grave without raising any uncommon emotion, or reminding them that they are themselves on the edge of the precipice, and that they must soon plunge into the gulf of eternity.

It seems to me remarkable that death increases our veneration for the good, and extenuates our hatred of the bad. Those virtues which once we envied, as Horace observes, because they eclipsed our own, can now no longer obstruct our reputation, and we have therefore no interest to suppress their praise.[4] That wickedness, which we feared for its malignity, is now become impotent, and the man whose name filled us with alarm, and rage, and indignation, can at last be considered only with pity, or contempt.

When a friend is carried to his grave, we at once find excuses for every weakness and palliations of every fault; we recollect a thousand endearments which before glided off our minds without impression, a thousand favors unrepaid, a thousand duties unperformed, and wish, vainly wish for his return, not so much that we may receive as that we may bestow happiness, and recompense that kindness which before we never understood.

There is not perhaps to a mind well instructed a more painful occur-

4. Horace, *Epistles,* II. i. 10–14.

rence than the death of one whom we have injured without reparation. Our crime seems now irretrievable, it is indelibly recorded, and the stamp of fate is fixed upon it. We consider with the most afflictive anguish the pain which we have given and now cannot alleviate, and the losses which we have caused and now cannot repair.

Of the same kind are the emotions which the death of an emulator or competitor produces. Whoever had qualities to alarm our jealousy, had excellence to deserve our fondness, and to whatever ardor of opposition interest may inflame us, no man ever outlived an enemy whom he did not then wish to have made a friend. Those who are versed in literary history know that the elder Scaliger was the redoubted antagonist of Cardan and Erasmus;[5] yet at the death of each of his great rivals he relented, and complained that they were snatched away from him before their reconciliation was completed.

Tune etiam moreris? Ah! quid me linquis, Erasme,
Ante meus quam sit conciliatus amor?

Art thou too fallen? ere anger could subside
And love return, has great Erasmus died?[6]

Such are the sentiments with which we finally review the effects of passion, but which we sometimes delay till we can no longer rectify our errors. Let us therefore make haste to do what we shall certainly at last wish to have done; let us return the caresses of our friends, and endeavor by mutual endearments to heighten that tenderness which is the balm of life. Let us be quick to repent of injuries while repentance may not be a barren anguish, and let us open our eyes to every rival excellence, and pay early and willingly those honors which justice will compel us to pay at last.

Athanatus.

No. 60.
Saturday, 13 October 1750.

Whose works the beautiful and base contain;
Of vice and virtue more instructive rules,
Than all the sober sages of the schools.
HORACE, *EPISTLES*, I.ii.3–4, TRANS. FRANCIS.

All joy or sorrow for the happiness or calamities of others is produced by an act of the imagination, that realizes the event however fictitious,

5. For the elder Scaliger, see Rambler no. 4, n. 3. Geronimo Cardano (1501–76), Italian mathematician, physician, and astrologer; Desiderius Erasmus (?1466–1536), great Dutch humanist.
6. *Heroes:* "Erasmus," 11. 1–2.

or approximates it[1] however remote, by placing us, for a time, in the condition of him whose fortune we contemplate; so that we feel, while the deception lasts, whatever motions would be excited by the same good or evil happening to ourselves.

Our passions are therefore more strongly moved, in proportion as we can more readily adopt the pains or pleasures proposed to our minds, by recognizing them as once our own, or considering them as naturally incident to our state of life. It is not easy for the most artful writer to give us an interest in happiness or misery which we think ourselves never likely to feel, and with which we have never yet been made acquainted. Histories of the downfall of kingdoms, and revolutions of empires, are read with great tranquillity; the imperial tragedy pleases common auditors only by its pomp of ornament and grandeur of ideas; and the man whose faculties have been engrossed by business, and whose heart never fluttered but at the rise or fall of stocks, wonders how the attention can be seized or the affections agitated by a tale of love.

Those parallel circumstances, and kindred images, to which we readily conform our minds, are, above all other writings, to be found in narratives of the lives of particular persons; and therefore no species of writing seems more worthy of cultivation than biography, since none can be more delightful or more useful, none can more certainly enchain the heart by irresistible interest, or more widely diffuse instruction to every diversity of condition.

The general and rapid narratives of history, which involve a thousand fortunes in the business of a day, and complicate innumerable incidents in one great transaction, afford a few lessons applicable to private life, which derives its comforts and its wretchedness from the right or wrong management of things which nothing but their frequency makes considerable, *Parva, si non fiant quotidie,* says Pliny,[2] and which can have no place in those relations[3] which never descend below the consultation of senates, the motions of armies, and the schemes of conspirators.

I have often thought that there has rarely passed a life of which a judicious and faithful narrative would not be useful. For not only every man has, in the mighty mass of the world, great numbers in the same condition with himself, to whom his mistakes and miscarriages, escapes and expedients, would be of immediate and apparent use; but there is such an uniformity in the state of man, considered apart from adventitious and separable decorations and disguises, that there is scarce any possibility of good or ill, but is common to human kind. A great part of the time of those who are placed at the greatest distance by fortune, or

1. Brings it near.
2. "Small things, if they did not happen every day" (Pliny the Younger, *Letters,* iii. 1).
3. Narratives.

by temper, must unavoidably pass in the same manner; and though, when the claims of nature are satisfied, caprice, and vanity, and accident, begin to produce discriminations and peculiarities, yet the eye is not very heedful or quick, which cannot discover the same causes still terminating their influence in the same effects, though sometimes accelerated, sometimes retarded, or perplexed by multiplied combinations. We are all prompted by the same motives, all deceived by the same fallacies, all animated by hope, obstructed by danger, entangled by desire, and seduced by pleasure.

It is frequently objected to relations of particular lives that they are not distinguished by any striking or wonderful vicissitudes. The scholar who passed his life among his books, the merchant who conducted only his own affairs, the priest whose sphere of action was not extended beyond that of his duty, are considered as no proper objects of public regard, however they might have excelled in their several stations, whatever might have been their learning, integrity, and piety. But this notion arises from false measures of excellence and dignity, and must be eradicated by considering that, in the esteem of uncorrupted reason, what is of most use is of most value.

It is, indeed, not improper to take honest advantages of prejudice, and to gain attention by a celebrated name; but the business of the biographer is often to pass slightly over those performances and incidents, which produce vulgar greatness, to lead the thoughts into domestic privacies, and display the minute details of daily life, where exterior appendages are cast aside, and men excel each other only by prudence and by virtue. The account of Thuanus[4] is, with great propriety, said by its author to have been written, that it might lay open to posterity the private and familiar character of that man, *cuius ingenium et candorem ex ipsius scriptis sunt olim semper miraturi,*[5] whose candor[6] and genius will to the end of time be by his writings preserved in admiration.

There are many invisible circumstances which, whether we read as inquirers after natural or moral knowledge, whether we intend to enlarge our science,[7] or increase our virtue, are more important than public occurrences. Thus Sallust, the great master of nature, has not forgot, in his account of Catiline, to remark that "his walk was now quick, and again slow," as an indication of a mind revolving something with violent commotion.[8] Thus the story of Melancthon[9] affords a

4. Jacques-Auguste de Thou, French historian, wrote *A History of his Own Time* (1604–20). The "account" Johnson quotes is by Nicolas Rigualt.

5. Johnson translates the Latin in the words that follow.

6. Sympathetic attitude toward others.

7. Learning.

8. Sallust, Roman historian (86–34 B.C.), wrote a history of Catiline's conspiracy against the Roman Republic.

9. Protestant theologian (1497–1560), associate of Luther in the early days of the Reformation; his life was written by his friend Joachim Camerarius.

striking lecture on the value of time, by informing us, that when he made an appointment, he expected not only the hour, but the minute to be fixed, that the day might not run out in the idleness of suspense; and all the plans and enterprises of DeWitt are not of less importance to the world, than that part of his personal character which represents him as "careful of his health and negligent of his life."[10]

But biography has often been allotted to writers who seem very little acquainted with the nature of their task, or very negligent about the performance. They rarely afford any other account than might be collected from public papers, but imagine themselves writing a life when they exhibit a chronological series of actions or preferments; and so little regard the manners or behavior of their heroes, that more knowledge may be gained of a man's real character by a short conversation with one of his servants, than from a formal and studied narrative, begun with his pedigree, and ended with his funeral.

If now and then they condescend to inform the world of particular facts, they are not always so happy as to select the most important. I know not well what advantage posterity can receive from the only circumstance by which Tickell has distinguished Addison from the rest of mankind, "the irregularity of his pulse":[11] nor can I think myself overpaid for the time spent in reading the life of Malherbe, by being enabled to relate, after the learned biographer, that Malherbe had two predominant opinions; one, that the looseness of a single woman might destroy all the boast of ancient descent; the other, that the French beggars made use very improperly and barbarously of the phrase, "noble gentleman," because either word included the sense of both.[12]

There are, indeed, some natural reasons why these narratives are often written by such as were not likely to give much instruction or delight, and why most accounts of particular persons are barren and useless. If a life be delayed till interest and envy are at an end, we may hope for impartiality, but must expect little intelligence; for the incidents which give excellence to biography are of a volatile and evanescent kind, such as soon escape the memory, and are rarely transmitted by tradition. We know how few can portray a living acquaintance except by his most prominent and observable particularities, and the grosser features of his mind; and it may be easily imagined how much of this little knowledge may be lost in imparting it, and how soon a succession of copies will lose all resemblance of the original.

If the biographer writes from personal knowledge, and makes haste to gratify the public curiosity, there is danger lest his interest, his fear,

10. Jan de Witt (1625–72), famous Dutch statesman. The comment on him is from Sir William Temple's "Essay upon the Cure of the Gout" (1680).

11. Thomas Tickell's life of Addison was prefaced to his edition of his friend's *Works* (1721).

12. The life of the French neoclassical poet François de Malherbe was written by his friend the Marquis de Racan (1651).

his gratitude, or his tenderness, overpower his fidelity, and tempt him to conceal, if not to invent. There are many who think it an act of piety to hide the faults or failings of their friends, even when they can no longer suffer by their detection; we therefore see whole ranks of characters adorned with uniform panegyric, and not to be known from one another, but by extrinsic and casual circumstances. "Let me remember," says Hale, "when I find myself inclined to pity a criminal, that there is likewise a pity due to the country."[13] If we owe regard to the memory of the dead, there is yet more respect to be paid to knowledge, to virtue, and to truth.

No. 74.
Saturday, 1 December 1750.

For nought tormented, she for nought torments.
HORACE, *EPISTLES*, I.xviii.15, TRANS. ELPHINSTON.

Men seldom give pleasure where they are not pleased themselves; it is necessary, therefore, to cultivate an habitual alacrity and cheerfulness that in whatever state we may be placed by providence, whether we are appointed to confer or receive benefits, to implore or to afford protection, we may secure the love of those with whom we transact. For though it is generally imagined that he who grants favors may spare any attention to his behavior, and that usefulness will always procure friends; yet it has been found that there is an art of granting requests, an art very difficult of attainment; that officiousness[1] and liberality may be so adulterated[2] as to lose the greater part of their effect; that compliance may provoke, relief may harass, and liberality distress.

No disease of the mind can more fatally disable it from benevolence,[3] the chief duty of social beings, than ill humor or peevishness; for though it breaks not out in paroxysms of outrage, nor bursts into clamor, turbulence, and bloodshed, it wears out happiness by slow corrosion, and small injuries incessantly repeated. It may be considered as the canker of life, that destroys its vigor, and checks its improvement, that creeps on with hourly depredations, and taints and vitiates what it cannot consume.

Peevishness, when it has been so far indulged as to outrun the motions[4] of the will, and discover[5] itself without premeditation, is a

13. For Hale, see *Rambler*, no. 14, n. 12. The quotation is from his biography by Gilbert Burnet (1682).

1. Eager helpfulness.
2. Mixed with some foreign substance.
3. Kindness or generosity in feeling and action; equivalent to St. Paul's use of "charity."
4. Proper reasons for action (?).
5. Reveal.

species of depravity in the highest degree disgusting and offensive, because no rectitude of intention, nor softness of address, can ensure a moment's exemption from affront and indignity. While we are courting the favor of a peevish man, and exerting ourselves in the most diligent civility, an unlucky syllable displeases, an unheeded circumstance ruffles and exasperates; and in the moment when we congratulate ourselves upon having gained a friend, our endeavors are frustrated at once, and all our assiduity forgotten in the casual tumult of some trifling irritation.

This troublesome impatience is sometimes nothing more than the symptom of some deeper malady. He that is angry without daring to confess his resentment, or sorrowful without the liberty of telling his grief, is too frequently inclined to give vent to the fermentations of his mind at the first passages that are opened, and to let his passions boil over upon those whom accident throws in his way. A painful and tedious course of sickness frequently produces such an alarming apprehension of the least increase of uneasiness as keeps the soul perpetually on the watch; such a restless and incessant solicitude as no care or tenderness can appease, and can only be pacified by the cure of the distemper and the removal of that pain by which it is excited.

Nearly approaching to this weakness is the captiousness[6] of old age. When the strength is crushed, the senses are dulled, and the common pleasures of life become insipid by repetition, we are willing to impute our uneasiness to causes not wholly out of our power, and please ourselves with fancying that we suffer by neglect, unkindness, or any evil which admits a remedy, rather than by the decays of nature, which cannot be prevented or repaired. We therefore revenge our pains upon those on whom we resolve to charge them; and too often drive mankind away at the time we have the greatest need of tenderness and assistance.

But though peevishness may sometimes claim our compassion as the consequence or concomitant of misery, it is very often found where nothing can justify or excuse its admission. It is frequently one of the attendants on the prosperous, and is employed by insolence in exacting homage, or by tyranny in harassing subjection. It is the offspring of idleness or pride; of idleness anxious for trifles, or pride unwilling to endure the least obstruction of her wishes. Those who have long lived in solitude indeed naturally contract this unsocial quality, because, having long had only themselves to please, they do not readily depart from their own inclinations; their singularities therefore are only blamable when they have imprudently or morosely withdrawn themselves from the world; but there are others, who have, without any necessity, nursed up this habit in their minds, by making implicit submissiveness

6. Faultfinding.

the condition of their favor, and suffering none to approach them but those who never speak but to applaud, or move but to obey.

He that gives himself up to his own fancy, and converses with none but such as he hires to lull him on the down of absolute authority, to soothe him with obsequiousness and regale him with flattery, soon grows too slothful for the labor of contest, too tender for the asperity of contradiction, and too delicate for the coarseness of truth; a little opposition offends, a little restraint enrages, and a little difficulty perplexes him; having been accustomed to see everything give way to his humor, he soon forgets his own littleness, and expects to find the world rolling at his beck, and all mankind employed to accommodate and delight him.

Tetrica had a large fortune bequeathed to her by an aunt, which made her very early independent, and placed her in a state of superiority to all about her. Having no superfluity of understanding, she was soon intoxicated by the flatteries of her maid, who informed her that ladies, such as she, had nothing to do but take pleasure their own way; that she wanted nothing from others, and had therefore no reason to value their opinion; that money was everything; and that they who thought themselves ill-treated should look for better usage among their equals.

Warm with these generous sentiments, Tetrica came forth into the world, in which she endeavored to force respect by haughtiness of mien and vehemence of language; but having neither birth, beauty, nor wit[7] in any uncommon degree, she suffered such mortifications from those who thought themselves at liberty to return her insults as reduced her turbulence to cooler malignity, and taught her to practice her arts of vexation only where she might hope to tyrannize without resistance. She continued from her twentieth to her fifty-fifth year to torment all her inferiors with so much diligence that she has formed a principle of disapprobation, and finds in every place something to grate her mind and disturb her quiet.

If she takes the air, she is offended with the heat or cold, the glare of the sun or the gloom of the clouds; if she makes a visit, the room in which she is to be received is too light or too dark, or furnished with something which she cannot see without aversion. Her tea is never of the right sort; the figures on the china give her disgust. Where there are children she hates the gabble of brats; where there are none, she cannot bear a place without some cheerfulness and rattle. If many servants are kept in a house, she never fails to tell how Lord Lavish was ruined by a numerous retinue; if few, she relates the story of a miser that made his company wait on themselves. She quarreled with one family, because she had an unpleasant view from their windows; with another, because

7. Intelligence; perceptiveness.

the squirrel leaped within two yards of her; and with a third, because she could not bear the noise of the parrot.

Of milliners and mantua-makers[8] she is the proverbial torment. She compels them to alter their work, then to unmake it, and contrive it after another fashion; then changes her mind, and likes it better as it was at first; then will have a small improvement. Thus she proceeds till no profit can recompense the vexation; they at last leave the clothes at her house, and refuse to serve her. Her maid, the only being that can endure her tyranny, professes to take her own course, and hear her mistress talk. Such is the consequence of peevishness; it can be borne only when it is despised.

It sometimes happens that too close an attention to minute exactness, or a too rigorous habit of examining everything by the standard of perfection, vitiates the temper rather than improves the understanding, and teaches the mind to discern faults with unhappy penetration. It is incident likewise to men of vigorous imagination to please themselves too much with futurities, and to fret because those expectations are disappointed which should never have been formed. Knowledge and genius are often enemies to quiet, by suggesting ideas of excellence which men and the performances of men cannot attain. But let no man rashly determine that his unwillingness to be pleased is a proof of understanding, unless his superiority appears from less doubtful evidence; for though peevishness may sometimes justly boast its descent from learning or from wit, it is much oftener of base extraction, the child of vanity, and nursling of ignorance.

No. 94.
Saturday, 9 February 1751.

Perpetual magistrate is he,
Who keeps strict justice full in sight;
Who bids the crowd at awful distance gaze,
And virtue's arms victoriously displays.
HORACE, *ODES*, IV.ix. 40–41, 43–44, TRANS. FRANCIS.

The resemblance of poetic numbers to the subject which they mention or describe, may be considered as general or particular; as consisting in the flow and structure of a whole passage taken together, or as comprised in the sound of some emphatical and descriptive words, or in the cadence[1] and harmony of single verses.

The general resemblance of the sound to the sense is to be found in every language which admits of poetry, in every author whose force of

8. Dressmakers.
1. The flow or movement.

fancy enables him to impress images strongly on his own mind, and whose choice and variety of language readily supplies him with just representations. To such a writer it is natural to change his measures with his subject, even without any effort of the understanding, or intervention of the judgment. To revolve[2] jollity and mirth necessarily tunes the voice of a poet to gay and sprightly notes, as it fires his eye with vivacity; and reflection on gloomy situations and disastrous events will sadden his numbers, as it will cloud his countenance. But in such passages there is only the similitude of pleasure to pleasure, and of grief to grief, without any immediate application to particular images. The same flow of joyous versification will celebrate the jollity of marriage, and the exultation of triumph; and the same languor of melody will suit the complaints of an absent lover, as of a conquered king.

It is scarcely to be doubted that on many occasions we make the music which we imagine ourselves to hear; that we modulate the poem by our own disposition, and ascribe to the numbers the effects of the sense. We may observe in life that it is not easy to deliver a pleasing message in an unpleasing manner, and that we readily associate beauty and deformity with those whom for any reason we love or hate. Yet it would be too daring to declare that all the celebrated adaptations of harmony are chimerical; that Homer had no extraordinary attention to the melody of his verse when he described a nuptial festivity:

> Νύμφας δ' ἐκ θαλάμων, δαίδων ὑπο λαμπομενάων,
> Ηγίνεον ἀνὰ ἄστυ, πολὺς δ' ὑμέναιος ὀρώρει.
>
> [*ILIAD*, XVIII.492–93]

> Here sacred pomp, and genial feast delight,
> And solemn dance, and hymeneal rite;
> Along the street the new-made brides are led,
> With torches flaming to the nuptial bed:
> The youthful dancers in a circle bound
> To the soft flute, and cittern's silver sound;
>
> POPE.

that Vida was merely fanciful, when he supposed Virgil endeavoring to represent by uncommon sweetness of numbers the adventitious beauty of Aeneas:

> *Os, humerosque Deo similis: namque ipsa decoram*
> *Caesariem nato genetrix, lumenque juventae*
> *Purpureum, et laetos oculis afflarat honores.*
>
> [*AENEID*, I.589–91.]

> The Trojan chief appeared in open sight,
> August in visage, and serenely bright.
> His mother goddess, with her hands divine,

2. Think about.

Had formed his curling locks, and made his temples shine;
And given his rolling eyes a sparkling grace,
And breathed a youthful vigor on his face;

DRYDEN.

or that Milton did not intend to exemplify the harmony which he mentions:

Fountains! and ye that warble as ye flow,
Melodious murmurs! warbling tune his praise.

[*PARADISE LOST*, V. 195–96.]

That Milton understood the force of sounds well adjusted, and knew the compass and variety of the ancient measures,[3] cannot be doubted, since he was both a musician and a critic; but he seems to have considered these conformities of cadence as either not often attainable in our language, or as petty excellencies unworthy of his ambition; for it will not be found that he has always assigned the same cast of numbers to the same subjects. He has given in two passages very minute descriptions of angelic beauty; but though the images are nearly the same, the numbers[4] will be found upon comparison very different.

And now a stripling cherub he appears,
Not of the prime, yet such as in his face
Youth smiled celestial, and to every limb
Suitable grace diffused, so well he feigned;
Under a coronet his flowing hair
In curls on either cheek played; wings he wore
Of many a colored plume, sprinkled with gold.

[III.636–42.]

Some of the lines of this description are remarkably defective in harmony, and therefore by no means correspondent with that symmetrical elegance and easy grace which they are intended to exhibit. The failure, however, is fully compensated by the representation of Raphael, which equally delights the ear and imagination.

A seraph winged: six wings he wore to shade
His lineaments divine; the pair that clad
Each shoulder broad, came mantling o'er his breast
With regal ornament: the middle pair
Girt like a starry zone his waist, and round
Skirted his loins and thighs, with downy gold,
And colors dipped in heaven: the third his feet
Shadowed from either heel with feathered mail,
Sky-tinctured grain![5] like Maia's son[6] he stood,

3. Greek and Roman meters.
4. The metrical arrangements.
5. Indelible blue color.
6. Hermes, the Greek god, represented with wings on his heels.

And shook his plumes, that heavenly fragrance filled
The circuit wide.

[V. 277-87]

The adumbration of particular and distinct images by an exact and perceptible resemblance of sound is sometimes studied, and sometimes casual. Every language has many words formed in imitation of the noises which they signify. Such are *stridor, balo,* and *boatus* in Latin;[7] and in English to *growl,* to *buzz,* to *hiss,* and to *jar.* Words of this kind give to a verse the proper similitude of sound, without much labor of the writer, and such happiness is therefore to be attributed rather to fortune than skill; yet they are sometimes combined with great propriety, and undeniably contribute to enforce the impression of the idea. We hear the passing arrow in this line of Virgil;

Et fugit *horrendum stridens* elapsa sagitta.

[*AENEID,* IX.632.]

Th' impetuous arrow whizzes on the wing;

POPE.

and the creaking of Hell gates, in the description by Milton:

Open fly
With impetuous recoil, and jarring sound
Th' infernal doors; and on their hinges grate
Harsh thunder.

[II.879–82.]

But many beauties of this kind which the moderns, and perhaps the ancients, have observed, seem to be the product of blind reverence acting upon fancy. Dionysius[8] himself tells us that the sound of Homer's verses sometimes exhibits the idea of corporeal bulk: is not this a discovery nearly approaching to that of the blind man, who after long inquiry into the nature of the scarlet color, found that it represented nothing so much as the clangor of a trumpet? The representative power of poetic harmony consists of sound and measure: of the force of the syllables singly considered, and of the time in which they are pronounced. Sound can resemble nothing but sound, and time can measure nothing but motion and duration.

The critics, however, have struck out other similitudes; nor is there any irregularity of numbers which credulous admiration cannot discover to be eminently beautiful. Thus the propriety of each of these lines has been celebrated by writers whose opinion the world has reason to regard,

Vertitur interea coelum, et ruit oceano nox.

[*AENEID,* II.250.]

7. Words indicating harsh, bleating, or roaring sounds respectively.

8. Dionysius of Halicarnassus, Greek critic living at Rome in the reign of Augustus. Johnson cites his treatise "On the Arrangement of Words."

Mean time the rapid heavens rowled down the light,
And on the shaded ocean rushed the night.

DRYDEN.

Sternitur, exanimisque tremens procumbit humi bos.

[*AENEID,* V.481.]

Down drops the beast, nor needs a second wound;
But sprawls in pangs of death, and spurns the ground.

DRYDEN.

Parturiunt montes, nascetur ridiculus mus.

[HORACE, *ART OF POETRY,* l. 139.]

The mountains labor, and a mouse is born.

ROSCOMMON.

If all these observations are just, there must be some remarkable conformity between the sudden succession of night to day, the fall of an ox under a blow, and the birth of a mouse from a mountain; since we are told of all these images that they are very strongly impressed by the same form and termination of the verse.

We may, however, without giving way to enthusiasm, admit that some beauties of this kind may be produced. A sudden stop at an unusual syllable may image the cessation of action, or the pause of discourse; and Milton has very happily imitated the repetitions of an echo,

I fled, and cried out *death:*
Hell trembled at the hideous name, and sighed
From all her caves, and back resounded *death.*

[II.787–89.]

The measure or time of pronouncing may be varied so as very strongly to represent not only the modes of external motion, but the quick or slow succession of ideas, and consequently the passions of the mind. This at least was the power of the spondaic and dactylic harmony,[9] but our language can reach no eminent diversities of sound. We can indeed sometimes, by encumbering and retarding the line, show the difficulty of a progress made by strong efforts and with frequent interruptions, or mark a slow and heavy motion. Thus Milton has imaged the toil of Satan struggling through chaos,

So he with difficulty and labor hard
Moved on: with difficulty and labor he;

[II.1021–22.]

9. Spondees and dactyls are much more frequent in Latin than in English verse.

thus he has described the leviathans or whales,

> Wallowing, unwieldly, enormous in their gait.[10]
>
> [VII.411.]

But he has at other times neglected such representations as may be observed in the volubility and levity of these lines, which express an action tardy and reluctant.

> Descent and fall
> To us is adverse. Who but felt of late,
> When the fierce foe hung on our broken rear
> Insulting, and pursued us through the deep,
> With what confusion and laborious flight
> We sunk thus low? Th' ascent is easy then.
>
> [II.76–81.]

In another place, he describes the gentle glide of ebbing waters in a line remarkably rough and halting.

> Tripping ebb; that stole
> With soft foot towards the deep, who now had stopped
> His sluices.
>
> [XI.847–49.]

It is not indeed to be expected, that the sound should always assist the meaning, but it ought never to counteract it; and therefore Milton has here certainly committed a fault like that of the player,[11] who looked on the earth when he implored the heavens, and to the heavens when he addressed the earth.

Those who are determined to find in Milton an assemblage of all the excellencies which have ennobled all other poets will perhaps be offended that I do not celebrate his versification in higher terms; for there are readers who discover that in this passage,

> So stretched out huge in length the arch-fiend lay,
>
> [I.209.]

a *long* form is described in a *long* line; but the truth is, that length of body is only mentioned in a *slow* line, to which it has only the resemblance of time to space, of an hour to a maypole.

The same turn of ingenuity might perform wonders upon the description of the ark:

> Then from the mountains hewing timber tall,
> Began to build a vessel of huge bulk;
> Measured by cubit, length, breadth, and height.
>
> [XI.728–30.]

10. Monstrous in their movements.
11. Actor.

In these lines the poet apparently designs to fix the attention upon bulk; but this is effected by the enumeration, not by the measure; for what analogy can there be between modulations of sound, and corporeal dimensions.

Milton, indeed, seems only to have regarded this species of embellishment so far as not to reject it when it came unsought; which would often happen to a mind so vigorous, employed upon a subject so various and extensive. He had, indeed, a greater and a nobler work to perform; a single sentiment of moral or religious truth, a single image of life or nature, would have been cheaply lost for a thousand echoes of the cadence to the sense; and he who had undertaken to "vindicate the ways of God to man,"[12] might have been accused of neglecting his cause, had he lavished much of his attention upon syllables and sounds.

No. 113.
Tuesday, 16 April 1751.

A sober man like thee to change his life!
What fury would possess thee with a wife?
JUVENAL, *SATIRES*. VI.28–29. TRANS. DRYDEN.

To The Rambler.

Sir,

I know not whether it is always a proof of innocence to treat censure with contempt. We owe so much reverence to the wisdom of mankind as justly to wish that our own opinion of our merit may be ratified by the concurrence of other suffrages;[1] and since guilt and infamy must have the same effect upon intelligences unable to pierce beyond external appearance, and influenced often rather by example than precept, we are obliged to refute a false charge, lest we should countenance the crime which we have never committed. To turn away from an accusation with supercilious silence is equally in the power of him that is hardened by villainy and inspirited by innocence. The wall of brass which Horace erects upon a clear conscience,[2] may be sometimes raised by impudence or power; and we should always wish to preserve the dignity of virtue by adorning her with graces which wickedness cannot assume.

For this reason I have determined no longer to endure, with either patient or sullen resignation, a reproach which is, at least in my opinion,

12. Instead of quoting *Paradise Lost*, i. 26 ("and justify the ways of God to men"), Johnson quotes Pope's *Essay on Man*, i. 16. Johnson often quoted inexactly from memory.
1. Opinions.
2. *Epistles*, I. i. 60–61.

unjust, but will lay my case honestly before you, that you or your readers may at length decide it.

Whether you will be able to preserve your boasted impartiality when you hear that I am considered as an adversary by half the female world, you may surely pardon me for doubting, notwithstanding the veneration to which you may imagine yourself entitled by your age, your learning, your abstraction,[3] or your virtue. Beauty, Mr. Rambler, has often overpowered the resolutions of the firm, and the reasonings of the wise, roused the old to sensibility, and subdued the rigorous to softness.

I am one of those unhappy beings, who have been marked out as husbands for many different women, and deliberated a hundred times on the brink of matrimony. I have discussed all the nuptial preliminaries so often that I can repeat the forms in which jointures[4] are settled, pin-money secured, and provisions for younger children ascertained; but am at last doomed by general consent to everlasting solitude, and excluded by an irreversible decree from all hopes of connubial felicity. I am pointed out by every mother as a man whose visits cannot be admitted without reproach; who raises hopes only to embitter disappointment, and makes offers only to seduce girls into a waste of that part of life in which they might gain advantageous matches, and become mistresses[5] and mothers.

I hope you will think that some part of this penal severity may justly be remitted, when I inform you that I never yet professed love to a woman without sincere intentions of marriage; that I have never continued an appearance of intimacy from the hour that my inclination changed, but to preserve her whom I was leaving from the shock of abruptness or the ignominy of contempt; that I always endeavored to give the ladies an opportunity of seeming to discard me; and that I never forsook a mistress for larger fortune or brighter beauty, but because I discovered some irregularity in her conduct or some depravity in her mind; not because I was charmed by another, but because I was offended by herself.

I was very early tired of that succession of amusements by which the thoughts of most young men are dissipated, and had not long glittered in the splendor of an ample patrimony before I wished for the calm of domestic happiness. Youth is naturally delighted with sprightliness and ardor, and therefore I breathed out the sighs of my first affection at the feet of the gay, the sparkling, the vivacious Ferocula. I fancied to myself a perpetual source of happiness in wit never exhausted, and spirit never depressed; looked with veneration on her readiness of expedients, contempt of difficulty, assurance of address, and promptitude

3. Intellectual ability to differentiate.
4. Marriage settlements providing for the wife in case she survives her husband.
5. Of households.

of reply; considered her as exempt by some prerogative of nature from the weakness and timidity of female minds; and congratulated myself upon a companion superior to all common troubles and embarrassments. I was, indeed, somewhat disturbed by the unshaken perseverance with which she enforced her demands of an unreasonable settlement;[6] yet I should have consented to pass my life in union with her, had not my curiosity led me to a crowd gathered in the street where I found Ferocula, in the presence of hundreds, disputing for sixpence with a chairman.[7] I saw her in so little need of assistance that it was no breach of the laws of chivalry to forbear interposition, and I spared myself the shame of owning her acquaintance. I forgot some point of ceremony at our next interview, and soon provoked her to forbid me her presence.

My next attempt was upon a lady of great eminence for learning and philosophy. I had frequently observed the barrenness and uniformity of connubial conversation, and therefore thought highly of my own prudence and discernment when I selected from a multitude of wealthy beauties, the deep-read Misothea, who declared herself the inexorable enemy of ignorant pertness and puerile levity; and scarcely condescended to make tea but for the linguist, the geometrician, the astronomer, or the poet. The queen of the Amazons was only to be gained by the hero who could conquer her in single combat;[8] and Misothea's heart was only to bless the scholar who could overpower her by disputation. Amidst the fondest transports of courtship she could call for a definition of terms, and treated every argument with contempt that could not be reduced to regular syllogism. You may easily imagine that I wished this courtship at an end; but when I desired her to shorten my torments, and fix the day of my felicity, we were led into a long conversation, in which Misothea endeavored to demonstrate the folly of attributing choice and self-direction to any human being. It was not difficult to discover the danger of committing myself for ever to the arms of one who might at any time mistake the dictates of passion or the calls of appetite for the decree of fate; or consider cuckoldom as necessary to the general system as a link in the everlasting chain of successive causes. I therefore told her that destiny had ordained us to part; and that nothing should have torn me from her but the talons of necessity.[9]

I then solicited the regard of the calm, the prudent, the economical Sophronia, a lady who considered wit as dangerous and learning as superfluous; and thought that the woman who kept her house clean and her accounts exact, took receipts for every payment, and could find

6. Financial guarantees to the wife.

7. Carrier of a sedan chair.

8. This statement is illustrated in the story that Theseus, ruler of Athens, subdued and married Hippolyta, queen of the Amazons.

9. In this ironic attack on determinism, Johnson treats "fate," "destiny," and "necessity" as equivalents.

them at a sudden call, inquired nicely after the condition of the tenants, read the price of stocks once a week, and purchased everything at the best market, could want[10] no accomplishments necessary to the happiness of a wise man. She discoursed with great solemnity on the care and vigilance which the superintendence of a family[11] demands; observed how many were ruined by confidence in servants; and told me that she never expected honesty but from a strong chest, and that the best storekeeper was the mistress's eye. Many such oracles of generosity she uttered, and made every day new improvements in her schemes for the regulation of her servants, and the distribution of her time. I was convinced that whatever I might suffer from Sophronia, I should escape poverty; and we therefore proceeded to adjust the settlements according to her own rule, "fair and softly." But one morning her maid came to me in tears to entreat my interest for a reconciliation to her mistress, who had turned her out at night for breaking six teeth in a tortoiseshell comb: she had attended her lady from a distant province, and having not lived long enough to save much money, was destitute among strangers, and though of a good family, in danger of perishing in the streets, or of being compelled by hunger to prostitution. I made no scruple of promising to restore her; but upon my first application to Sophronia was answered with an air which called for approbation, that if she neglected her own affairs, I might suspect her of neglecting mine; that the comb stood her in[12] three half-crowns; that no servant should wrong her twice; and that indeed, she took the first opportunity of parting with Phyllida, because, though she was honest, her constitution was bad, and she thought her very likely to fall sick. Of our conference I need not tell you the effect; it surely may be forgiven me, if on this occasion I forgot the decency of common forms.[13]

From two more ladies I was disengaged by finding that they entertained my rivals at the same time, and determined their choice by the liberality of our settlements. Another I thought myself justified in forsaking, because she gave my attorney a bribe to favor her in the bargain; another, because I could never soften her to tenderness, till she heard that most of my family had died young; and another, because to increase her fortune by expectations, she represented her sister as languishing and consumptive.

I shall in another letter give the remaining part of my history of courtship. I presume that I should hitherto have injured the majesty of female virtue, had I not hoped to transfer my affection to higher merit.

I am, etc.
Hymenaeus.

10. Lack.
11. Household.
12. Cost her.
13. Ordinary civilities.

No. 121.
Tuesday, 14 May 1751.

Away, ye imitators, servile herd!
HORACE, *EPISTLES*, I.xix. 19, TRANS. ELPHINSTON.

I have been informed by a letter, from one of the universities, that among the youth from whom the next swarm of reasoners is to learn philosophy, and the next flight of beauties to hear elegies and sonnets, there are many, who, instead of endeavoring by books and meditation to form their own opinions, content themselves with the secondary knowledge which a convenient bench in a coffee-house can supply; and, without any examination or distinction, adopt the criticisms and remarks which happen to drop from those who have risen, by merit or fortune, to reputation and authority.

These humble retailers of knowledge my correspondent stigmatizes with the name of Echoes; and seems desirous, that they should be made ashamed of lazy submission, and animated to attempts after new discoveries and original sentiments.

It is very natural for young men to be vehement, acrimonious, and severe. For, as they seldom comprehend at once all the consequences of a position, or perceive the difficulties by which cooler and more experienced reasoners are restrained from confidence, they form their conclusions with great precipitance. Seeing nothing that can darken or embarrass the question, they expect to find their own opinion universally prevalent, and are inclined to impute uncertainty and hesitation to want of honesty, rather than of knowledge. I may, perhaps, therefore be reproached by my lively correspondent, when it shall be found, that I have no inclination to persecute these collectors of fortuitous knowledge with the severity required; yet, as I am now too old to be much pained by hasty censure, I shall not be afraid of taking into protection those whom I think condemned without a sufficient knowledge of their cause.

He that adopts the sentiments of another, whom he has reason to believe wiser than himself, is only to be blamed, when he claims the honors which are not due but to the author, and endeavors to deceive the world into praise and veneration; for to learn is the proper business of youth; and whether we increase our knowledge by books or by conversation, we are equally indebted to foreign assistance.

The greater part of students are not born with abilities to construct systems,[1] or advance knowledge; nor can have any hope beyond that of becoming intelligent hearers in the schools of art,[2] of being able to

1. Philosophical theories.
2. Of the liberal arts, which included such studies as physics, logic, and ethics.

comprehend what others discover, and to remember what others teach. Even those to whom Providence has allotted greater strength of understanding can expect only to improve a single science.[3] In every other part of learning, they must be content to follow opinions which they are not able to examine; and, even in that which they claim as peculiarly their own, can seldom add more than some small particle of knowledge, to the hereditary stock devolved to them from ancient times, the collective labor of a thousand intellects.

In science which being fixed and limited admits of no other variety than such as arises from new methods of distribution, or new arts of illustration, the necessity of following the traces of our predecessors is indisputably evident; but there appears no reason why imagination should be subject to the same restraint. It might be conceived that of those who profess to forsake the narrow paths of truth every one may deviate towards a different point, since though rectitude is uniform and fixed, obliquity may be infinitely diversified. The roads of science are narrow, so that they who travel them must either follow or meet one another; but in the boundless regions of possibility which fiction claims for her dominion, there are surely a thousand recesses unexplored, a thousand flowers unplucked, a thousand fountains unexhausted, combinations of imagery yet unobserved, and races of ideal inhabitants not hitherto described.

Yet, whatever hope may persuade, or reason evince, experience can boast of very few additions to ancient fable. The wars of Troy, and the travels of Ulysses, have furnished almost all succeeding poets with incidents, characters, and sentiments. The Romans are confessed to have attempted little more than to display in their own tongue the inventions of the Greeks. There is, in all their writings, such a perpetual recurrence of allusions to the tales of the fabulous age, that they must be confessed often to want that power of giving pleasure which novelty supplies; nor can we wonder that they excelled so much in the graces of diction, when we consider how rarely they were employed in search of new thoughts.

The warmest admirers of the great Mantuan poet[4] can extol him for little more than the skill with which he has, by making his hero both a traveler and a warrior, united the beauties of the *Iliad* and *Odyssey* in one composition: yet his judgment was perhaps sometimes overborne by his avarice of the Homeric treasures; and, for fear of suffering a sparkling ornament to be lost, he has inserted it where it cannot shine with its original splendor.

When Ulysses visited the infernal regions, he found, among the heroes that perished at Troy, his competitor Ajax, who, when the arms

3. Field of knowledge.
4. Virgil, born near Mantua.

of Achilles were adjudged to Ulysses, died by his own hand in the madness of disappointment. He still appeared to resent, as on earth, his loss and disgrace. Ulysses endeavored to pacify him with praises and submission; but Ajax walked away without reply.[5] This passage has always been considered as eminently beautiful; because Ajax, the haughty chief, the unlettered soldier, of unshaken courage, of immovable constancy, but without the power of recommending his own virtues by eloquence, or enforcing his assertions by any other argument than the sword, had no way of making his anger known, but by gloomy sullenness and dumb ferocity. His hatred of a man whom he conceived to have defeated him only by volubility of tongue, was therefore naturally shown by silence more contemptuous and piercing than any words that so rude an orator could have found, and by which he gave his enemy no opportunity of exerting the only power in which he was superior.

When Aeneas is sent by Virgil to the shades,[6] he meets Dido the queen of Carthage, whom his perfidy had hurried to the grave; he accosts her with tenderness and excuses; but the lady turns away like Ajax in mute disdain. She turns away like Ajax, but she resembles him in none of those qualities which give either dignity or propriety to silence. She might, without any departure from the tenor of her conduct, have burst out like other injured women into clamor, reproach, and denunciation; but Virgil had his imagination full of Ajax, and therefore could not prevail on himself to teach Dido any other mode of resentment.

If Virgil could be thus seduced by imitation, there will be little hope that common wits should escape; and accordingly we find that besides the universal and acknowledged practice of copying the ancients, there has prevailed in every age a particular species of fiction. At one time all truth was conveyed in allegory; at another, nothing was seen but in a vision; at one period, all the poets followed sheep, and every event produced a pastoral; at another they busied themselves wholly in giving directions to a painter.[7]

It is indeed easy to conceive why any fashion should become popular, by which idleness is favored, and imbecility[8] assisted; but surely no man of genius can much applaud himself for repeating a tale with which the audience is already tired, and which could bring no honor to any but its inventor.

There are, I think, two schemes of writing on which the laborious wits of the present time employ their faculties. One is the adaptation of sense to all the rhymes which our language can supply to some word

5. *Odyssey*, xi. 541–67.
6. The underword, Hades. The following incident appears in the *Aeneid*, vi. 450–76.
7. "Advice to a Painter" was a popular 17th-century poetic genre.
8. Feebleness.

that makes the burden[9] of the stanza; but this, as it has been only used in a kind of amorous burlesque, can scarcely be censured with much acrimony. The other is the imitation of Spenser,[10] which, by the influence of some men of learning and genius, seems likely to gain upon the age, and therefore deserves to be more attentively considered.

To imitate the fictions and sentiments of Spenser can incur no reproach, for allegory is perhaps one of the most pleasing vehicles of instruction. But I am very far from extending the same respect to his diction or his stanza. His style was in his own time allowed to be vicious,[11] so darkened with old words and peculiarities of phrase, and so remote from common use, that Jonson boldly pronounces him "to have written no language."[12] His stanza is at once difficult and unpleasing; tiresome to the ear by its uniformity, and to the attention by its length. It was at first formed in imitation of the Italian poets, without due regard to the genius of our language. The Italians have little variety of termination, and were forced to contrive such a stanza as might admit the greatest number of similar rhymes; but our words end with so much diversity, that it is seldom convenient for us to bring more than two of the same sound together. If it be justly observed by Milton, that rhyme obliges poets to express their thoughts in improper terms,[13] these improprieties must always be multiplied, as the difficulty of rhyme is increased by long concatenations.[14]

The imitators of Spenser are indeed not very rigid censors of themselves, for they seem to conclude that when they have disfigured their lines with a few obsolete syllables, they have accomplished their design, without considering that they ought not only to admit old words, but to avoid new. The laws of imitation are broken by every word introduced since the time of Spenser, as the character of Hector is violated by quoting Aristotle in the play.[15] It would indeed be difficult to exclude from a long poem all modern phrases, though it is easy to sprinkle it with gleanings of antiquity. Perhaps, however, the style of Spenser might by long labor be justly copied; but life is surely given us for higher purposes than to gather what our ancestors have wisely thrown away, and to learn what is of no value, but because it has been forgotten.

9. Refrain.

10. The most notable contemporary imitation of Spenser was James Thomson's *Castle of Indolence* (1748).

11. Incorrect.

12. Ben Jonson's remark in *Timber* (1640).

13. In the Preface to *Paradise Lost* Milton speaks of rhyme as "the invention of a barbarous age," used by some modern poets "much to their own vexation, hindrance, and constraint to express many things otherwise, and for the most part worse than else they would have expressed them."

14. The Spenserian stanza of nine lines rhymes: ababbcbcc.

15. Hector quotes Aristotle in Shakespeare's *Troilus and Cressida,* II. ii. 166.

No. 125.
Tuesday, 28 May 1751.

But if, through weakness, or my want of art,
I can't to every different style impart
The proper strokes and colors it may claim,
Why am I honored with a poet's name?
HORACE, *ART OF POETRY*, LL. 86–87, TRANS. FRANCIS.

It is one of the maxims of the civil law that "definitions are hazardous." Things modified by human understandings, subject to varieties of complication, and changeable as experience advances knowledge, or accident influences caprice, are scarcely to be included in any standing form of expression, because they are always suffering some alteration of their state. Definition is, indeed, not the province of man; every thing is set above or below our faculties. The works and operations of nature are too great in their extent, or too much diffused in their relations, and the performances of art too inconstant and uncertain, to be reduced to any determinate idea. It is impossible to impress upon our minds an adequate and just representation of an object so great that we can never take it into our view, or so mutable that it is always changing under our eye, and has already lost its form while we are laboring to conceive it.

Definitions have been no less difficult or uncertain in criticism than in law. Imagination, a licentious and vagrant faculty, unsusceptible of limitations, and impatient of restraint, has always endeavored to baffle the logician, to perplex the confines of distinction, and burst the enclosures of regularity. There is therefore scarcely any species of writing, of which we can tell what is its essence, and what are its constituents; every new genius produces some innovation which, when invented and approved, subverts the rules which the practice of foregoing authors had established.

Comedy has been particularly unpropitious to definers; for though perhaps they might properly have contented themselves with declaring it to be "such a dramatic representation of human life as may excite mirth," they have embarrassed their definition with the means by which the comic writers attain their end, without considering that the various methods of exhilarating their audience, not being limited by nature, cannot be comprised in precept. Thus, some make comedy a representation of mean,[1] and others of bad men; some think that its essence consists in the unimportance, others in the fictitiousness, of the transaction. But any man's reflections will inform him that every dramatic composition which raises mirth is comic; and that, to raise mirth, it is by no means universally necessary that the personages

1. Lower-class.

should be either mean or corrupt, nor always requisite that the action should be trivial, nor ever, that it should be fictitious.

If the two kinds of dramatic poetry[2] had been defined only by their effects upon the mind, some absurdities might have been prevented with which the compositions of our greatest poets are disgraced, who, for want of some settled ideas and accurate distinctions, have unhappily confounded tragic with comic sentiments. They seem to have thought that as the meanness of personages constituted comedy, their greatness was sufficient to form a tragedy; and that nothing was necessary but that they should crowd the scene with monarchs and generals and guards; and make them talk, at certain intervals, of the downfall of kingdoms and the rout of armies. They have not considered that thoughts or incidents in themselves ridiculous grow still more grotesque by the solemnity of such characters; that reason and nature are uniform and inflexible; and that what is despicable and absurd will not, by any association with splended titles, become rational or great; that the most important affairs, by an intermixture of an unseasonable levity, may be made contemptible; and that the robes of royalty can give no dignity to nonsense or to folly.

"Comedy," says Horace, "sometimes raises her voice";[3] and tragedy may likewise on proper occasions abate her dignity; but as the comic personages can only depart from their familiarity of style when the more violent passions are put in motion, the heroes and queens of tragedy should never descend to trifle, but in the hours of ease, and intermissions of danger. Yet in the tragedy of *Don Sebastian,*[4] when the king of Portugal is in the hands of his enemy and, having just drawn the lot by which he is condemned to die, breaks out into a wild boast that his dust shall take possession of Africk, the dialogue proceeds thus between the captive and his conqueror:

Muley Moluch. What shall I do to conquer thee?
Seb. Impossible!
Souls know no conquerors.
M. Mol. I'll show thee for a monster through my Africk.
Seb. No, thou canst only show me for a man:
Africk is stored with monsters; man's a prodigy
Thy subjects have not seen.
M. Mol. Thou talk'st as if
Still at the head of battle.
Seb. Thou mistak'st,
For there I would not talk.
Benducar, the Minister. Sure he would sleep.

[I.i.]

2. Drama, i.e. comedy and tragedy.
3. *Art of Poetry,* l. 93.
4. By Dryden (1690).

This conversation, with the sly remark of the minister, can only be found not to be comic, because it wants the probability necessary to representations of common life, and degenerates too much towards buffoonery and farce.

The same play affords a smart return of the general to the emperor, who, enforcing his orders for the death of Sebastian, vents his impatience in this abrupt threat:

> No more replies,
> But see thou do'st it: or . . . .

To which Dorax answers,

> Choke in that threat: I can say "or" as loud.
>
> [III.i.]

A thousand instances of such impropriety might be produced, were not one scene in *Aureng-Zebe*[5] sufficient to exemplify it. Indamora, a captive queen, having Aureng-Zebe for her lover, employs Arimant, to whose charge she had been entrusted, and whom she had made sensible of her charms, to carry a message to his rival.

Arimant, *with a letter in his hand;* Indamora.

Arim. And I the messenger to him from you?
Your empire you to tyranny pursue:
You lay commands, both cruel and unjust,
To serve my rival, and betray my trust.
Ind. You first betrayed your trust in loving me:
And should not I my own advantage see?
Serving my love, you may my friendship gain:
You know the rest of your pretenses vain.
You must, my Arimant, you must be kind:
'Tis in your nature, and your noble mind.
Arim. I'll to the king, and straight my trust resign.
Ind. His trust you may, but you shall never mine.
Heaven made you love me for no other end,
But to become my confidant and friend:
As such, I keep no secret from your sight,
And therefore make you judge how ill I write:
Read it, and tell me freely then your mind,
If 'tis indited, as I meant it, kind.
Arim. *I ask not heaven my freedom to restore,* [Reading.
But only for your sake——I'll read no more.
And yet I must——
Less for my own than for your sorrow sad—— [Reading.
Another line like this would make me mad——
Heaven! she goes on—yet more—and yet more kind! [As reading.]

5. Dryden's *Aureng-Zebe* (1676).

Each sentence is a dagger to my mind.
See me this night—— [Reading.
Thank fortune who did such a friend provide;
For faithful Arimant shall be your guide.
Not only to be made an instrument,
But pre-engaged without my own consent!
Ind. Unknown t'engage you still augments my score,[6]
And gives you scope of meriting the more.
Arim. The best of men
Some interest in their actions must confess;
None merit, but in hope they may possess,
The fatal paper rather let me tear,
Than, like Bellerophon, my own sentence bear.[7]
Ind. You may; but 'twill not be your best advice:
'Twill only give me pains of writing twice.
You know you must obey me soon or late:
Why should you vainly struggle with your fate?
Arim. I thank thee, heaven! thou hast been wonderous kind!
Why am I thus to slavery designed,
And yet am cheated with a freeborn mind?
Or make thy orders with my reason suit,
Or let me live by sense, a glorious brute——
[*She frowns.*
You frown and I obey with speed before
That dreadful sentence comes, *See me no more.*
[III.i.]

In this scene, every circumstance concurs to turn tragedy to farce. The wild absurdity of the expedient; the contemptible subjection of the lover; the folly of obliging him to read the letter only because it ought to have been concealed from him; the frequent interruptions of amorous impatience; the faint expostulations of a voluntary slave; the imperious haughtiness of a tyrant without power; the deep reflection of the yielding rebel upon fate and free will; and his wise wish to lose his reason as soon as he finds himself about to do what he cannot persuade his reason to approve, are surely sufficient to awaken the most torpid risibility.

There is scarce a tragedy of the last century which has not debased its most important incidents, and polluted its most serious interlocutions with buffoonery and meanness; but though perhaps it cannot be pretended that the present age has added much to the force and efficacy of the drama, it has at least been able to escape many faults which either ignorance had overlooked, or indulgence had licensed. The later tragedies indeed have faults of another kind, perhaps more destructive

6. Bill, debt.

7. The Greek mythological hero Bellerophon was sent by his host to the latter's father-in-law with a letter asking that he be killed.

to delight, though less open to censure. That perpetual tumor of phrase with which every thought is now expressed by every personage, the paucity of adventures which regularity[8] admits, and the unvaried equality of flowing dialogue, has taken away from our present writers almost all that dominion over the passions which was the boast of their predecessors. Yet they may at least claim this commendation that they avoid gross faults, and that if they cannot often move terror or pity, they are always careful not to provoke laughter.

No. 156.
Saturday, 14 September 1751.

For wisdom ever echoes nature's voice.
JUVENAL, *SATIRES*, XIV. 321 [TRANS. JOHNSON].

Every government, say the politicians, is perpetually degenerating towards corruption, from which it must be rescued at certain periods by the resuscitation of its first principles, and the re-establishment of its original constitution. Every animal body, according to the methodic physicians,[1] is, by the predominance of some exuberant quality, continually declining towards disease and death, which must be obviated by a seasonable reduction of the peccant humor to the just equipoise which health requires.[2]

In the same manner the studies of mankind, all at least which not being subject to rigorous demonstration admit the influence of fancy and caprice, are perpetually tending to error and confusion. Of the great principles of truth which the first speculatists[3] discovered, the simplicity is embarrassed by ambitious additions, or the evidence obscured by inaccurate argumentation; and as they descend from one succession of writers to another, like light transmitted from room to room, they lose their strength and splendor, and fade at last in total evanescence.

The systems of learning therefore must be sometimes reviewed, complications analyzed into principles, and knowledge disentangled from opinion. It is not always possible without a close inspection to separate the genuine shoots of consequential reasoning which grow out of some radical[4] postulate from the branches which art has engrafted on it. The accidental prescriptions of authority, when time has pro-

8. The limitations prescribed by the unities of action, time, and place.
1. One of the three ancient schools of physicians.
2. According to ancient belief, bodily health depended upon a proper balance among four humors: blood, phlegm, black bile, yellow bile.
3. Theorists.
4. Basic, root.

cured them veneration, are often confounded with the laws of nature, and those rules are supposed coeval with reason of which the first rise cannot be discovered.

Criticism has sometimes permitted fancy to dictate the laws by which fancy ought to be restrained, and fallacy to perplex the principles by which fallacy is to be detected; her superintendance of others has betrayed her to negligence of herself; and, like the ancient Scythians, by extending her conquests over distant regions, she has left her throne vacant to her slaves.[5]

Among the laws of which the desire of extending authority, or ardor of promoting knowledge has prompted the prescription, all which writers have received, had not the same original right to our regard. Some are to be considered as fundamental and indispensable, others only as useful and convenient; some as dictated by reason and necessity, others as enacted by despotic antiquity; some as invincibly supported by their conformity to the order of nature and operations of the intellect; others as formed by accident, or instituted by example, and therefore always liable to dispute and alteration.

That many rules have been advanced without consulting nature or reason, we cannot but suspect, when we find it peremptorily decreed by the ancient masters that "only three speaking personages should appear at once upon the stage";[6] a law which, as the variety and intricacy of modern plays has made it impossible to be observed, we now violate without scruple, and, as experience proves, without inconvenience.

The original of this precept was merely accidental. Tragedy was a monody or solitary song in honor of Bacchus,[7] improved afterwards into a dialogue by the addition of another speaker; but the ancients, remembering that the tragedy was at first pronounced only by one, durst not for some time venture beyond two; at last when custom and impunity had made them daring, they extended their liberty to the admission of three, but restrained themselves by a critical edict from further exorbitance.

By what accident the number of acts was limited to five, I know not that any author has informed us; but certainly it is not determined by any necessity arising either from the nature of action or propriety of exhibition. An act is only the representation of such a part of the business of the play as proceeds in an unbroken tenor, or without any intermediate pause. Nothing is more evident than that of every real, and by consequence of every dramatic action, the intervals may be more or fewer than five; and indeed the rule is upon the English stage

5. This story about the Scythians, a barbarous people, comes from Herodotus, *History*, iv. 1–4.

6. Aristotle, *Poetics*, ch. iv, reports on the practice of Sophocles. Horace, *Art of Poetry*, 1. 192, recites what had come to be a rule.

7. Greek god of wine, and thus inspirer of music and poetry.

every day broken in effect, without any other mischief than that which arises from an absurd endeavor to observe it in appearance. Whenever the scene is shifted the act ceases, since some time is necessarily supposed to elapse while the personages of the drama change their place.

With no greater right to our obedience have the critics confined the dramatic action to a certain number of hours. Probability requires that the time of action should approach somewhat nearly to that of exhibition, and those plays will always be thought most happily conducted which crowd the greatest variety into the least space. But since it will frequently happen that some delusion must be admitted, I know not where the limits of imagination can be fixed. It is rarely observed that minds not prepossessed by mechanical[8] criticism feel any offence from the extension of the intervals between the acts; nor can I conceive it absurd or impossible that he who can multiply three hours into twelve or twenty-four might image with equal ease a greater number.

I know not whether he that professes to regard no other laws than those of nature will not be inclined to receive tragicomedy to his protection, whom, however generally condemned, her own laurels have hitherto shaded from the fulminations of criticism. For what is there in the mingled drama which impartial reason can condemn? The connection of important with trivial incidents, since it is not only common but perpetual in the world, may surely be allowed upon the stage, which pretends only to be the mirror of life. The impropriety of suppressing passions before we have raised them to the intended agitation, and of diverting the expectation from an event which we keep suspended only to raise it, may be speciously urged. But will not experience show this objection to be rather subtle than just? is it not certain that the tragic and comic affections have been moved alternately with equal force, and that no plays have oftener filled the eye with tears,.and the breast with palpitation, than those which are variegated with interludes of mirth?

I do not however think it safe to judge of works of genius merely by the event. These resistless vicissitudes[9] of the heart, this alternate prevalence of merriment and solemnity, may sometimes be more properly ascribed to the vigor of the writer than the justness of the design: and instead of vindicating tragicomedy by the success of Shakespeare, we ought perhaps to pay new honors to that transcendent and unbounded genius that could preside over the passions in sport; who, to actuate the affections, needed not the slow gradation of common means, but could fill the heart with instantaneous jollity or sorrow, and vary our disposition as he changed his scenes. Perhaps the effects even of Shakespeare's poetry might have been yet greater, had he not counteracted himself;

8. Rule-bound.
9. Alternations.

and we might have been more interested in the distresses of his heroes had we not been so frequently diverted by the jokes of his buffoons.

There are other rules more fixed and obligatory. It is necessary that of every play the chief action should be single; for since a play represents some transaction, through its regular maturation to its final event, two actions equally important must evidently constitute two plays.

As the design of tragedy is to instruct by moving the passions, it must always have a hero, a personage apparently and incontestably superior to the rest, upon whom the attention may be fixed, and the anxiety suspended. For though of two persons opposing each other with equal abilities and equal virtue, the auditor will inevitably in time choose his favorite, yet as that choice must be without any cogency of conviction, the hopes or fears which it raises will be faint and languid. Of two heroes acting in confederacy against a common enemy, the virtues or dangers will give little emotion, because each claims our concern with the same right, and the heart lies at rest between equal motives.

It ought to be the first endeavor of a writer to distinguish nature from custom, or that which is established because it is right, from that which is right only because it is established; that he may neither violate essential principles by a desire of novelty, nor debar himself from the attainment of beauties within his view by a needless fear of breaking rules which no literary dictator had authority to enact.

No. 158.
Saturday, 21 September 1751.

Critics yet contend,
And of their vain disputings find no end.
HORACE, *ART OF POETRY,* L. 78, TRANS. FRANCIS.

Criticism, though dignified from the earliest age by the labors of men eminent for knowledge and sagacity; and, since the revival of polite literature,[1] the favorite study of European scholars, has not yet attained the certainty and stability of science. The rules hitherto received are seldom drawn from any settled principle or self-evident postulate, or adapted to the natural and invariable constitution of things; but will be found upon examination the arbitrary edicts of legislators, authorized only by themselves, who, out of various means by which the same end may be attained, selected such as happened to occur to their own reflection, and then by a law which idleness and timidity were too willing to obey, prohibited new experiments of wit, restrained fancy from the indulgence of her innate inclination to

1. In the Renaissance.

hazard and adventure, and condemned all future flights of genius to pursue the path of the Maeonian eagle.[2]

This authority may be more justly opposed, as it is apparently derived from them whom they endeavor to control; for we owe few of the rules of writing to the acuteness of critics, who have generally no other merit than that having read the works of great authors with attention, they have observed the arrangement of their matter, or the graces of their expression, and then expected honor and reverence for precepts which they never could have invented: so that practice has introduced rules, rather than rules have directed practice.

For this reason the laws of every species of writing have been settled by the ideas of him who first raised it to reputation, without inquiry whether his performances were not yet susceptible of improvement. The excellencies and faults of celebrated writers have been equally recommended to posterity; and so far has blind reverence prevailed that even the number of their books has been thought worthy of imitation.[3]

The imagination of the first authors of lyric poetry was vehement and rapid, and their knowledge various and extensive.[4] Living in an age when science had been little cultivated, and when the minds of their auditors, not being accustomed to accurate inspection, were easily dazzled by glaring ideas,[5] they applied themselves to instruct rather by short sentences[6] and striking thoughts than by regular argumentation; and finding attention more successfully excited by sudden sallies and unexpected exclamations than by the more artful and placid beauties of methodical deduction, they loosed their genius to its own course, passed from one sentiment to another without expressing the intermediate ideas, and roved at large over the ideal world[7] with such lightness and agility that their footsteps are scarcely to be traced.

From this accidental peculiarity of the ancient writers the critics deduce the rules of lyric poetry, which they have set free from all the laws by which other compositions are confined, and allow to neglect the niceties of transition, to start into remote digressions, and to wander without restraint from one scene of imagery to another.

A writer of later times has, by the vivacity of his essays, reconciled mankind to the same licentiousness[8] in short dissertations;[9] and he

2. Homer, who supposedly was born in Maeonia.

3. Homer's *Iliad* and *Odyssey* each has twenty-four books, and Virgil's *Aeneid*, twelve. Spenser planned twelve for the *Faerie Queene*. Milton's *Paradise Lost* has twelve.

4. Presumably Johnson is referring to Greek and Roman lyric poets, though the rest of the paragraph suggests a work like Horace's *Art of Poetry*.

5. Striking images.

6. Aphorisms, epigrammatic sayings.

7. World of imagination.

8. Lawlessness.

9. Probably Francis Bacon in his *Essays* (1625), though Montaigne's *Essays* (1595) are professedly rambling.

therefore who wants skill to form a plan or diligence to pursue it needs only entitle his performance an essay to acquire the right of heaping together the collections of half his life without order, coherence, or propriety.

In writing, as in life, faults are endured without disgust when they are associated with transcendent merit, and may be sometimes recommended to weak judgments by the luster which they obtain from their union with excellence; but it is the business of those who presume to superintend the taste or morals of mankind to separate delusive combinations, and distinguish that which may be praised from that which can only be excused. As vices never promote happiness, though when overpowered by more active and more numerous virtues they cannot totally destroy it; so confusion and irregularity produce no beauty, though they cannot always obstruct the brightness of genius and learning. To proceed from one truth to another, and connect distant propositions by regular consequences, is the great prerogative of man. Independent and unconnected sentiments flashing upon the mind in quick succession may for a time delight by their novelty, but they differ from systematical reasoning as single notes from harmony, as glances of lightning from the radiance of the sun.

When rules are thus drawn rather from precedents than reason, there is danger not only from the faults of an author but from the errors of those who criticize his works; since they may often mislead their pupils by false representations, as the Ciceronians of the sixteenth century were betrayed into barbarisms by corrupt copies of their darling writer.[10]

It is established at present that the proemial[11] lines of a poem, in which the general subject is proposed, must be void of glitter and embellishment. "The first lines of *Paradise Lost,*" says Addison, "are perhaps as plain, simple, and unadorned as any of the whole poem, in which particular the author has conformed himself to the example of Homer and the precept of Horace."[12]

This observation seems to have been made by an implicit adoption of the common opinion without consideration either of the precept or example. Had Horace been consulted, he would have been found to direct only what should be comprised in the proposition, not how it should be expressed, and to have commended Homer in opposition to a meaner poet, not for the gradual elevation of his diction, but the

10. Erasmus in his *Ciceronianus* (1528) and Bacon in his *Advancement of Learning* (1605) criticized certain 16th-century humanists whose Latin ostentatiously imitated Cicero's. Some good 16th-century editions of Cicero were printed in Italy, but the first edition of his *Complete Works* in England did not appear until 1585; there, the lack of accurate grammars and even adequate dictionaries made it difficult to write correct classical Latin.

11. Prefatory.

12. *Spectator,* no. 203.

judicious expansion of his plan; for displaying unpromised events, not for producing unexpected elegancies.

Speciosa dehinc miracula promit,
Antiphaten Scyllamque, et cum Cyclope Charybdim.

[HORACE, *ART OF POETRY*, LL. 144–45.]

But from a cloud of smoke he breaks to light,
And pours his specious miracles to sight;
Antiphates his hideous feast devours,[13]
Charybdis[14] barks, and Polyphemus[15] roars.

FRANCIS.

If the exordial[16] verses of Homer be compared with the rest of the poem, they will not appear remarkable for plainness or simplicity, but rather eminently adorned and illuminated. . . .[17]

The man, for wisdom's various arts renowned,
Long exercised in woes, O muse! resound.
Who, when his arms had wrought the destined fall
Of sacred Troy, and razed her heaven-built wall,
Wandering from clime to clime, observant strayed,
Their manners noted, and their states surveyed.
On stormy seas unnumbered toils he bore,
Safe with his friends to gain his natal shore:
Vain toils! their impious folly dared to prey
On herds devoted to the god of day;[18]
The god vindictive doomed them never more
(Ah men unblessed) to touch that natal shore.
O snatch some portion of these acts from fate,
Celestial muse! and to our world relate.

POPE.

The first verses of the *Iliad* are in like manner particularly splendid, and the proposition[19] of the *Aeneid* closes with dignity and magnificence not often to be found even in the poetry of Virgil.

The intent of the introduction is to raise expectation and suspend it; something therefore must be discovered and something concealed;

13. King of the Laestrygonians, giants who slaughtered and ate Odysseus's men (*Odyssey*, x. 100–32).

14. A whirlpool which engulfed passing ships (in the Straits of Messina). Opposite was the monster Scylla, named in the Latin of Horace above. It was she who barked like a dog. (*Odyssey*, xii. 85–126, 426–46).

15. A one-eyed giant who ate some of Odysseus's men and subsequently was blinded by Odysseus (*Odyssey*, ix. 193–542).

16. Introductory.

17. Johnson here quotes the first ten lines of the *Odyssey* in Greek.

18. Apollo, the sun god, whose herds of cattle and sheep Odysseus's men killed and ate (*Odyssey*, xii. 260–419).

19. The introductory statement of the work's subject.

and the poet, while the fertility of his invention is yet unknown, may properly recommend himself by the grace of his language.

He that reveals too much or promises too little; he that never irritates the intellectual appetite, or that immediately satiates it, equally defeats his own purpose. It is necessary to the pleasure of the reader that the events should not be anticipated, and how then can his attention be invited but by grandeur of expression?

No. 168.
Saturday, 26 October 1751.

The tinsel glitter, and the specious mien
Delude the most; few pry behind the scene.
PHAEDRUS, *AESOP'S FABLES*, IV.ii. 5–7 [TRANS. JOHNSON].

It has been observed by Boileau that "a mean or common thought expressed in pompous diction generally pleases more than a new or noble sentiment delivered in low and vulgar language, because the number is greater of those whom custom has enabled to judge of words than whom study has qualified to examine things."[1]

This solution might satisfy if such only were offended with meanness of expression as are unable to distinguish propriety of thought, and to separate propositions or images from the vehicles by which they are conveyed to the understanding. But this kind of disgust is by no means confined to the ignorant or superficial; it operates uniformly and universally upon readers of all classes; every man, however profound or abstracted, perceives himself irresistibly alienated by low terms; they who profess the most zealous adherence to truth are forced to admit that she owes part of her charms to her ornaments, and loses much of her power over the soul, when she appears disgraced by a dress uncouth or ill-adjusted.

We are all offended by low terms, but are not disgusted alike by the same compositions, because we do not all agree to censure the same terms as low. No word is naturally or intrinsically meaner than another; our opinion therefore of words, as of other things arbitrarily and capriciously established, depends wholly upon accident and custom. The cottager thinks those apartments splendid and spacious, which an inhabitant of palaces will despise for their inelegance; and to him who has passed most of his hours with the delicate and polite, many expressions will seem sordid, which another, equally acute, may hear without offense; but a mean term never fails to displease him to whom it appears

1. *Critical Reflections on Longinus*, no. 9 (1694).

mean, as poverty is certainly and invariably despised, though he who is poor in the eyes of some, may by others be envied for his wealth.

Words become low by the occasions to which they are applied, or the general character of them who use them; and the disgust which they produce, arises from the revival of those images with which they are commonly united. Thus if, in the most solemn discourse, a phrase happens to occur which has been successfully employed in some ludicrous narrative, the gravest auditor finds it difficult to refrain from laughter, when they who are not prepossessed by the same accidental association are utterly unable to guess the reason of his merriment. Words which convey ideas of dignity in one age are banished from elegant writing or conversation in another, because they are in time debased by vulgar mouths, and can be no longer heard without the involuntary recollection of unpleasing images.

When Macbeth is confirming himself in the horrid purpose of stabbing his king, he breaks out amidst his emotions into a wish natural to a murderer,

> Come, thick night!
> And pall thee in the dunnest smoke of hell,
> That my keen knife see not the wound it makes;
> Nor heaven peep through the blanket of the dark,
> To cry, hold, hold![2]

In this passage is exerted all the force of poetry, that force which calls new powers into being, which embodies sentiment, and animates matter; yet perhaps scarce any man now peruses it without some disturbance of his attention from the counteraction of the words to the ideas. What can be more dreadful than to implore the presence of night, invested not in common obscurity, but in the smoke of hell? Yet the efficacy of this invocation is destroyed by the insertion of an epithet now seldom heard but in the stable, and *dun*[3] night may come or go without any other notice than contempt.

If we start into raptures when some hero of the *Iliad* tells us that **δόρυ μάινεται**, his lance rages with eagerness to destroy;[4] if we are alarmed at the terror of the soldiers commanded by Caesar to hew down the sacred grove, who dreaded, says Lucan, lest the ax aimed at the oak should fly back upon the striker,

> *Si robora sacra ferirent,*
> *In sua credebant redituras membra secures.*
>
> [*PHARSALIA*, III. 430–31.][5]

2. *Macbeth*, I.v.48–52.
3. "Dun" was a traditional name for a horse, especially one of a dull brown color.
4. Johnson translates the Greek words from *Iliad*, viii.111.
5. Lucan's *Pharsalia*, an epic poem (first century, A.D.) about the civil war between Caesar and Pompey.

None dares with impious steel the grove to rend,
Lest on himself the destined stroke[6] descend;

we cannot surely but sympathize with the horrors of a wretch about to murder his master, his friend, his benefactor, who suspects that the weapon will refuse its office,[7] and start back from the breast which he is preparing to violate. Yet this sentiment is weakened by the name of an instrument used by butchers and cooks in the meanest employments; we do not immediately conceive that any crime of importance is to be committed with a *knife;* or who does not, at last, from the long habit of connecting a knife with sordid offices, feel aversion rather than terror?

Macbeth proceeds to wish, in the madness of guilt, that the inspection of heaven may be intercepted, and that he may in the involutions[8] of infernal darkness escape the eye of Providence. This is the utmost extravagance of determined wickedness; yet this is so debased by two unfortunate words, that while I endeavor to impress on my reader the energy of the sentiment, I can scarce check my risibility, when the expression forces itself upon my mind; for who, without some relaxation of his gravity, can hear of the avengers of guilt "peeping through a blanket"?

These imperfections of diction are less obvious to the reader, as he is less acquainted with common usages; they are therefore wholly imperceptible to a foreigner, who learns our language from books, and will strike a solitary academic less forcibly than a modish lady.

Among the numerous requisites that must concur to complete an author, few are of more importance than an early entrance into the living world. The seeds of knowledge may be planted in solitude, but must be cultivated in public. Argumentation may be taught in colleges, and theories formed in retirement, but the artifice of embellishment, and the powers of attraction, can be gained only by general converse.

An acquaintance with prevailing customs and fashionable elegance is necessary likewise for other purposes. The injury that grand imagery suffers from unsuitable language, personal merit may fear from rudeness and indelicacy. When the success of Aeneas depended on the favor of the queen upon whose coasts he was driven, his celestial protectress thought him not sufficiently secured against rejection by his piety or bravery, but decorated him for the interview with preternatural beauty.[9] Whoever desires, for his writings or himself, what none can reasonably contemn,[10] the favor of mankind, must add grace to strength, and make his thoughts agreeable as well as useful. Many

6. Stroke of doom.
7. Function. Johnson has recurred to Macbeth.
8. Coverings, wrappings.
9. In book one of the *Aeneid,* when Aeneas arrives in the kingdom of Dido, Queen of Carthage, he is watched over by his mother, Venus.
10. Despise.

complain of neglect who never tried to attract regard. It cannot be expected that the patrons of science or virtue should be solicitous to discover excellencies which they who possess them shade and disguise. Few have abilities so much needed by the rest of the world as to be caressed[11] on their own terms; and he that will not condescend to recommend himself by external embellishments must submit to the fate of just sentiments meanly expressed, and be ridiculed and forgotten before he understood.

No. 179.
Tuesday, 3 December 1751.

Democritus would feed his spleen, and shake
His sides and shoulders till he felt them ache.[1]
JUVENAL, *SATIRES*, X. 33, TRANS. DRYDEN.

Every man, says Tully,[2] has two characters: one which he partakes with all mankind, and by which he is distinguished from brute animals; another which discriminates him from the rest of his own species, and impresses on him a manner and temper peculiar to himself; this particular character, if it be not repugnant to the laws of general humanity, it is always his business to cultivate and preserve.

Every hour furnishes some confirmation of Tully's precept. It seldom happens that an assembly of pleasure is so happily selected but that some one finds admission with whom the rest are deservedly offended; and it will appear on a close inspection, that scarce any man becomes eminently disagreeable but by a departure from his real character, and an attempt at something for which nature or education have left him unqualified.

Ignorance or dullness have indeed no power of affording delight, but they never give disgust except when they assume the dignity of knowledge, or ape the sprightliness of wit. Awkwardness and inelegance have none of those attractions by which ease and politeness take possession of the heart; but ridicule and censure seldom rise against them, unless they appear associated with that confidence which belongs only to long acquaintance with the modes of life, and to consciousness of unfailing propriety of behavior. Deformity itself is regarded with tenderness rather than aversion, when it does not attempt to deceive the sight by dress and decoration and to seize upon fictitious claims the prerogatives of beauty.

11. Praised, cherished.

1. Democritus (c.460-c.370 B.C.), known as the "laughing philosopher" from his reaction to human follies. The spleen was considered the source of many emotions, here of amused contempt.

2. Marcus Tullius Cicero. This paragraph derives from his *Of Moral Duties*, I. xxx.

He that stands to contemplate the crowds that fill the streets of a populous city will see many passengers whose air and motion it will be difficult to behold without contempt and laughter; but if he examines what are the appearances that thus powerfully excite his risibility, he will find among them neither poverty nor disease, nor any involuntary or painful defect. The disposition to derision and insult is awakened by the softness of foppery, the swell of insolence, the liveliness of levity, or the solemnity of grandeur; by the sprightly trip, the stately stalk, the formal strut, and the lofty mien, by gestures intended to catch the eye, and by looks elaborately formed as evidences of importance.

It has, I think, been sometimes urged in favor of affectation that it is only a mistake of the means to a good end, and that the intention with which it is practiced is always to please. If all attempts to innovate[3] the constitutional or habitual character have really proceeded from public spirit and love of others, the world has hitherto been sufficiently ungrateful, since no return but scorn has yet been made to the most difficult of all enterprises, a contest with nature; nor has any pity been shown to the fatigues of labor which never succeeded, and the uneasiness of disguise by which nothing was concealed.

It seems therefore to be determined by the general suffrage of mankind that he who decks himself in adscititious[4] qualities rather purposes to command applause than impart pleasure; and he is therefore treated as a man who by an unreasonable ambition usurps the place in society to which he has no right. Praise is seldom paid with willingness even to incontestable merit, and it can be no wonder that he who calls for it without desert is repulsed with universal indignation.

Affectation naturally counterfeits those excellencies which are placed at the greatest distance from possibility of attainment. We are conscious of our own defects, and eagerly endeavor to supply them by artificial excellence; nor would such efforts be wholly without excuse, were they not often excited by ornamental trifles, which he, that thus anxiously struggles for the reputation of possessing them, would not have been known to want, had not his industry quickened observation.

Gelasimus passed the first part of his life in academical privacy and rural retirement, without any other conversation[5] than that of scholars, grave, studious, and abstracted as himself. He cultivated the mathematical sciences with indefatigable diligence, discovered many useful theorems, discussed with great accuracy the resistance of fluids, and, though his priority was not generally acknowledged, was the first who fully explained all the properties of the catenarian curve.[6]

Learning, when it rises to eminence, will be observed in time what-

3. Alter.
4. Added (i.e. artificial).
5. Company.
6. Curve theoretically formed by a cable suspended from two points.

ever mists may happen to surround it. Gelasimus, in his forty-ninth year, was distinguished by those who have the rewards of knowledge in their hands, and called out to display his acquisitions[7] for the honor of his country, and add dignity by his presence to philosophical assemblies. As he did not suspect his unfitness for common affairs, he felt no reluctance to obey the invitation, and what he did not feel he had yet too much honesty to feign. He entered into the world as a larger and more populous college, where his performances would be more public and his renown farther extended; and imagined that he should find his reputation universally prevalent, and the influence of learning everywhere the same.

His merit introduced him to splendid tables and elegant acquaintance, but he did not find himself always qualified to join in the conversation. He was distressed by civilities which he knew not how to repay, and entangled in many ceremonial perplexities from which his books and diagrams could not extricate him. He was sometimes unluckily engaged in disputes with ladies, with whom algebraic axioms had no great weight, and saw many whose favor and esteem he could not but desire, to whom he was very little recommended by his theories of the tides, or his approximations to the quadrature[8] of the circle.

Gelasimus did not want penetration to discover that no charm was more generally irresistible than that of easy facetiousness and flowing hilarity. He saw that diversion was more frequently welcome than improvement, that authority and seriousness were rather feared than loved, and that the grave scholar was a kind of imperious ally, hastily dismissed when his assistance was no longer necessary. He came to a sudden resolution of throwing off those cumbrous ornaments of learning which hindered his reception, and commenced a man of wit and jocularity. Utterly unacquainted with every topic of merriment, ignorant of the modes and follies, the vices and virtues of mankind, and unfurnished with any ideas but such as Pappus and Archimedes[9] had given him, he began to silence all inquiries with a jest instead of a solution, extended his face with a grin which he mistook for a smile, and in the place of a scientific discourse retailed in a new language formed between the college and the tavern, the intelligence of the newspaper.

Laughter, he knew, was a token of alacrity, and, therefore, whatever he said, or heard, he was careful not to fail in that great duty of a wit.[10] If he asked or told the hour of the day, if he complained of heat or cold, stirred the fire, or filled a glass, removed his chair, or snuffed a candle,

7. Stores of learning.
8. Squaring.
9. Two famous Greek mathematicians.
10. Laughter often was regarded as ill-bred.

he always found some occasion to laugh. The jest was indeed a secret to all but himself, but habitual confidence in his own discernment hindered him from suspecting any weakness or mistake. He wondered that his wit was so little understood, but expected that his audience would comprehend it by degrees, and persisted all his life to show by gross buffoonery how little the strongest faculties can perform beyond the limits of their own province.

No. 188.
Saturday, 4 January 1752.

The more I honor thee, the less I love.
MARTIAL, *EPIGRAMS*, II. lv. 3 [TRANS. JOHNSON].

None of the desires dictated by vanity is more general or less blamable than that of being distinguished for the arts of conversation. Other accomplishments may be possessed without opportunity of exerting them, or wanted without danger that the defect can often be remarked; but as no man can live otherwise than in an hermitage without hourly pleasure or vexation from the fondness or neglect of those about him, the faculty of giving pleasure is of continual use. Few are more frequently envied than those who have the power of forcing attention wherever they come, whose entrance is considered as a promise of felicity, and whose departure is lamented, like the recess[1] of the sun from northern climates, as a privation of all that enlivens fancy or inspirits gaiety.

It is apparent that to excellence in this valuable art some peculiar qualifications are necessary; for everyone's experience will inform him that the pleasure which men are able to give in conversation holds no stated proportion to their knowledge or their virtue. Many find their way to the tables and the parties of those who never consider them as of the least importance in any other place; we have all, at one time or other, been content to love those whom we could not esteem, and been persuaded to try the dangerous experiment of admitting him for a companion whom we knew to be too ignorant for a counselor and too treacherous for a friend.

I question whether some abatement of character is not necessary to general acceptance. Few spend their time with much satisfaction under the eye of uncontestable superiority; and therefore among those whose presence is courted at assemblies of jollity there are seldom found men eminently distinguished for powers or acquisitions.[2] The wit whose

1. Recession.
2. Abilities or knowledge.

vivacity condemns slower tongues to silence, the scholar whose knowledge allows no man to fancy that he instructs him, the critic who suffers no fallacy to pass undetected, and the reasoner who condemns the idle to thought and the negligent to attention, are generally praised and feared, reverenced and avoided.

He that would please must rarely aim at such excellence as depresses his hearers in their own opinion, or debars them from the hope of contributing reciprocally to the entertainment of the company. Merriment, extorted by sallies of imagination, sprightliness of remark, or quickness of reply is too often what the Latins call the "Sardinian laughter," a distortion of the face without gladness of heart.

For this reason, no style of conversation is more extensively acceptable than the narrative. He who has stored his memory with slight anecdotes, private incidents, and personal particularities seldom fails to find his audience favorable. Almost every man listens with eagerness to contemporary history; for almost every man has some real or imaginary connection with a celebrated character, some desire to advance or oppose a rising name. Vanity often cooperates with curiosity. He that is a hearer in one place qualifies himself to become a speaker in another; for though he cannot comprehend a series of argument, or transport the volatile spirit of wit without evaporation, he yet thinks himself able to treasure up the various incidents of a story, and pleases his hopes with the information which he shall give to some inferior society.

Narratives are for the most part heard without envy, because they are not supposed to imply any intellectual qualities above the common rate. To be acquainted with facts not yet echoed by plebeian mouths may happen to one man as well as to another, and to relate them when they are known has in appearance so little difficulty that everyone concludes himself equal to the task.

But it is not easy, and in some situations of life not possible, to accumulate such a stock of materials as may support the expense of continual narration; and it frequently happens that they who attempt this method of ingratiating themselves please only at the first interview; and, for want of new supplies of intelligence, wear out their stories by continual repetition.

There would be, therefore, little hope of obtaining the praise of a good companion, were it not to be gained by more compendious methods; but such is the kindness of mankind to all except those who aspire to real merit and rational dignity that every understanding may find some way to excite benevolence; and whoever is not envied may learn the art of procuring love. We are willing to be pleased, but are not willing to admire; we favor the mirth or officiousness that solicits our regard, but oppose the worth or spirit that enforces it.

The first place among those that please, because they desire only to please, is due to the "merry fellow," whose laugh is loud, and whose voice is strong; who is ready to echo every jest with obstreperous approbation, and countenance every frolic with vociferations of applause. It is not necessary to a merry fellow to have in himself any fund of jocularity or force of conception; it is sufficient that he always appears in the highest exaltation of gladness, for the greater part of mankind are gay or serious by infection and follow without resistance the attraction of example.

Next to the merry fellow is the "good-natured man," a being generally without benevolence or any other virtue than such as indolence and insensibility confer. The characteristic of a good-natured man is to bear a joke; to sit unmoved and unaffected amidst noise and turbulence, profaneness and obscenity; to hear every tale without contradiction; to endure insult without reply; and to follow the stream of folly whatever course it shall happen to take. The good-natured man is commonly the darling of the petty wits, with whom they exercise themselves in the rudiments of raillery; for he never takes advantage of failings, nor disconcerts a puny satirist with unexpected sarcasms; but while the glass continues to circulate, contentedly bears the expense of uninterrupted laughter, and retires rejoicing at his own importance.

The "modest man" is a companion of a yet lower rank, whose only power of giving pleasure is not to interrupt it. The modest man satisfies himself with peaceful silence, which all his companions are candid[3] enough to consider as proceeding not from inability to speak but willingness to hear.

Many without being able to attain any general character of excellence have some single art of entertainment which serves them as a passport through the world. One I have known for fifteen years the darling of a weekly club, because every night precisely at eleven he begins his favorite song, and during the vocal performance by correspondent motions of his hand chalks out a giant upon the wall. Another has endeared himself to a long succession of acquaintances by sitting among them with his wig reversed; another by contriving to smut the nose of any stranger who was to be initiated in the club; another by purring like a cat and then pretending to be frighted; and another by yelping like a hound and calling to the drawers[4] to drive out the dog.

Such are the arts by which cheerfulness is promoted and sometimes friendship established; arts which those who despise them should not rigorously blame, except when they are practiced at the expense of innocence; for it is always necessary to be loved but not always necessary to be reverenced.

3. Good humored.
4. Bartenders or waiters.

No. 191.
Tuesday, 14 January 1752.

The youth . . .
Yielding like wax, th' impressive folly bears;
Rough to reproof, and slow to future cares.
HORACE, *ART OF POETRY*, L. 163, TRANS. FRANCIS.

To the Rambler.

Dear Mr. Rambler,
I have been four days confined to my chamber by a cold, which has already kept me from three plays, nine sales, five shows, and six card-tables, and put me seventeen visits behind hand; and the doctor tells my mamma that if I fret and cry it will settle in my head, and I shall not be fit to be seen these six weeks. But, dear Mr. Rambler, how can I help it? At this very time Melissa is dancing with the prettiest[1] gentleman;—she will breakfast with him tomorrow and then run to two auctions and hear compliments and have presents; then she will be dressed and visit and get a ticket to the play; then go to cards and win and come home with two flambeaux before her chair.[2] Dear Mr. Rambler, who can bear it?

My aunt has just brought me a bundle of your papers for my amusement. She says you are a philosopher, and will teach me to moderate my desires and look upon the world with indifference. But, dear sir, I do not wish nor intend to moderate my desires, nor can I think it proper to look upon the world with indifference till the world looks with indifference on me. I have been forced, however, to sit this morning a whole quarter of an hour with your paper before my face; but just as my aunt came in, Phyllida had brought me a letter from Mr. Trip, which I put within the leaves, and read about "absence" and "inconsolableness," and "ardor," and "irresistible passion," and "eternal constancy," while my aunt imagined that I was puzzling myself with your philosophy, and often cried out, when she saw me look confused, "If there is any word that you do not understand, child, I will explain it."

Dear soul! how old people that think themselves wise may be imposed upon! But it is fit that they should take their turn, for I am sure while they can keep poor girls close in the nursery they tyrannize over us in a very shameful manner, and fill our imaginations with tales of terror only to make us live in quiet subjection, and fancy that we can never be safe but by their protection.

I have a mamma and two aunts, who have all been formerly celebrated for wit and beauty, and are still generally admired by those that

1. Most charming or attractive.
2. Two torches to light the sedan chair she is carried in.

value themselves upon their understanding, and love to talk of vice and virtue, nature and simplicity, and beauty, and propriety; but if there was not some hope of meeting me, scarcely a creature would come near them that wears a fashionable coat. These ladies, Mr. Rambler, have had me under their government fifteen years and a half, and have all that time been endeavoring to deceive me by such representations of life as I now find not to be true; but I knew not whether I ought to impute them to ignorance or malice, as it is possible the world may be much changed since they mingled in general conversation.

Being desirous that I should love books, they told me that nothing but knowledge could make me an agreeable companion to men of sense, or qualify me to distinguish the superficial glitter of vanity from the solid merit of understanding; and that a habit of reading would enable me to fill up the vacuities of life without the help of silly or dangerous amusements, and preserve me from the snares of idleness and the inroads of temptation.

But their principal intention was to make me afraid of men, in which they succeeded so well for a time that I durst not look in their faces, or be left alone with them in a parlor; for they made me fancy that no man ever spoke but to deceive or looked but to allure; that the girl who suffered him that had once squeezed her hand to approach her a second time was on the brink of ruin; and that she who answered a billet[3] without consulting her relations gave love such power over her that she would certainly become either poor or infamous.

From the time that my leading strings were taken off, I scarce heard any mention of my beauty but from the milliner, the mantua-maker, and my own maid; for my mamma never said more when she heard me commended but "The girl is very well," and then endeavored to divert my attention by some inquiry after my needle or my book.

It is now three months since I have been suffered to pay and receive visits, to dance at public assemblies, to have a place kept for me in the boxes, and to play at Lady Racket's rout,[4] and you may easily imagine what I think of those who have so long cheated me with false expectations, disturbed me with fictitious terrors, and concealed from me all that I have found to make the happiness of woman.

I am so far from perceiving the usefulness or necessity of books that if I had not dropped all pretensions to learning I should have lost Mr. Trip, whom I once frighted into another box by retailing some of Dryden's remarks upon a tragedy; for Mr. Trip declares that he hates nothing like hard words, and I am sure there is not a better partner to be found; his very walk is a dance. I have talked once or twice among ladies about principles and ideas, but they put their fans before their

3. Billet-doux, love letter.
4. Fashionable evening party.

faces and told me I was too wise for them, who for their part never pretended to read anything but the playbill, and then asked me the price of my best head.[5]

Those vacancies of time which are to be filled up with books I have never yet obtained; for, consider, Mr. Rambler, I go to bed late and therefore cannot rise early; as soon as I am up I dress for the gardens; then walk in the park; then always go to some sale or show or entertainment at the Little Theater;[6] then must be dressed for dinner; then must pay my visits; then walk in the park; then hurry to the play; and from thence to the card table. This is the general course of the day when there happens nothing extraordinary; but sometimes I ramble into the country and come back again to a ball; sometimes I am engaged for a whole day and part of the night. If, at any time, I can gain an hour by not being at home, I have so many things to do, so many orders to give to the milliner, so many alterations to make in my clothes, so many visitants' names to read over, so many invitations to accept or refuse, so many cards to write, and so many fashions to consider, that I am lost in confusion, forced at last to let in company or step into my chair, and leave half my affairs to the direction of my maid.

This is the round of my day; and when shall I either stop my course or so change it as to want a book? I suppose it cannot be imagined that any of these diversions will be soon at an end. There will always be gardens and a park and auctions and shows and playhouses and cards; visits will always be paid and clothes always be worn; and how can I have time unemployed upon my hands?

But I am most at a loss to guess for what purpose they related such tragic stories of the cruelty, perfidy, and artifices of men who, if they ever were so malicious and destructive, have certainly now reformed their manners. I have not since my entrance into the world found one who does not profess himself devoted to my service, and ready to live or die as I shall command him. They are so far from intending to hurt me that their only contention is who shall be allowed most closely to attend and most frequently to treat me; when different places of entertainment or schemes of pleasure are mentioned, I can see the eyes sparkle and the cheeks glow of him whose proposals obtain my approbation; he then leads me off in triumph, adores my condescension, and congratulates himself that he has lived to the hour of felicity. Are these, Mr. Rambler, creatures to be feared? Is it likely that any injury will be done me by those who can enjoy life only while I favor them with my presence?

As little reason can I yet find to suspect them of stratagems and fraud. When I play at cards, they never take advantage of my mistakes nor exact from me a rigorous observation of the game. Even Mr.

5. Of hair.
6. In the Haymarket, which presented farces and other light entertainment.

Shuffle, a grave gentleman who has daughters older than myself, plays with me so negligently, that I am sometimes inclined to believe he loses his money by design, and yet he is so fond of play that he says he will one day take me to his house in the country that we may try by ourselves who can conquer. I have not yet promised him, but when the town grows a little empty I shall think upon it, for I want some trinkets, like Letitia's to my watch. I do not doubt my luck, but must study some means of amusing[7] my relations.

For all these distinctions I find myself indebted to that beauty which I was never suffered to hear praised, and of which therefore I did not before know the full value. This concealment was certainly an intentional fraud for my aunts have eyes like other people, and I am every day told that nothing but blindness can escape the influence of my charms. Their whole account of that world which they pretend to know so well has been only one fiction entangled with another; and though the modes of life oblige me to continue some appearances of respect, I cannot think that they, who have been so clearly detected in ignorance or imposture, have any right to the esteem, veneration, or obedience of, Sir,

Yours,
Bellaria.

No. 196.
Saturday, 1 February 1752.

The blessings flowing in with life's full tide
Down with our ebb of life decreasing glide.
HORACE, *ART OF POETRY*, LL. 175–76. TRANS. FRANCIS.

Baxter, in the narrative of his own life, has enumerated several opinions which, though he thought them evident and incontestable at his first entrance into the world, time and experience disposed him to change.[1]

Whoever reviews the state of his own mind from the dawn of manhood to its decline, and considers what he pursued or dreaded, slighted or esteemed at different periods of his age, will have no reason to imagine such changes of sentiment peculiar to any station or character. Every man, however careless and inattentive, has conviction forced upon him; the lectures of time obtrude themselves upon the most unwilling or dissipated[2] auditor; and by comparing our past with our present thoughts we perceive that we have changed our minds, though

7. Deceiving.

1. *Reliquiae Baxterianae (Baxter's Remains)*, ed. Matthew Sylvester (1696), i. 124–38. Richard Baxter was a seventeenth-century Presbyterian minister.

2. Scatterbrained.

perhaps we cannot discover when the alteration happened or by what causes it was produced.

This revolution of sentiments occasions a perpetual contest between the old and young. They who imagine themselves entitled to veneration by the prerogative of longer life are inclined to treat the notions of those whose conduct they superintend with superciliousness and contempt, for want of considering that the future and the past have different appearances; that the disproportion will always be great between expectation and enjoyment, between new possession and satiety; that the truth of many maxims of age gives too little pleasure to be allowed till it is felt; and that the miseries of life would be increased beyond all human power of endurance if we were to enter the world with the same opinions as we carry from it.

We naturally indulge those ideas that please us. Hope will predominate in every mind till it has been suppressed by frequent disappointments. The youth has not yet discovered how many evils are continually hovering about us, and when he is set free from the shackles of discipline looks abroad into the world with rapture; he sees an Elysian region open before him so variegated with beauty and so stored with pleasure, that his care is rather to accumulate good than to shun evil; he stands distracted by different forms of delight, and has no other doubt than which path to follow of those which all lead equally to the bowers of happiness.

He who has seen only the superficies of life believes every thing to be what it appears, and rarely suspects that external splendor conceals any latent sorrow or vexation. He never imagines that there may be greatness without safety, affluence without content, jollity without friendship, and solitude without peace. He fancies himself permitted to cull the blessings of every condition, and to leave its inconveniencies to the idle and the ignorant. He is inclined to believe no man miserable but by his own fault, and seldom looks with much pity upon failings or miscarriages because he thinks them willingly admitted or negligently incurred.

It is impossible, without pity and contempt, to hear a youth of generous sentiments and warm imagination declaring in the moment of openness and confidence his designs and expectations; because long life is possible he considers it as certain, and therefore promises himself all the changes of happiness and provides gratifications for every desire. He is for a time to give himself wholly to frolic and diversion, to range the world in search of pleasure, to delight every eye, to gain every heart, and to be celebrated equally for his pleasing levities and solid attainments, his deep reflections and his sparkling repartees. He then elevates his views to nobler enjoyments, and finds all the scattered excellencies of the female world united in a woman who prefers his addresses to wealth and titles; he is afterwards to engage in business, to dissipate difficulty, and overpower opposition; to climb by the mere force of merit to fame and greatness; and reward all those who countenanced his rise or paid due regard to his early excellence. At last he will retire in peace and honor; contract his views to domestic pleasures; form the manners of children like himself; observe how every year expands the beauty of his daughters, and how his sons catch ardor from their father's history; he will give laws to the neighborhood; dictate axioms to posterity; and leave the world an example of wisdom and of happiness.

With hopes like these, he sallies jocund into life; to little purpose is he told that the condition of humanity admits no pure and unmingled happiness; that the exuberant gaiety of youth ends in poverty or disease; that uncommon qualifications and contrarieties of excellence produce envy equally with applause; that whatever admiration and fondness may promise him, he must marry a wife like the wives of others, with some virtues and some faults, and be as often disgusted by her vices as delighted by her elegance; that if he adventures into the circle of action, he must expect to encounter men as artful, as daring, as resolute as himself; that of his children, some may be deformed and others vicious; some may disgrace him by their follies, some offend him by their insolence, and some exhaust him by their profusion.[3] He hears all this with obstinate incredulity, and wonders by what malignity old age is influenced that it cannot forbear to fill his ears with predictions of misery.

Among other pleasing errors of young minds is the opinion of their own importance. He that has not yet remarked how little attention his contemporaries can spare from their own affairs conceives all eyes turned upon himself, and imagines everyone that approaches him to be an enemy or a follower, an admirer or a spy. He therefore considers his fame as involved in the event of every action. Many of the virtues and vices of youth proceed from this quick[4] sense of reputation. This it is that gives firmness and constancy, fidelity and disinterestedness, and it is this that kindles resentment for slight injuries and dictates all the principles of sanguinary honor.[5]

But as time brings him forward into the world, he soon discovers that he only shares fame or reproach with innumerable partners; that he is left unmarked in the obscurity of the crowd; and that what he does, whether good or bad, soon gives way to new objects of regard. He then easily sets himself free from the anxieties of reputation, and considers praise or censure as a transient breath which, while he hears it, is passing away without any lasting mischief or advantage.

In youth, it is common to measure right and wrong by the opinion of

3. Spending of money.
4. Lively.
5. Principles of honor that lead to duels.

the world, and in age to act without any measure but interest, and to lose shame without substituting virtue.

Such is the condition of life that something is always wanting to happiness. In youth we have warm hopes which are soon blasted by rashness and negligence, and great designs which are defeated by inexperience. In age we have knowledge and prudence without spirit to exert, or motives to prompt them; we are able to plan schemes and regulate measures, but have not time remaining to bring them to completion.

No. 200.

Saturday, 15 February 1752.

No man expects (for who so much a sot,
Who has the times he lives in so forgot?)
What Seneca, what Piso[1] *used to send,*
To raise, or to support a sinking friend.
Those godlike men, to wanting virtue kind,
Bounty well-placed preferred, and well designed,
To all their titles, all that height of power,
Which turns the brains of fools, and fools alone adore.
When your poor client[2] *is condemned t'attend,*
'Tis all we ask, receive him as a friend:
Descend to this, and then we ask no more;
Rich to yourself, to all beside be poor.

JUVENAL, *SATIRES*, V. 108–13, TRANS. BOWLES.

To the Rambler.

Mr. Rambler,

Such is the tenderness or infirmity of many minds that when any affliction oppresses them, they have immediate recourse to lamentation and complaint, which, though it can only be allowed reasonable when evils admit of remedy, and then only when addressed to those from whom the remedy is expected, yet seems even in hopeless and incurable distresses to be natural, since those by whom it is not indulged, imagine that they give proof of extraordinary fortitude by suppressing it.

I am one of those who, with the Sancho of Cervantes, leave to higher characters the merit of suffering in silence, and give vent without scruple to any sorrow that swells in my heart.[3] It is therefore to me a severe aggravation of a calamity when it is such as in the common

1. Presumably Juvenal refers to the philosopher and dramatist Seneca, who was very wealthy; Piso may refer to his contemporary, C. Calpurnius Piso.
2. Dependent.
3. *Don Quixote*, part I, ch. viii.

opinion will not justify the acerbity of exclamation,[4] or support the solemnity of vocal grief. Yet many pains are incident to[5] a man of delicacy which the unfeeling world cannot be persuaded to pity, and which, when they are separated from their peculiar and personal circumstances, will never be considered as important enough to claim attention or deserve redress.

Of this kind will appear to gross and vulgar apprehensions the miseries which I endured in a morning visit to Prospero, a man lately raised to wealth by a lucky project, and too much intoxicated by sudden elevation, or too little polished by thought and conversation, to enjoy his present fortune with elegance and decency.

We set out in the world together; and for a long time mutually assisted each other in our exigencies, as either happened to have money or influence beyond his immediate necessities. You know that nothing generally endears men so much as participation of dangers and misfortunes; I therefore always considered Prospero as united with me in the strongest league of kindness, and imagined that our friendship was only to be broken by the hand of death. I felt at his sudden shoot of success an honest and disinterested joy; but as I want no part of his superfluities, am not willing to descend from that equality in which we hitherto have lived.

Our intimacy was regarded by me as a dispensation from ceremonial visits; and it was so long before I saw him at his new house that he gently complained of my neglect, and obliged me to come on a day appointed. I kept my promise, but found that the impatience of my friend arose not from any desire to communicate his happiness, but to enjoy his superiority.

When I told my name at the door, the footman went to see if his master was at home and, by the tardiness of return, gave me reason to suspect that time was taken to deliberate. He then informed me that Prospero desired my company, and showed the staircase carefully secured by mats from the pollution of my feet. The best apartments[6] were ostentatiously set open that I might have a distant view of the magnificence which I was not permitted to approach; and my old friend receiving me with all the insolence of condescension at the top of the stairs,[7] conducted me to a back room where he told me he always breakfasted when he had not great company.

On the floor where we sat, lay a carpet covered with a cloth, of which Prospero ordered his servant to lift up a corner, that I might contemplate the brightness of the colors, and the elegance of the texture, and asked me whether I had ever seen anything so fine before? I did

4. Sharpness of outcry.
5. Befall.
6. Rooms, suites.
7. Instead of coming to the door, or at least to the bottom of the stairs.

not gratify his folly with any outcries of admiration, but coldly bade the footman let down the cloth.

We then sat down and I began to hope that pride was glutted with persecution, when Prospero desired that I would give the servant leave to adjust the cover of my chair, which was slipped a little aside to show the damask; he informed me that he had bespoke[8] ordinary chairs for common use, but had been disappointed by his tradesman. I put the chair aside with my foot, and drew another so hastily that I was entreated not to rumple the carpet.

Breakfast was at last set,[9] and as I was not willing to indulge the peevishness that began to seize me, I commended the tea; Prospero then told me that another time I should taste his finest sort, but that he had only a very small quantity remaining, and reserved it for those whom he thought himself obliged to treat with particular respect.

While we were conversing upon such subjects as imagination happened to suggest, he frequently digressed into directions to the servant that waited, or made a slight inquiry after the jeweler or silversmith; and once as I was pursuing an argument with some degree of earnestness, he started from his posture of attention, and ordered that if Lord Lofty called on him that morning, he should be shown into the best parlor.

My patience was not yet wholly subdued. I was willing to promote his satisfaction, and therefore observed that the figures on the china were eminently pretty. Prospero had now an opportunity of calling for his Dresden china, which, says he, I always associate with my chased[10] teakettle. The cups were brought; I once resolved not to have looked upon them, but my curiosity prevailed. When I had examined them a little, Prospero desired me to set them down for they who were accustomed only to common dishes seldom handled china with much care. You will, I hope, commend my philosophy[11] when I tell you that I did not dash his baubles to the ground.

He was now so much elevated with his own greatness that he thought some humility necessary to avert the glance of envy, and therefore told me with an air of soft composure that I was not to estimate life by external appearance, that all these shining acquisitions had added little to his happiness, that he still remembered with pleasure the days in which he and I were upon the level, and had often, in the moment of reflection, been doubtful whether he should lose much by changing his condition for mine.

I began now to be afraid lest his pride should, by silence and submission, be emboldened to insults that could not easily be borne, and,

8. Ordered.
9. Served.
10. Embossed, engraved.
11. Calmness.

therefore, coolly considered how I should repress it without such bitterness of reproof as I was yet unwilling to use. But he interrupted my meditation by asking leave to be dressed, and told me that he had promised to attend some ladies in the park, and if I was going the same way would take me in his chariot.[12] I had no inclination to any other favors, and, therefore, left him without any intention of seeing him again, unless some misfortune should restore his understanding.

I am, etc.
Asper.

Though I am not wholly insensible of the provocations which my correspondent has received, I cannot altogether commend the keenness of his resentment, nor encourage him to persist in his resolution of breaking off all commerce[13] with his old acquaintance. One of the golden precepts of Pythagoras directs that "a friend should not be hated for little faults";[14] and surely he, upon whom nothing worse can be charged than that he mats his stairs and covers his carpet, and sets out his finery to show before those whom he does not admit to use it, has yet committed nothing that should exclude him from common degrees of kindness. Such improprieties often proceed rather from stupidity than malice. Those who thus shine only to dazzle, are influenced merely by custom and example, and neither examine nor are qualified to examine the motives of their own practice, or to state the nice limits between elegance and ostentation. They are often innocent of the pain which their vanity produces, and insult others when they have no worse purpose than to please themselves.

He that too much refines his delicacy will always endanger his quiet. Of those with whom nature and virtue oblige us to converse, some are ignorant of the arts of pleasing, and offend when they design to caress; some are negligent, and gratify themselves without regard to the quiet of another; some, perhaps, are malicious, and feel no greater satisfaction in prosperity than that of raising envy and trampling inferiority. But whatever be the motive of insult, it is always best to overlook it, for folly scarcely can deserve resentment, and malice is punished by neglect.

12. Coach.
13. Relations.
14. *Golden Precepts,* no. 7, by the Greek sixth-century B.C. philosopher.

Selections from *The Idler*

No. 3.
Saturday, 29 April 1758.[1]

It has long been the complaint of those who frequent the theaters that all the dramatic art has been long exhausted, and that the vicissitudes of fortune and accidents of life have been shown in every possible combination, till the first scene informs us of the last, and the play no sooner opens than every auditor knows how it will conclude. When a conspiracy is formed in a tragedy, we guess by whom it will be detected; when a letter is dropped in a comedy, we can tell by whom it will be found. Nothing is now left for the poet but character and sentiment, which are to make their way as they can, without the soft anxiety of suspense or the enlivening agitation of surprise.

A new paper lies under the same disadvantages as a new play. There is danger lest it be new without novelty. My earlier predecessors had their choice of vices and follies, and selected such as were most likely to raise merriment or attract attention; they had the whole field of life before them, untrodden and unsurveyed; characters of every kind shot up in their way, and those of the most luxuriant growth or most conspicuous colors were naturally cropped by the first sickle. They that follow are forced to peep into neglected corners, to note the casual[2] varieties of the same species, and to recommend themselves by minute industry and distinctions too subtle for common eyes.

Sometimes it may happen that the haste or negligence of the first inquirers has left enough behind to reward another search; sometimes

1. The epigraph from Statius (*Silvae*, IV. iv. 49–50) reads, "I charm my leisure hours with music."
2. Accidental.

new objects start up under the eye, and he that is looking for one kind of matter is amply gratified by the discovery of another. But still it must be allowed that as more is taken, less can remain, and every truth brought newly to light impoverishes the mine from which succeeding intellects are to dig their treasures.

Many philosophers[3] imagine that the elements themselves may be in time exhausted. That the sun, by shining long, will effuse all its light; and that, by the continual waste of aqueous particles, the whole earth will at last become a sandy desert.

I would not advise my readers to disturb themselves by contriving how they shall live without light and water. For the days of universal thirst and perpetual darkness are at a great distance. The ocean and the sun will last our time, and we may leave posterity to shift for themselves.

But if the stores of nature are limited, much more narrow bounds must be set to the modes of life; and mankind may want[4] a moral or amusing paper, many years before they shall be deprived of drink or daylight. This want, which to the busy and the inventive may seem easily remediable by some substitute or other, the whole race of Idlers will feel with all the sensibility that such torpid animals can suffer.

When I consider the innumerable multitudes that, having no motive of desire or determination of will, lie freezing in perpetual inactivity till some external impulse puts them in motion; who awake in the morning, vacant of thought, with minds gaping for the intellectual food which some kind essayist has been accustomed to supply; I am moved by the commiseration with which all human beings ought to behold the distresses of each other to try some expedients for their relief, and to inquire by what methods the listless may be actuated, and the empty be replenished.

There are said to be pleasures in madness known only to madmen. There are certainly miseries in idleness which the Idler only can conceive. These miseries I have often felt and often bewailed. I know, by experience, how welcome is every avocation that summons the thoughts to a new image; and how much languor and lassitude are relieved by that officiousness[5] which offers a momentary amusement to him who is unable to find it for himself.

It is naturally indifferent to this race of men what entertainment they receive, so they are but entertained. They catch, with equal eagerness, at a moral lecture, or the memoirs of a robber; a prediction of the appearance of a comet, or the calculation of the chances of a lottery.

They might therefore easily be pleased, if they consulted only their own minds; but those who will not take the trouble to think for themselves have always somebody that thinks for them; and the difficulty in writing is to please those from whom others learn to be pleased.

3. Here, scientists. 4. Lack. 5. Busy eagerness to help others.

Much mischief is done in the world with very little interest or design. He that assumes the character of a critic, and justifies his claim by perpetual censure, imagines that he is hurting none but the author, and him he considers as a pestilent animal whom every other being has a right to persecute; little does he think how many harmless men he involves in his own guilt by teaching them to be noxious without malignity, and to repeat objections which they do not understand; or how many honest minds he debars from pleasure by exciting an artificial fastidiousness, and making them too wise to concur with their own sensations. He who is taught by a critic to dislike that which pleased him in his natural state has the same reason to complain of his instructor as the madman to rail at his doctor, who, when he thought himself master of Peru, physicked him[6] to poverty.

If men will struggle against their own advantage, they are not to expect that the Idler will take much pains upon them; he has himself to please as well as them, and has long learned or endeavored to learn not to make the pleasure of others too necessary to his own.

No. 14.
Saturday, 15 July 1758.

When Diogenes received a visit in his tub from Alexander the Great and was asked, according to the ancient forms of royal courtesy, what petition he had to offer, "I have nothing," said he, "to ask, but that you would remove to the other side that you may not, by intercepting the sunshine, take from me what you cannot give me."[1]

Such was the demand of Diogenes from the greatest monarch of the earth which those, who have less power than Alexander, may with yet more propriety apply to themselves. He that does much good may be allowed to do sometimes a little harm. But if the opportunities of beneficence be denied by fortune, innocence should at least be vigilantly preserved.

It is well known that time once past never returns, and that the moment which is lost, is lost for ever. Time therefore ought, above all other kinds of property, to be free from invasion, and yet there is no man who does not claim the power of wasting that time which is the right of others.

This usurpation is so general that a very small part of the year is spent by choice; scarcely anything is done when it is intended, or obtained when it is desired. Life is continually ravaged by invaders; one steals away an hour and another a day; one conceals the robbery by hurrying

6. Cured him with medicine.

1. A well-known story found, among other places, in Plutarch's "Life of Alexander." Diogenes (?412–323 B.C.) was a Greek Cynic philosopher who lived in a tub.

us into business, another by lulling us with amusement; the depredation is continued through a thousand vicissitudes[2] of tumult and tranquillity, till having lost all we can lose no more.

This waste of the lives of men has been very frequently charged upon the great, whose followers linger from year to year in expectations, and die at last with petitions in their hands. Those who raise envy will easily incur censure. I know not whether statesmen and patrons do not suffer more reproaches than they deserve, and may not rather themselves complain that they are given up a prey to pretensions without merit and to importunity without shame.

The truth is that the inconveniencies of attendance are more lamented than felt. To the greater number solicitation is its own reward: to be seen in good company, to talk of familiarities with men of power, to be able to tell the freshest news, to gratify an inferior circle with predictions of increase or decline of favor, and to be regarded as a candidate for high offices, are compensations more than equivalent to the delay of favors, which perhaps he that begs them has hardly confidence to expect.

A man conspicuous in a high station who multiplies hopes that he may multiply dependents may be considered as a beast of prey, justly dreaded but easily avoided; his den is known, and they who would not be devoured need not approach it. The great danger of the waste of time is from caterpillars and moths, who are not resisted because they are not feared, and who work on with unheeded mischiefs and invisible encroachments.

He whose rank or merit procures him the notice of mankind must give up himself, in a great measure, to the convenience or humor of those that surround him. Every man who is sick of himself will fly to him for relief; he that wants to speak will require him to hear, and he that wants to hear will expect him to speak. Hour passes after hour, the noon succeeds to morning and the evening to noon while a thousand objects are forced upon his attention which he rejects as fast as they are offered, but which the custom of the world requires to be received with appearance of regard.

If we will have the kindness of others, we must endure their follies; he who cannot persuade himself to withdraw from society must be content to pay a tribute of his time to a multitude of tyrants: to the loiterer, who makes appointments which he never keeps; to the consulter, who asks advice which he never takes; to the boaster, who blusters only to be praised; to the complainer, who whines only to be pitied; to the projector,[3] whose happiness is to entertain his friends with expectations which all but himself know to be vain; to the economist,[4] who tells

2. Alternations.
3. An enthusiast for impractical schemes.
4. Manager of family or estate affairs.

of bargains and settlements; to the politician, who predicts the fate of battles and breach of alliances; to the usurer, who compares the different funds;[5] and to the talker, who talks only because he loves to be talking.

To put every man in possession of his own time and rescue the day from this succession of usurpers is beyond my power and beyond my hope. Yet perhaps some stop might be put to this unmerciful persecution, if all would seriously reflect that whoever pays a visit that is not desired, or talks longer than the hearer is willing to attend, is guilty of an injury which he cannot repair, and takes away that which he cannot give.

[No. 22.]

Saturday, 9 September 1758.[1]

Many naturalists are of opinion that the animals which we commonly consider as mute have the power of imparting their thoughts to one another. That they can express general sensations is very certain; every being that can utter sounds has a different voice for pleasure and for pain. The hound informs his fellows when he scents his game; the hen calls her chickens to their food by her cluck, and drives them from danger by her scream.

Birds have the greatest variety of notes; they have indeed a variety which seems almost sufficient to make a speech adequate to the purposes of a life which is regulated by instinct, and can admit little change or improvement. To the cries of birds, curiosity or superstition has been always attentive; many have studied the language of the feathered tribes, and some have boasted that they understood it.

The most skillful or most confident interpreters of the sylvan[2] dialogues have been commonly found among the philosophers of the East, in a country where the calmness of the air and the mildness of the seasons allow the student to pass a great part of the year in groves and bowers. But what may be done in one place by peculiar[3] opportunities may be performed in another by peculiar diligence. A shepherd of Bohemia has, by long abode in the forests, enabled himself to understand the voice of birds; at least he relates with great confidence a story of which the credibility may be considered by the learned.

"As I was sitting, (said he) within a hollow rock, and watching my sheep that fed in the valley, I heard two vultures interchangeably crying on the summit of the cliff. Both voices were earnest and deliberate.

5. Various government issues used to pay off the national debt.

1. This essay, no. 22 in the original serial publication, was omitted from the first collected edition of the *Idler*.

2. Woodland. 3. Particular.

My curiosity prevailed over my care of the flock; I climbed slowly and silently from crag to crag, concealed among the shrubs, till I found a cavity where I might sit and listen without suffering or giving disturbance.

"I soon perceived, that my labor would be well repaid; for an old vulture was sitting on a naked prominence, with her young about her, whom she was instructing in the arts of a vulture's life, and preparing, by the last lecture, for their final dismission to the mountains and the skies.

"'My children,' said the old vulture, 'you will the less want[4] my instructions because you have had my practice before your eyes; you have seen me snatch from the farm the household fowl, you have seen me seize the leveret[5] in the bush, and the kid in the pasture, you know how to fix your talons, and how to balance your flight when you are laden with your prey. But you remember the taste of more delicious food; I have often regaled you with the flesh of man.' 'Tell us,' said the young vultures, 'where man may be found, and how he may be known; his flesh is surely the natural food of a vulture. Why have you never brought a man in your talons to the nest?' 'He is too bulky,' said the mother; 'when we find a man, we can only tear away his flesh and leave his bones upon the ground.' 'Since man is so big,' said the young ones, 'how do you kill him. You are afraid of the wolf and of the bear, by what power are vultures superior to man, is man more defenseless than a sheep?' 'We have not the strength of man,' returned the mother, 'and I am sometimes in doubt whether we have the subtlety; and the vultures would seldom feast upon his flesh, had not nature, that devoted him to our uses, infused into him a strange ferocity, which I have never observed in any other being that feeds upon the earth. Two herds of men will often meet and shake the earth with noise, and fill the air with fire. When you hear noise and see fire which flashes along the ground, hasten to the place with your swiftest wing, for men are surely destroying one another; you will then find the ground smoking with blood and covered with carcasses, of which many are dismembered and mangled for the convenience of the vulture.' 'But when men have killed their prey,' said the pupil, 'why do they not eat it? When the wolf has killed a sheep he suffers not the vulture to touch it till he has satisfied himself. Is not man another kind of wolf?' 'Man,' said the mother, 'is the only beast who kills that which he does not devour, and this quality makes him so much a benefactor to our species.' 'If men kill our prey and lay it in our way,' said the young one, 'what need shall we have of laboring for ourselves.' 'Because man will, sometimes,' replied the mother, 'remain for a long time quiet in his den. The old vultures will tell you when you are to watch his motions. When you see men in great numbers moving

4. Need.
5. Young hare.

close together, like a flight of storks, you may conclude that they are hunting and that you will soon revel in human blood.' 'But still,' said the young one, 'I would gladly know the reason of this mutual slaughter. I could never kill what I could not eat.' 'My child,' said the mother, 'this is a question which I cannot answer, though I am reckoned the most subtle bird of the mountain. When I was young I used frequently to visit the aerie of an old vulture who dwelt upon the Carpathian rocks;[6] he had made many observations; he knew the places that afforded prey round his habitation, as far in every direction as the strongest wing can fly between the rising and setting of the summer sun; he had fed year after year on the entrails of men. His opinion was, that men had only the appearance of animal life, being really vegetables with a power of motion, and that as the boughs of an oak are dashed together by the storm that swine may fatten upon the falling acorns, so men are by some unaccountable power driven one against another, till they lose their motion, that vultures may be fed. Others think they have observed something of contrivance and policy among these mischievous beings, and those that hover more closely round them pretend that there is, in every herd, one that gives directions to the rest, and seems to be more eminently delighted with a wide carnage. What it is that entitles him to such pre-eminence we know not; he is seldom the biggest or the swiftest, but he shows by his eagerness and diligence that he is, more than any of the others, a friend to vultures.'"

No. 23.

Saturday, 23 September 1758.

Life has no pleasure higher or nobler than that of friendship. It is painful to consider that this sublime enjoyment may be impaired or destroyed by innumerable causes, and that there is no human possession of which the duration is less certain.

Many have talked, in very exalted language, of the perpetuity of friendship, of invincible constancy, and unalienable kindness; and some examples have been seen of men who have continued faithful to their earliest choice, and whose affection has predominated over changes of fortune and contrariety of opinion.

But these instances are memorable, because they are rare. The friendship which is to be practiced or expected by common mortals must take its rise from mutual pleasure, and must end when the power ceases of delighting each other.

Many accidents therefore may happen by which the ardor of kindness will be abated, without criminal baseness or contemptible inconstancy on either part. To give pleasure is not always in our power; and

6. A mountain range in eastern Europe.

little does he know himself who believes that he can be always able to receive it.

Those who would gladly pass their days together may be separated by the different course of their affairs; and friendship, like love, is destroyed by long absence, though it may be increased by short intermissions. What we have missed long enough to want it we value more when it is regained; but that which has been lost till it is forgotten, will be found at last with little gladness, and with still less if a substitute has supplied the place. A man deprived of the companion to whom he used to open his bosom, and with whom he shared the hours of leisure and merriment, feels the day at first hanging heavy on him; his difficulties oppress, and his doubts distract him; he sees time come and go without his wonted gratification, and all is sadness within and solitude about him. But this uneasiness never lasts long, necessity produces expedients, new amusements are discovered, and new conversation is admitted.

No expectation is more frequently disappointed than that which naturally arises in the mind from the prospect of meeting an old friend after long separation. We expect the attraction to be revived, and the coalition to be renewed; no man considers how much alteration time has made in himself, and very few inquire what effect it has had upon others. The first hour convinces them that the pleasure which they have formerly enjoyed is forever at an end; different scenes have made different impressions, the opinions of both are changed, and that similitude of manners[1] and sentiment is lost, which confirmed them both in the approbation of themselves.

Friendship is often destroyed by opposition of interest, not only by the ponderous and visible interest which the desire of wealth and greatness forms and maintains, but by a thousand secret and slight competitions, scarcely known to the mind upon which they operate. There is scarcely any man without some favorite trifle which he values above greater attainments, some desire of petty praise which he cannot patiently suffer to be frustrated. This minute ambition is sometimes crossed before it is known, and sometimes defeated by wanton petulance; but such attacks are seldom made without the loss of friendship; for whoever has once found the vulnerable part will always be feared, and the resentment will burn on in secret of which shame hinders the discovery.

This, however, is a slow malignity, which a wise man will obviate as inconsistent with quiet, and a good man will repress as contrary to virtue; but human happiness is sometimes violated by some more sudden strokes.

A dispute begun in jest, upon a subject which a moment before was

1. Habitual modes of behavior.

on both parts regarded with careless indifference, is continued by the desire of conquest, till vanity kindles into rage, and opposition rankles into enmity. Against this hasty mischief I know not what security can be obtained; men will be sometimes surprised into quarrels, and though they might both hasten to reconciliation as soon as their tumult has subsided, yet two minds will seldom be found together which can at once subdue their discontent or immediately enjoy the sweets of peace, without remembering the wounds of the conflict.

Friendship has other enemies. Suspicion is always hardening the cautious, and disgust repelling the delicate. Very slender differences will sometimes part those whom long reciprocation of civility or beneficence has united. Lonelove and Ranger retired into the country to enjoy the company of each other, and returned in six weeks cold and petulant; Ranger's pleasure was to walk in the fields, and Lonelove's to sit in a bower; each had complied with the other in his turn, and each was angry that compliance had been exacted.

The most fatal disease of friendship is gradual decay, or dislike hourly increased by causes too slender for complaint and too numerous for removal. Those who are angry may be reconciled; those who have been injured may receive a recompense; but when the desire of pleasing and willingness to be pleased is silently diminished, the renovation of friendship is hopeless; as, when the vital powers sink into languor, there is no longer any use of the physician.

No. 24.

Saturday, 30 September 1758.

When man sees one of the inferior creatures perched upon a tree or basking in the sunshine without any apparent endeavor or pursuit, he often asks himself or his companion, "on what that animal can be supposed to be thinking?"

Of this question, since neither bird nor beast can answer it, we must be content to live without the resolution. We know not how much the brutes recollect of the past or anticipate of the future; what power they have of comparing and preferring; or whether their faculties may not rest in motionless indifference till they are moved by the presence of their proper object or stimulated to act by corporal sensations.

I am the less inclined to these superfluous inquiries because I have always been able to find sufficient matter for curiosity in my own species. It is useless to go far in quest of that which may be found at home; a very narrow circle of observation will supply a sufficient number of men and women who might be asked with equal propriety, "on what they can be thinking?"

It is reasonable to believe that thought, like everything else, has its causes and effects; that it must proceed from something known, done, or suffered; and must produce some action or event. Yet how great is the number of those in whose minds no source of thought has ever been opened, in whose life no consequence of thought is ever discovered; who have learned nothing upon which they can reflect; who have neither seen nor felt anything which could leave its traces on the memory; who neither foresee nor desire any change of their condition, and have therefore neither fear, hope, nor design, and yet are supposed to be thinking beings.

To every act a subject is required. He that thinks must think upon something. But tell me, ye that pierce deepest into nature, ye that take the widest surveys of life, inform me, kind shades of Malebranche and of Locke,[1] what that something can be which excites and continues thought in maiden aunts with small fortunes; in younger brothers that live upon annuities; in traders retired from business; in soldiers absent from their regiments; or in widows that have no children?

Life is commonly considered as either active or contemplative; but surely this division, how long soever it has been received, is inadequate and fallacious. There are mortals whose life is certainly not active, for they do neither good nor evil, and whose life cannot be properly called contemplative: for they never attend either to the conduct of men or the works of nature, but rise in the morning, look round them till night in careless stupidity, go to bed and sleep, and rise again in the morning.

It has been lately a celebrated question in the schools of philosophy, "whether the soul always thinks?"[2] Some have defined the soul to be the "power of thinking," concluded that its essence consists in act; that if it should cease to act, it would cease to be; and that cessation of thought is but another name for extinction of mind. This argument is subtle but not conclusive; because it supposes what cannot be proved, that the nature of mind is properly defined. Others affect to disdain subtilty when subtilty will not serve their purpose, and appeal to daily experience. We spend many hours, they say, in sleep without the least remembrance of any thoughts which then passed in our minds; and since we can only by our own consciousness be sure that we think, why should we imagine that we have had thought of which no consciousness remains?

1. Nicolas de Malebranche (1638–1715), French philosopher, and John Locke (1632–1704), the most important English philosopher of his time.

2. René Descartes (1596–1650) maintained that the soul always thinks (see his *Reply to Objections V*, section 4). Locke, in his *Essay concerning Human Understanding*, wrote that he could not "conceive it any more necessary for the soul always to think than for the body always to move" (bk. II, ch. i, section 10). The following arguments arose from the views of Descartes and his followers.

This argument, which appeals to experience, may from experience be confuted. We every day do something which we forget when it is done, and know to have been done only by consequence. The waking hours are not denied to have been passed in thought, yet he that shall endeavor to recollect on one day the ideas of the former will only turn the eye of reflection upon vacancy; he will find that the greater part is irrevocably vanished, and wonder how the moments could come and go and leave so little behind them.

To discover only that the arguments on both sides are defective, and to throw back the tenet into its former uncertainty, is the sport of wanton or malevolent skepticism, delighting to see the sons of philosophy at work upon a task which never can be finished, at variance on a question that can never be decided. I shall suggest an argument, hitherto overlooked, which may perhaps determine the controversy.

If it be impossible to think without materials, there must necessarily be minds that do not always think; and whence shall we furnish materials for the meditation of the glutton between his meals, of the sportsman in a rainy month, of the annuitant between the days of quarterly payment, of the politician when the mails are detained by contrary winds.

But how frequent soever may be the examples of existence without thought, it is certainly a state not much to be desired. He that lives in torpid insensibility wants nothing of a carcass but putrefaction. It is the part of every inhabitant of the earth to partake the pains and pleasures of his fellow beings; and as in a road through a country desert and uniform the traveler languishes for want of amusement, so the passage of life will be tedious and irksome to him who does not beguile it by diversified ideas.

No. 31.

Saturday, 18 November 1758.

Many moralists have remarked that pride has of all human vices the widest dominion, appears in the greatest multiplicity of forms, and lies hid under the greatest variety of disguises; of disguises, which, like the moon's "veil of brightness," are both its "luster and its shade,"[1] and betray it to others, though they hide it from ourselves.

It is not my intention to degrade pride from this pre-eminence of mischief, yet I know not whether idleness may not maintain a very doubtful[2] and obstinate competition.

There are some that profess idleness in its full dignity, who call

1. From Samuel Butler's poem *Hudibras,* II (1664). i. 905–08.
2. Dubious (as to outcome).

themselves the "Idle," as Busiris in the play "calls himself the Proud";[3] who boast that they do nothing, and thank their stars that they have nothing to do; who sleep every night till they can sleep no longer, and rise only that exercise may enable them to sleep again; who prolong the reign of darkness by double curtains, and never see the sun but to "tell him how they hate his beams";[4] whose whole labor is to vary the postures of indulgence, and whose day differs from their night but as a couch or chair differs from a bed.

These are the true and open votaries of idleness, for whom she weaves the garlands of poppies, and into whose cup she pours the waters of oblivion; who exist in a state of unruffled stupidity,[5] forgetting and forgotten; who have long ceased to live, and at whose death the survivors can only say that they have ceased to breathe.

But idleness predominates in many lives where it is not suspected, for being a vice which terminates in itself, it may be enjoyed without injury to others, and is therefore not watched like fraud, which endangers property, or like pride which naturally seeks its gratifications in another's inferiority. Idleness is a silent and peaceful quality, that neither raises envy by ostentation, nor hatred by opposition; and therefore nobody is busy to censure or detect it.

As pride sometimes is hid under humility, idleness is often covered by turbulence and hurry. He that neglects his known duty and real employment naturally endeavors to crowd his mind with something that may bar out the remembrance of his own folly, and does anything but what he ought to do with eager diligence that he may keep himself in his own favor.

Some are always in a state of preparation, occupied in previous measures, forming plans, accumulating materials, and providing for the main affair. These are certainly under the secret power of idleness. Nothing is to be expected from the workman whose tools are for ever to be sought. I was once told by a great master that no man ever excelled in painting who was eminently curious[6] about pencils[7] and colors.

There are others to whom idleness dictates another expedient, by which life may be passed unprofitably away without the tediousness of many vacant hours. The art is to fill the day with petty business, to have always something in hand which may raise curiosity but not solicitude, and keep the mind in a state of action but not of labor.

This art has for many years been practiced by my old friend Sober with wonderful success.[8] Sober is a man of strong desires and quick imagination, so exactly balanced by the love of ease, that they can

3. Edward Young's *Busiris* (1719).
4. See *Paradise Lost*, iv. 37.
5. Stupor.
6. Fastidious.
7. Brushes.
8. The portrait of Sober is taken to resemble Johnson himself.

seldom stimulate him to any difficult undertaking; they have, however, so much power, that they will not suffer him to lie quite at rest, and though they do not make him sufficiently useful to others, they make him at least weary of himself.

Mr. Sober's chief pleasure is conversation; there is no end of his talk or his attention; to speak or to hear is equally pleasing; for he still fancies that he is teaching or learning something, and is free for the time from his own reproaches.

But there is one time at night when he must go home, that his friends may sleep; and another time in the morning, when all the world agrees to shut out interruption. These are the moments of which poor Sober trembles at the thought. But the misery of these tiresome intervals, he has many means of alleviating. He has persuaded himself that the manual arts are undeservedly overlooked; he has observed in many trades the effects of close thought and just ratiocination.[9] From speculation he proceeded to practice, and supplied himself with the tools of a carpenter, with which he mended his coal-box very successfully, and which he still continues to employ as he finds occasion.

He has attempted at other times the crafts of the shoemaker, tinman, plumber, and potter; in all these arts he has failed, and resolves to qualify himself for them by better information. But his daily amusement is chemistry. He has a small furnace, which he employs in distillation, and which has long been the solace of his life. He draws oils and waters, and essences and spirits, which he knows to be of no use; sits and counts the drops as they come from his retort, and forgets that, while a drop is falling, a moment flies away.

Poor Sober! I have often teased him with reproof, and he has often promised reformation; for no man is so much open to conviction as the Idler, but there is none on whom it operates so little. What will be the effect of this paper I know not; perhaps he will read it and laugh, and light the fire in his furnace; but my hope is that he will quit his trifles, and betake himself to rational and useful diligence.

No. 34.

Saturday, 9 December 1758.

To illustrate one thing by its resemblance to another has been always the most popular and efficacious art of instruction. There is indeed no other method of teaching that of which any one is ignorant but by means of something already known; and a mind so enlarged by contemplation and inquiry, that it has always many objects within its view, will seldom be long without some near and familiar image through

9. Correct reasoning.

which an easy transition may be made to truths more distant and obscure.

Of the parallels which have been drawn by wit and curiosity, some are literal and real, as between poetry and painting, two arts which pursue the same end, by the operation of the same mental faculties, and which differ only as the one represents things by marks permanent and natural, the other by signs accidental and arbitrary. The one therefore is more easily and generally understood, since similitude of form is immediately perceived; the other is capable of conveying more ideas, for men have thought and spoken of many things which they do not see.

Other parallels are fortuitous and fanciful, yet these have sometimes been extended to many particulars of resemblance by a lucky concurrence of diligence and chance. The animal "body" is composed of many members, united under the direction of one mind; any number of individuals connected for some common purpose is therefore called a body. From this participation of the same appellation arose the comparison of the body natural and body politic, of which, how far soever it has been deduced,[1] no end has hitherto been found.

In these imaginary similitudes, the same word is used at once in its primitive[2] and metaphorical sense. Thus health, ascribed to the body natural, is opposed to sickness; but attributed to the body politic stands as contrary to adversity. These parallels therefore have more of genius[3] but less of truth; they often please but they never convince.

Of this kind is a curious speculation frequently indulged by a philosopher of my acquaintance, who had discovered that the qualities requisite to conversation are very exactly represented by a bowl of punch.

Punch, says this profound investigator, is a liquor compounded of spirit and acid juices, sugar and water. The spirit, volatile and fiery, is the proper emblem of vivacity and wit, the acidity of the lemon will very aptly figure pungency of raillery and acrimony of censure; sugar is the natural representative of luscious adulation and gentle complaisance; and water is the proper hieroglyphic of easy prattle, innocent and tasteless.

Spirit alone is too powerful for use. It will produce madness rather than merriment; and instead of quenching thirst will inflame the blood. Thus wit too copiously poured out agitates the hearer with emotions rather violent than pleasing; every one shrinks from the force of its oppression, the company sits entranced and overpowered; all are astonished but nobody is pleased.

The acid juices give this genial liquor all its power of stimulating the

1. Drawn out.
2. Literal.
3. Ingenuity.

palate; and conversation would become dull and vapid, if negligence were not sometimes roused and sluggishness quickened by due severity of reprehension. But acids unmixed will distort the face and torture the palate; and he that has no other qualities than penetration and asperity, he whose constant employment is detection and censure, who looks only to find faults, and speaks only to punish them, will soon be dreaded, hated, and avoided.

The taste of sugar is generally pleasing, but it cannot long be eaten by itself. Thus meekness and courtesy will always recommend the first address, but soon pall and nauseate, unless they are associated with more sprightly qualities. The chief use of sugar is to temper the taste of other substances, and softness of behavior in the same manner mitigates the roughness of contradiction, and allays the bitterness of unwelcome truth.

Water is the universal vehicle by which are conveyed the particles necessary to sustenance and growth, by which thirst is quenched, and all the wants of life and nature are supplied. Thus all the business of the world is transacted by artless and easy talk, neither sublimed[4] by fancy, nor discolored by affectation, without either the harshness of satire, or the lusciousness of flattery. By this limpid vein of language curiosity is gratified, and all the knowledge is conveyed which one man is required to impart for the safety or convenience of another. Water is the only ingredient of punch which can be used alone, and with which man is content till fancy has framed an artificial want. Thus while we only desire to have our ignorance informed we are most delighted with the plainest diction; and it is only in the moments of idleness or pride that we call for the gratifications of wit or flattery.

He only will please long, who, by tempering the acid of satire with the sugar of civility, and allaying the heat of wit with the frigidity of humble chat, can make the true punch of conversation; and as that punch can be drank in the greatest quantity which has the largest proportion of water, so that companion will be oftenest welcome, whose talk flows out with inoffensive copiousness, and unenvied insipidity.[5]

I am, etc.

No. 36.

Saturday, 23 December 1758.

The great differences that disturb the peace of mankind are not about ends but means. We have all the same general desires, but how those desires shall be accomplished will forever be disputed. The ultimate purpose of government is temporal, and that of religion is eternal

4. Refined, exalted.
5. Literally, tastelessness, a technical term when applied to water.

happiness. Hitherto we agree; but here we must part, to try, according to the endless varieties of passion and understanding combined with one another, every possible form of government, and every imaginable tenet of religion.

We are told by Cumberland that "rectitude," applied to action or contemplation, is merely metaphorical; and that as a "right" line describes the shortest passage from point to point, so a "right" action effects a good design by the fewest means; and so likewise a "right" opinion is that which connects distant truths by the shortest train of intermediate propositions.[1]

To find the nearest way from truth to truth, or from purpose to effect, not to use more instruments where fewer will be sufficient, not to move by wheels and levers what will give way to the naked hand, is the great proof of a healthful and vigorous mind, neither feeble with helpless ignorance, nor overburdened with unwieldy knowledge.

But there are men to seem to think nothing so much the characteristic of a genius as to do common things in an uncommon manner: like Hudibras to "tell the clock by algebra,"[2] or like the lady in Dr. Young's satires, "to drink tea by stratagem."[3] To quit the beaten track only because it is known, and take a new path, however crooked or rough, because the straight was found out before.

Every man speaks and writes with intent to be understood, and it can seldom happen but he that understands himself might convey his notions to another if, content to be understood, he did not seek to be admired; but when once he begins to contrive how his sentiments may be received, not with most ease to his reader, but with most advantage to himself, he then transfers his consideration from words to sounds, from sentences to periods,[4] and as he grows more elegant becomes less intelligible.

It is difficult to enumerate every species of authors whose labors counteract themselves. The man of exuberance and copiousness, who diffuses every thought through so many diversities of expression, that it is lost like water in a mist. The ponderous dictator of sentences, whose notions are delivered in the lump, and are, like uncoined bullion, of more weight than use. The liberal illustrator who shows by examples and comparisons what was clearly seen when it was first proposed; and the stately son of demonstration, who proves with mathematical formality what no man has yet pretended to doubt.

There is a mode of style for which I know not that the masters of oratory have yet found a name, a style by which the most evident truths are so obscured that they can no longer be perceived, and the most

1. Richard Cumberland, *Treatise of the Laws of Nature* (1672).
2. *Hudibras*, I. i. 125–26.
3. Edward Young, *Love of Fame* (1728), vi. 188.
4. Carefully suspended sentence structures.

familiar propositions so disguised that they cannot be known. Every other kind of eloquence is the dress of sense, but this is the mask, by which a true master of his art will so effectually conceal it, that a man will as easily mistake his own positions if he meets them thus transformed, as he may pass in a masquerade his nearest acquaintance.

This style may be called the "terrific," for its chief intention is to terrify and amaze; it may be termed the "repulsive," for its natural effect is to drive away the reader; or it may be distinguished, in plain English, by the denomination of the "bugbear style," for it has more terror than danger, and will appear less formidable as it is more nearly approached.

A mother tells her infant that "two and two make four," the child remembers the proposition, and is able to count four to all the purposes of life, till the course of his education brings him among philosophers, who fright him from his former knowledge by telling him that four is a certain aggregate of units; that all numbers being only the repetition of an unit which, though not a number itself, is the parent, root, or original of all number, "four" is the denomination assigned to a certain number of such repetitions. The only danger is lest, when he first hears these dreadful sounds, the pupil should run away; if he has but the courage to stay till the conclusion, he will find that, when speculation[5] has done its worst, two and two still make four.

An illustrious example of this species of eloquence may be found in *Letters Concerning Mind.*[6] The author begins by declaring that "sorts of things are things that now are, have been, and shall be, and the things that strictly Are." In this position, except the last clause, in which he uses something of the scholastic language,[7] there is nothing but what every man has heard and imagines himself to know. But who would not believe that some wonderful novelty is presented to his intellect when he is afterwards told, in the true "bugbear" style, that "the Ares, in the former sense, are things that lie between the Have-beens and Shall-bes. The Have-beens are things that are past; the Shall-bes are things that are to come; and the things that Are, in the latter sense, are things that have not been, nor shall be, nor stand in the midst of such as are before them or shall be after them. The things that have been, and shall be, have respect to present, past, and future. Those likewise that now Are have moreover place; that, for instance, which is here, that which is to the east, that which is to the west."

All this, my dear reader, is very strange; but though it be strange, it is not new; survey these wonderful sentences again, and they will be found to contain nothing more than very plain truths, which till this author arose had always been delivered in plain language.

5. Theory.
6. By John Petvin (1750).
7. Metaphysical language, language of medieval scholastic philosophy.

No. 51.

Saturday, 7 April 1759.

It has been commonly remarked that eminent men are least eminent at home, that bright characters lose much of their splendor at a nearer view, and many who fill the world with their fame excite very little reverence among those that surround them in their domestic privacies.

To blame or to suspect is easy and natural. When the fact is evident and the cause doubtful, some accusation is always engendered between idleness and malignity. This disparity of general and familiar esteem is therefore imputed to hidden vices and to practices indulged in secret but carefully covered from the public eye.

Vice will indeed always produce contempt. The dignity of Alexander, though nations fell prostrate before him, was certainly held in little veneration by the partakers of his midnight revels, who had seen him in the madness of wine murder his friend, or set fire to the Persian palace at the instigation of a harlot;[1] and it is well remembered among us that the avarice of Marlborough kept him in subjection to his wife, while he was dreaded by France as her conqueror and honored by the Emperor as his deliverer.[2]

But though where there is vice there must be want of reverence, it is not reciprocally true that when there is want of reverence there is always vice. That awe which great actions or abilities impress will be inevitably diminished by acquaintance, though nothing either mean or criminal should be found.

Of men as of everything else we must judge according to our knowledge. When we see of a hero only his battles, or of a writer only his books, we have nothing to allay[3] our ideas of their greatness. We consider the one only as the guardian of his country and the other only as the instructor of mankind. We have neither opportunity nor motive to examine the minuter parts of their lives or the less apparent peculiarities of their characters; we name them with habitual respect, and forget what we still continue to know, that they are men like other mortals.

But such is the constitution of the world that much of life must be spent in the same manner by the wise and the ignorant, the exalted and

1. Alexander killed his friend Clitus in a drunken brawl, and set fire to the palace of Persepolis at the instigation of the courtesan Thaïs.

2. John Churchill, first Duke of Marlborough (1650–1722), had led the British forces in conjunction with those of the Netherlands and the Holy Roman Empire against the French in the War of the Spanish Succession. He was as notorious for his avarice as his wife Sarah, a close friend of Queen Anne, was for her imperious temper. The Duchess held profitable positions at Court.

3. Abate.

the low. Men, however distinguished by external accidents or intrinsic qualities, have all the same wants, the same pains, and, as far as the senses are consulted, the same pleasures. The petty cares and petty duties are the same in every station to every understanding, and every hour brings some occasion on which we all sink to the common level. We are all naked till we are dressed, and hungry till we are fed; and the general's triumph and sage's disputation end, like the humble labors of the smith or plowman, in a dinner or in sleep.

Those notions which are to be collected by reason in opposition to the senses will seldom stand forward in the mind, but lie treasured in the remoter repositories of memory, to be found only when they are sought. Whatever any man may have written or done, his precepts or his valor will scarcely overbalance the unimportant uniformity which runs through his time. We do not easily consider him as great whom our own eyes show us to be little nor labor to keep present to our thoughts the latent excellencies of him who shares with us all our weaknesses and many of our follies; who like us is delighted with slight amusements, busied with trifling employments, and disturbed by little vexations.

Great powers cannot be exerted but when great exigencies make them necessary. Great exigencies can happen but seldom, and therefore those qualities which have a claim to the veneration of mankind lie hid for the most part like subterranean treasures over which the foot passes as on common ground till necessity breaks open the golden cavern.

In the ancient celebrations of victory, a slave was placed on the triumphal car by the side of the general, who reminded him by a short sentence that he was a man. Whatever danger there might be lest a leader in his passage to the Capitol should forget the frailties of his nature, there was surely no need of such an admonition; the intoxication could not have continued long; he would have been at home but a few hours before some of his dependents would have forgot his greatness, and shown him that notwithstanding his laurels he was yet a man.

There are some who try to escape this domestic degradation, by laboring to appear always wise or always great; but he that strives against nature will forever strive in vain. To be grave of mien and slow of utterance; to look with solicitude and speak with hesitation is attainable at will; but the show of wisdom is ridiculous when there is nothing to cause doubt, as that of valor where there is nothing to be feared.

A man who has duly considered the condition of his being will contentedly yield to the course of things: he will not pant for distinction where distinction would imply no merit, but though on great occasions he may wish to be greater than others, he will be satisfied in common occurrences not to be less.

No. 60.
Saturday, 9 June 1759.

Criticism is a study by which men grow important and formidable at very small expense. The power of invention has been conferred by nature upon few, and the labor of learning those sciences[1] which may, by mere labor, be obtained, is too great to be willingly endured; but every man can exert such judgment as he has upon the works of others; and he whom nature has made weak, and idleness keeps ignorant, may yet support his vanity by the name of a critic.

I hope it will give comfort to great numbers who are passing through the world in obscurity when I inform them how easily distinction may be obtained. All the other powers of literature are coy and haughty, they must be long courted, and at last are not always gained; but criticism is a goddess easy of access and forward of advance, who will meet the slow and encourage the timorous; the want of meaning she supplies with words, and the want of spirit she recompenses with malignity.

This profession has one recommendation peculiar to itself, that it gives vent to malignity without real mischief. No genius was ever blasted by the breath of critics. The poison which, if confined, would have burst the heart, fumes away in empty hisses, and malice is set at ease with very little danger to merit. The critic is the only man whose triumph is without another's pain, and whose greatness does not rise upon another's ruin.

To a study at once so easy and so reputable, so malicious and so harmless, it cannot be necessary to invite my readers by a long or labored exhortation; it is sufficient, since all would be critics if they could, to show by one eminent example that all can be critics if they will.

Dick Minim, after the common course of puerile[2] studies, in which he was no great proficient, was put apprentice to a brewer, with whom he had lived two years, when his uncle died in the City and left him a large fortune in the stocks. Dick had for six months before used[3] the company of the lower players,[4] of whom he had learned to scorn a trade, and being now at liberty to follow his genius, he resolved to be a man of wit and humor. That he might be properly initiated in his new character, he frequented the coffee-houses near the theaters, where he listened very diligently, day after day, to those who talked of language and sentiments, and unities[5] and catastrophes,[6] till by slow degrees he

1. Branches of knowledge.
2. Childhood.
3. Frequented.
4. Actors.
5. The "rules" of action, time, and place.
6. Climaxes or turning points of drama.

began to think that he understood something of the stage, and hoped in time to talk himself.

But he did not trust so much to natural sagacity as wholly to neglect the help of books. When the theaters were shut, he retired to Richmond[7] with a few select writers, whose opinions he impressed upon his memory by unwearied diligence; and when he returned with other wits to the town, was able to tell, in very proper phrases, that the chief business of art is to copy nature; that a perfect writer is not to be expected, because genius decays as judgment increases; that the great art is the art of blotting, and that according to the rule of Horace every piece should be kept nine years.[8]

Of the great authors he now began to display the characters, laying down as an universal position that all had beauties and defects. His opinion was that Shakespeare, committing himself wholly to the impulse of nature, wanted that correctness which learning would have given him; and that Jonson,[9] trusting to learning, did not sufficiently cast his eye on nature. He blamed the stanza of Spenser, and could not bear the hexameters of Sidney. Denham and Waller he held the first reformers of English numbers, and thought that if Waller could have obtained the strength of Denham, or Denham the sweetness of Waller, there had been nothing wanting to complete a poet.[10] He often expressed his commiseration of Dryden's poverty, and his indignation at the age which suffered him to write for bread; he repeated with rapture the first lines of *All for Love,*[11] but wondered at the corruption of taste which could bear any thing so unnatural as rhyming tragedies. In Otway he found uncommon powers of moving the passions, but was disgusted by his general negligence, and blamed him for making a conspirator his hero, and never concluded his disquisition, without remarking how happily the sound of the clock is made to alarm the audience.[12] Southerne would have been his favorite, but that he mixes comic with tragic scenes, intercepts the natural course of the passions, and fills the mind with a wild confusion of mirth and melancholy.[13] The versification of Rowe he thought too melodious for the stage, and too little varied in different passions.[14] He made it the great fault of Congreve that all his persons were wits, and that he always wrote with more

7. A London suburb.

8. All standard critical clichés, as are the following opinions. See Alexander Pope's *Epistle to Augustus* (1737).

9. Ben Jonson.

10. Sir John Denham (1615–69) and Edmund Waller (1606–87), forerunners of Dryden and Pope in developing the rhetoric of the neo-classical couplet.

11. Dryden's most admired tragedy (1678).

12. In Thomas Otway's *Venice Preserved* (1682).

13. Thomas Southerne (1659–1746), best known for two tragedies, *The Fatal Marriage* (1694) and *Oroonoko* (1695).

14. Nicholas Rowe's "she-tragedies" were published between 1700 and 1715.

art than nature.[15] He considered *Cato*[16] rather as a poem than a play, and allowed Addison to be the complete master of allegory and grave humor, but paid no great deference to him as a critic. He thought the chief merit of Prior was in his easy tales and lighter poems, though he allowed that his *Solomon*[17] had many noble sentiments elegantly expressed. In Swift he discovered an inimitable vein of irony, and an easiness which all would hope and few would attain. Pope he was inclined to degrade from a poet to a versifier, and thought his numbers rather luscious[18] than sweet. He often lamented the neglect of *Phaedra and Hippolitus*,[19] and wished to see the stage under better regulations.[20]

These assertions passed commonly uncontradicted; and if now and then an opponent started up, he was quickly repressed by the suffrages[21] of the company, and Minim went away from every dispute with elation of heart and increase of confidence.

He now grew conscious of his abilities, and began to talk of the present state of dramatic poetry; wondered what was become of the comic genius which supplied our ancestors with wit and pleasantry, and why no writer could be found that durst now venture beyond a farce. He saw no reason for thinking that the vein of humor was exhausted, since we live in a country where liberty suffers every character to spread itself to its utmost bulk, and which therefore produces more originals than all the rest of the world together.[22] Of tragedy he concluded business[23] to be the soul, and yet often hinted that love predominates too much upon the modern stage.

He was now an acknowledged critic, and had his own seat in the coffee-house, and headed a party in the pit.[24] Minim has more vanity than ill-nature, and seldom desires to do much mischief; he will perhaps murmur a little in the ear of him that sits next him, but endeavors to influence the audience to favor by clapping when an actor exclaims "ye Gods," or laments the misery of his country.

By degrees he was admitted to rehearsals, and many of his friends are of opinion that our present poets are indebted to him for their happiest thoughts; by his contrivance the bell was rung twice in *Barbarossa*, and by his persuasion the author of *Cleone* concluded his play

15. William Congreve (1670–1729), the greatest writer of English comedy of manners. His *Way of the World* was first produced in 1700.

16. Addison's tragedy (1713).

17. Matthew Prior's long philosophic poem (1718).

18. Cloying.

19. Edmund Smith's tragedy (1707), admired by Addison.

20. The stage had been regulated (subjected to censorship) by the Licensing Act of 1737.

21. Opinions.

22. The comedy of "humors" dates from Ben Jonson. A humor character, or "original," is an eccentric figure who reflects the predominance of one of the four bodily humors: blood, phlegm, black bile, and yellow bile.

23. Action.

24. The floor of the theater, where seats were cheaper than in the boxes.

without a couplet;[25] for what can be more absurd, said Minim, than that part of a play should be rhymed and part written in blank verse? and by what acquisition of faculties is the speaker who never could find rhymes before, enabled to rhyme at the conclusion of an act!

He is the great investigator of hidden beauties, and is particularly delighted when he finds "the sound an echo to the sense."[26] He has read all our poets with particular attention to this delicacy of versification, and wonders at the supineness with which their works have been hitherto perused, so that no man has found the sound of a drum in this distich,[27]

> When pulpit, drum ecclesiastic,
> Was beat with fist instead of a stick;[28]

and that the wonderful lines upon honor and a bubble have hitherto passed without notice:

> Honor is like the glassy bubble,
> Which costs philosophers such trouble,
> Where one part cracked, the whole does fly,
> And wits are cracked to find out why.[29]

In these verses, says Minim, we have two striking accommodations of the sound to the sense. It is impossible to utter the two lines emphatically without an act like that which they describe: "bubble" and "trouble" causing a momentary inflation of the cheeks by the retention of the breath, which is afterwards forcibly emitted, as in the practice of "blowing bubbles." But the greatest excellence is in the third line, which is "cracked" in the middle to express a crack, and then shivers into monosyllables. Yet has this diamond lain neglected with common stones, and among the innumerable admirers of *Hudibras* the observation of this superlative passage has been reserved for the sagacity of Minim.

No. 61.

Saturday, 16 June 1759.

Mr. Minim had now advanced himself to the zenith of critical reputation; when he was in the pit, every eye in the boxes was fixed upon him; when he entered his coffee-house, he was surrounded by circles of candidates, who passed their novitiate of literature under his tuition;

25. John Brown's *Barbarossa* (1754), and Robert Dodsley's *Cleone* (1758). In Act III of *Barbarossa,* a bell tolling for the midnight watch serves as a signal for an uprising against Barbarossa. In Act V the bell tolls for the death of the hero, Selim.
26. See Pope, *Essay on Criticism,* l. 365.
27. Couplet.
28. *Hudibras,* I. i. 11–12.
29. *Hudibras,* II. ii. 385–88.

his opinion was asked by all who had no opinion of their own, and yet loved to debate and decide; and no composition was supposed to pass in safety to posterity till it had been secured by Minim's approbation.

Minim professes great admiration of the wisdom and munificence by which the academies of the Continent[1] were raised, and often wishes for some standard of taste, for some tribunal, to which merit may appeal from caprice, prejudice, and malignity. He has formed a plan for an academy of criticism, where every work of imagination may be read before it is printed, and which shall authoritatively direct the theaters what pieces to receive or reject, to exclude or to revive.

Such an institution would, in Dick's opinion, spread the fame of English literature over Europe, and make London the metropolis[2] of elegance and politeness, the place to which the learned and ingenious[3] of all countries would repair for instruction and improvement, and where nothing would any longer be applauded or endured that was not conformed to the nicest[4] rules, and finished with the highest elegance.

Till some happy conjunction of the planets shall dispose our princes or ministers to make themselves immortal by such an academy, Minim contents himself to preside four nights in a week in a critical society selected by himself, where he is heard without contradiction, and whence his judgment is disseminated through the great vulgar and the small.[5]

When he is placed in the chair of criticism, he declares loudly for the noble simplicity of our ancestors, in opposition to the petty refinements, and ornamental luxuriance. Sometimes he is sunk in despair, and perceives false delicacy daily gaining ground, and sometimes brightens his countenance with a gleam of hope, and predicts the revival of the true sublime.[6] He then fulminates his loudest censures against the monkish barbarity of rhyme;[7] wonders how beings that pretend to reason can be pleased with one line always ending like another; tells how unjustly and unnaturally sense is sacrificed to sound; how often the best thoughts are mangled by the necessity of confining or extending them to the dimensions of a couplet; and rejoices that genius has, in our days, shaken off the shackles which had encumbered it so long. Yet he allows that rhyme may sometimes be borne, if the lines be often broken and the pauses judiciously diversified.

From blank verse he makes an easy transition to Milton, whom he

1. Such as the French Academy, founded 1635; one of its purposes was to set standards for correct language.

2. Center, principal city.

3. Cultivated.

4. Most exact.

5. The commonplace people of both upper and lower classes. Johnson here adopts a line from Abraham Cowley's translation of Horace, *Odes,* III. i. 1–2.

6. The elevated and awe-inspiring—a quality sought for in the epic and great ode.

7. See Milton's Preface to *Paradise Lost.* (See *Rambler,* no. 121, n. 13.)

produces as an example of the slow advance of lasting reputation. Milton is the only writer whose books Minim can read forever without weariness. What cause it is that exempts this pleasure from satiety he has long and diligently inquired, and believes it to consist in the perpetual variation of the numbers,[8] by which the ear is gratified and the attention awakened. The lines that are commonly thought rugged and unmusical, he conceives to have been written to temper the melodious luxury of the rest, or to express things by a proper cadence: for he scarcely finds a verse that has not this favorite beauty; he declares that he could shiver in a hothouse when he reads that

> the ground
> Burns frore, and cold performs th' effect of fire.[9]

And that when Milton bewails his blindness, the verse,

> So thick a drop serene has quenched these orbs,[10]

has, he knows not how, something that strikes him with an obscure sensation like that which he fancies would be felt from the sound of darkness.

Minim is not so confident of his rules of judgment as not very eagerly to catch new light from the name of the author. He is commonly so prudent as to spare those whom he cannot resist, unless, as will sometimes happen, he finds the public combined against them. But a fresh pretender to fame he is strongly inclined to censure, till his own honor requires that he commend him. Till he knows the success of a composition, he entrenches himself in general terms; there are some new thoughts and beautiful passages, but there is likewise much which he would have advised the author to expunge. He has several favorite epithets, of which he has never settled the meaning, but which are very commodiously applied to books which he has not read, or cannot understand. One is "manly," another is "dry," another "stiff," and another "flimsy"; sometimes he discovers delicacy of style, and sometimes meets with "strange expressions."

He is never so great, or so happy, as when a youth of promising parts[11] is brought to receive his directions for the prosecution of his studies. He then puts on a very serious air; he advises the pupil to read none but the best authors and, when he finds one congenial to his own mind, to study his beauties but avoid his faults, and, when he sits down to write, to consider how his favorite author would think at the present time on the present occasion. He exhorts him to catch those moments when he finds his thoughts expanded and his genius exalted, but to take care lest imagination hurry him beyond the bounds of nature. He holds diligence the mother of success, yet enjoins him, with great ear-

8. Meter. 9. *Paradise Lost,* ii. 594–95.
10. *Paradise Lost,* iii. 25. 11. Abilities.

nestness, not to read more than he can digest, and not to confuse his mind by pursuing studies of contrary tendencies. He tells him, that every man has his genius, and that Cicero could never be a poet.[12] The boy retires illuminated, resolves to follow his genius,[13] and to think how Milton would have thought; and Minim feasts upon his own beneficence till another day brings another pupil.

No. 63.

Saturday, 30 June 1759.

The natural progress of the works of men is from rudeness[1] to convenience, from convenience to elegance, and from elegance to nicety.[2]

The first labor is enforced by necessity. The savage finds himself incommoded by heat and cold, by rain and wind; he shelters himself in the hollow of a rock, and learns to dig a cave where there was none before. He finds the sun and the wind excluded by the thicket, and when the accidents of the chase, or the convenience of pasturage leads him into more open places, he forms a thicket for himself by planting stakes at proper distances, and laying branches from one to another.

The next gradation of skill and industry produces a house, closed with doors, and divided by partitions; and apartments are multiplied and disposed according to the various degrees of power or invention; improvement succeeds improvement, as he that is freed from a greater evil grows impatient of a less, till ease in time is advanced to pleasure.

The mind set free from the importunities of natural want gains leisure to go in search of superfluous gratifications, and adds to the uses of habitation the delights of prospect. Then begins the reign of symmetry; orders of architecture[3] are invented, and one part of the edifice is conformed to another, without any other reason than that the eye may not be offended.

The passage is very short from elegance to luxury. Ionic and Corinthian columns are soon succeeded by gilt cornices, inlaid floors, and petty ornaments, which show rather the wealth than the taste of the possessor.

Language proceeds like everything else through improvement to degeneracy. The rovers[4] who first take possession of a country, having not many ideas, and those not nicely modified or discriminated, were contented if by general terms and abrupt sentences they could make

12. Cicero, famous for his prose, was often attacked as a mediocre poet.
13. Natural bent.
1. Roughness, crudeness.
2. Fastidious delicacy.
3. Classical styles, such as Doric, Ionic, and Corinthian.
4. Nomads.

their thoughts known to one another; as life begins to be more regulated and property to become limited, disputes must be decided and claims adjusted; the differences of things are noted, and distinctness and propriety of expression become necessary. In time, happiness and plenty give rise to curiosity, and the sciences are cultivated for ease and pleasure; to the arts which are now to be taught, emulation soon adds the art of teaching; and the studious and ambitious contend not only who shall think best, but who shall tell their thoughts in the most pleasing manner.

Then begin the arts of rhetoric and poetry, the regulation of figures,[5] the selection of words, the modulation of periods, the graces of transition, the complication of clauses, and all the delicacies of style and subtilties of composition, useful while they advance perspicuity and laudable while they increase pleasure, but easy to be refined by needless scrupulosity till they shall more embarrass the writer than assist the reader or delight him.

The first state is commonly antecedent to the practice of writing; the ignorant essays[6] of imperfect diction pass away with the savage generation that uttered them. No nation can trace their language beyond the second period, and even of that it does not often happen that many monuments remain.

The fate of the English tongue is like that of others. We know nothing of the scanty jargon of our barbarous ancestors, but we have specimens of our language when it began to be adapted to civil and religious purposes,[7] and find it such as might naturally be expected, artless and simple, unconnected[8] and concise. The writers seem to have desired little more than to be understood, and perhaps seldom aspired to the praise of pleasing. Their verses were considered chiefly as memorial,[9] and therefore did not differ from prose but by the measure[10] or the rhyme.

In this state, varied a little according to the different purposes or abilities of writers, our language may be said to have continued to the time of Gower,[11] whom Chaucer calls his master, and who, however obscured by his scholar's popularity, seems justly to claim the honor which has been hitherto denied him, of showing his countrymen that something more was to be desired, and that English verse might be exalted into poetry.

5. Special arrangements or devices of speech and thought: metaphor, hyperbole, repetition, parallel, inversion, antithesis, and the like.

6. Attempts.

7. The *Anglo-Saxon Chronicle,* for example, and the scriptural poems attributed to Caedmon.

8. Lacking in organization.

9. As records.

10. Meter.

11. John Gower (?1330–1408) wrote poems in Latin, French, and English.

From the time of Gower and Chaucer, the English writers have studied elegance, and advanced their language, by successive improvements to as much harmony as it can easily receive, and as much copiousness as human knowledge has hitherto required. These advances have not been made at all times with the same diligence or the same success. Negligence has suspended the course of improvement, or affectation turned it aside; time has elapsed with little change, or change has been made without amendment. But elegance has been long kept in view with attention as near to constancy as life permits, till every man now endeavors to excel others in accuracy, or outshine them in splendor of style, and the danger is lest care should too soon pass to affectation.

No. 70.

Saturday, 18 August 1759.

Few faults of style, whether real or imaginary, excite the malignity of a more numerous class of readers than the use of hard words.

If an author be supposed to involve his thoughts in voluntary obscurity, and to obstruct, by unnecessary difficulties, a mind eager in pursuit of truth; if he writes not to make others learned, but to boast the learning which he possesses himself, and wishes to be admired rather than understood, he counteracts the first end of writing, and justly suffers the utmost severity of censure, or the more afflictive severity of neglect.

But words are only hard to those who do not understand them, and the critic ought always to inquire whether he is incommoded by the fault of the writer, or by his own.

Every author does not write for every reader; many questions are such as the illiterate part of mankind can have neither interest nor pleasure in discussing, and which therefore it would be an useless endeavor to level with common minds, by tiresome circumlocutions or laborious explanations; and many subjects of general use may be treated in a different manner, as the book is intended for the learned or the ignorant. Diffusion[1] and explication are necessary to the instruction of those who, being neither able nor accustomed to think for themselves, can learn only what is expressly taught; but they who can form parallels, discover consequences, and multiply conclusions, are best pleased with involution[2] of argument and compression of thought; they desire only to receive the seeds of knowledge which they may branch out by their own power, to have the way to truth pointed out which they can then follow without a guide.

1. Diffuseness, prolixity.
2. Intricacy.

The Guardian directs one of his pupils "to think with the wise but speak with the vulgar."[3] This is a precept specious[4] enough, but not always practicable. Difference of thoughts will produce difference of language. He that thinks with more extent than another will want words of larger meaning; he that thinks with more subtilty will seek for terms of more nice[5] discrimination; and where is the wonder, since words are but the images of things, that he who never knew the originals should not know the copies?

Yet vanity inclines us to find faults anywhere rather than in ourselves. He that reads and grows no wiser seldom suspects his own deficiency; but complains of hard words and obscure sentences, and asks why books are written which cannot be understood.

Among the hard words which are no longer to be used, it has been long the custom to number terms of art.[6] "Every man," says Swift, "is more able to explain the subject of an art than its professors; a farmer will tell you, in two words that he has broken his leg; but a surgeon after a long discourse shall leave you as ignorant as you were before."[7] This could only have been said by such an exact observer of life in gratification of malignity or in ostentation of acuteness. Every hour produces instances of the necessity of terms of art. Mankind could never conspire in uniform affectation; it is not but by necessity that every science and every trade has its peculiar language. They that content themselves with general ideas may rest in general terms; but those whose studies or employments force them upon closer inspection must have names for particular parts and words by which they may express various modes of combination, such as none but themselves have occasion to consider.

Artists[8] are indeed sometimes ready to suppose that none can be strangers to words to which themselves are familiar, talk to an incidental inquirer as they talk to one another, and make their knowledge ridiculous by injudicious obtrusion. An art cannot be taught but by its proper terms, but it is not always necessary to teach the art.

That the vulgar express their thoughts clearly is far from true; and what perspicuity can be found among them proceeds not from the easiness of their language, but the shallowness of their thoughts. He that sees a building as a common spectator contents himself with relating that it is great or little, mean or splendid, lofty or low; all these words are intelligible and common, but they convey no distinct or limited ideas; if he attempts, without the terms of architecture, to delineate the parts, or enumerate the ornaments, his narration at once becomes unintelligible. The terms, indeed, generally displease, be-

3. *Guardian,* no, 24. *The Guardian* was a periodical founded by Steele (1713).
4. Plausible.
5. Precise.
6. Technical terms.
7. From Swift's "Letter to a Young Clergyman" (1721).
8. The practitioner of any occupation.

cause they are understood by few; but they are little understood only because few that look upon an edifice examine its parts, or analyze its columns into their members.

The state of every other art is the same; as it is cursorily surveyed or accurately examined, different forms of expression become proper. In morality it is one thing to discuss the niceties of the casuist,[9] and another to direct the practice of common life. In agriculture, he that instructs the farmer to plough and sow, may convey his notions without the words which he would find necessary in explaining to philosophers the process of vegetation; and if he, who has nothing to do but to be honest by the shortest way, will perplex his mind with subtile speculations; or if he whose task is to reap and thrash will not be contented without examining the evolution of the seed and circulation of the sap, the writers whom either shall consult are very little to be blamed, though it should sometimes happen that they are read in vain.

No. 71.

Saturday, 25 August 1759.[1]

Dick Shifter was born in Cheapside,[2] and having passed reputably through all the classes of St. Paul's School, has been for some years a student in the Temple.[3] He is of the opinion that intense application dulls the faculties, and thinks it necessary to temper the severity of the law by books that engage the mind but do not fatigue it. He has therefore made a copious collection of plays, poems, and romances, to which he has recourse when he fancies himself tired with statutes and reports, and he seldom inquires very nicely whether he is weary or idle.

Dick has received from his favorite authors very strong impressions of a country life; and though his furthest excursions have been to Greenwich on one side and Chelsea on the other,[4] he has talked for several years, with great pomp of language and elevation of sentiments, about a state too high for contempt and too low for envy, about homely quiet and blameless simplicity, pastoral delights and rural innocence.

His friends who had estates in the country often invited him to pass the summer among them, but something or other had always hindered

9. One trained to deal with difficult moral problems.

1. The motto from Tasso *(Aminta,* II. i. 17–18) reads, "The woods hide snakes, lions, and bears, within their lovely green foliage."

2. London district.

3. The Inner Temple, the Middle Temple, Gray's Inn, and Lincoln's Inn are four sets of buildings in London, known as the Inns of Court; they belong to four legal societies that have the exclusive right of admitting candidates to the bar.

4. Greenwich and Chelsea are southeast and southwest districts of London. In the eighteenth century they were suburbs.

him, and he considered that to reside in the house of another man was to incur a kind of dependence inconsistent with that laxity[5] of life which he had imaged as the chief good.

This summer he resolved to be happy, and procured a lodging to be taken for him at a solitary house situated about thirty miles from London, on the banks of a small river with corn fields before it and a hill on each side covered with wood. He concealed the place of his retirement that none might violate his obscurity, and promised himself many a happy day when he should hide himself among the trees, and contemplate the tumults and vexations of the town.

He stepped into the post chaise[6] with his heart beating and his eyes sparkling, was conveyed through many varieties of delightful prospects, saw hills and meadows, corn fields and pasture succeed each other, and for four hours charged none of his poets with fiction or exaggeration. He was now within six miles of happiness, when having never felt so much agitation before, he began to wish his journey at an end, and the last hour was passed in changing his posture, and quarreling with his driver.

An hour may be tedious but cannot be long; he at length alighted at his new dwelling, and was received as he expected; he looked round upon the hills and rivulets, but his joints were stiff and his muscles sore, and his first request was to see his bedchamber.

He rested well, and ascribed the soundness of his sleep to the stillness of the country. He expected from that time nothing but nights of quiet and days of rapture, and as soon as he had risen, wrote an account of his new state to one of his friends in the Temple.

"Dear Frank,

"I never pitied thee before. I am now as I could wish every man of wisdom and virtue to be, in the regions of calm content and placid meditation; with all the beauties of nature soliciting my notice, and all the diversities of pleasure courting my acceptance; the birds are chirping in the hedges, and the flowers blooming in the mead; the breeze is whistling in the woods, and the sun dancing on the water. I can now say with truth that a man capable of enjoying the purity of happiness is never more busy than in his hours of leisure, nor ever less solitary than in a place of solitude.

I am, dear Frank, etc."

When he had sent away his letter, he walked into the wood with some inconvenience from the furze that pricked his legs, and the briars that scratched his face; he at last sat down under a tree, and heard with great delight a shower, by which he was not wet, rattling among the branches;

5. Freedom.
6. An enclosed public carriage.

this, said he, is the true image of obscurity,[7] we hear of troubles and commotions, but never feel them.

His amusement did not overpower the calls of nature, and he therefore went back to order his dinner. He knew that the country produces whatever is eaten or drank, and imagining that he was now at the source of luxury, resolved to indulge himself with dainties which he supposed might be procured at a price next to nothing, if any price at all was expected; and intended to amaze the rustics with his generosity by paying more than they would ask. Of twenty dishes which he named, he was amazed to find that scarce one was to be had, and heard with astonishment and indignation that all the fruits of the earth were sold at a higher price than in the streets of London.

His meal was short and sullen, and he retired again to his tree to inquire how dearness[8] could be consistent with abundance, or how fraud should be practiced by simplicity. He was not satisfied with his own speculations, and returning home early in the evening went awhile from window to window, and found that he wanted something to do.

He inquired for a newspaper, and was told that farmers never minded news, but that they could send for it from the alehouse. A messenger was dispatched, who ran away at full speed, but loitered an hour behind the hedges, and at last coming back with his feet purposely bemired, instead of expressing the gratitude which Mr. Shifter expected for the bounty of a shilling, said that the night was wet, and the way dirty, and he hoped that his worship would not think it much to give him half a crown.[9]

Dick now went to bed with some abatement of his expectations; but sleep, I know not how, revives our hopes and rekindles our desires. He rose early in the morning, surveyed the landscape, and was pleased. He walked out, and passed from field to field without observing any beaten path, and wondered that he had not seen the shepherdesses dancing nor heard the swains piping to their flocks.

At last he saw some reapers and harvest-women at dinner. Here, said he, are the true Arcadians,[10] and advanced courteously towards them, as afraid of confusing them by the dignity of his presence. They acknowledged his superiority by no other token than that of asking him for something to drink. He imagined that he had now purchased the privilege of discourse, and began to descend to familiar questions, endeavoring to accommodate his discourse to the grossness of rustic understandings. The clowns[11] soon found that he did not know wheat from rye, and began to despise him; one of the boys, by pretending to

7. Inconspicuous retirement.
8. High prices.
9. A coin worth two and one half shillings.
10. Inhabitants of Arcadia, in classical literature the ideal pastoral world.
11. Yokels.

show him a bird's nest, decoyed him into a ditch, and one of the wenches sold him a bargain.[12]

This walk had given him no great pleasure, but he hoped to find other rustics less coarse of manners and less mischievous of disposition. Next morning he was accosted by an attorney who told him that unless he made Farmer Dobson satisfaction for trampling his grass, he had orders to indict him. Shifter was offended but not terrified, and telling the attorney that he was himself a lawyer talked so volubly of pettifoggers and barrators[13] that he drove him away.

Finding his walks thus interrupted, he was inclined to ride, and being pleased with the appearance of a horse that was grazing in a neighboring meadow, inquired the owner, who warranted him sound, and would not sell him but that he was too fine for a plain man. Dick paid down the price, and riding out to enjoy the evening, fell with his new horse into a ditch; they got out with difficulty, and as he was going to mount again, a countryman looked at the horse and perceived him to be blind. Dick went to the seller, and demanded back his money; but was told that a man who rented his ground must do the best for himself, that his landlord had his rent though the year was barren, and that whether horses had eyes or no, he should sell them to the highest bidder.

Shifter now began to be tired with rustic simplicity, and on the fifth day took possession again of his chambers,[14] and bade farewell to the regions of calm content and placid meditation.

No. 77.

Saturday, 6 October 1759.

Easy poetry is universally admired, but I know not whether any rule has yet been fixed by which it may be decided when poetry can be properly called easy; Horace has told us that it is such as "every reader hopes to equal, but after long labor finds unattainable."[1] This is a very loose description, in which only the effect is noted; the qualities which produce this effect remain to be investigated.

Easy poetry is that in which natural thoughts are expressed without violence to the language. The discriminating character of ease consists principally in the diction, for all true poetry requires that the sentiments be natural. Language suffers violence by harsh or by daring figures, by transposition, by unusual acceptations[2] of words, and by any

12. A game which consisted in tricking someone into asking a question to which the answer was "my ass."

13. Two types of shady lawyers.

14. Apartment (at the Temple).

1. *Art of Poetry*, ll. 240–42.

2. Meanings.

license which would be avoided by a writer of prose. Where any artifice appears in the construction of the verse, that verse is no longer easy. Any epithet which can be ejected without diminution of the sense, any curious iteration of the same word, and all unusual, though not ungrammatical, structure of speech destroy the grace of easy poetry.

The first lines of Pope's *Iliad* afford examples of many licenses which an easy writer must decline.

> Achilles' *wrath,* to Greece the *direful spring*
> Of woes unnumbered, *heavenly* Goddess sing,
> The wrath which *hurled* to Pluto's *gloomy reign*
> The souls of *mighty* chiefs untimely slain.

In the first couplet the language is distorted by inversions, clogged with superfluities, and clouded by a harsh metaphor; and in the second there are two words used in an uncommon sense,[3] and two epithets inserted only to lengthen the line; all these practices may in a long work easily be pardoned, but they always produce some degree of obscurity and ruggedness.

Easy poetry has been so long excluded by ambition of ornament, and luxuriance of imagery, that its nature seems now to be forgotten. Affectation, however opposite to ease, is sometimes mistaken for it, and those who aspire to gentle elegance collect female phrases[4] and fashionable barbarisms, and imagine that style to be easy which custom has made familiar. Such was the idea of the poet who wrote the following verses to a "Countess Cutting Paper."[5]

> Pallas grew *vap'rish*[6] *once and odd,*
> She would not *do the least right thing*
> Either for Goddess or for God,
> Nor work, nor play, nor paint, nor sing.
>
> Jove frowned, and "Use," he cried, "those eyes
> So skillful, and those hands so taper;[7]
> Do something exquisite and wise"—
> She bowed, obeyed him, and cut paper.
>
> This vexing him who gave her birth,
> Thought by all heaven a *burning shame,*
> *What does she next,* but bids on earth
> Her Burlington do just the same?

3. It is difficult to say which two words Johnson has in mind. "Reign" is a metonymy for "kingdom."

4. Expressions used by fashionable women, such as "vap'rish," "odd," "burning shame."

5. Pope, "On the Countess of Burlington Cutting Paper."

6. Vaporish: suffering from nervous depression.

7. Tapering, diminishing in size.

Pallas, you give yourself *strange airs;*
But sure you'll find it hard to spoil
The sense and taste, of one that bears
The name of Savile and of Boyle.[8]

Alas! one bad example shown,
How quickly all the sex pursue!
See, madam! see, the arts o'erthrown
Between John Overton[9] and *you.*

It is the prerogative of easy poetry to be understood as long as the language lasts; but modes of speech, which owe their prevalence only to modish folly, or to the eminence of those that use them, die away with their inventors, and their meaning in a few years is no longer known.

Easy poetry is commonly sought in petty compositions upon minute subjects; but ease, though it excludes pomp, will admit greatness. Many lines in Cato's soliloquy are at once easy and sublime.

'Tis the Divinity that stirs within us;
'Tis heaven itself that points out an hereafter,
And intimates eternity to man. . . .
If there's a power above us,
And that there is, all nature cries aloud
Through all her works, he must delight in virtue,
And that which he delights in must be happy.

[ADDISON, *CATO,* V.i. 7–9, 15–18.]

Nor is ease more contrary to wit than to sublimity; the celebrated stanza of Cowley,[10] on a lady elaborately dressed, loses nothing of its freedom by the spirit of the sentiment.

Th' adorning thee with so much art
Is but a barbarous skill,
'Tis like the poisoning of a dart
Too apt before to kill.

["THE WAITING MAID," LL. 13–16.]

Cowley seems to have possessed the power of writing easily beyond any other of our poets, yet his pursuit of remote thoughts led him often into harshness of expression. Waller often attempted, but seldom attained it; for he is too frequently driven into transpositions.[11] The poets, from the time of Dryden, have gradually advanced in embellishment, and consequently departed from simplicity and ease.

8. Both the Countess's family (Savile) and her husband's (Boyle) included a number of distinguished statesmen and scholars. Her husband was himself a well-known amateur architect.

9. John Overton (1640–1708) sold prints and drawings.

10. Abraham Cowley (1618–67), the most celebrated "metaphysical" (i.e. witty) poet of his time.

11. Inversions of normal word order.

To require from any author many pieces of easy poetry would be indeed to oppress him with too hard a task. It is less difficult to write a volume of lines swelled with epithets, brightened by figures, and stiffened by transpositions, than to produce a few couplets graced only by naked elegance and simple purity, which require so much care and skill that I doubt whether any of our authors has yet been able, for twenty lines together, nicely to observe the true definition of easy poetry.

No. 84.
Saturday, 24 November 1759.

Biography is, of the various kinds of narrative writing, that which is most eagerly read, and most easily applied to the purposes of life.

In romances, when the wild field of possibility lies open to invention, the incidents may easily be made more numerous, the vicissitudes more sudden, and the events more wonderful; but from the time of life when fancy begins to be overruled by reason and corrected by experience, the most artful tale raises little curiosity when it is known to be false; though it may, perhaps, be sometimes read as a model of a neat or elegant style, not for the sake of knowing what it contains, but how it is written; or those that are weary of themselves may have recourse to it as a pleasing dream, of which, when they awake, they voluntarily dismiss the images from their minds.

The examples and events of history press, indeed, upon the mind with the weight of truth; but when they are reposited in the memory, they are oftener employed for show than use, and rather diversify conversation than regulate life. Few are engaged in such scenes as give them opportunities of growing wiser by the downfall of statesmen or the defeat of generals. The stratagems of war, and the intrigues of courts, are read by far the greater part of mankind with the same indifference as the adventures of fabled heroes, or the revolutions of a fairy region. Between falsehood and useless truth there is little difference. As gold which he cannot spend will make no man rich, so knowledge which he cannot apply will make no man wise.

The mischievous consequences of vice and folly, of irregular desires and predominant passions, are best discovered[1] by those relations[2] which are leveled with the general surface of life, which tell not how any man became great, but how he was made happy; not how he lost the favor of his prince, but how he became discontented with himself.

Those relations are therefore commonly of most value in which the

1. Revealed.
2. Narratives.

writer tells his own story. He that recounts the life of another commonly dwells most upon conspicuous events, lessens the familiarity of his tale to increase its dignity, shows his favorite at a distance decorated and magnified like the ancient actors in their tragic dress,[3] and endeavors to hide the man that he may produce a hero.

But if it be true which was said by a French prince, "that no man was a hero to the servants of his chamber,"[4] it is equally true that every man is yet less a hero to himself. He that is most elevated above the crowd by the importance of his employments or the reputation of his genius feels himself affected by fame or business but as they influence his domestic life. The high and low, as they have the same faculties and the same senses, have no less similitude in their pains and pleasures. The sensations are the same in all, though produced by very different occasions. The prince feels the same pain when an invader seizes a province, as the farmer when a thief drives away his cow. Men thus equal in themselves will appear equal in honest and impartial biography; and those whom fortune or nature place at the greatest distance may afford instruction to each other.

The writer of his own life has at least the first qualification of an historian, the knowledge of the truth; and though it may be plausibly objected that his temptations to disguise it are equal to his opportunities of knowing it, yet I cannot but think that impartiality may be expected with equal confidence from him that relates the passages of his own life, as from him that delivers the transactions of another.

Certainty of knowledge not only excludes mistake but fortifies veracity. What we collect by conjecture, and by conjecture only can one man judge of another's motives or sentiments, is easily modified by fancy or by desire; as objects imperfectly discerned, take forms from the hope or fear of the beholder. But that which is fully known cannot be falsified but with reluctance of understanding, and alarm of conscience; of understanding, the lover of truth; of conscience, the sentinel of virtue.

He that writes the life of another is either his friend or his enemy, and wishes either to exalt his praise or aggravate his infamy; many temptations to falsehood will occur in the disguise of passions, too specious to fear much resistance. Love of virtue will animate panegyric, and hatred of wickedness embitter censure. The zeal of gratitude, the ardor of patriotism, fondness for an opinion, or fidelity to a party, may easily overpower the vigilance of a mind habitually well disposed, and prevail over unassisted and unfriended veracity.

But he that speaks of himself has no motive to falsehood or partiality except self-love, by which all have so often been betrayed that all are on

3. Greek actors of tragedy wore elevated boots and large masks, to command attention in the great outdoor theaters where they performed.

4. Proverbial phrase, sometimes attributed to Louis, Prince de Condé (1621–86).

the watch against its artifices. He that writes an apology for a single action, to confute an accusation, or recommend himself to favor, is indeed always to be suspected of favoring his own cause; but he that sits down calmly and voluntarily to review his life for the admonition of posterity, or to amuse himself, and leaves this account unpublished, may be commonly presumed to tell truth, since falsehood cannot appease his own mind, and fame will not be heard beneath the tomb.

No. 97.

Saturday, 23 February 1760.

It may, I think, be justly observed that few books disappoint their readers more than the narrations of travelers. One part of mankind is naturally curious to learn the sentiments, manners,[1] and condition of the rest; and every mind that has leisure or power to extend its views must be desirous of knowing in what proportion Providence has distributed the blessings of nature or the advantages of art among the several nations of the earth.

This general desire easily procures readers to every book from which it can expect gratification. The adventurer upon unknown coasts, and the describer of distant regions, is always welcomed as a man who has labored for the pleasure of others, and who is able to enlarge our knowledge and rectify our opinions; but when the volume is opened, nothing is found but such general accounts as leave no distinct idea behind them, or such minute enumerations as few can read with either profit or delight.

Every writer of travels should consider that, like all other authors, he undertakes either to instruct or please, or to mingle pleasure with instruction. He that instructs must offer to the mind something to be imitated or something to be avoided; he that pleases must offer new images to his reader, and enable him to form a tacit comparison of his own state with that of others.

The greater part of travelers tell nothing, because their method of traveling supplies them with nothing to be told. He that enters a town at night and surveys it in the morning and then hastens away to another place, and guesses at the manners of the inhabitants by the entertainment which his inn afforded him may please himself for a time with a hasty change of scenes and a confused remembrance of palaces and churches; he may gratify his eye with variety of landscapes; and regale his palate with a succession of vintages; but let him be contented to please himself without endeavor to disturb others. Why should he record excursions by which nothing could be learned, or wish to make a

1. Modes of behavior.

show of knowledge which, without some power of intuition unknown to other mortals, he never could attain.

Of those who crowd the world with their itineraries,[2] some have no other purpose than to describe the face of the country; those who sit idle at home and are curious to know what is done or suffered in distant countries may be informed by one of these wanderers that on a certain day he set out early with the caravan, and in the first hour's march saw towards the south a hill covered with trees, then passed over a stream which ran northward with a swift course, but which is probably dry in the summer months; that an hour after he saw something to the right which looked at a distance like a castle with towers, but which he discovered afterwards to be a craggy rock; that he then entered a valley in which he saw several trees tall and flourishing, watered by a rivulet not marked in the maps of which he was not able to learn the name; that the road afterward grew stony and the country uneven, where he observed among the hills many hollows worn by torrents, and was told that the road was passable only part of the year: that going on they found the remains of a building, once perhaps a fortress to secure the pass or to restrain the robbers, of which the present inhabitants can give no other account than that it is haunted by fairies; that they went to dine at the foot of a rock, and traveled the rest of the day along the banks of a river, from which the road turned aside towards evening and brought them within sight of a village, which was once a considerable town but which afforded them neither good victuals nor commodious lodging.

Thus he conducts his reader through wet and dry, over rough and smooth, without incidents, without reflection; and if he obtains his company for another day will dismiss him again at night equally fatigued with a like succession of rocks and streams, mountains and ruins.

This is the common style of those sons of enterprise who visit savage countries, and range through solitude and desolation; who pass a desert and tell that it is sandy; who cross a valley and find that it is green. There are others of more delicate sensibility that visit only the realms of elegance and softness; that wander through Italian palaces and amuse the gentle reader with catalogues of pictures; that hear masses in magnificent churches and recount the number of the pillars or variegations of the pavement. And there are yet others who, in disdain of trifles, copy inscriptions elegant and rude, ancient and modern; and transcribe into their book the walls of every edifice, sacred or civil. He that reads these books must consider his labor as its own reward, for he will find nothing on which attention can fix or which memory can retain.

He that would travel for the entertainment of others should remember that the great object of remark is human life. Every nation has

2. Books of travels.

something peculiar in its manufactures, its works of genius, its medicines, its agriculture, its customs, and its policy.[3] He only is a useful traveler who brings home something by which his country may be benefited; who procures some supply of want or some mitigation of evil, which may enable his readers to compare their condition with that of others, to improve it whenever it is worse, and whenever it is better to enjoy it.

No. 102.

Saturday, 29 March 1760.

It very seldom happens to man that his business is his pleasure. What is done from necessity is so often to be done when against the present inclination, and so often fills the mind with anxiety, that an habitual dislike steals upon us, and we shrink involuntarily from the remembrance of our task. This is the reason why almost every one wishes to quit his employment; he does not like another state, but is disgusted with his own.

From this unwillingness to perform more than is required of that which is commonly performed with reluctance, it proceeds that few authors write their own lives. Statesmen, courtiers, ladies, generals and seamen, have given to the world their own stories, and the events with which their different stations have made them acquainted. They retired to the closet[1] as to a place of quiet and amusement, and pleased themselves with writing, because they could lay down the pen whenever they were weary. But the author, however conspicuous or however important, either in the public eye or in his own, leaves his life to be related by his successors, for he cannot gratify his vanity but by sacrificing his ease.

It is commonly supposed that the uniformity of a studious life affords no matter for narration; but the truth is that of the most studious life a great part passes without study. An author partakes of the common condition of humanity; he is born and married like another man; he has hopes and fears, expectations and disappointments, griefs and joys, and friends and enemies, like a courtier or a statesman; nor can I conceive why his affairs should not excite curiosity as much as the whisper of a drawing room,[2] or the factions of a camp.

Nothing detains the reader's attention more powerfully than deep involutions of distress or sudden vicissitudes of fortune, and these might be abundantly afforded by memoirs of the sons of literature.[3]

3. Art of government.
1. Study.
2. That is, at Court.
3. Authors.

They are entangled by contracts which they know not how to fulfill, and obliged to write on subjects which they do not understand. Every publication is a new period of time from which some increase or declension of fame is to be reckoned. The gradations of a hero's life are from battle to battle, and of an author's from book to book.

Success and miscarriage have the same effects in all conditions. The prosperous are feared, hated and flattered; and the unfortunate avoided, pitied, and despised. No sooner is a book published than the writer may judge of the opinion of the world. If his acquaintance press round him in public places, or salute[4] him from the other side of the street; if invitations to dinner come thick upon him, and those with whom he dines keep him to supper;[5] if the ladies turn to him when his coat is plain, and the footmen serve him with attention and alacrity, he may be sure that his work has been praised by some leader of literary fashions.

Of declining reputation the symptoms are not less easily observed. If the author enters a coffee-house, he has a box[6] to himself; if he calls at a bookseller's, the boy turns his back; and, what is the most fatal of all prognostics, authors will visit him in a morning, and talk to him hour after hour of the malevolence of critics, the neglect of merit, the bad taste of the age, and the candor[7] of posterity.

All this modified and varied by accident and custom would form very amusing scenes of biography, and might recreate[8] many a mind which is very little delighted with conspiracies or battles, intrigues of a court or debates of a parliament: to this might be added all the changes of the countenance of a patron, traced from the first glow which flattery raises in his cheek, through ardor of fondness, vehemence of promise, magnificence of praise, excuse of delay, and lamentation of inability, to the last chill look of final dismission, when the one grows weary of soliciting and the other of hearing solicitation.

Thus copious are the materials which have been hitherto suffered to lie neglected, while the repositories of every family that has produced a soldier or a minister are ransacked, and libraries are crowded with useless folios of state papers which will never be read, and which contribute nothing to valuable knowledge.

I hope the learned will be taught to know their own strength and their value, and instead of devoting their lives to the honor of those who seldom thank them for their labors, resolve at last to do justice to themselves.

4. Greet.
5. In the eighteenth century, dinner was an afternoon meal and supper a light refreshment taken just before bedtime.
6. Booth.
7. Sympathetic attitude.
8. Entertain.

No. 103.

Saturday, 5 April 1760.[1]

Much of the pain and pleasure of mankind arises from the conjectures which everyone makes of the thoughts of others; we all enjoy praise which we do not hear, and resent contempt which we do not see. The Idler may therefore be forgiven if he suffers his imagination to represent to him what his readers will say or think when they are informed that they have now his last paper in their hands.

Value is more frequently raised by scarcity than by use. That which lay neglected when it was common rises in estimation as its quantity becomes less. We seldom learn the true want of what we have till it is discovered that we can have no more.

This essay will perhaps be read with care even by those who have not yet attended to any other; and he that finds this late attention recompensed will not forbear to wish that he had bestowed it sooner.

Though the Idler and his readers have contracted no close friendship, they are perhaps both unwilling to part. There are few things not purely evil of which we can say, without some emotion of uneasiness, "this is the last." Those who never could agree together shed tears when mutual discontent has determined them to final separation; of a place which has been frequently visited though without pleasure, the last look is taken with heaviness of heart; and the Idler, with all his chillness of tranquillity, is not wholly unaffected by the thought that his last essay is now before him.

This secret horror of the last is inseparable from a thinking being whose life is limited, and to whom death is dreadful. We always make a secret comparison between a part and the whole; the termination of any period of life reminds us that life itself has likewise its termination; when we have done anything for the last time, we involuntarily reflect that a part of the days allotted us is past, and that as more is past there is less remaining.

It is very happily and kindly provided that in every life there are certain pauses and interruptions, which force consideration upon the careless, and seriousness upon the light; points of time where one course of action ends and another begins; and by vicissitude of fortune, or alteration of employment, by change of place, or loss of friendship, we are forced to say of something, "this is the last."

An even and unvaried tenor of life always hides from our apprehension the approach of its end. Succession is not perceived but by variation; he that lives today as he lived yesterday, and expects that, as the present day is, such will be the morrow, easily conceives time as running

1. The motto for this *Idler* reads: "He bade him consider the final stage of a long life" (Juvenal, *Satires*, x. 275).

in a circle and returning to itself. The uncertainty of our duration is impressed commonly by dissimilitude of condition; it is only by finding life changeable that we are reminded of its shortness.

This conviction, however forcible at every new impression, is every moment fading from the mind; and partly by the inevitable incursion of new images, and partly by voluntary exclusion of unwelcome thoughts, we are again exposed to the universal fallacy; and we must do another thing for the last time, before we consider that the time is nigh when we shall do no more.

As the last *Idler* is published in that solemn week[2] which the Christian world has always set apart for the examination of the conscience, the review of life, the extinction of earthly desires, and the renovation of holy purposes, I hope that my readers are already disposed to view every incident with seriousness and improve it by meditation; and that when they see this series of trifles brought to a conclusion, they will consider that by outliving the *Idler,* they have passed weeks, months, and years which are now no longer in their power; that an end must in time be put to everything great as to everything little; that to life must come its last hour, and to this system of being its last day, the hour at which probation[3] ceases and repentance will be vain; the day in which every work of the hand and imagination of the heart shall be brought to judgment, and an everlasting futurity shall be determined.

2. The week preceding Easter.
3. The period of trial (i.e. human life).

Preface to A Dictionary of the English Language

It is the fate of those who toil at the lower employments of life to be rather driven by the fear of evil than attracted by the prospect of good; to be exposed to censure, without hope of praise; to be disgraced by miscarriage[1] or punished for neglect, where success would have been without applause and diligence without reward.

Among these unhappy mortals is the writer of dictionaries; whom mankind have considered not as the pupil but the slave of science, the pioneer[2] of literature, doomed only to remove rubbish and clear obstructions from the paths through which learning and genius press forward to conquest and glory, without bestowing a smile on the humble drudge that facilitates their progress. Every other author may aspire to praise; the lexicographer can only hope to escape reproach, and even this negative recompense has been yet granted to very few.

I have, notwithstanding this discouragement, attempted a dictionary of the English language which, while it was employed in the cultivation of every species of literature, has itself been hitherto neglected; suffered to spread, under the direction of chance, into wild exuberance; resigned to the tyranny of time and fashion; and exposed to the corruptions of ignorance, and caprices of innovation.

When I took the first survey of my undertaking, I found our speech copious without order, and energetic without rules: wherever I turned my view, there was perplexity to be disentangled and confusion to be regulated; choice was to be made out of boundless variety, without any established principle of selection; adulterations were to be detected without a settled test of purity; and modes of expression to be rejected or received without the suffrages[3] of any writers of classical reputation or acknowledged authority.

1. Failure.
2. Laborer.
3. Opinions.

Having therefore no assistance but from general grammar, I applied myself to the perusal of our writers; and noting whatever might be of use to ascertain or illustrate any word or phrase accumulated in time the materials of a dictionary, which, by degrees, I reduced to method, establishing to myself in the progress of the work such rules as experience and analogy suggested to me; experience, which practice and observation were continually increasing; and analogy, which, though in some words obscure, was evident in others.

In adjusting the orthography, which has been to this time unsettled and fortuitous, I found it necessary to distinguish those irregularities that are inherent in our tongue, and perhaps coeval with it, from others which the ignorance or negligence of later writers has produced. Every language has its anomalies which, though inconvenient and in themselves once unnecessary, must be tolerated among the imperfections of human things, and which require only to be registered that they may not be increased, and ascertained that they may not be confounded: but every language has likewise its improprieties and absurdities, which it is the duty of the lexicographer to correct or proscribe.

As language was at its beginning merely[4] oral, all words of necessary or common use were spoken before they were written; and while they were unfixed by any visible signs must have been spoken with great diversity, as we now observe those who cannot read catch sounds imperfectly and utter them negligently. When this wild and barbarous jargon was first reduced to an alphabet, every penman endeavored to express, as he could, the sounds which he was accustomed to pronounce or to receive, and vitiated in writing such words as were already vitiated in speech. The powers of the letters, when they were applied to a new language, must have been vague and unsettled, and therefore different hands would exhibit the same sound by different combinations.

From this uncertain pronunciation arise in a great part the various dialects of the same country, which will always be observed to grow fewer and less different as books are multiplied; and from this arbitrary representation of sounds by letters proceeds that diversity of spelling observable in the Saxon remains, and I suppose in the first books of every nation, which perplexes or destroys analogy, and produces anomalous formations that, being once incorporated, can never be afterward dismissed or reformed.

Of this kind are the derivatives *length* from *long, strength* from *strong, darling* from *dear, breadth* from *broad,* from *dry, drought,* and from *high, height,* which Milton, in zeal for analogy, writes *highth; Quid te exempta*

4. Entirely.

juvat spinis de pluribus una;[5] to change all would be too much, and to change one is nothing.

This uncertainty is most frequent in the vowels, which are so capriciously pronounced and so differently modified by accident or affectation, not only in every province but in every mouth, that to them, as is well known to etymologists, little regard is to be shown in the deduction of one language from another.

Such defects are not errors in orthography, but spots of barbarity impressed so deep in the English language that criticism can never wash them away: these, therefore, must be permitted to remain untouched; but many words have been altered by accident, or depraved[6] by ignorance, as the pronunciation of the vulgar has been weakly followed; and some still continue to be variously written, as authors differ in their care or skill: of these it was proper to inquire the true orthography, which I have always considered as depending on their derivation, and have therefore referred them to their original languages: thus I write *enchant, enchantment, enchanter,* after the French, and *incantation* after the Latin; thus *entire* is chosen rather than *intire,* because it passed to us not from the Latin *integer,* but from the French *entier.*

Of many words it is difficult to say whether they were immediately received from the Latin or the French, since at the time when we had dominions in France, we had Latin service in our churches. It is, however, my opinion, that the French generally supplied us; for we have few Latin words, among the terms of domestic use, which are not French; but many French, which are very remote from Latin.

Even in words of which the derivation is apparent, I have been often obliged to sacrifice uniformity to custom; thus I write, in compliance with a numberless majority, *convey* and *inveigh, deceit* and *receipt, fancy* and *phantom;* sometimes the derivative varies from the primitive, as *explain* and *explanation, repeat* and *repetition.*

Some combinations of letters having the same power are used indifferently without any discoverable reason of choice, as in *choak, choke; soap, sope; fewel, fuel,* and many others; which I have sometimes inserted twice, that those who search for them under either form may not search in vain.

In examining the orthography of any doubtful word, the mode of spelling by which it is inserted in the series of the dictionary is to be considered as that to which I give, perhaps not often rashly, the preference. I have left, in the examples, to every author his own practice unmolested, that the reader may balance suffrages and judge between

5. "What good does it do you to pluck out one of many thorns?" (Horace, *Epistles,* II. ii. 212).

6. Corrupted.

us: but this question is not always to be determined by reputed or by real learning; some men, intent upon greater things, have thought little on sounds and derivations; some, knowing in the ancient tongues, have neglected those in which our words are commonly to be sought. Thus Hammond[7] writes *fecibleness* for *feasibleness,* because I suppose he imagined it derived immediately from the Latin; and some words, such as *dependant, dependent; dependance, dependence,* vary their final syllable, as one or another language is present to the writer.

In this part of the work, where caprice has long wantoned without control, and vanity sought praise by petty reformation, I have endeavored to proceed with a scholar's reverence for antiquity, and a grammarian's regard to the genius of our tongue. I have attempted a few alterations, and among those few perhaps the greater part is from the modern to the ancient practice; and I hope I may be allowed to recommend to those whose thoughts have been perhaps employed too anxiously on verbal singularities, not to disturb, upon narrow views, or for minute propriety, the orthography of their fathers. It has been asserted that for the law to be *known* is of more importance than to be *right.* Change, says Hooker, is not made without inconvenience, even from worse to better.[8] There is in constancy and stability a general and lasting advantage, which will always overbalance the slow improvements of gradual correction. Much less ought our written language to comply with the corruptions of oral utterance, or copy that which every variation of time or place makes different from itself, and imitate those changes, which will again be changed, while imitation is employed in observing them.

This recommendation of steadiness and uniformity does not proceed from an opinion that particular combinations of letters have much influence on human happiness; or that truth may not be successfully taught by modes of spelling fanciful and erroneous: I am not yet so lost in lexicography, as to forget that *words are the daughters of earth, and that things are the sons of heaven.*[9] Language is only the instrument of science,[10] and words are but the signs of ideas: I wish, however, that the instrument might be less apt to decay, and that signs might be permanent, like the things which they denote.

In settling the orthography, I have not wholly neglected the pronunciation, which I have directed by printing an accent upon the acute[11] or elevated syllable. It will sometimes be found that the accent is placed by the author quoted on a different syllable from that marked in the alphabetical series; it is then to be understood that custom has varied,

7. Henry Hammond (d. 1660), author of *Paraphrase and Annotations on the New Testament.*
8. Richard Hooker (?1554–1600), *Laws of Ecclesiastical Polity,* IV. xiv.
9. The saying may be Johnson's.
10. Knowledge.
11. Stressed.

or that the author has, in my opinion, pronounced wrong. Short directions are sometimes given where the sound of letters is irregular; and if they are sometimes omitted, defect in such minute observations will be more easily excused than superfluity.

In the investigation both of the orthography and signification of words, their etymology was necessarily to be considered, and they were therefore to be divided into primitives and derivatives. A primitive word is that which can be traced no further to any English root; thus *circumspect, circumvent, circumstance, delude, concave,* and *complicate,* though compounds in the Latin are to us primitives. Derivatives are all those that can be referred to any word in English of greater simplicity.

The derivatives I have referred to their primitives, with an accuracy sometimes needless; for who does not see that *remoteness* comes from *remote, lovely* from *love, concavity* from *concave,* and *demonstrative* from *demonstrate*? but this grammatical exuberance the scheme of my work did not allow me to repress. It is of great importance in examining the general fabric of a language to trace one word from another, by noting the usual modes of derivation and inflection; and uniformity must be preserved in systematical works, though sometimes at the expense of particular propriety.

Among other derivatives I have been careful to insert and elucidate the anomalous plurals of nouns and preterits of verbs, which in the Teutonic dialects are very frequent and, though familiar to those who have always used them, interrupt and embarrass the learners of our language.

The two languages from which our primitives have been derived are the Roman and Teutonic: under the Roman I comprehend the French and provincial tongues;[12] and under the Teutonic range the Saxon, German, and all their kindred dialects. Most of our polysyllables are Roman, and our words of one syllable are very often Teutonic.

In assigning the Roman original, it has perhaps sometimes happened that I have mentioned only the Latin, when the word was borrowed from the French; and considering myself as employed only in the illustration of my own language, I have not been very careful to observe whether the Latin word be pure or barbarous, or the French elegant or obsolete.

For the Teutonic etymologies, I am commonly indebted to Junius and Skinner,[13] the only names which I have forborne to quote when I copied their books; not that I might appropriate their labors or usurp their honors, but that I might spare a perpetual repetition by one general acknowledgment. Of these, whom I ought not to mention but

12. Languages developed from Latin in what were provinces of the Roman Empire.

13. Francis Junius (1589–1677), author of *Etymologicum Anglicanum (English Etymologies)* (1743); and Stephen Skinner (1623–67), author of *Etymologicon Linguae Anglicanae (Etymological Dictionary of the English Language)* (1671).

with the reverence due to instructors and benefactors, Junius appears to have excelled in extent of learning, and Skinner in rectitude of understanding. Junius was accurately skilled in all the northern languages, Skinner probably examined the ancient and remoter dialects only by occasional inspection into dictionaries; but the learning of Junius is often of no other use than to show him a track by which he may deviate from his purpose, to which Skinner always presses forward by the shortest way. Skinner is often ignorant, but never ridiculous; Junius is always full of knowledge, but his variety distracts[14] his judgment and his learning is very frequently disgraced by his absurdities.

The votaries of the northern muses will not perhaps easily restrain their indignation when they find the name of Junius thus degraded by a disadvantageous comparison; but whatever reverence is due to his diligence or his attainments, it can be no criminal degree of censoriousness to charge that etymologist with want of judgment, who can seriously derive *dream* from *drama,* because *life is a drama and a drama is a dream,* and who declares with a tone of defiance that no man can fail to derive *moan* from *μόνος*, *monos, single* or *solitary,* who considers that grief naturally loves to be *alone.*[15]

Our knowledge of the northern literature is so scanty that of words undoubtedly Teutonic the original is not always to be found in any ancient language; and I have therefore inserted Dutch or German substitutes, which I consider not as radical but parallel, not as the parents but sisters of the English.

The words which are represented as thus related by descent or cognation[16] do not always agree in sense; for it is incident to words, as to their authors, to degenerate from[17] their ancestors, and to change their manners when they change their country. It is sufficient, in etymological inquiries, if the senses of kindred words be found such as may easily pass into each other, or such as may both be referred to one general idea.

The etymology, so far as it is yet known, was easily found in the volumes where it is particularly and professedly delivered; and, by proper attention to the rules of derivation, the orthography was soon adjusted. But to collect the words of our language was a task of greater difficulty: the deficiency of dictionaries was immediately apparent; and when they were exhausted, what was yet wanting must be sought by fortuitous and unguided excursions into books, and gleaned as industry should find or chance should offer it in the boundless chaos of a living speech. My search, however, has been either skillful or lucky for I have much augmented the vocabulary.

14. Confuses.
15. Johnson's long note, illustrating Junius's "etymological extravagance," is omitted.
16. Parallel derivation; kinship.
17. Change from the type or race of.

As my design was a dictionary, common or appellative,[18] I have omitted all words which have relation to proper names; such as *Arian, Socinian, Calvinist, Benedictine, Mahometan;* but have retained those of a more general nature, as *heathen, pagan.*

Of the terms of art[19] I have received such as could be found either in books of science or technical dictionaries; and have often inserted from philosophical[20] writers words which are supported perhaps only by a single authority, and which being not admitted into general use stand yet as candidates or probationers, and must depend for their adoption on the suffrage of futurity.

The words which our authors have introduced by their knowledge of foreign languages, or ignorance of their own, by vanity or wantonness, by compliance with fashion or lust of innovation, I have registered as they occurred, though commonly only to censure them, and warn others against the folly of naturalizing useless foreigners to the injury of the natives.

I have not rejected any by design, merely because they were unnecessary or exuberant;[21] but have received those which by different writers have been differently formed, as *viscid* and *viscidity, viscous* and *viscosity.*

Compounded or double words I have seldom noted, except when they obtain a signification different from that which the components have in their simple state. Thus *highwayman, woodman,* and *horsecourser,* require an explanation; but of *thieflike* or *coachdriver* no notice was needed, because the primitives contain the meaning of the compounds.

Words arbitrarily formed by a constant and settled analogy, like diminutive adjectives in *ish,* as *greenish, bluish,* adverbs in *ly,* as *dully, openly,* substantives in *ness,* as *vileness, faultiness,* were less diligently sought, and sometimes have been omitted when I had no authority that invited me to insert them; not that they are not genuine and regular offsprings of English roots, but because their relation to the primitive being always the same, their signification cannot be mistaken.

The verbal nouns in *ing,* such as the *keeping* of the castle, the *leading* of the army, are always neglected, or placed only to illustrate the sense of the verb, except when they signify things as well as actions, and have therefore a plural number, as *dwelling, living;* or have an absolute and abstract signification, as *coloring, painting, learning.*

The participles are likewise omitted unless, by signifying rather habit or quality than action, they take the nature of adjectives; as a *thinking* man, a man of prudence; a *pacing* horse, a horse that can pace: these I have ventured to call *participial adjectives.* But neither are these always

18. Of general meaning, as opposed to that of proper nouns.
19. Technical words.
20. Learned or scientific.
21. Overabundant.

inserted, because they are commonly to be understood without any danger of mistake by consulting the verb.

Obsolete words are admitted, when they are found in authors not obsolete, or when they have any force or beauty that may deserve revival.

As composition is one of the chief characteristics of a language, I have endeavored to make some reparation for the universal negligence of my predecessors, by inserting great numbers of compounded words, as may be found under *after, fore, new, night, fair,*[22] and many more. These, numerous as they are, might be multiplied, but that use and curiosity are here satisfied, and the frame of our language and modes of our combination are amply discovered.[23]

Of some forms of composition, such as that by which *re* is prefixed to note *repetition,* and *un* to signify *contrariety* or *privation,* all the examples cannot be accumulated, because the use of these particles, if not wholly arbitrary, is so little limited that they are hourly united to new words as occasion requires, or is imagined to require them.

There is another kind of composition more frequent in our language than perhaps in any other, from which arises to foreigners the greatest difficulty. We modify the signification of many verbs by a particle subjoined; as to *come off,* to escape by a fetch;[24] to *fall on,* to attack; to *fall off,* to apostatize; to *break off,* to stop abruptly; to *bear out,* to justify; to *fall in,* to comply; to *give over,* to cease; to *set off,* to embellish; to *set in,* to begin a continual tenor;[25] to *set out,* to begin a course or journey; to *take off,* to copy; with innumerable expressions of the same kind, of which some appear wildly irregular, being so far distant from the sense of the simple words that no sagacity will be able to trace the steps by which they arrived at the present use. These I have noted with great care; and though I cannot flatter myself that the collection is complete, I have perhaps so far assisted the students of our language that this kind of phraseology will be no longer insuperable; and the combinations of verbs and particles, by chance omitted, will be easily explained by comparison with those that may be found.

Many words yet stand supported only by the name of Bailey, Ainsworth, Phillips,[26] or the contracted Dict. for Dictionaries subjoined; of these I am not always certain that they are seen in any book but the works of lexicographers. Of such I have omitted many because I had never read them; and many I have inserted because they may perhaps exist, though they have escaped my notice: they are, however,

22. W. R. Keast suggests that *fair* was the printer's misreading of *semi.*

23. Revealed.

24. Trick.

25. Course.

26. Nathan Bailey was the author of a *Universal Etymological English Dictionary* (1721); Robert Ainsworth compiled a Latin-English *Thesaurus* (1736); Edward Phillips, Milton's nephew, wrote *A New World of English Words* (1658).

to be yet considered as resting only upon the credit of former dictionaries. Others which I considered as useful or know to be proper, though I could not at present support them by authorities, I have suffered to stand upon my own attestation, claiming the same privilege with my predecessors of being sometimes credited without proof.

The words, thus selected and disposed, are grammatically considered; they are referred to the different parts of speech; traced, when they are irregularly inflected, through their various terminations; and illustrated by observations, not indeed of great or striking importance, separately considered, but necessary to the elucidation of our language, and hitherto neglected or forgotten by English grammarians.

That part of my work on which I expect malignity[27] most frequently to fasten is the explanation; in which I cannot hope to satisfy those who are perhaps not inclined to be pleased, since I have not always been able to satisfy myself. To interpret a language by itself is very difficult; many words cannot be explained by synonyms because the idea signified by them has not more than one appellation; nor by paraphrase, because simple ideas[28] cannot be described. When the nature of things is unknown, or the notion unsettled and indefinite, and various in various minds, the words by which such notions are conveyed or such things denoted will be ambiguous and perplexed. And such is the fate of hapless lexicography that not only darkness, but light, impedes and distresses it; things may be not only too little, but too much known, to be happily illustrated. To explain requires the use of terms less abstruse than that which is to be explained, and such terms cannot always be found; for as nothing can be proved but by supposing something intuitively known and evident without proof, so nothing can be defined but by the use of words too plain to admit a definition.

Other words there are, of which the sense is too subtle and evanescent to be fixed in a paraphrase; such are all those which are by the grammarians termed expletives, and, in dead languages, are suffered to pass for empty sounds, of no other use than to fill a verse or to modulate a period,[29] but which are easily perceived in living tongues to have power and emphasis, though it be sometimes such as no other form of expression can convey.

My labor has likewise been much increased by a class of verbs too frequent in the English language, of which the signification is so loose and general, the use so vague and indeterminate, and the senses detorted[30] so widely from the first idea, that it is hard to trace them through the maze of variation, to catch them on the brink of utter inanity, to circumscribe them by any limitations, or interpret them by

27. Malice.
28. Sense perceptions or ideas incapable of division into parts.
29. Phrase or sentence.
30. Twisted in meaning.

any words of distinct and settled meaning; such are *bear, break, come, cast, fall, get, give, do, put, set, go, run, make, take, turn, throw.* If of these the whole power is not accurately delivered, it must be remembered that while our language is yet living, and variable by the caprice of every tongue that speaks it, these words are hourly shifting their relations, and can no more be ascertained in a dictionary than a grove, in the agitation of a storm, can be accurately delineated from its picture in the water.

The particles are among all nations applied with so great latitude that they are not easily reducible under any regular scheme of explication: this difficulty is not less, nor perhaps greater, in English than in other languages. I have labored them with diligence, I hope with success; such at least as can be expected in a task which no man, however learned or sagacious, has yet been able to perform.

Some words there are which I cannot explain because I do not understand them; these might have been omitted very often with little inconvenience, but I would not so far indulge my vanity as to decline this confession: for when Tully[31] owns himself ignorant whether *lessus,* in the *Twelve Tables,*[32] means a *funeral song,* or *mourning garment,* and Aristotle doubts whether οὐρεὺς in the *Iliad,* signifies a *mule,* or *muleteer,* I may surely, without shame, leave some obscurities to happier industry or future information.

The rigor of interpretative lexicography requires that the explanation, and the word explained, should be always reciprocal; this I have always endeavored, but could not always attain. Words are seldom exactly synonymous; a new term was not introduced but because the former was thought inadequate: names, therefore, have often many ideas,[33] but few ideas have many names. It was then necessary to use the proximate word, for the deficiency of single terms can very seldom be supplied by circumlocution; nor is the inconvenience great of such mutilated interpretations, because the sense may easily be collected entire from the examples.

In every word of extensive use, it was requisite to mark the progress of its meaning, and show by what gradations of intermediate sense it has passed from its primitive to its remote and accidental signification; so that every foregoing explanation should tend to that which follows, and the series be regularly concatenated[34] from the first notion to the last.

This is specious,[35] but not always practicable; kindred senses may be so interwoven that the perplexity[36] cannot be disentangled, nor any

31. Marcus Tullius Cicero.
32. An early Roman legal code.
33. Images; conceptions.
34. Linked together.
35. Plausible.
36. Intertwining.

reason be assigned why one should be ranged before the other. When the radical idea[37] branches out into parallel ramifications, how can a consecutive series be formed of senses in their nature collateral? The shades of meaning sometimes pass imperceptibly into each other; so that though on one side they apparently differ, yet it is impossible to mark the point of contact. Ideas of the same race, though not exactly alike, are sometimes so little different that no words can express the dissimilitude, though the mind easily perceives it when they are exhibited together; and sometimes there is such a confusion of acceptations that discernment is wearied and distinction puzzled, and perseverance herself hurries to an end by crowding together what she cannot separate.

These complaints of difficulty will, by those that have never considered words beyond their popular use, be thought only the jargon of a man willing to magnify his labors, and procure veneration to his studies by involution[38] and obscurity. But every art is obscure to those that have not learned it: this uncertainty of terms and commixture of ideas is well known to those who have joined philosophy with grammar; and if I have not expressed them very clearly, it must be remembered that I am speaking of that which words are insufficient to explain.

The original sense of words is often driven out of use by their metaphorical acceptations, yet must be inserted for the sake of a regular origination. Thus I know not whether *ardor* is used for *material heat,* or whether *flagrant,* in English, ever signifies the same with *burning;* yet such are the primitive ideas of these words, which are therefore set first though without examples, that the figurative senses may be commodiously[39] deduced.

Such is the exuberance of signification which many words have obtained that it was scarcely possible to collect all their senses; sometimes the meaning of derivatives must be sought in the mother term, and sometimes deficient explanations of the primitive may be supplied in the train of derivation. In any case of doubt or difficulty, it will be always proper to examine all the words of the same race; for some words are slightly passed over to avoid repetition, some admitted easier and clearer explanation than others, and all will be better understood as they are considered in greater variety of structures and relations.

All the interpretations of words are not written with the same skill or the same happiness: things equally easy in themselves are not all equally easy to any single mind. Every writer of a long work commits errors where there appears neither ambiguity to mislead nor obscurity to confound him; and in a search like this, many felicities of expression will be casually overlooked, many convenient parallels will be forgot-

37. Root; basic meaning.
38. Intricacy.
39. Conveniently.

ten, and many particulars will admit improvement from a mind utterly unequal to the whole performance.

But many seeming faults are to be imputed rather to the nature of the undertaking than the negligence of the performer. Thus some explanations are unavoidably reciprocal or circular, as *hind, the female of the stag; stag, the male of the hind:* sometimes easier words are changed into harder, as *burial* into *sepulture* or *interment, drier* into *desiccative, dryness* into *siccity* or *aridity, fit* into *paroxysm;* for the easiest word, whatever it be, can never be translated into one more easy. But easiness and difficulty are merely relative, and if the present prevalence of our language should invite foreigners to this dictionary, many will be assisted by those words which now seem only to increase or produce obscurity. For this reason I have endeavored frequently to join a Teutonic and Roman interpretation, as to *cheer,* to *gladden* or *exhilarate,* that every learner of English may be assisted by his own tongue.

The solution of all difficulties and the supply of all defects must be sought in the examples subjoined to the various senses of each word, and ranged according to the time of their authors.

When first I collected these authorities, I was desirous that every quotation should be useful to some other end than the illustration of a word; I therefore extracted from philosophers principles of science; from historians remarkable facts; from chemists complete processes; from divines striking exhortations; and from poets beautiful descriptions. Such is design while it is yet at a distance from execution. When the time called upon me to range this accumulation of elegance and wisdom into an alphabetical series, I soon discovered that the bulk of my volumes would fright away the student, and was forced to depart from my scheme of including all that was pleasing or useful in English literature, and reduce my transcripts very often to clusters of words in which scarcely any meaning is retained; thus to the weariness of copying, I was condemned to add the vexation of expunging. Some passages I have yet spared which may relieve the labor of verbal searches, and intersperse with verdure and flowers the dusty deserts of barren philology.

The examples, thus mutilated, are no longer to be considered as conveying the sentiments or doctrine of their authors; the word for the sake of which they are inserted, with all its appendant clauses, has been carefully preserved; but it may sometimes happen, by hasty detruncation, that the general tendency of the sentence may be changed: the divine may desert his tenets, or the philosopher his system.

Some of the examples have been taken from writers who were never mentioned as masters of elegance or models of style; but words must be sought where they are used; and in what pages, eminent for purity, can terms of manufacture or agriculture be found? Many quotations serve no other purpose than that of proving the bare existence of words, and are therefore selected with less scrupulousness than those which are to teach their structures and relations.

My purpose was to admit no testimony of living authors, that I might not be misled by partiality, and that none of my cotemporaries might have reason to complain; nor have I departed from this resolution but when some performance of uncommon excellence excited my veneration, when my memory supplied me, from late books, with an example that was wanting, or when my heart, in the tenderness of friendship, solicited admission for a favorite name.

So far have I been from any care to grace my pages with modern decorations that I have studiously endeavored to collect examples and authorities from the writers before the Restoration, whose works I regard as "the wells of English undefiled,"[40] as the pure sources of genuine diction. Our language, for almost a century, has, by the concurrence of many causes, been gradually departing from its original Teutonic character, and deviating towards a Gallic structure and phraseology, from which it ought to be our endeavor to recall it by making our ancient volumes the groundwork of style, admitting among the additions of later times only such as may supply real deficiencies, such as are readily adopted by the genius[41] of our tongue, and incorporate easily with our native idioms.

But as every language has a time of rudeness[42] antecedent to perfection, as well as of false refinement and declension,[43] I have been cautious lest my zeal for antiquity might drive me into times too remote and crowd my book with words now no longer understood. I have fixed Sidney's work for the boundary beyond which I make few excursions. From the authors which rose in the time of Elizabeth, a speech might be formed adequate to all the purposes of use and elegance. If the language of theology were extracted from Hooker and the translation of the Bible; the terms of natural knowledge[44] from Bacon; the phrases of policy, war, and navigation from Raleigh; the dialect of poetry and fiction from Spenser and Sidney; and the diction of common life from Shakespeare, few ideas would be lost to mankind for want of English words in which they might be expressed.

It is not sufficient that a word is found unless it be so combined as that its meaning is apparently[45] determined by the tract[46] and tenor of the sentence; such passages I have therefore chosen, and when it happened that any author gave a definition of a term or such an explanation as is equivalent to a definition, I have placed his authority as a

40. Spenser's praise of Chaucer (*Faerie Queene,* IV. ii. 2).
41. Native character.
42. Barbarism.
43. Degeneration.
44. Science.
45. Obviously.
46. Continuity (that is, context).

supplement to my own, without regard to the chronological order that is otherwise observed.

Some words, indeed, stand unsupported by any authority, but they are commonly derivative nouns or adverbs, formed from their primitives by regular and constant analogy, or names of things seldom occurring in books, or words of which I have reason to doubt[47] the existence.

There is more danger of censure from the multiplicity than paucity of examples; authorities will sometimes seem to have been accumulated without necessity or use, and perhaps some will be found which might, without loss, have been omitted. But a work of this kind is not hastily to be charged with superfluities: those quotations which to careless or unskillful perusers appear only to repeat the same sense will often exhibit to a more accurate examiner diversities of signification or, at least, afford different shades of the same meaning: one will show the word applied to persons, another to things; one will express an ill, another a good, and a third a neutral sense; one will prove the expression genuine from an ancient author; another will show it elegant from a modern: a doubtful authority is corroborated by another of more credit; an ambiguous sentence is ascertained by a passage clear and determinate; the word, how often soever repeated, appears with new associates and in different combinations, and every quotation contributes something to the stability or enlargement of the language.

When words are used equivocally, I receive them in either sense; when they are metaphorical, I adopt them in their primitive acceptation.

I have sometimes, though rarely, yielded to the temptation of exhibiting a genealogy of sentiments, by showing how one author copied the thoughts and diction of another: such quotations are indeed little more than repetitions which might justly be censured, did they not gratify the mind by affording a kind of intellectual history.

The various syntactical structures occurring in the examples have been carefully noted; the license or negligence with which many words have been hitherto used has made our style capricious and indeterminate; when the different combinations of the same word are exhibited together, the preference is readily given to propriety, and I have often endeavored to direct the choice.

Thus have I labored by settling the orthography, displaying the analogy, regulating the structures, and ascertaining the signification of English words, to perform all the parts of a faithful lexicographer: but I have not always executed my own scheme or satisfied my own expectations. The work, whatever proofs of diligence and attention it may exhibit, is yet capable of many improvements: the orthography which I recommend is still controvertible, the etymology which I adopt is un-

47. Suspect. Alternatively, Johnson may have intended to write, "I have no reason to doubt . . ." as W. R. Keast suggests.

certain and perhaps frequently erroneous; the explanations are sometimes too much contracted and sometimes too much diffused, the significations are distinguished rather with subtilty than skill, and the attention is harassed with unnecessary minuteness.

The examples are too often injudiciously truncated, and perhaps sometimes, I hope very rarely, alleged in a mistaken sense; for in making this collection I trusted more to memory than, in a state of disquiet and embarrassment, memory can contain, and purposed to supply at the review what was left incomplete in the first transcription.

Many terms appropriated to particular occupations, though necessary and significant, are undoubtedly omitted; and of the words most studiously considered and exemplified, many senses have escaped observation.

Yet these failures, however frequent, may admit extenuation and apology. To have attempted much is always laudable, even when the enterprise is above the strength that undertakes it: to rest below his own aim is incident to everyone whose fancy is active, and whose views are comprehensive; nor is any man satisfied with himself because he has done much, but because he can conceive little. When first I engaged in this work, I resolved to leave neither words nor things unexamined, and pleased myself with a prospect of the hours which I should revel away in feasts of literature, with the obscure recesses of northern learning which I should enter and ransack;[48] the treasures with which I expected every search into those neglected mines to reward my labor, and the triumph with which I should display my acquisitions to mankind. When I had thus inquired into the original of words, I resolved to show likewise my attention to things; to pierce deep into every science, to inquire the nature of every substance of which I inserted the name, to limit every idea by a definition strictly logical, and exhibit every production of art or nature in an accurate description, that my book might be in place of all other dictionaries whether appellative or technical. But these were the dreams of a poet doomed at last to wake a lexicographer. I soon found that it is too late to look for instruments when the works calls for execution, and that whatever abilities I had brought to my task, with those I must finally perform it. To deliberate whenever I doubted, to inquire whenever I was ignorant, would have protracted the undertaking without end, and perhaps without much improvement; for I did not find by my first experiments[49] that what I had not of my own was easily to be obtained: I saw that one inquiry only gave occasion to another, that book referred to book, that to search was not always to find, and to find was not always to be informed; and that thus to pursue perfection was, like the first inhabitants of Arcadia, to

48. Little was known in Johnson's time of the relation of English to its Germanic cognates.

49. Experiences.

chase the sun, which, when they had reached the hill where he seemed to rest, was still beheld at the same distance from them.

I then contracted my design, determining to confide in myself, and no longer to solicit auxiliaries which produced more encumbrance than assistance: by this I obtained at least one advantage, that I set limits to my work, which would in time be ended though not completed.

Despondency has never so far prevailed as to depress me to negligence; some faults will at last appear to be the effects of anxious diligence and persevering activity. The nice[50] and subtle ramifications of meaning were not easily avoided by a mind intent upon accuracy, and convinced of the necessity of disentangling combinations and separating similitudes. Many of the distinctions which to common readers appear useless and idle will be found real and important by men versed in the school of philosophy,[51] without which no dictionary shall ever be accurately compiled or skillfully examined.

Some senses, however, there are which, though not the same, are yet so nearly allied that they are often confounded. Most men think indistinctly, and therefore cannot speak with exactness; and consequently some examples might be indifferently put to either signification: this uncertainty is not to be imputed to me, who do not form but register the language; who do not teach men how they should think, but relate how they have hitherto expressed their thoughts.

The imperfect sense of some examples I lamented but could not remedy, and hope they will be compensated by innumerable passages selected with propriety, and preserved with exactness; some shining with sparks of imagination, and some replete with treasures of wisdom.

The orthography and etymology, though imperfect, are not imperfect for want of care, but because care will not always be successful, and recollection or information come too late for use.

That many terms of art and manufacture are omitted must be frankly acknowledged; but for this defect I may boldly allege that it was unavoidable: I could not visit caverns to learn the miner's language, nor take a voyage to perfect my skill in the dialect of navigation, nor visit the warehouses of merchants and shops of artificers to gain the names of commodities, utensils, tools, and operations, of which no mention is found in books; what favorable accident or easy inquiry brought within my reach has not been neglected; but it had been a hopeless labor to glean up words by courting living information, and contesting with the sullenness of one and the roughness of another.

To furnish the academicians della Crusca[52] with words of this kind, a series of comedies called *La Fiera*, or *The Fair*, was professedly written

50. Exact, precise.

51. Scholastic (medieval) philosophy, which emphasized accuracy of terminology.

52. The Accademia della Crusca was founded at Florence in 1582 to standardize the Italian language.

by Buonarroti;[53] but I had no such assistant, and therefore was content to want[54] what they must have wanted likewise, had they not luckily been so supplied.

Nor are all words which are not found in the vocabulary to be lamented as omissions. Of the laborious and mercantile part of the people, the diction is in a great measure casual and mutable; many of their terms are formed for some temporary or local convenience, and though current at certain times and places are in others utterly unknown. This fugitive cant,[55] which is always in a state of increase or decay, cannot be regarded as any part of the durable materials of a language, and therefore must be suffered to perish with other things unworthy of preservation.

Care will sometimes betray to the appearance of negligence. He that is catching opportunities which seldom occur, will suffer those to pass by unregarded which he expects hourly to return; he that is searching for rare and remote things will neglect those that are obvious and familiar: thus many of the most common and cursory[56] words have been inserted with little illustration, because in gathering the authorities I forbore to copy those which I thought likely to occur whenever they were wanted. It is remarkable that, in reviewing my collection, I found the word "sea" unexemplified.

Thus it happens that in things difficult there is danger from ignorance, and in things easy from confidence; the mind, afraid of greatness and disdainful of littleness, hastily withdraws herself from painful searches, and passes with scornful rapidity over tasks not adequate to her powers, sometimes too secure for caution and again too anxious for vigorous effort; sometimes idle in a plain path, and sometimes distracted in labyrinths and dissipated[57] by different intentions.

A large work is difficult because it is large, even though all its parts might singly be performed with facility; where there are many things to be done, each must be allowed its share of time and labor in the proportion only which it bears to the whole; nor can it be expected that the stones which form the dome of a temple should be squared and polished like the diamond of a ring.

Of the event of this work, for which, having labored it with so much application, I cannot but have some degree of parental fondness, it is natural to form conjectures. Those who have been persuaded to think well of my design will require that it should fix our language and put a stop to those alterations which time and chance have hitherto been suffered to make in it without opposition. With this consequence I will

53. Michelangelo Buonarroti, the great sculptor, painter, and poet.
54. Do without.
55. Evanescent specialized language.
56. Words passed over rapidly.
57. Diffused, diverted.

confess that I flattered myself for a while; but now begin to fear that I have indulged expectation which neither reason nor experience can justify. When we see men grow old and die at a certain time one after another, from century to century, we laugh at the elixir that promises to prolong life to a thousand years; and with equal justice may the lexicographer be derided, who being able to produce no example of a nation that has preserved their words and phrases from mutability, shall imagine that his dictionary can embalm his language and secure it from corruption and decay, that it is in his power to change sublunary nature, and clear the world at once from folly, vanity, and affectation.

With this hope, however, academies have been instituted to guard the avenues of their languages, to retain fugitives[58] and repulse intruders; but their vigilance and activity have hitherto been vain; sounds are too volatile and subtle for legal restraints; to enchain syllables and to lash the wind are equally the undertakings of pride, unwilling to measure its desires by its strength. The French language has visibly changed under the inspection of the Academy,[59] the style of Amelot's translation of Father Paul is observed by Le Courayer[60] to be "un peu passé";[61] and no Italian will maintain that the diction of any modern writer is not perceptibly different from that of Boccace, Machiavel, or Caro.[62]

Total and sudden transformations of a language seldom happen; conquests and migrations are now very rare: but there are other causes of change which, though slow in their operation, and invisible in their progress, are perhaps as much superior to human resistance, as the revolutions of the sky, or intumescence[63] of the tide. Commerce, however necessary, however lucrative, as it depraves the manners, corrupts the language; they that have frequent intercourse with strangers, to whom they endeavor to accommodate themselves, must in time learn a mingled dialect, like the jargon which serves the traffickers[64] on the Mediterranean and Indian coasts. This will not always be confined to the exchange, the warehouse, or the port, but will be communicated by degrees to other ranks of the people, and be at last incorporated with the current speech.

There are likewise internal causes equally forcible. The language most likely to continue long without alteration would be that of a nation raised a little, and but a little above barbarity, secluded from strangers, and totally employed in procuring the conveniencies of life; either

58. Ephemeral words.

59. The French Academy was founded in 1635 to stabilize the French language.

60. Paolo Sarpi's *History of the Council of Trent* was translated into French by Amelot in 1683 and by Le Courayer in 1736.

61. "Somewhat old-fashioned."

62. Boccaccio (1313–75); Machiavelli (1469–1527); Annibale Caro (1507–66).

63. Rising.

64. Traders.

without books or, like some of the Mahometan countries, with very few: men thus busied and unlearned, having only such words as common use requires, would perhaps long continue to express the same notions by the same signs. But no such constancy can be expected in a people polished by arts and classed by subordination,[65] where one part of the community is sustained and accommodated by the labor of the other. Those who have much leisure to think will always be enlarging the stock of ideas, and every increase of knowledge, whether real or fancied, will produce new words or combinations of words. When the mind is unchained from necessity, it will range after convenience; when it is left at large in the fields of speculation, it will shift opinions; as any custom is disused, the words that expressed it must perish with it; as any opinion grows popular, it will innovate speech in the same proportion as it alters practice.

As by the cultivation of various sciences, a language is amplified, it will be more furnished with words deflected from their original sense; the geometrician will talk of a courtier's zenith, or the eccentric[66] virtue of a wild hero, and the physician of sanguine expectations and phlegmatic[67] delays. Copiousness of speech will give opportunities to capricious choice, by which some words will be preferred and others degraded; vicissitudes of fashion will enforce the use of new or extend the signification of known terms. The tropes of poetry will make hourly encroachments, and the metaphorical will become the current sense: pronunciation will be varied by levity or ignorance, and the pen must at length comply with the tongue; illiterate writers will at one time or other, by public infatuation, rise into renown, who, not knowing the original import of words, will use them with colloquial licentiousness, confound distinction, and forget propriety.[68] As politeness increases, some expressions will be considered as too gross and vulgar for the delicate, others as too formal and ceremonious for the gay and airy; new phrases are therefore adopted, which must for the same reasons, be in time dismissed. Swift, in his petty[69] treatise on the English language,[70] allows that new words must sometimes be introduced, but proposes that none should be suffered to become obsolete. But what makes a word obsolete more than general agreement to forbear it? and how shall it be continued when it conveys an offensive idea, or recalled again into the mouths of mankind when it has once become unfamiliar by disuse and unpleasing by unfamiliarity?

65. Divided into distinct social classes.
66. Off-center, irregular.
67. Obsolete medical terms, "sanguine" referring to a physical temperament dominated by blood, "phlegmatic" to a temperament dominated by phlegm: the first was characteristically hopeful; the second, lethargic.
68. Suitableness.
69. Little.
70. *A Proposal for Correcting, Improving, and Ascertaining the English Tongue* (1712).

There is another cause of alteration more prevalent than any other, which yet in the present state of the world cannot be obviated. A mixture of two languages will produce a third distinct from both, and they will always be mixed where the chief part of education, and the most conspicuous accomplishment, is skill in ancient or in foreign tongues. He that has long cultivated another language will find its words and combinations crowd upon his memory; and haste or negligence, refinement or affectation, will obtrude borrowed terms and exotic expressions.

The great pest of speech is frequency of translation. No book was ever turned from one language into another without imparting something of its native idiom; this is the most mischievous and comprehensive innovation; single words may enter by thousands and the fabric of the tongue continue the same, but new phraseology changes much at once; it alters not the single stones of the building but the order [70a] of the columns. If an academy should be established for the cultivation of our style, which I, who can never wish to see dependence multiplied, hope the spirit of English liberty will hinder or destroy, let them, instead of compiling grammars and dictionaries, endeavor, with all their influence, to stop the license of translators, whose idleness and ignorance, if it be suffered to proceed, will reduce us to babble a dialect of France.

If the changes that we fear be thus irresistible, what remains but to acquiesce with silence, as in the other insurmountable distresses of humanity? It remains that we retard what we cannot repel, that we palliate what we cannot cure. Life may be lengthened by care, though death cannot be ultimately defeated: tongues, like governments, have a natural tendency to degeneration; we have long preserved our constitution, let us make some struggles for our language.

In hope of giving longevity to that which its own nature forbids to be immortal, I have devoted this book, the labor of years, to the honor of my country, that we may no longer yield the palm[71] of philology without a contest to the nations of the Continent. The chief glory of every people arises from its authors: whether I shall add anything by my own writings to the reputation of English literature must be left to time: much of my life has been lost under the pressures of disease; much has been trifled away; and much has always been spent in provision for the day that was passing over me; but I shall not think my employment useless or ignoble if by my assistance foreign nations and distant ages gain access to the propagators of knowledge, and understand the teachers of truth; if my labors afford light to the repositories of science, and add celebrity to Bacon, to Hooker, to Milton, and to Boyle.[72]

70a. Style, such as Doric, Ionic, etc.

71. Prize.

72. Robert Boyle, 17th-century scientist, one of the founders of the Royal Society.

When I am animated by this wish, I look with pleasure on my book, however defective, and deliver it to the world with the spirit of a man that has endeavored well. That it will immediately become popular I have not promised to myself: a few wild blunders and risible absurdities, from which no work of such multiplicity was ever free, may for a time furnish folly with laughter, and harden ignorance in contempt; but useful diligence will at last prevail, and there never can be wanting some who distinguish desert,[73] who will consider that no dictionary of a living tongue ever can be perfect, since while it is hastening to publication some words are budding and some falling away; that a whole life cannot be spent upon syntax and etymology, and that even a whole life would not be sufficient; that he whose design includes whatever language can express, must often speak of what he does not understand; that a writer will sometimes be hurried by eagerness to the end, and sometimes faint with weariness under a task, which Scaliger[74] compares to the labors of the anvil and the mine; that what is obvious is not always known, and what is known is not always present; that sudden fits of inadvertency will surprise vigilance, slight avocations will seduce attention, and casual eclipses of the mind will darken learning; and that the writer shall often in vain trace his memory at the moment of need for that which yesterday he knew with intuitive readiness, and which will come uncalled into his thoughts tomorrow.

In this work, when it shall be found that much is omitted, let it not be forgotten that much likewise is performed; and though no book was ever spared out of tenderness to the author, and the world is little solicitous to know whence proceeded the faults of that which it condemns; yet it may gratify curiosity to inform it, that the *English Dictionary* was written with little assistance of the learned, and without any patronage of the great; not in the soft obscurities of retirement or under the shelter of academic bowers, but amidst inconvenience and distraction, in sickness and in sorrow. It may repress the triumph of malignant criticism to observe that if our language is not here fully displayed, I have only failed in an attempt which no human powers have hitherto completed. If the lexicons of ancient tongues, now immutably fixed and comprised in a few volumes, are yet, after the toil of successive ages, inadequate and delusive; if the aggregated knowledge, and cooperating diligence of the Italian academicians did not secure them from the censure of Beni;[75] if the embodied critics of France, when fifty years had been spent upon their work,[76] were obliged to

73. Merit.

74. Joseph Justus Scaliger (1540–1609), professor at Geneva and Leyden, one of the greatest of classical scholars. Johnson alludes to a Latin poem by Scaliger, *Against the Compilers of Lexicons.*

75. Paolo Beni, Italian critic of the Renaissance.

76. The first edition of the French Academy's *Dictionary* did not appear until 1694, about sixty years after the Academy's founding.

change its economy[77] and give their second edition another form, I may surely be contented without the praise of perfection, which, if I could obtain, in this gloom of solitude, what would it avail me? I have protracted my work till most of those whom I wished to please have sunk into the grave, and success and miscarrriage are empty sounds: I therefore dismiss it with frigid tranquillity, having little to fear or hope from censure or from praise.

77. Principles of organization.

Preface to The Plays of William Shakespeare

That praises are without reason lavished on the dead, and that the honors due only to excellence are paid to antiquity, is a complaint likely to be always continued by those who, being able to add nothing to truth, hope for eminence from the heresies of paradox; or those who, being forced by disappointment upon consolatory expedients, are willing to hope from posterity what the present age refuses and flatter themselves that the regard which is yet denied by envy will be at last bestowed by time.

Antiquity, like every other quality that attracts the notice of mankind, has undoubtedly votaries that reverence it not from reason, but from prejudice. Some seem to admire indiscriminately whatever has been long preserved, without considering that time has sometimes cooperated with chance; all perhaps are more willing to honor past than present excellence; and the mind contemplates genius through the shades of age, as the eye surveys the sun through artificial opacity. The great contention of criticism is to find the faults of the moderns and the beauties of the ancients. While an author is yet living, we estimate his powers by his worst performance; and when he is dead, we rate them by his best.

To works, however, of which the excellence is not absolute and definite, but gradual and comparative; to works not raised upon principles demonstrative and scientific but appealing wholly to observation and experience, no other test can be applied than length of duration and continuance of esteem. What mankind have long possessed they have often examined and compared; and if they persist to value the possession, it is because frequent comparisons have confirmed opinion in its favor. As among the works of nature no man can properly call a river deep or a mountain high, without the knowledge of many mountains and many rivers; so, in the productions of genius, nothing can be styled excellent till it has been compared with other works of the same kind. Demonstration immediately displays its power and has nothing to hope or fear from the flux of years; but works tentative and experimental must be estimated by their proportion to the general and collective ability of man, as it is discovered in a long succession of endeavors. Of the first building that was raised, it might be with certainty determined that it was round or square, but whether it was spacious or lofty must have been referred to time. The Pythagorean scale of numbers[1] was at once discovered to be perfect; but the poems of Homer we yet know not to transcend the common limits of human intelligence but by remarking that nation after nation, and century after century, has been able to do little more than transpose his incidents, new-name his characters, and paraphrase his sentiments.

The reverence due to writings that have long subsisted arises, therefore, not from any credulous confidence in the superior wisdom of past ages or gloomy persuasion of the degeneracy of mankind, but is the consequence of acknowledged and indubitable positions that what has been longest known has been most considered, and what is most considered is best understood.

The poet of whose works I have undertaken the revision[2] may now begin to assume the dignity of an ancient and claim the privilege of established fame and prescriptive veneration.[3] He has long outlived his century, the term commonly fixed as the test of literary merit. Whatever advantages he might once derive from personal allusions, local customs, or temporary opinions have for many years been lost; and every topic of merriment or motive of sorrow which the modes of artificial[4] life afforded him now only obscure the scenes which they once illuminated. The effects of favor and competition are at an end; the tradition of his friendships and his enmities have perished; his works support no opinion with arguments nor supply any faction with invectives; they can neither indulge vanity nor gratify malignity,[5] but are read without any other reason than the desire of pleasure and are therefore praised only as pleasure is obtained; yet, thus unassisted by interest[6] or passion, they have passed through variations of taste and changes of manners, and, as they devolved from one generation to another, have received new honors at every transmission.

But because human judgment, though it be gradually gaining upon certainty, never becomes infallible; and approbation, though long continued, may yet be only the approbation of prejudice or fashion; it is

1. The Greek philosopher Pythagoras discovered that the principal intervals of the musical scale corresponded to numerical ratios.
2. Edition.
3. Veneration acquired through time.
4. Social, as contrasted to natural and unchanging.
5. Malice.
6. Self-interest.

proper to inquire by what peculiarities of excellence Shakespeare has gained and kept the favor of his countrymen.

Nothing can please many, and please long, but just representations of general nature. Particular manners[7] can be known to few, and therefore few only can judge how nearly they are copied. The irregular combinations of fanciful invention may delight awhile by that novelty of which the common satiety of life sends us all in quest; but the pleasures of sudden wonder are soon exhausted, and the mind can only repose on the stability of truth.

Shakespeare is, above all writers, at least above all modern writers, the poet of nature, the poet that holds up to his readers a faithful mirror of manners and of life. His characters are not modified by the customs of particular places, unpracticed by the rest of the world; by the peculiarities of studies or professions which can operate but upon small numbers; or by the accidents of transient fashions or temporary opinions: they are the genuine progeny of common humanity, such as the world will always supply, and observation will always find. His persons act and speak by the influence of those general passions and principles by which all minds are agitated and the whole system of life is continued in motion. In the writings of other poets a character is too often an individual; in those of Shakespeare it is commonly a species.

It is from this wide extension of design that so much instruction is derived. It is this which fills the plays of Shakespeare with practical axioms and domestic wisdom. It was said of Euripides that every verse was a precept;[8] and it may be said of Shakespeare that from his works may be collected a system of civil and economical prudence.[9] Yet his real power is not shown in the splendor of particular passages, but by the progress of his fable[10] and the tenor of his dialogue; and he that tries to recommend him by select quotations will succeed like the pedant in Hierocles,[11] who, when he offered his house for sale, carried a brick in his pocket as a specimen.

It will not easily be imagined how much Shakespeare excels in accommodating his sentiments to real life but by comparing him with other authors. It was observed of the ancient schools of declamation that the more diligently they were frequented, the more was the student disqualified for the world, because he found nothing there which he should ever meet in any other place.[12] The same remark may be

7. Temporary modes of behavior.

8. By Cicero in his *Letters to his Friends* (xvi. 8).

9. Public and private conduct.

10. Plot.

11. Neo-Platonic critic of the fifth century A.D., who wrote a *Commentary on the "Golden Verses"* of Pythagoras.

12. Petronius, who lived in the first century A.D., wrote: "I believe that colleges make complete fools of our young men, because they see and hear nothing of ordinary life there" (*Satyricon*, i. 1).

applied to every stage but that of Shakespeare. The theater, when it is under any other direction, is peopled by such characters as were never seen, conversing in a language which was never heard, upon topics which will never arise in the commerce of mankind. But the dialogue of this author is often so evidently determined by the incident which produces it, and is pursued with so much ease and simplicity, that it seems scarcely to claim the merit of fiction, but to have been gleaned by diligent selection out of common conversation and common occurrences.

Upon every other stage the universal agent is love, by whose power all good and evil is distributed and every action quickened or retarded. To bring a lover, a lady, and a rival into the fable; to entangle them in contradictory obligations, perplex them with oppositions of interest, and harass them with violence of desires inconsistent with each other; to make them meet in rapture and part in agony, to fill their mouths with hyperbolical joy and outrageous sorrow, to distress them as nothing human ever was distressed, to deliver them as nothing human ever was delivered, is the business of a modern dramatist. For this, probability is violated, life is misrepresented, and language is depraved.[13] But love is only one of many passions; and as it has no great influence upon the sum of life, it has little operation in the dramas of a poet who caught his ideas from the living world and exhibited only what he saw before him. He knew that any other passion, as it was regular or exorbitant, was a cause of happiness or calamity.

Characters thus ample and general were not easily discriminated and preserved, yet perhaps no poet ever kept his personages more distinct from each other. I will not say with Pope that every speech may be assigned to the proper speaker,[14] because many speeches there are which have nothing characteristical; but, perhaps, though some may be equally adapted to every person, it will be difficult to find any that can be properly transferred from the present possessor to another claimant. The choice is right, when there is reason for choice.

Other dramatists can only gain attention by hyperbolical or aggravated[15] characters, by fabulous and unexampled excellence or depravity, as the writers of barbarous romances invigorated the reader by a giant and a dwarf; and he that should form his expectations of human affairs from the play, or from the tale, would be equally deceived. Shakespeare has no heroes; his scenes are occupied only by men, who act and speak as the reader thinks that he should himself have spoken or acted on the same occasion. Even where the agency is supernatural, the dialogue is level with life. Other writers disguise the most natural passions and most frequent incidents, so that he who contemplates

13. Debased.
14. In Pope's Preface to his edition of Shakespeare's plays (1725).
15. Exaggerated.

them in the book will not know them in the world. Shakespeare approximates[16] the remote and familiarizes the wonderful; the event which he represents will not happen but, if it were possible, its effects would probably be such as he has assigned; and it may be said that he has not only shown human nature as it acts in real exigences, but as it would be found in trials to which it cannot be exposed.

This, therefore, is the praise of Shakespeare, that his drama is the mirror of life; that he who has mazed[17] his imagination in following the phantoms which other writers raise up before him may here be cured of his delirious ecstasies by reading human sentiments in human language, by scenes from which a hermit may estimate the transactions of the world and a confessor[18] predict the progress of the passions.

His adherence to general nature has exposed him to the censure of critics who form their judgments upon narrower principles. Dennis and Rymer think his Romans not sufficiently Roman and Voltaire censures his kings as not completely royal.[19] Dennis is offended that Menenius, a senator of Rome, should play the buffoon;[20] and Voltaire perhaps thinks decency violated when the Danish usurper is represented as a drunkard.[21] But Shakespeare always makes nature predominate over accident; and, if he preserves the essential character, is not very careful of distinctions superinduced and adventitious. His story requires Romans or kings, but he thinks only on men. He knew that Rome, like every other city, had men of all dispositions; and wanting a buffoon, he went into the senate house for that which the senate house would certainly have afforded him. He was inclined to show an usurper and a murderer not only odious, but despicable; he therefore added drunkenness to his other qualities, knowing that kings love wine like other men, and that wine exerts its natural power upon kings. These are the petty cavils of petty minds; a poet overlooks the casual distinction of country and condition, as a painter, satisfied with the figure, neglects the drapery.

The censure which he has incurred by mixing comic and tragic scenes, as it extends to all his works, deserves more consideration. Let the fact be first stated and then examined.

Shakespeare's plays are not in the rigorous and critical sense either tragedies or comedies, but compositions of a distinct kind; exhibiting the real state of sublunary nature, which partakes of good and evil, joy

16. Literally, brings near.

17. Confused.

18. A (celibate) priest (?).

19. John Dennis, author of *An Essay on the Genius and Writings of Shakespeare* (1712); Thomas Rymer, author of *A Short View of Tragedy* (1693). Voltaire's criticism of Shakespeare appears in his *Appeal to All the Nations of Europe* (1761).

20. In *Coriolanus,* Menenius describes himself as a buffoon (II. i).

21. "The king doth wake tonight and takes his rouse,
Keeps wassail, and the swaggering upspring reels . . ."
(*Hamlet* I. iv. 8–9).

and sorrow, mingled with endless variety of proportion and innumerable modes of combination; and expressing the course of the world, in which the loss of one is the gain of another; in which, at the same time, the reveler is hasting to his wine, and the mourner burying his friend; in which the malignity of one is sometimes defeated by the frolic of another; and many mischiefs and many benefits are done and hindered without design.

Out of this chaos of mingled purposes and casualties[22] the ancient poets, according to the laws which custom had prescribed, selected some the crimes of men and some their absurdities; some the momentous vicissitudes of life, and some the lighter occurrences; some the terrors of distress, and some the gaieties of prosperity. Thus rose the two modes of imitation, known by the names of *tragedy* and *comedy*, compositions intended to promote different ends by contrary means, and considered as so little allied that I do not recollect among the Greeks or Romans a single writer who attempted both.

Shakespeare has united the powers of exciting laughter and sorrow not only in one mind but in one composition. Almost all his plays are divided between serious and ludicrous characters, and, in the successive evolutions of the design, sometimes produce seriousness and sorrow, and sometimes levity and laughter.

That this is a practice contrary to the rules of criticism will be readily allowed; but there is always an appeal open from criticism to nature. The end of writing is to instruct; the end of poetry is to instruct by pleasing.[23] That the mingled drama may convey all the instruction of tragedy or comedy cannot be denied, because it includes both in its alternations of exhibition and approaches nearer than either to the appearance of life, by showing how great machinations and slender designs may promote or obviate one another, and the high and the low cooperate in the general system by unavoidable concatenation.

It is objected that by this change of scenes the passions are interrupted in their progression, and that the principal event, being not advanced by a due gradation of preparatory incidents, wants at last the power to move, which constitutes the perfection of dramatic poetry. This reasoning is so specious[24] that it is received as true even by those who in daily experience feel it to be false. The interchanges of mingled scenes seldom fail to produce the intended vicissitudes[25] of passion. Fiction cannot move so much but that the attention may be easily transferred; and though it must be allowed that pleasing melancholy be sometimes interrupted by unwelcome levity, yet let it be considered

22. Events.

23. This critical commonplace was a Renaissance development from such classical sources as the statement by Horace (*Art of Poetry*, 11. 343–44) that poetry either instructs or entertains or, best of all, does both.

24. Plausible.

25. Alternations.

likewise that melancholy is often not pleasing, and that the disturbance of one man may be the relief of another; that different auditors have different habitudes; and that, upon the whole, all pleasure consists in variety.

The players, who in their edition divided our author's works into comedies, histories, and tragedies,[26] seem not to have distinguished the three kinds by any very exact or definite ideas.

An action which ended happily to the principal persons, however serious or distressful through its intermediate incidents, in their opinion constituted a comedy. This idea of a comedy continued long amongst us; and plays were written which, by changing the catastrophe, were tragedies today and comedies tomorrow.

Tragedy was not in those times a poem of more general dignity or elevation than comedy; it required only a calamitous conclusion, with which the common criticism of the age was satisfied, whatever lighter pleasure it afforded in its progress.

History was a series of actions with no other than chronological succession, independent on each other, and without any tendency to introduce or regulate the conclusion. It is not always very nicely distinguished from tragedy. There is not much nearer approach to unity of action in the tragedy of *Antony and Cleopatra* than in the history of *Richard the Second.* But a history might be continued through many plays; as it had no plan, it had no limits.

Through all these denominations of the drama, Shakespeare's mode of composition is the same: an interchange of seriousness and merriment, by which the mind is softened at one time and exhilarated at another. But whatever be his purpose, whether to gladden or depress, or to conduct the story, without vehemence or emotion, through tracts of easy and familiar dialogue, he never fails to attain his purpose; as he commands us, we laugh or mourn, or sit silent with quiet expectation, in tranquillity without indifference.

When Shakespeare's plan is understood, most of the criticisms of Rymer and Voltaire vanish away. The play of *Hamlet* is opened, without impropriety, by two sentinels; Iago bellows at Brabantio's window without injury to the scheme of the play, though in terms which a modern audience would not easily endure; the character of Polonius is seasonable and useful; and the gravediggers themselves may be heard with applause.[27]

Shakespeare engaged in dramatic poetry with the world open before him; the rules of the ancients were yet known to few; the public judg-

26. John Heminges and Henry Condell, actors in Shakespeare's company, published the first collected edition (the First Folio) of his plays (1623).

27. To Rymer the language in the opening scene of *Othello* sounded like something out of Bedlam: "in a play one should speak like a man of business" *(A Short View).* For Voltaire's views of *Hamlet* and *Othello,* see his *Appeal.*

ment was unformed; he had no example of such fame as might force him upon imitation, nor critics of such authority as might restrain his extravagance; he therefore indulged his natural disposition; and his disposition, as Rymer has remarked, led him to comedy. In tragedy he often writes, with great appearance of toil and study, what is written at last with little felicity; but in his comic scenes he seems to produce, without labor, what no labor can improve. In tragedy he is always struggling after some occasion to be comic; but in comedy he seems to repose, or to luxuriate, as in a mode of thinking congenial to his nature. In his tragic scenes there is always something wanting, but his comedy often surpasses expectation or desire. His comedy pleases by the thoughts and the language, and his tragedy for the greater part by incident and action. His tragedy seems to be skill, his comedy to be instinct.

The force of his comic scenes has suffered little diminution, from the changes made by a century and a half, in manners or in words. As his personages act upon principles arising from genuine passion very little modified by particular forms, their pleasures and vexations are communicable to all times and to all places; they are natural and therefore durable. The adventitious peculiarities of personal habits are only superficial dyes, bright and pleasing for a little while, yet soon fading to a dim tinct, without any remains of former luster; but the discriminations of true passion are the colors of nature; they pervade the whole mass and can only perish with the body that exhibits them. The accidental compositions of heterogeneous modes are dissolved by the chance which combined them; but the uniform simplicity of primitive[28] qualities neither admits increase nor suffers decay. The sand heaped by one flood is scattered by another, but the rock always continues in its place. The stream of time, which is continually washing the dissoluble fabrics of other poets, passes without injury by the adamant of Shakespeare.

If there be, what I believe there is, in every nation a style which never becomes obsolete, a certain mode of phraseology so consonant and congenial to the analogy[29] and principles of its respective language as to remain settled and unaltered; this style is probably to be sought in the common intercourse of life, among those who speak only to be understood without ambition of elegance. The polite are always catching modish innovations, and the learned depart from established forms of speech in hope of finding or making better; those who wish for distinction forsake the vulgar[30] when the vulgar is right; but there is a conversation above grossness and below refinement where propriety resides, and where this poet seems to have gathered his comic dialogue.

28. Basic.
29. Basic properties.
30. Ordinary.

He is therefore more agreeable to the ears of the present age than any other author equally remote, and among his other excellencies deserves to be studied as one of the original masters of our language.

These observations are to be considered not as unexceptionably constant, but as containing general and predominant truth. Shakespeare's familiar dialogue is affirmed to be smooth and clear, yet not wholly without ruggedness or difficulty; as a country may be eminently fruitful though it has spots unfit for cultivation; his characters are praised as natural, though their sentiments are sometimes forced and their actions improbable; as the earth upon the whole is spherical, though its surface is varied with protuberances and cavities.

Shakespeare with his excellencies has likewise faults, and faults sufficient to obscure and overwhelm any other merit. I shall show them in the proportion in which they appear to me, without envious malignity or superstitious veneration. No question can be more innocently discussed than a dead poet's pretensions to renown; and little regard is due to that bigotry which sets candor[31] higher than truth.

His first defect is that to which may be imputed most of the evil in books or in men. He sacrifices virtue to convenience and is so much more careful to please than to instruct that he seems to write without any moral purpose. From his writings indeed a system of social duty may be selected, for he that thinks reasonably must think morally; but his precepts and axioms drop casually from him; he makes no just distribution of good or evil, nor is always careful to show in the virtuous a disapprobation of the wicked; he carries his persons indifferently through right and wrong and at the close dismisses them without further care and leaves their examples to operate by chance. This fault the barbarity of his age cannot extenuate; for it is always a writer's duty to make the world better, and justice is a virtue independent on time or place.

The plots are often so loosely formed that a very slight consideration may improve them, and so carelessly pursued that he seems not always to comprehend his own design. He omits opportunities of instructing or delighting which the train of his story seems to force upon him, and apparently rejects those exhibitions which would be more affecting, for the sake of those which are more easy.

It may be observed that in many of his plays the latter part is evidently neglected. When he found himself near the end of his work and in view of his reward, he shortened the labor to snatch the profit. He therefore remits his efforts where he should most vigorously exert them, and his catastrophe is improbably produced or imperfectly represented.

31. Kindness, readiness to overlook faults. "Bigotry" means "blind zeal" or Shakespeare-worship.

He had no regard to distinction of time or place but gives to one age or nation, without scruple, the customs, institutions, and opinions of another, at the expense not only of likelihood but of possibility. These faults Pope has endeavored, with more zeal than judgment, to transfer to his imagined interpolators.[32] We need not wonder to find Hector quoting Aristotle,[33] when we see the loves of Theseus and Hippolyta combined with the Gothic mythology of fairies.[34] Shakespeare, indeed, was not the only violator of chronology, for in the same age Sidney, who wanted not[35] the advantages of learning, has, in his *Arcadia,* confounded the pastoral with the feudal times, the days of innocence, quiet, and security, with those of turbulence, violence, and adventure.[36]

In his comic scenes he is seldom very successful when he engages his characters in reciprocations of smartness and contests of sarcasm; their jests are commonly gross and their pleasantry licentious; neither his gentlemen nor his ladies have much delicacy nor are sufficiently distinguished from his clowns by any appearance of refined manners. Whether he represented the real conversation of his time is not easy to determine. The reign of Elizabeth is commonly supposed to have been a time of stateliness, formality, and reserve; yet perhaps the relaxations of that severity were not very elegant. There must, however, have been always some modes of gaiety preferable to others, and a writer ought to choose the best.

In tragedy his performance seems constantly to be worse as his labor is more. The effusions of passion which exigence forces out are for the most part striking and energetic; but whenever he solicits his invention or strains his faculties, the offspring of his throes is tumor, meanness,[37] tediousness, and obscurity.

In narration he affects a disproportionate pomp of diction and a wearisome train of circumlocution and tells the incident imperfectly in many words which might have been more plainly delivered in few. Narration in dramatic poetry is naturally tedious, as it is unanimated and inactive and obstructs the progress of the action; it should therefore always be rapid and enlivened by frequent interruption. Shakespeare found it an encumbrance and, instead of lightening it by brevity, endeavored to recommend it by dignity and splendor.

His declamations or set speeches are commonly cold and weak, for

32. Pope blamed certain of Shakespeare's "faults" on those who first published his plays.

33. *Troilus and Cressida,* II. ii. 166–67.

34. In *A Midsummer Night's Dream,* Shakespeare introduces the Greek figures of Theseus and Hippolyta along with those of Oberon and Titania, king and queen of the fairies.

35. Did not lack.

36. Pastoral poetry dealt traditionally with the Golden Age.

37. Baseness.

his power was the power of nature; when he endeavored, like other tragic writers, to catch opportunities of amplification and, instead of inquiring what the occasion demanded, to show how much his stores of knowledge could supply, he seldom escapes without the pity or resentment of his reader.

It is incident to him to be now and then entangled with an unwieldy sentiment, which he cannot well express and will not reject; he struggles with it awhile and, if it continues stubborn, comprises it in words such as occur and leaves it to be disentangled and evolved[38] by those who have more leisure to bestow upon it.

Not that always where the language is intricate the thought is subtle, or the image always great where the line is bulky; the equality of words to things is very often neglected, and trivial sentiments and vulgar ideas disappoint the attention to which they are recommended by sonorous epithets and swelling figures.[39]

But the admirers of this great poet have most reason to complain when he approaches nearest to his highest excellence and seems fully resolved to sink them in dejection and mollify them with tender emotions by the fall of greatness, the danger of innocence, or the crosses of love. What he does best, he soon ceases to do. He is not long soft and pathetic without some idle conceit[40] or contemptible equivocation. He no sooner begins to move than he counteracts himself; and terror and pity, as they are rising in the mind, are checked and blasted by sudden frigidity.

A quibble[41] is to Shakespeare what luminous vapors[42] are to the traveler; he follows it at all adventures; it is sure to lead him out of his way and sure to engulf him in the mire. It has some malignant power over his mind, and its fascinations are irresistible. Whatever be the dignity or profundity of his disquisition, whether he be enlarging knowledge or exalting affection, whether he be amusing attention with incidents or enchaining it in suspense, let but a quibble spring up before him and he leaves his work unfinished. A quibble is the golden apple for which he will always turn aside from his career or stoop from his elevation.[43] A quibble, poor and barren as it is, gave him such delight that he was content to purchase it by the sacrifice of reason, propriety, and truth. A quibble was to him the fatal Cleopatra for which he lost the world and was content to lose it.

It will be thought strange that in enumerating the defects of this writer I have not yet mentioned his neglect of the unities, his violation

38. Set forth in orderly sequence.
39. Elaborate figures of speech.
40. Play on words.
41. Pun.
42. Will-o'-the-wisps; marsh gases.
43. In Greek legend, Atalanta was tricked into losing a race, because she stooped to pick up golden apples in her path.

of those laws which have been instituted and established by the joint authority of poets and critics.

For his other deviations from the art of writing, I resign him to critical justice without making any other demand in his favor than that which must be indulged to all human excellence: that his virtues be rated with his failings. But from the censure which this irregularity may bring upon him, I shall, with due reverence to that learning which I must oppose, adventure to try how I can defend him.

His histories, being neither tragedies nor comedies, are not subject to any of their laws; nothing more is necessary to all the praise which they expect than that the changes of action be so prepared as to be understood, that the incidents be various and affecting, and the characters consistent, natural, and distinct. No other unity is intended, and therefore none is to be sought.

In his other works he has well enough preserved the unity of action. He has not, indeed, an intrigue[44] regularly perplexed[45] and regularly unraveled; he does not endeavor to hide his design only to discover[46] it, for this is seldom the order of real events, and Shakespeare is the poet of nature; but his plan has commonly, what Aristotle requires, a beginning, a middle, and an end,[47] one event is concatenated with another, and the conclusion follows by easy consequence. There are perhaps some incidents that might be spared, as in other poets there is much talk that only fills up time upon the stage; but the general system makes gradual advances, and the end of the play is the end of expectation.

To the unities of time and place he has shown no regard; and perhaps a nearer view of the principles on which they stand will diminish their value and withdraw from them the veneration which, from the time of Corneille,[48] they have very generally received, by discovering that they have given more trouble to the poet than pleasure to the auditor.

The necessity of observing the unities of time and place arises from the supposed necessity of making the drama credible. The critics hold it impossible that an action of months or years can be possibly believed to pass in three hours; or that the spectator can suppose himself to sit in the theater while ambassadors go and return between distant kings, while armies are levied and towns besieged, while an exile wanders and returns, or till he whom they saw courting his mistress shall lament the untimely fall of his son. The mind revolts from evident falsehood, and fiction loses its force when it departs from the resemblance of reality.

From the narrow limitation of time necessarily arises the contraction

44. Plot.

45. Complicated.

46. Reveal.

47. *Poetics*, ch. 8.

48. Corneille's "Essay on the Three Unities" was published in an edition of his plays in 1660.

of place. The spectator, who knows that he saw the first act at Alexandria, cannot suppose that he sees the next at Rome,[49] at a distance to which not the dragons of Medea could, in so short a time, have transported him;[50] he knows with certainty that he has not changed his place; and he knows that place cannot change itself; that what was a house cannot become a plain; that what was Thebes can never be Persepolis.

Such is the triumphant language with which a critic exults over the misery of an irregular poet and exults commonly without resistance or reply. It is time, therefore, to tell him by the authority of Shakespeare, that he assumes, as an unquestionable principle, a position which, while his breath is forming it into words, his understanding pronounces to be false. It is false, that any representation is mistaken for reality; that any dramatic fable in its materiality was ever credible, or, for a single moment, was ever credited.

The objection arising from the impossibility of passing the first hour at Alexandria and the next at Rome supposes that when the play opens the spectator really imagines himself at Alexandria and believes that his walk to the theater has been a voyage to Egypt, and that he lives in the days of Antony and Cleopatra. Surely he that imagines this may imagine more. He that can take the stage at one time for the palace of the Ptolemies may take it in half an hour for the promontory of Actium. Delusion, if delusion be admitted, has no certain limitation; if the spectator can be once persuaded that his old acquaintance[51] are Alexander and Caesar, that a room illuminated with candles is the plain of Pharsalia or the bank of Granicus,[52] he is in a state of elevation above the reach of reason or of truth, and from the heights of empyrean poetry may despise the circumscriptions of terrestrial nature. There is no reason why a mind thus wandering in ecstasy should count the clock, or why an hour should not be a century in that calenture[53] of the brains that can make the stage a field.

The truth is that the spectators are always in their senses and know from the first act to the last that the stage is only a stage, and that the players are only players. They come to hear a certain number of lines recited with just gesture and elegant modulation. The lines relate to some action, and an action must be in some place; but the different actions that complete a story may be in places very remote from each other; and where is the absurdity of allowing that space to represent first Athens and then Sicily which was always known to be neither Sicily nor Athens, but a modern theater.

49. As in Shakespeare's *Antony and Cleopatra.*
50. In Euripides' *Medea,* Medea flies away in a chariot drawn by dragons.
51. Such as Johnson's friend and one-time pupil, David Garrick.
52. Scenes of celebrated victories of Julius Caesar and Alexander the Great.
53. Fever.

By supposition, as place is introduced, time may be extended; the time required by the fable elapses for the most part between the acts; for, of so much of the action as is represented, the real and poetical duration is the same. If in the first act preparations for war against Mithridates are represented to be made in Rome, the event of the war may, without absurdity, be represented in the catastrophe as happening in Pontus; we know that there is neither war nor preparation for war; we know that we are neither in Rome nor Pontus; that neither Mithridates nor Lucullus are before us.[54] The drama exhibits successive imitations of successive actions; and why may not the second imitation represent an action that happened years after the first if it be so connected with it that nothing but time can be supposed to intervene? Time is, of all modes of existence, most obsequious to the imagination; a lapse of years is as easily conceived as a passage of hours. In contemplation we easily contract the time of real actions and therefore willingly permit it to be contracted when we only see their imitation.

It will be asked how the drama moves if it is not credited. It is credited with all the credit due to a drama. It is credited, whenever it moves, as a just picture of a real original; as representing to the auditor what he would himself feel if he were to do or suffer what is there feigned to be suffered or to be done. The reflection that strikes the heart is not that the evils before us are real evils, but that they are evils to which we ourselves may be exposed. If there be any fallacy, it is not that we fancy[55] the players, but that we fancy ourselves unhappy for a moment; but we rather lament the possibility than suppose the presence of misery, as a mother weeps over her babe when she remembers that death may take it from her. The delight of tragedy proceeds from our consciousness of fiction; if we thought murders and treasons real, they would please no more.

Imitations produce pain or pleasure not because they are mistaken for realities, but because they bring realities to mind. When the imagination is recreated[56] by a painted landscape, the trees are not supposed capable to give us shade, or the fountains coolness; but we consider how we should be pleased with such fountains playing beside us and such woods waving over us. We are agitated in reading the history of *Henry the Fifth*, yet no man takes his book for the field of Agincourt. A dramatic exhibition is a book recited with concomitants that increase or diminish its effect. Familiar[57] comedy is often more powerful in the theater than on the page; imperial tragedy is always less. The humor of

54. Probably a reference to Nathaniel Lee's tragedy *Mithridates* (1678). Mithridates was king of Pontus in Asia Minor, and Lucullus his successful Roman adversary.

55. Imagine.

56. Delighted.

57. Domestic.

Petruchio[58] may be heightened by grimace; but what voice or what gesture can hope to add dignity or force to the soliloquy of Cato?[59]

A play read affects the mind like a play acted. It is therefore evident that the action is not supposed to be real; and it follows that between the acts a longer or shorter time may be allowed to pass, and that no more account of space or duration is to be taken by the auditor of a drama than by the reader of a narrative, before whom may pass in an hour the life of a hero or the revolutions of an empire.

Whether Shakespeare knew the unities and rejected them by design, or deviated from them by happy ignorance, it is, I think, impossible to decide and useless to inquire. We may reasonably suppose that when he rose to notice, he did not want the counsels and admonitions of scholars and critics, and that he at last deliberately persisted in a practice which he might have begun by chance. As nothing is essential to the fable but unity of action, and as the unities of time and place arise evidently from false assumptions, and, by circumscribing the extent of the drama, lessen its variety, I cannot think it much to be lamented that they were not known by him, or not observed; nor, if such another poet could arise, should I very vehemently reproach him that his first act passed at Venice and his next in Cyprus.[60] Such violations of rules merely positive[61] become the comprehensive genius of Shakespeare, and such censures are suitable to the minute and slender criticism of Voltaire:

> Non usque adeo permiscuit imis
> Longus summa dies, ut non, si voce Metelli
> Serventur leges, malint a Caesare tolli.[62]

Yet when I speak thus slightly of dramatic rules, I cannot but recollect how much wit and learning may be produced against me; before such authorities I am afraid to stand, not that I think the present question one of those that are to be decided by mere authority, but because it is to be suspected that these precepts have not been so easily received but for better reasons than I have yet been able to find. The result of my inquiries, in which it would be ludicrous to boast of impartiality, is that the unities of time and place are not essential to a just[63] drama; that, though they may sometimes conduce to pleasure, they are always to be sacrificed to the nobler beauties of variety and instruction; and that a play written with nice observation of critical rules is to be contemplated as an elaborate curiosity, as the product of superfluous

58. In *The Taming of the Shrew.*
59. Cato contemplates suicide in this famous speech (Addison, *Cato,* V. i).
60. As in *Othello,* Acts I - II.
61. Man made.
62. "The passage of time does not change things so much that one would not prefer to have the laws flouted by a Caesar than saved by a Metellus" (Lucan's *Pharsalia,* iii. 138–40, an epic poem on the Roman civil wars).
63. Correctly written.

and ostentatious art, by which is shown rather what is possible than what is necessary.

He that, without diminution of any other excellence, shall preserve all the unities unbroken deserves the like applause with the architect who shall display all the orders of architecture[64] in a citadel without any deduction from its strength; but the principal beauty of a citadel is to exclude the enemy, and the greatest graces of a play are to copy nature and instruct life.

Perhaps what I have here not dogmatically but deliberatively written may recall the principles of the drama to a new examination. I am almost frightened at my own temerity and, when I estimate the fame and the strength of those that maintain the contrary opinion, am ready to sink down in reverential silence; as Aeneas withdrew from the defense of Troy when he saw Neptune shaking the wall and Juno heading the besiegers.[65]

Those whom my arguments cannot persuade to give their approbation to the judgment of Shakespeare will easily, if they consider the condition of his life, make some allowance for his ignorance.

Every man's performances, to be rightly estimated, must be compared with the state of the age in which he lived and with his own particular opportunities; and though to a reader a book be not worse or better for the circumstances of the author, yet as there is always a silent reference of human works to human abilities, and as the inquiry how far man may extend his designs, or how high he may rate his native force, is of far greater dignity than in what rank we shall place any particular performance, curiosity is always busy to discover the instruments as well as to survey the workmanship, to know how much is to be ascribed to original powers and how much to casual and adventitious help. The palaces of Peru or Mexico were certainly mean and incommodious habitations if compared to the houses of European monarchs; yet who could forbear to view them with astonishment who remembered that they were built without the use of iron?

The English nation, in the time of Shakespeare, was yet struggling to emerge from barbarity. The philology[66] of Italy had been transplanted hither in the reign of Henry the Eighth; and the learned languages had been successfully cultivated by Lily, Linacre, and More; by Pole, Cheke, and Gardiner; and afterwards by Smith, Clerk, Haddon, and Ascham.[67] Greek was now taught to boys in the principal schools; and those who united elegance with learning read with great diligence the Italian and Spanish poets. But literature was yet confined to professed scholars, or to men and women of high rank. The public was gross and

64. Doric, Ionic, and Corinthian are the main classical orders.
65. *Aeneid*, ii. 610–14.
66. Literary scholarship.
67. Various 16th-century humanist scholars.

dark; and to be able to read and write was an accomplishment still valued for its rarity.

Nations, like individuals, have their infancy. A people newly awakened to literary curiosity, being yet unacquainted with the true state of things, knows not how to judge of that which is proposed as its resemblance. Whatever is remote from common appearances is always welcome to vulgar, as to childish, credulity; and of a country unenlightened by learning, the whole people is the vulgar. The study of those who then aspired to plebeian learning was laid out upon adventures, giants, dragons, and enchantments. *The Death of Arthur* was the favorite volume.[68]

The mind which has feasted on the luxurious wonders of fiction has no taste for the insipidity of truth. A play which imitated only the common occurrences of the world would, upon the admirers of *Palmerin* and *Guy of Warwick,*[69] have made little impression; he that wrote for such an audience was under the necessity of looking round for strange events and fabulous transactions; and that incredibility by which maturer knowledge is offended was the chief recommendation of writings to unskillful curiosity.

Our author's plots are generally borrowed from novels; and it is reasonable to suppose that he chose the most popular, such as were read by many and related by more; for his audience could not have followed him through the intricacies of the drama had they not held the thread to the story in their hands.

The stories which we now find only in remoter authors were in his time accessible and familiar. The fable of *As You Like It,* which is supposed to be copied from Chaucer's *Gamelyn,*[70] was a little pamphlet of those times; and old Mr. Cibber[71] remembered the tale of *Hamlet* in plain English prose, which the critics have now to seek in Saxo Grammaticus.[72]

His English histories he took from English chronicles and English ballads; and as the ancient writers were made known to his countrymen by versions,[73] they supplied him with new subjects; he dilated some of Plutarch's lives into plays, when they had been translated by North.[74]

His plots, whether historical or fabulous, are always crowded with

68. Sir Thomas Malory's *Morte D'Arthur* (first printed, 1485).

69. The tales of Palmerin were Spanish romances that were translated into English (1588–96). *The History of Guy of Warwick* was a popular English medieval verse romance.

70. A 14th-century verse romance formerly attributed to Chaucer.

71. Colley Cibber, actor, dramatist, and Poet Laureate, here distinguished from his son, Theophilus.

72. Saxo Grammaticus' partly mythical *History of the Danes* was published in Latin in 1514.

73. Translations.

74. Thomas North's translations (1579) of Plutarch's *Lives of the Noble Grecians and Romans* was an important source for Shakespeare's Roman history plays: *Julius Caesar, Antony and Cleopatra, Coriolanus* and *Timon of Athens.*

incidents by which the attention of a rude[75] people was more easily caught than by sentiment or argumentation; and such is the power of the marvelous, even over those who despise it, that every man finds his mind more strongly seized by the tragedies of Shakespeare than of any other writer. Others please us by particular speeches; but he always makes us anxious for the event and has perhaps excelled all but Homer in securing the first purpose of a writer, by exciting restless and unquenchable curiosity and compelling him that reads his work to read it through.

The shows and bustle with which his plays abound have the same original.[76] As knowledge advances, pleasure passes from the eye to the ear, but returns, as it declines, from the ear to the eye. Those to whom our author's labors were exhibited had more skill in pomps or processions than in poetical language and perhaps wanted some visible and discriminated[77] events as comments on the dialogue. He knew how he should most please; and whether his practice is more agreeable to nature, or whether his example has prejudiced the nation, we still find that on our stage something must be done as well as said, and inactive declamation is very coldly heard, however musical or elegant, passionate or sublime.

Voltaire expresses his wonder that our author's extravagances are endured by a nation which has seen the tragedy of *Cato*. Let him be answered that Addison speaks the language of poets; and Shakespeare, of men. We find in *Cato* innumerable beauties which enamor us of its author, but we see nothing that acquaints us with human sentiments or human actions; we place it with the fairest and the noblest progeny which judgment propagates by conjunction with learning; but *Othello* is the vigorous and vivacious offspring of observation impregnated by genius. *Cato* affords a splendid exhibition of artificial and fictitious manners and delivers just and noble sentiments, in diction easy, elevated, and harmonious, but its hopes and fears communicate no vibration to the heart; the composition refers us only to the writer; we pronounce the name of *Cato,* but we think on Addison.

The work of a correct and regular writer is a garden accurately formed and diligently planted, varied with shades, and scented with flowers; the composition of Shakespeare is a forest, in which oaks extend their branches, and pines tower in the air, interspersed sometimes with weeds and brambles, and sometimes giving shelter to myrtles and to roses; filling the eye with awful pomp and gratifying the mind with endless diversity. Other poets display cabinets of precious rarities, minutely finished, wrought into shape, and polished into brightness.

75. Unlearned.
76. Origin.
77. Distinctly portrayed or presented.

Shakespeare opens a mine which contains gold and diamonds in unexhaustible plenty, though clouded by incrustations, debased by impurities, and mingled with a mass of meaner minerals.

It has been much disputed whether Shakespeare owed his excellence to his own native force, or whether he had the common helps of scholastic education, the precepts of critical science, and the examples of ancient authors.

There has always prevailed a tradition that Shakespeare wanted learning, that he had no regular education, nor much skill in the dead languages. Jonson, his friend, affirms that "he had small Latin, and less Greek,"[78] who, besides that he had no imaginable temptation to falsehood, wrote at a time when the character and acquisitions of Shakespeare were known to multitudes. His evidence ought therefore to decide the controversy, unless some testimony of equal force could be opposed.

Some have imagined that they have discovered deep learning in many imitations of old writers; but the examples which I have known urged were drawn from books translated in his time; or were such easy coincidences of thought as will happen to all who consider the same subjects; or such remarks on life or axioms of morality as float in conversation and are transmitted through the world in proverbial sentences.

I have found it remarked that in this important sentence, "Go before, I'll follow," we read a translation of, *I prae, sequar.*[79] I have been told that when Caliban, after a pleasing dream, says, "I cried to sleep again,"[80] the author imitates Anacreon,[81] who had, like every other man, the same wish on the same occasion.

There are a few passages which may pass for imitations, but so few that the exception only confirms the rule; he obtained them from accidental quotations or by oral communication and, as he used what he had, would have used more if he had obtained it.

The *Comedy of Errors* is confessedly taken from the *Menaechmi* of Plautus; from the only play of Plautus which was then in English.[82] What can be more probable than that he who copied that would have copied more; but that those which were not translated were inaccessible?

78. The quotation is from Ben Jonson's poem "To the Memory of My Beloved . . . Mr. William Shakespeare."

79. Johnson is ironic about the critic Zachary Grey's solemn suggestion that this line from *Richard III* (I. i. 144) must be a translation of a line from a Latin comedy by Terence (190–159 B.C.) which means, "Go, I will follow."

80. *The Tempest,* III. ii. 155: "I cried to dream again."

81. Greek lyric poet of the 6th century B.C.

82. An English translation of *The Twins* by Plautus (254–184 B.C.), the Roman playwright, was published in 1595, too late for Shakespeare to have used it in *The Comedy of Errors* (c. 1592). The translation may have circulated in manuscript.

Whether he knew the modern languages is uncertain. That his plays have some French scenes proves but little; he might easily procure them to be written, and probably, even though he had known the language in the common degree, he could not have written it without assistance. In the story of *Romeo and Juliet* he is observed to have followed the English translation, where it deviates from the Italian; but this on the other part proves nothing against his knowledge of the original. He was to copy, not what he knew himself, but what was known to his audience.

It is most likely that he had learned Latin sufficiently to make him acquainted with construction, but that he never advanced to an easy perusal of the Roman authors. Concerning his skill in modern languages, I can find no sufficient ground of determination; but as no imitations of French or Italian authors have been discovered, though the Italian poetry was then high in esteem, I am inclined to believe that he read little more than English and chose for his fables only such tales as he found translated.

That much knowledge is scattered over his works is very justly observed by Pope; but it is often such knowledge as books did not supply. He that will understand Shakespeare must not be content to study him in the closet,[83] he must look for his meaning sometimes among the sports of the field, and sometimes among the manufactures of the shop.

There is, however, proof enough that he was a very diligent reader, nor was our language then so indigent of books but that he might very liberally indulge his curiosity without excursion into foreign literature. Many of the Roman authors were translated, and some of the Greek; the Reformation had filled the kingdom with theological learning; most of the topics of human disquisition had found English writers; and poetry had been cultivated not only with diligence but success. This was a stock of knowledge sufficient for a mind so capable of appropriating and improving it.

But the greater part of his excellence was the product of his own genius. He found the English stage in a state of the utmost rudeness; no essays either in tragedy or comedy had appeared from which it could be discovered to what degree of delight either one or other might be carried. Neither character nor dialogue were yet understood. Shakespeare may be truly said to have introduced them both amongst us and in some of his happier scenes to have carried them both to the utmost height.

By what gradations of improvement he proceeded is not easily known; for the chronology of his works is yet unsettled. Rowe is of opinion that "perhaps we are not to look for his beginning, like those of other writers, in his least perfect works; art had so little and nature so

83. Private room.

large a share in what he did, that for aught I know," says he, "the performances of his youth, as they were the most vigorous, were the best."[84] But the power of nature is only the power of using to any certain purpose the materials which diligence procures or opportunity supplies. Nature gives no man knowledge, and, when images are collected by study and experience, can only assist in combining or applying them. Shakespeare, however favored by nature, could impart only what he had learned; and as he must increase his ideas, like other mortals, by gradual acquisition, he, like them, grew wiser as he grew older, could display life better, as he knew it more, and instruct with more efficacy, as he was himself more amply instructed.

There is a vigilance of observation and accuracy of distinction which books and precepts cannot confer; from this almost all original and native excellence proceeds. Shakespeare must have looked upon mankind with perspicacity, in the highest degree curious and attentive. Other writers borrow their characters from preceding writers and diversify them only by the accidental appendages of present manners; the dress is a little varied, but the body is the same. Our author had both matter and form to provide; for, except the characters of Chaucer, to whom I think he is not much indebted, there were no writers in English, and perhaps not many in other modern languages, which showed life in its native colors.

The contest about the original benevolence or malignity of man had not yet commenced.[85] Speculation had not yet attempted to analyze the mind, to trace the passions to their sources, to unfold the seminal principles of vice and virtue, or sound the depths of the heart for the motives of action. All those inquiries, which from that time that human nature became the fashionable study have been made sometimes with nice discernment but often with idle subtilty, were yet unattempted. The tales with which the infancy of learning was satisfied exhibited only the superficial appearances of action, related the events but omitted the causes, and were formed for such as delighted in wonders rather than in truth. Mankind was not then to be studied in the closet; he that would know the world was under the necessity of gleaning his own remarks by mingling as he could in its business and amusements.

Boyle congratulated himself upon his high birth, because it favored his curiosity by facilitating his access.[86] Shakespeare had no such ad-

84. Nicholas Rowe published the first life of Shakespeare, with his edition of the plays (1709).

85. Thomas Hobbes's *Leviathan* (1651) suggested that the political state arose because men required it to protect themselves from one another's natural "malignity." Hobbes's pessimism was opposed in England by the Earl of Shaftesbury's *Inquiry Concerning Virtue or Merit* (1709), and in France by J. J. Rousseau's *Essay on the Origin . . . of Inequality* (1754). To oversimplify, Shaftesbury believed that men had an innate moral sense; Rousseau, that men lost their natural benevolence as they moved from the savage state to the civilized.

86. The chemist, Robert Boyle (1627–91), was son of the Earl of Cork.

vantage; he came to London a needy adventurer and lived for a time by very mean employments. Many works of genius and learning have been performed in states of life that appear very little favorable to thought or to inquiry; so many that he who considers them is inclined to think that he sees enterprise and perseverance predominating over all external agency and bidding help and hindrance vanish before them. The genius of Shakespeare was not to be depressed by the weight of poverty nor limited by the narrow conversation to which men in want are inevitably condemned; the incumbrances of his fortune were shaken from his mind, "as dewdrops from a lion's mane."[87]

Though he had so many difficulties to encounter and so little assistance to surmount them, he has been able to obtain an exact knowledge of many modes of life and many casts of native dispositions, to vary them with great multiplicity, to mark them by nice distinctions, and to show them in full view by proper combinations. In this part of his performances he had none to imitate, but has himself been imitated by all succeeding writers; and it may be doubted whether from all his successors more maxims of theoretical knowledge or more rules of practical prudence can be collected than he alone has given to his country.

Nor was his attention confined to the actions of men; he was an exact surveyor of the inanimate world; his descriptions have always some peculiarities gathered by contemplating things as they really exist. It may be observed that the oldest poets of many nations preserve their reputation, and that the following generations of wit, after a short celebrity, sink into oblivion. The first, whoever they may be, must take their sentiments and descriptions immediately from knowledge; the resemblance is therefore just, their descriptions are verified by every eye, and their sentiments acknowledged by every breast. Those whom their fame invites to the same studies copy partly them and partly nature, till the books of one age gain such authority as to stand in the place of nature to another, and imitation, always deviating a little, becomes at last capricious and casual. Shakespeare, whether life or nature be his subject, shows plainly that he has seen with his own eyes; he gives the image which he receives, not weakened or distorted by the intervention of any other mind; the ignorant feel his representations to be just, and the learned see that they are complete.

Perhaps it would not be easy to find any author, except Homer, who invented so much as Shakespeare, who so much advanced the studies which he cultivated, or effused so much novelty upon his age or country. The form, the characters, the language, and the shows of the English drama are his. "He seems," says Dennis, "to have been the very original of our English tragical harmony, that is, the harmony of blank

87. *Troilus and Cressida*, III. iii. 224.

verse, diversified often by dissyllable and trisyllable terminations. For the diversity distinguishes it from heroic harmony,[88] and by bringing it nearer to common use makes it more proper to gain attention and more fit for action and dialogue. Such verse we make when we are writing prose; we make such verse in common conversation."

I know not whether this praise is rigorously just. The dissyllable termination, which the critic rightly appropriates to the drama, is to be found—though, I think, not in *Gorboduc*,[89] which is confessedly before our author—yet in *Hieronimo*,[90] of which the date is not certain, but which there is reason to believe at least as old as his earliest plays. This, however, is certain, that he is the first who taught either tragedy or comedy to please, there being no theatrical piece of any older writer of which the name is known except to antiquaries and collectors of books which are sought because they are scarce, and would not have been scarce, had they been much esteemed.

To him we must ascribe the praise, unless Spenser may divide it with him, of having first discovered to how much smoothness and harmony the English language could be softened. He has speeches, perhaps sometimes scenes, which have all the delicacy of Rowe, without his effeminacy.[91] He endeavors indeed commonly to strike by the force and vigor of his dialogue, but he never executes his purpose better than when he tries to soothe by softness.

Yet it must be at last confessed that as we owe everything to him, he owes something to us; that, if much of his praise is paid by perception and judgment, much is likewise given by custom and veneration. We fix our eyes upon his graces and turn them from his deformities and endure in him what we should in another loathe and despise. If we endured without praising, respect for the father of our drama might excuse us; but I have seen in the book of some modern critic[92] a collection of anomalies, which show that he has corrupted language by every mode of depravation, but which his admirer has accumulated as a monument of honor.

He has scenes of undoubted and perpetual excellence; but perhaps not one play which, if it were now exhibited as the work of a contemporary writer, would be heard to the conclusion. I am indeed far from thinking that his works were wrought to his own ideas of perfection; when they were such as would satisfy the audience, they satisfied the writer. It is seldom that authors, though more studious of fame than Shakespeare, rise much above the standard of their own age; to add a

88. The harmony of the heroic couplet.

89. An early English tragedy, by Thomas Norton and Thomas Sackville, performed in 1561.

90. Thomas Kyd's *Spanish Tragedy*, commonly called *Hieronimo* (1592).

91. Rowe, besides editing Shakespeare, wrote "she-tragedies" in blank verse. Johnson admired Rowe's *The Fair Penitent* (1703).

92. John Upton, author of *Critical Observations on Shakespeare* (1746).

little to what is best will always be sufficient for present praise, and those who find themselves exalted into fame are willing to credit their encomiasts and to spare the labor of contending with themselves.

It does not appear that Shakespeare thought his works worthy of posterity, that he levied any ideal[93] tribute upon future times, or had any further prospect than of present popularity and present profit. When his plays had been acted, his hope was at an end; he solicited no addition of honor from the reader. He therefore made no scruple to repeat the same jests in many dialogues, or to entangle different plots by the same knot of perplexity, which may at least be forgiven him by those who recollect that of Congreve's four comedies two are concluded by a marriage in a mask, by a deception which perhaps never happened, and which, whether likely or not, he did not invent.[94]

So careless was this great poet of future fame that, though he retired to ease and plenty while he was yet little "declined into the vale of years,"[95] before he could be disgusted with fatigue or disabled by infirmity, he made no collection of his works nor desired to rescue those that had been already published from the depravations that obscured them or secure to the rest a better destiny, by giving them to the world in their genuine state.

Of the plays which bear the name of Shakespeare in the late editions, the greater part were not published till about seven years after his death; and the few which appeared in his life are apparently thrust into the world without the care of the author and therefore probably without his knowledge.[96]

Of all the publishers, clandestine or professed, the negligence and unskillfulness has by the late revisers[97] been sufficiently shown. The faults of all are indeed numerous and gross and have not only corrupted many passages perhaps beyond recovery but have brought others into suspicion which are only obscured by obsolete phraseology or by the writer's unskillfulness and affectation. To alter is more easy than to explain, and temerity is a more common quality than diligence. Those who saw that they must employ conjecture to a certain degree were willing to indulge it a little further. Had the author published his own works, we should have sat quietly down to disentangle his intricacies and clear his obscurities; but now we tear what we cannot loose and eject what we happen not to understand.

93. Imaginary (he entertained no idea of tribute).

94. William Congreve (1670–1729), whose *The Old Bachelor* and *Love for Love* are described here.

95. *Othello,* III. iii. 265.

96. About half of Shakespeare's plays were published during his lifetime in separate quarto editions.

97. Nicholas Rowe's edition of Shakespeare was published in 1709, Pope's in 1725, Lewis Theobald's in 1733, Sir Thomas Hanmer's in 1743–44, and the Rev. William Warburton's in 1747.

The faults are more than could have happened without the concurrence of many causes. The style of Shakespeare was in itself ungrammatical, perplexed, and obscure; his works were transcribed for the players by those who may be supposed to have seldom understood them; they were transmitted by copiers equally unskillful, who still multiplied errors; they were perhaps sometimes mutilated by the actors, for the sake of shortening the speeches, and were at last printed without correction of the press.

In this state they remained, not as Dr. Warburton supposes, because they were unregarded,[98] but because the editor's art was not yet applied to modern languages, and our ancestors were accustomed to so much negligence of English printers that they could very patiently endure it. At last an edition was undertaken by Rowe; not because a poet was to be published by a poet, for Rowe seems to have thought very little on correction or explanation; but that our author's works might appear like those of his fraternity, with the appendages of a life and recommendatory preface. Rowe has been clamorously blamed for not performing what he did not undertake; and it is time that justice be done him, by confessing that though he seems to have had no thought of corruption beyond the printer's errors, yet he has made many emendations, if they were not made before, which his successors have received without acknowledgment, and which, if they had produced them, would have filled pages and pages with censures of the stupidity by which the faults were committed, with displays of the absurdities which they involved, with ostentatious expositions of the new reading, and self-congratulations on the happiness of discovering it.

As of the other editors I have preserved the prefaces, I have likewise borrowed the author's life from Rowe, though not written with much elegance or spirit; it relates, however, what is now to be known, and therefore deserves to pass through all succeeding publications.

The nation had been for many years content enough with Mr. Rowe's performance, when Mr. Pope made them acquainted with the true state of Shakespeare's text, showed that it was extremely corrupt, and gave reason to hope that there were means of reforming it. He collated the old copies, which none had thought to examine before, and restored many lines to their integrity; but, by a very compendious[99] criticism, he rejected whatever he disliked and thought more of amputation than of cure.

I know not why he is commended by Dr. Warburton for distinguishing the genuine from the spurious plays. In his choice he exerted no judgment of his own; the plays which he received were given by Heming and Condell, the first editors; and those which he rejected, though,

98. In the Preface to his edition, Warburton blames the neglect of Shakespeare on "the stubborn nonsense with which he was encrusted."

99. Summary.

according to the licentiousness[1] of the press in those times, they were printed during Shakespeare's life, with his name, had been omitted by his friends and were never added to his works before the edition of 1664, from which they were copied by the later printers.

This was a work which Pope seems to have thought unworthy of his abilities, being not able to suppress his contempt of "the dull duty of an editor."[2] He understood but half his undertaking. The duty of a collator is indeed dull, yet, like other tedious tasks, is very necessary; but an emendatory critic would ill discharge his duty without qualities very different from dullness. In perusing a corrupted piece, he must have before him all possibilities of meaning, with all possibilities of expression. Such must be his comprehension of thought and such his copiousness of language. Out of many readings possible, he must be able to select that which best suits with the state, opinions, and modes of language prevailing in every age and with his author's particular cast of thought and turn of expression. Such must be his knowledge and such his taste. Conjectural criticism demands more than humanity possesses, and he that exercises it with most praise has very frequent need of indulgence. Let us now be told no more of the dull duty of an editor.

Confidence is the common consequence of success. They whose excellence of any kind has been loudly celebrated are ready to conclude that their powers are universal. Pope's edition fell below his own expectations, and he was so much offended when he was found to have left anything for others to do that he passed the latter part of his life in a state of hostility with verbal[3] criticism.

I have retained all his notes, that no fragment of so great a writer may be lost. His Preface, valuable alike for elegance of composition and justness of remark, and containing a general criticism on his author so extensive that little can be added and so exact that little can be disputed, every editor has an interest to suppress, but that every reader would demand its insertion.

Pope was succeeded by Theobald, a man of narrow comprehension and small acquisitions, with no native and intrinsic splendor of genius, with little of the artificial light of learning, but zealous for minute accuracy and not negligent in pursuing it. He collated the ancient copies and rectified many errors. A man so anxiously scrupulous might have been expected to do more, but what little he did was commonly right.

In his reports of copies and editions he is not to be trusted without examination. He speaks sometimes indefinitely of copies, when he has only one. In his enumeration of editions, he mentions the two first Folios as of high, and the Third Folio as of middle authority; but the

1. Laxness.
2. Pope's Preface to his edition.
3. Textual, bibliographical.

truth is that the First is equivalent to all others, and that the rest only deviate from it by the printer's negligence.[4] Whoever has any of the Folios has all, excepting those diversities which mere reiteration of editions will produce. I collated them all at the beginning, but afterwards used only the First.

Of his notes I have generally retained those which he retained himself in his second edition, except when they were confuted by subsequent annotators or were too minute to merit preservation. I have sometimes adopted his restoration of a comma, without inserting the panegyric in which he celebrated himself for his achievement. The exuberant excrescence of his diction I have often lopped, his triumphant exultations over Pope and Rowe I have sometimes suppressed, and his contemptible ostentation I have frequently concealed; but I have in some places shown him, as he would have shown himself, for the reader's diversion, that the inflated emptiness of some notes may justify or excuse the contraction of the rest.

Theobald, thus weak and ignorant, thus mean and faithless, thus petulant and ostentatious, by the good luck of having Pope for his enemy, has escaped, and escaped alone, with reputation, from this undertaking.[5] So willingly does the world support those who solicit favor, against those who command reverence; and so easily is he praised whom no man can envy.

Our author fell then into the hands of Sir Thomas Hanmer, the Oxford editor, a man, in my opinion, eminently qualified by nature for such studies. He had, what is the first requisite to emendatory criticism, that intuition by which the poet's intention is immediately discovered, and that dexterity of intellect which dispatches its work by the easiest means. He had undoubtedly read much; his acquaintance with customs, opinions, and traditions, seems to have been large; and he is often learned without show. He seldom passes what he does not understand, without an attempt to find or to make a meaning, and sometimes hastily makes what a little more attention would have found. He is solicitous to reduce to grammar what he could not be sure that his author intended to be grammatical. Shakespeare regarded more the series of ideas than of words; and his language, not being designed for the reader's desk, was all that he desired it to be if it conveyed his meaning to the audience.

Hanmer's care of the meter has been too violently censured. He found the measures reformed in so many passages by the silent labors of some editors, with the silent acquiescence of the rest, that he thought himself allowed to extend a little further the license which had already

4. The First Folio is the players' edition of 1623. The Second appeared in 1632, the Third in 1663, and a second issue of the Third the following year.

5. Theobald's severe criticism of Pope in *Shakespeare Restored* led Pope to make him the pre-eminent dunce in the *Dunciad* of 1728.

been carried so far without reprehension; and of his corrections in general, it must be confessed that they are often just, and made commonly with the least possible violation of the text.

But by inserting his emendations, whether invented or borrowed, into the page without any notice of varying copies, he has appropriated the labor of his predecessors and made his own edition of little authority. His confidence indeed, both in himself and others, was too great; he supposes all to be right that was done by Pope and Theobald; he seems not to suspect a critic of fallibility; and it was but reasonable that he should claim what he so liberally granted.

As he never writes without careful inquiry and diligent consideration, I have received all his notes and believe that every reader will wish for more.

Of the last editor it is more difficult to speak. Respect is due to high place, tenderness to living reputation, and veneration to genius and learning; but he cannot be justly offended at that liberty of which he has himself so frequently given an example, nor very solicitous what is thought of notes which he ought never to have considered as part of his serious employments, and which, I suppose, since the ardor of composition is remitted, he no longer numbers among his happy effusions.[6]

The original and predominant error of his commentary is acquiescence in his first thoughts; that precipitation which is produced by consciousness of quick discernment; and that confidence which presumes to do, by surveying the surface, what labor only can perform, by penetrating the bottom. His notes exhibit sometimes perverse interpretations and sometimes improbable conjectures; he at one time gives the author more profundity of meaning than the sentence admits and at another discovers absurdities where the sense is plain to every other reader. But his emendations are likewise often happy and just, and his interpretation of obscure passages learned and sagacious.

Of his notes, I have commonly rejected those against which the general voice of the public has exclaimed, or which their own incongruity immediately condemns, and which, I suppose, the author himself would desire to be forgotten. Of the rest, to part I have given the highest approbation, by inserting the offered reading in the text; part I have left to the judgment of the reader, as doubtful, though specious; and part I have censured without reserve, but I am sure without bitterness of malice, and, I hope, without wantonness of insult.

It is no pleasure to me, in revising my volumes, to observe how much paper is wasted in confutation. Whoever considers the revolutions of learning and the various questions of greater or less importance upon which wit and reason have exercised their powers, must lament the unsuccessfulness of inquiry and the slow advances of truth, when he

6. Warburton, Bishop of Gloucester, was a formidable antagonist in both literary and theological controversy.

reflects that great part of the labor of every writer is only the destruction of those that went before him. The first care of the builder of a new system is to demolish the fabrics which are standing. The chief desire of him that comments an author is to show how much other commentators have corrupted and obscured him. The opinions prevalent in one age as truths above the reach of controversy are confuted and rejected in another and rise again to reception in remoter times. Thus the human mind is kept in motion without progress. Thus sometimes truth and error, and sometimes contrarieties of error, take each other's place by reciprocal invasion. The tide of seeming knowledge which is poured over one generation retires and leaves another naked and barren; the sudden meteors of intelligence which for a while appear to shoot their beams into the regions of obscurity, on a sudden withdraw their luster and leave mortals again to grope their way.

These elevations and depressions of renown and the contradictions to which all improvers of knowledge must forever be exposed, since they are not escaped by the highest and brightest of mankind, may surely be endured with patience by critics and annotators, who can rank themselves but as the satellites of their authors. "How canst thou beg for life," says Achilles to his captive, "when thou knowest that thou art now to suffer only what must another day be suffered by Achilles?"[7]

Dr. Warburton had a name sufficient to confer celebrity on those who could exalt themselves into antagonists, and his notes have raised a clamor too loud to be distinct. His chief assailants are the authors of *The Canons of Criticism* and of the *Revisal of Shakespeare's Text*,[8] of whom one ridicules his errors with airy petulance, suitable enough to the levity of the controversy; the other attacks them with gloomy malignity, as if he were dragging to justice an assassin or incendiary. The one stings like a fly, sucks a little blood, takes a gay flutter, and returns for more; the other bites like a viper and would be glad to leave inflammations and gangrene behind him. When I think on one, with his confederates, I remember the danger of Coriolanus, who was afraid that "girls with spits, and boys with stones, should slay him in puny battle,"[9] when the other crosses my imagination, I remember the prodigy in *Macbeth:*

> A falcon towering in his pride of place,
> Was by a mousing owl hawked at and killed.[10]

Let me, however, do them justice. One is a wit,[11] and one a scholar. They have both shown acuteness sufficient in the discovery of faults

7. Homer, *Iliad,* xxi. 106–14.

8. Seven editions of Thomas Edwards' *Canons of Criticism* were published between 1748 and 1765. Benjamin Heath's *Revisal* appeared in 1765.

9. *Coriolanus,* IV. iv. 5–6: "Lest that thy wives with spits and boys with stones/ In puny battle slay me."

10. *Macbeth,* II. iv. 12–13.

11. A clever intellectual.

and have both advanced some probable interpretations of obscure passages; but when they aspire to conjecture and emendation, it appears how falsely we all estimate our own abilities, and the little which they have been able to perform might have taught them more candor to the endeavors of others.

Before Dr. Warburton's edition, *Critical Observations on Shakespeare* had been published by Mr. Upton, a man skilled in languages and acquainted with books, but who seems to have had no great vigor of genius or nicety of taste. Many of his explanations are curious and useful, but he, likewise, though he professed to oppose the licentious confidence of editors and adhere to the old copies, is unable to restrain the rage of emendation, though his ardor is ill seconded by his skill. Every cold empiric,[12] when his heart is expanded by a successful experiment, swells into a theorist, and the laborious collator at some unlucky moment frolics in conjecture.

Critical, Historical, and Explanatory Notes have been likewise published upon Shakespeare by Dr. Grey,[13] whose diligent perusal of the old English writers has enabled him to make some useful observations. What he undertook he has well enough performed, but as he neither attempts judicial nor emendatory criticism, he employs rather his memory than his sagacity. It were to be wished that all would endeavor to imitate his modesty who have not been able to surpass his knowledge.

I can say with great sincerity of all my predecessors, what I hope will hereafter be said of me, that not one has left Shakespeare without improvement; nor is there one to whom I have not been indebted for assistance and information. Whatever I have taken from them, it was my intention to refer to its original author, and it is certain that what I have not given to another, I believed when I wrote it to be my own. In some perhaps I have been anticipated; but if I am ever found to encroach upon the remarks of any other commentator, I am willing that the honor, be it more or less, should be transferred to the first claimant, for his right, and his alone, stands above dispute; the second can prove his pretensions only to himself, nor can himself always distinguish invention, with sufficient certainty, from recollection.

They have all been treated by me with candor, which they have not been careful of observing to one another. It is not easy to discover from what cause the acrimony of a scholiast[14] can naturally proceed. The subjects to be discussed by him are of very small importance; they involve neither property nor liberty, nor favor the interest of sect or party. The various readings of copies and different interpretations of a passage seem to be questions that might exercise the wit without engaging the passions. But whether it be that "small things make mean men

12. A practitioner, sometimes a quack, without a knowledge of professional theory.
13. Zachary Grey, *Critical, Historical . . . Notes* (1754).
14. One who annotates the classics.

proud,"[15] and vanity catches small occasions; or that all contrariety of opinion, even in those that can defend it no longer, makes proud men angry; there is often found in commentators a spontaneous strain of invective and contempt, more eager and venomous than is vented by the most furious controvertist in politics against those whom he is hired to defame.

Perhaps the lightness of the matter may conduce to the vehemence of the agency; when the truth to be investigated is so near to inexistence as to escape attention, its bulk is to be enlarged by rage and exclamation. That to which all would be indifferent in its original state may attract notice when the fate of a name is appended to it. A commentator has indeed great temptations to supply by turbulence what he wants of dignity, to beat his little gold to a spacious surface, to work that to foam which no art or diligence can exalt[16] to spirit.

The notes which I have borrowed or written are either illustrative, by which difficulties are explained; or judicial, by which faults and beauties are remarked; or emendatory, by which depravations are corrected.

The explanations transcribed from others, if I do not subjoin any other interpretation, I suppose commonly to be right, at least I intend by acquiescence to confess that I have nothing better to propose.

After the labors of all the editors, I found many passages which appeared to me likely to obstruct the greater number of readers, and thought it my duty to facilitate their passage. It is impossible for an expositor not to write too little for some and too much for others. He can only judge what is necessary by his own experience; and, how long soever he may deliberate, will at last explain many lines which the learned will think impossible to be mistaken and omit many for which the ignorant will want his help. These are censures merely relative and must be quietly endured. I have endeavored to be neither superfluously copious nor scrupulously reserved, and hope that I have made my author's meaning accessible to many who before were frighted from perusing him, and contributed something to the public, by diffusing innocent and rational pleasure.

The complete explanation of an author not systematic and consequential[17] but desultory and vagrant, abounding in casual allusions and light hints, is not to be expected from any single scholiast. All personal reflections, when names are suppressed, must be in a few years irrecoverably obliterated; and customs too minute to attract the notice of law, such as modes of dress, formalities of conversation, rules of visits, disposition of furniture, and practices of ceremony, which naturally find places in familiar dialogue, are so fugitive and unsub-

15. *2 Henry VI,* IV. i. 106: "Small things make base men proud."
16. Refine (a metaphor taken from chemistry).
17. Proceeding in logical sequence.

stantial that they are not easily retained or recovered. What can be known will be collected by chance from the recesses of obscure and obsolete papers perused commonly with some other view. Of this knowledge every man has some, and none has much; but when an author has engaged the public attention, those who can add anything to his illustration communicate their discoveries, and time produces what had eluded diligence.

To time I have been obliged to resign many passages which, though I did not understand them, will perhaps hereafter be explained; having, I hope, illustrated some which others have neglected or mistaken, sometimes by short remarks or marginal directions, such as every editor has added at his will, and often by comments more laborious than the matter will seem to deserve; but that which is most difficult is not always most important, and to an editor nothing is a trifle by which his author is obscured.

The poetical beauties or defects I have not been very diligent to observe. Some plays have more and some fewer judicial observations, not in proportion to their difference of merit, but because I gave this part of my design to chance and to caprice. The reader, I believe, is seldom pleased to find his opinion anticipated; it is natural to delight more in what we find or make than in what we receive. Judgment, like other faculties, is improved by practice, and its advancement is hindered by submission to dictatorial decisions, as the memory grows torpid by the use of a table-book.[18] Some initiation is, however, necessary. Of all skill, part is infused by precept, and part is obtained by habit; I have therefore shown so much as may enable the candidate of criticism to discover the rest.

To the end of most plays I have added short strictures, containing a general censure of faults or praise of excellence; in which I know not how much I have concurred with the current opinion; but I have not, by any affectation of singularity, deviated from it. Nothing is minutely and particularly examined, and therefore it is to be supposed that in the plays which are condemned there is much to be praised, and in those which are praised much to be condemned.

The part of criticism in which the whole succession of editors has labored with the greatest diligence, which has occasioned the most arrogant ostentation and excited the keenest acrimony, is the emendation of corrupted passages, to which the public attention, having been first drawn by the violence of contention between Pope and Theobald, has been continued by the persecution which, with a kind of conspiracy, has been since raised against all the publishers[19] of Shakespeare.

That many passages have passed in a state of depravation through all the editions is indubitably certain; of these the restoration is only to be

18. Memorandum book.
19. Editors.

attempted by collation of copies or sagacity of conjecture. The collator's province is safe and easy, the conjecturer's perilous and difficult. Yet as the greater part of the plays are extant only in one copy, the peril must not be avoided nor the difficulty refused.

Of the readings which this emulation of amendment has hitherto produced, some from the labors of every publisher I have advanced into the text; those are to be considered as in my opinion sufficiently supported; some I have rejected without mention, as evidently erroneous; some I have left in the notes without censure or approbation, as resting in equipoise between objection and defense; and some, which seemed specious but not right, I have inserted with a subsequent animadversion.

Having classed the observations of others, I was at last to try what I could substitute for their mistakes and how I could supply their omissions. I collated such copies as I could procure and wished for more, but have not found the collectors of these rarities very communicative.[20] Of the editions which chance or kindness put into my hands I have given an enumeration, that I may not be blamed for neglecting what I had not the power to do.

By examining the old copies, I soon found that the later publishers, with all their boasts of diligence, suffered many passages to stand unauthorized, and contented themselves with Rowe's regulation of the text even where they knew it to be arbitrary and with a little consideration might have found it to be wrong. Some of these alterations are only the ejection of a word for one that appeared to him more elegant or more intelligible. These corruptions I have often silently rectified; for the history of our language and the true force of our words can only be preserved by keeping the text of authors free from adulteration. Others, and those very frequent, smoothed the cadence or regulated the measure; on these I have not exercised the same rigor; if only a word was transposed or a particle inserted or omitted, I have sometimes suffered the line to stand; for the inconstancy of the copies is such as that some liberties may be easily permitted. But this practice I have not suffered to proceed far, having restored the primitive diction wherever it could for any reason be preferred.

The emendations which comparison of copies supplied I have inserted in the text; sometimes, where the improvement was slight, without notice, and sometimes with an account of the reasons of the change.

Conjecture, though it be sometimes unavoidable, I have not wantonly nor licentiously indulged. It has been my settled principle that the reading of the ancient books is probably true and therefore is not to be disturbed for the sake of elegance, perspicuity, or mere improvement of the sense. For though much credit is not due to the fidelity, nor any

20. An indirect hit at Garrick, who owned a number of old editions.

to the judgment, of the first publishers, yet they who had the copy before their eyes were more likely to read it right than we who read it only by imagination. But it is evident that they have often made strange mistakes by ignorance or negligence, and that therefore something may be properly attempted by criticism, keeping the middle way between presumption and timidity.

Such criticism I have attempted to practice, and, where any passage appeared inextricably perplexed, have endeavored to discover how it may be recalled to sense with least violence. But my first labor is always to turn the old text on every side and try if there be any interstice through which light can find its way; nor would Huetius[21] himself condemn me as refusing the trouble of research for the ambition of alteration. In this modest industry I have not been unsuccessful. I have rescued many lines from the violations of temerity and secured many scenes from the inroads of correction. I have adopted the Roman sentiment, that it is more honorable to save a citizen than to kill an enemy, and have been more careful to protect than to attack.

I have preserved the common distribution of the plays into acts, though I believe it to be in almost all the plays void of authority. Some of those which are divided in the later editions have no division in the First Folio, and some that are divided in the Folio have no division in the preceding copies. The settled mode of the theater requires four intervals in the play; but few, if any, of our author's compositions can be properly distributed in that manner. An act is so much of the drama as passes without intervention of time or change of place. A pause makes a new act. In every real, and therefore in every imitative action, the intervals may be more or fewer, the restriction of five acts being accidental and arbitrary. This Shakespeare knew, and this he practiced; his plays were written and at first printed in one unbroken continuity and ought now to be exhibited with short pauses interposed as often as the scene is changed or any considerable time is required to pass. This method would at once quell a thousand absurdities.

In restoring the author's works to their integrity, I have considered the punctuation as wholly in my power; for what could be their care of colons and commas who corrupted words and sentences? Whatever could be done by adjusting points[22] is therefore silently performed, in some plays with much diligence, in others with less; it is hard to keep a busy eye steadily fixed upon evanescent atoms or a discursive mind upon evanescent truth.

The same liberty has been taken with a few particles or other words of slight effect. I have sometimes inserted or omitted them without notice. I have done that sometimes which the other editors have done always, and which indeed the state of the text may sufficiently justify.

21. Pierre Huet, author of *On Interpretation* (1661).
22. Punctuation.

The greater part of readers, instead of blaming us for passing trifles, will wonder that on mere trifles so much labor is expended, with such importance of debate, and such solemnity of diction. To these I answer with confidence that they are judging of an art which they do not understand; yet cannot much reproach them with their ignorance nor promise that they would become in general, by learning criticism, more useful, happier, or wiser.

As I practiced conjecture more, I learned to trust it less; and after I had printed a few plays, resolved to insert none of my own readings in the text. Upon this caution I now congratulate myself, for every day increases my doubt of my emendations.

Since I have confined my imagination to the margin,[23] it must not be considered as very reprehensible if I have suffered it to play some freaks in its own dominion. There is no danger in conjecture if it be proposed as conjecture; and while the text remains uninjured, those changes may be safely offered which are not considered even by him that offers them as necessary or safe.

If my readings are of little value, they have not been ostentatiously displayed or importunately obtruded. I could have written longer notes, for the art of writing notes is not of difficult attainment. The work is performed, first by railing at the stupidity, negligence, ignorance, and asinine tastelessness of the former editors, and showing, from all that goes before and all that follows, the inelegance and absurdity of the old reading; then by proposing something which to superficial readers would seem specious, but which the editor rejects with indignation; then by producing the true reading, with a long paraphrase, and concluding with loud acclamations on the discovery and a sober wish for the advancement and prosperity of genuine criticism.

All this may be done, and perhaps done sometimes without impropriety. But I have always suspected that the reading is right which requires many words to prove it wrong; and the emendation wrong that cannot without so much labor appear to be right. The justness of a happy restoration strikes at once, and the moral precept may be well applied to criticism, *quod dubitas ne feceris.*[24]

To dread the shore which he sees spread with wrecks is natural to the sailor. I had before my eye so many critical adventures ended in miscarriage that caution was forced upon me. I encountered in every page wit struggling with its own sophistry, and learning confused by the multiplicity of its views. I was forced to censure those whom I admired and could not but reflect, while I was dispossessing their emendations, how soon the same fate might happen to my own, and how many of the readings which I have corrected may be by some other editor defended or established.

23. To footnotes (rather than insert emendations into the text).
24. "When in doubt, refrain."

Critics I saw, that others' names efface,
And fix their own with labor in the place;
Their own, like others, soon their place resigned,
Or disappeared and left the first behind.

POPE.[25]

That a conjectural critic should often be mistaken, cannot be wonderful,[26] either to others or himself, if it be considered that in his art there is no system, no principal and axiomatical truth that regulates subordinate positions. His chance of error is renewed at every attempt; an oblique view of the passage, a slight misapprehension of a phrase, a casual inattention to the parts connected, is sufficient to make him not only fail, but fail ridiculously; and when he succeeds best, he produces perhaps but one reading of many probable, and he that suggests another will always be able to dispute his claims.

It is an unhappy state in which danger is hid under pleasure. The allurements of emendation are scarcely resistible. Conjecture has all the joy and all the pride of invention, and he that has once started a happy change is too much delighted to consider what objections may rise against it.

Yet conjectural criticism has been of great use in the learned world; nor is it my intention to depreciate a study that has exercised so many mighty minds, from the revival of learning to our own age, from the bishop of Aleria[27] to English Bentley.[28] The critics on ancient authors have, in the exercise of their sagacity, many assistances which the editor of Shakespeare is condemned to want. They are employed upon grammatical and settled languages, whose construction contributes so much to perspicuity that Homer has fewer passages unintelligible than Chaucer. The words have not only a known regimen[29] but invariable quantities,[30] which direct and confine the choice. There are commonly more manuscripts than one; and they do not often conspire in the same mistakes. Yet Scaliger could confess to Salmasius how little satisfaction his emendations gave him. *Illudunt nobis conjecturae nostrae, quarum nos pudet, posteaquam in meliores codices incidimus.*[31] And Lipsius could complain that critics were making faults by trying to remove them. *Ut olim vitiis, ita nunc remediis laboratur.*[32] And indeed, where mere conjecture is to be used, the emendations of Scaliger and Lipsius, notwithstanding

25. *Temple of Fame*, ll. 37–40, with slight variation.
26. Surprising.
27. Johannes Andreas, 15th-century classical scholar.
28. The great 18th-century editor of classical texts, Richard Bentley.
29. Grammatical properties, case, agreement, etc.
30. Long and short syllables.
31. "Our emendations make us feel foolish and ashamed when, later, we come upon better manuscripts," wrote Joseph Scaliger, the 16th-century French scholar, to his friend Claude de Saumaise.
32. "As once one suffered from defects, now one suffers from corrections." Justus Lipsius edited Latin texts in the 16th century.

their wonderful sagacity and erudition, are often vague and disputable, like mine or Theobald's.

Perhaps I may not be more censured for doing wrong than for doing little; for raising in the public expectations which at last I have not answered. The expectation of ignorance is indefinite, and that of knowledge is often tyrannical. It is hard to satisfy those who know not what to demand, or those who demand by design what they think impossible to be done. I have indeed disappointed no opinion more than my own; yet I have endeavored to perform my task with no slight solicitude. Not a single passage in the whole work has appeared to me corrupt which I have not attempted to restore; or obscure which I have not endeavored to illustrate. In many I have failed, like others; and from many, after all my efforts, I have retreated and confessed the repulse. I have not passed over, with affected superiority, what is equally difficult to the reader and to myself, but, where I could not instruct him, have owned my ignorance. I might easily have accumulated a mass of seeming learning upon easy scenes; but it ought not to be imputed to negligence that, where nothing was necessary, nothing has been done, or that, where others have said enough, I have said no more.

Notes are often necessary, but they are necessary evils. Let him that is yet unacquainted with the powers of Shakespeare and who desires to feel the highest pleasure that the drama can give, read every play, from the first scene to the last, with utter negligence of all his commentators. When his fancy is once on the wing, let it not stoop at[33] correction or explanation. When his attention is strongly engaged, let it disdain alike to turn aside to the name of Theobald and of Pope. Let him read on through brightness and obscurity, through integrity and corruption; let him preserve his comprehension of the dialogue and his interest in the fable. And when the pleasures of novelty have ceased, let him attempt exactness and read the commentators.

Particular passages are cleared by notes, but the general effect of the work is weakened. The mind is refrigerated by interruption; the thoughts are diverted from the principal subject; the reader is weary, he suspects not why, and at last throws away the book which he has too diligently studied.

Parts are not to be examined till the whole has been surveyed; there is a kind of intellectual remoteness necessary for the comprehension of any great work in its full design and in its true proportions; a close approach shows the smaller niceties, but the beauty of the whole is discerned no longer.

It is not very grateful[34] to consider how little the succession of editors has added to this author's power of pleasing. He was read, admired,

33. Descend to, pounce upon.
34. Gratifying.

studied, and imitated, while he was yet deformed with all the improprieties which ignorance and neglect could accumulate upon him; while the reading was yet not rectified nor his allusions understood; yet then did Dryden pronounce that "Shakespeare was the man who of all modern and perhaps ancient poets had the largest and most comprehensive soul."

> All the images of nature were still present to him, and he drew them not laboriously but luckily; when he describes anything, you more than see it, you feel it too. Those who accuse him to have wanted learning give him the greater commendation; he was naturally learned; he needed not the spectacles of books to read nature; he looked inwards and found her there. I cannot say he is everywhere alike; were he so, I should do him injury to compare him with the greatest of mankind. He is many times flat and insipid; his comic wit degenerating into clenches,[35] his serious swelling into bombast. But he is always great when some great occasion is presented to him; no man can say he ever had a fit subject for his wit and did not then raise himself as high above the rest of poets,
>
> Quantum lenta solent inter viburna cupressi.[36]

It is to be lamented that such a writer should want a commentary; that his language should become obsolete or his sentiments obscure. But it is vain to carry wishes beyond the condition of human things; that which must happen to all has happened to Shakespeare, by accident and time; and more than has been suffered by any other writer since the use of types[37] has been suffered by him through his own negligence of fame, or perhaps by that superiority of mind which despised its own performances when it compared them with its powers, and judged those works unworthy to be preserved which the critics of following ages were to contend for the fame of restoring and explaining.

Among these candidates of inferior fame, I am now to stand the judgment of the public; and wish that I could confidently produce my commentary as equal to the encouragement which I have had the honor of receiving. Every work of this kind is by its nature deficient, and I should feel little solicitude about the sentence were it to be pronounced only by the skillful and the learned.

35. Puns.

36. Dryden, *An Essay of Dramatic Poesy* (1668). His Latin quotation is from Virgil's *Eclogues*, i. 25; "Just as cypresses stand out among the twining viburnum bushes."

37. Practice of printing.

Lives of the Poets

Abraham Cowley
1618–1667

The life of Cowley, notwithstanding the penury of English biography, has been written by Dr. Sprat,[1] an author whose pregnancy of imagination and elegance of language have deservedly set him high in the ranks of literature; but his zeal of friendship, or ambition of eloquence, has produced a funeral oration rather than a history: he has given the character, not the life of Cowley; for he writes with so little detail that scarcely anything is distinctly known, but all is shown confused and enlarged through the mist of panegyric.

Abraham Cowley was born in the year one thousand six hundred and eighteen. His father was a grocer, whose condition Dr. Sprat conceals under the general appellation of a citizen; and, what would probably not have been less carefully suppressed, the omission of his name in the register of St. Dunstan's parish gives reason to suspect that his father was a sectary.[2] Whoever he was, he died before the birth of his son, and consequently left him to the care of his mother; whom Wood[3] represents as struggling earnestly to procure him a literary education, and who, as she lived to the age of eighty, had her solicitude rewarded by seeing her son eminent, and, I hope, by seeing him fortunate, and partaking his prosperity. We know at least, from Sprat's account, that he always acknowledged her care, and justly paid the dues of filial gratitude.

In the window of his mother's apartment lay Spenser's *Faerie Queene;* in which he very early took delight to read, till, by feeling the charms of

1. Thomas Sprat, *An Account of the Life and Writings of Mr. Abraham Cowley* (1668).
2. The will of Thomas Cowley, Abraham's father, describes him as a stationer of the parish of St. Michael le Querne, Cheapside. The early records of this parish are lost, so that Johnson's suspicion that the father was a "sectary"—a member of a dissenting Protestant sect rather than the Church of England—cannot be corroborated.
3. Anthony à Wood, *Athenae Oxonienses* (1691–92).

verse, he became, as he relates,[4] irrecoverably a poet. Such are the accidents which, sometimes remembered and perhaps sometimes forgotten, produce that particular designation of mind, and propensity for some certain science or employment, which is commonly called genius. The true genius is a mind of large general powers, accidentally determined to some particular direction. Sir Joshua Reynolds, the great painter of the present age, had the first fondness for his art excited by the perusal of Richardson's treatise.[5]

By his mother's solicitation he was admitted into Westminster school, where he was soon distinguished. "He was wont," says Sprat, to relate "that he had this defect in his memory at that time, that his teachers never could bring it to retain the ordinary rules of grammar."

This is an instance of the natural desire of man to propagate a wonder. It is surely very difficult to tell anything as it was heard, when Sprat could not refrain from amplifying a commodious incident, though the book to which he prefixed his narrative contained its confutation. A memory admitting some things, and rejecting others, an intellectual digestion that concocted[6] the pulp of learning, but refused the husks, had the appearance of an instinctive elegance, of a particular provision made by nature for literary politeness. But in the author's own honest relation, the marvel vanishes: he was, he says, such "an enemy to all constraint that his master never could prevail on him to learn the rules without book."[7] He does not tell that he could not learn the rules, but that, being able to perform his exercises without them, and being an "enemy to constraint," he spared himself the labor.

Among the English poets, Cowley, Milton, and Pope might be said "to lisp in numbers,"[8] and have given such early proofs, not only of powers of language, but of comprehension of things, as to more tardy minds seems scarcely credible. But of the learned puerilities[9] of Cowley there is no doubt, since a volume of his poems was not only written but printed in his thirteenth year, containing, with other poetical compositions, "The Tragical History of Pyramus and Thisbe," written when he was ten years old; and "Constantia and Philetus," written two years after.[10]

While he was yet at school he produced a comedy called *Love's Riddle,* though it was not published till he had been some time at Cambridge. This comedy is of the pastoral kind, which requires no acquaintance

4. In his essay "Of Myself." Cowley's "Several Discourses by Way of Essay, in Verse and Prose" were first published posthumously (1668) in Thomas Sprat's edition of Cowley's *Works*.

5. Jonathan Richardson, *An Essay on the Theory of Painting* (1715).

6. Turned into nutriment.

7. By memory ("Of Myself").

8. Adapted from Pope, *Epistle to Dr. Arbuthnot,* l. 128.

9. Childhood productions.

10. *Poetical Blossoms,* Cowley's first volume of poems, was published in 1633, when Cowley was 15.

with the living world, and therefore the time at which it was composed adds little to the wonders of Cowley's minority.

In 1636, he was removed to Cambridge, where he continued his studies with great intenseness; for he is said to have written, while he was yet a young student, the greater part of his *Davideis,*[11] a work of which the materials could not have been collected without the study of many years but by a mind of the greatest vigor and activity.

Two years after his settlement at Cambridge he published *Love's Riddle,* with a poetical dedication to Sir Kenelm Digby;[12] of whose acquaintance all his contemporaries seem to have been ambitious; and *Naufragium Joculare,*[13] a comedy written in Latin, but without due attention to the ancient models; for it is not loose verse, but mere prose. It was printed, with a dedication in verse to Dr. Comber, master of the college;[14] but having neither the facility of a popular nor the accuracy of a learned work, it seems to be now universally neglected.

At the beginning of the Civil War, as the Prince[15] passed through Cambridge in his way to York, he was entertained with the representation of *The Guardian,* a comedy, which Cowley says was neither written nor acted, but rough-drawn by him, and repeated by the scholars. That this comedy was printed during his absence from his country, he appears to have considered as injurious to his reputation, though, during the suppression of the theaters, it was sometimes privately acted with sufficient approbation.

In 1643, being now master of arts, he was, by the prevalence of the parliament, ejected from Cambridge, and sheltered himself at St. John's College in Oxford; where, as is said by Wood, he published a satire called "The Puritan and Papist," which was only inserted in the last collection of his works; and so distinguished himself by the warmth of his loyalty, and the elegance of his conversation, that he gained the kindness and confidence of those who attended the King, and amongst others of Lord Falkland, whose notice cast a luster on all to whom it was extended.[16]

About the time when Oxford was surrendered to the parliament, he followed the Queen to Paris[17] where he became secretary to the Lord Jermyn, afterwards Earl of St. Albans, and was employed in such correspondence as the royal cause required, and particularly in ciphering and deciphering the letters that passed between the King and Queen: an employment of the highest confidence and honor. So wide was his

11. An epic poem in heroic couplets about the biblical King David (1656).
12. Diplomat, privateer, and miscellaneous author.
13. *The Laughable Shipwreck.*
14. Trinity College, Cambridge.
15. The Prince of Wales, later Charles II.
16. Lucius Cary, second Viscount Falkland, Secretary of State under Charles I.
17. The Queen was Henrietta Maria, wife of Charles I. Oxford surrendered in June, 1646.

province of intelligence that, for several years, it filled all his days and two or three nights in the week.

In the year 1647, his *Mistress* was published; for he imagined, as he declared in his Preface to a subsequent edition, that "poets are scarce thought freemen of their company without paying some duties, or obliging themselves to be true to love."

This obligation to amorous ditties owes, I believe, its original to the fame of Petrarch, who, in an age rude and uncultivated, by his tuneful homage to his Laura, refined the manners of the lettered world, and filled Europe with love and poetry.[18] But the basis of all excellence is truth: he that professes love ought to feel its power. Petrarch was a real lover, and Laura doubtless deserved his tenderness. Of Cowley, we are told by Barnes,[19] who had means enough of information, that, whatever he may talk of his own inflammability, and the variety of characters by which his heart was divided, he in reality was in love but once, and then never had resolution to tell his passion.

This consideration cannot but abate, in some measure, the reader's esteem for the work and the author. To love excellence is natural; it is natural likewise for the lover to solicit reciprocal regard by an elaborate display of his own qualifications. The desire of pleasing has in different men produced actions of heroism, and effusions of wit; but it seems as reasonable to appear the champion as the poet of an "airy nothing,"[20] and to quarrel as to write for what Cowley might have learned from his master Pindar to call the "dream of a shadow."[21]

It is surely not difficult, in the solitude of a college, or in the bustle of the world, to find useful studies and serious employment. No man needs to be so burthened with life as to squander it in voluntary dreams of fictitious occurrences. The man that sits down to suppose himself charged with treason or peculation, and heats his mind to an elaborate purgation of his character from crimes which he was never within the possibility of committing, differs only by the infrequency of his folly from him who praises beauty which he never saw, complains of jealousy which he never felt; supposes himself sometimes invited, and sometimes forsaken; fatigues his fancy, and ransacks his memory, for images which may exhibit the gaiety of hope, or the gloominess of despair, and dresses his imaginary Chloris or Phyllis sometimes in flowers fading as her beauty, and sometimes in gems lasting as her virtues.

At Paris, as secretary to Lord Jermyn, he was engaged in transacting things of real importance with real men and real women, and at that

18. Francesco Petrarca, or Petrarch (1304–74), an exile at Avignon from the political wars of Florence; his *Verses on the Life and Death of his Lady Laura* were inspired by the wife of Count Hugues de Sade, whom he first saw in 1327; she died in 1348.

19. Joshua Barnes, Preface to his edition of Anacreon (1705).

20. Shakespeare, *A Midsummer Night's Dream,* V. i. 16.

21. Cowley, "Life and Fame," l. 7, echoing Pindar, *Pythian Odes,* viii. 95.

time did not much employ his thoughts upon phantoms of gallantry. Some of his letters to Mr. Bennet, afterwards Earl of Arlington, from April to December in 1650, are preserved in *Miscellanea Aulica*, a collection of papers published by Brown.[22] These letters, being written like those of other men whose mind is more on things than words, contribute no otherwise to his reputation than as they show him to have been above the affectation of unseasonable elegance, and to have known that the business of a statesman can be little forwarded by flowers of rhetoric.

One passage, however, seems not unworthy of some notice. Speaking of the Scotch treaty then in agitation:[23]

"The Scotch treaty," says he, "is the only thing now in which we are vitally concerned; I am one of the last hopers, and yet cannot now abstain from believing that an agreement will be made: all people upon the place incline to that of union. The Scotch will moderate something of the rigor of their demands; the mutual necessity of an accord is visible, the King is persuaded of it. And to tell you the truth (which I take to be an argument above all the rest), Virgil has told the same thing to that purpose."[24]

This expression from a secretary of the present time would be considered as merely ludicrous, or at most as an ostentatious display of scholarship; but the manners of that time were so tinged with superstition that I cannot but suspect Cowley of having consulted on this great occasion the Virgilian lots, and to have given some credit to the answer of his oracle.[25]

Some years afterwards, "business," says Sprat, "passed of course into other hands"; and Cowley, being no longer useful at Paris, was in 1656 sent back into England that, "under pretense of privacy and retirement, he might take occasion of giving notice of the posture of things in this nation."

Soon after his return to London, he was seized by some messengers of the usurping powers, who were sent out in quest of another man; and, being examined, was put into confinement, from which he was not dismissed without the security of a thousand pounds given by Dr. Scarburgh.[26]

This year he published his poems, with a preface, in which he seems to have inserted something, suppressed in subsequent editions, which was interpreted to denote some relaxation of his loyalty. In this preface

22. This work *(A Courtier's Miscellany)*, subtitled *A Collection of State Treatises*, was edited by Thomas Brown in 1702.

23. Charles II was proclaimed King of Scotland in February 1649. The Scottish parliament sent representatives to the Netherlands to negotiate with him.

24. By the treaty eventually concluded, Charles agreed to the major Scottish demands.

25. The Virgilian "lots" *(sortes Vergilianae)* were consulted by picking a passage of Virgil at random and applying it to the situation in question.

26. Dr. Charles Scarburgh, later physician to Charles II.

he declares, that "his desire had been for some days past, and did still very vehemently continue, to retire himself to some of the American plantations, and to forsake this world forever."

From the obloquy which the appearance of submission to the usurpers brought upon him, his biographer has been very diligent to clear him, and indeed it does not seem to have lessened his reputation. His wish for retirement we can easily believe to be undissembled; a man harassed in one kingdom, and persecuted in another, who, after a course of business that employed all his days and half his nights in ciphering and deciphering, comes to his own country and steps into a prison, will be willing enough to retire to some place of quiet, and of safety. Yet let neither our reverence for a genius, nor our pity for a sufferer, dispose us to forget that, if his activity was virtue, his retreat was cowardice.

He then took upon himself the character of physician, still, according to Sprat, with intention "to dissemble the main design of his coming over," and, as Mr. Wood relates, "complying with the men then in power (which was much taken notice of by the royal party), he obtained an order to be created Doctor of Physic, which being done to his mind (whereby he gained the ill will of some of his friends), he went into France again, having made a copy of verses on Oliver's death."[27]

This is no favorable representation, yet even in this not much wrong can be discovered. How far he complied with the men in power is to be inquired before he can be blamed. It is not said that he told them any secrets, or assisted them by intelligence, or any other act. If he only promised to be quiet, that they in whose hands he was might free him from confinement, he did what no law of society prohibits.

The man whose miscarriage in a just cause has put him in the power of his enemy may, without any violation of his integrity, regain his liberty, or preserve his life, by a promise of neutrality: for the stipulation gives the enemy nothing which he had not before; the neutrality of a captive may be always secured by his imprisonment or death. He that is at the disposal of another may not promise to aid him in any injurious act, because no power can compel active obedience. He may engage to do nothing, but not to do ill.

There is reason to think that Cowley promised little. It does not appear that his compliance gained him confidence enough to be trusted without security, for the bond of his bail was never canceled; nor that it made him think himself secure, for at that dissolution of government which followed the death of Oliver, he returned into France, where he resumed his former station, and stayed till the Restoration.

27. Oliver Cromwell, ruler of England as Lord Protector, died in 1658. Doctor of Physic means Doctor of Medicine.

"He continued," says his biographer, "under these bonds till the general deliverance"; it is therefore to be supposed that he did not go to France, and act again for the King, without the consent of his bondsman; that he did not show his loyalty at the hazard of his friend, but by his friend's permission.

Of the verses on Oliver's death, in which Wood's narrative seems to imply something encomiastic there has been no appearance. There is a discourse concerning his government, indeed, with verses intermixed, but such as certainly gained its author no friends among the abettors of usurpation.[28]

A Doctor of Physic, however, he was made at Oxford, in December 1657; and in the commencement of the Royal Society, of which an account has been published by Dr. Birch,[29] he appears busy among the experimental philosophers[30] with the title of Dr. Cowley.

There is no reason for supposing that he ever attempted practice; but his preparatory studies have contributed something to the honor of his country. Considering botany as necessary to a physician, he retired into Kent to gather plants; and as the predominance of a favorite study affects all subordinate operations of the intellect, botany in the mind of Cowley turned into poetry. He composed in Latin several books on plants, of which the first and second display the qualities of herbs, in elegiac verse; the third and fourth the beauties of flowers in various measures; and in the fifth and sixth, the uses of trees in heroic numbers.[31]

At the same time were produced from the same university, the two great poets, Cowley and Milton, of dissimilar genius, of opposite principles; but concurring in the cultivation of Latin poetry, in which the English, till their works and May's poem[32] appeared, seemed unable to contest the palm with any other of the lettered nations.

If the Latin performances of Cowley and Milton be compared, for May I hold to be superior to both, the advantage seems to lie on the side of Cowley. Milton is generally content to express the thoughts of the ancients in their language; Cowley, without much loss of purity or elegance, accommodates the diction of Rome to his own conceptions.

At the Restoration,[33] after all the diligence of his long service, and

28. *A Vision, Concerning His Late Pretended Highness, Cromwell the Wicked* (1661), reprinted in Cowley's *Works* (1668) as "A Discourse by Way of Vision concerning the Government of Oliver Cromwell."

29. Dr. Thomas Birch, *History of the Royal Society of London* (1756–57). Cowley was elected a member in 1661.

30. Scientists.

31. Latin elegiac verse is written in alternating hexameters and pentameters, heroic (epic) verse in hexameters.

32. Thomas May, Secretary for the Parliament in 1646, had published in 1640 a Latin poem, *Supplementum Lucani (Supplement to Lucan),* a parallel from English history to the Roman poet Lucan's *Pharsalia,* an epic about the civil war between Pompey and Caesar.

33. Of Charles II, in 1660.

with consciousness not only of the merit of fidelity, but of the dignity of great abilities, he naturally expected ample preferments; and, that he might not be forgotten by his own fault, wrote a "Song of Triumph."[34] But this was a time of such general hope that great numbers were inevitably disappointed; and Cowley found his reward very tediously delayed. He had been promised by both Charles the First and Second the Mastership of the Savoy;[35] but "he lost it," says Wood, "by certain persons, enemies to the Muses."

The neglect of the court was not his only mortification; having, by such alteration as he thought proper, fitted his old comedy of *The Guardian* for the stage, he produced it to the public under the title of *The Cutter of Coleman Street.* It was treated on the stage with great severity, and was afterwards censured as a satire on the king's party.

Mr. Dryden, who went with Mr. Sprat to the first exhibition, related to Mr. Dennis,[36] "that when they told Cowley how little favor had been shown him, he received the news of his ill success not with so much firmness as might have been expected from so great a man."

What firmness they expected, or what weakness Cowley discovered,[37] cannot be known. He that misses his end will never be as much pleased as he that attains it, even when he can impute no part of his failure to himself; and when the end is to please the multitude, no man perhaps has a right, in things admitting of gradation and comparison, to throw the whole blame upon his judges, and totally to exclude diffidence and shame by a haughty consciousness of his own excellence.

For the rejection of this play, it is difficult now to find the reason: it certainly has, in a very great degree, the power of fixing attention and exciting merriment. From the charge of disaffection he exculpates himself in his preface, by observing how unlikely it is that, having followed the royal family through all their distresses, "he should choose the time of their restoration to begin a quarrel with them." It appears, however, from the *Theatrical Register* of Downes the prompter,[38] to have been popularly considered as a satire on the Royalists.

That he might shorten this tedious suspense, he published his pretensions and his discontent, in an ode called "The Complaint," in which he styles himself the *melancholy* Cowley. This met with the usual fortune of complaints, and seems to have excited more contempt than pity.

34. "Ode upon His Majesty's Restoration," published 31 May 1660, two days after Restoration Day.

35. The Hospital of the Savoy, a charitable institution for the care of the poor.

36. John Dennis (1657–1734), literary critic.

37. Revealed.

38. John Downes was prompter to Sir William Davenant's company at the theater in Lincoln's Inn Fields in 1661: he published his *Roscius Anglicanus* [*English Actor*], *or An Historical Review of the Stage* in 1708.

These unlucky incidents are brought, maliciously enough, together in some stanzas, written about that time, on the choice of a Laureate; a mode of satire, by which, since it was first introduced by Suckling,[39] perhaps every generation of poets has been teased:

> Savoy-missing Cowley came into the court,
> Making apologies for his bad play;
> Every one gave him so good a report,
> That Apollo gave heed to all he could say;
> Now would he have had, 'tis thought, a rebuke,
> Unless he had done some notable folly;
> Writ verses unjustly in praise of Sam Tuke,[40]
> Or printed his pitiful "Melancholy."

His vehement desire of retirement now came again upon him. "Not finding," says the morose Wood, "that preferment conferred upon him which he expected, while others for their money carried away most places, he retired discontented into Surrey."

"He was now," says the courtly Sprat, "weary of the vexations and formalities of an active condition. He had been perplexed with a long compliance to foreign manners. He was satiated with the arts of a court; which sort of life, though his virtue made it innocent[41] to him, yet nothing could make it quiet. Those were the reasons that moved him to follow the violent inclination of his own mind, which, in the greatest throng of his former business, had still called upon him, and represented to him the true delights of solitary studies, of temperate pleasures, and a moderate revenue below the malice and flatteries of fortune."

So differently are things seen, and so differently are they shown; but actions are visible, through motives are secret. Cowley certainly retired; first to Barn Elms, and afterwards to Chertsey, in Surrey. He seems, however, to have lost part of his dread of the "hum of men."[42] He thought himself now safe enough from intrusion, without the defense of mountains and oceans; and, instead of seeking shelter in America, wisely went only so far from the bustle of life as that he might easily find his way back, when solitude should grow tedious. His retreat was at first but slenderly accommodated;[43] yet he soon obtained, by the interest of

39. Sir John Suckling, "A Session of the Poets" (1646). The following quotation is from "The Session of the Poets," an anonymous satire modeled after Suckling's poem; see *Poems on Affairs of State*, ed. G. de F. Lord i (1963). 330.

40. Cowley praises Sir Samuel Tuke in the poem "On Colonel Tuke's Tragi-Comedy of *The Adventures of Five Hours*."

41. Harmless.

42. "And the busy hum of men," Milton, "L'Allegro," l. 118. Barn Elms was a house or estate in East Surrey near London.

43. Fitted out.

the Earl of St. Albans and the Duke of Buckingham,[44] such a lease of the Queen's lands as afforded him an ample income.

By the lover of virtue and of wit it will be solicitously asked, if he now was happy. Let them peruse one of his letters accidently preserved by Peck,[45] which I recommend to the consideration of all that may hereafter pant for solitude.

> To Dr. Thomas Sprat.
>
> Chertsey, 21 May 1665.
>
> The first night that I came hither I caught so great a cold, with a defluxion of rheum,[46] as made me keep my chamber ten days. And, two after, had such a bruise on my ribs with a fall, that I am yet unable to move or turn myself in my bed. This is my personal fortune here to begin with. And, besides, I can get no money from my tenants, and have my meadows eaten up every night by cattle put in by my neighbors. What this signifies, or may come to in time, God knows; if it be ominous, it can end in nothing less than hanging. Another misfortune has been, and stranger than all the rest, that you have broke your word with me, and failed to come, even though you told Mr. Bois that you would. This is what they call *monstri simile.*[47] I do hope to recover my late hurt so far within five or six days (though it be uncertain yet whether I shall ever recover it) as to walk about again. And then, methinks, you and I and the Dean[48] might be very merry upon St. Anne's Hill. You might very conveniently come hither the way of Hampton Town, lying there one night. I write this in pain, and can say no more: *verbum sapienti.*[49]

He did not long enjoy the pleasure or suffer the uneasiness of solitude; for he died at the Porch House in Chertsey in 1667, in the 49th year of his age.

He was buried with great pomp near Chaucer and Spenser; and King Charles pronounced, "That Mr. Cowley had not left a better man behind him in England." He is represented by Dr. Sprat as the most amiable of mankind; and this posthumous praise may be safely credited, as it has never been contradicted by envy or by faction.

Such are the remarks and memorials which I have been able to add to the narrative of Dr. Sprat; who, writing when the feuds of the Civil War were yet recent, and the minds of either party easily irritated, was obliged to pass over many transactions in general expressions, and to leave curiosity often unsatisfied. What he did not tell cannot, however,

44. George Villiers, second Duke of Buckingham (1628–87), principal author of *The Rehearsal* (1671), a burlesque drama ridiculing Dryden. He is the Zimri of Dryden's *Absalom and Achitophel* (1681).
45. Francis Peck, *Memoirs of Oliver Cromwell* (1740).
46. Watery or mucous discharge.
47. "A devil of a thing," a monstrous calamity, Terence, *The Eunuch,* 1. 334.
48. Possibly a neighbor.
49. "A word to the wise," Terence, *Phormio,* 1. 542.

now be known. I must therefore recommend the perusal of his work, to which my narration can be considered only as a slender supplement.

Cowley, like other poets who have written with narrow views, and, instead of tracing intellectual pleasure to its natural sources in the mind of man, paid their court to temporary prejudices,[50] has been at one time too much praised, and too much neglected at another.

Wit, like all other things subject by their nature to the choice of man, has its changes and fashions, and at different times takes different forms. About the beginning of the seventeenth century appeared a race of writers that may be termed the metaphysical poets; of whom, in a criticism on the works of Cowley, it is not improper to give some account.

The metaphysical poets were men of learning, and to show their learning was their whole endeavor; but, unluckily resolving to show it in rhyme, instead of writing poetry, they only wrote verses, and very often such verses as stood the trial of the finger better than of the ear; for the modulation was so imperfect, that they were only found to be verses by counting the syllables.

If the father of criticism has rightly denominated poetry **τέχνη μιμητικὴ**, *an imitative art,*[51] these writers will, without great wrong, lose their right to the name of poets; for they cannot be said to have imitated anything; they neither copied nature nor life; neither painted the forms of matter, nor represented the operations of intellect.

Those, however, who deny them to be poets, allow them to be wits. Dryden confesses of himself and his contemporaries, that they fall below Donne in wit, but maintains that they surpass him in poetry.[52]

If wit be well described by Pope, as being "that which has been often thought, but was never before so well expressed,"[53] they certainly never attained, nor ever sought it; for they endeavored to be singular in their thoughts, and were careless of their diction. But Pope's account of wit is undoubtedly erroneous: he depresses it below its natural dignity, and reduces it from strength of thought to happiness of language.

If by a more noble and more adequate conception that be considered as wit, which is at once natural and new, that which, though not obvious is, upon its first production, acknowledged to be just; if it be that which he that never found it wonders how he missed; to wit of this kind the metaphysical poets have seldom risen. Their thoughts are often new, but seldom natural; they are not obvious, but neither are they just; and the reader, far from wondering that he missed them, wonders more frequently by what perverseness of industry they were ever found.

50. Fashions. 51. Aristotle, *Poetics, passim.*

52. Dryden, Dedication of *Eleanora* (1692), and Dedication of the translation of Juvenal (1693).

53. Adapted from Pope, *Essay on Criticism,* 1. 298.

But wit, abstracted from its effects upon the hearer, may be more rigorously and philosophically considered as a kind of *discordia concors*:[54] a combination of dissimilar images, or discovery of occult resemblances in things apparently unlike. Of wit, thus defined, they have more than enough. The most heterogeneous ideas[55] are yoked by violence together; nature and art are ransacked for illustrations, comparisons, and allusions; their learning instructs, and their subtilty surprises; but the reader commonly thinks his improvement dearly bought, and, though he sometimes admires, is seldom pleased.

From this account of their compositions it will be readily inferred that they were not successful in representing or moving the affections. As they were wholly employed on something unexpected and surprising, they had no regard to that uniformity of sentiment which enables us to conceive and to excite the pains and the pleasures of other minds: they never inquired what, on any occasion, they should have said or done; but wrote rather as beholders than partakers of human nature; as beings looking upon good and evil, impassive and at leisure; as Epicurean deities making remarks on the actions of men, and the vicissitudes of life, without interest and without emotion.[56] Their courtship was void of fondness, and their lamentation of sorrow. Their wish was only to say what they hoped had been never said before.

Nor was the sublime more within their reach than the pathetic;[57] for they never attempted that comprehension and expanse of thought which at once fills the whole mind, and of which the first effect is sudden astonishment, and the second rational admiration. Sublimity is produced by aggregation, and littleness by disperson. Great thoughts are always general, and consist in positions not limited by exceptions, and in descriptions not descending to minuteness. It is with great propriety that subtilty, which in its original import means exility[58] of particles, is taken in its metaphorical meaning for nicety[59] of distinction. Those writers who lay on the watch for novelty could have little hope of greatness; for great things cannot have escaped former observation. Their attempts were always analytic; they broke every image into fragments, and could no more represent, by their slender conceits[60] and labored particularities, the prospects of nature or the scenes of life,

54. "Harmony made out of discord."
55. Images, as well as thoughts.
56. The gods, as the Greek philosopher Epicurus explained them, took no part in human affairs.
57. The sublime and the pathetic comprised two sets of emotions, which 18th-century poets often tried to arouse. The sublime included terror, amazement, and awe; the pathetic included love, sympathy, and melancholy.
58. Fineness.
59. Delicacy.
60. Elaborate, often extravagant, similes and metaphors.

than he who dissects a sunbeam with a prism can exhibit the wide effulgence of a summer noon.

What they wanted however of the sublime, they endeavored to supply by hyperbole; their amplification had no limits; they left not only reason but fancy behind them; and produced combinations of confused magnificence, that not only could not be credited but could not be imagined.

Yet great labor, directed by great abilities, is never wholly lost: if they frequently threw away their wit upon false conceits, they likewise sometimes struck out unexpected truth: if their conceits were far-fetched, they were often worth the carriage. To write on their plan, it was at least necessary to read and think. No man could be born a metaphysical poet, nor assume the dignity of a writer, by descriptions copied from descriptions, by imitations borrowed from imitations, by traditional imagery, and hereditary similes, by readiness of rhyme, and volubility of syllables.

In perusing the works of this race of authors, the mind is exercised either by recollection or inquiry; either something already learned is to be retrieved, or something new is to be examined. If their greatness seldom elevates, their acuteness often surprises; if the imagination is not always gratified, at least the powers of reflection and comparison are employed; and in the mass of materials which ingenious absurdity has thrown together, genuine wit and useful knowledge may be sometimes found, buried perhaps in grossness of expression, but useful to those who know their value; and such as, when they are expanded to perspicuity, and polished to elegance, may give luster to works which have more propriety though less copiousness of sentiment.

This kind of writing, which was, I believe, borrowed from Marino[61] and his followers, had been recommended by the example of Donne, a man of very extensive and various knowledge; and by Jonson, whose manner resembled that of Donne more in the ruggedness of his lines than in the cast of his sentiments.

When their reputation was high they had undoubtedly more imitators than time has left behind. Their immediate successors, of whom any remembrance can be said to remain, were Suckling, Waller, Denham, Cowley, Cleveland,[62] and Milton. Denham and Waller sought another way to fame, by improving the harmony[63] of our numbers. Milton tried the metaphysic style only in his lines upon Hobson the Carrier.[64] Cowley adopted it, and excelled his predecessors, having as

61. Giambattista Marini (or Marino) (1569–1625), Italian poet.

62. Edmund Waller (1606–87), Sir John Denham (1615–69), John Cleveland (1613–58).

63. Smoothness.

64. Milton wrote two poems on the death of Thomas Hobson, driver of the weekly coach between Cambridge and London.

much sentiment, and more music. Suckling neither improved versification, nor abounded in conceits. The fashionable style remained chiefly with Cowley; Suckling could not reach it, and Milton disdained it.

Critical remarks are not easily understood without examples; and I have therefore collected instances of the modes of writing by which this species of poets, for poets they were called by themselves and their admirers, was eminently distinguished.

As the authors of this race were perhaps more desirous of being admired than understood, they sometimes drew their conceits from recesses of learning not very much frequented by common readers of poetry. Thus Cowley on knowledge:

> The sacred tree midst the fair orchard grew;
> The phoenix Truth did on it rest,
> And built his perfumed nest,
> That right Porphyrian tree[65] which did true logic show.
> Each leaf did learned notions give,
> And th' apples were demonstrative:
> So clear their color and divine,
> The very shade they cast did other lights outshine.[66]

On Anacreon continuing a lover in his old age:

> Love was with thy life entwined,
> Close as heat with fire is joined;
> A powerful brand prescribed the date
> Of thine, like Meleager's fate.[67]
> Th' antiperistasis[68] of age
> More inflamed thy amorous rage.[69]

In the following verses we have an allusion to a rabbinical opinion concerning manna:

> Variety I ask not: give me one
> To live perpetually upon.
> The person Love does to us fit,
> Like manna, has the taste of all in it.[70]

Thus Donne shows his medicinal knowledge in some encomiastic verses:

65. Porphyry, third-century A.D. philosopher, devised a chart or genealogical tree for "man" as an entity, which served as a model for logical categorization.

66. "The Tree of Knowledge," ll. 1–8.

67. The Fates decreed at his birth that Meleager, son of the king of Calydon, would die as soon as a certain log that was on the fire was consumed.

68. Resistance.

69. "Elegy upon Anacreon," ll. 33–38. Anacreon was a Greek poet of the sixth century B.C., noted for his songs, usually in praise of love and wine.

70. "Resolved to be Beloved," ll. 21–24.

In every thing there naturally grows
A balsamum to keep it fresh and new,
If 'twere not injured by extrinsic blows;
Your youth and beauty are this balm in you.
But you, of learning and religion,
And virtue and such ingredients, have made
A mithridate,[71] whose operation
Keeps off, or cures what can be done or said.[72]

Though the following lines of Donne, on the last night of the year, have something in them too scholastic,[73] they are not inelegant:

This twilight of two years, not past nor next,
Some emblem is of me, or I of this,
Who, meteor-like, of stuff and form perplexed,[74]
Whose what and where, in disputation is,
If I should call me any thing, should miss.

I sum the years and me, and find me not
Debtor to th' old, nor creditor to the new,
That cannot say, my thanks I have forgot,
Nor trust I this with hopes; and yet scarce true
This bravery[75] is, since these times showed me you.

DONNE[76]

Yet more abstruse and profound is Donne's reflection upon man as a microcosm:

If men be worlds, there is in every one
Something to answer in some proportion
All the world's riches: and in good men, this
Virtue our form's form, and our soul's soul is.[77]

Of thoughts so far-fetched, as to be not only unexpected but unnatural, all their books are full.

To a lady, who wrote posies for rings:

They, who above do various circles find,
Say, like a ring th' equator heaven does bind.
When heaven shall be adorned by thee
(Which then more heaven than 'tis, will be),
'Tis thou must write the posy there,

71. Antidote.
72. "To the Countess of Bedford" ("Reason is our soul's left hand"), 11. 21–28.
73. Pertaining to the "schoolmen," the medieval philosophers.
74. Intermingled.
75. Fine show, melancholy boast.
76. "To the Countess of Bedford" ("This twilight of two years"), 11. 1–10.
77. "To Mr. R. W.," 11. 29–32.

For it wanteth one as yet,
Though the sun pass through't twice a year,
The sun, which is esteemed the god of wit.

COWLEY.[78]

The difficulties which have been raised about identity in philosophy are by Cowley with still more perplexity applied to love:

Five years ago (says story) I loved you.
For which you call me most inconstant now;
Pardon me, madam, you mistake the man;
For I am not the same that I was then;
No flesh is now the same 'twas then in me,
And that my mind is changed yourself may see.
The same thoughts to retain still, and intents,
Were more inconstant far; for accidents
Must of all things most strangely inconstant prove,
If from one subject they t'another move;
My members then, the father members were
From whence these take their birth, which now are here.
If then this body love what th' other did,
'Twere incest, which by nature is forbid.[79]

The love of different women is, in geographical poetry, compared to travels through different countries:

Hast thou not found, each woman's breast
(The land where thou hast traveled)
Either by savages possessed,
Or wild, and uninhabited?
What joy could'st take, or what repose,
In countries so uncivilized as those?
Lust, the scorching Dog Star,[80] here
Rages with immoderate heat;
Whilst Pride, the rugged Northern Bear,[81]
In others makes the cold too great.
And where these are temperate known,
The soil's all barren sand, or rocky stone.

COWLEY.[82]

A lover, burnt up by his affection, is compared to Egypt:

The fate of Egypt I sustain,
And never feel the dew of rain,

78. "To a Lady," 11. 25–32. Cowley puns on "posies" (mottoes) and "poesies."
79. "Inconstancy," 11. 1–14.
80. Sirius, associated with the heat of late summer and with madness.
81. Ursa Major, a constellation, one side of which points to the Pole Star.
82. "The Welcome," 11. 13–24.

From clouds which in the head appear;
  But all my too much moisture owe
  To overflowings of the heart below.

COWLEY[83]

The lover supposes his lady acquainted with the ancient laws of augury and rites of sacrifice:

And yet this death of mine, I fear,
Will ominous to her appear:
  When sound in every other part,
Her sacrifice is found without an heart.
  For the last tempest of my death
Shall sigh out that too, with my breath.[84]

That the chaos was harmonized, has been recited of old,[85] but whence the different sounds arose, remained for a modern to discover:

Th' ungoverned parts no correspondence knew,
An artless war from thwarting motions grew:
Till they to number and fixed rules were brought. . . .
Water and air he for the tenor chose,
Earth made the bass, the treble flame arose.

COWLEY[86]

The tears of lovers are always of great poetical account; but Donne has extended them into worlds. If the lines are not easily understood, they may be read again.

On a round ball
A workman, that hath copies by, can lay
An Europe, Afric, and an Asia,
And quickly make that, which was nothing, all.
    So doth each tear,
    Which thee doth wear,
A globe, yea world, by that impression grow,
Till thy tears mixed with mine do overflow
This world, by waters sent from thee my heaven dissolved so.[87]

On reading the following lines, the reader may perhaps cry out—"Confusion worse confounded."[88]

Here lies a she sun, and a he moon here,
  She gives the best light to his sphere,

83. "Sleep," 11. 10–14.
84. Cowley, "The Concealment," 11. 23–28.
85. As in Ovid, *Metamorphoses,* i. 21–31.
86. *Davideis,* i. 453–55, 457–58.
87. "A Valediction: Of Weeping," 11. 10–18.
88. *Paradise Lost,* ii. 996.

Or each is both, and all, and so
They unto one another nothing owe.

DONNE.[89]

Who but Donne would have thought that a good man is a telescope?

Though God be our true glass, through which we see
All, since the being of all things is he,
Yet are the trunks, which do to us derive
Things, in proportion fit, by perspective,
Deeds of good men; for by their living here,
Virtues, indeed remote, seem to be near.[90]

Who would imagine it possible that in a very few lines so many remote ideas could be brought together?

Since 'tis my doom, Love's undershrieve,[91]
Why this reprieve?
Why doth my She advowson[92] fly
Incumbency?

To sell thyself dost thou intend
By candle's end,
And hold the contrast thus in doubt,
Life's taper out?[93]
Think but how soon the market fails,
Your sex lives faster than the males;
As if to measure age's span,
The sober Julian were th' account of man,
Whilst you live by the fleet Gregorian.[94]

CLEVELAND.[95]

Of enormous and disgusting[96] hyperboles, these may be examples:

By every wind, that comes this way,
Send me at least a sigh or two,
Such and so many I'll repay
As shall themselves make winds to get to you.[97]

COWLEY.

89. "An Epithalamion on the Lady Elizabeth . . ." 11. 85–88.
90. "Obsequies to the Lord Harrington," 11. 35–40.
91. Deputy sheriff.
92. One presented to an ecclesiastical post.
93. Success at an auction went to the last person to bid before the candle expired. "Contrast," in the previous line, means "contention."
94. The Gregorian calendar is about eleven minutes shorter than the Julian.
95. "To Julia, to Expedite her Promise," 11. 1–4, 10–18.
96. Perverse and displeasing.
97. "Friendship in Absence," 11. 39–42.

In tears I'll waste these eyes,
By love so vainly fed;
So lust of old the Deluge punished.

COWLEY[98]

All armed in brass, the richest dress of war,
(A dismal glorious sight) he shone afar.
The sun himself started with sudden fright,
To see his beams return so dismal bright.

COWLEY.

An universal consternation:

His bloody eyes he hurls round, his sharp paws
Tear up the ground; then runs he wild about,
Lashing his angry tail and roaring out.
Beasts creep into their dens, and tremble there;
Trees, though no wind is stirring, shake with fear;
Silence and horror fill the place around:
Echo itself dares scarce repeat the sound.

COWLEY[99]

Their fictions were often violent and unnatural.

Of his mistress bathing:

The fish around her crowded, as they do
To the false light that treacherous fishers show,
And all with as much ease might taken be,
As she at first took me:
For ne'er did light so clear
Among the waves appear,
Though every night the sun himself set there.

COWLEY.[1]

The poetical effect of a lover's name upon glass:

My name engraved herein
Doth contribute my firmness to this glass;
Which, ever since that charm, hath been
As hard as that which graved it was.

DONNE.[2]

Their conceits were sometimes slight and trifling.

On an inconstant woman:

He enjoys thy calmy sunshine now,
And no breath stirring hears,

98. "The Despair," 11. 4–6.
99. *Davideis,* iii. 387–90; i. 635–39.
1. "Bathing in the River," 11. 1–7.
2. "A Valediction: Of my Name in the Window," 11. 1–4.

In the clear heaven of thy brow,
No smallest cloud appears.
He sees thee gentle, fair and gay,
And trusts the faithless April of thy May.

COWLEY.[3]

Upon a paper written with the juice of lemon and read by the fire:

Nothing yet in thee is seen;
But when a genial heat warms thee within,
A newborn wood of various lines there grows;
Here buds an L, and there a B,
Here sprouts a V, and there a T,
And all the flourishing letters stand in rows.

COWLEY.[4]

As they sought only for novelty, they did not much inquire whether their allusions were to things high or low, elegant or gross; whether they compared the little to the great, or the great to the little.

Physic and chirurgery[5] for a lover:

Gently, ah gently, madam, touch
The wound, which you yourself have made;
That pain must needs be very much,
Which makes me of your hand afraid.
Cordials of pity give me now,
For I too weak for purgings grow.

COWLEY.[6]

The world and a clock:

Mahol,[7] th' inferior world's fantastic face,
Through all the turns of matter's maze did trace;
Great Nature's well-set clock in pieces took;
On all the springs and smallest wheels did look.
Of life and motion; and with equal art
Made up again the whole of every part.

COWLEY.[8]

A coal pit has not often found its poet; but that it may not want its due honor, Cleveland has paralleled it with the sun:

The moderate value of our guiltless ore
Makes no man atheist, and no woman whore;

3. "Ode in Imitation of Horace's *Ode,* I. v," 11. 19–24.
4. "Written in Juice of Lemon," 11. 31–36.
5. Surgery.
6. "Counsel," 11. 1–6.
7. Mahol is a figure mentioned briefly in 2 Kings 4:31. The passage quoted above is part of a longer one in Cowley's *Davideis* describing a fanciful "prophets college" founded by Samuel. Cowley explains in a note that he conceives Mahol as a "Reader of Natural Philosophy" in the college.
8. *Davideis,* i. 741–46.

Yet why should hallowed vestal's sacred shrine[9]
Deserve more honor than a flaming mine?
These pregnant wombs of heat would fitter be
Than a few embers, for a deity.
Had he our pits, the Persian would admire
No sun,[10] but warm's devotion at our fire:
He'd leave the trotting whipster,[11] and prefer
Our profound Vulcan[12] 'bove that wagoner.
For wants he heat or light? or would have store
Of both? 'tis here: and what can suns give more?
Nay, what's the sun but, in a different name,
A coal pit rampant, or a mine on flame!
Then let this truth reciprocally run,
The sun's heaven's coalery, and coals our sun.[13]

Death, a voyage:

No family
E'er rigged a soul for heaven's discovery,
With whom more venturers might boldly dare
Venture their stakes, with him in joy to share.

DONNE[14]

Their thoughts and expressions were sometimes grossly absurd, and such as no figures[15] or license can reconcile to the understanding.

A lover neither dead nor alive:

Then down I laid my head,
Down on cold earth; and for a while was dead,
And my freed soul to a strange somewhere fled:
Ah, sottish soul, said I,
When back to its cage again I saw it fly;
Fool to resume her broken chain!
And row her galley here again!
Fool, to that body to return
Where it condemned and destined is to burn!
Once dead, how can it be,
Death should a thing so pleasant seem to thee,
That thou should'st come to live it o'er again in me?

COWLEY[16]

9. An allusion to the Roman shrine of Vesta, the goddess of the hearth, whose sacred flame was guarded by the vestal virgins.

10. The followers of Zoroaster worshiped Mithras, the sun god.

11. The sun god in his chariot; also "wagoner," in the next line.

12. Roman god of fire; "profound" means "of the depths."

13. *News from Newcastle,* ll. 21–36. The poem appears in early editions of Cleveland's *Poems* but is not accepted as Cleveland's by modern editors.

14. "Elegy on the L.C.," ll. 13–16. Professor Helen Gardner supplies an improved title: "A Funeral Elegy, to L.C."

15. (Theory of) imagery.

16. "The Despair," ll. 25–36.

A lover's heart, a hand grenado:

Woe to her stubborn heart, if once mine come
  Into the self-same room,
  'Twill tear and blow up all within,
Like a grenado shot into a magazin.[17]
Then shall Love keep the ashes, and torn parts,
  Of both our broken hearts:
  Shall out of both one new one make;
From her's th' allay; from mine, the metal take.

COWLEY.[18]

The poetical propagation of light:

The Prince's favor is diffused o'er all,
From which all fortunes, names, and natures fall;
Then from those wombs of stars, the bride's bright eyes,
  At every glance a constellation flies,
And sows the court with stars, and doth prevent[19]
  In light and power, the all-eyed firmament:
First her eye kindles other ladies' eyes,
  Then from their beams their jewels' lusters rise;
And from their jewels torches do take fire,
And all is warmth, and light, and good desire.

DONNE.[20]

They were in very little care to clothe their notions with elegance of dress, and therefore miss the notice and the praise which are often gained by those, who think less, but are more diligent to adorn their thoughts.

That a mistress beloved is fairer in idea than in reality is by Cowley thus expressed:

Thou in my fancy dost much higher stand,
Than women can be placed by Nature's hand;
And I must needs, I'm sure, a loser be,
To change thee, as thou 'rt there, for very thee.[21]

That prayer and labor should cooperate, are thus taught by Donne:

In none but us are such mixed engines found,
As hands of double office: for the ground
We till with them; and them to heaven we raise;
Who prayerless labors, or, without this, prays,
Doth but one half, that's none.[22]

17. (Powder) magazine.
18. "The Given Heart," 11. 9–16. "Allay" in the last line means "alloy."
19. Outdo.
20. "Eclogue, 1613," 11. 23–32.
21. "Against Fruition," 11. 17–20.
22. "To the Countess of Bedford" ("T' have written then"), 11. 43–47.

By the same author, a common topic, the danger of procrastination, is thus illustrated:

> That which I should have begun
> In my youth's morning, now late must be done;
> And I, as giddy travelers must do,
> Which stray or sleep all day, and having lost
> Light and strength, dark and tired must then ride post.[23]

All that man has to do is to live and die; the sum of humanity is comprehended by Donne in the following lines:

> Think in how poor a prison thou didst lie;
> After, enabled but to suck and cry.
> Think, when 'twas grown to most, 'twas a poor inn,
> A province packed up in two yards of skin,
> And that usurped, or threatened with a rage
> Of sicknesses, or their true mother, age.
> But think that death hath now enfranchised thee;
> Thou hast thy expansion now, and liberty;
> Think, that a rusty piece discharged is flown
> In pieces, and the bullet is his own,
> And freely flies: this to thy soul allow,
> Think thy shell broke, think thy soul hatched but now.[24]

They were sometimes indelicate and disgusting. Cowley thus apostrophizes beauty:

> Thou tyrant, which leav'st no man free!
> Thou subtle thief, from whom nought safe can be!
> Thou murtherer, which hast killed, and devil, which
> wouldst damn me![25]

Thus he addresses his mistress:

> Thou who, in many a propriety,[26]
> So truly art the sun to me,
> Add one more likeness, which I'm sure you can,
> And let me and my sun beget a man.[27]

Thus he represents the meditations of a lover:

> Though in thy thoughts scarce any tracks have been
> So much as of original sin,
> Such charms thy beauty wears as might

23. "To Mr. B. B.," 11. 10–14. "Post" means by relays of horses kept at each post station, i.e. hastily.

24. *The Second Anniversary*, 11. 173–84.

25. "Beauty," 11. 34–36.

26. Property, trait.

27. "The Parting," 11. 21–24. The sun was supposed to beget creatures from mud or slime.

Desires in dying confessed saints excite.
Thou with strange adultery
Dost in each breast a brothel keep;
Awake, all men do lust for thee,
And some enjoy thee when they sleep.

[COWLEY.][28]

The true taste of tears:

Hither with crystal vials, lovers, come,
And take my tears, which are Love's wine,
And try your mistress' tears at home;
For all are false, that taste not just like mine.

DONNE.[29]

This is yet more indelicate:

As the sweet sweat of roses in a still,
As that which from chafed musk-cat's pores doth trill,
As the almighty balm of th' early East;
Such are the sweat drops of my mistress' breast.
And on her neck her skin such luster sets,
They seem no sweat drops, but pearl coronets:
Rank sweaty froth thy mistress' brow defiles.

DONNE.[30]

Their expressions sometimes raise horror, when they intend perhaps to be pathetic:

As men in hell are from diseases free,
So from all other ills am I,
Free from their known formality:[31]
But all pains eminently lie in thee.

COWLEY.[32]

They were not always strictly curious whether the opinions from which they drew their illustrations were true; it was enough that they were popular. Bacon[33] remarks that some falsehoods are continued by tradition, because they supply commodious allusions.

It gave a piteous groan, and so it broke;
In vain it something would have spoke:

28. "The Innocent Ill," 11. 12–19. In the second line, "not even" is understood before "so much."
29. "Twickenham Garden," 11. 19–22.
30. "Elegy VIII," 11. 1–7.
31. The characteristic property by which something is defined.
32. "The Usurpation," 11. 33–36.
33. Francis Bacon (1561–1626), Viscount St. Albans, Lord Chancellor, essayist, philosopher, and scientist. See his *Advancement of Learning* (1605), II. i. 3.

The love within too strong for 't was,
Like poison put into a Venice glass.

COWLEY[34]

In forming descriptions, they looked out not for images, but for conceits. Night has been a common subject, which poets have contended to adorn. Dryden's Night[35] is well known; Donne's is as follows:

Thou seest me here at midnight, now all rest:
Time's dead low-water; when all minds divest
Tomorrow's business, when the laborers have
Such rest in bed, that their last churchyard grave,
Subject to change, will scarce be a type[36] of this,
Now when the client, whose last hearing is
Tomorrow, sleeps; when the condemned man,
Who, when he opes his eyes, must shut them then
Again by death, although sad watch he keep,
Doth practice dying by a little sleep,
Thou at this midnight seest me.[37]

It must be however confessed of these writers that if they are upon common subjects often unnecessarily and unpoetically subtle; yet where scholastic speculation[38] can be properly admitted, their copiousness and acuteness may justly be admired. What Cowley has written upon hope shows an unequaled fertility of invention:

  Hope, whose weak being ruined is,
  Alike if it succeed, and if it miss;
Whom good or ill does equally confound,
And both the horns of Fate's dilemma wound.
  Vain shadow, which dost vanish quite,
  Both at full noon and perfect night!
  The stars have not a possibility
  Of blessing thee;
If things then from their end we happy call,
'Tis Hope is the most hopeless thing of all.
  Hope, thou bold taster of delight,
  Who, whilst thou should'st but taste, devour'st it quite!
  Thou bring'st us an estate, yet leav'st us poor,
  By clogging it with legacies before!
  The joys which we entire should wed,
  Come deflowered virgins to our bed;

34. "The Heartbreaking," ll. 1–4. Venetian glass, fragile and expensive, was supposed to crack when poison was put into it.
35. *The Indian Emperor,* III. ii. 1–6.
36. Foreshadowing representation.
37. "Obsequies to the Lord Harrington," ll. 15–25.
38. Theory.

Good fortunes without gain imported be,
  Such mighty custom's paid to thee:
For joy, like wine, kept close, does better taste;
If it take air before, its spirits waste.[39]

To the following comparison of a man that travels, and his wife that stays at home, with a pair of compasses, it may be doubted whether absurdity or ingenuity has the better claim:

Our two souls therefore, which are one,
  Though I must go, endure not yet
A breach, but an expansion,
  Like gold to airy thinness beat.

If they be two, they are two so
  As stiff twin compasses are two;
Thy soul the fixed foot, makes no show
  To move, but doth, if th' other do.

And though it in the center sit,
  Yet when the other far doth roam,
It leans, and hearkens after it,
  And grows erect, as that comes home.

Such wilt thou be to me, who must
  Like th' other foot, obliquely run.
Thy firmness makes my circle just,
  And makes me end, where I begun.

DONNE.[40]

In all these examples it is apparent that whatever is improper or vicious is produced by a voluntary deviation from nature in pursuit of something new and strange; and that the writers fail to give delight, by their desire of exciting admiration.

Having thus endeavored to exhibit a general representation of the style and sentiments of the metaphysical poets, it is now proper to examine particularly the works of Cowley, who was almost the last of that race, and undoubtedly the best.

His *Miscellanies* contain a collection of short compositions, written some as they were dictated by a mind at leisure, and some as they were called forth by different occasions; with great variety of style and sentiment, from burlesque levity to awful[41] grandeur. Such an assemblage of diversified excellence no other poet has hitherto afforded. To choose the best, among many good, is one of the most hazardous attempts of criticism. I know not whether Scaliger himself has persuaded

39. "Against Hope," 11. 1–20.
40. "A Valediction: Forbidding Mourning," 11. 21–36.
41. Awe-inspiring.

many readers to join with him in his preference of the two favorite odes, which he estimates in his raptures at the value of a kingdom.[42] I will, however, venture to recommend Cowley's first piece,[43] which ought to be inscribed "To my Muse," for want of which the second couplet is without reference. When the title is added, there will still remain a defect; for every piece ought to contain in itself whatever is necessary to make it intelligible. Pope has some epitaphs without names; which are therefore epitaphs to be let,[44] occupied indeed for the present, but hardly appropriated.[45]

The ode on wit is almost without a rival. It was about the time of Cowley that "wit," which had been till then used for "intellection," in contradistinction to "will," took the meaning, whatever it be, which it now bears.

Of all the passages in which poets have exemplified their own precepts, none will easily be found of greater excellence than that in which Cowley condemns exuberance of wit:

> Yet 'tis not to adorn and gild each part,
>   That shows more cost than art.
> Jewels at nose and lips but ill appear;
>   Rather than all things wit, let none be there.
>   Several lights will not be seen,
>   If there be nothing else between.
> Men doubt, because they stand so thick i' th' sky,
> If those be stars which paint the galaxy.[46]

In his verses to Lord Falkland, whom every man of his time was proud to praise, there are, as there must be in all Cowley's compositions, some striking thoughts; but they are not well wrought. His elegy on Sir Henry Wotton[47] is vigorous and happy: the series of thoughts is easy and natural, and the conclusion, though a little weakened by the intrusion of Alexander,[48] is elegant and forcible.

It may be remarked, that in this elegy, and in most of his encomiastic poems, he has forgotten or neglected to name his heroes.

In his poem on the death of Hervey,[49] there is much praise but little passion, a very just and ample delineation of such virtues as a studious privacy admits, and such intellectual excellence as a mind not yet called

42. Julius Caesar Scaliger (1484–1558), whose *Poetics* (1561), Bk. vi, thus praises two of Horace's *Odes* (III, ix;IV. iii).

43. "The Motto."

44. For rent.

45. Assigned to a particular person.

46. "Ode: Of Wit," 11. 33–40.

47. Sir Henry Wotton (1568–1639), poet, ambassador to Venice, and Provost (headmaster) of Eton.

48. Alexander the Great. Cowley represents Wotton as lamenting that, like Alexander, he had only one world to conquer—i.e. the world of art.

49. William Hervey, a Cambridge University friend.

forth to action can display. He knew how to distinguish, and how to commend the qualities of his companion; but when he wishes to make us weep, he forgets to weep himself, and diverts his sorrow by imagining how his crown of bays,[50] if he had it, would "crackle" in the "fire." It is the odd fate of this thought to be worse for being true. The bay leaf crackles remarkably as it burns; as therefore this property was not assigned it by chance, the mind must be thought sufficiently at ease that could attend to such minuteness of physiology. But the power of Cowley is not so much to move the affections as to exercise the understanding.

"The Chronicle" is a composition unrivaled and alone: such gaiety of fancy, such facility of expression, such varied similitude, such a succession of images, and such a dance of words, it is in vain to expect except from Cowley. His strength always appears in his agility; his volatility is not the flutter of a light, but the bound of an elastic mind. His levity never leaves his learning behind it; the moralist, the politician, and the critic, mingle their influence even in this airy frolic of genius. To such a performance Suckling could have brought the gaiety, but not the knowledge; Dryden could have supplied the knowledge, but not the gaiety.

The verses to Davenant,[51] which are vigorously begun, and happily concluded, contain some hints of criticism very justly conceived and happily expressed. Cowley's critical abilities have not been sufficiently observed: the few decisions and remarks which his prefaces and his notes on the *Davideis* supply, were at that time accessions to English literature, and show such skill as raises our wish for more examples.

The lines from Jersey[52] are a very curious and pleasing specimen of the familiar descending to the burlesque.

His two metrical disquisitions *for* and *against* reason are no mean specimens of metaphysical poetry. The stanzas against knowledge produce little conviction. In those which are intended to exalt the human faculties, reason has its proper task assigned it: that of judging, not of things revealed, but of the reality of revelation. In the verses *for* reason is a passage which Bentley,[53] in the only English verses which he is known to have written, seems to have copied, though with the inferiority of an imitator.

> The holy Book like the eighth sphere[54] does shine
> With thousand lights of truth divine,
> So numberless the stars that to our eye

50. Wreath appropriate to a distinguished poet.

51. Sir William Davenant (1606–68), playwright and poet.

52. In "An Answer to a Copy of Verses Sent Me from Jersey," Cowley deplores the low estate of poetry on the island.

53. Richard Bentley (1662–1742), the most famous classical scholar of the period.

54. In Ptolemaic astronomy, the eighth of the spheres (hollow orbs which revolved around the earth) contained the fixed stars.

> It makes all but one galaxy:
> Yet Reason must assist too; for in seas
> So vast and dangerous as these,
> Our course by stars above we cannot know
> Without the compass too below.[55]

After this says Bentley:

> Who travels in religious jars,[56]
> Truth mixed with error, clouds with rays,
> With Whiston[57] wanting pyx[58] and stars,
> In the wide ocean sinks or strays.[59]

Cowley seems to have had, what Milton is believed to have wanted, the skill to rate his own performances by their just value, and has therefore closed his *Miscellanies* with the verses upon Crashaw,[60] which apparently excel all that have gone before them, and in which there are beauties which common authors may justly think not only above their attainment, but above their ambition.

To the *Miscellanies* succeed the *Anacreontics,* or paraphrastical translations of some little poems which pass, however justly, under the name of Anacreon. Of those songs dedicated to festivity and gaiety, in which even the morality is voluptuous, and which teach nothing but the enjoyment of the present day, he has given rather a pleasing than a faithful representation, having retained their sprightliness, but lost their simplicity. The Anacreon of Cowley, like the Homer of Pope, has admitted the decoration of some modern graces, by which he is undoubtedly made more amiable to common readers, and perhaps, if they would honestly declare their own perceptions, to far the greater part of those whom courtesy and ignorance are content to style the learned.

These little pieces will be found more finished in their kind than any other of Cowley's works. The diction shows nothing of the mold of time, and the sentiments are at no great distance from our present habitudes of thought. Real mirth must be always natural, and nature is uniform. Men have been wise in very different modes, but they have always laughed the same way.

Levity of thought naturally produced familiarity of language, and the familiar part of language continues long the same: the dialogue of comedy, when it is transcribed from popular manners and real life, is read from age to age with equal pleasure. The artifice of inversion, by

55. Cowley, "Reason," ll. 33–40.
56. Disputes.
57. William Whiston (1667–1752), an eccentric theologian.
58. Mariner's compass.
59. Bentley, "A Reply," ll. 13–16.
60. Richard Crashaw (?1612–49), friend of Cowley, Roman Catholic metaphysical and devotional poet, author of *Steps to the Temple* (1646).

which the established order of words is changed, or of innovation, by which new words or new meanings of words are introduced, is practiced not by those who talk to be understood, but by those who write to be admired.

The *Anacreontics* therefore of Cowley give now all the pleasure which they ever gave. If he was formed by nature for one kind of writing more than for another, his power seems to have been greatest in the familiar and the festive.

The next class of his poems is called *The Mistress,* of which it is not necessary to select any particular pieces for praise or censure. They have all the same beauties and faults, and nearly in the same proportion. They are written with exuberance of wit, and with copiousness of learning; and it is truly asserted by Sprat that the plenitude of the writer's knowledge flows in upon his page, so that the reader is commonly surprised into some improvement. But, considered as the verses of a lover, no man that has ever loved will much commend them. They are neither courtly nor pathetic, have neither gallantry nor fondness. His praises are too far-sought, and too hyperbolical, either to express love, or to excite it: every stanza is crowded with darts and flames, with wounds and death, with mingled souls, and with broken hearts.

The principal artifice by which *The Mistress* is filled with conceits is very copiously displayed by Addison.[61] Love is by Cowley, as by other poets, expressed metaphorically by flame and fire; and that which is true of real fire is said of love, or figurative fire, the same word in the same sentence retaining both significations. Thus, "observing the cold regard of his mistress's eyes, and at the same time their power of producing love in him, he considers them as burning-glasses made of ice. Finding himself able to live in the greatest extremities of love, he concludes the torrid zone to be habitable. Upon the dying of a tree, on which he had cut his loves, he observes that his flames had burnt up and withered the tree."[62]

These conceits Addison calls mixed wit; that is, wit which consists of thoughts true in one sense of the expression, and false in the other. Addison's representation is sufficiently indulgent. That confusion of images may entertain for a moment; but being unnatural, it soon grows wearisome. Cowley delighted in it, as much as if he had invented it; but, not to mention the ancients, he might have found it full-blown in modern Italy.

> Aspice quam variis distringar Vesbia curis,
>   Uror, et heu! nostro manat ab igne liquor;

61. *Spectator*, no. 62.
62. "The Vain Love," 11. 1–4; "The Request," 1. 32; "The Tree," 11. 5–6, respectively.

Sum Nilus, sumque Aetna simul; restringite flammas
O lacrimae, aut lacrimas ebibe flamma meas.[63]

One of the severe theologians of that time censured him as having published "a book of profane and lascivious verses."[64] From the charge of profaneness, the constant tenor of his life, which seems to have been eminently virtuous, and the general tendency of his opinions, which discover no irreverence of religion, must defend him; but that the accusation of lasciviousness is unjust, the perusal of his works will sufficiently evince.

Cowley's *Mistress* has no power of seduction: "she plays round the head, but comes not at the heart."[65] Her beauty and absence, her kindness and cruelty, her disdain and inconstancy, produce no correspondence of emotion. His poetical account of the virtues[66] of plants, and colors of flowers, is not perused with more sluggish frigidity. The compositions are such as might have been written for penance by a hermit, or for hire by a philosophical rhymer who had only heard of another sex; for they turn the mind only on the writer, whom, without thinking on a woman but as the subject for his task, we sometimes esteem as learned, and sometimes despise as trifling, always admire as ingenious, and always condemn as unnatural.

The *Pindaric Odes* are now to be considered; a species of composition which Cowley thinks Pancirolus[67] might have counted "in his list of the lost inventions of antiquity," and which he has made a bold and vigorous attempt to recover.

The purpose with which he has paraphrased an *Olympic* and *Nemean Ode* is by himself sufficiently explained. His endeavor was not to show "precisely what Pindar spoke, but his manner of speaking."[68] He was therefore not at all restrained to his expressions, nor much to his sentiments; nothing was required of him, but not to write as Pindar would not have written.

Of the *Olympic Ode* the beginning is, I think, above the original in

63. "See, Vesbia, how diverse the cares by which I am distracted. I burn, and alas! moisture drips from my fire. I am the Nile and Mt. Etna at the same time; oh, tears, put out my flames, or flame consume my tears" (Jacopo Sannazaro, "To Vesbia," *Epigrams*, 1526).

64. Edmund Elys, *Exclamation . . . against an Apology . . . for Mr. Cowley's Lascivious and Profane Verses* (1670).

65. Based on Pope, *Essay on Man*, iv. 254.

66. Powers, properties.

67. Guido Panciroli (1523–99), lawyer and scholar, was the author of a treatise published in a Latin translation (1599–1602), in the original Italian (1612), and in an English translation, *The History of Many Memorable Things Lost* (1715).

68. Preface to *Pindaric Odes* (1656). Pindar (518–438 B.C.), Theban poet, great author of Greek choral lyrics, especially paeans, dithyrambs, and epinicia (victory odes), the last divided into four groups, celebrating victories in the Olympian, the Pythian, the Nemean, and the Isthmian Games.

elegance, and the conclusion below it in strength. The connection is supplied with great perspicuity, and the thoughts, which to a reader of less skill seem thrown together by chance, are concatenated[69] without any abruption. Though the English ode cannot be called a translation, it may be very properly consulted as a commentary.

The spirit of Pindar is indeed not everywhere equally preserved. The following pretty lines are not such as his "deep mouth"[70] was used[71] to pour:

> Great Rhea's son. . .[72]
> If in Olympus' top where thou
> Sitt'st to behold thy sacred show,
> If in Alpheus' silver flight,[73]
> If in my verse thou take delight,
> My verse, great Rhea's son, which is
> Lofty as that, and smooth as this.[74]

In the *Nemean Ode* the reader must, in mere justice to Pindar, observe that whatever is said of "the original new moon, her tender forehead and her horns,"[75] is superadded by his paraphrast, who has many other plays of words and fancy unsuitable to the original, as,

> The table, free for every guest,
> No doubt will thee admit,
> And feast more upon thee, than thou on it.[76]

He sometimes extends his author's thoughts without improving them. In the *Olympionic* an oath is mentioned in a single word, and Cowley spends three lines in swearing by the "Castalian stream."[77] We are told of Theron's bounty, with a hint that he had enemies, which Cowley thus enlarges in rhyming prose:

> But in this thankless world the giver
> Is envied even by the receiver;
> 'Tis now the cheap and frugal fashion
> Rather to hide than own the obligation:
> Nay, 'tis much worse than so;
> It now an artifice does grow
> Wrongs and injuries to do,
> Lest men should think we owe.[78]

69. Linked.
70. Horace, *Odes*, IV. ii. 7.
71. Accustomed.
72. Zeus.
73. One of the largest rivers in Greece; it flows by the plain of Olympia.
74. *The Second Olympic Ode of Pindar*, 11. 29, 31–36. Here as often elsewhere, Johnson's quotation is only approximate.
75. *The First Nemean Ode of Pindar*, 11. 5–6.
76. Ibid., ll. 54–56.
77. A spring on Mt. Parnassus, sacred to the Muses.
78. *Second Olympic Ode*, ll. 180–188. Theron was ruler of Acragas in Sicily in the 5th century B.C.

It is hard to conceive that a man of the first rank in learning and wit, when he was dealing out such minute morality in such feeble diction, could imagine, either waking or dreaming, that he imitated Pindar.

In the following odes, where Cowley chooses his own subjects, he sometimes rises to dignity truly Pindaric, and, if some deficiencies of language be forgiven, his strains are such as those of the Theban bard were to his contemporaries:

Begin the song, and strike the living lyre:
Lo how the years to come, a numerous and well-fitted choir,
All hand in hand do decently advance,
And to my song with smooth and equal measure dance;
While the dance lasts, how long soe'er it be,
My music's voice shall bear it company;
Till all gentle notes be drowned
In the last trumpet's dreadful sound.[79]

After such enthusiasm, who will not lament to find the poet conclude with lines like these!

But stop, my Muse . . . .
Hold thy Pindaric Pegasus closely in,
Which does to rage begin . . . .
'Tis an unruly and a hard-mouthed horse . . . .
'Twill no unskillful touch endure,
But flings writer and reader too that sits not sure.[80]

The fault of Cowley, and perhaps of all the writers of the metaphysical race, is that of pursuing his thoughts to their last ramifications, by which he loses the grandeur of generality; for of the greatest things the parts are little; what is little can be but pretty, and by claiming dignity becomes ridiculous. Thus all the power of description is destroyed by a scrupulous enumeration; and the force of metaphors is lost, when the mind by the mention of particulars is turned more upon the original than the secondary sense, more upon that from which the illustration is drawn than that to which it is applied.

Of this we have a very eminent example in the ode entitled "The Muse," who goes to "take the air" in an intellectual chariot, to which he harnesses Fancy and Judgment, Wit and Eloquence, Memory and Invention: how he distinguished Wit from Fancy, or how Memory could properly contribute to Motion, he has not explained; we are however content to suppose that he could have justified his own fiction, and wish to see the Muse begin her career; but there is yet more to be done.

79. "The Resurrection," ll. 13–20.

80. "The Resurrection," ll. 52, 54–55, 57, 63–64. Pegasus, a winged horse, with his hoof created the fountain Hippocrene on Mt. Helicon, sacred to the Muses. Pegasus represents lofty poetic inspiration.

Let the *postilion* Nature mount, and let
The *coachman* Art be set;
And let the airy *footmen,* running all beside,
Make a long row of goodly pride;
Figures, conceits, raptures, and sentences,[81]
In a well-worded dress,
And innocent loves, and pleasant truths, and useful lies,
In all their gaudy *liveries.*[82]

Every mind is now disgusted with this cumber of magnificence; yet I cannot refuse myself the four next lines:

Mount, glorious queen, thy traveling throne,
And bid it to put on;
For long though cheerful is the way,
And life, alas! allows but one ill winter's day.

In the same ode, celebrating the power of the Muse, he gives her prescience, or, in poetical language, the foresight of events hatching in futurity; but having once an egg in his mind, he cannot forbear to show us that he knows what an egg contains:

Thou into the close nests of Time dost peep,
And there with piercing eye
Through the firm shell and the thick white dost spy
Years to come a-forming lie,
Close in their sacred secundine asleep.[83]

The same thought is more generally, and therefore more poetically, expressed by Casimir, a writer who has many of the beauties and faults of Cowley:

Omnibus mundi Dominator horis
Aptat urgendas per inane pennas,
Pars adhuc nido latet, et futuros
Crescit in annos.[84]

Cowley, whatever was his subject, seems to have been carried by a kind of destiny, to the light and the familiar, or to conceits which require still more ignoble epithets. A slaughter in the Red Sea, "new dyes the water's name";[85] and England, during the Civil War, was "Albion no more, nor to be named from white."[86] It is surely by some

81. Aphorisms.
82. "The Muse," 11. 8–15.
83. "Secundine" in this passage seems to refer to the inner coat of an egg in an early stage of growth.
84. "At every season the Creator of the world makes wings for flying through the void; some still lie concealed in the nest, and grow for future years" (Maciej Sarbiewski, 1595–1640, *Odes,* I. iv).
85. *The Plagues of Egypt,* 1. 362.
86. "To Dr. Scarburgh," 1. 6.

fascination not easily surmounted, that a writer professing to revive "the noblest and highest writing in verse,"[87] makes this address to the new year:

> Nay, if thou lov'st me, gentle year,
> Let not so much as love be there,
> Vain, fruitless love I mean; for, gentle year,
> Although I fear,
> There's of this caution little need,
> Yet, gentle year, take heed
> How thou dost make
> Such a mistake;
> Such love I mean alone
> As by thy cruel predecessors has been shown;
> For, though I have too much cause to doubt it,
> I fain would try, for once, if life can live without it.[88]

The reader of this will be inclined to cry out with Prior—

> Ye critics, say,
> How poor to this was Pindar's style![89]

Even those who cannot perhaps find in the Isthmian or Nemean songs what antiquity has disposed them to expect, will at least see that they are ill represented by such puny poetry; and all will determine that if this be the old Theban strain, it is not worthy of revival.

To the disproportion and incongruity of Cowley's sentiments must be added the uncertainty and looseness of his measures.[90] He takes the liberty of using in any place a verse of any length, from two syllables to twelve. The verses of Pindar have, as he observes, very little harmony to a modern ear; yet by examining the syllables we perceive them to be regular, and have reason enough for supposing that the ancient audiences were delighted with the sound. The imitator ought therefore to have adopted what he found, and to have added what was wanting: to have preserved a constant return of the same numbers,[91] and to have supplied smoothness of transition and continuity of thought.

It is urged by Dr. Sprat that the "irregularity of numbers is the very thing" which makes "that kind of poesy fit for all manner of subjects." But he should have remembered that what is fit for everything can fit nothing well. The great pleasure of verse arises from the known measure of the lines and uniform structure of the stanzas, by which the voice is regulated, and the memory relieved.

87. Preface to *Pindaric Odes*.
88. "To the New Year," ll. 37–48.
89. Matthew Prior, "An English Ballad on the Taking of Namur," ll. 95–96.
90. Prosody.
91. Metrical patterns. Pindar's poems are written in regular stanzas, either in a single form repeated or in repeated triads, each consisting of strophe, antistrophe, and epode. No two of his poems are metrically the same.

If the Pindaric style be, what Cowley thinks it, "the highest and noblest kind of writing in verse,"[92] it can be adapted only to high and noble subjects; and it will not be easy to reconcile the poet with the critic, or to conceive how that can be the highest kind of writing in verse, which, according to Sprat, "is chiefly to be preferred for its near affinity to prose."

This lax and lawless versification so much concealed the deficiencies of the barren, and flattered the laziness of the idle, that it immediately overspread our books of poetry; all the boys and girls caught the pleasing fashion, and they that could do nothing else could write like Pindar. The rights of antiquity were invaded, and disorder tried to break into the Latin: a poem on the Sheldonian Theater, in which all kinds of verse are shaken together, is unhappily inserted in the *Musae Anglicanae.*[93] Pindarism prevailed above half a century; but at last died gradually away, and other imitations supply its place.

The *Pindaric Odes* have so long enjoyed the highest degree of poetical reputation that I am not willing to dismiss them with unabated censure; and surely though the mode of their composition be erroneous, yet many parts deserve at least that admiration which is due to great comprehension of knowledge, and great fertility of fancy. The thoughts are often new, and often striking; but the greatness of one part is disgraced by the littleness of another; and total negligence of language gives the noblest conceptions the appearance of a fabric august in the plan, but mean in the materials. Yet surely those verses are not without a just claim to praise, of which it may be said with truth that no man but Cowley could have written them.

The *Davideis* now remains to be considered; a poem which the author designed to have extended to twelve books, merely, as he makes no scruple of declaring, because the *Aeneid* had that number; but he had leisure or perseverance only to write the third part. Epic poems have been left unfinished by Virgil, Statius,[94] Spenser, and Cowley. That we have not the whole *Davideis* is, however, not much to be regretted; for in this undertaking Cowley is, tacitly at least, confessed to have miscarried. There are not many examples of so great a work, produced by an author generally read and generally praised, that has crept through a century with so little regard. Whatever is said of Cowley is meant of his other works. Of the *Davideis* no mention is made; it never appears in books, nor emerges in conversation. By the *Spectator* it has once been quoted,[95] by Rymer it has once been praised,[96] and by Dryden, in *Mac-*

92. Preface to *Pindaric Odes.*

93. Corbett Owen's "Pindaric Song on the Sheldonian Theater" (1669) reappears in the *Musae Anglicanae* (*The English Muses,* 1761). The Sheldonian Theater is the major Oxford auditorium.

94. Statius (A.D. c.40–c.96) left only one book and a part of a second of his *Achilleid.*

95. *Spectator,* no. 590.

96. Thomas Rymer, in the Preface to his translation of Rapin's *Reflections on Aristotle's Treatise of Poesie* (1674).

Flecknoe, it has once been imitated;[97] nor do I recollect much other notice from its publication till now, in the whole succession of English literature.

Of this silence and neglect, if the reason be inquired, it will be found partly in the choice of the subject, and partly in the performance of the work.

Sacred history has been always read with submissive reverence, and an imagination overawed and controlled. We have been accustomed to acquiesce in the nakedness and simplicity of the authentic narrative, and to repose on its veracity with such humble confidence as suppresses curiosity. We go with the historian as he goes, and stop with him when he stops. All amplification is frivolous and vain; all addition to that which is already sufficient for the purposes of religion seems not only useless, but in some degree profane.

Such events as were produced by the visible interposition of divine power are above the power of human genius to dignify. The miracle of Creation, however it may teem with images, is best described with little diffusion of language: "He spake the word, and they were made."[98]

We are told that Saul "was troubled with an evil spirit";[99] from this Cowley takes an opportunity of describing Hell, and telling the history of Lucifer, who was, he says,

> Once general of a gilded host of sprites,[1]
> Like Hesper[2] leading forth the spangled nights;
> But down like lightning, which him struck, he came,
> And roared at his first plunge into the flame.[3]

Lucifer makes a speech to the inferior agents of mischief, in which there is something of heathenism, and therefore of impropriety; and, to give efficacy to his words, concludes by lashing "his breast with his long tail."[4] Envy, after a pause, steps out, and among other declarations of her zeal utters these lines:

> Do thou but threat, loud storms shall make reply,
> And thunder echo't to the trembling sky.
> Whilst raging seas swell to so bold an height,
> As shall the fire's proud element affright.
> Th' old drudging sun, from his long-beaten way,
> Shall at thy voice start, and misguide the day.
> The jocund orbs shall break their measured pace,
> And stubborn poles change their allotted place.

97. *MacFlecknoe,* ll. 72–73, parodies *Davideis,* i. 79–80.
98. See Psalms 33:9; 148:15.
99. 1 Samuel 16:14.
1. Spirits.
2. The evening star.
3. *Davideis,* i. 93–96.
4. *Davideis,* i. 143.

Heaven's gilded troops shall flutter here and there;
Leaving their boasting songs tuned to a sphere.[5]

Every reader feels himself weary with this useless talk of an allegorical being.

It is not only when the events are confessedly miraculous that fancy and fiction lose their effect: the whole system of life, while the theocracy was yet visible, has an appearance so different from all other scenes of human action that the reader of the sacred volume habitually considers it as the peculiar[6] mode of existence of a distinct species of mankind that lived and acted with manners uncommunicable; so that it is difficult even for imagination to place us in the state of them whose story is related, and by consequence their joys and griefs are not easily adopted, nor can the attention be often interested in anything that befalls them.

To the subject, thus originally indisposed to the reception of poetical embellishments, the writer brought little that could reconcile impatience, or attract curiosity. Nothing can be more disgusting than a narrative spangled with conceits, and conceits are all that the *Davideis* supplies.

One of the great sources of poetical delight is description, or the power of presenting pictures to the mind. Cowley gives inferences instead of images, and shows not what may be supposed to have been seen, but what thoughts the sight might have suggested. When Virgil describes the stone which Turnus lifted against Aeneas, he fixes the attention on its bulk and weight:

Saxum circumspicit ingens,
Saxum antiquum, ingens, campo quod forte jacebat
Limes agro positus, litem ut discerneret arvis.[7]

Cowley says of the stone with which Cain slew his brother,

I saw him fling the stone, as if he meant
At once his murther and his monument.

Of the sword taken from Goliah, he says,

A sword so great, that it was only fit
To cut off his great head that came with it.[8]

5. *Davideis*, i. 175–84. In the last lines, Cowley refers to the beliefs that each of the spheres (of sun, moon, the various planets, and the fixed stars), revolving around the earth, was guided by an angel, and that the spheres, moving in harmony, made a "music of the spheres," inaudible to humans.

6. Special.

7. "Looking around him, he sees a huge stone, an old, huge stone, which was lying by chance on the plain, placed to mark boundaries, and to settle quarrels about land" (*Aeneid*, xii. 896–98).

8. *Davideis*, i. 201–02; iii. 13–14.

Other poets describe death by some of its common appearances; Cowley says, with a learned allusion to sepulchral lamps, real or fabulous,

> 'Twixt his right ribs deep pierced the furious blade,
> And opened wide those secret vessels where
> Life's light goes out, when first they let in air.

But he has allusions vulgar as well as learned. In a visionary succession of kings:

> Joas[9] at first does bright and glorious show,
> In life's fresh morn his fame does early crow.[10]

Describing an undisciplined army, after having said with elegance,

> His forces seemed no army, but a crowd
> Heartless, unarmed, disorderly, and loud;

he gives them a fit of the ague.

The allusions however are not always to vulgar things: he offends by exaggeration as much as by diminution:

> The king was placed alone, and o'er his head
> A well-wrought heaven of silk and gold was spread.[11]

Whatever he writes is always polluted with some conceit:

> Where the sun's fruitful beams give metals birth,
> Where he the growth of fatal gold does see,
> Gold, which alone more influence has than he.[12]

In one passage he starts a sudden question, to the confusion of philosophy:

> Ye learned heads, whom ivy garlands grace,
> Why does that twining plant the oak embrace?
> The oak, for courtship most of all unfit,
> And rough as are the winds that fight with it.

His expressions have sometimes a degree of meanness that surpasses expectation:

> Nay, gentle guests, he cries, since now you're in,[13]
> The story of your gallant friend begin.[14]

In a simile descriptive of the morning:

9. King of Judah (2 Kings 11).
10. *Davideis,* iv. 587–89, ii. 600–01.
11. *Davideis,* iv. 719–20; ii. 349–50.
12. *Davideis,* i. 72–74. The sun supposedly engendered gold and other minerals.
13. You're involved (in your narrative).
14. *Davideis,* ii. 58–61; iii. 309–10.

As glimmering stars just at th' approach of day,
Cashiered by troops, at last drop all away.[15]

The dress of Gabriel deserves attention:

He took for skin a cloud most soft and bright,
That e'er the midday sun pierced through with light;
Upon his cheeks a lively blush he spread,
Washed from the morning beauties' deepest red;
An harmless flattering meteor shone for hair,
And fell adown his shoulders with loose care;
He cuts out a silk mantle from the skies,
Where the most sprightly azure pleased the eyes;
This he with starry vapors sprinkles all,
Took in their prime ere they grow ripe and fall;
Of a new rainbow, ere it fret or fade,
The choicest piece cut out, a scarf is made.[16]

This is a just specimen of Cowley's imagery: what might in general expressions be great and forcible, he weakens and makes ridiculous by branching it into small parts. That Gabriel was invested with the softest or brightest colors of the sky, we might have been told, and been dismissed to improve the idea in our different proportions of conception; but Cowley could not let us go till he had related where Gabriel got first his skin, and then his mantle, then his lace, and then his scarf, and related it in the terms of the mercer and tailor.

Sometimes he indulges himself in a digression, always conceived with his natural exuberance, and commonly, even where it is not long, continued till it is tedious:

I' the library a few choice authors stood,
Yet 'twas well stored; for that small store was good;
Writing, man's spiritual physic, was not then
Itself, as now, grown a disease of men.
Learning (young virgin) but few suitors knew;
The common prostitute she lately grew,
And with the spurious brood loads now the press;
Laborious effects of idleness.[17]

As the *Davideis* affords only four books, though intended to consist of twelve, there is no opportunity for such criticisms as epic poems commonly supply. The plan of the whole work is very imperfectly shown by the third part. The duration of an unfinished action cannot be known. Of characters either not yet introduced, or shown but upon few occasions, the full extent and the nice discriminations cannot be ascertained. The fable is plainly implex,[18] formed rather from the *Odyssey*

15. *Davideis*, iv. 402–03. "Cashiered" means "dismissed."
16. *Davideis*, ii. 796–807.
17. *Davideis*, i. 707–14.
18. Involved; having a complicated plot.

than the *Iliad*; and many artifices of diversification are employed with the skill of a man acquainted with the best models. The past is recalled by narration, and the future anticipated by vision: but he has been so lavish of his poetical art, that it is difficult to imagine how he could fill eight books more without practicing again the same modes of disposing his matter; and perhaps the perception of this growing incumbrance inclined him to stop. By this abruption,[19] posterity lost more instruction than delight. If the continuation of the *Davideis* can be missed, it is for the learning that had been diffused over it, and the notes in which it had been explained.

Had not his characters been depraved[20] like every other part by improper decorations, they would have deserved uncommon praise. He gives Saul both the body and mind of a hero:

> His way once chose, he forward thrust outright,
> Nor turned aside for danger or delight.[21]

And the different beauties of the lofty Merab and the gentle Michal are very justly conceived and strongly painted.[22]

Rymer has declared the *Davideis* superior to the *Jerusalem* of Tasso, "which," says he, "the poet, with all his care, has not totally purged from pedantry."[23] If by pedantry is meant that minute knowledge which is derived from particular sciences and studies, in opposition to the general notions supplied by a wide survey of life and nature, Cowley certainly errs by introducing pedantry far more frequently than Tasso. I know not, indeed, why they should be compared; for the resemblance of Cowley's work to Tasso's is only that they both exhibit the agency of celestial and infernal spirits, in which however they differ widely; for Cowley supposes them commonly to operate upon the mind by suggestion; Tasso represents them as promoting or obstructing events by external agency.

Of particular passages that can be properly compared, I remember only the description of Heaven, in which the different manner of the two writers is sufficiently discernible. Cowley's is scarcely description, unless it be possible to describe by negatives; for he tells us only what there is not in Heaven. Tasso endeavors to represent the splendors and pleasures of the regions of happiness. Tasso affords images, and Cowley sentiments. It happens, however, that Tasso's description affords some reason for Rymer's censure. He says of the Supreme Being,

19. Breaking off.
20. Disfigured.
21. *Davideis,* iv. 360–61.
22. *Davideis,* iii. 652–94. Merab and Michal were daughters of Saul. Michal married David (1 Samuel 18).
23. Thomas Rymer, Preface to Rapin's *Reflections.* Torquato Tasso wrote the epic poem *Jerusalem Delivered* (1581).

Ha sotto i piedi e Fato e la Natura,
Ministri umili, e'l moto e ch'il misura.[24]

The second line has in it more of pedantry than perhaps can be found in any other stanza of the poem.

In the perusal of the *Davideis,* as of all Cowley's works, we find wit and learning unprofitably squandered. Attention has no relief; the affections are never moved; we are sometimes surprised but never delighted, and find much to admire but little to approve. Still, however, it is the work of Cowley, of a mind capacious by nature and replenished by study.

In the general review of Cowley's poetry it will be found that he wrote with abundant fertility, but negligent or unskillful selection; with much thought, but with little imagery; that he is never pathetic and rarely sublime, but always either ingenious or learned, either acute or profound.

It is said by Denham in his elegy,

To him no author was unknown;
Yet what he writ was all his own.[25]

This wide position requires less limitation, when it is affirmed of Cowley, than perhaps of any other poet—he read much, and yet borrowed little.

His character of writing was indeed not his own: he unhappily adopted that which was predominant. He saw a certain way to present praise, and not sufficiently inquiring by what means the ancients have continued to delight through all the changes of human manners, he contented himself with a deciduous laurel, of which the verdure in its spring was bright and gay, but which time has been continually stealing from his brows.

He was in his own time considered as of unrivaled excellence. Clarendon represents him as having taken a flight beyond all that went before him,[26] and Milton is said to have declared that the three greatest English poets were Spenser, Shakespeare, and Cowley.

His manner he had in common with others, but his sentiments were his own. Upon every subject he thought for himself; and such was his copiousness of knowledge that something at once remote and applicable rushed into his mind; yet it is not likely that he always rejected a commodious[27] idea merely because another had used it: his known wealth was so great that he might have borrowed without loss of credit.

24. "Fate and Nature sit at his feet,/ Humble ministers, motion and that which measures it" (*Jerusalem Delivered,* IX. lvi. 7–8).

25. "On Mr. Abraham Cowley," ll. 29–30.

26. Edward Hyde, Lord Chancellor and first Earl of Clarendon (1609–74), *Life . . . of Clarendon* (1759), p. 16.

27. Convenient.

In his elegy on Sir Henry Wotton, the last lines have such resemblance to the noble epigram of Grotius[28] upon the death of Scaliger that I cannot but think them copied from it, though they are copied by no servile hand.

One passage in his *Mistress* is so apparently borrowed from Donne, that he probably would not have written it, had it not mingled with his own thoughts so as that he did not perceive himself taking it from another.

Although I think thou never found wilt be,
  Yet I'm resolved to search for thee;
  The search itself rewards the pains.
So, though the chemic his great secret miss[29]
(For neither it in art nor nature is),
  Yet things well worth his toil he gains:
  And does his charge and labor pay
With good unsought experiments by the way.

COWLEY.[30]

Some that have deeper digged Love's mine than I,
Say, where his centric happiness doth lie:
  I have loved, and got, and told;
But should I love, get, tell, till I were old,
I should not find that hidden mystery;
  Oh, 'tis imposture all:
And as no chemic yet th' elixir got,
But glorifies[31] his pregnant pot,
If by the way to him befall
Some odoriferous thing, or medicinal,
  So lovers dream a rich and long delight
  But get a winter-seeming summer's night.[32]

Jonson and Donne, as Dr. Hurd remarks,[33] were then in the highest esteem.

It is related by Clarendon that Cowley always acknowledged his obligation to the learning and industry of Jonson, but I have found no traces of Jonson in his works; to emulate Donne appears to have been his purpose: and from Donne he may have learned that familiarity with religious images, and that light allusion to sacred things, by which readers far short of sanctity are frequently offended; and which would not be borne in the present age, when devotion, perhaps not more fervent, is more delicate.

28. Hugo Grotius (1583–1645), dramatist and founder of international law.
29. Alchemists strove to discover the "elixir," a substance supposed to have almost miraculous powers of curing disease.
30. "Maidenhead," ll. 25–32.
31. Praises excessively.
32. "Love's Alchemy," ll. 1–12.
33. Richard Hurd (1720–1808), Bishop of Worcester, edited Cowley's *Select Works*.

Having produced one passage taken by Cowley from Donne, I will recompense him by another which Milton seems to have borrowed from him. He says of Goliah,

> His spear, the trunk was of a lofty tree,
> Which Nature meant some tall ship's mast should be.

Milton of Satan,

> His spear, to equal which the tallest pine
> Hewn on Norwegian hills, to be the mast
> Of some great admiral, were but a wand,
> He walked with.[34]

His diction was in his own time censured as negligent. He seems not to have known, or not to have considered, that words being arbitrary must owe their power to association, and have the influence, and that only, which custom has given them. Language is the dress of thought; and as the noblest mien, or most graceful action, would be degraded and obscured by a garb appropriated to the gross employments of rustics or mechanics,[35] so the most heroic sentiments will lose their efficacy, and the most splendid ideas drop their magnificence, if they are conveyed by words used commonly upon low and trivial occasions, debased by vulgar mouths, and contaminated by inelegant applications.

Truth indeed is always truth, and reason is always reason; they have an intrinsic and unalterable value, and constitute that intellectual gold which defies destruction: but gold may be so concealed in baser matter that only a chemist can recover it; sense may be so hidden in unrefined and plebeian words that none but philosophers can distinguish it; and both may be so buried in impurities as not to pay the cost of their extraction.

The diction, being the vehicle of the thoughts, first presents itself to the intellectual eye; and if the first appearance offends, a further knowledge is not often sought. Whatever professes to benefit by pleasing, must please at once. The pleasures of the mind imply something sudden and unexpected; that which elevates must always surprise. What is perceived by slow degrees may gratify us with the consciousness of improvement, but will never strike with the sense of pleasure.

Of all this, Cowley appears to have been without knowledge, or without care. He makes no selection of words, nor seeks any neatness of phrase: he has no elegances either lucky or elaborate; as his endeavors were rather to impress sentences upon the understanding than images on the fancy, he has few epithets, and those scattered without peculiar propriety or nice adaptation. It seems to follow from the necessity of

34. *Davideis*, iii. 393–94; *Paradise Lost*, i. 292–95.
35. Workmen, a term often used derogatorily.

the subject, rather than the care of the writer, that the diction of his heroic poem is less familiar than that of his slightest writings. He has given not the same numbers, but the same diction, to the gentle Anacreon and the tempestuous Pindar.

His versification seems to have had very little of his care; and if what he thinks be true, that his numbers are unmusical only when they are ill read, the art of reading them is at present lost; for they are commonly harsh to modern ears. He has indeed many noble lines, such as the feeble care of Waller never could produce. The bulk of his thoughts sometimes swelled his verse to unexpected and inevitable grandeur; but his excellence of this kind is merely fortuitous: he sinks willingly down to his general carelessness, and avoids with very little care either meanness or asperity.

His contractions are often rugged and harsh:

> One flings a mountain, and its rivers too
> Torn up with 't.[36]

His rhymes are very often made by pronouns or particles, or the like unimportant words, which disappoint the ear and destroy the energy of the line.

His combination of different measures is sometimes dissonant and unpleasing; he joins verses together, of which the former does not slide easily into the latter.

The words *do* and *did*, which so much degrade in present estimation the line that admits them, were in the time of Cowley little censured or avoided; how often he used them, and with how bad an effect, at least to our ears, will appear by a passage, in which every reader will lament to see just and noble thoughts defrauded of their praise by inelegance of language:

> Where honor or where conscience *does* not bind,
>   No other law shall shackle me;
>   Slave to myself I ne'er will be;
> Nor shall my future actions be confined
>   By my own present mind.
> Who by resolves and vows engaged *does* stand
>   For days that yet belong to fate,
> *Does* like an unthrift mortgage his estate
>   Before it falls into his hand;
>   The bondman[37] of the cloister so,
> All that he *does* receive *does* always owe.
> And still as Time comes in, it goes away,
>   Not to enjoy, but debts to pay!
> Unhappy slave, and pupil to a bell!

36. *Davideis*, iii. 379–80.
37. Serf; one bound to service. Possibly Cowley means a monk.

Which his hours' work as well as hours *does* tell:
Unhappy till the last, the kind releasing knell.[38]

His heroic lines are often formed of monosyllables; but yet they are sometimes sweet and sonorous.

He says of the Messiah,

Round the whole earth his dreaded name shall sound,
And reach to worlds that must not yet be found.

In another place, of David,

Yet bid him go securely, when he sends;
'Tis Saul that is his foe, and we his friends.
The man who has his God, no aid can lack;
And we who bid him go, will bring him back.[39]

Yet amidst his negligence he sometimes attempted an improved and scientific versification; of which it will be best to give his own account subjoined to this line,

Nor can the glory contain itself in th' endless space.

I am sorry that it is necessary to admonish the most part of readers that it is not by negligence that this verse is so loose, long, and, as it were, vast; it is to paint in the number the nature of the thing which it describes, which I would have observed in divers other places of this poem, that else will pass for very careless verses: as before,

And overruns the neighb'ring fields with violent course.

In the second book,

Down a precipice deep, down he casts them all.

And

And fell a-down his shoulders with loose care.

In the third,

Brass was his helmet, his boots brass, and o'er
His breast a thick plate of strong brass he wore.

In the fourth,

Like some fair pine o'erlooking all th' ignobler wood.

And,

Some from the rocks cast themselves down headlong.[40]

38. "Ode: Upon Liberty," ll. 95–110.
39. *Davideis*, i. 832–33; i. 429–32.
40. *Davideis*, i. 354; i. 60; ii. 610; ii. 801; iii. 391–92; iv. 351; iv. 982.

> And many more: but it is enough to instance in a few. The thing is that the disposition of words and numbers should be such, as that, out of the order and sound of them, the things themselves may be represented. This the Greeks were not so accurate as to bind themselves to; neither have our English poets observed it, for aught I can find. The Latins (*qui musas colunt severiores*)[41] sometimes did it, and their prince, Virgil, always: in whom the examples are innumerable, and taken notice of by all judicious men, so that it is superfluous to collect them.[42]

I know not whether he has, in many of these instances, attained the representation or resemblance that he purposes. Verse can imitate only sound and motion. A *boundless* verse, a *headlong* verse, and a verse of *brass* or of *strong brass,* seem to comprise very incongruous and unsociable ideas. What there is peculiar in the sound of the line expressing *loose care,* I cannot discover; nor why the *pine* is *taller* in an alexandrine[43] than in ten syllables.

But, not to defraud him of his due praise, he has given one example of representative versification which perhaps no other English line can equal:

> Begin, be bold, and venture to be wise.
> He who defers this work from day to day,
> Does on a river's bank expecting stay
> Till the whole stream that stopped him shall be gone,
> *Which runs, and as it runs, for ever shall run on.*[44]

Cowley was, I believe, the first poet that mingled alexandrines at pleasure with the common heroic of ten syllables, and from him Dryden borrowed the practice, whether ornamental or licentious. He considered the verse of twelve syllables as elevated and majestic, and has therefore deviated into that measure when he supposes the voice heard of the Supreme Being.

The author of the *Davideis* is commended by Dryden for having written it in couplets, because he discovered that any staff[45] was too lyrical for an heroic poem; but this seems to have been known before by May and Sandys, the translators of the *Pharsalia* and the *Metamorphoses.*

In the *Davideis* are some hemistichs, or verses left imperfect by the author, in imitation of Virgil, whom he supposes not to have intended to complete them: that this opinion is erroneous may be probably concluded, because this truncation is imitated by no subsequent Roman

41. "Who court the sterner Muses" (Martial, *Epigrams,* IX. xi. 17).
42. *Davideis,* "Notes upon the First Book."
43. An iambic hexameter line.
44. Cowley's translation of Horace's *Epistle,* I. ii. 40–43, which appears in his essay, "The Danger of Procrastination."
45. Stanzaic form.

poet; because Virgil himself filled up one broken line in the heat of recitation; because in one the sense is now unfinished; and because all that can be done by a broken verse, a line intersected by a caesura and a full stop will equally effect.

Of triplets[46] in his *Davideis* he makes no use, and perhaps did not at first think them allowable; but he appears afterwards to have changed his mind, for in the "Verses on the Government of Cromwell" he inserts them liberally with great happiness.[47]

After so much criticism on his poems, the essays which accompany them must not be forgotten. What is said by Sprat of his conversation, that no man could draw from it any suspicion of his excellence in poetry, may be applied to these compositions. No author ever kept his verse and his prose at a greater distance from each other. His thoughts are natural, and his style has a smooth and placid equability, which has never yet obtained its due commendation. Nothing is far-sought, or hard-labored; but all is easy without feebleness, and familiar without grossness.

It has been observed by Felton, in his *Essay on the Classics,* that Cowley was beloved by every muse that he courted; and that he has rivaled the ancients in every kind of poetry but tragedy.[48]

It may be affirmed, without any encomiastic fervor, that he brought to his poetic labors a mind replete with learning, and that his pages are embellished with all the ornaments which books could supply; that he was the first who imparted to English numbers the enthusiasm of the greater ode, and the gaiety of the less;[49] that he was equally qualified for sprightly sallies, and for lofty flights; that he was among those who freed translation from servility, and, instead of following his author at a distance, walked by his side; and that if he left versification yet improvable, he left likewise from time to time such specimens of excellence as enabled succeeding poets to improve it.

46. Three rhyming lines, instead of the usual couplet.

47. These "Verses," which occur at the end of Cowley's essay, "On the Government of Cromwell," contain only two triplets.

48. Henry Felton, *A Dissertation on Reading the Classics* (1713).

49. Respectively, the odes of Pindar and of Anacreon.

John Milton
1608–1674

The life of Milton has been already written in so many forms, and with such minute inquiry, that I might perhaps more properly have contented myself with the addition of a few notes to Mr. Fenton's elegant abridgment,[1] but that a new narrative was thought necessary to the uniformity of this edition.

John Milton was by birth a gentleman, descended from the proprietors of Milton near Thame in Oxfordshire, one of whom forfeited his estate in the times of York and Lancaster. Which side he took I know not; his descendant inherited no veneration for the White Rose.[2]

His grandfather John[3] was keeper of the forest of Shotover, a zealous papist, who disinherited his son because he had forsaken the religion of his ancestors.

His father, John, who was the son disinherited, had recourse for his support to the profession of a scrivener.[4] He was a man eminent for his skill in music, many of his compositions being still to be found; and his reputation in his profession was such that he grew rich, and retired to an estate. He had probably more than common literature,[5] as his son addresses him in one of his most elaborate Latin poems.[6] He married a gentlewoman of the name of Caston,[7] a Welsh family, by whom he had two sons, John the poet, and Christopher who studied the law, and adhered, as the law taught him, to the King's party, for which he was

1. Elijah Fenton wrote a life of Milton for his edition of *Paradise Lost* (1725).

2. The White Rose was the emblem of the House of York, and the Red Rose, of Lancaster. Johnson thinks of the Stuarts (Charles I, etc.) as descendents of the House of York.

3. Johnson's account of Milton's ancestry is inaccurate. The most reliable modern biography is William R. Parker's *Milton* (1968).

4. Copyist, notary, money lender, and contract lawyer.

5. Learning.

6. "Ad Patrem" ("To His Father").

7. Sarah Jeffrey. Probably Castons were among her ancestors.

awhile persecuted; but having, by his brother's interest, obtained permission to live in quiet, he supported himself so honorably by chamber-practice,[8] that soon after the accession of King James, he was knighted and made a judge; but his constitution being too weak for business, he retired before any disreputable compliances became necessary.[9]

He had likewise a daughter Anne, whom he married with a considerable fortune to Edward Phillips, who came from Shrewsbury, and rose in the Crown Office to be secondary;[10] by him she had two sons, John and Edward, who were educated by the poet, and from whom is derived the only authentic account of his domestic manners.[11]

John, the poet, was born in his father's house, at the Spread Eagle in Bread Street, December 9, 1608, between six and seven in the morning. His father appears to have been very solicitous about his education; for he was instructed at first by private tuition under the care of Thomas Young, who was afterwards chaplain to the English merchants at Hamburg; and of whom we have reason to think well, since his scholar considered him as worthy of an epistolary elegy.[12]

He was then sent to St. Paul's School, under the care of Mr. Gill; and removed, in the beginning of his sixteenth year, to Christ's College in Cambridge, where he entered a sizar, February 12, 1624.[13]

He was at this time eminently skilled in the Latin tongue; and he himself, by annexing the dates to his first compositions, a boast of which the learned Politian[14] had given him an example, seems to commend the earliness of his own proficiency to the notice of posterity. But the products of his vernal fertility have been surpassed by many, and particularly by his contemporary Cowley. Of the powers of the mind it is difficult to form an estimate: many have excelled Milton in their first essays who never rose to works like *Paradise Lost.*

At fifteen, a date which he uses till he is sixteen,[15] he translated or versified two Psalms, 114 and 136, which he thought worthy of the public eye; but they raise no great expectations; they would in any numerous school have obtained praise, but not excited wonder.

Many of his Elegies appear to have been written in his eighteenth year,[16] by which it appears that he had then read the Roman authors

8. Private practice, often as a consultant to other lawyers.

9. Christopher Milton was knighted in 1686; James II (1685–88), a Roman Catholic, tried to make the courts subservient to his views.

10. Second in charge of the Crown Office in the Court of Chancery.

11. John Phillips was Milton's secretary; Edward appended a biography to his edition of *Letters of State, written by Mr. John Milton* (1694).

12. "Elegy IV."

13. Milton entered as a commoner (regular student) rather than as a sizar (scholarship student). The correct date is 1625.

14. Angelo Poliziano, 15th-century Italian poet.

15. Instead of the usual phrase, "in his sixteenth year."

16. Some of Milton's Elegies, written in Latin, were composed when he was seventeen, and some at a later age.

with very nice discernment. I once heard Mr. Hampton, the translator of Polybius,[17] remark what I think is true, that Milton was the first Englishman who, after the revival of letters, wrote Latin verses with classic elegance. If any exceptions can be made, they are very few: Haddon and Ascham,[18] the pride of Elizabeth's reign, however they may have succeeded in prose, no sooner attempt verses than they provoke derision. If we produced anything worthy of notice before the Elegies of Milton, it was perhaps Alabaster's *Roxana*.[19]

Of these exercises which the rules of the University required, some were published by him in his maturer years. They had been undoubtedly applauded; for they were such as few can perform: yet there is reason to suspect that he was regarded in his College with no great fondness. That he obtained no fellowship is certain; but the unkindness with which he was treated was not merely negative. I am ashamed to relate what I fear is true, that Milton was one of the last students in either university that suffered the public indignity of corporal correction.

It was, in the violence of controversial hostility, objected to him that he was expelled: this he steadily denies, and it was apparently not true; but it seems plain from his own verses to Diodati,[20] that he had incurred "rustication," a temporary dismission into the country, with perhaps the loss of a term:

> Me tenet urbs reflua quam Thamesis alluit unda,
> Meque nec invitum patria dulcis habet.
> Jam nec arundiferum mihi cura revisere Camum
> Nec dudum *vetiti* me *laris* angit amor. . . .
> Nec duri libet usque minas perferre magistri
> Caeteraque ingenio non subeunda meo.
> Si sit hoc *exilium* patrios adiisse penates,
> Et vacuum curis otia grata sequi,
> Non ego vel *profugi* nomen sortemve recuso,
> Laetus et *exilii* conditione fruor.[21]

I cannot find any meaning but this, which even kindness and reverence can give to the term, *vetiti laris*, "a habitation from which he is

17. James Hampton's translation of the Greek historian Polybius (2nd century B.C.) appeared in 1756–61.

18. Walter Haddon (1516–72), Protestant theologian; Roger Ascham (1515–68), tutor to Queen Elizabeth I.

19. William Alabaster's Latin tragedy *Roxana* (written c. 1592, published 1632).

20. Charles Diodati (?1608–38), a physician and Milton's close friend.

21. "The city holds me that the Thames washes with its tides, and I rest willingly in the sweet place of my birth. Nor am I now anxious to revisit the river Cam with its reeds, nor longing for the habitation forbidden to me. . . . I do not care to be continually threatened by a harsh master, or to suffer other things repugnant to my spirit. If it is exile to be again in my paternal home, and free from care, to make use of welcome leisure, then I do not object to an exile's name or fate, but gladly rejoice in my state of banishment" ("Elegy I," ll. 9–12, 15–20).

excluded"; or how *exile* can be otherwise interpreted. He declares yet more, that he is weary of enduring "the threats of a rigorous master, and something else, which a temper like his cannot undergo." What was more than threat was probably punishment. This poem, which mentions his *exile*, proves likewise that it was not perpetual; for it concludes with a resolution of returning some time to Cambridge. And it may be conjectured from the willingness with which he has perpetuated the memory of his exile that its cause was such as gave him no shame.

He took both the usual degrees; that of Bachelor in 1628,[22] and that of Master in 1632; but he left the university with no kindness for its institution, alienated either by the injudicious severity of his governors, or his own captious perverseness. The cause cannot now be known, but the effect appears in his writings. His scheme of education, inscribed to Hartlib,[23] supersedes all academical instruction, being intended to comprise the whole time which men usually spend in literature, from their entrance upon grammar, "till they proceed, as it is called, masters of arts." And in his discourse *On the Likeliest Way to Remove Hirelings out of the Church,* he ingeniously proposes that

> the profits of the lands forfeited by the act for superstitious uses should be applied to such academies all over the land, where languages and arts may be taught together; so that youth may be at once brought up to a competency of learning and an honest trade, by which means such of them as had the gift, being enabled to support themselves (without tithes) by the latter, may, by the help of the former, become worthy preachers.[24]

One of his objections to academical education, as it was then conducted, is that men designed for orders[25] in the Church were permitted to act plays, "writhing and unboning their clergy limbs to all the antic and dishonest gestures of Trinculos,[26] buffoons and bawds, prostituting the shame of that ministry which they had, or were near having, to the eyes of courtiers and court-ladies, their grooms and mademoiselles."[27]

This is sufficiently peevish in a man, who, when he mentions his exile from the college, relates, with great luxuriance, the compensation

22. 1629.

23. Milton's *Of Education* (1644) is addressed to Samuel Hartlib, writer on education, agriculture, religion.

24. Johnson abstracts from a section of Milton's essay, the title of which is *Considerations Touching the Likeliest Means,* etc. (1659).

25. Holy Orders.

26. Probably a character in Thomas Tomkis's comedy *Albumazar* (1615), rather than Trinculo in Shakespeare's *The Tempest.*

27. From *An Apology against a Pamphlet Called A Modest Confutation of the Animadversions upon the Remonstrant against Smectymnuus* (1642). See below, pp. 394–95.

which the pleasures of the theater afford him.[28] Plays were therefore only criminal when they were acted by academics.

He went to the university with a design of entering into the church, but in time altered his mind; for he declared that whoever became a clergyman must "subscribe slave, and take an oath withal, which unless he took with a conscience that could retch, he must straight perjure himself. He thought it better to prefer a blameless silence before the [sacred] office of speaking, bought and begun with servitude and forswearing."[29]

These expressions are, I find, applied to the subscription of the Articles;[30] but it seems more probable that they relate to canonical obedience. I know not any of the Articles which seem to thwart his opinions; but the thoughts of obedience, whether canonical or civil, raised his indignation.

His unwillingness to engage in the ministry, perhaps not yet advanced to a settled resolution of declining it, appears in a letter to one of his friends, who had reproved his suspended and dilatory life, which he seems to have imputed to an insatiable curiosity, and fantastic luxury of various knowledge.[31] To this he writes a cool and plausible answer, in which he endeavors to persuade him that the delay proceeds not from the delights of desultory study, but from the desire of obtaining more fitness for his task; and that he goes on, "not taking thought of being late, so it give advantage to be more fit."[32]

When he left the university, he returned to his father, then residing at Horton in Buckinghamshire, with whom he lived five years; in which time he is said to have read all the Greek and Latin writers. With what limitations this universality is to be understood, who shall inform us?

It might be supposed that he who read so much should have done nothing else; but Milton found time to write the masque of *Comus*, which was presented at Ludlow, then the residence of the Lord President of Wales, in 1634; and had the honor of being acted by the Earl of Bridgewater's sons and daughter.[33] The fiction is derived from Homer's Circe;[34] but we never can refuse to any modern the liberty of borrowing from Homer:

a quo ceu fonte perenni
Vatum Pieriis ora rigantur aquis.[35]

28. "Elegy I," ll. 27–46.
29. *The Reason of Church Government* (1642), bk. ii.
30. Subscription to the Thirty-Nine Articles (of faith) was required of Anglican clergymen.
31. Indulgence in pursuing various branches of knowledge.
32. *Letter to a Friend,* second draft.
33. John Egerton, first Earl of Bridgewater, was Lord President of Wales.
34. The witch who turns men into beasts (*Odyssey,* bk. x), an allegorical example of sensuality.
35. "From whom, as from an eternal fountain, the lips of bards are bedewed with the waters of the Pierian spring" (Ovid, *The Loves,* III. ix. 25–26).

His next production was "Lycidas," an elegy, written in 1637, on the death of Mr. King, the son of Sir John King, secretary for Ireland in the time of Elizabeth, James, and Charles.[36] King was much a favorite at Cambridge, and many of the wits joined to do honor to his memory. Milton's acquaintance with the Italian writers may be discovered by a mixture of longer and shorter verses, according to the rules of Tuscan poetry, and his malignity to the Church by some lines which are interpreted as threatening its extermination.

He is supposed about this time to have written his "Arcades"; for while he lived at Horton he used sometimes to steal from his studies a few days, which he spent at Harefield, the house of the Countess Dowager of Derby, where the "Arcades" made part of a dramatic entertainment.[37]

He began now to grow weary of the country; and had some purpose of taking chambers in the Inns of Court, when the death of his mother set him at liberty to travel, for which he obtained his father's consent, and Sir Henry Wotton's directions, with the celebrated precept of prudence, "i pensieri stretti, ed il viso sciolto," "thoughts close, and looks loose."[38]

In 1638 he left England, and went first to Paris; where, by the favor of Lord Scudamore,[39] he had the opportunity of visiting Grotius,[40] then residing at the French court as ambassador from Christina of Sweden. From Paris he hasted into Italy, of which he had with particular diligence studied the language and literature; and, though he seems to have intended a very quick perambulation of the country, stayed two months at Florence; where he found his way into the academies, and produced his compositions with such applause as appears to have exalted him in his own opinion, and confirmed him in the hope, that, "by labor and intense study, which," says he, "I take to be my portion in this life, joined with a strong propensity of nature," he might "leave something so written to aftertimes, as they should not willingly let it die."[41]

It appears, in all his writings, that he had the usual concomitant of great abilities, a lofty and steady confidence in himself, perhaps not without some contempt of others; for scarcely any man ever wrote so much, and praised so few. Of his praise he was very frugal; as he set its value high, and considered his mention of a name as a security against the waste of time, and a certain preservative from oblivion.

36. Elizabeth I (1558–1603), James I (1603–25), Charles I (1625–49).

37. "Arcades," a short masque, was published in 1645. There is no evidence that the Countess Dowager of Derby entertained Milton.

38. Wotton to Milton, April 13, 1638. Wotton had been English ambassador to Venice.

39. John Scudamore, first Viscount Scudamore, English ambassador to France.

40. Hugo Grotius (1583–1645), famous Dutch scholar and founder of international law.

41. *The Reason of Church Government*, bk. ii.

At Florence he could not indeed complain that his merit wanted distinction. Carlo Dati presented him with an encomiastic inscription, in the tumid lapidary style;[42] and Francini wrote him an ode, of which the first stanza is only empty noise; the rest are perhaps too diffuse on common topics, but the last is natural and beautiful.[43]

From Florence he went to Siena, and from Siena to Rome, where he was again received with kindness by the learned and the great. Holstenius, the keeper of the Vatican Library, who had resided three years at Oxford, introduced him to Cardinal Barberini; and he, at a musical entertainment, waited for him at the door, and led him by the hand into the assembly. Here Selvaggi praised him in a distich, and Salsilli in a tetrastich; neither of them of much value.[44] The Italians were gainers by this literary commerce; for the encomiums with which Milton repaid Salsilli,[45] though not secure against a stern grammarian, turn the balance indisputably in Milton's favor.

Of these Italian testimonies, poor as they are, he was proud enough to publish them before his poems; though he says, he cannot be suspected but to have known that they were said "non tam de se, quam supra se."[46]

At Rome, as at Florence, he stayed only two months; a time indeed sufficient if he desired only to ramble with an explainer of its antiquities or to view palaces and count pictures, but certainly too short for the contemplation of learning, policy, or manners.[47]

From Rome he passed on to Naples, in company of a hermit; a companion from whom little could be expected, yet to him Milton owed his introduction to Manso, Marquis of Villa, who had been before the patron of Tasso.[48] Manso was enough delighted with his accomplishments to honor him with a sorry distich, in which he commends him for everything but his religion; and Milton, in return, addressed him in a Latin poem, which must have raised an high opinion of English elegance and literature.[49]

His purpose was now to have visited Sicily and Greece, but hearing of the differences between the king and parliament, he thought it proper to hasten home rather than pass his life in foreign amusements while his countrymen were contending for their rights. He therefore came back to Rome, though the merchants informed him of plots laid against him by the Jesuits, for the liberty of his conversations on reli-

42. Swollen, commemorative style.

43. Antonio Francini's ode in Italian is prefixed to the Latin poems of Milton (1645), as are Dati's Latin testimonial, and the epigrams of Salsilli and Selvaggi mentioned below.

44. A distich is a couplet; a tetrastich is a four-line stanza.

45. "Stanzas to Salsilli, a Roman Poet, as He Lay Ill," in Latin.

46. "Not so much about him as above him" (Milton's introductory note to his Latin poems).

47. Learning, statesmanship, or customary behavior.

48. Torquato Tasso, author of the Italian epic poem, *Jerusalem Delivered* (1581).

49. "Mansus."

gion. He had sense enough to judge that there was no danger, and therefore kept on his way, and acted as before, neither obtruding nor shunning controversy. He had perhaps given some offense by visiting Galileo, then a prisoner in the Inquisition for philosophical heresy; and at Naples he was told by Manso that, by his declarations on religious questions, he had excluded himself from some distinctions which he should otherwise have paid him. But such conduct, though it did not please, was yet sufficiently safe; and Milton stayed two months more at Rome, and went on to Florence without molestation.

From Florence he visited Lucca. He afterwards went to Venice; and having sent away a collection of music and other books traveled to Geneva, which he probably considered as the metropolis of orthodoxy. Here he reposed, as in a congenial element, and became acquainted with John Diodati[50] and Frederick Spanheim,[51] two learned professors of divinity. From Geneva he passed through France, and came home, after an absence of a year and three months.

At his return he heard of the death of his friend Charles Diodati; a man whom it is reasonable to suppose of great merit, since he was thought by Milton worthy of a poem, entitled *Epitaphium Damonis* written with the common but childish imitation of pastoral life.[52]

He now hired a lodging at the house of one Russell, a tailor in St. Bride's Churchyard, and undertook the education of John and Edward Phillips, his sister's sons. Finding his rooms too little, he took a house and garden in Aldersgate Street, which was not then so much out of the world as it is now; and chose his dwelling at the upper end of a passage that he might avoid the noise of the street. Here he received more boys, to be boarded and instructed.

Let not our veneration for Milton forbid us to look with some degree of merriment on great promises and small performance, on the man who hastens home because his countrymen are contending for their liberty, and, when he reaches the scene of action, vapors away his patriotism in a private boarding school. This is the period of his life from which all his biographers seem inclined to shrink. They are unwilling that Milton should be degraded to a schoolmaster; but, since it cannot be denied that he taught boys, one finds out that he taught for nothing, and another that his motive was only zeal for the propagation of learning and virtue; and all tell what they do not know to be true, only to excuse an act which no wise man will consider as in itself disgraceful. His father was alive; his allowance was not ample; and he supplied its deficiencies by an honest and useful employment.

50. Theologian, uncle of Milton's friend Charles Diodati.

51. There is no evidence that Milton met Frederick Spanheim, the scholar and theologian.

52. *Damon's Epitaph* (Damon being a common pastoral name). The poem makes clear that Milton was still abroad when he heard of Diodati's death.

It is told that in the art of education he performed wonders; and a formidable list is given of the authors, Greek and Latin, that were read in Aldersgate Street by youth between ten and fifteen or sixteen years of age. Those who tell or receive these stories should consider that nobody can be taught faster than he can learn. The speed of the horseman must be limited by the power of his horse. Every man that has ever undertaken to instruct others can tell what slow advances he has been able to make, and how much patience it requires to recall vagrant inattention, to stimulate sluggish indifference, and to rectify absurd misapprehension.

The purpose of Milton, as it seems, was to teach something more solid than the common literature of schools, by reading those authors that treat of physical subjects; such as the georgic,[53] and astronomical treatises of the ancients. This was a scheme of improvement which seems to have busied many literary projectors[54] of that age. Cowley, who had more means than Milton of knowing what was wanting to the embellishments of life, formed the same plan of education in his imaginary college.[55]

But the truth is that the knowledge of external nature, and the sciences[56] which that knowledge requires or includes, are not the great or the frequent business of the human mind. Whether we provide for action or conversation, whether we wish to be useful or pleasing, the first requisite is the religious and moral knowledge of right and wrong; the next is an acquaintance with the history of mankind, and with those examples which may be said to embody truth and prove by events the reasonableness of opinions. Prudence[57] and justice are virtues and excellences of all times and of all places; we are perpetually moralists, but we are geometricians only by chance. Our intercourse with intellectual nature is necessary; our speculations upon matter are voluntary and at leisure. Physiological learning[58] is of such rare emergence that one man may know another half his life without being able to estimate his skill in hydrostatics or astronomy, but his moral and prudential character immediately appears.

Those authors, therefore, are to be read at schools that supply most axioms of prudence, most principles of moral truth, and most materials for conversation; and these purposes are best served by poets, orators, and historians.

Let me not be censured for this digression as pedantic or paradoxical; for if I have Milton against me, I have Socrates on my side. It was his

53. A type of poem, like Virgil's *Georgics,* dealing with agricultural occupations. The Greek word *georgos* means "farmer."

54. A term, often derogatory, for persons advancing new schemes or methods.

55. In his "Proposition for the Advancement of Experimental Philosophy" (1661).

56. Branches of learning.

57. Proper conduct in the world.

58. Natural science.

labor to turn philosophy from the study of nature to speculations upon life, but the innovators whom I oppose are turning off attention from life to nature. They seem to think that we are placed here to watch the growth of plants, or the motions of the stars. Socrates was rather of opinion that what we had to learn was how to do good, and avoid evil.

"Οττι τοι ἐν μεγάροισι κακόν τ' ἀγαθόν τε τέτυκται.[59]

Of institutions we may judge by their effects. From this wonder-working academy, I do not know that there ever proceeded any man very eminent for knowledge; its only genuine product, I believe, is a small history of poetry, written in Latin by his nephew Phillips, of which perhaps none of my readers has ever heard.[60]

That in his school, as in everything else which he undertook, he labored with great diligence, there is no reason for doubting. One part of his method deserves general imitation. He was careful to instruct his scholars in religion. Every Sunday was spent upon theology, of which he dictated a short system,[61] gathered from the writers that were then fashionable in the Dutch universities.

He set his pupils an example of hard study and spare diet; only now and then he allowed himself to pass a day of festivity and indulgence with some gay gentlemen of Gray's Inn.[62]

He now began to engage in the controversies of the times, and lent his breath to blow the flames of contention. In 1641 he published a treatise *Of Reformation,* in two books, against the established Church; being willing to help the Puritans, who were, he says, "inferior to the prelates in learning."[63]

Hall, Bishop of Norwich, had published an *Humble Remonstrance,* in defense of episcopacy; to which in 1641 six[64] ministers, of whose names the first letters made the celebrated word *Smectymnuus,* gave their answer. Of this answer a confutation was attempted by the learned Ussher;[65] and to the confutation Milton published a reply, entitled, *Of Prelatical Episcopacy, and whether It May Be Deduced from the Apostolical Times, by Virtue of those Testimonies which are Alleged to that Purpose in some Late Treatises, One whereof Goes under the Name of James Lord Bishop of Armagh.*

I have transcribed this title, to show, by his contemptuous mention of

59. "What evil and what good has been wrought in thy halls" (*Odyssey,* iv. 392).

60. Edward Phillips, *A Short Treatise on the Dramatic Songs of the Ancient Poets* (1669), an edition of a popular student manual on the composition of Latin verse.

61. Coherent account.

62. One of the Inns of Court, residences for lawyers and law students.

63. In *A Second Defense of the People of England* (1654). Milton says that the Puritans were inferior to the Anglicans in "eloquence," rather than in learning.

64. Five: Stephen Marshall, Edmund Calamy, Thomas Young, Matthew Newcomen, William Spurstow. See above, p. 388 and n. 27. During 1641–42 Milton published four contributions to this controversy.

65. James Ussher, Archbishop of Armagh, noted for his study of biblical chronology.

Ussher, that he had now adopted the puritanical savageness of manners. His next work was *The Reason of Church Government Urged against Prelacy, by Mr. John Milton,* 1642. In this book he discovers, not with ostentatious exultation, but with calm confidence, his high opinion of his own powers; and promises to undertake something, he yet knows not what, that may be of use and honor to his country. "This," says he, "is not to be obtained but by devout prayer to that Eternal Spirit that can enrich with all utterance and knowledge, and sends out his seraphim with the hallowed fire of his altar, to touch and purify the lips of whom he pleases. To this must be added, industrious and select reading, steady observation, and insight into all seemly and generous arts and affairs; till which in some measure be compassed, I refuse not to sustain this expectation." From a promise like this, at once fervid, pious, and rational, might be expected the *Paradise Lost.*

He published the same year two more pamphlets, upon the same question.[66] To one of his antagonists, who affirms that he was "vomited out of the university,"[67] he answers, in general terms: "The Fellows of the College wherein I spent some years, at my parting, after I had taken two degrees, as the manner is, signified many times how much better it would content them that I should stay. . . . As for the common approbation or dislike of that place, as now it is, that I should esteem or disesteem myself the more for that, too simple is the answerer, if he think to obtain with me. Of small practice were the physician who could not judge, by what she and her sister[68] have of long time vomited, that the worser stuff she strongly keeps in her stomach, but the better she is ever kecking at,[69] and is queasy: she vomits now out of sickness; but before it be well with her, she must vomit by strong physic. . . . The University, in the time of her better health, and my younger judgment, I never greatly admired, but now much less."

This is surely the language of a man who thinks that he has been injured. He proceeds to describe the course of his conduct, and the train of his thoughts; and, because he has been suspected of incontinence, gives an account of his own purity: "That if I be justly charged," says he, "with this crime, it may come upon me with tenfold shame."[70]

The style of his piece is rough, and such perhaps was that of his antagonist. This roughness he justifies, by great examples, in a long digression. Sometimes he tries to be humorous: "Lest I should take him for some chaplain in hand, some squire of the body to his prelate,[71] one

66. *Animadversions upon the Remonstrant's Defense against Smectymnuus* (1641), and *An Apology against a Pamphlet.*

67. Preface to *A Modest Confutation of a Slanderous and Scurrilous Libel* (1642), attributed to Bishop Joseph Hall.

68. Oxford University.

69. Retching at; rejecting with distaste.

70. *An Apology against a Pamphlet.*

71. Bishop.

who serves not at the altar only but at the Court-cupboard,[72] he will bestow on us a pretty model of himself; and sets me out half a dozen phthisical[73] mottoes, wherever he had them, hopping short in the measure of convulsion fits; in which labor the agony of his wit having scaped narrowly, instead of well-sized periods, he greets us with a quantity of thumb-ring posies. . . . And thus ends this section, or rather dissection of himself."[74] Such is the controversial merriment of Milton; his gloomy seriousness is yet more offensive. Such is his malignity, "that hell grows darker at his frown."[75]

His father, after Reading was taken by Essex,[76] came to reside in his house; and his school increased. At Whitsuntide, in his thirty-fifth year, he married Mary,[77] the daughter of Mr. Powell, a Justice of the Peace in Oxfordshire. He brought her to town with him, and expected all the advantages of a conjugal life. The lady, however, seems not much to have delighted in the pleasures of spare diet and hard study; for, as Phillips relates, "having for a month led a philosophical life, after having been used at home to a great house, and much company and joviality, her friends, possibly by her own desire, made earnest suit to have her company the remaining part of the summer; which was granted, upon a promise of her return at Michaelmas."

Milton was too busy to much miss his wife; he pursued his studies; and now and then visited the Lady Margaret Ley, whom he has mentioned in one of his sonnets. At last Michaelmas arrived; but the lady had no inclination to return to the sullen gloom of her husband's habitation, and therefore very willingly forgot her promise. He sent her a letter, but had no answer; he sent more with the same success.[78] It could be alleged that letters miscarry; he therefore dispatched a messenger, being by this time too angry to go himself. His messenger was sent back with some contempt. The family of the lady were Cavaliers.[79]

In a man whose opinion of his own merit was like Milton's, less provocation than this might have raised violent resentment. Milton soon determined to repudiate her for disobedience; and, being one of those who could easily find arguments to justify inclination, published (in 1644)[80] *The Doctrine and Discipline of Divorce;* which was followed by *The Judgment of Martin Bucer, concerning Divorce;*[81] and the next year, his

72. As a servant at Court; courtier.

73. Asthmatic.

74. "Himself" is Milton's antagonist; "posies" are mottoes for rings.

75. See *Paradise Lost,* ii. 719–20.

76. The third Earl of Essex, a Parliamentary general, captured Reading on April 27, 1643.

77. He married Mary Powell in the summer of 1642.

78. Outcome.

79. Royalists, in the Civil Wars against the Parliamentary (Roundhead) party.

80. Actually 1643.

81. Bucer, a German theologian and Professor of Divinity at Cambridge, had defended divorce in his *On the Reign of Christ* (1557), which Milton recasts in this work.

Tetrachordon: Expositions upon the Four Chief Places of Scripture which Treat of Marriage.

This innovation was opposed, as might be expected, by the clergy, who, then holding their famous assembly at Westminster, procured that the author should be called before the Lords; "but that House," says Wood, "whether approving the doctrine, or not favoring his accusers, did soon dismiss him."[82]

There seems not to have been much written against him, nor anything by any writer of eminence. The antagonist that appeared is styled by him, "a servingman turned solicitor."[83] Howell in his *Letters*[84] mentions the new doctrine with contempt; and it was, I suppose, thought more worthy of derision than of confutation. He complains of his neglect in two sonnets, of which the first is contemptible, and the second not excellent.[85]

From this time it is observed that he became an enemy to the Presbyterians, whom he had favored before.[86] He that changes his party by his humor is not more virtuous than he that changes it by his interest; he loves himself rather than truth.

His wife and her relations now found that Milton was not an unresisting sufferer of injuries; and perceiving that he had begun to put his doctrine in practice, by courting a young woman of great accomplishments, the daughter of one Doctor Davis, who was however not ready to comply, they resolved to endeavor a reunion. He went sometimes to the house of one Blackborough, his relation, in the lane of St. Martin's-le-Grand, and at one of his usual visits was surprised to see his wife come from another room, and implore forgiveness on her knees. He resisted her entreaties for a while; "but partly," says Phillips, "his own generous nature, more inclinable to reconciliation than to perseverance in anger or revenge, and partly the strong intercession of friends on both sides, soon brought him to an act of oblivion and a firm league of peace." It were injurious to omit that Milton afterwards received her father and her brothers in his own house, when they were distressed, with other Royalists.

He published about the same time his *Areopagitica, a Speech of Mr. John Milton for the Liberty of Unlicensed Printing.* The danger of such unbounded liberty, and the danger of bounding it, have produced a problem in the science of government, which human understanding seems hitherto unable to solve. If nothing may be published but what civil authority shall have previously approved, power must always be

82. Anthony à Wood, *Athenae Oxonienses* (1691–92).
83. *Colasterion: A Reply to a Nameless Answer* . . . (1645). A solicitor is a lawyer.
84. James Howell in his *Familiar Letters* (1645–55).
85. "Sonnets XI and XII."
86. The Parliamentary party was composed mainly of Presbyterians and various Independent sects.

the standard of truth; if every dreamer of innovations may propagate his projects, there can be no settlement; if every murmurer at government may diffuse discontent, there can be no peace; and if every skeptic in theology may teach his follies, there can be no religion. The remedy against these evils is to punish the authors; for it is yet allowed that every society may punish, though not prevent, the publication of opinions which that society shall think pernicious; but this punishment, though it may crush the author, promotes the book; and it seems not more reasonable to leave the right of printing unrestrained, because writers may be afterwards censured, than it would be to sleep with doors unbolted, because by our laws we can hang a thief.

But whatever were his engagements, civil or domestic, poetry was never long out of his thoughts. About this time (1645) a collection of his Latin and English poems appeared, in which the "Allegro" and "Penseroso," with some others, were first published.

He had taken a larger house in Barbican for the reception of scholars; but the numerous relations of his wife, to whom he generously granted refuge for a while, occupied his rooms. In time, however, they went away; "and the house again," says Phillips, "now looked like a house of the Muses only, though the accession of scholars was not great. Possibly his having proceeded so far in the education of youth, may have been the occasion of his adversaries calling him pedagogue and schoolmaster; whereas it is well known he never set up for a public school to teach all the young fry of a parish, but only was willing to impart his learning and knowledge to relations and the sons of gentlemen who were his intimate friends; and that neither his writings nor his way of teaching ever savored in the least of pedantry."

Thus laboriously does his nephew extenuate what cannot be denied, and what might be confessed without disgrace. Milton was not a man who could become mean[87] by a mean employment. This, however, his warmest friends seem not to have found; they therefore shift and palliate. He did not sell literature to all comers at an open shop; he was a chamber-milliner,[88] and measured his commodities only to his friends.

Phillips, evidently impatient of viewing him in this state of degradation, tells us that it was not long continued; and, to raise his character again, has a mind to invest him with military splendor: "He is much mistaken," he says, "if there was not about this time a design of making him an adjutant-general in Sir William Waller's army. But the new-modeling of the army proved an obstruction to the design." An event cannot be set at a much greater distance than by having been only "designed, about some time," if a man "be not much mistaken." Milton shall be a pedagogue no longer; for, if Phillips be not much mistaken, somebody at some time designed him for a soldier.

87. Low, vulgar.

88. A milliner who carries on business in a private house, not in a shop.

About the time that the army was new-modeled (1645) he removed to a smaller house in Holborn, which opened backward into Lincoln's Inn Fields. He is not known to have published anything afterwards till the King's death, when, finding his murderers condemned by the Presbyterians, he wrote a treatise to justify it, and "to compose the minds of the people."[89]

He made some *Remarks on the Articles of Peace between Ormonde and the Irish Rebels.*[90] While he contented himself to write, he perhaps did only what his conscience dictated; and if he did not very vigilantly watch the influence of his own passions, and the gradual prevalence of opinions, first willingly admitted and then habitually indulged, if objections, by being overlooked, were forgotten, and desire superinduced conviction, he yet shared only the common weakness of mankind, and might be no less sincere than his opponents. But as faction seldom leaves a man honest, however it might find him, Milton is suspected of having interpolated the book called *Eikon Basilike,* which the Council of State, to whom he was now made Latin Secretary, employed him to censure, by inserting a prayer taken from Sidney's *Arcadia,* and imputing it to the King; whom he charges, in his *Eikonoklastes,* with the use of this prayer as with a heavy crime, in the indecent language with which prosperity had emboldened the advocates for rebellion to insult all that is venerable or great: "Who would have imagined so little fear in him of the true all-seeing Deity—as, immediately before his death, to pop into the hands of the grave bishop that attended him, as a special relic of his saintly exercises, a prayer stolen word for word from the mouth of a heathen woman praying to a heathen god?"[91]

The papers which the King gave to Dr. Juxon[92] on the scaffold the regicides took away, so that they were at least the publishers of this prayer; and Dr. Birch,[93] who had examined the question with great care, was inclined to think them the forgers. The use of it by adaptation was innocent; and they who could so noisily censure it, with a little extension of their malice could contrive what they wanted to accuse.

King Charles the Second, being now sheltered in Holland, employed Salmasius,[94] Professor of Polite Learning at Leyden, to write a defense of his father and of monarchy; and, to excite his industry, gave him, as

89. *The Tenure of Kings and Magistrates* (1649).

90. *Observations upon the Articles of Peace with the Irish Rebels* (1649). The first Duke of Ormonde was chief of the Royalist forces in Ireland.

91. *Eikon Basilike (The King's Image)* was published immediately after Charles I's execution in 1649. Milton, who attacked it in *Eikonoklastes (The Image Breaker),* seems to be innocent of interpolating the prayer from Sir Philip Sidney's *Arcadia* (1590), a long pastoral romance.

92. William Juxon, Bishop of London.

93. Thomas Birch, *An Historical and Critical Account of the Life and Writings of Mr. John Milton* (1738). He revised his views on the possible forgery in the 1753 edition.

94. Claude de Saumaise (1588–1653), French scholar.

was reported, a hundred jacobuses.[95] Salmasius was a man of skill in languages, knowledge of antiquity, and sagacity of emendatory criticism, almost exceeding all hope of human attainment; and having, by excessive praises, been confirmed in great confidence of himself, though he probably had not much considered the principles of society or the rights of government, undertook the employment without distrust of his own qualifications; and, as his expedition in writing was wonderful, in 1649 published *Defensio Regis.*[96]

To this Milton was required to write a sufficient answer; which he performed (1651) in such a manner, that Hobbes declared himself unable to decide whose language was best, or whose arguments were worst.[97] In my opinion, Milton's periods are smoother, neater, and more pointed; but he delights himself with teasing his adversary as much as with confuting him. He makes a foolish allusion of Salmasius, whose doctrine he considers as servile and unmanly, to the stream of Salmacis, which whoever entered left half his virility behind him.[98] Salmasius was a Frenchman, and was unhappily married to a scold. "Tu es Gallus," says Milton, "et, ut aiunt, nimium gallinaceus."[99] But his supreme pleasure is to tax his adversary, so renowned for criticism, with vicious[1] Latin. He opens his book with telling that he has used *persona,* which, according to Milton, signifies only a *mask,* in a sense not known to the Romans, by applying it as we apply *person.* But as Nemesis is always on the watch, it is memorable that he has enforced the charge of a solecism by an expression in itself grossly solecistical, when, for one of those supposed blunders, he says, as Ker, and I think some one before him, has remarked, "propino te grammatistis tuis *vapulandum.*"[2] From *vapulo,* which has a passive sense, *vapulandus* can never be derived. No man forgets his original trade: the rights of nations, and of kings, sink into questions of grammar, if grammarians discuss them.

Milton when he undertook this answer was weak of body and dim of sight; but his will was forward, and what was wanting of health was supplied by zeal. He was rewarded with a thousand pounds, and his book was much read; for paradox, recommended by spirit and elegance, easily gains attention; and he who told every man that he was equal to his king could hardly want an audience.

That the performance of Salmasius was not dispersed with equal rapidity, or read with equal eagerness, is very credible. He taught only the stale doctrine of authority and the unpleasing duty of submission;

95. A jacobus was worth twenty shillings.
96. *A Defense of the King.*
97. Thomas Hobbes, the philosopher, in *Behemoth* (1679).
98. See Ovid, *Metamorphoses,* iv. 285–388.
99. "You are Gallic and, so they say, exceedingly henpecked."
1. Defective.
2. "I turn you over to your fellow grammarians to be beaten" (John Ker, *Select Remarks on Latin,* 1709).

and he had been so long not only the monarch but the tyrant of literature that almost all mankind were delighted to find him defied and insulted by a new name, not yet considered as anyone's rival. If Christina, as is said, commended the *Defense of the People,*[3] her purpose must be to torment Salmasius, who was then at her Court; for neither her civil station nor her natural character could dispose her to favor the doctrine, who was by birth a queen, and by temper despotic.

That Salmasius was, from the appearance of Milton's book, treated with neglect, there is not much proof; but to a man so long accustomed to admiration, a little praise of his antagonist would be sufficiently offensive, and might incline him to leave Sweden, from which, however, he was dismissed, not with any mark of contempt, but with a train of attendance scarce less than regal.

He prepared a reply, which, left as it was imperfect, was published by his son in the year of the Restoration.[4] In the beginning, being probably most in pain for his Latinity, he endeavors to defend his use of the word *persona*; but, if I remember right, he misses a better authority than any that he has found, that of Juvenal in his fourth Satire:

> Quid agas cum dira et foedior omni
> Crimine *persona* est?[5]

As Salmasius reproached Milton with losing his eyes in the quarrel, Milton delighted himself with the belief that he had shortened Salmasius's life, and both perhaps with more malignity than reason. Salmasius died at the Spa, September 3, 1653; and as controvertists are commonly said to be killed by their last dispute, Milton was flattered with the credit of destroying him.

Cromwell had now dismissed the parliament by the authority of which he had destroyed monarchy, and commenced monarch himself, under the title of Protector, but with kingly and more than kingly power.[6] That his authority was lawful never was pretended; he himself founded his right only in necessity; but Milton, having now tasted the honey of public employment, would not return to hunger and philosophy, but, continuing to exercise his office under a manifest usurpation, betrayed to his power that liberty which he had defended. Nothing can be more just than that rebellion should end in slavery; that he, who had justified the murder of his king, for some acts which to him seemed unlawful, should now sell his services, and his flatteries, to a tyrant, of whom it was evident that he could do nothing lawful.

He had now been blind for some years; but his vigor of intellect was

3. Milton's answer to Salmasius; in Latin, *Pro Populo Anglicano Defensio.*
4. 1660.
5. "What can you do about someone whose person is more foul and monstrous than any crime charged against him?" (ll. 14–15).
6. December 16, 1653, having rid himself of the remains of Parliament.

such that he was not disabled to discharge his office of Latin Secretary or continue his controversies. His mind was too eager to be diverted, and too strong to be subdued.

About this time his first wife died in childbed[7] having left him three daughters. As he probably did not much love her, he did not long continue the appearance of lamenting her; but after a short time married Katherine, the daughter of one Captain Woodcock of Hackney; a woman doubtless educated in opinions like his own. She died within a year, of childbirth, or some distemper that followed it; and her husband has honored her memory with a poor sonnet.[8]

The first reply to Milton's *Defensio Populi* was published in 1651, called *Apologia pro Rege et Populo Anglicano, contra Johannis Polypragmatici (alias Miltoni) Defensionem Destructivam Regis et Populi.*[9] Of this the author was not known; but Milton and his nephew Phillips, under whose name he published an answer so much corrected by him that it might be called his own, imputed it to Bramhall;[10] and, knowing him no friend to regicides, thought themselves at liberty to treat him as if they had known what they only suspected.

Next year appeared *Regii Sanguinis Clamor ad Coelum.*[11] Of this the author was Peter du Moulin, who was afterwards prebendary of Canterbury; but Morus, or More,[12] a French minister, having the care of its publication, was treated as the writer by Milton in his *Defensio Secunda,*[13] and overwhelmed by such violence of invective that he began to shrink under the tempest, and gave his persecutors the means of knowing the true author. Du Moulin was now in great danger; but Milton's pride operated against his malignity; and both he and his friends were more willing that Du Moulin should escape than that he should be convicted of mistake.

In this *Second Defense* he shows that his eloquence is not merely satirical; the rudeness of his invective is equalled by the grossness of his flattery.

> Deserimur, Cromuelle, tu solus superes, ad te summa nostrarum rerum rediit, in te solo consistit, insuperabili tuae virtuti cedimus cuncti, nemine vel obloquente, nisi qui aequales inaequalis ipse honores sibi quaerit, aut digniori concessos invidet, aut non intelligit nihil esse in societate hominum magis vel Deo gratum, vel rationi consentaneum, esse in civitate nihil

7. 1652.

8. "Sonnet XIX" : "Methought I saw my late espoused saint. . . ."

9. *Defense of the King and the English People against John Busybody's (alias Milton's) Defense, which Would Destroy King and People.*

10. John Bramhall, Archbishop of Armagh. The actual author was John Rowland, a Royalist clergyman.

11. *The Cry of the King's Blood to Heaven.*

12. Alexander More (or Morus) wrote only its dedication to Charles II.

13. The *Second Defense* (the first being the *Defense of the People of England*).

aequius, nihil utilius, quam potiri rerum dignissimum. Eum te agnoscunt omnes, Cromuelle, ea tu civis maximus et gloriosissimus, dux publici consilii, exercituum fortissimorum imperator, pater patriae gessisti. Sic tu spontanea bonorum omnium et animitus missa voce salutaris.[14]

Caesar, when he assumed the perpetual dictatorship, had not more servile or more elegant flattery. A translation may show its servility; but its elegance is less attainable. Having exposed the unskillfulness or selfishness of the former government, "We were left," says Milton, "to ourselves: the whole national interest fell into your hands, and subsists only in your abilities. To your virtue, overpowering and resistless, every man gives way, except some who, without equal qualifications, aspire to equal honors, who envy the distinctions of merit greater than their own; or who have yet to learn that in the coalition of human society nothing is more pleasing to God or more agreeable to reason than that the highest mind should have the sovereign power. Such, Sir, are you by general confession; such are the things achieved by you, the greatest and most glorious of our countrymen, the director of our public councils, the leader of unconquered armies, the father of your country; for by that title does every good man hail you, with sincere and voluntary praise."

Next year, having defended all that wanted defense, he found leisure to defend himself. He undertook his own vindication against More, whom he declares in his title to be justly called the author of the *Regii Sanguinis Clamor.* In this there is no want of vehemence nor eloquence, nor does he forget his wonted wit. "Morus es? an Momus? an uterque idem est?"[15] He then remembers that *Morus* is Latin for a mulberry tree, and hints at the known transformation:

Poma alba ferebat
Quae post nigra tulit Morus.[16]

14. "Cromwell, we are deserted; you alone remain; the sovereign authority of the state is returned into your hands, and subsists only in you. To your invincible virtue we all give place, all but such, who without equal ability are desirous of equal honors; who look with envy upon the honors bestowed upon others more worthy than themselves, or who know not, that there is nothing in human society more pleasing to God, or more agreeable to reason, that there is nothing more just in a state, nothing more useful, than that the most worthy should possess the sovereign power. That you are such, Cromwell, that such have been your deeds, is acknowledged by all—you, who are the greatest and most glorious of our citizens, the director of the public counsels, the leader of the bravest of armies, the father of your country: for by this title do all good men hail you with spontaneous voice sent forth from the heart" (trans. Burnett, rev. Hadas). Compare Johnson's translation below. Johnson's note attacking Milton's use of "gloriosissimus" is omitted.

15. "Are you Morus or Momus? Or are both one and the same?" (*Milton's Defense of Himself,* 1655). Momus, the Greek god of ridicule, personifies faultfinding.

16. "Morus once had borne white fruit, but afterwards bore black" (misquoted from Ovid, *Metamorphoses,* iv. 51–52). Johnson changes Milton's *qui* (masc.) = *Morus* (fool) back to Ovid's *quae* (fem.) = *morus* (mulberry tree).

With this piece ended his controversies; and he from this time gave himself up to his private studies and his civil employment.

As Secretary to the Protector he is supposed to have written the Declaration of the reasons for a war with Spain. His agency was considered as of great importance; for when a treaty with Sweden was artfully suspended, the delay was publicly imputed to Mr. Milton's indisposition; and the Swedish agent was provoked to express his wonder, that only one man in England could write Latin and that man blind.

Being now forty-seven years old, and seeing himself disencumbered from external interruptions, he seems to have recollected his former purposes, and to have resumed three great works which he had planned for his future employment: an epic poem, the history of his country, and a dictionary of the Latin tongue.

To collect a dictionary seems a work of all others least practicable in a state of blindness, because it depends upon perpetual and minute inspection and collation. Nor would Milton probably have begun it, after he had lost his eyes; but, having had it always before him, he continued it, says Phillips, "almost to his dying day; but the papers were so discomposed and deficient that they could not be fitted for the press." The compilers of the Latin dictionary printed at Cambridge had the use of those collections in three folios; but what was their fate afterwards is not known.

To compile a history from various authors, when they can only be consulted by other eyes, is not easy, nor possible but with more skillful and attentive help than can be commonly obtained; and it was probably the difficulty of consulting and comparing that stopped Milton's narrative at the Conquest;[17] a period at which affairs were not yet very intricate, nor authors very numerous.

For the subject of his epic poem, after much deliberation, "long choosing, and beginning late,"[18] he fixed upon *Paradise Lost*; a design so comprehensive that it could be justified only by success. He had once designed to celebrate King Arthur, as he hints in his verses to Mansus; but "Arthur was reserved," says Fenton, "to another destiny."[19]

It appears by some sketches of poetical projects left in manuscript, and to be seen in a library at Cambridge, that he had digested his thoughts on this subject into one of those wild dramas which were anciently called mysteries; and Phillips had seen what he terms part of a tragedy, beginning with the first ten lines of Satan's address to the sun.[20] These mysteries consist of allegorical persons, such as Justice,

17. The Norman Conquest of England, begun in 1066.

18. *Paradise Lost,* ix. 26.

19. Sir Richard Blackmore wrote two bad epics, *Prince Arthur* (1695) and *King Arthur* (1697). For Fenton, see the first note to this "Life."

20. *Paradise Lost,* iv. 32–41.

Mercy, Faith.[21] Of the tragedy or mystery of *Paradise Lost* there are two plans:

The Persons.

Michael.
Chorus of Angels.
Heavenly Love.
Lucifer.
Adam,
Eve, } with the Serpent.
Conscience.
Death.
Labor,
Sickness,
Discontent,
Ignorance,
with others; } Mutes.
Faith.
Hope.
Charity.

The Persons.

Moses.
Divine Justice, Wisdom,
Heavenly Love.
The Evening Star, Hesperus.
Chorus of Angels.
Lucifer.
Adam.
Eve.
Conscience.
Labor,
Sickness,
Discontent,
Ignorance,
Fear,
Death; } Mutes.
Faith.
Hope.
Charity.

Paradise Lost.

The Persons.

Moses προλογίζει,[22] recounting how he assumed his true body; that it corrupts not, because it is with God in the mount; declares the like of Enoch and Elijah;[23] besides the purity of the place, that certain pure winds, dews, and clouds, preserves it from corruption; whence exhorts to the sight of God; tells they cannot see Adam in the state of innocence, by reason of their sin.

Justice,
Mercy,
Wisdom, } debating what should become of man, if he fall.
Chorus of Angels singing a hymn of the Creation.

Act II.

Heavenly Love.
Evening Star.
Chorus sing the marriage song, and describe Paradise.

21. What Johnson calls "mysteries" are now called morality plays: they use allegorical figures. Mystery plays deal with stories from the Bible or of saints' lives.
22. "Delivers the prologue."
23. Both Enoch (Hebrews 11:5) and Elijah (2 Kings 2:11) were taken up to Heaven alive.

Act III

Lucifer, contriving Adam's ruin.
Chorus fears for Adam, and relates Lucifer's rebellion and fall.

Act IV.

Adam, } fallen.
Eve, }
Conscience cites them to God's examination.
Chorus bewails, and tells the good Adam has lost.

Act V.

Adam and Eve driven out of Paradise.
————presented by an angel with
Labor, Grief, Hatred, Envy, War, Famine, } Mutes.
Pestilence, Sickness, Discontent, Ignorance, }
Fear, Death,
To whom he gives their names. Likewise Winter, Heat, Tempest, etc.
Faith, }
Hope, } comfort him, and instruct him.
Charity, }
Chorus briefly concludes.

Such was his first design, which could have produced only an allegory, or mystery. The following sketch seems to have attained more maturity.

Adam Unparadised:

The angel Gabriel, either descending or entering; showing, since this globe was created, his frequency as much on earth as in heaven; describes Paradise. Next, the Chorus, showing the reason of his coming to keep his watch in Paradise, after Lucifer's rebellion, by command from God; and withal expressing his desire to see and know more concerning this excellent new creature, man. The angel Gabriel, as by his name signifying a prince of power,[24] tracing Paradise with a more free office[25] passes by the station of the Chorus, and, desired by them, relates what he knew of man; as the creation of Eve, with their love and marriage. After this, Lucifer appears, after his overthrow; bemoans himself, seeks revenge on man. The Chorus prepare resistance at his first approach. At last, after discourse of enmity on either side, he departs: whereat the Chorus sings of the battle and victory in heaven against him and his accomplices: as before, after the first act, was sung a hymn of the creation. Here again may appear Lucifer, relating and insulting in what he had done to the destruction of man. Man next, and Eve having by this time been seduced by the Serpent, appears confusedly covered with leaves. Conscience, in a

24. In Hebrew, Gabriel means "man of God."
25. Taking his course through Paradise more freely because of his official duty.

> shape,[26] accuses him; Justice cites him to the place whither Jehovah called for him. In the meanwhile, the Chorus entertains the stage, and is informed by some angel the manner of the Fall. Here the Chorus bewails Adam's fall; Adam then and Eve return; accuse one another; but especially Adam lays the blame to his wife; is stubborn in his offense. Justice appears, reasons with him, convinces him. The Chorus admonisheth Adam, and bids him beware of Lucifer's example of impenitence. The angel is sent to banish them out of Paradise; but before causes to pass before his eyes, in shapes, a mask of all the evils of this life and world. He is humbled, relents, despairs: at last appears Mercy, comforts him, promises the Messiah; then calls in Faith, Hope, and Charity; instructs him; he repents, gives God the glory, submits to his penalty. The Chorus briefly concludes. Compare this with the former draught.

These are very imperfect rudiments of *Paradise Lost;* but it is pleasant to see great works in their seminal state, pregnant with latent possibilities of excellence; nor could there be any more delightful entertainment than to trace their gradual growth and expansion, and to observe how they are sometimes suddenly advanced by accidental hints, and sometimes slowly improved by steady meditation.

Invention is almost the only literary labor which blindness cannot obstruct, and therefore he naturally solaced his solitude by the indulgence of his fancy and the melody of his numbers.[27] He had done what he knew to be necessarily previous to poetical excellence; he had made himself acquainted with "seemly arts and affairs";[28] his comprehension was extended by various knowledge, and his memory stored with intellectual treasures. He was skillful in many languages, and had by reading and composition attained the full mastery of his own. He would have wanted[29] little help from books, had he retained the power of perusing them.

But while his greater designs were advancing, having now, like many other authors, caught the love of publication, he amused himself, as he could, with little productions. He sent to the press (1658) a manuscript of Ralegh,[30] called the *Cabinet Council;* and next year gratified his malevolence to the clergy, by a *Treatise of Civil Power in Eccesiastical Cases,* and *The Means of Removing Hirelings out of the Church.*

Oliver was now dead; Richard was constrained to resign:[31] the system of extemporary government, which had been held together only by force, naturally fell into fragments when that force was taken away; and Milton saw himself and his cause in equal danger. But he had still

26. Visible form. 27. Verses.
28. *Reason of Church Government.* See p. 395.
29. Needed. 30. Sir Walter Ralegh (?1552–1618).
31. Richard Cromwell, Oliver's son, became Protector September 4, 1658, and abdicated May 25, 1659.

hope of doing something. He wrote letters, which Toland has published,[32] to such men as he thought friends to the new Commonwealth; and even in the year of the Restoration he "bated no jot of heart or hope,"[33] but was fantastical enough to think that the nation, agitated as it was, might be settled by a pamphlet, called *A Ready and Easy Way to Establish a Free Commonwealth*; which was, however, enough considered to be both seriously and ludicrously answered.

The obstinate enthusiasm of the commonwealthmen was very remarkable. When the King was apparently returning, Harrington, with a few associates as fanatical as himself, used to meet, with all the gravity of political importance, to settle an equal government by rotation;[34] and Milton, kicking when he could strike no longer, was foolish enough to publish, a few weeks before the Restoration, notes upon a sermon preached by one Griffiths,[35] entitled *The Fear of God and the King.* To these notes an answer was written by L'Estrange,[36] in a pamphlet petulantly called *No Blind Guides.*

But whatever Milton could write, or men of greater activity could do, the King was now about to be restored with the irresistible approbation of the people. He was therefore no longer Secretary, and was consequently obliged to quit the house which he held by his office; and proportioning his sense of danger to his opinion of the importance of his writings, thought it convenient to seek some shelter, and hid himself for a time in Bartholomew Close by West Smithfield.

I cannot but remark a kind of respect, perhaps unconsciously, paid to this great man by his biographers: every house in which he resided is historically mentioned, as if it were an injury to neglect naming any place that he honored by his presence.

The King,[37] with lenity of which the world has had perhaps no other example, declined to be the judge or avenger of his own or his father's wrongs, and promised to admit into the Act of Oblivion all, except those whom the parliament should except; and the parliament doomed none to capital punishment but the wretches who had immediately cooperated in the murder of the King. Milton was certainly not one of them; he had only justified what they had done.

This justification was indeed sufficiently offensive; and (June 16) an order was issued to seize Milton's *Defense,* and Goodwin's *Obstructors of Justice,* another book of the same tendency, and burn them by the common hangman.[38] The attorney general was ordered to prosecute

32. *A Complete Collection of the . . . Works of Milton,* ed. John Toland (1694–98), which includes a life of Milton.

33. See "To Mr. Cyriack Skinner," ll. 7–8.

34. James Harrington, political theorist. His club was called *The Rota.*

35. Matthew Griffith, Royalist clergyman.

36. Sir Roger L'Estrange, pamphleteer.

37. Charles II.

38. John Goodwin, a Dissenting clergyman, defended the execution of Charles I in his *Obstructors,* as Milton did in his first *Defense of the People.*

the authors; but Milton was not seized, nor perhaps very diligently pursued.

Not long after (August 19)[39] the flutter of innumerable bosoms was stilled by an Act which the King, that his mercy might want no recommendation of elegance, rather called an *act of oblivion* than of *grace*. Goodwin was named, with nineteen more, as incapacitated for any public trust; but of Milton there was no exception.

Of this tenderness shown to Milton, the curiosity of mankind has not forborne to inquire the reason. Burnet thinks he was forgotten;[40] but this is another instance which may confirm Dalrymple's observation who says, "that whenever Burnet's narrations are examined, he appears to be mistaken."[41]

Forgotten he was not; for his prosecution was ordered; it must be therefore by design that he was included in the general oblivion. He is said to have had friends in the House[42] such as Marvell, Morrice, and Sir Thomas Clarges;[43] and undoubtedly a man like him must have had influence. A very particular story of his escape is told by Richardson in his memoirs, which he received from Pope, as delivered by Betterton, who might have heard it from Davenant.[44] In the war between the King and Parliament, Davenant was made prisoner, and condemned to die; but was spared at the request of Milton. When the turn of success brought Milton into the like danger, Davenant repaid the benefit by appearing in his favor. Here is a reciprocation of generosity and gratitude so pleasing that the tale makes its own way to credit. But if help were wanted, I know not where to find it. The danger of Davenant is certain from his own relation;[45] but of his escape there is no account. Betterton's narration can be traced no higher; it is not known that he had it from Davenant. We are told that the benefit exchanged was life for life; but it seems not certain that Milton's life ever was in danger. Goodwin, who had committed the same kind of crime, escaped with incapacitation; and as exclusion from public trust is a punishment which the power of government can commonly inflict without the help of a particular law, it required no great interest to exempt Milton from a censure little more than verbal. Something may be reasonably ascribed to veneration and compassion—to veneration of his abilities, and compassion for his distresses—which made it fit to forgive his

39. August 29, 1660.

40. Gilbert Burnet, Bishop of Salisbury, in his *History of His Own Times* (1724–34), i. 163.

41. Sir John Dalyrmple, *Memoirs of Great Britain and Ireland* (1771–73), i. 34 n.

42. House of Commons.

43. Andrew Marvell, the poet; Sir William Morrice, Secretary of State; Sir Thomas Clarges, brother-in-law of General Monck, who had been very influential in restoring Charles II to his throne.

44. Jonathan Richardson, *Explanatory Notes and Remarks on Milton's "Paradise Lost"* (1734). Sir William Davenant was a playwright, Thomas Betterton, an actor.

45. In the "Postscript" (dated 1650) to Davenant's epic poem, *Gondibert*.

malice for his learning. He was now poor and blind; and who would pursue with violence an illustrious enemy, depressed by fortune, and disarmed by nature?

The publication of the Act of Oblivion put him in the same condition with his fellow subjects. He was, however, upon some pretense not now known, in the custody of the sergeant[46] in December; and, when he was released, upon his refusal of the fees demanded, he and the sergeant were called before the House. He was now safe within the shade of oblivion, and knew himself to be as much out of the power of a griping officer as any other man. How the question was determined is not known. Milton would hardly have contended, but that he knew himself to have right on his side.

He then removed to Jewin Street, near Aldersgate Street; and being blind, and by no means wealthy, wanted a domestic companion and attendant; and therefore, by the recommendation of Dr. Paget,[47] married Elizabeth Minshull, of a gentleman's family in Cheshire, probably without a fortune. All his wives were virgins; for he has declared that he thought it gross and indelicate to be a second husband:[48] upon what other principles his choice was made cannot now be known, but marriage afforded not much of his happiness. The first wife left him in disgust,[49] and was brought back only by terror; the second, indeed, seems to have been more a favorite, but her life was short. The third, as Phillips relates,[50] oppressed his children in his lifetime, and cheated them at his death.

Soon after his marriage, according to an obscure story, he was offered the continuance of his employment, and, being pressed by his wife to accept it, answered, "You, like other women, want to ride in your coach; my wish is to live and die an honest man." If he considered the Latin Secretary as exercising any of the powers of government, he that had shared authority either with the Parliament or Cromwell, might have forborne to talk very loudly of his honesty; and if he thought the office purely ministerial, he certainly might have honestly retained it under the King. But this tale has too little evidence to deserve a disquisition; large offers and sturdy rejections are among the common topics of falsehood.

He had so much either of prudence or gratitude that he forebore to disturb the new settlement with any of his political or ecclesiastical opinions, and from this time devoted himself to poetry and literature. Of his zeal for learning in all its parts he gave a proof by publishing, the

46. The sergeant-at-arms of the House of Commons, James Norfolk.
47. Nathan Paget, physician, and a cousin of Elizabeth Minshull.
48. *An Apology against a Pamphlet.* Johnson himself married a widow.
49. Distaste.
50. The source is Thomas Birch, not Phillips.

next year (1661), *Accidence Commenced Grammar*;[51] a little book which has nothing remarkable, but that its author, who had been lately defending the supreme powers of his country and was then writing *Paradise Lost*, could descend from his elevation to rescue children from the perplexity of grammatical confusion, and the trouble of lessons unnecessarily repeated.

About this time Ellwood the Quaker, being recommended to him as one who would read Latin to him, for the advantage of his conversation, attended him every afternoon, except on Sundays. Milton, who, in his letter to Hartlib, had declared, that "to read Latin with an English mouth is as ill a hearing as Law French,"[52] required that Ellwood should learn and practice the Italian pronunciation, which, he said, was necessary, if he would talk with foreigners. This seems to have been a task troublesome without use. There is little reason for preferring the Italian pronunciation to our own, except that it is more general; and to teach it to an Englishman is only to make him a foreigner at home. He who travels, if he speaks Latin, may so soon learn the sounds which every native gives it, that he need make no provision before his journey; and if strangers visit us, it is their business to practice such conformity to our modes as they expect from us in their own countries. Ellwood complied with the directions, and improved himself by his attendance; for he relates, that Milton, having a curious ear, knew by his voice when he read what he did not understand, and would stop him, and "open the most difficult passages."[53]

In a short time he took a house in the Artillery Walk, leading to Bunhill Fields; the mention of which concludes the register of Milton's removals and habitations. He lived longer in this place than in any other.

He was now busied by *Paradise Lost*. Whence he drew the original design has been variously conjectured, by men who cannot bear to think themselves ignorant of that which, at last, neither diligence nor sagacity can discover. Some find the hint in an Italian tragedy. Voltaire tells a wild and unauthorized story of a farce seen by Milton in Italy, which opened thus: "Let the rainbow be the fiddlestick of the fiddle of Heaven."[54] It has been already shown that the first conception was a tragedy or mystery, not of a narrative, but a dramatic work, which he is supposed to have begun to reduce to its present form about the time (1655) when he finished his dispute with the defenders of the King.

51. First published in 1669. "Accidence" comprises the basic elements of a subject, such as the inflections of words.

52. *Of Education*. The English anglicized the pronunciation of Latin, as lawyers do French legal phrases.

53. *Life of Ellwood*, ed. Joseph Wyeth (1714), p. 135.

54. From the play *Adamo* by Giovanni Battista Andreini; see Voltaire's *Essay on Epic Poetry* (1727).

He long before had promised to adorn his native country by some great performance, while he had yet perhaps no settled design, and was stimulated only by such expectations as naturally arose from the survey of his attainments, and the consciousness of his powers. What he should undertake, it was difficult to determine. He was "long choosing, and began late."[54a]

While he was obliged to divide his time between his private studies and affairs of state, his poetical labor must have been often interrupted; and perhaps he did little more in that busy time than construct the narrative, adjust the episodes, proportion the parts, accumulate images and sentiments, and treasure in his memory, or preserve in writing, such hints as books or meditation would supply. Nothing particular is known of his intellectual operations while he was a statesman; for, having every help and accommodation at hand, he had no need of uncommon expedients.

Being driven from all public stations he is yet too great not to be traced by curiosity to his retirement, where he has been found by Mr. Richardson, the fondest of his admirers, sitting "before his door in a grey coat of coarse cloth, in warm sultry weather, to enjoy the fresh air; and so, as well as in his own room, receiving the visits of people of distinguished parts as well as quality." His visitors of high quality must now be imagined to be few; but men of parts might reasonably court the conversation of a man so generally illustrious, that foreigners are reported by Wood to have visited the house in Bread Street where he was born.

According to another account, he was seen in a small house, "neatly enough dressed in black clothes, sitting in a room hung with rusty green; pale but not cadaverous, with chalkstones in his hands. He said, that if it were not for the gout, his blindness would be tolerable."[55]

In the intervals of his pain, being made unable to use the common exercises, he used to swing in a chair, and sometimes played upon an organ.

He was now confessedly and visibly employed upon his poem, of which the progress might be noted by those with whom he was familiar; for he was obliged, when he had composed as many lines as his memory would conveniently retain, to employ some friend in writing them, having, at least for part of the time, no regular attendant. This gave opportunity to observations and reports.

Mr. Phillips observes that there was a very remarkable circumstance in the composure[56] of *Paradise Lost,* "which I have a particular reason," says he, "to remember; for whereas I had the perusal of it from the very beginning, for some years, as I went from time to time to visit him, in

54a. See *Paradise Lost,* ix. 26.

55. This account is quoted by Richardson. Chalkstones are chalklike concretions in the joints, caused by gout.

56. Composition.

parcels of ten, twenty, or thirty verses at a time (which, being written by whatever hand came next, might possibly want correction as to the orthography and pointing),[57] having, as the summer came on, not been showed any for a considerable while, and desiring the reason thereof, was answered that his vein never happily flowed but from the autumnal equinox to the vernal; and that whatever he attempted at other times was never to his satisfaction, though he courted his fancy never so much; so that, in all the years he was about this poem, he may be said to have spent half his time therein."

Upon this relation Toland remarks that in his opinion Phillips has mistaken the time of the year; for Milton, in his elegies, declares that with the advance of the spring he feels the increase of his poetical force, "redeunt in carmina vires."[58] To this it is answered, that Phillips could hardly mistake time so well marked; and it may be added, that Milton might find different times of the year favorable to different parts of life. Mr. Richardson conceives it impossible that "such a work should be suspended for six months, or for one. It may go on faster or slower, but it must go on." By what necessity it must continually go on, or why it might not be laid aside and resumed, it is not easy to discover.

This dependance of the soul upon the seasons, those temporary and periodical ebbs and flows of intellect, may, I suppose, justly be derided as the fumes of vain imagination. "Sapiens dominabitur astris."[59] The author that thinks himself weatherbound will find, with a little help from hellebore,[60] that he is only idle or exhausted. But while this notion has possession of the head, it produces the inability which it supposes. Our powers owe much of their energy to our hopes; "possunt quia posse videntur."[61] When success seems attainable, diligence is enforced; but when it is admitted that the faculties are suppressed by a cross wind or a cloudy sky, the day is given up without resistance; for who can contend with the course of nature?

From such prepossessions Milton seems not to have been free. There prevailed in his time an opinion that the world was in its decay, and that we have had the misfortune to be produced in the decrepitude of nature. It was suspected that the whole creation languished, that neither trees nor animals had the height or bulk of their predecessors, and that everything was daily sinking by gradual diminution. Milton appears to suspect that souls partake of the general degeneracy, and is not without some fear that his book is to be written in "an age too late"[62] for heroic poesy.

57. Punctuation.

58. "Strength comes back to my songs" ("Elegy V," 1.5).

59. "The stars will rule the wise [but God rules them]" (Robert Burton, *Anatomy of Melancholy,* I. ii. 1. 4).

60. A plant used to cure mental illness.

61. "They are strong because they think themselves strong" (*Aeneid,* v. 231).

62. *Paradise Lost,* ix. 44.

Another opinion wanders about the world, and sometimes finds reception among wise men—an opinion that restrains the operations of the mind to particular regions, and supposes that a luckless mortal may be born in a degree of latitude too high or too low for wisdom or for wit. From this fancy, wild as it is, he had not wholly cleared his head when he feared lest the "climate" of his country might be "too cold"[63] for flights of imagination.

Into a mind already occupied by such fancies, another not more reasonable might easily find its way. He that could fear lest his genius had fallen upon too old a world, or too chill a climate, might consistently magnify to himself the influence of the seasons, and believe his faculties to be vigorous only half the year.

His submission to the seasons was at least more reasonable than his dread of decaying nature, or a frigid zone, for general causes must operate uniformly in a general abatement of mental power; if less could be performed by the writer, less likewise would content the judges of his work. Among this lagging race of frosty grovelers he might still have risen into eminence by producing something which "they should not willingly let die." However inferior to the heroes who were born in better ages, he might still be great among his contemporaries, with the hope of growing every day greater in the dwindle of posterity: he might still be the giant of the pygmies, the one-eyed monarch of the blind.

Of his artifices of study or particular hours of composition we have little account, and there was perhaps little to be told. Richardson, who seems to have been very diligent in his inquiries, but discovers always a wish to find Milton discriminated from other men, relates that "he would sometimes lie awake whole nights, but not a verse could he make; and on a sudden his poetical faculty would rush upon him with an *impetus* or *oestrum*,[64] and his daughter was immediately called to secure what came. At other times he would dictate perhaps forty lines in a breath, and then reduce them to half the number."

These bursts of light and involutions[65] of darkness, these transient and involuntary excursions and retrocessions of invention, having some appearance of deviation from the common train of nature, are eagerly caught by the lovers of a wonder. Yet something of this inequality happens to every man in every mode of exertion, manual or mental. The mechanic cannot handle his hammer and his file at all times with equal dexterity; there are hours, he knows not why, when "his hand is out."[66] By Mr. Richardson's relation, casually conveyed, much regard

63. Adapted from *Paradise Lost,* ix. 44–45.
64. Vehement impulse.
65. Coverings.
66. *Love's Labor's Lost,* IV. i. 127.

cannot be claimed. That, in his intellectual hour, Milton called for his daughter "to secure what came," may be questioned; for unluckily it happens to be known that his daughters were never taught to write,[67] nor would he have been obliged, as is universally confessed, to have employed any casual visitor in disburthening his memory, if his daughter could have performed the office.

The story of reducing his exuberance has been told of other authors, and, though doubtless true of every fertile and copious mind, seems to have been gratuitously transferred to Milton

What he has told us, and we cannot now know more, is that he composed much of his poem in the night and morning, I suppose before his mind was disturbed with common business; and that he poured out with great fluency his "unpremeditated verse."[68] Versification free, like his, from the distresses of rhyme, must by a work so long be made prompt and habitual; and, when his thoughts were once adjusted, the words would come at his command.

At what particular times of his life the parts of his work were written cannot often be known. The beginning of the third book shows that he had lost his sight; and the introduction to the seventh that the return of the King had clouded him with discountenance, and that he was offended by the licentious festivity of the Restoration. There are no other internal notes of time. Milton, being now cleared from all effects of his disloyalty, had nothing required from him but the common duty of living in quiet, to be rewarded with the common right of protection; but this, which, when he skulked from the approach of his King, was perhaps more than he hoped, seems not to have satisfied him, for no sooner is he safe than he finds himself in danger, "fallen on evil days and evil tongues, and with darkness and with danger compassed round."[69] This darkness, had his eyes been better employed, had undoubtedly deserved compassion; but to add the mention of danger was ungrateful and unjust. He was fallen indeed on "evil days"; the time was come in which regicides could no longer boast their wickedness. But of "evil tongues" for Milton to complain required impudence at least equal to his other powers—Milton, whose warmest advocates must allow that he never spared any asperity of reproach or brutality of insolence.

But the charge itself seems to be false, for it would be hard to recollect any reproach cast upon him, either serious or ludicrous, through the whole remaining part of his life. He pursued his studies or his amusements without persecution, molestation, or insult. Such is the

67. One of Milton's daughters, Deborah, is said to have served as his scribe (John Aubrey, *Brief Lives*).

68. *Paradise Lost,* ix. 24.

69. Adapted from *Paradise Lost,* vii. 25–27.

reverence paid to great abilities, however misused: they who contemplated in Milton the scholar and the wit were contented to forget the reviler of his King.

When the plague (1665) raged in London, Milton took refuge at Chalfont in Bucks,[70] where Ellwood, who had taken the house for him, first saw a complete copy of *Paradise Lost,* and, having perused it, said to him, "Thou hast said a great deal upon *Paradise Lost*; what hast thou to say upon *Paradise Found*?"

Next year, when the danger of infection had ceased, he returned to Bunhill Fields, and designed the publication of his poem. A license was necessary, and he could expect no great kindness from a chaplain of the Archbishop of Canterbury. He seems, however, to have been treated with tenderness; for though objections were made to particular passages, and among them to the simile of the sun eclipsed in the first book,[71] yet the license was granted; and he sold his copy, April 27, 1667, to Samuel Simmons, for an immediate payment of five pounds, with a stipulation to receive five pounds more when thirteen hundred should be sold of the first edition, and again, five pounds after the sale of the same number of the second edition, and another five pounds after the same sale of the third. None of the three editions were to be extended beyond fifteen hundred copies.

The first edition was ten books, in a small quarto. The titles were varied from year to year; and an advertisement and the arguments of the books[72] were omitted in some copies, and inserted in others.

The sale gave him in two years a right to his second payment, for which the receipt was signed April 26, 1669. The second edition was not given till 1674; it was printed in small octavo, and the number of books was increased to twelve, by a division of the seventh and twelfth,[73] and some other small improvements were made. The third edition was published in 1678; and the widow, to whom the copy was then to devolve, sold all her claims to Simmons for eight pounds, according to her receipt given Dec. 21, 1680. Simmons had already agreed to transfer the whole right to Brabazon Aylmer for twenty-five pounds; and Aylmer sold to Jacob Tonson half, August 17, 1683, and half, March 24, 1690,[74] at a price considerably enlarged. In the history of *Paradise Lost* a deduction thus minute will rather gratify than fatigue.

The slow sale and tardy reputation of this poem have been always mentioned as evidences of neglected merit and of the uncertainty of literary fame, and inquiries have been made and conjectures offered about the causes of its long obscurity and late reception. But has the

70. Buckinghamshire, close to London.
71. Ll. 594–99.
72. Prose summaries prefixed to each book of *Paradise Lost.*
73. Tenth.
74. 1691.

case been truly stated? Have not lamentation and wonder been lavished on an evil that was never felt?

That in the reigns of Charles and James the *Paradise Lost* received no public acclamations is readily confessed. Wit and literature were on the side of the court; and who that solicited favor or fashion would venture to praise the defender of the regicides? All that he himself could think his due, from "evil tongues" in "evil days," was that reverential silence which was generously preserved. But it cannot be inferred that his poem was not read or not, however unwillingly, admired.

The sale, if it be considered, will justify the public. Those who have no power to judge of past times but by their own should always doubt their conclusions. The call for books was not in Milton's age what it is in the present. To read was not then a general amusement; neither traders nor often gentlemen thought themselves disgraced by ignorance. The women had not then aspired to literature, nor was every house supplied with a closet[75] of knowledge. Those, indeed, who professed learning were not less learned than at any other time; but of that middle race of students who read for pleasure or accomplishment and who buy the numerous products of modern typography, the number was then comparatively small. To prove the paucity of readers, it may be sufficient to remark that the nation had been satisfied, from 1623 to 1664, that is, forty-one years, with only two editions of the works of Shakespeare, which probably did not together make one thousand copies.[76]

The sale of thirteen hundred copies in two years, in opposition to so much recent enmity and to a style of versification new to all and disgusting to many, was an uncommon example of the prevalence of genius. The demand did not immediately increase; for many more readers than were supplied at first the nation did not afford. Only three thousand were sold in eleven years; for it forced its way without assistance: its admirers did not dare to publish their opinion, and the opportunities now given of attracting notice by advertisements were then very few; the means of proclaiming the publication of new books have been produced by that general literature which now pervades the nation through all its ranks.

But the reputation and price of the copy still advanced, till the Revolution[77] put an end to the secrecy of love, and *Paradise Lost* broke into open view with sufficient security of kind reception.

Fancy can hardly forbear to conjecture with what temper Milton

75. Study, small library.

76. That is, there were three editions of Shakespeare's collected plays: the First Folio of 1623, the Second of 1632, and the Third of 1663, reissued the following year. Johnson may have considered the Second Folio a second impression of the First.

77. The Glorious Revolution of 1688, in which the deposed James II was succeeded by William and Mary.

surveyed the silent progress of his work, and marked his reputation stealing its way in a kind of subterraneous current through fear and silence. I cannot but conceive him calm and confident, little disappointed, not at all dejected, relying on his own merit with steady consciousness, and waiting without impatience the vicissitudes of opinion, and the impartiality of a future generation.

In the meantime he continued his studies, and supplied the want of sight by a very odd expedient, of which Phillips gives the following account:

Mr. Phillips tells us, "that though our author had daily about him one or other to read, some persons of man's estate, who, of their own accord, greedily catched at the opportunity of being his readers that they might as well reap the benefit of what they read to him as oblige him by the benefit of their reading, and others of younger years were sent by their parents to the same end; yet excusing only the eldest daughter, by reason of her bodily infirmity and difficult utterance of speech (which, to say truth, I doubt[78] was the principal cause of excusing her), the other two were condemned to the performance of reading and exactly pronouncing of all the languages of whatever book he should at one time or other, think fit to peruse, viz. the Hebrew (and I think the Syriac), the Greek, the Latin, the Italian, Spanish, and French. All which sorts of books to be confined to read, without understanding one word, must needs be a trial of patience almost beyond endurance. Yet it was endured by both for a long time, though the irksomeness of this employment could not be always concealed, but broke out more and more into expressions of uneasiness; so that at length they were all, even the eldest also, sent out to learn some curious and ingenious sorts of manufacture that are proper for women to learn; particularly embroideries in gold or silver."

In the scene of misery which this mode of intellectual labor sets before our eyes, it is hard to determine whether the daughters or the father are most to be lamented. A language not understood can never be so read as to give pleasure, and very seldom so as to convey meaning. If few men would have had resolution to write books with such embarrassments, few likewise would have wanted ability to find some better expedient.

Three years after his *Paradise Lost* (1667), he published his *History of England,* comprising the whole fable of Geoffrey of Monmouth,[79] and continued to the Norman invasion. Why he should have given the first part, which he seems not to believe, and which is universally rejected, it

78. Suspect. Anne, Milton's eldest daughter, was lame.

79. Author of the Latin *History of the Kings of Britain* (c. 1135), in large part a fictional reconstruction of early British history.

is difficult to conjecture. The style is harsh; but it has something of rough vigor, which perhaps may often strike, though it cannot please.

On this history the licenser again fixed his claws, and before he would transmit it to the press tore out several parts. Some censures of the Saxon monks were taken away, lest they should be applied to the modern clergy; and a character of the Long Parliament, and Assembly of Divines, was excluded, of which the author gave a copy to the Earl of Anglesey, and which, being afterwards published, has been since inserted in its proper place.[80]

The same year were printed *Paradise Regained* and *Samson Agonistes*, a tragedy written in imitation of the ancients, and never designed by the author for the stage. As these poems were published by another bookseller, it has been asked whether Simmons was discouraged from receiving them by the slow sale of the former. Why a writer changed his bookseller a hundred years ago I am far from hoping to discover. Certainly he who in two years sells thirteen hundred copies of a volume in quarto, bought for two payments of five pounds each, has no reason to repent his purchase.

When Milton showed *Paradise Regained* to Ellwood, "This," said he, "is owing to you; for you put it in my head by the question you put to me at Chalfont, which otherwise I had not thought of."

His last poetical offspring was his favorite. He could not, as Ellwood relates, endure to hear *Paradise Lost* preferred to *Paradise Regained*. Many causes may vitiate a writer's judgment of his own works. On that which has cost him much labor he sets a high value, because he is unwilling to think that he has been diligent in vain; what has been produced without toilsome efforts is considered with delight as a proof of vigorous faculties and fertile invention; and the last work, whatever it be, has necessarily most of the grace of novelty. Milton, however it happened, had this prejudice, and had it to himself.

To that multiplicity of attainments and extent of comprehension that entitle this great author to our veneration may be added a kind of humble dignity, which did not disdain the meanest services to literature. The epic poet, the controvertist, the politician, having already descended to accommodate children with a book of rudiments, now in the last years of his life composed a book of logic, for the initiation of students in philosophy, and published (1672) *Artis Logicae Plenior Institutio ad Petri Rami Methodum Concinnata*, that is, *A New Scheme of Logic, according to the Method of Ramus*.[81] I know not whether even in this book

80. Milton's *Character of the Long Parliament and Assembly of Divines* was first printed in 1681. The "Long Parliament" sat from 1640 to 1648. The Westminster Assembly of Divines (1643–49) was called to reform religion. The third Earl of Anglesey (1614–86) was a friend of Milton's.

81. Petrus Ramus (1515–72), famous French logician.

he did not intend an act of hostility against the universities; for Ramus was one of the first oppugners of the old philosophy who disturbed with innovations the quiet of the schools.[82]

His polemical disposition again revived. He had now been safe so long that he forgot his fears, and published a *Treatise of True Religion, Heresy, Schism, Toleration, and the Best Means to Prevent the Growth of Popery.*

But this little tract is modestly written, with respectful mention of the Church of England, and an appeal to the Thirty-nine Articles. His principle of toleration is agreement in the sufficiency of the Scriptures, and he extends it to all who, whatever their opinions are, profess to derive them from the sacred books. The papists appeal to other testimonies, and are therefore in his opinion not to be permitted the liberty of either public or private worship; for though they plead conscience, "we have no warrant," he says, "to regard conscience which is not grounded in Scripture."

Those who are not convinced by his reasons may be perhaps delighted with his wit. The term "Roman Catholic" is, he says, "one of the Pope's bulls; it is particular universal, or catholic schismatic."[83]

He has, however, something better. As the best preservative against Popery he recommends the diligent perusal of the Scriptures; a duty from which he warns the busy part of mankind not to think themselves excused.

He now reprinted his juvenile poems with some additions.

In the last year of his life he sent to the press, seeming to take delight in publication, a collection of *Familiar Epistles* in Latin; to which, being too few to make a volume, he added some academical exercises, which perhaps he perused with pleasure, as they recalled to his memory the days of youth; but for which nothing but veneration for his name could now procure a reader.

When he had attained his sixty-sixth year, the gout, with which he had been long tormented, prevailed over the enfeebled powers of nature. He died by a quiet and silent expiration, about the tenth of November 1674, at his house in Bunhill Fields, and was buried next his father in the chancel of St. Giles at Cripplegate. His funeral was very splendidly and numerously attended.

Upon his grave there is supposed to have been no memorial; but in our time a monument has been erected in Westminster Abbey "To the Author of Paradise Lost," by Mr. Benson, who has in the inscription bestowed more words upon himself than upon Milton.[84]

82. The "old philosophy . . . of the schools" was the scholastic philosophy developed in the Middle Ages.

83. Milton plays on two meanings of "bull": 1) a papal decree, 2) a self-contradictory remark.

84. William Benson, politician and literary patron, erected this monument in 1737.

When the inscription for the monument of Philips, in which he was said to be *soli Miltono secundus,*[85] was exhibited to Dr. Sprat, then Dean of Westminster, he refused to admit it; the name of Milton was, in his opinion, too detestable to be read on the wall of a building dedicated to devotion. Atterbury,[86] who succeeded him, being author of the inscription, permitted its reception. "And such has been the change of public opinion," said Dr. Gregory,[87] from whom I heard this account, "that I have seen erected in the church a statue of that man, whose name I once knew considered as a pollution of its walls."

Milton has the reputation of having been in his youth eminently beautiful, so as to have been called the Lady of his college. His hair, which was of a light brown, parted at the foretop, and hung down upon his shoulders, according to the picture which he has given of Adam. He was, however, not of the heroic stature, but rather below the middle size, according to Mr. Richardson, who mentions him as having narrowly escaped from being "short and thick." He was vigorous and active, and delighted in the exercise of the sword, in which he is related to have been eminently skillful. His weapon was, I believe, not the rapier but the backsword,[88] of which he recommends the use in his book on education.

His eyes are said never to have been bright; but, if he was a dexterous fencer, they must have been once quick.

His domestic habits, so far as they are known, were those of a severe student. He drank little strong drink of any kind, and fed without excess in quantity, and in his earlier years without delicacy of choice. In his youth he studied late at night; but afterwards changed his hours, and rested in bed from nine to four in the summer, and five in the winter. The course of his day was best known after he was blind. When he first rose he heard a chapter in the Hebrew Bible, and then studied till twelve; then took some exercise for an hour; then dined; then played on the organ, and sung, or heard another sing; then studied to six; then entertained his visitors till eight; then supped, and, after a pipe of tobacco and a glass of water, went to bed.

So is his life described; but this even tenor appears attainable only in colleges. He that lives in the world will sometimes have the succession of his practice broken and confused. Visitors, of whom Milton is represented to have had great numbers, will come and stay unseasonably; business, of which every man has some, must be done when others will do it.

85. "Second only to Milton." John Philips (1676–1709), author of Miltonic parodies, *The Splendid Shilling* (1705) and *Cyder* (1708).

86. Francis Atterbury (1662–1732), later Bishop of Rochester. Thomas Sprat (1635–1713), the biographer of Cowley, preceded Atterbury both as Dean and as Bishop.

87. Perhaps David Gregory, Dean of Christ Church, Oxford.

88. A sword with only one cutting edge.

When he did not care to rise early, he had something read to him by his bedside; perhaps at this time his daughters were employed. He composed much in the morning, and dictated in the day, sitting obliquely in an elbow-chair with his leg thrown over the arm.

Fortune appears not to have had much of his care. In the Civil Wars he lent his personal estate to the Parliament; but when, after the contest was decided, he solicited repayment, he met not only with neglect, but "sharp rebuke";[89] and, having tired both himself and his friends, was given up to poverty and hopeless indignation, till he showed how able he was to do greater service. He was then made Latin Secretary, with two hundred pounds a year; and had a thousand pounds for his *Defense of the People*. His widow, who after his death, retired to Nantwich in Cheshire, and died about 1729,[90] is said to have reported that he lost two thousand pounds by entrusting it to a scrivener; and that, in the general depredation upon the Church, he had grasped an estate of about sixty pounds a year belonging to Westminster Abbey, which, like other sharers of the plunder of rebellion, he was afterwards obliged to return. Two thousand pounds, which he had placed in the Excise Office,[91] were also lost. There is yet no reason to believe that he was ever reduced to indigence. His wants, being few, were competently supplied. He sold his library before his death, and left his family fifteen hundred pounds; on which his widow laid hold, and only gave one hundred to each of his daughters.[92]

His literature was unquestionably great. He read all the languages which are considered either as learned or polite: Hebrew, with its two dialects, Greek, Latin, Italian, French, and Spanish. In Latin his skill was such as places him in the first rank of writers and critics; and he appears to have cultivated Italian with uncommon diligence. The books in which his daughter, who used to read to him, represented him as most delighting, after Homer, which he could almost repeat, were Ovid's *Metamorphoses* and Euripides. His Euripides is, by Mr. Cradock's kindness, now in my hands: the margin is sometimes noted; but I have found nothing remarkable.[93]

Of the English poets he set most value upon Spenser, Shakespeare, and Cowley. Spenser was apparently his favorite; Shakespeare he may easily be supposed to like, with every other skillful reader, but I should not have expected that Cowley, whose ideas of excellence were differ-

89. Preface to his *Character of the Long Parliament.*

90. She died in 1727.

91. A bank, which failed at the Restoration. The two thousand pounds lost in this failure may be the same two thousand mentioned just above.

92. According to W. R. Parker, Milton probably left about nine hundred pounds, of which his widow received the usual two-thirds.

93. Milton's copy of Euripides, then owned by Joseph Cradock, is now in the Bodleian Library, Oxford.

ent from his own, would have had much of his approbation. His character of Dryden, who sometimes visited him, was, that he was a good rhymist, but no poet.[94]

His theological opinions are said to have been first Calvinistical; and afterwards, perhaps when he began to hate the Presbyterians, to have tended towards Arminianism.[95] In the mixed questions of theology and government, he never thinks that he can recede far enough from popery, or prelacy; but what Baudius says of Erasmus seems applicable to him, "magis habuit quod fugeret, quam quod sequeretur."[96] He had determined rather what to condemn than what to approve. He has not associated himself with any denomination of Protestants: we know rather what he was not, than what he was. He was not of the Church of Rome; he was not of the Church of England.

To be of no church is dangerous. Religion, of which the rewards are distant and which is animated only by faith and hope, will glide by degrees out of the mind unless it be invigorated and reimpressed by external ordinances, by stated calls to worship, and the salutary influence of example. Milton, who appears to have had full conviction of the truth of Christianity, and to have regarded the Holy Scriptures with the profoundest veneration, to have been untainted by an heretical peculiarity of opinion, and to have lived in a confirmed belief of the immediate and occasional agency[97] of Providence, yet grew old without any visible worship. In the distribution of his hours, there was no hour of prayer, either solitary or with his household; omitting public prayers, he omitted all.

Of this omission the reason has been sought, upon a supposition which ought never to be made, that men live with their own approbation and justify their conduct to themselves. Prayer certainly was not thought superfluous by him, who represents our first parents as praying acceptably in the state of innocence, and efficaciously after their fall. That he lived without prayer can hardly be affirmed; his studies and meditations were an habitual prayer. The neglect of it in his family was probably a fault for which he condemned himself, and which he intended to correct, but that death, as too often happens, intercepted his reformation.

His political notions were those of an acrimonious and surly republican, for which it is not known that he gave any better reason than that

94. Reported by Thomas Newton, ed. *Paradise Lost* (1749), I. lvi–lvii. "Rhymist" here means one who writes in rhyme.

95. Derived from the doctrines of the Dutch theologian, Jacobus Arminius (1560–1609), who denied predestination.

96. The Latin is translated freely in the next sentence. It is taken from the *Letters* of Dominic Baudius (1561–1613). Desiderius Erasmus (?1466–1536), the Dutch humanist, was noted for his Catholicism which verged on Protestantism.

97. Direct intervention on some occasions.

"a popular government was the most frugal; for the trappings of a monarchy would set up an ordinary commonwealth."[98] It is surely very shallow policy that supposes money to be the chief good; and even this, without considering that the support and expense of a court is for the most part only a particular kind of traffic, by which money is circulated without any national impoverishment.

Milton's republicanism was, I am afraid, founded in an envious hatred of greatness, and a sullen desire of independence; in petulance impatient of control, and pride disdainful of superiority. He hated monarchs in the state and prelates in the church; for he hated all whom he was required to obey. It is to be suspected that his predominant desire was to destroy rather than establish, and that he felt not so much the love of liberty as repugnance to authority.

It has been observed that they who most loudly clamor for liberty do not most liberally grant it. What we know of Milton's character in domestic relations is that he was severe and arbitrary. His family consisted of women; and there appears in his books something like a Turkish contempt of females, as subordinate and inferior beings. That his own daughters might not break the ranks, he suffered them to be depressed by a mean and penurious education. He thought woman made only for obedience, and man only for rebellion.

Of his family some account may be expected. His sister, first married to Mr. Phillips, afterwards married Mr. Agar, a friend of her first husband, who succeeded him in the Crown Office. She had by her first husband Edward and John, the two nephews whom Milton educated; and by her second, two daughters.

His brother, Sir Christopher, had two daughters, Mary and Catherine, and a son Thomas, who succeeded Agar in the Crown Office, and left a daughter living in 1749 in Grosvenor Street.

Milton had children only by his first wife: Anne, Mary, and Deborah. Anne, though deformed, married a master builder, and died of her first child. Mary died single. Deborah married Abraham Clark, a weaver in Spitalfields, and lived seventy-six years, to August, 1727. This is the daughter of whom public mention has been made.[99] She could repeat the first lines of Homer, the *Metamorphoses,* and some of Euripides, by having often read them. Yet here incredulity is ready to make a stand. Many repetitions are necessary to fix in the memory lines not understood; and why should Milton wish or want to hear them so often? These lines were at the beginning of the poems. Of a book written in a language not understood the beginning raises no more attention than the end, and as those that understand it know commonly the beginning best, its rehearsal will seldom be necessary. It is not likely

98. Quoted from John Toland's *Life of Milton.*

99. A letter about her appeared in *The Gentleman's Magazine,* 46 (1776), 200.

that Milton required any passage to be so much repeated as that his daughter could learn it; nor likely that he desired the initial lines to be read at all; nor that the daughter, weary of the drudgery of pronouncing unideal sounds,[1] would voluntarily commit them to memory.

To this gentlewoman Addison made a present, and promised some establishment; but died soon after. Queen Caroline[2] sent her fifty guineas. She had seven sons and three daughters; but none of them had any children, except her son Caleb and her daughter Elizabeth. Caleb went to Fort St. George in the East Indies, and had two sons, of whom nothing is now known. Elizabeth married Thomas Foster, a weaver in Spitalfields, and had seven children, who all died. She kept a petty grocer's or chandler's shop, first at Holloway, and afterwards in Cock Lane near Shoreditch Church. She knew little of her grandfather, and that little was not good. She told of his harshness to his daughters, and his refusal to have them taught to write; and, in opposition to other accounts, represented him as delicate, though temperate, in his diet.

In 1750, April 5, *Comus* was played for her benefit. She had so little acquaintance with diversion or gaiety that she did not know what was intended when a benefit was offered her. The profits of the night were only one hundred and thirty pounds, though Dr. Newton[3] brought a large contribution; and twenty pounds were given by Tonson,[4] a man who is to be praised as often as he is named. Of this sum one hundred pounds was placed in the stocks, after some debate between her and her husband in whose name it should be entered; and the rest augmented their little stock, with which they removed to Islington. This was the greatest benefaction that *Paradise Lost* ever procured the author's descendants; and to this he who has now attempted to relate his life had the honor of contributing a Prologue.

In the examination of Milton's poetical works I shall pay so much regard to time as to begin with his juvenile productions. For his early pieces he seems to have had a degree of fondness not very laudable: what he has once written he resolves to preserve, and gives to the public an unfinished poem, which he broke off because he was "nothing satisfied with what he had done,"[5] supposing his readers less nice[6] than himself. These preludes to his future labors are in Italian, Latin, and English. Of the Italian I cannot pretend to speak as a critic, but I have heard them commended by a man well qualified to decide their merit. The Latin pieces are lusciously elegant; but the delight which they

1. Sounds conveying no idea.
2. (1683–1737), wife of George II.
3. Thomas Newton, Bishop of Bristol, editor and biographer of Milton.
4. Jacob Tonson, publisher and great-nephew of the Jacob Tonson who bought the rights to *Paradise Lost*.
5. Milton's note on "The Passion."
6. Discriminating.

afford is rather by the exquisite imitation of the ancient writers, by the purity of the diction, and the harmony of the numbers, than by any power of invention or vigor of sentiment. They are not all of equal value; the elegies excel the odes, and some of the exercises on Gunpowder Treason might have been spared.[7]

The English poems, though they make no promises of *Paradise Lost,* have this evidence of genius, that they have a cast original and unborrowed. But their peculiarity is not excellence: if they differ from verses of others, they differ for the worse; for they are too often distinguished by repulsive harshness; the combination of words are new, but they are not pleasing; the rhymes and epithets seem to be laboriously sought and violently applied.

That in the early parts of his life he wrote with much care appears from his manuscripts, happily preserved at Cambridge, in which many of his smaller works are found as they were first written, with the subsequent corrections. Such relics show how excellence is acquired: what we hope ever to do with ease we may learn first to do with diligence.

Those who admire the beauties of this great poet sometimes force their own judgment into false approbation of his little pieces, and prevail upon themselves to think that admirable which is only singular. All that short compositions can commonly attain is neatness and elegance. Milton never learned the art of doing little things with grace; he overlooked the milder excellence of suavity and softness: he was a "lion" that had no skill "in dandling the kid."[8]

One of the poems on which much praise has been bestowed is "Lycidas"; of which the diction is harsh, the rhymes uncertain, and the numbers unpleasing. What beauty there is we must therefore seek in the sentiments and images. It is not to be considered as the effusion of real passion; for passion runs not after remote allusions and obscure opinions. Passion plucks no berries from the myrtle and ivy, nor calls upon Arethuse and Mincius,[9] nor tell of rough "satyrs" and "fauns with cloven heel."[10] Where there is leisure for fiction there is little grief.

In this poem there is no nature, for there is no truth; there is no art, for there is nothing new. Its form is that of a pastoral, easy, vulgar,[11] and therefore disgusting: whatever images it can supply, are long ago exhausted; and its inherent improbability always forces dissatisfaction on the mind. When Cowley tells of Hervey that they studied to-

7. Several poems celebrating the failure of the Gunpowder Plot, devised by Guy Fawkes and a few other Roman Catholics to blow up the Houses of Parliament on November 5, 1605, while the King was present.

8. See *Paradise Lost,* iv. 343–44.

9. A Sicilian fountain appearing in an Idyl of Theocritus and a river in Lombardy described by Virgil in an Eclogue, both invoked by Milton in "Lycidas," ll. 85–86.

10. "Lycidas," l. 34.

11. Commonplace.

gether,[12] it is easy to suppose how much he must miss the companion of his labors, and the partner of his discoveries; but what image of tenderness can be excited by these lines?

> We drove afield, and both together heard
> What time the grey fly winds her sultry horn,
> Battening our flocks with the fresh dews of night.[13]

We know that they never drove afield, and that they had no flocks to batten; and though it be allowed that the representation may be allegorical, the true meaning is so uncertain and remote that it is never sought because it cannot be known when it is found.

Among the flocks and copses and flowers appear the heathen deities, Jove and Phoebus, Neptune and Aeolus, with a long train of mythological imagery, such as a college easily supplies. Nothing can less display knowledge or less exercise invention than to tell how a shepherd has lost his companion and must now feed his flocks alone, without any judge of his skill in piping; and how one god asks another god what is become of Lycidas, and how neither god can tell. He who thus grieves will excite no sympathy; he who thus praises will confer no honor.

This poem has yet a grosser fault. With these trifling fictions are mingled the most awful[14] and sacred truths, such as ought never to be polluted with such irreverend combinations. The shepherd likewise is now a feeder of sheep, and afterwards an ecclesiastical pastor, a superintendent of a Christian flock. Such equivocations are always unskillful; but here they are indecent, and at least approach to impiety, of which, however, I believe the writer not to have been conscious.

Such is the power of reputation justly acquired that its blaze drives away the eye from nice examination. Surely no man could have fancied that he read "Lycidas" with pleasure, had he not known its author.

Of the two pieces, "L'Allegro" and "Il Penseroso," I believe opinion is uniform; every man that reads them, reads them with pleasure. The author's design is not, what Theobald has remarked,[15] merely to show how objects derive their colors from the mind, by representing the operation of the same things upon the gay and the melancholy temper, or upon the same man as he is differently disposed; but rather how, among the successive variety of appearances, every disposition of mind takes hold on those by which it may be gratified.

The *cheerful* man hears the lark in the morning; the *pensive* man hears the nightingale in the evening. The *cheerful* man sees the cock strut, and hears the horn and hounds echo in the woods; then walks "not un-

12. "On the Death of Mr. William Hervey." Hervey was a young friend of Cowley's at Cambridge.
13. "Lycidas," ll. 27–29.
14. Awe-inspiring.
15. Lewis Theobald, in his Preface to *The Works of Shakespeare* (1734), vol. i.

seen"[16] to observe the glory of the rising sun or listen to the singing milkmaid, and view the labors of the plowman and the mower; then casts his eyes about him over scenes of smiling plenty, and looks up to the distant tower, the residence of some fair inhabitant: thus he pursues rural gaiety through a day of labor or of play, and delights himself at night with the fanciful narratives of superstitious ignorance.

The *pensive* man at one time walks "unseen"[17] to muse at midnight; and at another hears the sullen curfew. If the weather drives him home, he sits in a room lighted only by "glowing embers";[18] or by a lonely lamp outwatches the North Star to discover the habitation of separate souls, and varies the shades of meditation by contemplating the magnificent or pathetic scenes of tragic and epic poetry. When the morning comes, a morning gloomy with rain and wind, he walks into the dark trackless woods, falls asleep by some murmuring water, and with melancholy enthusiasm expects some dream of prognostication or some music played by aerial performers.

Both Mirth and Melancholy are solitary, silent inhabitants of the breast that neither receive nor transmit communication; no mention is therefore made of a philosophical friend or a pleasant companion. The seriousness does not arise from any participation of calamity, nor the gaiety from the pleasures of the bottle.

The man of *cheerfulness* having exhausted the country tries what "towered cities"[19] will afford, and mingles with scenes of splendor, gay assemblies, and nuptial festivities; but he mingles a mere spectator as, when the learned comedies of Jonson or the wild dramas of Shakespeare are exhibited, he attends the theater.[20]

The *pensive* man never loses himself in crowds, but walks the cloister or frequents the cathedral. Milton probably had not yet forsaken the Church.

Both his characters delight in music; but he seems to think that cheerful notes would have obtained from Pluto a complete dismission of Eurydice, of whom solemn sounds only procured a conditional release.[21]

For the old age of Cheerfulness he makes no provision; but Melancholy he conducts with great dignity to the close of life. His Cheerfulness is without levity, and his Pensiveness without asperity.

16. "L'Allegro," l. 57.
17. "Il Penseroso," l. 65.
18. L. 79.
19. "L'Allegro," l. 117.
20. Milton praises Jonson's comedies as "learned," and Shakespeare's plays as the products of fancy ("L'Allegro," ll. 132–34).
21. Through the power of his music, Orpheus persuaded Pluto, ruler of the underworld, to release his wife Eurydice. Her release, however, was conditional. Orpheus was told not to look back at her while conducting her out of Hades, and when he disobeyed she disappeared forever.

Through these two poems the images are properly selected and nicely distinguished, but the colors[22] of the diction seem not sufficiently discriminated. I know not whether the characters are kept sufficiently apart. No mirth can, indeed, be found in his melancholy; but I am afraid that I always meet some melancholy in his mirth. They are two noble efforts of imagination.

The greatest of his juvenile performances is the masque of *Comus*, in which may very plainly be discovered the dawn or twilight of *Paradise Lost*. Milton appears to have formed very early that system of diction and mode of verse which his maturer judgment approved, and from which he never endeavored nor desired to deviate.

Nor does *Comus* afford only a specimen of his language: it exhibits likewise his power of description and his vigor of sentiment, employed in the praise and defense of virtue. A work more truly poetical is rarely found; allusions, images, and descriptive epithets, embellish almost every period[23] with lavish decoration. As a series of lines, therefore, it may be considered as worthy of all the admiration with which the votaries have received it.

As a drama it is deficient. The action is not probable. A masque, in those parts where supernatural intervention is admitted, must indeed be given up to all the freaks of imagination; but so far as the action is merely human it ought to be reasonable, which can hardly be said of the conduct of the two brothers, who, when their sister sinks with fatigue in a pathless wilderness, wander both away together in search of berries too far to find their way back, and leave a helpless lady to all the sadness and danger of solitude. This however is a defect overbalanced by its convenience.

What deserves more reprehension is that the prologue spoken in the wild wood by the Attendant Spirit is addressed to the audience; a mode of communication so contrary to the nature of dramatic representation that no precedents can support it.

The discourse of the Spirit is too long, an objection that may be made to almost all the following speeches; they have not the spriteliness of a dialogue animated by reciprocal contention, but seem rather declamations deliberately composed and formally repeated on a moral question. The auditor therefore listens as to a lecture, without passion, without anxiety.

The song of Comus has airiness and jollity; but, what may recommend Milton's morals as well as his poetry, the invitations to pleasure are so general that they excite no distinct images of corrupt enjoyment, and take no dangerous hold on the fancy.

22. Verbal qualities, varieties of expression.
23. Sentence.

The following soliloquies of Comus and the Lady are elegant, but tedious. The song[24] must owe much to the voice, if it ever can delight. At last the Brothers enter, with too much tranquillity; and when they have feared lest their sister should be in danger, and hoped that she is not in danger, the Elder makes a speech in praise of chastity, and the Younger finds how fine it is to be a philosopher.

Then descends the Spirit in form of a shepherd; and the Brother, instead of being in haste to ask his help, praises his singing, and inquires his business in that place. It is remarkable that at this interview the Brother is taken with a short fit of rhyming. The Spirit relates that the Lady is in the power of Comus, the Brother moralizes again, and the Spirit makes a long narration, of no use because it is false, and therefore unsuitable to a good being.

In all these parts the language is poetical and the sentiments are generous, but there is something wanting to allure attention.

The dispute between the Lady and Comus is the most animated and affecting scene of the drama, and wants nothing but a brisker reciprocation of objections and replies to invite attention and detain it.

The songs are vigorous, and full of imagery; but they are harsh in their diction, and not very musical in their numbers.

Throughout the whole the figures[25] are too bold, and the language too luxuriant for dialogue: it is a drama in the epic style, inelegantly splendid, and tediously instructive.

The *Sonnets* were written in different parts of Milton's life upon different occasions. They deserve not any particular criticism; for of the best it can only be said that they are not bad, and perhaps only the eighth and the twenty-first are truly entitled to this slender commendation.[26] The fabric of a sonnet, however adapted to the Italian language, has never succeeded in ours which, having greater variety of termination, requires the rhymes to be often changed.

Those little pieces may be dispatched without much anxiety; a greater work calls for greater care. I am now to examine *Paradise Lost,* a poem which, considered with respect to design, may claim the first place, and with respect to performance the second,[27] among the productions of the human mind.

By the general consent of critics the first praise of genius is due to the writer of an epic poem, as it requires an assemblage of all the powers which are singly sufficient for other compositions. Poetry is the art of uniting pleasure with truth, by calling imagination to the help of reason. Epic poetry undertakes to teach the most important truths by the

24. "The Lady's Song," ll. 230–43.

25. Rhetorical figures, such as metaphors and similes.

26. The sonnets beginning "Captain, or colonel, or knight in arms," and "Cyriack, whose grandsire on the Royal Bench."

27. Presumably Johnson gives first place in "performance" to the *Iliad.*

most pleasing precepts, and therefore relates some great event in the most affecting manner. History must supply the writer with the rudiments of narration, which he must improve and exalt by a nobler art, must animate by dramatic energy, and diversify by retrospection and anticipation; morality must teach him the exact bounds and different shades of vice and virtue; from policy and the practice of life he has to learn the discriminations of character and the tendency of the passions, either single or combined; and physiology[28] must supply him with illustrations and images. To put these materials to poetical use is required an imagination capable of painting nature and realizing fiction. Nor is he yet a poet till he has attained the whole extension of his language, distinguished all the delicacies of phrase, and all the colors of words, and learned to adjust their different sounds to all the varieties of metrical modulation.

Bossu is of opinion that the poet's first work is to find a *moral,* which his fable is afterwards to illustrate and establish.[29] This seems to have been the process only of Milton: the moral of other poems is incidental and consequent; in Milton's only it is essential and intrinsic. His purpose was the most useful and the most arduous: "to vindicate the ways of God to man";[30] to show the reasonableness of religion, and the necessity of obedience to the Divine Law.

To convey this moral there must be a *fable,* a narration artfully constructed so as to excite curiosity and surprise expectation. In this part of his work Milton must be confessed to have equaled every other poet. He has involved in his account of the Fall of Man the events which preceded, and those that were to follow it: he has interwoven the whole system of theology with such propriety that every part appears to be necessary, and scarcely any recital is wished shorter for the sake of quickening the progress of the main action.

The subject of an epic poem is naturally an event of great importance. That of Milton is not the destruction of a city, the conduct[31] of a colony, or the foundation of an empire. His subject is the fate of worlds, the revolutions of heaven and of earth; rebellion against the Supreme King raised by the highest order of created beings; the overthrow of their host and the punishment of their crime; the creation of a new race of reasonable creatures; their original happiness and innocence, their forfeiture of immortality, and their restoration to hope and peace.

Great events can be hastened or retarded only by persons of elevated dignity. Before the greatness displayed in Milton's poem all other greatness shrinks away. The weakest of his agents are the highest and

28. Study and description of natural objects.

29. René Le Bossu, *Treatise on the Epic Poem* (1675).

30. *Paradise Lost,* i. 26 reads, "justify the ways of God to men." Johnson has quoted Pope, *Essay on Man,* i. 16.

31. Guidance in transit and establishment.

noblest of human beings, the original parents of mankind; with whose actions the elements consented,[32] on whose rectitude or deviation of will depended the state of terrestrial nature and the condition of all the future inhabitants of the globe.

Of the other agents in the poem the chief are such as it is irreverence to name on slight occasions. The rest are lower powers,

> of which the least could wield
> Those elements, and arm him with the force
> Of all their regions;[33]

powers which only the control of Omnipotence restrains from laying creation waste, and filling the vast expanse of space with ruin and confusion. To display the motives and actions of beings thus superior, so far as human reason can examine them or human imagination represent them, is the task which this mighty poet has undertaken and performed.

In the examination of epic poems much speculation is commonly employed upon the *characters.* The characters in the *Paradise Lost* which admit of examination are those of angels and of man; of angels good and evil, of man in his innocent and sinful state.

Among the angels the virtue of Raphael is mild and placid, of easy condescension[34] and free communication; that of Michael is regal and lofty, and, as may seem, attentive to the dignity of his own nature. Abdiel and Gabriel appear occasionally, and act as every incident requires; the solitary fidelity of Abdiel is very amiably painted.

Of the evil angels the characters are more diversified. To Satan, as Addison observes, such sentiments are given as suit "the most exalted and most depraved being."[35] Milton has been censured, by Clarke, for the impiety which sometimes breaks from Satan's mouth.[36] For there are thoughts, as he justly remarks, which no observation of character can justify, because no good man would willingly permit them to pass, however transiently, through his own mind. To make Satan speak as a rebel, without any such expressions as might taint the reader's imagination, was indeed one of the great difficulties in Milton's undertaking, and I cannot but think that he has extricated himself with great happiness. There is in Satan's speeches little that can give pain to a pious ear. The language of rebellion cannot be the same with that of obedience. The malignity of Satan foams in haughtiness and obstinacy; but his expressions are commonly general, and no otherwise offensive than as they are wicked.

32. Worked in harmony.
33. *Paradise Lost,* vi. 221–23.
34. Dealing with one's inferiors easily (the phrase is not derogatory).
35. *Spectator,* no. 303.
36. John Clarke, *An Essay upon Study* (1731), p. 204.

The other chiefs of the celestial rebellion are very judiciously discriminated in the first and second books; and the ferocious character of Moloch appears, both in the battle and the council, with exact consistency.[37]

To Adam and to Eve are given during their innocence such sentiments as innocence can generate and utter. Their love is pure benevolence and mutual veneration; their repasts are without luxury and their diligence without toil. Their addresses to their Maker have little more than the voice of admiration and gratitude. Fruition left them nothing to ask, and innocence left them nothing to fear.

But with guilt enter distrust and discord, mutual accusation, and stubborn self-defense; they regard each other with alienated minds, and dread their Creator as the avenger of their transgression. At last they seek shelter in his mercy, soften to repentance, and melt in supplication. Both before and after the Fall the superiority of Adam is diligently sustained.

Of the *probable* and the *marvelous,* two parts of a vulgar[38] epic poem which immerge[39] the critic in deep consideration, the *Paradise Lost* requires little to be said. It contains the history of a miracle, of Creation and Redemption; it displays the power and the mercy of the Supreme Being; the probable therefore is marvelous, and the marvelous is probable. The substance of the narrative is truth; and as truth allows no choice, it is, like necessity, superior to rule. To the accidental or adventitious parts, as to everything human, some slight exceptions may be made. But the main fabric is immovably supported.

It is justly remarked by Addison that this poem has, by the nature of its subject, the advantage above all others, that it is universally and perpetually interesting.[40] All mankind will, through all ages, bear the same relation to Adam and to Eve, and must partake of that good and evil which extend to themselves.

Of the *machinery,* so called from Θεὸς ἀπὸ μηχανῆς,[41] by which is meant the occasional interposition of supernatural power, another fertile topic of critical remarks, here is no room to speak, because everything is done under the immediate and visible direction of Heaven; but the rule is so far observed that no part of the action could have been accomplished by any other means.

Of *episodes,*[42] I think there are only two, contained in Raphael's relation of the war in heaven and Michael's prophetic account of the

37. *Paradise Lost,* vi. 354–62; ii. 43–105.

38. Ordinary or secular.

39. Immerse.

40. See *Spectator,* nos. 267 and 273.

41. "The god in the machine" (Aristotle, *Poetics,* ch. 15). In Euripides' *Medea,* for example, Medea escapes, after murdering her children, in the chariot of her grandfather the Sun.

42. Digressions from the main action.

changes to happen in this world. Both are closely connected with the great action; one was necessary to Adam as a warning, the other as a consolation.

To the completeness or *integrity* of the design nothing can be objected; it has distinctly and clearly what Aristotle requires, a beginning, a middle, and an end.[43] There is perhaps no poem of the same length from which so little can be taken without apparent mutilation. Here are no funeral games,[44] nor is there any long description of a shield.[45] The short digressions at the beginning of the third, seventh, and ninth books, might doubtless be spared; but superfluities so beautiful who would take away? or who does not wish that the author of the *Iliad* had gratified succeeding ages with a little knowledge of himself? Perhaps no passages are more frequently or more attentively read than those extrinsic paragraphs; and, since the end of poetry is pleasure, that cannot be unpoetical with which all are pleased.

The questions, whether the action of the poem be strictly *one,* whether the poem can be properly termed *heroic,* and who is the hero, are raised by such readers as draw their principles of judgment rather from books than from reason. Milton, though he entitled *Paradise Lost* only a "poem," yet calls it himself "heroic song."[46] Dryden, petulantly and indecently,[47] denies the heroism of Adam, because he was overcome;[48] but there is no reason why the hero should not be unfortunate except established practice, since success and virtue do not go necessarily together. Cato is the hero of Lucan;[49] but Lucan's authority will not be suffered by Quintilian to decide.[50] However, if success be necessary, Adam's deceiver was at last crushed; Adam was restored to his Maker's favor, and therefore may securely resume his human rank.

After the scheme and fabric of the poem must be considered its component parts, the sentiments and the diction.

The *sentiments,* as expressive of manners or appropriated to characters, are for the greater part unexceptionably just.

Splendid passages containing lessons of morality or precepts of prudence occur seldom. Such is the original formation of this poem that as it admits no human manners till the Fall, it can give little assistance to human conduct. Its end is to raise the thoughts above sublunary

43. *Poetics,* ch. 7.

44. As in *Iliad,* xxiii. 257–897; *Aeneid,* v. 104–603. *Paradise Lost* does, however, include an episode of epic games, the diversions of the fallen angels (bk. ii) during the absence of Satan on his journey to discover the world of man.

45. *Iliad,* xviii. 478–608.

46. *Paradise Lost,* ix. 25.

47. In violation of (literary) propriety.

48. In the Dedication of his translation of the *Aeneid* (1697).

49. Of Lucan's *Pharsalia* (65 A.D.). Cato fights on the side of Pompey, who is defeated by Caesar.

50. Quintilian (c.35–c.100), most famous of Roman writers on rhetoric, in his *Institutes of Oratory,* X. i. 90, thinks Lucan better for imitation by the orator than by the poet.

cares or pleasures. Yet the praise of that fortitude, with which Abdiel maintained his singularity of virtue against the scorn of multitudes,[51] may be accommodated to all times; and Raphael's reproof of Adam's curiosity after the planetary motions, with the answer returned by Adam,[52] may be confidently opposed[53] to any rule of life which any poet has delivered.

The thoughts which are occasionally called forth in the progress are such as could only be produced by an imagination in the highest degree fervid and active, to which materials were supplied by incessant study and unlimited curiosity. The heat of Milton's mind might be said to sublimate[54] his learning, to throw off into his work the spirit of science, unmingled with its grosser parts.

He had considered creation in its whole extent, and his descriptions are therefore learned. He had accustomed his imagination to unrestrained indulgence, and his conceptions therefore were extensive. The characteristic quality of his poem is sublimity. He sometimes descends to the elegant, but his element is the great. He can occasionally invest himself with grace; but his natural port[55] is gigantic loftiness. He can please when pleasure is required; but it is his peculiar power to astonish.

He seems to have been well acquainted with his own genius, and to know what it was that nature had bestowed upon him more bountifully than upon others: the power of displaying the vast, illuminating the splendid, enforcing the awful, darkening the gloomy, and aggravating the dreadful: he therefore chose a subject on which too much could not be said, on which he might tire his fancy without the censure of extravagance.

The appearances of nature and the occurrences of life did not satiate his appetite of greatness. To paint things as they are requires a minute attention, and employs the memory rather than the fancy. Milton's delight was to sport in the wide regions of possibility; reality was a scene too narrow for his mind. He sent his faculties out upon discovery into worlds where only imagination can travel, and delighted to form new modes of existence, and furnish sentiment and action to superior beings, to trace the counsels[56] of hell, or accompany the choirs of heaven.

But he could not be always in other worlds: he must sometimes revisit earth, and tell of things visible and known. When he cannot raise wonder by the sublimity of his mind, he gives delight by its fertility.

Whatever be his subject he never fails to fill the imagination. But his

51. *Paradise Lost,* v. 800–904.
52. *Paradise Lost,* viii. 66–197.
53. Compared.
54. Refine, as in chemistry.
55. Manner, bearing.
56. Both "counsels" (advice, suggestions) and the actual councils which take place in Hell.

images and descriptions of the scenes or operations of nature do not seem to be always copied from original form, nor to have the freshness, raciness, and energy of immediate observation. He saw nature, as Dryden expresses it, "through the spectacles of books";[57] and on most occasions calls learning to his assistance. The garden of Eden brings to his mind the vale of Enna, where Proserpine was gathering flowers. Satan makes his way through fighting elements, like Argo between the Cyanean rocks, or Ulysses between the two Sicilian whirlpools, when he shunned Charybdis "on the larboard."[58] The mythological allusions have been justly censured, as not being always used with notice of their vanity; but they contribute variety to the narration, and produce an alternate exercise of the memory and the fancy.

His similes are less numerous and more various than those of his predecessors. But he does not confine himself within the limits of rigorous comparison: his great excellence is amplitude, and he expands the adventitious image beyond the dimensions which the occasion required. Thus, comparing the shield of Satan to the orb of the Moon, he crowds the imagination with the discovery of the telescope and all the wonders which the telescope discovers.[59]

Of his moral sentiments it is hardly praise to affirm that they excel those of all other poets; for this superiority he was indebted to his acquaintance with the sacred writings. The ancient epic poets, wanting the light of Revelation, were very unskillful teachers of virtue: their principal characters may be great, but they are not amiable. The reader may rise from their works with a greater degree of active or passive fortitude, and sometimes of prudence; but he will be able to carry away few precepts of justice, and none of mercy.

From the Italian writers it appears that the advantages of even Christian knowledge may be possessed in vain. Ariosto's pravity[60] is generally known; and though the *Deliverance of Jerusalem* may be considered as a sacred subject, the poet has been very sparing of moral instruction.

In Milton every line breathes sanctity of thought and purity of manners, except when the train of the narration requires the introduction of the rebellious spirits; and even they are compelled to acknowledge their subjection to God in such a manner as excites reverence and confirms piety.

Of human beings there are but two; but those two are the parents of mankind, venerable before their fall for dignity and innocence, and

57. *An Essay of Dramatic Poesy* (1668)—*Essays,* ed. W. P. Ker, i. 80: "Shakespeare needed not the spectacles of books to read Nature."

58. *Paradise Lost,* iv. 268–72; ii. 1016–20.

59. Reveals. The passage is *Paradise Lost,* i. 284–91.

60. Moral corruption. Ludovico Ariosto's *Orlando Furioso (Orlando Mad),* the greatest Italian romantic epic, was published in 1532. Torquato Tasso is the author of the *Deliverance of Jerusalem* (1575), next mentioned.

amiable after it for repentance and submission. In their first state their affection is tender without weakness, and their piety sublime without presumption. When they have sinned they show how discord begins in mutual frailty, and how it ought to cease in mutual forbearance; how confidence of the divine favor is forfeited by sin, and how hope of pardon may be obtained by penitence and prayer. A state of innocence we can only conceive, if indeed in our present misery it be possible to conceive it; but the sentiments and worship proper to a fallen and offending being we have all to learn, as we have all to practice.

The poet, whatever be done, is always great. Our progenitors in their first state conversed with angels; even when folly and sin had degraded them, they had not in their humiliation "the port of mean suitors";[61] and they rise again to reverential regard, when we find that their prayers were heard.

As human passions did not enter the world before the Fall, there is in the *Paradise Lost* little opportunity for the pathetic; but what little there is has not been lost. That passion which is peculiar to rational nature, the anguish arising from the consciousness of transgression and the horrors attending the sense of the divine displeasure, are very justly described and forcibly impressed. But the passions are moved only on one occasion; sublimity is the general prevailing quality in this poem—sublimity variously modified, sometimes descriptive, sometimes argumentative.[62]

The defects and faults of *Paradise Lost,* for faults and defects every work of man must have, it is the business of impartial criticism to discover. As in displaying the excellence of Milton I have not made long quotations, because of selecting beauties there had been no end, I shall in the same general manner mention that which seems to deserve censure; for what Englishman can take delight in transcribing passages, which, if they lessen the reputation of Milton, diminish in some degree the honor of our country?

The generality of my scheme does not admit the frequent notice of verbal inaccuracies; which Bentley, perhaps better skilled in grammar than in poetry, has often found, though he sometimes made them, and which he imputed to the obtrusions of a reviser whom the author's blindness obliged him to employ.[63] A supposition rash and groundless, if he thought it true; and vile and pernicious if, as is said, he in private allowed it to be false.

The plan of *Paradise Lost* has this inconvenience, that it comprises

61. *Paradise Lost,* xi. 8–9.

62. Pertaining to the subject or theme (argument). For the pathetic and the sublime, see the "Life of Cowley," p. 348, n. 57.

63. The Cambridge classical scholar Richard Bentley used his talent for emendation in an edition of *Paradise Lost* (1732), where he attributed "faults" to an imaginary reviser of the poem.

neither human actions nor human manners. The man and woman who act and suffer are in a state which no other man or woman can ever know. The reader finds no transaction in which he can be engaged, beholds no condition in which he can by any effort of imagination place himself; he has, therefore, little natural curiosity or sympathy.

We all, indeed, feel the effects of Adam's disobedience; we all sin like Adam, and like him must all bewail our offenses; we have restless and insidious enemies in the fallen angels, and in the blessed spirits we have guardians and friends; in the redemption of mankind we hope to be included: in the description of heaven and hell we are surely interested, as we are all to reside hereafter either in the regions of horror or of bliss.

But these truths are too important to be new: they have been taught to our infancy; they have mingled with our solitary thoughts and familiar conversation, and are habitually interwoven with the whole texture of life. Being therefore not new, they raise no unaccustomed emotion in the mind; what we knew before, we cannot learn; what is not unexpected, cannot surprise.

Of the ideas suggested by these awful scenes, from some we recede with reverence, except when stated hours require their association; and from others we shrink with horror, or admit them only as salutary inflictions, as counterpoises to our interests and passions. Such images rather obstruct the career of fancy than incite it.

Pleasure and terror are indeed the genuine sources of poetry; but poetical pleasure must be such as human imagination can at least conceive, and poetical terror such as human strength and fortitude may combat. The good and evil of eternity are too ponderous for the wings of wit; the mind sinks under them in passive helplessness, content with calm belief and humble adoration.

Known truths, however, may take a different appearance, and be conveyed to the mind by a new train of intermediate images. This Milton has undertaken, and performed with pregnancy and vigor of mind peculiar to himself. Whoever considers the few radical positions[64] which the Scriptures afforded him will wonder by what energetic operation he expanded them to such extent and ramified them to so much variety, restrained as he was by religious reverence from licentiousness of fiction.

Here is a full display of the united force of study and genius; of a great accumulation of materials, with judgment to digest and fancy to combine them: Milton was able to select from nature, or from story, from ancient fable or from modern science, whatever could illustrate or adorn his thoughts. An accumulation of knowledge impregnated his mind, fermented by study and exalted by imagination.[65]

64. Small amount of basic material.

65. Fermented (brewed) and exalted (refined) are used in a quasi-chemical sense.

It has been therefore said, without an indecent hyperbole, by one of his encomiasts,[66] that in reading *Paradise Lost* we read a book of universal knowledge.

But original deficience cannot be supplied. The want of human interest is always felt. *Paradise Lost* is one of the books which the reader admires and lays down, and forgets to take up again. None ever wished it longer than it is. Its perusal is a duty rather than a pleasure. We read Milton for instruction, retire harassed and overburdened, and look elsewhere for recreation; we desert our master, and seek for companions.

Another inconvenience of Milton's design is that it requires the description of what cannot be described, the agency of spirits. He saw that immateriality supplied no images, and that he could not show angels acting but by instruments of action; he therefore invested them with form and matter. This, being necessary, was therefore defensible; and he should have secured the consistency of his system by keeping immateriality out of sight, and enticing his reader to drop it from his thoughts. But he has unhappily perplexed his poetry with his philosophy. His infernal and celestial powers are sometimes pure spirit and sometimes animated body. When Satan walks with his lance upon the "burning marl," he has a body; when, in his passage between hell and the new world he is in danger of sinking in the vacuity and is supported by a gust of rising vapors, he has a body; when he animates the toad, he seems to be mere spirit that can penetrate matter at pleasure; when he "starts up in his own shape," he has at least a determined form; and when he is brought before Gabriel he has "a spear and a shield," which he had the power of hiding in the toad, though the arms of the contending angels are evidently material.[67]

The vulgar inhabitants of Pandaemonium, being "incorporeal spirits," are "at large though without number" in a limited space; yet in the battle when they were overwhelmed by mountains their armor hurt them, "crushed in upon their substance, now grown gross by sinning." This likewise happened to the uncorrupted angels, who were overthrown "the sooner for their arms, for unarmed they might easily as spirits have evaded by contraction or remove." Even as spirits they are hardly spiritual; for "contraction" and "remove" are images of matter; but if they could have escaped without their armor, they might have escaped from it and left only the empty cover to be battered. Uriel, when he rides on a sunbeam, is material; Satan is material when he is afraid of the prowess of Adam.[68]

The confusion of spirit and matter which pervades the whole narra-

66. Samuel Barrow, in his Latin poem, "On Paradise Lost," prefixed to the second edition of the poem (1674).

67. See *Paradise Lost,* i. 296; ii. 927–38; iv. 799–809; iv. 819; iv. 989–90.

68. See *Paradise Lost,* i. 789–91; vi. 656–61; vi. 595–97; iv. 555–56; ix. 482–88.

tion of the war of heaven fills it with incongruity; and the book in which it is related is, I believe, the favorite of children, and gradually neglected as knowledge is increased.

After the operation of immaterial agents which cannot be explained may be considered that of allegorical persons, which have no real existence. To exalt causes into agents, to invest abstract ideas with form and animate them with activity has always been the right of poetry. But such airy beings are for the most part suffered only to do their natural office, and retire. Thus Fame tells a tale, and Victory hovers over a general or perches on a standard; but Fame and Victory can do no more. To give them any real employment or ascribe to them any material agency is to make them allegorical no longer, but to shock the mind by ascribing effects to nonentity. In the *Prometheus* of Aeschylus we see Violence and Strength, and in the *Alcestis* of Euripides we see Death, brought upon the stage, all as active persons of the drama; but no precedents can justify absurdity.

Milton's allegory of Sin and Death is undoubtedly faulty. Sin is indeed the mother of Death, and may be allowed to be the portress of hell; but when they stop the journey of Satan, a journey described as real, and when Death offers him battle, the allegory is broken. That Sin and Death should have shown the way to hell might have been allowed; but they cannot facilitate the passage by building a bridge, because the difficulty of Satan's passage is described as real and sensible,[69] and the bridge ought to be only figurative. The hell assigned to the rebellious spirits is described as not less local than the residence of man. It is placed in some distant part of space, separated from the regions of harmony and order by a chaotic waste and an unoccupied vacuity; but Sin and Death worked up a "mole of aggravated[70] soil," cemented with "asphaltus"; a work too bulky for ideal architects.[71]

This unskillful allegory appears to me one of the greatest faults of the poem; and to this there was no temptation, but the author's opinion of its beauty.

To the conduct of the narrative some objections may be made. Satan is with great expectation brought before Gabriel in Paradise, and is suffered to go away unmolested. The creation of man is represented as the consequence of the vacuity left in heaven by the expulsion of the rebels, yet Satan mentions it as a report "rife in heaven" before his departure.[72]

To find sentiments for the state of innocence was very difficult; and something of anticipation perhaps is now and then discovered. Adam's discourse of dreams seems not to be the speculation of a new-created

69. Material.
70. Milton wrote "aggregated": collected, massed together.
71. *Paradise Lost,* x. 282–305.
72. *Paradise Lost,* vii. 150–61; i. 650–54.

being. I know not whether his answer to the angel's reproof for curiosity does not want something of propriety: it is the speech of a man acquainted with many other men. Some philosophical notions, especially when the philosophy is false, might have been better omitted. The angel, in a comparison, speaks of "timorous deer,"[73] before deer were yet timorous, and before Adam could understand the comparison.

Dryden remarks, that Milton has some flats among his elevations.[74] This is only to say that all the parts are not equal. In every work one part must be for the sake of others; a palace must have passages, a poem must have transitions. It is no more to be required that wit should always be blazing than that the sun should always stand at noon. In a great work there is a vicissitude of luminous and opaque parts, as there is in the world a succession of day and night. Milton, when he has expatiated[75] in the sky, may be allowed sometimes to revisit earth; for what other author ever soared so high or sustained his flight so long?

Milton, being well versed in the Italian poets, appears to have borrowed often from them; and, as every man catches something from his companions, his desire of imitating Ariosto's levity has disgraced his work with the "Paradise of Fools";[76] a fiction not in itself ill-imagined, but too ludicrous for its place.

His play on words, in which he delights too often; his equivocations, which Bentley endeavors to defend by the example of the ancients; his unnecessary and ungraceful use of terms of art,[77] it is not necessary to mention, because they are easily remarked and generally censured, and at last bear so little proportion to the whole that they scarcely deserve the attention of a critic.

Such are the faults of that wonderful performance, *Paradise Lost;* which he who can put in balance with its beauties must be considered not as nice but as dull, as less to be censured for want of candor[78] than pitied for want of sensibility.

Of *Paradise Regained* the general judgment seems now to be right, that it is in many parts elegant, and everywhere instructive. It was not to be supposed that the writer of *Paradise Lost* could ever write without great effusions of fancy and exalted precepts of wisdom. The basis of *Paradise Regained* is narrow; a dialogue without action can never please like an union of the narrative and dramatic powers. Had this poem been written, not by Milton but by some imitator, it would have claimed and received universal praise.

If *Paradise Regained* has been too much depreciated, *Samson Agonistes*

73. *Paradise Lost,* vi. 857 ("timorous flock"). The angel is Raphael.
74. "On Translation," printed as Preface to Dryden's *Second Miscellany* (1685).
75. Wandered freely.
76. *Paradise Lost,* iii. 444–97.
77. Technical terms.
78. Lack of sympathetic attention.

has in requital been too much admired. It could only be by long prejudice[79] and the bigotry of learning that Milton could prefer the ancient tragedies with their encumbrance of a chorus to the exhibitions of the French and English stages; and it is only by a blind confidence in the reputation of Milton that a drama can be praised in which the intermediate parts have neither cause nor consequence, neither hasten nor retard the catastrophe.

In this tragedy are however many particular beauties, many just sentiments and striking lines; but it wants that power of attracting the attention which a well-connected plan produces.

Milton would not have excelled in dramatic writing; he knew human nature only in the gross, and had never studied the shades of character, nor the combinations of concurring or the perplexity of contending passions. He had read much and knew what books could teach; but had mingled little in the world, and was deficient in the knowledge which experience must confer.

Through all his greater works there prevails an uniform peculiarity of *diction,* a mode and cast of expression which bears little resemblance to that of any former writer, and which is so far removed from common use that an unlearned reader, when he first opens his book, finds himself surprised by a new language.

This novelty has been, by those who can find nothing wrong in Milton, imputed to his laborious endeavors after words suitable to the grandeur of his ideas. "Our language," says Addison, "sunk under him."[80] But the truth is that, both in prose and verse, he had formed his style by a perverse and pedantic principle. He was desirous to use English words with a foreign idiom. This in all his prose is discovered and condemned, for there judgment operates freely, neither softened by the beauty nor awed by the dignity of his thoughts; but such is the power of his poetry that his call is obeyed without resistance, the reader feels himself in captivity to a higher and a nobler mind, and criticism sinks in admiration.

Milton's style was not modified by his subject: what is shown with greater extent in *Paradise Lost* may be found in *Comus.* One source of his peculiarity was his familiarity with the Tuscan poets: the disposition of his words is, I think, frequently Italian; perhaps sometimes combined with other tongues. Of him, at last, may be said what Jonson says of Spenser, that "he wrote no language,"[81] but has formed what Butler calls a "Babylonish dialect,"[82] in itself harsh and barbarous, but made by exalted genius and extensive learning the vehicle of so much in-

79. Prejudgment, prepossession.

80. *Spectator,* no. 297.

81. Ben Jonson, *Timber, or Discoveries* (1640), no. 116 (ed. Maurice Castèlain, 1906): "Spenser, in affecting the ancients, writ no language."

82. Samuel Butler, *Hudibras,* I. i. 93.

struction and so much pleasure that, like other lovers, we find grace in its deformity.

Whatever be the faults of his diction he cannot want the praise of copiousness and variety; he was master of his language in its full extent, and has selected the melodious words with such diligence that from his book alone the art of English poetry might be learned.

After his diction, something must be said of his versification. "The measure," he says, "is the English heroic verse without rhyme."[83] Of this mode he had many examples among the Italians, and some in his own country. The Earl of Surrey is said to have translated one of Virgil's books without rhyme,[84] and besides our tragedies a few short poems had appeared in blank verse; particularly one tending to reconcile the nation to Ralegh's wild attempt upon Guiana, and probably written by Ralegh himself.[85] These petty performances cannot be supposed to have much influenced Milton, who more probably took his hint from Trissino's *Italia Liberata;*[86] and, finding blank verse easier than rhyme, was desirous of persuading himself that it is better.

"Rhyme," he says, and says truly, "is no necessary adjunct of true poetry."[87] But perhaps of poetry as a mental operation meter or music is no necessary adjunct: it is however by the music of meter that poetry has been discriminated in all languages, and in languages melodiously constructed with a due proportion of long and short syllables, meter is sufficient. But one language cannot communicate its rules to another; where meter is scanty and imperfect some help is necessary. The music of the English heroic line strikes the ear so faintly that it is easily lost, unless all the syllables of every line cooperate together; this cooperation can be only obtained by the preservation of every verse unmingled with another as a distinct system of sounds, and this distinctness is obtained and preserved by the artifice of rhyme. The variety of pauses, so much boasted by the lovers of blank verse, changes the measures of an English poet to the periods of a declaimer; and there are only a few skillful and happy readers of Milton who enable their audience to perceive where the lines end or begin. "Blank verse," said an ingenious critic, "seems to be verse only to the eye."[88]

Poetry may subsist without rhyme, but English poetry will not often please; nor can rhyme ever be safely spared but where the subject is able to support itself. Blank verse makes some approach to that which is

83. Preface to *Paradise Lost.*

84. Henry Howard, Earl of Surrey (?1517–47), translated the *Aeneid,* books ii and iv, into blank verse.

85. "Of Guiana, an Epic Song" (1596) is by George Chapman. Sir Walter Ralegh had headed an expedition in 1595 to look for the fabled Eldorado in what is now Venezuela.

86. Giovanni Giorgio Trissino's epic, *Italy Delivered from the Goths* (1547–48).

87. Preface to *Paradise Lost.*

88. William Locke (1732–1810), art collector, identified in Boswell's *Life of Johnson* under the year 1781. The remark seems to have been made in conversation.

called the "lapidary style," has neither the easiness of prose nor the melody of numbers, and therefore tires by long continuance. Of the Italian writers without rhyme, whom Milton alleges as precedents,[89] not one is popular; what reason could urge in its defense has been confuted by the ear.

But, whatever be the advantage of rhyme I cannot prevail on myself to wish that Milton had been a rhymer, for I cannot wish his work to be other than it is; yet like other heroes he is to be admired rather than imitated. He that thinks himself capable of astonishing may write blank verse, but those that hope only to please must condescend to rhyme.

The highest praise of genius is original invention. Milton cannot be said to have contrived the structure of an epic poem, and therefore owes reverence to that vigor and amplitude of mind to which all generations must be indebted for the art of poetical narration, for the texture of the fable, the variation of incidents, the interposition of dialogue, and all the stratagems that surprise and enchain attention. But of all the borrowers from Homer Milton is perhaps the least indebted. He was naturally a thinker for himself, confident of his own abilities and disdainful of help or hindrance; he did not refuse admission to the thought or images of his predecessors, but he did not seek them. From his contemporaries he neither courted nor received support; there is in his writings nothing by which the pride of other authors might be gratified or favor gained; no exchange of praise, nor solicitation of support. His great works were performed under discountenance and in blindness, but difficulties vanished at his touch; he was born for whatever is arduous; and his work is not the greatest of heroic poems, only because it is not the first.

89. Preface to *Paradise Lost.*

Jonathan Swift
1667–1745

An account of Dr. Swift has been already collected, with great diligence and acuteness, by Dr. Hawkesworth, according to a scheme which I laid before him in the intimacy of our friendship. I cannot therefore be expected to say much of a life concerning which I had long since communicated my thoughts to a man capable of dignifying his narration with so much elegance of language and force of sentiment.[1]

Jonathan Swift was, according to an account said to be written by himself, the son of Jonathan Swift, an attorney, and was born at Dublin on St. Andrew's Day,[2] 1667: according to his own report, as delivered by Pope to Spence,[3] he was born at Leicester, the son of a clergyman, who was minister of a parish in Herefordshire. During his life the place of his birth was undetermined.[4] He was contented to be called an Irishman by the Irish, but would occasionally call himself an Englishman. The question may, without much regret, be left in the obscurity in which he delighted to involve it.

Whatever was his birth, his education was Irish. He was sent at the age of six to the school at Kilkenny, and in his fifteenth year (1682) was admitted into the University of Dublin.

In his academical studies he was either not diligent or not happy. It must disappoint every reader's expectation that, when at the usual time he claimed the Bachelorship of Arts, he was found by the examiners too conspicuously deficient for regular admission, and obtained his

1. Dr. John Hawkesworth's *Life of Swift* was published in 1755. Johnson had collaborated with Hawkesworth in a periodical called *The Adventurer* in 1752–54.

2. November 30.

3. Joseph Spence (1699–1768), whose *Anecdotes,* derived notably from conversations with Pope, are an important source for literary history.

4. Swift was born posthumously in Dublin, but his mother spent most of her life in Leicester. His paternal grandfather was a Herefordshire clergyman.

degree at last by *special favor,*[5] a term used in that university to denote want of merit.

Of this disgrace it may be easily supposed that he was much ashamed, and shame had its proper effect in producing reformation. He resolved from that time to study eight hours a day, and continued his industry for seven years, with what improvement is sufficiently known. This part of his story well deserves to be remembered; it may afford useful admonition and powerful encouragement to men whose abilities have been made for a time useless by their passions or pleasures, and who, having lost one part of life in idleness, are tempted to throw away the remainder in despair.

In this course of daily application he continued three years longer at Dublin; and in this time, if the observation and memory of an old companion may be trusted, he drew the first sketch of his *Tale of a Tub.*

When he was about one-and-twenty (1688), being by the death of Godwin Swift his uncle, who had supported him, left without subsistence, he went to consult his mother, who then lived at Leicester, about the future course of his life, and by her direction solicited the advice and patronage of Sir William Temple,[6] who had married one of Mrs. Swift's relations, and whose father, Sir John Temple, Master of the Rolls in Ireland, had lived in great familiarity of friendship with Godwin Swift, by whom Jonathan had been to that time maintained.

Temple received with sufficient kindness the nephew of his father's friend, with whom he was, when they conversed together, so much pleased that he detained him two years in his house. Here he became known to King William, who sometimes visited Temple when he was disabled by the gout, and, being attended by Swift in the garden, showed him how to cut asparagus in the Dutch way.

King William's notions were all military, and he expressed his kindness to Swift by offering to make him a captain of horse.

When Temple removed to Moor Park, he took Swift with him; and when he was consulted by the Earl of Portland about the expedience of complying with a bill then depending[7] for making parliaments triennial, against which King William was strongly prejudiced, after having in vain tried to show the Earl that the proposal involved nothing dangerous to royal power, he sent Swift for the same purpose to the King. Swift, who probably was proud of his employment, and went with all the confidence of a young man, found his arguments and his art of displaying them made totally ineffectual by the predetermination of the King; and used to mention this disappointment as his first antidote against vanity.

Before he left Ireland he contracted a disorder, as he thought, by

5. Like Swift himself, Johnson overstates the want of academic merit.
6. (1628–99), diplomat and essayist.
7. Pending.

eating too much fruit. The original of diseases is commonly obscure. Almost every boy eats as much fruit as he can get, without any great inconvenience. The disease of Swift was giddiness with deafness, which attacked him from time to time, began very early, pursued him through life, and at last sent him to the grave, deprived of reason.[8]

Being much oppressed at Moor Park by this grievous malady, he was advised to try his native air, and went to Ireland; but, finding no benefit, returned to Sir William, at whose house he continued his studies, and is known to have read, among other books, Cyprian and Irenaeus.[9] He thought exercise of great necessity, and used to run half a mile up and down a hill every two hours.

It is easy to imagine that the mode in which his first degree was conferred left him no great fondness for the University of Dublin, and therefore he resolved to become a Master of Arts at Oxford. In the testimonial which he produced the words of disgrace were omitted; and he took his Master's degree (July 5, 1692) with such reception and regard as fully contented him.

While he lived with Temple, he used to pay his mother at Leicester an yearly visit. He traveled on foot unless some violence of weather drove him into a wagon, and at night he would go to a penny lodging, where he purchased clean sheets for sixpence. This practice Lord Orrery imputes to his innate love of grossness and vulgarity: some may ascribe it to his desire of surveying human life through all its varieties; and others, perhaps with equal probability, to a passion which seems to have been deep fixed in his heart—the love of a shilling.

In time he began to think that his attendance at Moor Park deserved some other recompense than the pleasure, however mingled with improvement, of Temple's conversation; and grew so impatient that (1694) he went away in discontent.

Temple, conscious of having given reason for complaint, is said to have made him Deputy Master of the Rolls in Ireland; which, according to his kinsman's account,[10] was an office which he knew him not able to discharge. Swift therefore resolved to enter into the Church, in which he had at first no higher hopes than of the chaplainship to the factory[11] at Lisbon; but, being recommended to Lord Capel,[12] he obtained the prebend[13] of Kilroot in Connor of about a hundred pounds a year.

But the infirmities of Temple made a companion like Swift so necessary that he invited him back, with a promise to procure him English

8. Swift suffered from Ménière's disease, a disturbance of the inner ear.
9. Two early Christian writers.
10. His "cousin" Deane Swift's *Essay upon Swift* (1755).
11. English trading post.
12. Lord Lieutenant of Ireland, its governor.
13. Parish dependent on a cathedral or other church.

preferment,[14] in exchange for the prebend, which he desired him to resign. With this request Swift complied, having perhaps equally repented their separation, and they lived on together with mutual satisfaction; and, in the four years that passed between his return and Temple's death, it is probable that he wrote the *Tale of a Tub* and the *Battle of the Books*.

Swift began early to think, or to hope, that he was a poet, and wrote Pindaric odes to Temple, to the King, and to the Athenian Society, a knot of obscure men, who published a periodical pamphlet of answers to questions sent, or supposed to be sent, by letters. I have been told that Dryden, having perused these verses, said, "Cousin Swift, you will never be a poet"; and that this denunciation was the motive of Swift's perpetual malevolence to Dryden.

In 1699 Temple died, and left a legacy with his manuscripts to Swift, for whom he had obtained from King William a promise of the first prebend that should be vacant at Westminster or Canterbury.

That this promise might not be forgotten, Swift dedicated to the King the posthumous works with which he was entrusted; but neither the dedication, nor tenderness for the man whom he once had treated with confidence and fondness, revived in King William the remembrance of his promise. Swift awhile attended the Court, but soon found his solicitations hopeless.

He was then invited by the Earl of Berkeley[15] to accompany him into Ireland as his private secretary; but after having done the business till their arrival at Dublin, he then found that one Bushe had persuaded the Earl that a clergyman was not a proper secretary, and had obtained the office for himself. In a man like Swift such circumvention and inconstancy must have excited violent indignation.

But he had yet more to suffer. Lord Berkeley had the disposal of the deanery of Derry, and Swift expected to obtain it, but by the secretary's influence, supposed to have been secured by a bribe, it was bestowed on somebody else; and Swift was dismissed with the livings of Laracor and Rathbeggan in the diocese of Meath, which together did not equal half the value of the deanery.[16]

At Laracor he increased the parochial duty by reading prayers on Wednesdays and Fridays, and performed all the offices of his profession with great decency and exactness.

Soon after his settlement at Laracor he invited to Ireland the unfortunate Stella, a young woman whose name was Johnson, the daughter

14. Office, position.
15. One of the three Lord Justices of Ireland, who ruled in the absence of the Lord Lieutenant.
16. Johnson follows Swift's own account here, but Swift was never seriously considered for the Dean's position.

of the steward of Sir William Temple, who, in consideration of her father's virtues, left her a thousand pounds. With her came Mrs. Dingley, whose whole fortune was twenty-seven pounds a year for her life. With these ladies he passed his hours of relaxation, and to them he opened his bosom; but they never resided in the same house, nor did he see either without a witness. They lived at the parsonage when Swift was away, and when he returned, removed to a lodging or to the house of a neighboring clergyman.

Swift was not one of those minds which amaze the world with early pregnancy: his first work, except his few poetical essays, was the *Dissensions in Athens and Rome,* published (1701) in his thirty-fourth year.[17] After its appearance, paying a visit to some bishop, he heard mention made of the new pamphlet that Burnet[18] had written, replete with political knowledge. When he seemed to doubt Burnet's right to the work he was told by the Bishop that he was "a young man," and, still persisting to doubt, that he was "a very positive young man."

Three years afterward (1704) was published the *Tale of a Tub*: of this book charity may be persuaded to think that it might be written by a man of a peculiar character, without ill intention; but it is certainly of dangerous example.[19] That Swift was its author, though it be universally believed, was never owned by himself, nor very well proved by any evidence; but no other claimant can be produced, and he did not deny it when Archbishop Sharp and the Duchess of Somerset, by showing it to the Queen, debarred him from a bishopric.[20]

When this wild work first raised the attention of the public, Sacheverell, meeting Smalridge, tried to flatter him by seeming to think him the author; but Smalridge answered with indignation, "Not all that you and I have in the world, nor all that ever we shall have, should hire me to write the *Tale of a Tub.*"[21]

The digressions relating to Wotton and Bentley must be confessed to discover want of knowledge, or want of integrity; he did not understand the two controversies, or he willingly misrepresented them. But

17. The *Dissensions* is a "parallel history," in which a discussion of politics in ancient Athens and Rome presented obvious parallels to quarrels between modern Whigs and Tories.

18. Gilbert Burnet (1643–1715), Bishop of Salisbury, prominent ecclesiastic and historian.

19. The *Tale* satirizes the Roman Catholic, the Anglican, and the Dissenting churches—and much else, in digressions on critics, on ancient and modern learning, and on madness.

20. Johnson overdramatizes the harmful effect that the *Tale of a Tub* had on Swift's career. Swift was scarcely considered as a candidate for a bishopric.

21. Henry Sacheverell (?1674–1724), inflammatory Tory preacher; George Smalridge (1663–1719), Bishop of Bristol. Smalridge seemed perhaps a likely author of the *Tale* because he had participated in an earlier attack by the "Ancients" on Bentley: *Dr. Bentley's Dissertation . . . Examined* (1698).

wit can stand its ground against truth only a little while. The honors due to learning have been justly distributed by the decision of posterity.[22]

The Battle of the Books is so like the *Combat des Livres,*[23] which the same question concerning the Ancients and Moderns had produced in France, that the improbability of such a coincidence of thoughts without communication is not, in my opinion, balanced by the anonymous protestation prefixed, in which all knowledge of the French book is peremptorily disowned.

For some time after Swift was probably employed in solitary study, gaining the qualifications requisite for future eminence. How often he visited England, and with what diligence he attended his parishes, I know not. It was not till about four years afterwards that he became a professed author; and then one year (1708) produced *The Sentiments of a Church-of-England Man;* the ridicule of astrology, under the name of "Bickerstaff"; the *Argument against Abolishing Christianity;* and the defense of the *Sacramental Test.*[24]

The Sentiments of a Church-of-England Man is written with great coolness, moderation, ease, and perspicuity. The *Argument against Abolishing Christianity* is a very happy and judicious irony. One passage in it deserves to be selected:

> If Christianity were once abolished, how could the freethinkers, the strong reasoners, and the men of profound learning be able to find another subject so calculated, in all points, whereon to display their abilities? What wonderful productions of wit should we be deprived of from those whose genius, by continual practice, hath been wholly turned upon raillery and invectives against religion, and would therefore never be able to shine, or distinguish themselves, upon any other subject? We are daily complaining of the great decline of wit among us, and would take away the greatest, perhaps the only topic we have left. Who would ever have suspected Asgill for a wit, or Toland for a philosopher, if the inexhaustible stock of Christianity had not been at hand to provide them with materials? What other subject, through all art or nature, could have produced Tindal for a profound author, or

22. William Wotton (1666–1727) and Richard Bentley (1662–1742) were scholars who defended the "Moderns" in debates concerning the relative merits of ancient and modern learning. Swift makes them representatives of modern pedantry (*A Tale of a Tub,* Section III, "A Digression Concerning Critics"; Section V, "A Digression in the Modern Kind").

23. Johnson refers to François de Callières' *Poetic History of the Newly Declared War between the Ancients and the Moderns* (1688).

24. The Sacramental Test Statute provided that only communicants of the Anglican Church could hold civil or military offices or be elected to Parliament. A London cobbler named John Partridge published an almanac of astrological predictions. Swift's parody under the name of Isaac Bickerstaff (1708) foretold the death of Partridge, and in subsequent Bickerstaff papers he contended that Partridge was actually dead.

> furnished him with readers?[25] It is the wise choice of the subject that alone adorns and distinguishes the writer. For had an hundred such pens as these been employed on the side of religion, they would have immediately sunk into silence and oblivion.

The reasonableness of a *test* is not hard to be proved; but perhaps it must be allowed that the proper test has not been chosen.

The attention paid to the papers published under the name of "Bickerstaff" induced Steele, when he projected *The Tatler,* to assume an appellation which had already gained possession of the reader's notice.

In the year following he wrote *A Project for the Advancement of Religion,* addressed to Lady Berkeley, by whose kindness it is not unlikely that he was advanced to his benefices. To this project, which is formed with great purity of intention, and displayed with sprightliness and elegance, it can only be objected that, like many projects, it is, if not generally impracticable, yet evidently hopeless, as it supposes more zeal, concord, and perseverance than a view of mankind gives reason for expecting.

He wrote likewise this year a "Vindication of Bickerstaff," and an explanation of an "Ancient Prophecy," part written after the facts, and the rest never completed, but well planned to excite amazement.[26]

Soon after began the busy and important part of Swift's life. He was employed (1710) by the Primate of Ireland to solicit the Queen for a remission of the First Fruits and Twentieth Parts to the Irish clergy.[27] With this purpose he had recourse to Mr. Harley,[28] to whom he was mentioned as a man neglected and oppressed by the last ministry because he had refused to cooperate with some of their schemes. What he had refused has never been told; what he had suffered was, I suppose, the exclusion from a bishopric by the remonstrances of Sharp, whom he describes as "the harmless tool of others' hate," and whom he represents as afterwards "suing for pardon."[28a]

Harley's designs and situation were such as made him glad of an auxiliary so well qualified for his service; he therefore soon admitted him to familiarity, whether ever to confidence some have made a doubt; but it would have been difficult to excite his zeal without persuading him that he was trusted, and not very easy to delude him by false persuasions.

25. John Asgill, John Toland, and Matthew Tindal wrote deistic works which the House of Commons ordered to be burned.

26. Johnson wrongly implies that Swift's "A Famous Prediction of Merlin" was an explanation of an historical document. Swift himself wrote the "ancient" prophecy.

27. The Irish Church paid the English Crown the entire profits of the first year of a benefice (the "First Fruits") and one-twentieth of the succeeding annual profits (the "Twentieth Parts"). Swift persuaded the Queen to remit these dues.

28. Robert Harley (later first Earl of Oxford), Chancellor of the Exchequer and head of the Tory ministry.

28a. "The Author upon Himself," ll. 51–52.

He was certainly admitted to those meetings in which the first hints and original plan of action are supposed to have been formed, and was one of the sixteen ministers, or agents of the ministry, who met weekly at each others' houses, and were united by the name of "Brother."

Being not immediately considered as an obdurate Tory, he conversed indiscriminately with all the wits, and was yet the friend of Steele, who in *The Tatler,* which began in 1710,[29] confesses the advantages of his conversation, and mentions something contributed by him to his paper. But he was now immerging into political controversy; for the same year produced *The Examiner,*[30] of which Swift wrote thirty-three papers. In argument he may be allowed to have the advantage; for where a wide system of conduct, and the whole of a public character is laid open to inquiry, the accuser, having the choice of facts, must be very unskillful if he does not prevail; but with regard to wit, I am afraid none of Swift's papers will be found equal to those by which Addison opposed him.

Early in the next year he published a *Proposal for Correcting, Improving, and Ascertaining the English Tongue, in a Letter to the Earl of Oxford,* written without much knowledge of the general nature of language, and without any accurate inquiry into the history of other tongues. The certainty and stability which, contrary to all experience, he thinks attainable, he proposes to secure by instituting an academy; the decrees of which every man would have been willing, and many would have been proud to disobey, and which, being renewed by successive elections, would in a short time have differed from itself.

He wrote in the same year a *Letter to the October Club,* a number of Tory gentlemen sent from the country to Parliament, who formed themselves into a club to the number of about a hundred, and met to animate the zeal and raise the expectations of each other. They thought, with great reason, that the ministers were losing opportunities; that sufficient use was not made of the ardor of the nation; they called loudly for more changes and stronger efforts, and demanded the punishment of part, and the dismission of the rest,[31] of those whom they considered as public robbers.

Their eagerness was not gratified by the Queen or by Harley. The Queen was probably slow because she was afraid, and Harley was slow because he was doubtful: he was a Tory only by necessity or for convenience, and when he had power in his hands had no settled purpose for which he should employ it; forced to gratify to a certain degree the

29. It began April 12, 1709.

30. A Tory periodical which rivaled Addison's *Whig Examiner.*

31. Swift's *Some Advice . . . to the October Club* (1712) was addressed to a group of country Tories who were pressing the Tory ministry to punish the chiefs of the Whig ministry which had resigned in 1710, and to get rid of the Whig holdovers.

Tories who supported him, but unwilling to make his reconcilement to the Whigs utterly desperate, he corresponded at once with the two expectants of the Crown,[32] and kept, as has been observed, the succession undetermined. Not knowing what to do he did nothing; and with the fate of a double-dealer at last he lost his power, but kept his enemies.

Swift seems to have concurred in opinion with the October Club; but it was not in his power to quicken the tardiness of Harley, whom he stimulated as much as he could, but with little effect. He that knows not whither to go is in no haste to move. Harley, who was perhaps not quick by nature, became yet more slow by irresolution, and was content to hear that dilatoriness lamented as natural, which he applauded in himself as politic.

Without the Tories, however, nothing could be done, and as they were not to be gratified they must be appeased; and the conduct of the Minister, if it could not be vindicated, was to be plausibly excused.

Swift now attained the zenith of his political importance: he published (1712)[33] *The Conduct of the Allies,* ten days before the Parliament assembled. The purpose was to persuade the nation to a peace, and never had any writer more success. The people, who had been amused with bonfires and triumphal processions, and looked with idolatry on the General[34] and his friends who, as they thought, had made England the arbitress of nations, were confounded between shame and rage when they found that "mines had been exhausted and millions destroyed,"[35] to secure the Dutch or aggrandize the Emperor, without any advantage to ourselves; that we had been bribing our neighbors to fight their own quarrel, and that amongst our enemies we might number our allies.

That is no longer doubted of which the nation was then first informed, that the war was unnecessarily protracted to fill the pockets of Marlborough, and that it would have been continued without end if he could have continued his annual plunder. But Swift, I suppose, did not yet know what he has since written, that a commission was drawn which would have appointed him General for life, had it not become ineffectual by the resolution of Lord Cowper, who refused the Seal.[36]

"Whatever is received," say the schools,[37] "is received in proportion

32. The Elector of Hanover, later George I; and James Edward, the "Old Pretender."

33. The title page is dated 1711.

34. John Churchill, Duke of Marlborough, who commanded the English forces in the War of the Spanish Succession. England, Holland, the Emperor of the Holy Roman Empire, Portugal, and several German states banded together in a war against France and Spain.

35. This quotation has not been traced.

36. William Cowper, the Lord Chancellor, refused to affix the Great Seal, which was necessary to make the appointment official.

37. Medieval (scholastic) philosophers.

to the recipient." The power of a political treatise depends much upon the disposition of the people: the nation was then combustible, and a spark set it on fire. It is boasted that between November and January eleven thousand were sold; a great number at that time, when we were not yet a nation of readers. To its propagation certainly no agency of power or influence was wanting. It furnished arguments for conversation, speeches for debate, and materials for parliamentary resolutions.

Yet, surely, whoever surveys this wonder-working pamphlet with cool perusal will confess that its efficacy was supplied by the passions of its readers; that it operates by the mere weight of facts, with very little assistance from the hand that produced them.

This year (1712) he published his *Reflections on the Barrier Treaty*, which carries on the design of his *Conduct of the Allies*, and shows how little regard in that negotiation had been shown to the interest of England, and how much of the conquered country had been demanded by the Dutch.[38]

This was followed by *Remarks on the Bishop of Sarum's Introduction to his Third Volume of the History of the Reformation*, a pamphlet which Burnet published as an alarm to warn the nation of the approach of Popery. Swift, who seems to have disliked the Bishop with something more than political aversion, treats him like one whom he is glad of an opportunity to insult.

Swift, being now the declared favorite and supposed confidant of the Tory ministry, was treated by all that depended on the Court with the respect which dependents know how to pay. He soon began to feel part of the misery of greatness; he that could say he knew him considered himself as having fortune in his power. Commissions, solicitations, remonstrances crowded about him; he was expected to do every man's business, to procure employment for one, and to retain it for another. In assisting those who addressed him, he represents himself as sufficiently diligent; and desires to have others believe, what he probably believed himself, that by his interposition many Whigs of merit, and among them Addison and Congreve, were continued in their places. But every man of known influence has so many petitions which he cannot grant, that he must necessarily offend more than he gratifies, because the preference given to one affords all the rest a reason for complaint. "When I give away a place," said Louis XIV, "I make a hundred discontented, and one ungrateful."

Much has been said of the equality and independence which he preserved in his conversation with the ministers, of the frankness of his remonstrances, and the familiarity of his friendship. In accounts of this kind a few single incidents are set against the general tenor of behavior.

38. The English agreed to a treaty in which they gained little, but the Dutch were allowed to garrison a number of towns in the Spanish Netherlands (modern Belgium) as a barrier against the French.

No man, however, can pay a more servile tribute to the great than by suffering his liberty in their presence to aggrandize him in his own esteem. Between different ranks of the community there is necessarily some distance: he who is called by his superior to pass the interval may properly accept the invitation, but petulance and obtrusion are rarely produced by magnanimity, nor have often any nobler cause than the pride of importance and the malice of inferiority. He who knows himself necessary may set, while that necessity lasts, a high value upon himself, as, in a lower condition, a servant eminently skillful may be saucy; but he is saucy only because he is servile. Swift appears to have preserved the kindness of the great when they wanted him no longer; and therefore it must be allowed that the childish freedom, to which he seems enough inclined, was overpowered by his better qualities.

His disinterestedness has been likewise mentioned; a strain of heroism which would have been in his condition romantic[39] and superfluous. Ecclesiastical benefices, when they become vacant, must be given away; and the friends of power may, if there be no inherent disqualification, reasonably expect them. Swift accepted (1713) the deanery of St. Patrick,[40] the best preferment that his friends could venture to give him. That ministry was in a great degree supported by the clergy, who were not yet reconciled to the author of the *Tale of a Tub* and would not, without much discontent and indignation, have borne to see him installed in an English cathedral.

He refused, indeed, fifty pounds from Lord Oxford, but he accepted afterwards a draft of a thousand upon the Exchequer, which was intercepted by the Queen's death, and which he resigned, as he says himself, "multa gemens" (with many a groan).

In the midst of his power and his politics he kept a journal of his visits, his walks, his interviews with ministers, and quarrels with his servant, and transmitted it to Mrs. Johnson and Mrs. Dingley, to whom he knew that whatever befell him was interesting, and no accounts could be too minute.[41] Whether these diurnal trifles were properly exposed to eyes which had never received any pleasure from the presence of the Dean may be reasonably doubted. They have, however, some odd attraction: the reader, finding frequent mention of names which he has been used to consider as important, goes on in hope of information; and, as there is nothing to fatigue attention, if he is disappointed he can hardly complain. It is easy to perceive from every page that though ambition pressed Swift into a life of bustle, the wish for a life of ease was always returning.

He went to take possession of his deanery as soon as he had obtained it; but he was not suffered to stay in Ireland more than a fortnight

39. Exaggerated.
40. In Dublin.
41. Later published as the *Journal to Stella*.

before he was recalled to England, that he might reconcile Lord Oxford and Lord Bolingbroke,[42] who began to look on one another with malevolence, which every day increased, and which Bolingbroke appeared to retain in his last years.

Swift contrived an interview, from which they both departed discontented; he procured a second, which only convinced him that the feud was irreconcilable: he told them his opinion, that all was lost. This denunciation was contradicted by Oxford, but Bolingbroke whispered that he was right.

Before this violent dissension had shattered the ministry, Swift had published, in the beginning of the year (1714), *The Public Spirit of the Whigs,* in answer to *The Crisis,* a pamphlet for which Steele was expelled from the House of Commons. Swift was now so far alienated from Steele as to think him no longer entitled to decency, and therefore treats him sometimes with contempt, and sometimes with abhorrence.

In this pamphlet the Scotch were mentioned in terms so provoking to that irritable nation that, resolving "not to be offended with impunity," the Scotch Lords in a body[43] demanded an audience of the Queen, and solicited reparation. A proclamation was issued, in which three hundred pounds was offered for discovery of the author. From this storm he was, as he relates, "secured by a sleight," of what kind, or by whose prudence, is not known; and such was the increase of his reputation that the Scottish nation "applied again that he would be their friend."

He was become so formidable to the Whigs that his familiarity with the ministers was clamored at in Parliament, particularly by two men, afterwards of great note, Aislabie and Walpole.[44]

But, by the disunion of his great friends, his importance and his designs were now at an end; and seeing his services at last useless, he retired about June (1714) into Berkshire, where, in the house of a friend, he wrote what was then suppressed, but has since appeared under the title of *Free Thoughts on the Present State of Affairs.*

While he was waiting in this retirement for events which time or chance might bring to pass, the death of the Queen broke down at once the whole system of Tory politics; and nothing remained but to withdraw from the implacability of triumphant Whiggism, and shelter himself in unenvied obscurity.

The accounts of his reception in Ireland, given by Lord Orrery and Dr. Delany,[45] are so different that the credit of the writers, both undoubtedly veracious, cannot be saved but by supposing, what I think is

42. Henry St. John (1678–1751), first Viscount Bolingbroke, and Secretary of State.

43. The sixteen Representative Peers of Scotland who sat in the House of Lords.

44. John Aislabie, Chancellor of the Exchequer, 1718–20; Sir Robert Walpole, Prime Minister and Chancellor of the Exchequer, 1715–17, 1721–42.

45. John Boyle, fifth Earl of Orrery, and Patrick Delany, whose accounts of Swift were published respectively in 1752 and 1754.

true, that they speak of different times. When Delany says that he was received with respect, he means for the first fortnight, when he came to take legal possession; and when Lord Orrery tells that he was pelted by the populace, he is to be understood of the time when, after the Queen's death, he became a settled resident.

The Archbishop of Dublin gave him at first some disturbance in the exercise of his jurisdiction; but it was soon discovered that between prudence and integrity he was seldom in the wrong; and that, when he was right, his spirit did not easily yield to opposition.

Having so lately quitted the tumults of a party and the intrigues of a court, they still kept his thoughts in agitation, as the sea fluctuates a while when the storm has ceased. He therefore filled his hours with some historical attempts, relating to the "Change of the Ministers," and the "Conduct of the Ministry." He likewise is said to have written a *History of the Four Last Years of Queen Anne,* which he began in her lifetime, and afterwards labored with great attention, but never published. It was after his death in the hands of Lord Orrery and Dr. King. A book under that title was published, with Swift's name, by Dr. Lucas; of which I can only say that it seemed by no means to correspond with the notions that I had formed of it, from a conversation which I once heard between the Earl of Orrery and old Mr. Lewis.[46]

Swift now, much against his will, commenced Irishman for life, and was to contrive how he might be best accommodated[47] in a country where he considered himself as in a state of exile. It seems that his first recourse was to piety. The thoughts of death rushed upon him at this time with such incessant importunity, that they took possession of his mind when he first waked for many years together.

He opened his house by a public table[48] two days a week, and found his entertainments gradually frequented by more and more visitants of learning among the men, and of elegance among the women. Mrs. Johnson had left the country, and lived in lodgings not far from the deanery. On his public days she regulated the table, but appeared at it as a mere guest, like other ladies.

On other days he often dined, at a stated price, with Mr. Worrall, a clergyman of his cathedral, whose house was recommended by the peculiar[49] neatness and pleasantry of his wife. To this frugal mode of living he was first disposed by care to pay some debts which he had contracted, and he continued it for the pleasure of accumulating money. His avarice, however, was not suffered to obstruct the claims of his dignity; he was served in plate, and used to say that he was the

46. Erasmus Lewis, Swift's close friend. The version of the *History* published by Dr. Charles Lucas at London and Dublin in 1758 agrees closely with several extant manuscript copies endorsed or corrected in Swift's hand.

47. Made comfortable.

48. A meal to which guests could come without a formal invitation.

49. Particular.

poorest gentleman in Ireland that eat upon plate,[50] and the richest that lived without a coach.

How he spent the rest of his time, and how he employed his hours of study, has been inquired with hopeless curiosity. For who can give an account of another's studies? Swift was not likely to admit any to his privacies, or to impart a minute account of his business or his leisure.

Soon after (1716), in his forty-ninth year, he was privately married to Mrs. Johnson by Dr. Ashe, Bishop of Clogher, as Dr. Madden told me, in the garden.[51] The marriage made no change in their mode of life; they lived in different houses, as before: nor did she ever lodge in the deanery but when Swift was seized with a fit of giddiness. "It would be difficult," says Lord Orrery, "to prove that they were ever afterwards together without a third person."

The Dean of St. Patrick's lived in a private manner, known and regarded only by his friends till, about the year 1720, he, by a pamphlet, recommended to the Irish the use, and consequently the improvement, of their manufacture. For a man to use the productions of his own labor is surely a natural right, and to like best what he makes himself is a natural passion. But to excite this passion, and enforce this right, appeared so criminal to those who had an interest in the English trade that the printer was imprisoned; and, as Hawkesworth justly observes, the attention of the public being by this outrageous resentment turned upon the proposal, the author was by consequence made popular.

In 1723 died Mrs. Vanhomrigh,[52] a woman made unhappy by her admiration of wit, and ignominiously distinguished by the name of *Vanessa,* whose conduct has been already sufficiently discussed, and whose history is too well known to be minutely repeated. She was a young woman fond of literature, whom *Decanus,* the Dean, called *Cadenus* by transposition of the letters, took pleasure in directing and instructing; till, from being proud of his praise, she grew fond of his person. Swift was then about forty-seven, at an age when vanity is strongly excited by the amorous attention of a young woman. If it be said that Swift should have checked a passion which he never meant to gratify, recourse must be had to that extenuation which he so much despised, "men are but men": perhaps, however, he did not at first know his own mind, and, as he represents himself, was undetermined. For his admission of her courtship, and his indulgence of her hopes

50. Ate upon fine tableware, silver or perhaps china.

51. Swift's "marriage" to Stella has been a persistent subject of scholarly debate. His latest, careful biographer, Irvin Ehrenpreis, maintains that he did not marry her.

52. Esther Vanhomrigh, daughter of a wealthy mayor of Dublin. She was Swift's friend and in a sense his pupil, at London, from 1708 (when she was about eighteen) until their rupture in 1723, which led to her death. This unhappy relationship produced Swift's poem *Cadenus and Vanessa,* written in 1713, published in 1726 by a direction left in her will.

after his marriage to Stella, no other honest plea can be found than that he delayed a disagreeable discovery from time to time, dreading the immediate bursts of distress, and watching for a favorable moment. She thought herself neglected, and died of disappointment; having ordered by her will the poem to be published, in which Cadenus had proclaimed her excellence, and confessed his love. The effect of the publication upon the Dean and Stella is thus related by Delany.

> I have good reason to believe that they both were greatly shocked and distressed (though it may be differently) upon this occasion. The Dean made a tour to the south of Ireland, for about two months, at this time, to dissipate[53] his thoughts, and give place to[54] obloquy. And Stella retired (upon the earnest invitation of the owner) to the house of a cheerful, generous, good-natured friend of the Dean's, whom she also much loved and honored. There my informer often saw her; and, I have reason to believe, used his utmost endeavors to relieve, support, and amuse her in this sad situation.
>
> One little incident he told me of, on that occasion, I think I shall never forget. As her friend was an hospitable, open-hearted man, well-beloved and largely acquainted, it happened one day that some gentlemen dropped in to dinner, who were strangers to Stella's situation; and as the poem of *Cadenus and Vanessa* was then the general topic of conversation, one of them said, "Surely that Vanessa must be an extraordinary woman that could inspire the Dean to write so finely upon her." Mrs. Johnson smiled, and answered, "that she thought that point not quite so clear; for it was well known the Dean could write finely upon a broomstick."[55]

The great acquisition of esteem and influence was made by the *Drapier's Letters* in 1724. One Wood, of Wolverhampton in Staffordshire, a man enterprising and rapacious, had, as is said, by a present to the Duchess of Munster,[56] obtained a patent empowering him to coin one hundred and eighty thousand pounds of halfpence and farthings for the kingdom of Ireland, in which there was a very inconvenient and embarrassing scarcity of copper coin; so that it was possible to run in debt upon the credit of a piece of money; for the cook or keeper of an alehouse could not refuse to supply a man that had silver in his hand, and the buyer would not leave his money without change.

The project was therefore plausible. The scarcity, which was already great, Wood took care to make greater by agents who gathered up the old halfpence; and was about to turn his brass into gold by pouring the treasures of his new mint upon Ireland, when Swift, finding that the metal was debased to an enormous degree, wrote *Letters*, under the

53. Distract.
54. Retreat from.
55. Stella was alluding to Swift's humorous "Meditation upon a Broomstick."
56. Mistress of George I.

name of "M. B. Drapier," to show the folly of receiving, and the mischief that must ensue by giving, gold and silver for coin worth perhaps not a third part of its nominal value.

The nation was alarmed; the new coin was universally refused; but the governors of Ireland considered resistance to the King's patent as highly criminal; and one Whitshed, then Chief Justice, who had tried the printer of the former pamphlet, and sent out the jury nine times, till by clamor and menaces they were frighted into a special verdict, now presented the Drapier, but could not prevail on the grand jury to find the bill.[57]

Lord Carteret[58] and the Privy Council published a proclamation, offering three hundred pounds for discovering the author of the "Fourth Letter." Swift had concealed himself from his printers, and trusted only his butler, who transcribed the paper. The man, immediately after the appearance of the proclamation, strolled from the house, and stayed out all night and part of the next day. There was reason enough to fear that he had betrayed his master for the reward; but he came home, and the Dean ordered him to put off his livery and leave the house, "for," says he, "I know that my life is in your power, and I will not bear, out of fear, either your insolence or negligence." The man excused his fault with great submission, and begged that he might be confined in the house while it was in his power to endanger his master; but the Dean resolutely turned him out, without taking farther notice of him, till the term of information had expired, and then received him again. Soon afterwards he ordered him and the rest of the servants into his presence, without telling his intentions, and bade them take notice that their fellow-servant was no longer Robert the butler, but that his integrity had made him Mr. Blakeney, verger of St. Patrick's, an officer whose income was between thirty and forty pounds a year; yet he still continued for some years to serve his old master as his butler.[58a]

Swift was known from this time by the appellation of "The Dean." He was honored by the populace as the champion, patron, and instructor of Ireland; and gained such power as, considered both in its extent and duration, scarcely any man has ever enjoyed without greater wealth or higher station.

He was from this important year the oracle of the traders and the idol of the rabble, and by consequence was feared and courted by all to whom the kindness of the traders or the populace was necessary. The Drapier was a sign;[59] the Drapier was a health; and which way soever

57. Approve the indictment. Swift published five *Drapier's Letters* between April and December of 1724. He put his initials to a sixth, first published in 1735.

58. Lord Lieutenant.

58a. The butler's name was Blakely, and the story is unreliable.

59. Tavern sign.

the eye or the ear was turned, some tokens were found of the nation's gratitude to the Drapier.

The benefit was indeed great; he had rescued Ireland from a very oppressive and predatory invasion; and the popularity which he had gained he was diligent to keep by appearing forward and zealous on every occasion where the public interest was supposed to be involved. Nor did he much scruple to boast his influence; for when, upon some attempts to regulate the coin, Archbishop Boulter, then one of the Justices,[60] accused him of exasperating the people, he exculpated himself by saying, "If I had lifted up my finger, they would have torn you to pieces."

But the pleasure of popularity was soon interrupted by domestic misery. Mrs. Johnson, whose conversation was to him the great softener of the ills of life, began in the year of the Drapier's triumph to decline; and two years afterwards was so wasted with sickness that her recovery was considered as hopeless.

Swift was then in England, and had been invited by Lord Bolingbroke to pass the winter with him in France; but this call of calamity hastened him to Ireland, where perhaps his presence contributed to restore her to imperfect and tottering health.

He was now so much at ease that (1727) he returned to England, where he collected three volumes of *Miscellanies* in conjunction with Pope, who prefixed a querulous and apologetical Preface.

This important year sent likewise into the world *Gulliver's Travels,*[61] a production so new and strange that it filled the reader with a mingled emotion of merriment and amazement. It was received with such avidity that the price of the first edition was raised before the second could be made; it was read by the high and the low, the learned and illiterate. Criticism was for awhile lost in wonder: no rules of judgment were applied to a book written in open defiance of truth and regularity. But when distinctions came to be made, the part which gave least pleasure was that which describes the Flying Island, and that which gave most disgust must be the history of the Houyhnhnms.

While Swift was enjoying the reputation of his new work the news of the King's death arrived; and he kissed the hands of the new King and Queen[62] three days after their accession.

By the Queen, when she was Princess, he had been treated with some distinction, and was well received by her in her exaltation; but whether she gave hopes which she never took care to satisfy, or he formed expectations which she never meant to raise, the event was that he always afterwards thought on her with malevolence, and particularly

60. Lord Justices.
61. Published in 1726.
62. George II and Queen Caroline. George I died in 1727.

charged her with breaking her promise of some medals which she engaged to send him.

I know not whether she had not in her turn some reason for complaint. A letter was sent her, not so much entreating as requiring her patronage of Mrs. Barber, an ingenious Irishwoman, who was then begging subscriptions for her poems. To this letter was subscribed the name of Swift, and it has all the appearances of his diction and sentiments; but it was not written in his hand, and had some little improprieties. When he was charged with this letter he laid hold of the inaccuracies, and urged the improbability of the accusation, but never denied it: he shuffles between cowardice and veracity, and talks big when he says nothing.

He seemed desirous enough of recommencing courtier, and endeavored to gain the kindness of Mrs. Howard, remembering what Mrs. Masham had performed in former times;[63] but his flatteries were, like those of other wits, unsuccessful; the lady either wanted power, or had no ambition of poetical immortality.

He was seized not long afterwards by a fit of giddiness, and again heard of the sickness and danger of Mrs. Johnson. He then left the house of Pope, as it seems, with very little ceremony, finding that "two sick friends cannot live together," and did not write to him till he found himself at Chester.[64]

He returned to a home of sorrow: poor Stella was sinking into the grave, and, after a languishing decay of about two months, died in her forty-fourth year on January 28, 1728. How much he wished her life his papers show; nor can it be doubted that he dreaded the death of her whom he loved most, aggravated by the consciousness that himself had hastened it.

Beauty and the power of pleasing, the greatest external advantages that woman can desire or possess, were fatal to the unfortunate Stella. The man whom she had the misfortune to love was, as Delany observes, fond of singularity, and desirous to make a mode of happiness for himself different from the general course of things and order of Providence. From the time of her arrival in Ireland he seems resolved to keep her in his power, and therefore hindered a match sufficiently advantageous by accumulating unreasonable demands and prescribing conditions that could not be performed.[65] While she was at her own disposal he did not consider his possession as secure; resentment, ambition, or caprice might separate them; he was therefore resolved to make "assurance double sure,"[65a] and to appropriate her by a private

63. Henrietta Howard, Countess of Suffolk, was the mistress of George II; Abigail Masham, Lady Masham, was Queen Anne's favorite during the last years of her reign.

64. Well along on the journey to Ireland.

65. Johnson exaggerates Swift's efforts to hinder a marriage between Stella and Dr. William Tisdall, an Irish clergyman.

65a. *Macbeth,* IV. i. 83.

marriage, to which he had annexed the expectation of all the pleasures of perfect friendship, without the uneasiness of conjugal restraint. But with this state poor Stella was not satisfied; she never was treated as a wife, and to the world she had the appearance of a mistress. She lived sullenly on, in hope that in time he would own and receive her; but the time did not come till the change of his manners and depravation[66] of his mind made her tell him, when he offered to acknowledge her, that "it was too late." She then gave up herself to sorrowful resentment, and died under the tyranny of him by whom she was in the highest degree loved and honored.

What were her claims to this eccentric tenderness, by which the laws of nature were violated to retain her, curiosity will inquire; but how shall it be gratified? Swift was a lover; his testimony may be suspected. Delany and the Irish saw with Swift's eyes and therefore add little confirmation. That she was virtuous, beautiful, and elegant in a very high degree, such admiration from such a lover makes it very probable; but she had not much literature, for she could not spell her own language; and of her wit, so loudly vaunted, the smart sayings which Swift himself has collected afford no splendid specimen.

The reader of Swift's *Letter to a Lady on her Marriage* may be allowed to doubt whether his opinion of female excellence ought implicitly[67] to be admitted; for if his general thoughts on women were such as he exhibits, a very little sense in a lady would enrapture and a very little virtue would astonish him. Stella's supremacy, therefore, was perhaps only local; she was great because her associates were little.

In some remarks lately published on the *Life of Swift*,[68] this marriage is mentioned as fabulous or doubtful; but, alas! poor Stella, as Dr. Madden told me, related her melancholy story to Dr. Sheridan when he attended her as a clergyman to prepare her for death; and Delany mentions it not with doubt, but only with regret. Swift never mentioned her without a sigh.

The rest of his life was spent in Ireland, in a country to which not even power almost despotic, nor flattery almost idolatrous, could reconcile him. He sometimes wished to visit England, but always found some reason of delay. He tells Pope, in the decline of life, that he hopes once more to see him; "but if not," says he, "we must part, as all human beings have parted."

After the death of Stella his benevolence was contracted and his severity exasperated; he drove his acquaintance from his table and wondered why he was deserted. But he continued his attention to the public, and wrote from time to time such directions, admonitions, or

66. Deterioration, corruption.
67. Fully.
68. Johnson refers to *Biographical Anecdotes of Dean Swift,* in a supplementary volume (1779) to Hawkesworth's *Life of Swift* (1755).

censures as the exigency of affairs, in his opinion, made proper, and nothing fell from his pen in vain.

In a short poem on the Presbyterians, whom he always regarded with detestation, he bestowed one stricture upon Bettesworth, a lawyer eminent for his insolence to the clergy, which, from very considerable reputation, brought him into immediate and universal contempt. Bettesworth, enraged at his disgrace and loss, went to Swift and demanded whether he was the author of that poem. "Mr. Bettesworth," answered he, "I was in my youth acquainted with great lawyers, who, knowing my disposition to satire, advised me that if any scoundrel or blockhead whom I had lampooned should ask, 'Are you the author of this paper?' I should tell him that I was not the author; and therefore I tell you, Mr. Bettesworth, that I am not the author of these lines."

Bettesworth was so little satisfied with this account that he publicly professed his resolution of a violent and corporal revenge; but the inhabitants of St. Patrick's district embodied themselves in the Dean's defense. Bettesworth declared in Parliament that Swift had deprived him of twelve hundred pounds a year.

Swift was popular awhile by another mode of beneficence. He set aside some hundreds to be lent in small sums to the poor, from five shillings, I think, to five pounds. He took no interest, and only required that, at repayment, a small fee should be given to the accomptant; but he required that the day of promised payment should be exactly kept. A severe and punctilious temper is ill qualified for transactions with the poor; the day was often broken and the loan was not repaid. This might have been easily foreseen, but for this Swift had made no provision of patience or pity. He ordered his debtors to be sued. A severe creditor has no popular character; what then was likely to be said of him who employs the catchpoll[69] under the appearance of charity? The clamor against him was loud and the resentment of the populace outrageous; he was therefore forced to drop his scheme and own the folly of expecting punctuality from the poor.

His asperity continually increasing condemned him to solitude, and his resentment of solitude sharpened his asperity. He was not, however, totally deserted: some men of learning and some women of elegance often visited him, and he wrote from time to time either verse or prose; of his verses he willingly gave copies, and is supposed to have felt no discontent when he saw them printed. His favorite maxim was "Vive la bagatelle";[70] he thought trifles a necessary part of life, and perhaps found them necessary to himself. It seems impossible to him to be idle, and his disorders made it difficult or dangerous to be long seriously studious or laboriously diligent. The love of ease is always gaining upon age, and he had one temptation to petty amusements peculiar to him-

69. A law officer who arrests for debt.
70. "Long live trifles!"

self: whatever he did he was sure to hear applauded; and such was his predominance over all that approached, that all their applauses were probably sincere. He that is much flattered soon learns to flatter himself: we are commonly taught our duty by fear or shame, and how can they act upon the man who hears nothing but his own praises?

As his years increased, his fits of giddiness and deafness grew more frequent, and his deafness made conversation difficult; they grew likewise more severe, till in 1736, as he was writing a poem called *The Legion Club,* he was seized with a fit so painful and so long continued, that he never after thought it proper to attempt any work of thought or labor.

He was always careful of his money and was therefore no liberal entertainer, but was less frugal of his wine than of his meat. When his friends of either sex came to him in expectation of a dinner his custom was to give every one a shilling, that they might please themselves with their provision. At last his avarice grew too powerful for his kindness; he would refuse a bottle of wine, and in Ireland no man visits where he cannot drink.

Having thus excluded conversation, and desisted from study, he had neither business nor amusement; for having, by some ridiculous resolution or mad vow, determined never to wear spectacles, he could make little use of books in his later years; his ideas, therefore, being neither renovated by discourse, nor increased by reading, wore gradually away, and left his mind vacant to the vexations of the hour, till at last his anger was heightened into madness.

He, however, permitted one book to be published, which had been the production of former years: *Polite Conversation,* which appeared in 1738. The *Directions for Servants* was printed soon after his death. These two performances show a mind incessantly attentive, and, when it was not employed upon great things, busy with minute occurrences. It is apparent that he must have had the habit of noting whatever he observed; for such a number of particulars could never have been assembled by the power of recollection.

He grew more violent; and his mental powers declined, till (1741) it was found necessary that legal guardians should be appointed of his person and fortune. He now lost distinction.[71] His madness was compounded of rage and fatuity. The last face that he knew was that of Mrs. Whiteway,[72] and her he ceased to know in a little time. His meat was brought him cut into mouthfuls; but he would never touch it while the servant stayed, and at last, after it had stood perhaps an hour, would eat it walking; for he continued his old habit, and was on his feet ten hours a day.

Next year (1742) he had an inflammation in his left eye, which swelled

71. The capacity for clear intellectual perception.
72. Martha Whiteway, Swift's first cousin and the manager of his household.

it to the size of an egg, with boils in other parts; he was kept long waking with the pain, and was not easily restrained by five attendants from tearing out his eye.

The tumor at last subsided; and a short interval of reason ensuing, in which he knew his physician and his family, gave hopes of his recovery; but in a few days he sunk into lethargic stupidity,[73] motionless, heedless, and speechless. But it is said that, after a year of total silence, when his housekeeper, on the 30th of November, told him that the usual bonfires and illuminations were preparing to celebrate his birthday, he answered, "It is all folly; they had better let it alone."

It is remembered that he afterwards spoke now and then, or gave some intimation of a meaning; but at last sunk into perfect silence, which continued till about the end of October, 1744[74] when, in his seventy-eighth year, he expired without a struggle.

When Swift is considered as an author it is just to estimate his powers by their effects. In the reign of Queen Anne he turned the stream of popularity against the Whigs, and must be confessed to have dictated for a time the political opinions of the English nation. In the succeeding reign he delivered Ireland from plunder and oppression; and showed that wit, confederated with truth, had such force as authority was unable to resist. He said truly of himself that Ireland "was his debtor."[75] It was from the time when he first began to patronize the Irish that they may date their riches and prosperity. He taught them first to know their own interest, their weight, and their strength, and gave them spirit to assert that equality with their fellow-subjects to which they have ever since been making vigorous advances, and to claim those rights which they have at last established. Nor can they be charged with ingratitude to their benefactor, for they reverenced him as a guardian and obeyed him as a dictator.

In his works he has given very different specimens both of sentiment and expression. His *Tale of a Tub* has little resemblance to his other pieces. It exhibits a vehemence and rapidity of mind, a copiousness of images, and vivacity of diction, such as he afterwards never possessed or never exerted. It is of a mode so distinct and peculiar that it must be considered by itself; what is true of that is not true of anything else which he has written.

In his other works is found an equable tenor of easy language, which rather trickles than flows. His delight was in simplicity. That he has in his works no metaphor, as has been said, is not true; but his few metaphors seem to be received rather by necessity than choice. He studied purity; and though perhaps all his strictures are not exact, yet it

73. Stupor.
74. Swift died October 19, 1745.
75. See *Verses on the Death of Dr. Swift,* l. 483.

is not often that solecisms can be found: and whoever depends on his authority may generally conclude himself safe. His sentences are never too much dilated or contracted; and it will not be easy to find any embarrassment in the complication of his clauses, any inconsequence in his connections, or abruptness in his transitions.

His style was well suited to his thoughts, which are never subtilized by nice disquisitions, decorated by sparkling conceits,[76] elevated by ambitious sentences,[77] or variegated by far-sought learning. He pays no court to the passions; he excites neither surprise nor admiration; he always understands himself, and his reader always understands him: the peruser of Swift wants little previous knowledge; it will be sufficient that he is acquainted with common words and common things; he is neither required to mount elevations nor to explore profundities; his passage is always on a level, along solid ground, without asperities,[78] without obstruction.

This easy and safe conveyance of meaning it was Swift's desire to attain, and for having attained he deserves praise, though perhaps not the highest praise. For purposes merely didactic, when something is to be told that was not known before, it is the best mode; but against that inattention by which known truths are suffered to lie neglected, it makes no provision; it instructs, but does not persuade.

By his political education he was associated with the Whigs; but he deserted them when they deserted their principles, yet without running into the contrary extreme; he continued throughout his life to retain the disposition which he assigns to the "Church-of-England Man," of thinking commonly with the Whigs of the State, and with the Tories of the Church.

He was a churchman rationally zealous; he desired the prosperity and maintained the honor of the clergy; of the Dissenters he did not wish to infringe the toleration, but he opposed their encroachments.

To his duty as Dean he was very attentive. He managed the revenues of his church with exact economy; and it is said by Delany that more money was, under his direction, laid out in repairs than had ever been in the same time since its first erection. Of his choir he was eminently careful; and, though he neither loved nor understood music, took care that all the singers were well qualified, admitting none without the testimony of skillful judges.

In his church he restored the practice of weekly communion, and distributed the sacramental elements in the most solemn and devout manner with his own hand. He came to church every morning, preached commonly in his turn, and attended the evening anthem, that it might not be negligently performed.

76. Brilliant metaphors, wit.
77. Maxims, aphorisms.
78. Rough places.

He read the service "rather with a strong, nervous[79] voice than in a graceful manner; his voice was sharp and high-toned, rather than harmonious."

He entered upon the clerical state with hope to excel in preaching; but complained that, from the time of his political controversies, "he could only preach pamphlets." This censure of himself, if judgment be made from those sermons which have been published, was unreasonably severe.

The suspicions of his irreligion proceeded in a great measure from his dread of hypocrisy: instead of wishing to seem better, he delighted in seeming worse than he was. He went in London to early prayers lest he should be seen at church; he read prayers to his servants every morning with such dexterous secrecy that Dr. Delany was six months in his house before he knew it. He was not only careful to hide the good which he did, but willingly incurred the suspicion of evil which he did not. He forgot what himself had formerly asserted,[80] that hypocrisy is less mischievous than open impiety. Dr. Delany, with all his zeal for his honor, has justly condemned this part of his character.

The person of Swift had not many recommendations. He had a kind of muddy complexion, which, though he washed himself with oriental scrupulosity, did not look clear. He had a countenance sour and severe, which he seldom softened by any appearance of gaiety. He stubbornly resisted any tendency to laughter.

To his domestics he was naturally rough; and a man of a rigorous temper, with that vigilance of minute attention which his works discover, must have been a master that few could bear. That he was disposed to do his servants good on important occasions is no great mitigation; benefaction can be but rare, and tyrannic peevishness is perpetual. He did not spare the servants of others. Once, when he dined alone with the Earl of Orrery, he said, of one that waited in the room, "That man has, since we sat to the table, committed fifteen faults." What the faults were Lord Orrery, from whom I heard the story, had not been attentive enough to discover. My number may perhaps not be exact.

In his economy he practiced a peculiar and offensive parsimony, without disguise or apology. The practice of saving being once necessary, became habitual, and grew first ridiculous, and at last detestable. But his avarice, though it might exclude pleasure, was never suffered to encroach upon his virtue. He was frugal by inclination, but liberal by principle; and if the purpose to which he destined his little accumulations be remembered, with his distribution of occasional charity, it will perhaps appear that he only liked one mode of expense better than another, and saved merely that he might have something to give. He

79. Energetic.
80. In *A Project for the Advancement of Religion* (1709).

did not grow rich by injuring his successors, but left both Laracor and the Deanery more valuable than he found them.

With all this talk of his covetousness and generosity it should be remembered that he was never rich. The revenue of his Deanery was not much more than seven hundred a year.

His beneficence was not graced with tenderness or civility; he relieved without pity, and assisted without kindness; so that those who were fed by him could hardly love him.

He made a rule to himself to give but one piece at a time, and therefore always stored his pocket with coins of different value.

Whatever he did, he seemed willing to do in a manner peculiar to himself, without sufficiently considering that singularity, as it implies a contempt of the general practice, is a kind of defiance which justly provokes the hostility of ridicule; he, therefore, who indulges peculiar habits is worse than others, if he be not better.

Of his humor, a story told by Pope may afford a specimen:

> Dr. Swift has an odd, blunt way that is mistaken by strangers for ill-nature.—'Tis so odd, that there's no describing it but by facts. I'll tell you one that first comes into my head. One evening Gay[81] and I went to see him: you know how intimately we were all acquainted. On our coming in, "Hey-day, gentlemen (says the Doctor), what's the meaning of this visit? How came you to leave all the great lords, that you are so fond of, to come hither to see a poor Dean?"—"Because we would rather see you than any of them."—"Ay, any one that did not know [you] so well as I do, might believe you. But since you are come, I must get some supper for you, I suppose."—"No, Doctor, we have supped already."—"Supped already? that's impossible! why, 'tis not eight o'clock yet. That's very strange; but, if you had not supped, I must have got something for you. Let me see, what should I have had? A couple of lobsters; ay, that would have done very well, two shillings; tarts, a shilling; but you will drink a glass of wine with me, though you supped so much before your usual time only to spare my pocket?"—"No, we had rather talk with you than drink with you."—"But if you had supped with me, as in all reason you ought to have done, you must then have drunk with me.—A bottle of wine, two shillings—two and two is four, and one is five: just two and sixpence apiece. There, Pope, there's half a crown for you, and there's another for you, Sir; for I won't save anything by you, I am determined."—This was all said and done with his usual seriousness on such occasions; and, in spite of everything we could say to the contrary, he actually obliged us to take the money.

In the intercourse of familiar life he indulged his disposition to petulance and sarcasm, and thought himself injured if the licentiousness of

81. John Gay (1685–1732), poet and dramatist.

his raillery, the freedom of his censures, or the petulance of his frolics, were resented or repressed. He predominated over his companions with very high ascendency, and probably would bear none over whom he could not predominate. To give him advice was, in the style of his friend Delany, "to venture to speak to him." This customary superiority soon grew too delicate for truth; and Swift, with all his penetration, allowed himself to be delighted with low flattery.

On all common occasions he habitually affects a style of arrogance, and dictates rather than persuades. This authoritative and magisterial language he expected to be received as his peculiar mode of jocularity; but he apparently flattered his own arrogance by an assumed imperiousness, in which he was ironical only to the resentful, and to the submissive sufficiently serious.

He told stories with great felicity, and delighted in doing what he knew himself to do well; he was therefore captivated by the respectful silence of a steady listener, and told the same tales too often.

He did not, however, claim the right of talking alone; for it was his rule, when he had spoken a minute, to give room by a pause for any other speaker. Of time, on all occasions, he was an exact computer, and knew the minutes required to every common operation.

It may be justly supposed that there was in his conversation, what appears so frequently in his letters, an affectation of familiarity with the great, an ambition of momentary equality sought and enjoyed by the neglect of those ceremonies which custom has established as the barriers between one order of society and another. This transgression of regularity was by himself and his admirers termed greatness of soul. But a great mind disdains to hold anything by courtesy, and therefore never usurps what a lawful claimant may take away. He that encroaches on another's dignity puts himself in his power: he is either repelled with helpless indignity, or endured by clemency and condescension.

Of Swift's general habits of thinking, if his letters can be supposed to afford any evidence, he was not a man to be either loved or envied. He seems to have wasted life in discontent, by the rage of neglected pride, and the languishment of unsatisfied desire. He is querulous and fastidious, arrogant and malignant; he scarcely speaks of himself but with indignant lamentations, or of others but with insolent superiority when he is gay, and with angry contempt when he is gloomy. From the letters that pass between him and Pope, it might be inferred that they, with Arbuthnot[82] and Gay, had engrossed all the understanding and virtue of mankind; that their merits filled the world; or that there was no hope of more. They show the age involved in darkness, and shade the picture with sullen emulation.

When the Queen's death drove him into Ireland, he might be al-

82. Dr. John Arbuthnot (1667–1735), physician and satirist.

lowed to regret for a time the interception of his views, the extinction of his hopes, and his ejection from gay scenes, important employment, and splendid friendships; but when time had enabled reason to prevail over vexation the complaints, which at first were natural, became ridiculous because they were useless. But querulousness was now grown habitual, and he cried out when he probably had ceased to feel. His reiterated wailings persuaded Bolingbroke that he was really willing to quit his deanery for an English parish; and Bolingbroke procured an exchange, which was rejected; and Swift still retained the pleasure of complaining.[83]

The greatest difficulty that occurs, in analyzing his character, is to discover by what depravity of intellect he took delight in revolving ideas[84] from which almost every other mind shrinks with disgust. The ideas of pleasure, even when criminal, may solicit the imagination; but what has disease, deformity, and filth upon which the thoughts can be allured to dwell? Delany is willing to think that Swift's mind was not much tainted with this gross corruption before his long visit to Pope. He does not consider how he degrades his hero by making him at fifty-nine the pupil of turpitude, and liable to the malignant influence of an ascendant mind. But the truth is that Gulliver had described his Yahoos before the visit; and he that had formed those images had nothing filthy to learn.

I have here given the character of Swift as he exhibits himself to my perception; but now let another be heard who knew him better. Dr. Delany, after long acquaintance, describes him to Lord Orrery in these terms:

> My Lord, when you consider Swift's singular, peculiar, and most variegated vein of wit, always rightly intended (although not always so rightly directed), delightful in many instances, and salutary, even where it is most offensive; when you consider his strict truth, his fortitude in resisting oppression and arbitrary power; his fidelity in friendship, his sincere love and zeal for religion, his uprightness in making right resolutions, and his steadiness in adhering to them; his care of his church, its choir, its economy, and its income; his attention to all those that preached in his cathedral, in order to[85] their amendment in pronunciation and style; as also his remarkable attention to the interest of his successors, preferably to his own present emoluments; [his] invincible patriotism, even to a country which he did not love; his very various, well-devised, well-judged, and extensive charities, throughout his life, and his whole fortune (to say nothing of his wife's) conveyed to the same Christian purposes at his death—charities from which he could enjoy no honor, advantage, or

83. The exchange would have involved a substantial decrease in Swift's income.
84. In his *Dictionary* (1755) Johnson defines "idea" as "mental imagination."
85. That is, in order to promote.

satisfaction of any kind in this world. When you consider his ironical and humorous, as well as his serious schemes, for the promotion of true religion and virtue, his success in soliciting for the First Fruits and Twentieths, to the unspeakable benefit of the Established Church of Ireland;[86] and his felicity (to rate it no higher) in giving occasion to the building of fifty new churches in London.

All this considered, the character of his life will appear like that of his writings; they will both bear to be reconsidered and re-examined with the utmost attention, and always discover new beauties and excellences upon every examination.

They will bear to be considered as the sun, in which the brightness will hide the blemishes; and whenever petulant ignorance, pride, malice, malignity, or envy interposes to cloud or sully his fame, I will take upon me to pronounce that the eclipse will not last long.

To conclude—no man ever deserved better of any country than Swift did of his. A steady, persevering, inflexible friend; a wise, a watchful, and a faithful counselor, under many severe trials and bitter persecutions, to the manifest hazard both of his liberty and fortune.

He lived a blessing, he died a benefactor, and his name will ever live an honor to Ireland.

In the poetical works of Dr. Swift there is not much upon which the critic can exercise his powers. They are often humorous, almost always light, and have the qualities which recommend such compositions, easiness and gaiety. They are, for the most part, what their author intended. The diction is correct, the numbers[87] are smooth, and the rhymes exact. There seldom occurs a hard-labored expression or a redundant epithet; all his verses exemplify his own definition of a good style: they consist of "proper words in proper places."[88]

To divide this collection into classes, and show how some pieces are gross, and some are trifling, would be to tell the reader what he knows already, and to find faults of which the author could not be ignorant, who certainly wrote often not to his judgment, but his humor.

It was said, in a Preface to one of the Irish editions, that Swift had never been known to take a single thought from any writer, ancient or modern. This is not literally true; but perhaps no writer can easily be found that has borrowed so little, or that in all his excellences and all his defects has so well maintained his claim to be considered as original.

86. The Anglican Church, established by law as the official religion.
87. Measures, meter.
88. In his *Letter to a Young Gentleman Lately Entered into Holy Orders* (1721).

Alexander Pope
1688–1744

Alexander Pope was born in London, May 22,[1] 1688, of parents whose rank or station was never ascertained: we are informed that they were of "gentle blood";[2] that his father was of a family of which the Earl of Downe was the head,[3] and that his mother was the daughter of William Turner, Esquire, of York, who had likewise three sons, one of whom had the honor of being killed, and the other of dying, in the service of Charles the First; the third was made a general officer in Spain, from whom the sister inherited what sequestrations and forfeitures had left in the family.[4]

This and this only is told by Pope; who is more willing, as I have heard observed, to show what his father was not, than what he was. It is allowed that he grew rich by trade; but whether in a shop or on the Exchange was never discovered, till Mr. Tyers told, on the authority of Mrs. Rackett, that he was a linen-draper in the Strand.[5] Both parents were Papists.

Pope was from his birth of a constitution tender and delicate; but is said to have shown remarkable gentleness and sweetness of disposition. The weakness of his body continued through his life, but the mildness of his mind perhaps ended with his childhood. His voice, when he was young, was so pleasing that he was called in fondness the "little nightingale."

Being not sent early to school he was taught to read by an aunt, and when he was seven or eight years old became a lover of books. He first

1. May 21.
2. Pope, *Epistle to Dr. Arbuthnot,* l. 388 and its note.
3. Pope was not related to the Earl of Downe.
4. The property of Royalists (those who adhered to Charles I in the Civil Wars) was often sequestered (seized as security against legal claims) or forfeited under the Commonwealth.
5. Mrs. Rackett was Pope's half sister. Thomas Tyers wrote a pamphlet, *An Historical Rhapsody on Mr. Pope* (1782). "Till . . . Strand" was added in the 1783 edition.

learned to write by imitating printed books; a species of penmanship in which he retained great excellence through his whole life, though his ordinary hand was not elegant.

When he was about eight he was placed in Hampshire under Taverner, a Romish priest, who, by a method very rarely practiced, taught him the Greek and Latin rudiments together. He was now first regularly initiated in poetry by the perusal of Ogilby's Homer, and Sandys's Ovid: Ogilby's assistance he never repaid with any praise; but of Sandys he declared, in his notes to the *Iliad,* that English poetry owed much of its present beauty to his translations. Sandys very rarely attempted original composition.

From the care of Taverner, under whom his proficiency was considerable, he was removed to a school at Twyford near Winchester, and again to another school about Hyde Park Corner; from which he used sometimes to stroll to the playhouse, and was so delighted with theatrical exhibitions that he formed a kind of play from Ogilby's *Iliad,* with some verses of his own intermixed, which he persuaded his schoolfellows to act, with the addition of his master's gardener, who personated Ajax.

At the two last schools he used to represent himself as having lost part of what Taverner had taught him, and on his master at Twyford he had already exercised his poetry in a lampoon. Yet under those masters he translated more than a fourth part of the *Metamorphoses.* If he kept the same proportion in his other exercises it cannot be thought that his loss was great.

He tells of himself in his poems that "he lisped in numbers,"[6] and used to say that he could not remember the time when he began to make verses. In the style of fiction it might have been said of him as of Pindar, that when he lay in his cradle, "the bees swarmed about his mouth."[7]

About the time of the Revolution[8] his father, who was undoubtedly disappointed by the sudden blast of popish prosperity, quitted his trade, and retired to Binfield in Windsor Forest, with about twenty thousand pounds, for which, being conscientiously determined not to entrust it to the government, he found no better use than that of locking it up in a chest and taking from it what his expenses required; and his life was long enough to consume a great part of it before his son came to the inheritance.[9]

To Binfield Pope was called by his father when he was about twelve years old; and there he had for a few months the assistance of one

6. *Epistle to Dr. Arbuthnot,* 1. 128. As often, Johnson quotes inexactly.

7. Pausanias, *Description of Greece,* IX. xxiii. 2–3.

8. The Glorious Revolution of 1688 by which James II, a Roman Catholic, was deposed. He was succeeded by William and Mary.

9. The Popes did not move to Binfield until about 1700; the sum was perhaps ten thousand pounds, and the story of the chest is unreliable.

Deane, another priest, of whom he learned only to construe a little of Tully's *Offices.*[10] How Mr. Deane could spend with a boy who had translated so much of Ovid, some months over a small part of Tully's *Offices,* it is now vain to inquire.

Of a youth so successfully employed, and so conspicuously improved, a minute account must be naturally desired; but curiosity must be contented with confused, imperfect, and sometimes improbable intelligence. Pope, finding little advantage from external help, resolved thenceforward to direct himself, and at twelve formed a plan of study which he completed with little other incitement than the desire of excellence.

His primary and principal purpose was to be a poet, with which his father accidentally concurred, by proposing subjects and obliging him to correct his performances by many revisals; after which the old gentleman, when he was satisfied, would say, "these are good rhymes."

In his perusal of the English poets he soon distinguished the versification of Dryden, which he considered as the model to be studied, and was impressed with such veneration for his instructer that he persuaded some friends to take him to the coffee-house which Dryden frequented, and pleased himself with having seen him.

Dryden died May 1, 1701,[11] some days before Pope was twelve: so early must he therefore have felt the power of harmony and the zeal of genius. Who does not wish that Dryden could have known the value of the homage that was paid him, and foreseen the greatness of his young admirer?

The earliest of Pope's productions is his "Ode on Solitude," written before he was twelve,[12] in which there is nothing more than other forward boys have attained, and which is not equal to Cowley's performances at the same age.

His time was now spent wholly in reading and writing. As he read the classics he amused himself with translating them; and at fourteen made a version of the first book of the *Thebais,*[13] which, with some revision, he afterwards published. He must have been at this time, if he had no help, a considerable proficient in the Latin tongue.

By Dryden's *Fables,* which had then been not long published, and were much in the hands of poetical readers, he was tempted to try his own skill in giving Chaucer a more fashionable appearance, and put *January and May,*[14] and the *Prologue of the Wife of Bath,* into modern English. He translated likewise the *Epistle of Sappho to Phaon* from Ovid,

10. Marcus Tullius Cicero's *De Officiis,* a treatise on the duties of a virtuous man. The priest may have been William Mannock rather than Thomas Deane, who apparently conducted one of the schools previously mentioned.

11. 1700.

12. The poem seems to have been revised later before publication in 1717.

13. An epic poem by the Latin poet Statius (A.D. c. 40 - c. 96).

14. "The Merchant's Tale."

to complete the version[15] which was before imperfect, and wrote some other small pieces, which he afterwards printed.

He sometimes imitated the English poets, and professed to have written at fourteen his poem upon "Silence," after Rochester's "Nothing."[16] He had now formed his versification, and in the smoothness of his numbers surpassed his original; but this is a small part of his praise: he discovers[17] such acquaintance both with human life and public affairs as is not easily conceived to have been attainable by a boy of fourteen in Windsor Forest.

Next year he was desirous of opening to himself new sources of knowledge, by making himself acquainted with modern languages, and removed for a time to London that he might study French and Italian, which, as he desired nothing more than to read them, were by diligent application soon despatched. Of Italian learning he does not appear to have ever made much use in his subsequent studies.

He then returned to Binfield, and delighted himself with his own poetry. He tried all styles, and many subjects. He wrote a comedy, a tragedy, an epic poem, with panegyrics on all the princes of Europe; and, as he confesses, "thought himself the greatest genius that ever was."[18] Self-confidence is the first requisite to great undertakings; he, indeed, who forms his opinion of himself in solitude, without knowing the powers of other men, is very liable to error; but it was the felicity of Pope to rate himself at his real value.

Most of his puerile[19] productions were by his maturer judgment afterwards destroyed; "Alcander," the epic poem, was burnt by the persuasion of Atterbury.[20] The tragedy was founded on the legend of St. Geneviève.[21] Of the comedy there is no account.

Concerning his studies it is related that he translated Tully *On Old Age*; and that, besides his books of poetry and criticism, he read Temple's *Essays* and Locke *On Human Understanding.*[22] His reading, though his favorite authors are not known, appears to have been sufficiently extensive and multifarious; for his early pieces show, with sufficient evidence, his knowledge of books.

He that is pleased with himself easily imagines that he shall please others. Sir William Trumbull, who had been Ambassador at Constantinople, and Secretary of State, when he retired from business fixed his

15. Translation. Ovid's *Epistles* had been translated by Dryden and others (1680).

16. A well-known poem by John Wilmot, second Earl of Rochester (1648–80).

17. Reveals.

18. Quoted by William Warburton in the Preface to his edition of Pope's *Works* (1751).

19. Juvenile.

20. Francis Atterbury, Bishop of Rochester (1662–1732).

21. Patron saint of Paris, who, according to tradition, saved the city from the Huns by her prayers, and converted its conqueror Clovis, leader of the Franks, to Christianity.

22. Sir William Temple (1628–99), diplomat and a patron of Swift. John Locke (1632–1704), the greatest philosopher of contemporary England.

residence in the neighborhood of Binfield. Pope, not yet sixteen, was introduced to the statesman of sixty, and so distinguished himself that their interviews ended in friendship and correspondence. Pope was through his whole life ambitious of splendid acquaintance, and he seems to have wanted neither diligence nor success in attracting the notice of the great; for from his first entrance into the world, and his entrance was very early, he was admitted to familiarity with those whose rank or station made them most conspicuous.

From the age of sixteen the life of Pope as an author may be properly computed. He now wrote his *Pastorals,* which were shown to the poets and critics of that time; as they well deserved they were read with admiration, and many praises were bestowed upon them and upon the Preface, which is both elegant and learned in a high degree: they were, however, not published till five years afterwards.

Cowley, Milton, and Pope are distinguished among the English poets by the early exertion of their powers; but the works of Cowley alone were published in his childhood, and therefore of him only can it be certain that his puerile performances received no improvement from his maturer studies.

At this time began his acquaintance with Wycherley, a man who seems to have had among his contemporaries his full share of reputation, to have been esteemed without virtue, and caressed without good-humor. Pope was proud of his notice, Wycherley wrote verses in his praise,[23] which he was charged by Dennis with writing to himself,[24] and they agreed for a while to flatter one another. It is pleasant to remark how soon Pope learned the cant[25] of an author, and began to treat critics with contempt, though he had yet suffered nothing from them.

But the fondness of Wycherley was too violent to last. His esteem of Pope was such that he submitted some poems to his revision; and when Pope, perhaps proud of such confidence, was sufficiently bold in his criticisms and liberal in his alterations, the old scribbler was angry to see his pages defaced, and felt more pain from the detection than content from the amendment of his faults. They parted; but Pope always considered him with kindness, and visited him a little time before he died.

Another of his early correspondents was Mr. Cromwell, of whom I have learned nothing particular but that he used to ride a-hunting in a tie-wig.[26] He was fond, and perhaps vain, of amusing himself with

23. William Wycherley (1640–1716), dramatist, wrote "To My Friend, Mr. Pope, on His Pastorals."

24. John Dennis (1657–1734), an often shrewd and always opinionated critic, in his *Reflections upon "An Essay upon Criticism"* (1711).

25. Jargon.

26. Henry Cromwell (?1659–1728), a man of fashion. A tie-wig gathers the hair in back with a ribbon.

poetry and criticism, and sometimes sent his performances to Pope, who did not forbear such remarks as were now and then unwelcome. Pope, in his turn, put the juvenile version of Statius into his hands for correction.

Their correspondence afforded the public its first knowledge of Pope's epistolary powers; for his letters were given by Cromwell to one Mrs. Thomas, and she many years afterwards sold them to Curll, who inserted them in a volume of his *Miscellanies.*[27]

Walsh, a name yet preserved among the minor poets, was one of his first encouragers.[28] His regard was gained by the *Pastorals,* and from him Pope received the counsel by which he seems to have regulated his studies. Walsh advised him to correctness,[29] which, as he told him, the English poets had hitherto neglected, and which therefore was left to him as a basis of fame; and, being delighted with rural poems, recommended to him to write a pastoral comedy, like those which are read so eagerly in Italy; a design which Pope probably did not approve, as he did not follow it.

Pope had now declared himself a poet; and, thinking himself entitled to poetical conversation, began at seventeen to frequent Will's, a coffee-house on the north side of Russell Street in Covent Garden, where the wits of that time used to assemble, and where Dryden had, when he lived, been accustomed to preside.

During this period of his life he was indefatigably diligent, and insatiably curious; wanting health for violent, and money for expensive pleasures, and having certainly excited in himself very strong desires of intellectual eminence, he spent much of his time over his books: but he read only to store his mind with facts and images, seizing all that his authors presented with undistinguishing voracity, and with an appetite for knowledge too eager to be nice.[30] In a mind like his, however, all the faculties were at once involuntarily improving. Judgment is forced upon us by experience. He that reads many books must compare one opinion or one style with another; and when he compares, must necessarily distinguish, reject, and prefer. But the account given by himself of his studies was that from fourteen to twenty he read only for amusement, from twenty to twenty-seven for improvement and instruction; that in the first part of this time he desired only to know, and in the second he endeavored to judge.

The *Pastorals,* which had been for some time handed about among poets and critics, were at last printed (1709) in Tonson's *Miscellany,* in a

27. The "unspeakable" Edmund Curll (1675–1747), an unscrupulous publisher, included these as "Familiar Letters" in his *Miscellanea* (1727).

28. William Walsh (1663–1708).

29. Literary "decorum," or the proper matching of manner with matter: accuracy in diction, imagery, and versification.

30. Fastidious.

volume which began with the *Pastorals* of Philips,[31] and ended with those of Pope.

The same year was written the *Essay on Criticism,* a work which displays such extent of comprehension, such nicety of distinction, such acquaintance with mankind, and such knowledge both of ancient and modern learning as are not often attained by the maturest age and longest experience. It was published about two years afterwards, and being praised by Addison in *The Spectator*[32] with sufficient liberality, met with so much favor as enraged Dennis, "who," he says,

> found himself attacked, without any manner of provocation on his side, and attacked in his person, instead of his writings, by one who was wholly a stranger to him, at a time when all the world knew he was persecuted by fortune; and not only saw that this was attempted in a clandestine manner, with the utmost falsehood and calumny, but found that all this was done by a little affected hypocrite, who had nothing in his mouth at the same time but truth, candor,[33] friendship, good nature, humanity, and magnanimity.[34]

How the attack was clandestine is not easily perceived, nor how his person is depreciated;[35] but he seems to have known something of Pope's character, in whom may be discovered an appetite to talk too frequently of his own virtues.

The pamphlet is such as rage might be expected to dictate. He supposes himself to be asked two questions: whether the *Essay* will succeed, and who or what is the author.

Its success he admits to be secured by the false opinions then prevalent; the author he concludes to be "young and raw."

> First, because he discovers a sufficiency[36] beyond his little ability, and hath rashly undertaken a task infinitely above his force. Secondly, while this little author struts, and affects the dictatorian air, he plainly shows that at the same time he is under the rod; and while he pretends to give law to others, is a pedantic slave to authority and opinion. Thirdly, he hath, like schoolboys, borrowed both from living and dead. Fourthly, he knows not his own mind, and frequently contradicts himself. Fifthly, he is almost perpetually in the wrong.

All these positions he attempts to prove by quotations and remarks;

31. Ambrose Philips (?1675–1749), known as "Namby-Pamby" from his poems addressed to children and his use of childish diction.

32. No. 253, December 20, 1711.

33. Kindliness.

34. Dennis, *Reflections.*

35. The *Essay* appeared anonymously, and Dennis, author of a bombastic play entitled *Appius and Virginia* (1709), was caricatured as Appius (11. 585–87), an author waxing angry at each word of criticism.

36. Reveals a self-confidence.

but his desire to do mischief is greater than his power. He has, however, justly critized some passages: in these lines,

> There are whom heaven has blessed with store of wit,
> Yet want as much again to manage it;
> For wit and judgment ever are at strife:[37]

it is apparent that "wit" has two meanings, and that what is wanted, though called "wit," is truly judgment. So far Dennis is undoubtedly right; but, not content with argument, he will have a little mirth, and triumphs over the first couplet in terms too elegant to be forgotten. "By the way, what rare numbers[38] are here! Would not one swear that this youngster had espoused some antiquated Muse, who had sued out a divorce on account of impotence from some superannuated sinner, and, having been p-xed[39] by her former spouse, has got the gout in her decrepit age, which makes her hobble so damnably." This was the man who would reform a nation sinking into barbarity.

In another place Pope himself allowed that Dennis had detected one of those blunders which are called "bulls."[40] The first edition had this line:

> What is this wit . . . ?
> Where wanted,[41] scorned; and envied where acquired?[42]

"How," says the critic, "can wit be *scorned* where it is not? Is not this a figure[43] frequently employed in Hibernian land? The person that wants this wit may indeed be scorned, but the scorn shows the honor which the contemner[44] has for wit." Of this remark Pope made the proper use, by correcting the passage.

I have preserved, I think, all that is reasonable in Dennis's criticism; it remains that justice be done to his delicacy.

> For his acquaintance (says Dennis) he names Mr. Walsh, who had by no means the qualification which this author reckons absolutely necessary to a critic, it being very certain that he was, like this essayer, a very indifferent poet; he loved to be well dressed; and I remember a little young gentleman whom Mr. Walsh used to take into his company, as a double foil to his person and capacity. . . . Inquire between Sunninghill and Oakingham for a young, short, squab[45] gentleman, the very bow of the God of Love, and tell me whether he be a proper author to make personal reflections? . . . He may extol the ancients, but he has reason to

37. *An Essay on Criticism,* 11. 80–82.

38. Verses.

39. Poxed: infected with the great pox (syphilis).

40. Self-contradictory statements. The Irish were supposed to be particularly prone to them.

41. Lacking.

42. Ll. 500, 503. Pope corrected this bull in the second edition of his poem, 1713.

43. Figure of speech. 44. Despiser. 45. Squat.

> thank the gods that he was born a modern; for had he been born of Grecian parents, and his father consequently had by law had the absolute disposal of him, his life had been no longer than that of one of his poems, the life of half a day. . . .[46] Let the person of a gentleman of his parts[47] be never so contemptible, his inward man is ten times more ridiculous; it being impossible that his outward form, though it be that of downright monkey, should differ so much from human shape, as his unthinking immaterial part does from human understanding.

Thus began the hostility between Pope and Dennis, which, though it was suspended for a short time, never was appeased. Pope seems, at first, to have attacked him wantonly;[48] but though he always professed to despise him, he discovers, by mentioning him very often, that he felt his force or his venom.

Of this *Essay* Pope declared that he did not expect the sale to be quick, because "not one gentleman in sixty, even of liberal education, could understand it."[49] The gentlemen, and the education of that time, seem to have been of a lower character than they are of this. He mentioned a thousand copies as a numerous impression.

Dennis was not his only censurer; the zealous Papists thought the monks treated with too much contempt, and Erasmus[50] too studiously praised; but to these objections he had not much regard.

The *Essay* has been translated into French by Hamilton, author of the *Comte de Grammont,* whose version was never printed, by Robethon, secretary to the King for Hanover,[51] and by Resnel; and commented by Dr. Warburton, who has discovered in it such order and connection as was not perceived by Addison, nor, as is said, intended by the author.

Almost every poem consisting of precepts is so far arbitrary and immethodical that many of the paragraphs may change places with no apparent inconvenience; for of two or more positions, depending upon some remote and general principle, there is seldom any cogent reason why one should precede the other. But for the order in which they stand, whatever it be, a little ingenuity may easily give a reason. "It is possible," says Hooker, "that by long circumduction, from any one truth all truth may be inferred."[52] Of all homogeneous truths at least, of all truths respecting the same general end, in whatever series they may be produced, a concatenation[53] by intermediate ideas may be

46. Exposure of unwanted infants was a practice of the ancient Greeks and a theme in Greek drama (e.g. *Oedipus the King*). Pope suffered from spinal deformation.

47. Physical makeup, but ordinarily used to mean "abilities."

48. Without reason.

49. Pope to John Caryll, July 19, 1711.

50. Pope regarded Desiderius Erasmus (?1466–1536), the great Dutch humanist, as a model of religious moderation.

51. George I, Elector of Hanover and King of England (ruled 1714–27).

52. Richard Hooker, *Laws of Ecclesiastical Polity* (1597), II. i. 2.

53. Connection.

formed, such as, when it is once shown, shall appear natural; but if this order be reversed, another mode of connection equally specious may be found or made. Aristotle is praised for naming fortitude first of the cardinal virtues,[54] as that without which no other virtue can steadily be practiced; but he might, with equal propriety, have placed prudence and justice before it, since without prudence, fortitude is mad; without justice, it is mischievous.

As the end of method is perspicuity, that series is sufficiently regular that avoids obscurity; and where there is no obscurity it will not be difficult to discover method.

In *The Spectator*[55] was published the "Messiah," which he first submitted to the perusal of Steele, and corrected in compliance with his criticisms.

It is reasonable to infer, from his letters, that the verses on "The Unfortunate Lady" were written about the time when his *Essay* was published. The lady's name and adventures I have sought with fruitless inquiry.

I can therefore tell no more than I have learned from Mr. Ruffhead, who writes with the confidence of one who could trust his information.[56] She was a woman of eminent rank and large fortune, the ward of an uncle who, having given her a proper education, expected like other guardians that she should make at least an equal match; and such he proposed to her, but found it rejected in favor of a young gentleman of inferior condition.[57]

Having discovered the correspondence between the two lovers, and finding the young lady determined to abide by her own choice, he supposed that separation might do what can rarely be done by arguments, and sent her into a foreign country, where she was obliged to converse only with those from whom her uncle had nothing to fear.

Her lover took care to repeat his vows; but his letters were intercepted and carried to her guardian, who directed her to be watched with still greater vigilance; till of this restraint she grew so impatient that she bribed a woman-servant to procure her a sword, which she directed to her heart.

From this account, given with evident intention to raise the lady's character, it does not appear that she had any claim to praise, nor much to compassion. She seems to have been impatient, violent, and ungovernable. Her uncle's power could not have lasted long; the hour of liberty and choice would have come in time. But her desires were too hot for delay, and she liked self-murder better than suspense.

54. *Nicomachean Ethics,* iii. 6–9.

55. No. 378, May 14, 1712.

56. Owen Ruffhead's *Life of Pope* (1769) was based on materials supplied by Warburton, Pope's literary executor. It was one of Johnson's principal sources. This passage, however, Ruffhead derived from William Ayre's *Memoirs of Pope* (1745).

57. Social position.

Nor is it discovered that the uncle, whoever he was, is with much justice delivered to posterity as a "false guardian";[58] he seems to have done only that for which a guardian is appointed: he endeavored to direct his niece till she should be able to direct herself. Poetry has not often been worse employed than in dignifying the amorous fury of a raving girl.

Not long after, he wrote *The Rape of the Lock,* the most airy, the most ingenious, and the most delightful of all his compositions, occasioned by a frolic of gallantry, rather too familiar, in which Lord Petre cut off a lock of Mrs. Arabella Fermor's hair. This, whether stealth or violence, was so much resented that the commerce of the two families, before very friendly, was interrupted. Mr. Caryll, a gentleman who, being secretary to King James's Queen, had followed his mistress into France,[59] and who being the author of *Sir Salomon Single,* a comedy, and some translations, was entitled to the notice of a wit, solicited Pope to endeavor a reconciliation by a ludicrous poem, which might bring both the parties to a better temper. In compliance with Caryll's request, though his name was for a long time marked only the first and last letter, C—l, a poem of two cantos was written (1711), as is said, in a fortnight, and sent to the offended lady, who liked it well enough to show it; and with the usual process of literary transactions, the author, dreading a surreptitious edition, was forced to publish it.[60]

The event is said to have been such as was desired; the pacification and diversion of all to whom it related, except Sir George Browne, who complained with some bitterness that, in the character of Sir Plume, he was made to talk nonsense. Whether all this be true, I have some doubt; for at Paris, a few years ago, a niece of Mrs. Fermor, who presided in an English convent, mentioned Pope's work with very little gratitude, rather as an insult than an honor; and she may be supposed to have inherited the opinion of her family.

At its first appearance it was termed by Addison *merum sal.*[61] Pope, however, saw that it was capable of improvement; and, having luckily contrived to borrow his machinery from the Rosicrucians, imparted the scheme with which his head was teeming to Addison, who told him that his work, as it stood, was "a delicious little thing," and gave him no encouragement to retouch it.

This has been too hastily considered as an instance of Addison's jealousy; for as he could not guess the conduct of the new design, or the possibilities of pleasure comprised in a fiction of which there had been no examples, he might very reasonably and kindly persuade the

58. "Elegy to the Memory of an Unfortunate Lady," 1.29.

59. Mary of Modena, wife of James II, went into exile with him in 1688. Her secretary, the dramatist, was the uncle of the Caryll who urged Pope to write the poem.

60. The threat of unauthorized editions often served as a convenient pretext for publication.

61. "Pure wit." See Lucretius, *On the Nature of Things,* iv. 1162.

author to acquiesce in his own prosperity, and forbear an attempt which he considered as an unnecessary hazard.

Addison's counsel was happily rejected. Pope foresaw the future efflorescence of imagery then budding in his mind and resolved to spare no art or industry of cultivation. The soft luxuriance of his fancy was already shooting, and all the gay varieties of diction were ready at his hand to color and embellish it.

His attempt was justified by its success. *The Rape of the Lock* stands forward, in the classes of literature, as the most exquisite example of ludicrous poetry. Berkeley[62] congratulated him upon the display of powers more truly poetical than he had shown before; with elegance of description and justness of precepts, he had now exhibited boundless fertility of invention.

He always considered the intermixture of the machinery[63] with the action as his most successful exertion of poetical art. He indeed could never afterwards produce anything of such unexampled excellence. Those performances which strike with wonder are combinations of skillful genius with happy casualty;[64] and it is not likely that any felicity, like the discovery of a new race of preternatural agents, should happen twice to the same man.

Of this poem the author was, I think, allowed to enjoy the praise for a long time without disturbance. Many years afterwards Dennis published some *Remarks* upon it,[65] with very little force, and with no effect; for the opinion of the public was already settled, and it was no longer at the mercy of criticism.

About this time he published *The Temple of Fame,* which, as he tells Steele in their correspondence, he had written two years before;[66] that is, when he was only twenty-two years old, an early time of life for so much learning and so much observation as that work exhibits.

On this poem Dennis afterwards published some remarks of which the most reasonable is that some of the lines represent "motion" as exhibited by "sculpture."[67]

Of the *Epistle from Eloisa to Abelard,* I do not know the date.[68] His first inclination to attempt a composition of that tender kind arose, as Mr. Savage told me,[69] from his perusal of Prior's *Nut-Brown Maid.*[70] How much he has surpassed Prior's work it is not necessary to mention, when perhaps it may be said with justice that he has excelled every

62. The philosopher, George Berkeley, Bishop of Cloyne (1685–1753).
63. Of the sylphs and gnomes, the poem's supernatural agents.
64. Chance, accident.
65. *Remarks on Mr. Pope's "Rape of the Lock"* (1728).
66. Pope to Steele, November 16, 1712. *The Temple of Fame* was published in 1715.
67. *Remarks upon Pope's Homer* (1717).
68. It was published in the first collected edition of Pope's *Works* (1717).
69. Richard Savage (?1697–1743), Pope's protégé and Johnson's friend.
70. Matthew Prior (1664–1721), diplomat and poet. His *Henry and Emma* is an imitation of this old ballad.

composition of the same kind. The mixture of religious hope and resignation gives an elevation and dignity to disappointed love, which images merely natural cannot bestow. The gloom of a convent strikes the imagination with far greater force than the solitude of a grove.

This piece was, however, not much his favorite in his latter years, though I never heard upon what principle he slighted it.

In the next year (1713) he published *Windsor Forest;* of which part was, as he relates, written at sixteen, about the same time as his *Pastorals,* and the latter part was added afterwards: where the addition begins, we are not told. The lines relating to the Peace confess their own date.[71] It is dedicated to Lord Lansdowne, who was then high in reputation and influence among the Tories;[72] and it is said that the conclusion of the poem gave great pain to Addison, both as a poet and a politician. Reports like this are often spread with boldness very disproportionate to their evidence. Why should Addison receive any particular disturbance from the last lines of *Windsor Forest?* If contrariety of opinion could poison a politician, he would not live a day; and as a poet, he must have felt Pope's force of genius much more from many other parts of his works.

The pain that Addison might feel it is not likely that he would confess; and it is certain that he so well suppressed his discontent that Pope now thought himself his favorite; for having been consulted in the revisal of *Cato,* he introduced it by a Prologue; and, when Dennis published his *Remarks,*[73] undertook not indeed to vindicate but to revenge his friend, by *A Narrative of the Frenzy of John Dennis.*

There is reason to believe that Addison gave no encouragement to this disingenuous hostility; for, says Pope, in a letter to him, "indeed your opinion, that 'tis entirely to be neglected would be my own in my own case; but I felt more warmth here than I did when I first saw his book against myself (though indeed in two minutes it made me heartily merry)." Addison was not a man on whom such cant of sensibility could make much impression. He left the pamphlet to itself, having disowned it to Dennis, and perhaps did not think Pope to have deserved much by his officiousness.

This year was printed in *The Guardian*[74] the ironical comparison between the *Pastorals* of Philips and Pope: a composition of artifice, criticism, and literature, to which nothing equal will easily be found. The superiority of Pope is so ingeniously dissembled, and the feeble lines of Philips so skillfully preferred, that Steele, being deceived, was unwilling to print the paper lest Pope should be offended. Addision

71. The Peace of Utrecht (April 1713) ended the War of the Spanish Succession. The lines relating to it are 355–422.

72. George Granville, first Baron Lansdowne (1666–1735) was Secretary at War in 1710, and held other government positions.

73. *Remarks on "Cato, a Tragedy"* (1713).

74. No. 40 of this periodical (1713).

immediately saw the writer's design, and, as it seems, had malice enough to conceal his discovery, and to permit a publication which, by making his friend Philips ridiculous, made him forever an enemy to Pope.[75]

It appears that about this time Pope had a strong inclination to unite the art of painting with that of poetry, and put himself under the tuition of Jervas.[76] He was nearsighted, and therefore not formed by nature for a painter: he tried, however, how far he could advance, and sometimes persuaded his friends to sit. A picture of Betterton[77] supposed to be drawn by him was in the possession of Lord Mansfield:[78] if this was taken from the life, he must have begun to paint earlier, for Betterton was now dead. Pope's ambition of this new art produced some encomiastic verses to Jervas, which certainly show his power as a poet, but I have been told that they betray his ignorance of painting.

He appears to have regarded Betterton with kindness and esteem; and after his death published, under his name, a version into modern English of Chaucer's *Prologues,* and one of his *Tales,* which, as was related by Mr. Harte, were believed to have been the performance of Pope himself by Fenton, who made him a gay offer of five pounds, if he would show them in the hand of Betterton.[79]

The next year (1713) produced a bolder attempt, by which profit was sought as well as praise. The poems which he had hitherto written, however they might have diffused his name, had made very little addition to his fortune. The allowance which his father made him, though, proportioned to what he had, it might be liberal, could not be large; his religion hindered him from the occupation of any civil employment,[80] and he complained that he wanted even money to buy books.

He therefore resolved to try how far the favor of the public extended, by soliciting a subscription to a version of the *Iliad,* with large notes.

To print by subscription was, for some time, a practice peculiar to the English. The first considerable work for which this expedient was employed is said to have been Dryden's *Virgil,* and it had been tried again with great success when *The Tatlers* were collected into volumes.

There was reason to believe that Pope's attempt would be successful. He was in the full bloom of reputation, and was personally known to almost all whom dignity of employment or splendor of reputation had

75. Pope wrote this essay.

76. Charles Jervas (1675–1739), portrait painter.

77. Thomas Betterton (?1635–1710), actor. Pope copied Sir Godfrey Kneller's portrait of Betterton.

78. William Murray, first Earl of Mansfield (1705–93), Lord Chief Justice of the Court of the King's Bench. He was a friend of Pope.

79. Probably Pope did no more than revise Betterton's work.

80. Catholics were prohibited from holding public office, from being doctors or lawyers, or the like.

made eminent; he conversed indifferently with both parties, and never disturbed the public with his political opinions; and it might be naturally expected, as each faction then boasted its literary zeal, that the great men, who on other occasions practiced all the violence of opposition, would emulate each other in their encouragement of a poet who had delighted all, and by whom none had been offended.

With those hopes, he offered an English *Iliad* to subscribers, in six volumes in quarto, for six guineas; a sum, according to the value of money at that time, by no means inconsiderable, and greater than I believe to have been ever asked before. His proposal, however, was very favorably received, and the patrons of literature were busy to recommend his undertaking, and promote his interest. Lord Oxford,[81] indeed, lamented that such a genius should be wasted upon a work not original; but proposed no means by which he might live without it: Addison recommended caution and moderation, and advised him not to be content with the praise of half the nation, when he might be universally favored.

The greatness of the design, the popularity of the author, and the attention of the literary world, naturally raised such expectations of the future sale, that the booksellers made their offers with great eagerness; but the highest bidder was Bernard Lintot, who became proprietor on condition of supplying, at his own expense, all the copies which were to be delivered to subscribers, or presented to friends, and paying two hundred pounds for every volume.

Of the quartos it was, I believe, stipulated that none should be printed but for the author, that the subscription might not be depreciated; but Lintot impressed the same pages upon a small folio, and paper perhaps a little thinner; and sold exactly at half the price, for half a guinea each volume, books so little inferior to the quartos, that, by a fraud of trade, those folios, being afterwards shortened by cutting away the top and bottom, were sold as copies printed for the subscribers.

Lintot printed two hundred and fifty on royal paper[82] in folio for two guineas a volume; of the small folio, having printed seventeen hundred and fifty copies of the first volume, he reduced the number in the other volumes to a thousand.

It is unpleasant to relate that the bookseller, after all his hopes and all his liberality, was, by a very unjust and illegal action, defrauded of his profit. An edition of the English *Iliad* was printed in Holland in duodecimo, and imported clandestinely for the gratification of those who were impatient to read what they could not yet afford to buy. This fraud could only be counteracted by an edition equally cheap and more

81. Robert Harley, first Earl of Oxford, Lord Treasurer and head of the Tory Ministry at this time.

82. Printer's paper measuring 25" x 20".

commodious,[83] and Lintot was compelled to contract his folio at once into a duodecimo, and lose the advantage of an intermediate gradation.[84] The notes, which in the Dutch copies were placed at the end of each book, as they had been in the large volumes, were now subjoined to the text in the same page, and are therefore more easily consulted. Of this edition two thousand five hundred were first printed, and five thousand a few weeks afterwards; but indeed great numbers were necessary to produce considerable profit.

Pope, having now emitted his proposals, and engaged not only his own reputation, but in some degree that of his friends who patronized his subscription, began to be frighted at his own undertaking; and finding himself at first embarrassed with difficulties, which retarded and oppressed him, he was for a time timorous and uneasy; had his nights disturbed by dreams of long journeys through unknown ways, and wished, as he said, "that somebody would hang him."[85]

This misery, however, was not of long continuance; he grew by degrees more acquainted with Homer's images and expressions, and practice increased his facility of versification. In a short time he represents himself as despatching regularly fifty verses a day, which would show him by an easy computation the termination of his labor.

His own diffidence was not his only vexation. He that asks a subscription soon finds that he has enemies. All who do not encourage him defame him. He that wants money will rather be thought angry than poor, and he that wishes to save his money conceals his avarice by his malice. Addison had hinted his suspicion that Pope was too much a Tory; and some of the Tories suspected his principles because he had contributed to *The Guardian,* which was carried on by Steele.

To those who censured his politics were added enemies yet more dangerous, who called in question his knowledge of Greek, and his qualifications for a translator of Homer.[86] To these he made no public opposition, but in one of his letters[87] escapes from them as well as he can. At an age like his, for he was not more than twenty-five, with an irregular education, and a course of life of which much seems to have passed in conversation, it is not very likely that he overflowed with Greek. But when he felt himself deficient he sought assistance; and what man of learning would refuse to help him? Minute inquiries into the force of words are less necessary in translating Homer than other poets, because his positions[88] are general, and his representations natural, with very little dependence on local or temporary customs, on

83. Serviceable.

84. The intermediate gradation would have been an edition in octavo.

85. Joseph Spence (1699–1768), *Observations* (first published 1820), ed J. M. Osborn (1966), #197.

86. Such as Dennis, *Remarks on Pope's Homer.*

87. To Addison, January 30, 1714.

88. Propositions, assertions.

those changeable scenes of artificial[89] life, which, by mingling original with accidental notions, and crowding the mind with images which time effaces, produce ambiguity in diction, and obscurity in books. To this open display of unadulterated nature it must be ascribed that Homer has fewer passages of doubtful meaning than any other poet either in the learned or in modern languages. I have read of a man who being, by his ignorance of Greek, compelled to gratify his curiosity with the Latin printed on the opposite page, declared that from the rude simplicity of the lines literally rendered, he formed nobler ideas of the Homeric majesty than from the labored elegance of polished versions.

Those literal translations were always at hand, and from them he could easily obtain his author's sense with sufficient certainty; and among the readers of Homer the number is very small of those who find much in the Greek more than in the Latin, except the music of the numbers.

If more help was wanting, he had the poetical translation of Eobanus Hessus, an unwearied writer of Latin verses; he had the French Homers of La Valterie and Dacier, and the English of Chapman, Hobbes, and Ogilby.[90] With Chapman, whose work, though now totally neglected, seems to have been popular almost to the end of the last century, he had very frequent consultations, and perhaps never translated any passage till he had read his version, which indeed he has been sometimes suspected of using instead of the original.

Notes were likewise to be provided; for the six volumes would have been very little more than six pamphlets without them. What the mere perusal of the text could suggest, Pope wanted no assistance to collect or methodize; but more was necessary; many pages were to be filled, and learning must supply materials to wit and judgment. Something might be gathered from Dacier; but no man loves to be indebted to his contemporaries, and Dacier was accessible to common readers. Eustathius[91] was therefore necessarily consulted. To read Eustathius, of whose work there was then no Latin version, I suspect Pope, if he had been willing, not to have been able; some other was therefore to be found, who had leisure as well as abilities, and he was doubtless most readily employed who would do much work for little money.

The history of the notes has never been traced. Broome, in his preface to his poems, declares himself the commentator "in part upon the *Iliad*"; and it appears from Fenton's letter, preserved in the Museum, that Broome was at first engaged in consulting Eustathius;[92] but that after a time, whatever was the reason, he desisted: another man of

89. Civilized.

90. The dates of these translations of the *Iliad* are: Hessus, 1540; La Valterie, 1681; Dacier, 1699–1711; Chapman, 1611; Hobbes, 1676; Ogilby, 1660.

91. A 12th-century Byzantine commentator.

92. William Broome (1689–1745) and Elijah Fenton (1683–1730) later translated half of Pope's version of the *Odyssey* between them.

Cambridge was then employed, who soon grew weary of the work; and a third, that was recommended by Thirlby, is now discovered to have been Jortin, a man since well known to the learned world,[93] who complained that Pope, having accepted and approved his performance, never testified any curiosity to see him, and who professed to have forgotten the terms on which he worked. The terms which Fenton uses are very mercantile: "I think at first sight that his performance is very commendable, and have sent word for him to finish the 17th book, and to send it with his demands for his trouble. I have here enclosed the specimen; if the rest come before the return, I will keep them till I receive your order."

Broome then offered his service a second time, which was probably accepted, as they had afterwards a closer correspondence. Parnell[94] contributed the "Life of Homer," which Pope found so harsh that he took great pains in correcting it; and by his own diligence, with such help as kindness or money could procure him, in somewhat more than five years he completed his version of the *Iliad,* with the notes. He began it in 1712, his twenty-fifty year, and concluded it in 1718, his thirtieth year.

When we find him translating fifty lines a day, it is natural to suppose that he would have brought his work to a more speedy conclusion. The *Iliad,* containing less than sixteen thousand verses, might have been despatched in less than three hundred and twenty days by fifty verses in a day. The notes, compiled with the assistance of his mercenaries, could not be supposed to require more time than the text. According to this calculation, the progress of Pope may seem to have been slow; but the distance is commonly very great between actual performances and speculative possibility. It is natural to suppose that as much as has been done today may be done tomorrow; but on the morrow some difficulty emerges, or some external impediment obstructs. Indolence, interruption, business, and pleasure, all take their turns of retardation; and every long work is lengthened by a thousand causes that can, and ten thousand that cannot, be recounted. Perhaps no extensive and multifarious performance was ever effected within the term originally fixed in the undertaker's mind. He that runs against time has an antagonist not subject to casualties.

The encouragement given to this translation, though report seems to have overrated it, was such as the world has not often seen. The subscribers were five hundred and seventy-five. The copies for which subscriptions were given were six hundred and fifty-four; and only six hundred and sixty were printed. For those copies Pope had nothing to

93. John Jortin (1698–1770), D.D., author of a life of Erasmus, and of critical and theological tracts. Styan Thirlby was his tutor at Cambridge. Fenton's letter to Pope about Jortin was written in September, 1718.

94. Thomas Parnell (1679–1718), poet and member of the Scriblerus Club together with Pope, Swift, Gay, and Arbuthnot.

pay; he therefore received, including the two hundred pounds a volume, five thousand three hundred and twenty pounds four shillings, without deduction, as the books were supplied by Lintot.

By the success of his subscription Pope was relieved from those pecuniary distresses with which, notwithstanding his popularity, he had hitherto struggled. Lord Oxford had often lamented his disqualification for public employment, but never proposed a pension. While the translation of Homer was in its progress, Mr. Craggs, then secretary of state, offered to procure him a pension which, at least during his ministry, might be enjoyed with secrecy. This was not accepted by Pope, who told him, however, that if he should be pressed with want of money, he would send to him for occasional supplies. Craggs was not long in power, and was never solicited for money by Pope, who disdained to beg what he did not want.

With the product of this subscription, which he had too much discretion to squander, he secured his future life from want, by considerable annuities. The estate of the Duke of Buckingham was found to have been charged with five hundred pounds a year, payable to Pope, which doubtless his translation enabled him to purchase.

It cannot be unwelcome to literary curiosity that I deduce thus minutely the history of the English *Iliad*. It is certainly the noblest version of poetry which the world has ever seen; and its publication must therefore be considered as one of the great events in the annals of learning.

To those who have skill to estimate the excellence and difficulty of this great work, it must be very desirable to know how it was performed, and by what gradations it advanced to correctness. Of such an intellectual process the knowledge has very rarely been attainable; but happily there remains the original copy of the *Iliad*, which, being obtained by Bolingbroke[95] as a curiosity, descended from him to Mallet, and is now by the solicitation of the late Dr. Maty reposited in the Museum.[96]

Between this manuscript, which is written upon accidental fragments of paper, and the printed edition, there must have been an intermediate copy, that was perhaps destroyed as it returned from the press.

From the first copy I have procured a few transcripts, and shall exhibit first the printed lines; then, in a smaller print, those of the manuscripts, with all their variations. Those words in the small print which are given in italics, are cancelled in the copy, and the words placed under them adopted in their stead.

95. Henry St. John, first Viscount Bolingbroke (1678–1751), Tory political writer, deistic thinker, statesman, Pope's "guide, philosopher, and friend" (*Essay on Man*, iv. 390).

96. The British Museum (now called the British Library), of which Mathew Maty (1718–76) was the principal librarian.

The beginning of the first book stands thus:

The wrath of Peleus' son,[97] the direful spring
Of all the Grecian woes, O Goddess, sing!
That wrath which hurled to Pluto's gloomy reign
The souls of mighty chiefs untimely slain.

The stern Pelides' *rage,* O Goddess, sing!
wrath
Of all the woes *of Greece* the fatal spring,
Grecian
That strewed with *warriors* dead the Phrygian plain,
heroes
And *peopled the dark hell with heroes* slain;
filled the shady hell with chiefs untimely

Whose limbs, unburied on the naked shore,
Devouring dogs and hungry vultures tore,
Since great Achilles and Atrides[98] strove;
Such was the sovereign doom,[99] and such the will of Jove.

Whose limbs, unburied on the hostile shore,
Devouring dogs and greedy vultures tore,
Since first Atrides and Achilles strove;
Such was the sovereign doom, and such the will of Jove.

Declare, O Muse, in what ill-fated hour
Sprung the fierce strife, from what offended power!
Latona's son[1] a dire contagion spread,
And heaped the camp with mountains of the dead;
The King of men his reverend priest defied,
And for the King's offense the people died.

Declare, O Goddess! what offended power
Enflamed their *rage,* in that *ill-omened* hour;
anger fatal, hapless
Phoebus himself the *dire* debate procured,
fierce
T' avenge the wrongs his injured priest endured;
For this the God a dire infection spread,
And heaped the camp with millions of the dead:
The King of men the sacred sire defied,
And for the King's offense the people died.

For Chryses sought with costly gifts to gain
His captive daughter from the victor's chain;
Suppliant the venerable father stands,
Apollo's awful ensigns grace his hands,

97. Achilles, also called Pelides (son of Peleus).
98. Agamemnon (son of Atreus), King of the Greeks.
99. Judgment.
1. Phoebus Apollo loosed a plague on the Greek camp because the Greeks would not take ransom for Chryseis, his priest's daughter. The plague forced Agamemnon to release her, and he recompensed himself by taking Briseis, Achilles' captive, away from him.

By these he begs, and, lowly bending down,
Extends the scepter and the laurel crown.

For Chryses sought by *presents to regain*
costly gifts to gain
His captive daughter from the victor's chain;
Suppliant the venerable father stands,
Apollo's awful ensigns graced his hands,
By these he begs and, lowly bending down,
The golden scepter and the laurel crown,
Presents the scepter
For these as ensigns of his God he bare,
The God that sends his golden shafts afar;
Then low on earth, the venerable man,
Suppliant before the brother kings[2] began.

He sued to all, but chief implored for grace
The brother kings of Atreus' royal race;
Ye kings and warriors, may your vows be crowned,
And Troy's proud walls lie level with the ground;
May Jove restore you, when your toils are o'er,
Safe to the pleasures of your native shore.

To all he sued, but chief implored for grace
The brother kings of Atreus' royal race;
Ye *sons of Atreus,* may your vows be crowned,
kings and warriors
Your labors, by the Gods be all your labors crowned,
So may the Gods your arms with conquest bless,
And Troy's proud walls *lie* level with the ground;
Till laid
And crown your labors with deserved success;
May Jove restore you, when your toils are o'er
Safe to the pleasures of your native shore.

But, oh! relieve a wretched parent's pain,
And give Chryseis to these arms again;
If mercy fail, yet let my present move,
And dread avenging Phoebus, son of Jove.

But, oh! relieve a hapless parent's pain,
And give my daughter to these arms again;
Receive my gifts; if mercy fails, yet let my present move,
And fear *the God that deals his darts around,*
avenging Phoebus, son of Jove.

The Greeks, in shouts, their joint assent declare
The priest to reverence, and release the fair.
Not so Atrides; he, with kingly pride,
Repulsed the sacred sire, and thus replied.

He said, the Greeks their joint assent declare,
The father said, the generous Greeks relent,

2. Agamemnon and his brother, Menelaus.

T' accept the ransom, and release the fair;
Revere the priest, and speak their joint assent:
Not so *the tyrant;* he, with kingly pride,
Atrides,
Repulsed the sacred sire, and thus replied.
[Not so the tyrant. Dryden.][3]

Of these lines, and of the whole first book, I am told that there was yet a former copy, more varied and more deformed with interlineations.

The beginning of the second book varies very little from the printed page, and is therefore set down without any parallel: the few slight differences do not require to be elaborately displayed.

Now pleasing sleep had sealed each mortal eye;
Stretched in their tents the Grecian leaders lie;
Th' Immortals slumbered on their thrones above,
All but the ever-watchful eye of Jove.
To honor Thetis' son[4] he bends his care,
And plunge the Greeks in all the woes of war.
Then bids an empty phantom rise to sight,
And thus *commands* the vision of the night:
directs
Fly hence, delusive dream, and, light as air,
To Agamemnon's royal tent repair;
Bid him in arms draw forth th' embattled train,
March all his legions to the dusty plain.
Now tell the King 'tis given him to destroy
Declare even now
The lofty *walls* of wide-extended Troy;
towers
For now no more the Gods with Fate contend;
At Juno's suit the heavenly factions end.
Destruction *hovers* o'er yon devoted[5] wall,
hangs
And nodding Ilium[6] waits th' impending fall.

Invocation to the Catalogue of Ships.

Say, Virgins, seated round the throne divine,
All-knowing Goddesses! immortal Nine!
Since earth's wide regions, heaven's unmeasured height,
And hell's abyss, hide nothing from your sight
(We, wretched mortals! lost in doubts below,
But guess by rumor, and but boast we know),
Oh! say what heroes, fired by thirst of fame
Or urged by wrongs, to Troy's destruction came!

3. Dryden's translation of the *Iliad,* i. 523.
4. Achilles.
5. Doomed.
6. Tottering Ilium (Troy).

To count them all demands a thousand tongues,
A throat of brass and adamantine lungs.

Now, Virgin Goddesses, immortal Nine!
That round Olympus' heavenly summit shine,
Who see through heaven and earth, and hell profound,
And all things know, and all things can resound;
Relate what armies sought the Trojan land,
What nations followed, and what chiefs command
(For doubtful Fame distracts[7] mankind below,
And nothing can we tell, and nothing know);
Without your aid, to count th' unnumbered train
A thousand mouths, a thousand tongues were vain.

Book V. v. 1

But Pallas now Tydides' soul inspires,[8]
Fills with her force, and warms with all her fires:
Above the Greeks his deathless fame to raise,
And crown her hero with distinguished praise.
High on his helm celestial lightnings play,
His beamy shield emits a living ray;
Th' unwearied blaze incessant streams supplies,
Like the red star that fires th' autumnal skies.

But Pallas now Tydides' soul inspires,
Fills with her *rage,* and warms with all her fires;
force,
O'er all the Greeks decrees his fame to raise,
Above the Greeks *her warrior's* fame to raise,
his deathless
And crown her hero with *immortal* praise:
distinguished
Bright from his beamy *crest* the lightnings play,
High on helm
From his broad buckler flashed the living ray,
High on his helm celestial lightnings play,
His beamy shield emits a living ray.
The Goddess with her breath the flame supplies,
Bright as the star whose fires in Autumn rise;
Her breath divine thick streaming flames supplies,
Bright as the star that fires th' autumnal skies.[9]

When first he rears his radiant orb to sight,
And bathed in ocean shoots a keener light.
Such glories Pallas on the chief bestowed,
Such from his arms the fierce effulgence flowed;
Onward she drives him furious to engage,
Where the fight burns, and where the thickest rage.

7. Rumor perplexes.
8. The goddess Pallas Athena now instigates the Greek hero Diomedes to action.
9. Two lines not in the manuscript (according to G. B. Hill) are omitted here.

When fresh he rears his radiant orb to sight,
And gilds old Ocean with a blaze of light,
Bright as the star that fires th' autumnal skies,
Fresh from the deep, and gilds the seas and skies.
Such glories Pallas on her chief bestowed,
Such sparkling rays from his bright armor flowed,
Such from his arms the fierce effulgence flowed.
Onward she drives him *headlong* to engage,
furious
Where the *war bleeds,* and where the *fiercest* rage.
fight burns thickest

The sons of Dares first the combat sought,
A wealthy priest, but rich without a fault;
In Vulcan's fane the father's days were led,
The sons to toils of glorious battle bred;

There lived a Trojan—Dares was his name,
The priest of Vulcan, rich, yet void of blame;
The sons of Dares first the combat sought,
A wealthy priest, but rich without a fault.

Conclusion of Book VIII. v. 687

As when the moon, refulgent lamp of night,
O'er heaven's clear azure spreads her sacred light;
When not a breath disturbs the deep serene,
And not a cloud o'ercasts the solemn scene;
Around her throne the vivid planets roll,
And stars unnumbered gild the glowing pole:
O'er the dark trees a yellower verdure shed,
And tip with silver every mountain's head;
Then shine the vales—the rocks in prospect rise,
A flood of glory bursts from all the skies;
The conscious swains,[10] rejoicing in the sight,
Eye the blue vault, and bless the useful light.
So many flames before proud Ilion blaze,
And lighten glimmering Xanthus[11] with their rays;
The long reflection of the distant fires
Gleam on the walls, and tremble on the spires:
A thousand piles the dusky horrors gild,
And shoot a shady luster o'er the field;
Full fifty guards each flaming pile attend,
Whose umbered arms by fits thick flashes send;
Loud neigh the coursers o'er their heaps of corn,[12]
And ardent warriors wait the rising morn.

As when in stillness of the silent night,
As when the moon in all her luster bright,

10. Shepherds perceiving (this).
11. A river near Troy (Ilium or Ilion).
12. Grain.

As when the moon, refulgent lamp of night,
O'er heaven's *clear* azure *sheds* her *silver* light;
pure spreads sacred
As still in air the trembling luster stood,
And o'er its golden border shoots a flood;
When *no loose gale* disturbs the deep serene,
not a breath
And *no dim* cloud o'ercasts the solemn scene;
not a
Around her silver throne the planets glow,
And stars unnumbered trembling beams bestow;
Around her throne the vivid planets roll,
And stars unnumbered gild the glowing pole:
Clear gleams of light o'er the dark trees are seen,
o'er the dark trees a yellow sheds,
O'er the dark trees a yellower *green* they shed
gleam
verdure
And tip with silver all the *mountain* heads:
forest
And tip with silver every mountain's head.
The valleys open, and the forests rise,
The vales appear, the rocks in prospect rise,
All Nature stands revealed before our eyes;
A flood of glory bursts from all the skies.
The conscious shepherd, joyful at the sight,
Eyes the blue vault, and numbers every light.
The conscious *swains, rejoicing at the* sight,
shepherds, gazing with delight,
Eye the blue vault, and bless the *vivid* light.
glorious
useful
So many flames before *the navy* blaze,
proud Ilion
And lighten glimmering Xanthus with their rays,
Wide o'er the fields to Troy extend the gleams,
And tip the distant spires with fainter beams;
The long reflections of the distant fires
Gild the high walls, and tremble on the spires,
Gleam on the walls, and tremble on the spires;
A thousand fires at distant stations bright,
Gild the dark prospect, and dispel the night.

Of these specimens every man who has cultivated poetry, or who delights to trace the mind from the rudeness of its first conceptions to the elegance of its last, will naturally desire a greater number; but most other readers are already tired, and I am not writing only to poets and philosophers.

The *Iliad* was published volume by volume, as the translation proceeded; the four first books appeared in 1715. The expectation of this work was undoubtedly high, and every man who had connected his name with criticism, or poetry, was desirous of such intelligence as might enable him to talk upon the popular topic. Halifax,[13] who, by having been first a poet, and then a patron of poetry, had acquired the right of being a judge, was willing to hear some books while they were yet unpublished. Of this rehearsal Pope afterwards gave the following account:

> The famous Lord Halifax was rather a pretender to taste than really possessed of it. When I had finished the two or three first books of my translation of the *Iliad,* that Lord desired to have the pleasure of hearing them read at his house. Addison, Congreve, and Garth,[14] were there at the reading. In four or five places Lord Halifax stopped me very civilly, and with a speech each time, much of the same kind, "I beg your pardon, Mr. Pope; but there is something in that passage that does not quite please me. Be so good as to mark the place, and consider it a little at your leisure. I'm sure you can give it a little turn." I returned from Lord Halifax's with Dr. Garth, in his chariot; and, as we were going along, was saying to the Doctor that my Lord had laid me under a good deal of difficulty by such loose and general observations; that I had been thinking over the passages almost ever since, and could not guess at what it was that offended his Lordship in either of them. Garth laughed heartily at my embarrassment; said, I had not been long enough acquainted with Lord Halifax to know his way yet; that I need not puzzle myself about looking those places over and over, when I got home. "All you need to do (says he) is to leave them just as they are; call on Lord Halifax two or three months hence, thank him for his kind observations on those passages, and then read them to him as altered. I have known him much longer than you have, and will be answerable for the event." I followed his advice; waited on Lord Halifax some time after; said, I hoped he would find his objections to those passages removed; read them to him exactly as they were at first; and his Lordship was extremely pleased with them, and cried out, "Ay, now they are perfectly right: nothing can be better."[15]

It is seldom that the great or the wise suspect that they are despised or cheated. Halifax, thinking this a lucky opportunity of securing immortality, made some advances of favor and some overtures of advantage to Pope, which he seems to have received with sullen coldness. All our knowledge of this transaction is derived from a single letter (December 1, 1714), in which Pope says,

> I am obliged to you, both for the favors you have done me, and those you intend me. I distrust neither your will nor your memory, when it is to do good; and if I ever become troublesome or solicitous, it must not be out of expectation, but out of gratitude.

13. Charles Montagu, first Earl of Halifax (1661–1715).
14. Sir Samuel Garth (1661–1719), physician and poet.
15. Spence, *Observations,* #204.

> Your Lordship may cause me to live agreeably in the town, or contentedly in the country, which is really all the difference I set between an easy fortune and a small one. It is indeed a high strain of generosity in you to think of making me easy all my life, only because I have been so happy as to divert you some few hours; but, if I may have leave to add it is because you think me no enemy to my native country, there will appear a better reason; for I must of consequence be very much (as I sincerely am) yours, etc.

These voluntary[15a] offers, and this faint acceptance, ended without effect. The patron was not accustomed to such frigid gratitude, and the poet fed his own pride with the dignity of independence. They probably were suspicious of each other. Pope would not dedicate till he saw at what rate his praise was valued; he would be "troublesome out of gratitude, not expectation." Halifax thought himself entitled to confidence; and would give nothing, unless he knew what he should receive. Their commerce had its beginning in hope of praise on one side, and of money on the other, and ended because Pope was less eager of money than Halifax of praise. It is not likely that Halifax had any personal benevolence to Pope; it is evident that Pope looked on Halifax with scorn and hatred.

The reputation of this great work failed of gaining him a patron; but it deprived him of a friend. Addison and he were now at the head of poetry and criticism; and both in such a state of elevation, that, like the two rivals in the Roman state, one could no longer bear an equal, nor the other a superior. Of the gradual abatement of kindness between friends, the beginning is often scarcely discernible by themselves, and the process is continued by petty provocations, and incivilities sometimes peevishly returned, and sometimes contemptuously neglected, which would escape all attention but that of pride, and drop from any memory but that of resentment. That the quarrel of those two wits should be minutely deduced, is not to be expected from a writer to whom, as Homer says, "nothing but rumor has reached, and who has no personal knowledge."[16]

Pope doubtless approached Addison, when the reputation of their wit first brought them together, with the respect due to a man whose abilities were acknowledged, and who, having attained that eminence to which he was himself aspiring, had in his hands the distribution of literary fame. He paid court with sufficient diligence by his Prologue to *Cato,* by his abuse of Dennis, and, with praise yet more direct, by his poem on the "Dialogues on Medals," of which the immediate publication was then intended.[17] In all this there was no hypocrisy; for he confessed that he found in Addison something more pleasing than in any other man.

15a. Carefully calculated.
16. *Iliad,* ii. 485–86.
17. It was not published until 1721, two years after Addison's death.

It may be supposed that as Pope saw himself favored by the world, and more frequently compared his own powers with those of others, his confidence increased, and his submission lessened; and that Addison felt no delight from the advances of a young wit, who might soon contend with him for the highest place. Every great man, of whatever kind be his greatness, has among his friends those who officiously, or insidiously, quicken his attention to offences, heighten his disgust, and stimulate his resentment. Of such adherents Addison doubtless had many, and Pope was now too high to be without them.

From the emission and reception of the Proposals for the *Iliad,* the kindness of Addison seems to have abated. Jervas the painter once pleased himself (August 20, 1714) with imagining that he had re-established their friendship; and wrote to Pope that Addison once suspected him of too close a confederacy with Swift, but was now satisfied with his conduct. To this Pope answered, a week after, that his engagements to Swift were such as his services in regard to the subscription demanded, and that the Tories never put him under the necessity of asking leave to be grateful. "But," says he, "as Mr. Addison must be *the judge* in what regards himself, and seems to be no very just one in regard to me, so I must own to you I expect nothing but civility from him." In the same letter he mentions Philips as having been busy to kindle animosity between them; but, in a letter to Addison, he expresses some consciousness of behavior inattentively deficient in respect.

Of Swift's industry in promoting the subscription there remains the testimony of Kennett, no friend to either him or Pope.

> Nov. 2, 1713, Dr. Swift came into the coffee-house, and had a bow from everybody but me, who, I confess, could not but despise him. When I came to the antechamber to wait, before prayers, Dr. Swift was the principal man of talk and business, and acted as master of requests. Then he instructed a young nobleman that the best poet in England was Mr. Pope (a Papist), who had begun a translation of Homer into English verse, for which he must have them all subscribe; "for," says he, "the author shall not begin to print till I have a thousand guineas for him."[18]

About this time it is likely that Steele, who was, with all his political fury, good natured and officious, procured an interview between these angry rivals, which ended in aggravated malevolence.[19] On this occasion, if the reports be true, Pope made his complaint with frankness and spirit, as a man undeservedly neglected or opposed; and Addison affected a contemptuous unconcern, and, in a calm even voice, reproached Pope with his vanity, and, telling him of the improvements

18. White Kennett, Bishop of Peterborough (1660–1728), in his diary.
19. This meeting may never have occurred.

which his early works had received from his own remarks and those of Steele, said that he, being now engaged in public business,[20] had no longer any care for his poetical reputation; nor had any other desire with regard to Pope than that his[20a] should not, by too much arrogance, alienate the public.

To this Pope is said to have replied with great keenness and severity, upbraiding Addison with perpetual dependence,[21] and with the abuse of those qualifications[22] which he had obtained at the public cost, and charging him with mean endeavors to obstruct the progress of rising merit. The contest rose so high that they parted at last without any interchange of civility.

The first volume of Homer was (1715) in time published; and a rival version of the first *Iliad,* for rivals the time of their appearance inevitably made them, was immediately printed, with the name of Tickell.[23] It was soon perceived that among the followers of Addison, Tickell had the preference, and the critics and poets divided into factions. "I," says Pope, "have the town, that is, the mob, on my side; but it is not uncommon for the smaller party to supply by industry what it wants in numbers.—I appeal to the people as my rightful judges, and, while they are not inclined to condemn me, shall not fear the highfliers at Button's."[24] This opposition he immediately imputed to Addison, and complained of it in terms sufficiently resentful to Craggs, their common friend.

When Addison's opinion was asked he declared the versions to be both good, but Tickell's the best that had ever been written; and sometimes said that they were both good, but that Tickell had more of Homer.

Pope was now sufficiently irritated; his reputation and his interest were at hazard. He once intended to print together the four versions of Dryden, Maynwaring,[25] Pope, and Tickell, that they might be readily compared, and fairly estimated. This design seems to have been defeated by the refusal of Tonson,[26] who was the proprietor of the other three versions.

Pope intended at another time a rigorous criticism of Tickell's translation, and had marked a copy, which I have seen, in all places that appeared defective. But while he was thus meditating defense or re-

20. Addison held various high political offices in the Whig administration which came into power on the accession of George I in 1714.

20a. A mistake for "he" (?).

21. Reliance on, or subordination to, others (Addison's political friends).

22. Positions.

23. Addison may have prompted and revised the translation of the first book of the *Iliad* by Thomas Tickell (1685–1740).

24. To James Craggs, July 15, 1715. Button's Coffee-house was patronized by Addison and his friends. "Highfliers" are ambitious or pretentious people.

25. Arthur Maynwaring's translation of most of the *Iliad,* i, was published in 1704.

26. Jacob Tonson (1656–1736), well-known publisher.

venge his adversary sunk before him without a blow; the voice of the public was not long divided, and the preference was universally given to Pope's performance.

He was convinced, by adding one circumstance to another, that the other translation was the work of Addison himself; but if he knew it in Addison's lifetime it does not appear that he told it. He left his illustrious antagonist to be punished by what has been considered as the most painful of all reflections, the remembrance of a crime perpetrated in vain.

The other circumstances of their quarrel were thus related by Pope:

> Philips seemed to have been encouraged to abuse me in coffeehouses and conversations, and Gildon wrote a thing about Wycherley,[27] in which he had abused both me and my relations very grossly. Lord Warwick[28] himself told me one day that it was in vain for me to endeavor to be well with Mr. Addison; that his jealous temper would never admit of a settled friendship between us; and, to convince me of what he had said, assured me that Addison had encouraged Gildon to publish those scandals, and had given him ten guineas after they were published. The next day, while I was heated with what I had heard, I wrote a letter to Mr. Addison, to let him know that I was not unacquainted with this behaviour of his; that if I was to speak severely to him, in return for it, it should [not] be in such a dirty way; that I should rather tell him himself fairly of his faults, and allow his good qualities; and that it should be something in the following manner. I then adjoined the first sketch of what has since been called my satire on Addison.[29] Mr. Addison used me very civilly ever after.[30]

The verses on Addison, when they were sent to Atterbury, were considered by him as the most excellent of Pope's performances; and the writer was advised, since he knew where his strength lay, not to suffer it to remain unemployed.

This year (1715) being by the subscription enabled to live more by choice, having persuaded his father to sell their estate at Binfield, he purchased, I think only for his life, that house at Twickenham to which his residence afterwards procured so much celebration, and removed thither with his father and mother.[31]

Here he planted the vines and the quincunx which his verses mention, and being under the necessity of making a subterraneous passage to a garden on the other side of the road he adorned it with fossil

27. Charles Gildon, *Memoirs of Wycherley* (1718).
28. Addison's stepson.
29. Later incorporated in Pope's *Epistle to Dr. Arbuthnot,* ll. 193–214.
30. Spence, *Observations,* #165–66.
31. Pope moved to Twickenham on the Thames, west of London, in 1718, more than a year after his father's death.

bodies, and dignified it with the title of a grotto: a place of silence and retreat, from which he endeavored to persuade his friends and himself that cares and passions could be excluded.

A grotto is not often the wish or pleasure of an Englishman, who has more frequent need to solicit than exclude the sun; but Pope's excavation was requisite as an entrance to his garden, and, as some men try to be proud of their defects, he extracted an ornament from an inconvenience, and vanity produced a grotto where necessity enforced a passage. It may be frequently remarked of the studious and speculative[32] that they are proud of trifles, and that their amusements seem frivolous and childish; whether it be that men conscious of great reputation think themselves above the reach of censure, and safe in the admission of negligent indulgences, or that mankind expect from elevated genius an uniformity of greatness, and watch its degradation with malicious wonder; like him who having followed with his eye an eagle into the clouds should lament that she ever descended to a perch.

While the volumes of his Homer were annually published he collected his former works (1717) into one quarto volume, to which he prefixed a Preface, written with great sprightliness and elegance, which was afterwards reprinted, with some passages subjoined that he at first omitted; other marginal additions of the same kind he made in the later editions of his poems. Waller remarks that poets lose half their praise, because the reader knows not what they have blotted.[33] Pope's voracity of fame taught him the art of obtaining the accumulated honor both of what he had published, and of what he had suppressed.

In this year his father died suddenly, in his seventy-fifth year,[34] having passed twenty-nine years in privacy. He is not known but by the character which his son has given him.[35] If the money with which he retired was all gotten by himself, he had traded very successfully in times when sudden riches were rarely attainable.

The publication of the *Iliad* was at last completed in 1720. The splendor and success of this work raised Pope many enemies, that endeavored to depreciate his abilities. Burnet, who was afterwards a judge of no mean reputation, censured him in a piece called *Homerides* before it was published; Duckett likewise endeavored to make him ridiculous.[36] Dennis was the perpetual persecutor of all his studies. But, whoever his critics were, their writings are lost, and the names which are preserved are preserved in *The Dunciad.*

32. Philosophic.

33. Edmund Waller (1606–87), "Upon the Earl of Roscommon's Translation of Horace," ll. 41–42.

34. Actually he was 71.

35. *Epistle to Dr. Arbuthnot,* ll. 388–405; *Imitations of Horace, Epistles,* II. ii. 54–67.

36. Thomas Burnet and George Duckett collaborated on two pamphlets, both called *Homerides* (1715, 1716).

In this disastrous year (1720) of national infatuation, when more riches than Peru can boast were expected from the South Sea, when the contagion of avarice tainted every mind, and even poets panted after wealth, Pope was seized with the universal passion, and ventured some of his money. The stock rose in its price, and he for a while thought himself "the lord of thousands."[37] But this dream of happiness did not last long, and he seems to have waked soon enough to get clear with the loss only of what he once thought himself to have won, and perhaps not wholly of that.

Next year he published some select poems of his friend Dr. Parnell, with a very elegant Dedication to the Earl of Oxford, who, after all his struggles and dangers, then lived in retirement, still under the frown of a victorious faction, who could take no pleasure in hearing his praise.

He gave the same year (1721) an edition of Shakespeare.[38] His name was now of so much authority that Tonson thought himself entitled, by annexing it, to demand a subscription of six guineas for Shakespeare's plays in six quarto volumes; nor did his expectation much deceive him; for of seven hundred and fifty which he printed, he dispersed a great number at the price proposed. The reputation of that edition indeed sunk afterwards so low, that one hundred and forty copies were sold at sixteen shillings each.

On this undertaking, to which Pope was induced by a reward of two hundred and seventeen pounds, twelve shillings, he seems never to have reflected afterwards without vexation; for Theobald, a man of heavy diligence, with very slender powers, first in a book called *Shakespeare Restored,* and then in a formal edition,[39] detected his deficiencies with all the insolence of victory; and, as he was now high enough to be feared and hated, Theobald had from others all the help that could be supplied, by the desire of humbling a haughty character.

From this time Pope became an enemy to editors, collators, commentators, and verbal critics,[40] and hoped to persuade the world that he miscarried in this undertaking only by having a mind too great for such minute employment.

Pope in his edition undoubtedly did many things wrong, and left many things undone; but let him not be defrauded of his due praise: he was the first that knew, at least the first that told, by what helps the text might be improved. If he inspected the early editions negligently, he taught others to be more accurate. In his Preface he expanded with great skill and elegance the character which had been given of Shake-

37. *Imitations of Horace, Satires,* II. ii. 134. The South Sea Bubble was the greatest speculative boom and crash of the century.

38. The edition appeared in 1725.

39. Lewis Theobald's *Shakespeare Restored* appeared in 1726, and his edition of Shakespeare in 1734.

40. Critics "minutely exact in words" (Johnson's *Dictionary*).

speare by Dryden; and he drew the public attention upon his works, which, though often mentioned, had been little read.

Soon after the appearance of the *Iliad,* resolving not to let the general kindness cool, he published proposals for a translation of the *Odyssey,* in five volumes, for five guineas. He was willing, however, now to have associates in his labor, being either weary with toiling upon another's thoughts, or having heard, as Ruffhead relates, that Fenton and Broome had already begun the work, and liking better to have them confederates than rivals.

In the patent,[41] instead of saying that he had "translated" the *Odyssey,* as he had said of the *Iliad,* he says that he had "undertaken" a translation; and in the proposals the subscription is said to be "not solely for his own use but for that of two of his friends who have assisted him in this work."

In 1723, while he was engaged in this new version, he appeared before the Lords at the memorable trial of Bishop Atterbury,[42] with whom he had lived in great familiarity and frequent correspondence. Atterbury had honestly recommended to him the study of the Popish controversy,[43] in hope of his conversion; to which Pope answered in a manner that cannot much recommend his principles or his judgment. In questions and projects of learning, they agreed better. He was called at the trial to give an account of Atterbury's domestic life and private employment, that it might appear how little time he had left for plots. Pope had but few words to utter, and in those few he made several blunders.

His letters to Atterbury express the utmost esteem, tenderness, and gratitude: "perhaps," says he, "it is not only in this world that I may have cause to remember the Bishop of Rochester." At their last interview in the Tower, Atterbury presented him with a Bible.

Of the *Odyssey* Pope translated only twelve books; the rest were the work of Broome and Fenton: the notes were written wholly by Broome, who was not over-liberally rewarded. The public was carefully kept ignorant of the several shares, and an account was subjoined at the conclusion, which is now known not to be true.

The first copy of Pope's books, with those of Fenton, are to be seen in the Museum. The parts of Pope are less interlined than the *Iliad,* and the latter books of the *Iliad* less than the former. He grew dexterous by practice, and every sheet enabled him to write the next with more facility. The books of Fenton have very few alterations by the hand of Pope. Those of Broome have not been found; but Pope complained, as it is reported, that he had much trouble in correcting them.

41. A writ granting copyright.

42. Atterbury was convicted of treasonable correspondence with the Jacobites, whom he joined in Paris after being exiled.

43. Controversy between Catholics and Protestants.

His contract with Lintot was the same as for the *Iliad,* except that only one hundred pounds were to be paid him for each volume. The number of subscribers was five hundred and seventy-four, and of copies eight hundred and nineteen; so that his profit, when he had paid his assistants, was still very considerable.[44] The work was finished in 1725, and from that time he resolved to make no more translations.

The sale did not answer Lintot's expectation, and he then pretended to discover something of fraud in Pope, and commenced, or threatened, a suit in Chancery.

On the English *Odyssey* a criticism was published by Spence, at that time Prelector[45] of Poetry at Oxford; a man whose learning was not very great, and whose mind was not very powerful. His criticism, however, was commonly just; what he thought, he thought rightly, and his remarks were recommended by his coolness and candor. In him Pope had the first experience of a critic without malevolence, who thought it as much his duty to display beauties as expose faults; who censured with respect, and praised with alacrity.

With this criticism Pope was so little offended that he sought the acquaintance of the writer, who lived with him from that time in great familiarity, attended him in his last hours, and compiled memorials of his conversation. The regard of Pope recommended him to the great and powerful, and he obtained very valuable preferments in the Church.

Not long after, Pope was returning home from a visit in a friend's coach which, in passing a bridge, was overturned into the water; the windows were closed, and being unable to force them open, he was in danger of immediate death, when the postilion snatched him out by breaking the glass, of which the fragments cut two of his fingers in such a manner that he lost their use.

Voltaire, who was then in England, sent him a letter of consolation. He had been entertained by Pope at his table, where he talked with so much grossness that Mrs. Pope was driven from the room. Pope discovered, by a trick, that he was a spy for the Court, and never considered him as a man worthy of confidence.[46]

He soon afterwards (1727) joined with Swift, who was then in England, to publish three volumes of *Miscellanies,* in which amongst other things, he inserted the "Memoirs of a Parish Clerk," in ridicule of Burnet's importance in his own *History,*[47] and a "Debate upon Black and White Horses," written in all the formalities of a legal process by

44. Johnson's account of these financial details is unreliable. Of the fifty-eight hundred pounds received, Pope kept five thousand.

45. Lecturer. He wrote *An Essay on Pope's "Odyssey"* (1726–27).

46. The story goes that Pope deliberately misinformed Voltaire as to who had written a certain attack on Walpole, and Voltaire repeated this information to Walpole.

47. Gilbert Burnet, Bishop of Salisbury (1643–1715), wrote *A History of His Own Times* (first volume published in 1724).

the assistance, as is said, of Mr. Fortescue, afterwards Master of the Rolls.[48] Before these *Miscellanies* is a preface signed by Swift and Pope, but apparently written by Pope, in which he makes a ridiculous and romantic[49] complaint of the robberies committed upon authors by the clandestine seizure and sale of their papers. He tells, in tragic strains, how "the cabinets of the sick and the closets of the dead have been broke open and ransacked"; as if those violences were often committed for papers of uncertain and accidental value, which are rarely provoked by real treasures, as if epigrams and essays were in danger where gold and diamonds are safe. A cat hunted for his musk is, according to Pope's account, but the emblem of a wit winded by booksellers.

His complaint, however, received some attestation, for the same year the letters written by him to Mr. Cromwell in his youth were sold by Mrs. Thomas to Curll, who printed them.

In these *Miscellanies* was first published *The Art of Sinking in Poetry*, which, by such a train of consequences as usually passes in literary quarrels, gave in a short time, according to Pope's account, occasion to *The Dunciad.*

In the following year (1728) he began to put Atterbury's advice in practice, and showed his satirical powers by publishing *The Dunciad*, one of his greatest and most elaborate performances, in which he endeavored to sink into contempt all the writers by whom he had been attacked, and some others whom he thought unable to defend themselves.

At the head of the Dunces he placed poor Theobald, whom he accused of ingratitude, but whose real crime was supposed to be that of having revised[50] Shakespeare more happily than himself. This satire had the effect which he intended, by blasting the characters which it touched. Ralph,[51] who, unnecessarily interposing in the quarrel, got a place in a subsequent edition, complained that for a time he was in danger of starving, as the booksellers had no longer any confidence in his capacity.

The prevalence of this poem was gradual and slow: the plan, if not wholly new, was little understood by common readers. Many of the allusions required illustration; the names were often expressed only by the initial and final letters, and, if they had been printed at length, were such as few had known or recollected. The subject itself had nothing generally interesting; for whom did it concern to know that one or another scribbler was a dunce? If therefore it had been possible for those who were attacked to conceal their pain and their resentment, *The Dunciad* might have made its way very slowly in the world.

48. The Mastership of the Rolls was one of several high legal offices held by Pope's friend William Fortescue (1687–1749).

49. Extravagant.

50. Edited.

51. James Ralph, journalist and poet, attacked Pope in his poem *Sawney* (1728).

This, however, was not to be expected: every man is of importance to himself, and therefore, in his own opinion, to others, and, supposing the world already acquainted with all his pleasures and his pains, is perhaps the first to publish injuries or misfortunes which had never been known unless related by himself, and at which those that hear them will only laugh; for no man sympathizes with the sorrows of vanity.

The history of *The Dunciad* is very minutely related by Pope himself, in a Dedication which he wrote to Lord Middlesex[52] in the name of Savage.

> I will relate the . . . war of the "dunces" (for so it has been commonly called), which began in the year 1727, and ended in 1730.
>
> When Dr. Swift and Mr. Pope thought it proper, for reasons specified in the Preface to their *Miscellanies,* to publish such little pieces of theirs as had casually got abroad, there was added to them *The Treatise of the Bathos, or The Art of Sinking in Poetry.* It happened that in one chapter of this piece the several species of bad poets were ranged in classes, to which were prefixed almost all the letters of the alphabet (the greatest part of them at random); but such was the number of poets eminent in that art that some one or other took every letter to himself: all fell into so violent a fury that, for half a year or more, the common newspapers (in most of which they had some property, as being hired writers) were filled with the most abusive falsehoods and scurrilities they could possibly devise. A liberty no way to be wondered at in those people and in those papers that for many years during the uncontrolled license of the press had aspersed almost all the great characters of the age; and this with impunity, their own persons and names being utterly secret and obscure.
>
> This gave Mr. Pope the thought that he had now some opportunity of doing good, by detecting and dragging into light these common enemies of mankind; since to invalidate this universal slander it sufficed to show what contemptible men were the authors of it. He was not without hopes that, by manifesting the dullness of those who had only malice to recommend them, either the booksellers would not find their account in employing them, or the men themselves, when discovered, want courage to proceed in so unlawful an occupation. This it was that gave birth to *The Dunciad;* and he thought it an happiness that, by the late flood of slander on himself, he had acquired such a peculiar[53] right over their names as was necessary to this design.
>
> On the 12th of March, 1729, at St. James's, that poem was presented to the King and Queen[54] (who had before been pleased

52. Charles Sackville, Earl of Middlesex, later second Duke of Dorset (1711–69).
53. Particular.
54. George II (ruled 1727–1760) and Caroline (1683–1737).

to read it) by the Right Honorable Sir Robert Walpole;[55] and some days after the whole impression was taken and dispersed by several noblemen and persons of the first distinction.

It is certainly a true observation that no people are so impatient of censure as those who are the greatest slanderers, which was wonderfully exemplified on this occasion. On the day the book was first vended a crowd of authors besieged the shop; entreaties, advices, threats of law and battery, nay cries of treason, were all employed to hinder the coming out of *The Dunciad:* on the other side, the booksellers and hawkers made as great efforts to procure it. What could a few poor authors do against so great a majority as the public? There was no stopping a torrent with a finger, so out it came.

Many ludicrous circumstances attended it. The "dunces" (for by this name they were called) held weekly clubs to consult of hostilities against the author: one wrote a letter to a great minister, assuring him Mr. Pope was the greatest enemy the government had; and another bought his image in clay to execute him in effigy, with which sad sort of satisfaction the gentlemen were a little comforted.

Some false editions of the book having an owl in their frontispiece,[56] the true one, to distinguish it, fixed in its stead an ass laden with authors. Then another surreptitious one being printed with the same ass, the new edition in octavo returned for distinction to the owl again. Hence arose a great contest of booksellers against booksellers and advertisements against advertisements; some recommending the edition of the owl, and others the edition of the ass; by which names they came to be distinguished, to the great honor also of the gentlemen of *The Dunciad.*[57]

Pope appears by this narrative to have contemplated his victory over the Dunces with great exultation; and such was his delight in the tumult which he had raised, that for a while his natural sensibility was suspended, and he read reproaches and invectives without emotion, considering them only as the necessary effects of that pain which he rejoiced in having given.

It cannot, however, be concealed that, by his own confession, he was the aggressor, for nobody believes that the letters in *The Bathos* were placed at random; and it may be discovered that, when he thinks himself concealed, he indulges the common vanity of common men, and triumphs in those distinctions which he had affected to despise. He is proud that his book was presented to the King and Queen by the Right Honorable Sir Robert Walpole; he is proud that they had read it before; he is proud that the edition was taken off by the nobility and persons of the first distinction.

55. Walpole served as Prime Minister from 1715 to 1717 and from 1721 to 1742.
56. Pope himself published these "false editions."
57. *A Collection of Pieces . . . on Occasion of "The Dunciad"* (1732), Dedication.

The edition of which he speaks was, I believe, that, which by telling in the text the names and in the notes the characters of those whom he had satirized, was made intelligible and diverting.[58] The critics had now declared their approbation of the plan, and the common reader began to like it without fear; those who were strangers to petty literature, and therefore unable to decipher initials and blanks, had now names and persons brought within their view, and delighted in the visible effect of those shafts of malice, which they had hitherto contemplated as shot into the air.

Dennis, upon the fresh provocation now given him, renewed the enmity which had for a time been appeased by mutual civilities, and published remarks, which he had till then suppressed, upon *The Rape of the Lock.* Many more grumbled in secret, or vented their resentment in the newspapers by epigrams or invectives.

Duckett, indeed, being mentioned as loving Burnet with "pious passion,"[59] pretended that his moral character was injured, and for some time declared his resolution to take vengeance with a cudgel. But Pope appeased him, by changing "pious passion" to "cordial friendship," and by a note, in which he vehemently disclaims the malignity of meaning imputed to the first expression.

Aaron Hill, who was represented as diving for the prize,[60] expostulated with Pope in a manner so much superior to all mean solicitation, that Pope was reduced to sneak and shuffle, sometimes to deny and sometimes to apologize: he first endeavors to wound, and is then afraid to own that he meant a blow.

The Dunciad, in the complete edition, is addressed to Dr. Swift: of the notes, part was written by Dr. Arbuthnot, and an apologetical letter was prefixed, signed by Cleland,[61] but supposed to have been written by Pope.

After this general war upon dullness he seems to have indulged himself a while in tranquillity; but his subsequent productions prove that he was not idle. He published (1731) a poem *On Taste,* in which he very particularly and severely criticizes the house, furniture, the gardens, and the entertainments of Timon, a man of great wealth and little taste. By Timon he was universally supposed, and by the Earl of Burlington, to whom the poem is addressed, was privately said, to mean the Duke of Chandos; a man perhaps too much delighted with pomp and show, but of a temper kind and beneficent, and who had consequently the voice of the public in his favor.

A violent outcry was therefore raised against the ingratitude and

58. The first edition of *The Dunciad* (1728), published in the previous year, had not provided names in full.

59. *The Dunciad* (1728), iii. 137. The change mentioned below appeared in only one of the early editions.

60. *The Dunciad* (1728), ii. 273. Aaron Hill (1685–1750), dramatist and poet.

61. William Cleland (?1674–1741). "Apologetical" means explanatory.

treachery of Pope, who was said to have been indebted to the patronage of Chandos for a present of a thousand pounds, and who gained the opportunity of insulting him by the kindness of his invitation.

The receipt of the thousand pounds Pope publicly denied;[62] but from the reproach which the attack on a character so amiable brought upon him, he tried all means of escaping. The name of Cleland was again employed in an apology, by which no man was satisfied; and he was at last reduced to shelter his temerity behind dissimulation, and endeavor to make that disbelieved which he never had confidence openly to deny. He wrote an exculpatory letter to the Duke, which was answered with great magnanimity, as by a man who accepted his excuse without believing his professions. He said that to have ridiculed his taste or his buildings had been an indifferent action in another man, but that in Pope, after the reciprocal kindness that had been exchanged between them, it had been less easily excused.[63]

Pope, in one of his letters, complaining of the treatment which his poem had found, "owns that such critics can intimidate him, nay almost persuade him to write no more, which is a compliment this age deserves."[64] The man who threatens the world is always ridiculous; for the world can easily go on without him, and in a short time will cease to miss him. I have heard of an idiot who used to revenge his vexations by lying all night upon the bridge. "There is nothing," says Juvenal, "that a man will not believe in his own favor."[65] Pope had been flattered till he thought himself one of the moving powers in the system of life. When he talked of laying down his pen, those who sat round him entreated and implored, and self-love did not suffer him to suspect that they went away and laughed.

The following year deprived him of Gay, a man whom he had known early, and whom he seemed to love with more tenderness than any other of his literary friends. Pope was now forty-four years old; an age at which the mind begins less easily to admit new confidence and the will to grow less flexible, and when therefore the departure of an old friend is very acutely felt.

In the next year he lost his mother, not by an unexpected death, for she had lasted to the age of ninety-three; but she did not die unlamented.[66] The filial piety of Pope was in the highest degree amiable and exemplary; his parents had the happiness of living till he was at the summit of poetical reputation, till he was at ease in his fortune, and without a rival in his fame, and found no diminution of his respect or tenderness. Whatever was his pride, to them he was obedient; and

62. *Epistle to Dr. Arbuthnot,* l. 375 n. The sum alleged was five hundred pounds.

63. Johnson's summary of Chandos's letter is misleading, and modern scholars tend to reject the identification of Timon with Chandos.

64. To Richard Boyle, third Earl of Burlington, January 1732.

65. *Satires,* iv. 70.

66. See *Epistle to Dr. Arbuthnot,* ll. 408–13.

whatever was his irritability, to them he was gentle. Life has, among its soothing and quiet comforts, few things better to give than such a son.

One of the passages of Pope's life, which seems to deserve some inquiry, was a publication of letters between him and many of his friends, which falling into the hands of Curll, a rapacious bookseller of no good fame, were by him printed and sold. This volume containing some letters from noblemen, Pope incited a prosecution against him in the House of Lords for breach of privilege, and attended himself to stimulate the resentment of his friends. Curll appeared at the bar, and, knowing himself in no great danger, spoke of Pope with very little reverence. "He has," said Curll, "a knack at versifying, but in prose I think myself a match for him." When the orders of the House were examined, none of them appeared to have been infringed; Curll went away triumphant, and Pope was left to seek some other remedy.

Curll's account was, that one evening a man in a clergyman's gown, but with a lawyer's band,[67] brought and offered to sale a number of printed volumes, which he found to be Pope's epistolary correspondence; that he asked no name, and was told none, but gave the price demanded, and thought himself authorized to use his purchase to his own advantage.

That Curll gave a true account of the transaction, it is reasonable to believe, because no falsehood was ever detected; and when some years afterwards I mentioned it to Lintot, the son of Bernard,[68] he declared his opinion to be that Pope knew better than anybody else how Curll obtained the copies, because another parcel was at the same time sent to himself, for which no price had ever been demanded, as he made known his resolution not to pay a porter, and consequently not to deal with a nameless agent.

Such care had been taken to make them public that they were sent at once to two booksellers: to Curll, who was likely to seize them as a prey, and to Lintot, who might be expected to give Pope information of the seeming injury. Lintot, I believe, did nothing; and Curll did what was expected. That to make them public was the only purpose may be reasonably supposed, because the numbers offered to sale by the private messengers showed that hope of gain could not have been the motive of the impression.[69]

It seems that Pope, being desirous of printing his letters, and not knowing how to do, without imputation of vanity, what has in this country been done very rarely, contrived an appearance of compulsion: that when he could complain that his letters were surreptitiously published, he might decently and defensively publish them himself.

Pope's private correspondence thus promulgated filled the nation

67. Neckband.
68. Henry Lintot (1703–58), publisher.
69. Six hundred and fifty copies were offered.

with praises of his candor, tenderness, and benevolence, the purity of his purposes, and the fidelity of his friendship. There were some letters which a very good or a very wise man would wish suppressed; but, as they had been already exposed, it was impracticable now to retract them.

From the perusal of those letters, Mr. Allen[70] first conceived the desire of knowing him, and with so much zeal did he cultivate the friendship which he had newly formed, that when Pope told his purpose of vindicating[71] his own property by a genuine edition, he offered to pay the cost.

This, however, Pope did not accept; but in time solicited a subscription for a quarto volume, which appeared (1737), I believe, with sufficient profit. In the Preface he tells that his letters were reposited in a friend's library, said to be the Earl of Oxford's,[72] and that the copy thence stolen was sent to the press. The story was doubtless received with different degrees of credit. It may be suspected that the Preface to the *Miscellanies* was written to prepare the public for such an incident; and to strengthen this opinion, James Worsdale, a painter, who was employed in clandestine negotiations, but whose veracity was very doubtful, declared that he was the messenger who carried by Pope's direction the books to Curll.

When they were thus published and avowed, as they had relation to recent facts, and persons either then living or not yet forgotten, they may be supposed to have found readers; but as the facts were minute, and the characters being either private or literary were little known or little regarded, they awakened no popular kindness or resentment: the book never became much the subject of conversation; some read it as contemporary history, and some perhaps as a model of epistolary language; but those who read it did not talk of it. Not much therefore was added by it to fame or envy; nor do I remember that it produced either public praise or public censure.

It had, however, in some degree the recommendation of novelty. Our language has few letters, except those of statesmen. Howell indeed, about a century ago, published his letters, which are commended by Morhoff, and which alone of his hundred volumes continue his memory.[73] Loveday's *Letters* were printed only once;[74] those of Herbert and Suckling are hardly known.[75] Mrs. Philips' (Orinda's) are equally

70. Ralph Allen (1694–1764), who made a fortune by setting up a secondary postal route system. Pope praised him in the *Epilogue to the Satires*, i. 135.

71. Laying claim to.

72. The son of Robert Harley, Pope's early friend.

73. James Howell published his *Familiar Letters* in 1645–55. D. G. Morhoff was a German professor of poetry.

74. The *Letters* of Robert Loveday went through several editions after they were first printed in 1659.

75. No separate editions had been published of letters by the poets George Herbert (1593–1633) and Sir John Suckling (1609–42).

neglected,[76] and those of Walsh seem written as exercises, and were never sent to any living mistress or friend. Pope's epistolary excellence had an open field; he had no English rival, living or dead.

Pope is seen in this collection as connected with the other contemporary wits, and certainly suffers no disgrace in the comparison; but it must be remembered that he had the power of favoring himself: he might have originally had publication in his mind, and have written with care, or have afterwards selected those which he had most happily conceived, or most diligently labored; and I know not whether there does not appear something more studied and artificial in his productions than the rest, except one long letter by Bolingbroke, composed with all the skill and industry of a professed author.[77] It is indeed not easy to distinguish affectation from habit; he that has once studiously formed a style rarely writes afterwards with complete ease. Pope may be said to write always with his reputation in his head; Swift perhaps like a man who remembered that he was writing to Pope; but Arbuthnot like one who lets thoughts drop from his pen as they rise into his mind.

Before these *Letters* appeared he published the first part of what he persuaded himself to think a system of ethics, under the title of an *Essay on Man,* which, if his letter to Swift (of Sept. 14, 1725) be rightly explained by the commentator,[78] had been eight years under his consideration, and of which he seems to have desired the success with great solicitude. He had now many open and doubtless many secret enemies. The Dunces were yet smarting with the war, and the superiority which he publicly arrogated disposed the world to wish his humiliation.

All this he knew, and against all this he provided. His own name, and that of his friend to whom the work is inscribed, were in the first editions carefully suppressed;[79] and the poem, being of a new kind, was ascribed to one or another as favor determined or conjecture wandered: it was given, says Warburton, to every man except him only who could write it. Those who like only when they like the author, and who are under the dominion of a name, condemned it; and those admired it who are willing to scatter praise at random, which while it is unappropriated excites no envy. Those friends of Pope that were trusted with the secret went about lavishing honors on the new-born poet, and hinting that Pope was never so much in danger from any former rival.

To those authors whom he had personally offended, and to those whose opinion the world considered as decisive, and whom he sus-

76. Katherine Philips (1631–64), minor poet, whose letters of *Orinda to Poliarchus* appeared in 1705.

77. To Swift, August 1723.

78. Warburton, whose 1751 edition of Pope's *Works* included voluminous and sometimes inaccurate or far-fetched notes.

79. The *Essay on Man* is addressed to Bolingbroke, who is called Laelius in the first two editions.

pected of envy or malevolence, he sent his *Essay* as a present before publication that they might defeat their own enmity by praises, which they could not afterwards decently retract.

With these precautions, in 1733 was published the first part of the *Essay on Man.* There had been for some time a report that Pope was busy upon a system of morality, but this design was not discovered in the new poem, which had a form and a title with which its readers were unacquainted. Its reception was not uniform: some thought it a very imperfect piece, though not without good lines. While the author was unknown some, as will always happen, favored him as an adventurer, and some censured him as an intruder, but all thought him above neglect: the sale increased, and editions were multiplied.

The subsequent editions of the first Epistle exhibited two memorable corrections. At first, the poet and his friend

> Expatiate freely o'er this scene of man,
> A mighty maze of *walks without a plan.*[80]

For which he wrote afterwards,

> A mighty maze, *but not without a plan:*

for, if there were no plan, it was in vain to describe or to trace the maze.

The other alteration was of these lines:

> And spite of pride, *and in thy reason's spite,*
> One truth is clear, whatever is, is right;[81]

but having afterwards discovered, or been shown, that the *truth* which subsisted *in spite of reason* could not be very *clear,* he substituted

> And spite of pride, *in erring reason's spite.*

To such oversights will the most vigorous mind be liable when it is employed at once upon argument and poetry.

The second and third Epistles were published, and Pope was, I believe, more and more suspected of writing them; at last, in 1734, he avowed the fourth, and claimed the honor of a moral poet.

In the conclusion it is sufficiently acknowledged that the doctrine of the *Essay on Man* was received from Bolingbroke, who is said to have ridiculed Pope, among those who enjoyed his confidence, as having adopted and advanced principles of which he did not perceive the consequence, and as blindly propagating opinions contrary to his own.[82] That those communications had been consolidated into a scheme regularly drawn, and delivered to Pope, from whom it returned only transformed from prose to verse, has been reported, but

80. i. 5–6.
81. i. 293–94.
82. Modern scholars discount Johnson's interpretation of the relationship between Bolingbroke's views and Pope's.

hardly can be true. The *Essay* plainly appears the fabric of a poet: what Bolingbroke supplied could be only the first principles; the order, illustration, and embellishments must all be Pope's.

These principles it is not my business to clear from obscurity, dogmatism, or falsehood, but they were not immediately examined; philosophy and poetry have not often the same readers, and the *Essay* abounded in splendid amplifications and sparkling sentences,[83] which were read and admired with no great attention to their ultimate purpose: its flowers caught the eye which did not see what the gay foliage concealed, and for a time flourished in the sunshine of universal approbation. So little was any evil discovered that, as innocence is unsuspicious, many read it for a manual of piety.

Its reputation soon invited a translator. It was first turned into French prose, and afterwards by Resnel into verse. Both translations fell into the hands of Crousaz, who first, when he had the version in prose, wrote a general censure, and afterwards reprinted Resnel's version with particular remarks upon every paragraph.[84]

Crousaz was a professor of Switzerland, eminent for his treatise of logic, and his *Examen de Pyrrhonisme,*[85] and, however little known or regarded here, was no mean[86] antagonist. His mind was one of those in which philosophy and piety are happily united. He was accustomed to argument and disquisition, and perhaps was grown too desirous of detecting faults; but his intentions were always right, his opinions were solid, and his religion pure.

His incessant vigilance for the promotion of piety disposed him to look with distrust upon all metaphysical systems of theology, and all schemes of virtue and happiness purely rational, and therefore it was not long before he was persuaded that the positions of Pope, as they terminated for the most part in natural religion,[87] were intended to draw mankind away from revelation, and to represent the whole course of things as a necessary concatenation of indissoluble fatality; and it is undeniable that in many passages a religious eye may easily discover expressions not very favorable to morals or to liberty.

About this time Warburton began to make his appearance in the first ranks of learning. He was a man of vigorous faculties, a mind fervid and vehement, supplied by incessant and unlimited inquiry, with wonderful extent and variety of knowledge, which yet had not oppressed his imagination nor clouded his perspicacity. To every work he brought a memory full fraught, together with a fancy fertile of original combi-

83. Aphorisms.

84. Jean-Pierre de Crousaz, *Examination of Pope's Essay* (1737), and *Commentary on the Verse Translation of Resnel* (1738).

85. *Examination of Pyrrhonism* (1733). Pyrrhonism is a form of philosophical skepticism, named after Pyrrho of Elis (c. 360–c. 270 B.C.).

86. Vulgar, commonplace.

87. Worship of God that dispenses with Christian revelation.

nations, and at once exerted the powers of the scholar, the reasoner, and the wit. But his knowledge was too multifarious to be always exact, and his pursuits were too eager to be always cautious. His abilities gave him an haughty confidence which he disdained to conceal or mollify, and his impatience of opposition disposed him to treat his adversaries with such contemptuous superiority as made his readers commonly his enemies, and excited against the advocate the wishes of some who favored the cause. He seems to have adopted the Roman Emperor's determination, *oderint dum metuant;*[88] he used no allurements of gentle language, but wished to compel rather than persuade.

His style is copious without selection, and forcible without neatness; he took the words that presented themselves: his diction is coarse and impure, and his sentences are unmeasured.

He had, in the early part of his life, pleased himself with the notice of inferior wits and corresponded with the enemies of Pope. A letter was produced, when he had perhaps himself forgotten it, in which he tells Concanen,[89] "Dryden I observe borrows for want of leisure, and Pope for want of genius; Milton out of pride, and Addison out of modesty."[90] And when Theobald published Shakespeare, in opposition to Pope, the best notes were supplied by Warburton.

But the time was now come when Warburton was to change his opinion, and Pope was to find a defender in him who had contributed so much to the exaltation of his rival.

The arrogance of Warburton excited against him every artifice of offense, and therefore it may be supposed that his union with Pope was censured as hypocritical inconstancy; but surely to think differently at different times of poetical merit may be easily allowed. Such opinions are often admitted and dismissed without nice examination. Who is there that has not found reason for changing his mind about questions of greater importance?

Warburton, whatever was his motive, undertook without solicitation to rescue Pope from the talons of Crousaz, by freeing him from the imputation of favoring fatality or rejecting revelation, and from month to month continued a vindication of the *Essay on Man* in the literary journal of that time, called *The Republic of Letters.*

Pope, who probably began to doubt the tendency of his own work, was glad that the positions of which he perceived himself not to know the full meaning, could by any mode of interpretation be made to mean well. How much he was pleased with his gratuitous defender the following letter evidently shows:—

88. "Let them hate me, so long as they fear me," a remark attributed to the Emperor Caligula by the biographer Suetonius ("Caligula," ch. 30, in *Lives of the Twelve Caesars).*

89. Matthew Concanen (1701–49), one of the Dunces.

90. January 2, 1727. The letter is printed in John and J. B. Nichols, *Illustrations of the Literary History of the Eighteenth Century* (1817–58), ii. 195–98.

March 24, 1743[91]

Sir,

I have just received from Mr. R.[92] two more of your "Letters." It is in the greatest hurry imaginable that I write this, but I cannot help thanking you in particular for your "Third Letter," which is so extremely clear, short, and full, that I think Mr. Crousaz ought never to have another answer, and deserved not so good an one. I can only say you do him too much honor and me too much right, so odd as the expression seems; for you have made my system as clear as I ought to have done, and could not. It is indeed the same system as mine, but illustrated with a ray of your own, as they say our natural body is the same still when it is glorified. I am sure I like it better than I did before, and so will every man else. I know I meant just what you explain, but I did not explain my own meaning so well as you. You understand me as well as I do myself, but you express me better than I could express myself. Pray accept the sincerest acknowledgments. I cannot but wish these letters were put together in one book, and intend (with your leave) to procure a translation of part at least of all of them into French, but I shall not proceed a step without your consent and opinion, etc.

By this fond and eager acceptance of an exculpatory comment Pope testified that, whatever might be the seeming or real import of the principles which he had received from Bolingbroke, he had not intentionally attacked religion; and Bolingbroke, if he meant to make him without his own consent an instrument of mischief, found him now engaged with his eyes open on the side of truth.

It is known that Bolingbroke concealed from Pope his real opinions. He once discovered them to Mr. Hooke,[93] who related them again to Pope, and was told by him that he must have mistaken the meaning of what he heard; and Bolingbroke, when Pope's uneasiness incited him to desire an explanation, declared that Hooke had misunderstood him.

Bolingbroke hated Warburton, who had drawn his pupil from him; and a little before Pope's death they had a dispute, from which they parted with mutual aversion.

From this time Pope lived in the closest intimacy with his commentator, and amply rewarded his kindness and his zeal; for he introduced him to Mr. Murray,[94] by whose interest he became preacher at Lincoln's Inn,[95] and to Mr. Allen, who gave him his niece and his estate, and by consequence a bishopric. When he died he left him the property

91. The correct date is April 11, 1739.

92. Jacob Robinson, who published the "Letters" of Warburton, mentioned below, in *The Works of the Learned* (not, as Johnson says, in the defunct *Republic of Letters*).

93. Nathaniel Hooke (d. 1763), biographer and historian.

94. William Murray, later Lord Chief Justice and first Earl of Mansfield.

95. One of the four "Inns of Court," which have the right to admit laws students to the bar.

of his works, a legacy which may be reasonably estimated at four thousand pounds.

Pope's fondness for the *Essay on Man* appeared by his desire of its propagation. Dobson, who had gained reputation by his version of Prior's *Solomon,* was employed by him to translate it into Latin verse, and was for that purpose some time at Twickenham; but he left his work, whatever was the reason, unfinished, and, by Benson's invitation, undertook the longer task of *Paradise Lost.* Pope then desired his friend to find a scholar who should turn his *Essay* into Latin prose; but no such performance has ever appeared.

Pope lived at this time "among the great,"[96] with that reception and respect to which his works entitled him, and which he had not impaired by any private misconduct or factious partiality. Though Bolingbroke was his friend, Walpole was not his enemy, but treated him with so much consideration as, at his request, to solicit and obtain from the French Minister an abbey for Mr. Southcote, whom he considered himself as obliged to reward, by this exertion of his interest, for the benefit which he had received from his attendance in a long illness.[97]

It was said that, when the Court was at Richmond, Queen Caroline had declared her intention to visit him. This may have been only a careless effusion, thought on no more: the report of such notice, however, was soon in many mouths; and, if I do not forget or misapprehend Savage's account, Pope, pretending to decline what was not yet offered, left his house for a time, not, I suppose, for any other reason than lest he should be thought to stay at home in expectation of an honor which would not be conferred. He was, therefore, angry at Swift, who represents him as "refusing the visits of a Queen,"[98] because he knew that what had never been offered had never been refused.

Beside the general system of morality supposed to be contained in the *Essay on Man,* it was his intention to write distinct poems upon the different duties or conditions of life; one of which is the *Epistle to Lord Bathurst* (1733) *on the Use of Riches,* a piece on which he declared great labor to have been bestowed.

Into this poem some incidents are historically thrown, and some known characters are introduced, with others of which it is difficult to say how far they are real or fictitious; but the praise of Kyrle, "the Man of Ross," deserves particular examination, who, after a long and pompous enumeration of his public works and private charities, is said to have diffused all those blessings from "five hundred a year."[99] Won-

96. Pope, *Imitations of Horace, Satires,* II. i. 133.

97. Thomas Southcote (1670–1748), priest. The French Prime Minister was Cardinal Fleury (1653–1743).

98. "A Libel on Dr. Delany," l. 74: "refusing" for "refused." See Pope to Swift, March 4, 1730.

99. *Epistle to Bathurst,* l. 280.

ders are willingly told and willingly heard. The truth is that Kyrle was a man of known integrity and active benevolence, by whose solicitation the wealthy were persuaded to pay contributions to his charitable schemes; this influence he obtained by an example of liberality exerted to the utmost extent of his power, and was thus enabled to give more than he had. This account Mr. Victor[1] received from the minister of the place, and I have preserved it that the praise of a good man, being made more credible, may be more solid. Narrations of romantic and impracticable virtue will be read with wonder, but that which is unattainable is recommended in vain: that good may be endeavored it must be shown to be possible.

This is the only piece in which the author has given a hint of his religion by ridiculing the ceremony of burning the Pope, and by mentioning with some indignation the inscription on the Monument.[2]

When this poem was first published, the dialogue, having no letters of direction, was perplexed and obscure. Pope seems to have written with no very distinct idea, for he calls that an *Epistle to Bathurst* in which Bathurst is introduced as speaking.[3]

He afterwards (1734) inscribed to Lord Cobham his *Characters of Men*, written with close attention to the operations of the mind and modifications[3a] of life. In this poem he has endeavored to establish and exemplify his favorite theory of the "ruling passion," by which he means an original direction of desire to some particular object, an innate affection which gives all action a determinate and invariable tendency, and operates upon the whole system of life either openly or more secretly by the intervention of some accidental or subordinate propension.

Of any passion thus innate and irresistible the existence may reasonably be doubted. Human characters are by no means constant; men change by change of place, of fortune, of acquaintance; he who is at one time a lover of pleasure is at another a lover of money. Those indeed who attain any excellence commonly spend life in one pursuit, for excellence is not often gained upon easier terms. But to the particular species of excellence, men are directed not by an ascendant planet or predominating humor, but by the first book which they read, some early conversation which they heard, or some accident which excited ardor and emulation.

It must be at least allowed that this "ruling passion," antecedent to reason and observation, must have an object independent on human

1. Benjamin Victor, theater manager.

2. Until 1831, this column commemorating the Great Fire of London (1666) bore an inscription stating that the fire was set by Catholics. The Pope was burned in effigy on November 17, the date of Elizabeth I's accession to the throne.

3. Warburton, apparently with Pope's permission, converted the poem into a dialogue.

3a. Modes.

contrivance, for there can be no natural desire of artificial good. No man therefore can be born, in the strict acceptation, a lover of money, for he may be born where money does not exist; nor can he be born, in a moral sense, a lover of his country, for society, politically regulated, is a state contradistinguished from a state of nature, and any attention to that coalition of interests which makes the happiness of a country is possible only to those whom inquiry and reflection have enabled to comprehend it.

This doctrine is in itself pernicious as well as false; its tendency is to produce the belief of a kind of moral predestination or overruling principle which cannot be resisted: he that admits it is prepared to comply with every desire that caprice or opportunity shall excite, and to flatter himself that he submits only to the lawful dominion of nature in obeying the resistless authority of his "ruling passion."

Pope has formed his theory with so little skill that, in the examples by which he illustrates and confirms it, he has confounded passions, appetites, and habits.

To the *Characters of Men* he added soon after, in an Epistle supposed to have been addressed to Martha Blount, but which the last edition has taken from her, the *Characters of Women.*[4] This poem, which was labored with great diligence, and, in the author's opinion, with great success, was neglected at its first publication, as the commentator supposes, because the public was informed by an advertisement that it contained "no character drawn from the life"; an assertion which Pope probably did not expect or wish to have been believed, and which he soon gave his readers sufficient reason to distrust, by telling them in a note that the work was imperfect, because part of his subject was "vice too high"[5] to be yet exposed.

The time, however, soon came in which it was safe to display the Duchess of Marlborough under the name of Atossa, and her character was inserted with no great honor to the writer's gratitude.[6]

He published from time to time (between 1730 and 1740) imitations of different poems of Horace, generally with his name, and once, as was suspected, without it.[7] What he was upon moral principles ashamed to own, he ought to have suppressed. Of these pieces it is useless to settle the dates, as they had seldom much relation to the times, and perhaps had been long in his hands.

This mode of imitation, in which the ancients are familiarized by

4. Warburton greatly disliked Martha Blount; he added a note to his edition of 1751 saying that the Lady addressed in the poem was imaginary.

5. *Of the Characters of Women,* n. to l. 199. "Vice too high" is quoted from *Imitations of Horace, Satires,* II. i. 60.

6. It is likely that the portrait of Atossa was drawn from more than one model. Sarah Jennings (1660–1744), wife of the great Duke of Marlborough, was a friend and supposed patron of Pope.

7. *Sober Advice from Horace* (1734) was published anonymously.

adapting their sentiments to modern topics, by making Horace say of Shakespeare what he originally said of Ennius, and accommodating his satires on Pantolabus and Nomentanus to the flatterers and prodigals of our own time, was first practiced in the reign of Charles the Second by Oldham[8] and Rochester; at least I remember no instances more ancient. It is a kind of middle composition between translation and original design, which pleases when the thoughts are unexpectedly applicable and the parallels lucky. It seems to have been Pope's favorite amusement, for he has carried it further than any former poet.

He published likewise a revival in smoother numbers of Dr. Donne's *Satires*, which was recommended to him by the Duke of Shrewsbury and the Earl of Oxford. They made no great impression on the public. Pope seems to have known their imbecility,[9] and therefore suppressed them while he was yet contending to rise in reputation, but ventured them when he thought their deficiencies more likely to be imputed to Donne than to himself.

The *Epistle to Dr. Arbuthnot,* which seems to be derived in its first design from Boileau's address, *A Son Esprit,*[10] was published in January, 1735, about a month before the death of him to whom it is inscribed. It is to be regretted that either honor or pleasure should have been missed by Arbuthnot, a man estimable for his learning, amiable for his life, and venerable for his piety.

Arbuthnot was a man of great comprehension, skillful in his profession, versed in the sciences, acquainted with ancient literature, and able to animate his mass of knowledge by a bright and active imagination; a scholar with great brilliancy of wit; a wit, who, in the crowd of life, retained and discovered a noble ardor of religious zeal.

In this poem Pope seems to reckon with the public. He vindicates himself from censures; and with dignity, rather than arrogance, enforces his own claims to kindness and respect.

Into this poem are interwoven several paragraphs which had been before printed as a fragment, and among them the satirical lines upon Addison, of which the last couplet has been twice corrected. It was at first,

> Who would not smile if such a man there be?
> Who would not laugh if Addison were he?

Then,

> Who would not grieve if such a man there be?
> Who would not laugh if Addison were he?

At last it is,

8. John Oldham (1653–83), satirical poet.
9. Feebleness.
10. *To his Spirit, Satire IX* by Nicholas Boileau-Despréaux (1636–1711), celebrated French critic and poet.

Who but must laugh if such a man there be?
Who would not weep if Atticus were he?[11]

He was at this time at open war with Lord Hervey, who had distinguished himself as a steady adherent to the Ministry; and, being offended with a contemptuous answer to one of his pamphlets, had summoned Pulteney to a duel.[12] Whether he or Pope made the first attack perhaps cannot now be easily known: he had written an invective against Pope, whom he calls, "Hard as thy heart, and as thy birth obscure," and hints that his father was a "hatter."[13] To this Pope wrote a reply in verse and prose; the verses are in this poem,[14] and the prose, though it was never sent, is printed among his Letters, but to a cool reader of the present time exhibits nothing but tedious malignity.[15]

His last satires of the general kind were two *Dialogues,* named from the year in which they were published, *Seventeen Hundred and Thirty-eight.* In these poems many are praised, and many are reproached. Pope was then entangled in the Opposition; a follower of the Prince of Wales, who dined at his house, and the friend of many who obstructed and censured the conduct of the Ministers.[16] His political partiality was too plainly shown; he forgot the prudence with which he passed, in his earlier years, uninjured and unoffending through much more violent conflicts of faction.

In the first *Dialogue,* having an opportunity of praising Allen of Bath, he asked his leave to mention him as a man not illustrious by any merit of his ancestors, and called him in his verses "low-born Allen." Men are seldom satisfied with praise introduced or followed by any mention of defect. Allen seems not to have taken any pleasure in his epithet, which was afterwards softened into "humble Allen."[17]

In the second *Dialogue* he took some liberty with one of the Foxes, among others; which Fox, in a reply to Lyttleton,[18] took an opportunity of repaying, by reproaching him with the friendship of a lampooner, who scattered his ink without fear or decency, and against whom he hoped the resentment of the legislature would quickly be discharged.

11. Ll. 213–14.

12. In the duel (1731) between Hervey and a leader of the Opposition, William Pulteney, neither was much injured. Hervey had great influence with Queen Caroline.

13. *Verses to the Imitator of Horace* (1733), l. 20, now thought to be a joint effort by Hervey and Lady Mary Wortley Montagu.

14. Hervey is caricatured as Sporus (*Epistle to Dr. Arbuthnot,* ll. 305–33).

15. Pope's *Letter to a Noble Lord* was first published in *Works* (1751).

16. Frederick, Prince of Wales (1707–51), was a center of the Opposition party in Parliament. His father, George II, supported the Ministry.

17. *Epilogue to the Satires,* i. 135.

18. Henry Fox, later Baron Holland, a follower of Walpole, is glanced at in Pope's *Epilogue to the Satires,* i. 71 and ii. 166–80, the latter passage including a "filthy simile." Pope's friend George (later Baron) Lyttelton was an Opposition Whig, Secretary to the Prince of Wales (1737), and an eager opponent of Walpole. He was a poet and patron of literature. His parliamentary exchange with Fox is narrated by Johnson in his "Life of Lyttelton," para. 8.

About this time Paul Whitehead, a small poet, was summoned before the Lords for a poem called *Manners*, together with Dodsley, his publisher. Whitehead, who hung loose upon society, skulked and escaped; but Dodsley's shop and family made his appearance necessary. He was, however, soon dismissed; and the whole process was probably intended rather to intimidate Pope than to punish Whitehead.

Pope never afterwards attempted to join the patriot with the poet, nor drew his pen upon statesmen. That he desisted from his attempts of reformation is imputed, by his commentator,[19] to his despair of prevailing over the corruption of the time. He was not likely to have been ever of opinion that the dread of his satire would countervail the love of power or of money: he pleased himself with being important and formidable, and gratified sometimes his pride, and sometimes his resentment; till at last he began to think he should be more safe if he were less busy.

The *Memoirs of Scriblerus*, published about this time,[20] extend only to the first book of a work, projected in concert by Pope, Swift, and Arbuthnot, who used to meet in the time of Queen Anne, and denominated themselves the "Scriblerus Club." Their purpose was to censure the abuses of learning by a fictitious life of an infatuated scholar.[21] They were dispersed; the design was never completed; and Warburton laments its miscarriage as an event very disastrous to polite letters.[22]

If the whole may be estimated by this specimen, which seems to be the production of Arbuthnot, with a few touches perhaps by Pope, the want of more will not be much lamented, for the follies which the writer ridicules are so little practiced that they are not known; nor can the satire be understood but by the learned: he raises phantoms of absurdity, and then drives them away. He cures diseases that were never felt.

For this reason this joint production of three great writers has never obtained any notice from mankind; it has been little read, or when read has been forgotten, as no man could be wiser, better, or merrier, by remembering it.

The design cannot boast of much originality; for, besides its general resemblance to *Don Quixote*, there will be found in it particular imitations of the *History of Mr. Oufle*.[23]

Swift carried so much of it into Ireland as supplied him with hints for his *Travels*;[24] and with those the world might have been contented, though the rest had been suppressed.

Pope had sought for images and sentiments in a region not known to have been explored by many other of the English writers; he had

19. Warburton.
20. In April, 1741.
21. Scriblerus is a pedant "infatuated" with his own learning and scholarly talent.
22. Belles-lettres; literature.
23. By Laurent Bordelon. The French original appeared in 1710.
24. *Gulliver's Travels* (1726).

consulted the modern writers of Latin poetry, a class of authors whom Boileau endeavored to bring into contempt, and who are too generally neglected. Pope, however, was not ashamed of their acquaintance, nor ungrateful for the advantages which he might have derived from it. A small selection from the Italians who wrote in Latin had been published at London, about the latter end of the last century, by a man who concealed his name, but whom his Preface shows to have been well qualified for his undertaking.[25] This collection Pope amplified by more than half, and (1740) published it in two volumes, but injuriously omitted his predecessor's Preface. To these books, which had nothing but the mere text, no regard was paid; the authors were still neglected, and the editor was neither praised nor censured.

He did not sink into idleness; he had planned a work which he considered as subsequent to his *Essay on Man,* of which he has given this account to Dr. Swift.

> March 25, 1736.
>
> If ever I write any more Epistles in verse one of them shall be addressed to you. I have long concerted it, and begun it; but I would make what bears your name as finished as my last work ought to be, that is to say, more finished than any of the rest. The subject is large, and will divide into four Epistles, which naturally follow the *Essay on Man,* viz. 1. Of the extent and limits of human reason and science. 2. A view of the useful and therefore attainable, and of the unuseful and therefore unattainable arts. 3. Of the nature, ends, application, and use of different capacities. 4. Of the use of learning, of the science of the world, and of wit. It will conclude with a satire against the misapplication of all these, exemplified by pictures, characters, and examples.

This work in its full extent, being now afflicted with an asthma, and finding the powers of life gradually declining, he had no longer courage to undertake; but, from the materials which he had provided, he added, at Warburton's request, another book to *The Dunciad,* of which the design is to ridicule such studies as are either hopeless or useless, as either pursue what is unattainable, or what, if it be attained, is of no use.

When this book was printed (1742) the laurel had been for some time upon the head of Cibber;[26] a man whom it cannot be supposed that Pope could regard with much kindness or esteem, though in one of the *Imitations of Horace* he has liberally enough praised *The Careless Husband.*[27] In *The Dunciad,* among other worthless scribblers, he had mentioned Cibber, who, in his *Apology,* complains of the great poet's un-

25. *Anthology, or a Selection of Latin Poems Written by Italians* (1684), edited by Francis Atterbury, who had been a close friend of Pope. See p. 505.

26. Colley Cibber (1671–1757), dramatist and theater manager, was made Poet Laureate in 1730.

27. *Imitations of Horace, Epistles,* II. i. 91–92.

kindness as more injurious, "because," says he, "I never have offended him."[28]

It might have been expected that Pope should have been, in some degree, mollified by this submissive gentleness; but no such consequence appeared. Though he condescended to commend Cibber once, he mentioned him afterwards contemptuously in one of his *Satires,* and again in his *Epistle to Arbuthnot,*[29] and in the fourth book of *The Dunciad* attacked him with acrimony, to which the provocation is not easily discoverable. Perhaps he imagined that, in ridiculing the Laureate, he satirized those by whom the laurel had been given, and gratified that ambitious petulance with which he affected to insult the great.

The severity of this satire left Cibber no longer any patience. He had confidence enough in his own powers to believe that he could disturb the quiet of his adversary, and doubtless did not want instigators, who, without any care about the victory, desired to amuse themselves by looking on the contest. He therefore gave the town a pamphlet,[30] in which he declares his resolution from that time never to bear another blow without returning it, and to tire out his adversary by perseverance, if he cannot conquer him by strength.

The incessant and unappeasable malignity of Pope he imputes to a very distant cause. After the *Three Hours after Marriage*[31] had been driven off the stage, by the offense which the mummy and crocodile gave the audience, while the exploded[32] scene was yet fresh in memory, it happened that Cibber played Bayes in *The Rehearsal;*[33] and, as it had been usual to enliven the part by the mention of any recent theatrical transactions, he said that he once thought to have introduced his lovers disguised in a mummy and a crocodile. "This," says he, "was received with loud claps, which indicated contempt of the play." Pope, who was behind the scenes, meeting him as he left the stage, attacked him, as he says, with all the virulence of a "wit out of his senses"; to which he replied "that he would take no other notice of what was said by so particular[34] a man than to declare that, as often as he played that part, he would repeat the same provocation."

He shows his opinion to be that Pope was one of the authors of the

28. *Apology for the Life of Colley Cibber* (1740).

29. *Imitations of Horace, Satires,* II. i. 34; *Epistle to Dr. Arbuthnot,* ll. 97, 373. These two poems were published before *Epistles,* II. i, in which Cibber is supposedly praised.

30. *A Letter to Mr. Pope* (1742).

31. By Gay, with the assistance of Arbuthnot and Pope (1717). In it, two young lovers were introduced in the disguises of a mummy and a crocodile.

32. Hissed off the stage.

33. A play (1671) by George Villiers, second Duke of Buckingham, and others, presumably intended to attack Dryden as Bayes (the Poet Laureate). In *Three Hours,* Cibber had played a role that satirized himself.

34. Odd, singular.

play which he so zealously defended, and adds an idle story of Pope's behavior at a tavern.[35]

The pamphlet was written with little power of thought or language, and, if suffered to remain without notice, would have been very soon forgotten. Pope had now been enough acquainted with human life to know, if his passion had not been too powerful for his understanding, that from a contention like his with Cibber the world seeks nothing but diversion, which is given at the expense of the higher character. When Cibber lampooned Pope, curiosity was excited; what Pope would say of Cibber nobody inquired, but in hope that Pope's asperity might betray his pain and lessen his dignity.

He should, therefore, have suffered the pamphlet to flutter and die, without confessing that it stung him. The dishonor of being shown as Cibber's antagonist could never be compensated by the victory. Cibber had nothing to lose; when Pope had exhausted all his malignity upon him, he would rise in the esteem both of his friends and his enemies. Silence only could have made him despicable: the blow which did not appear to be felt would have been struck in vain.

But Pope's irascibility prevailed, and he resolved to tell the whole English world that he was at war with Cibber; and to show that he thought him no common adversary he prepared no common vengeance: he published a new edition of *The Dunciad,* in which he degraded Theobald from his painful pre-eminence, and enthroned Cibber in his stead. Unhappily the two heroes were of opposite characters, and Pope was unwilling to lose what he had already written; he has therefore depraved his poem by giving to Cibber the old books, the cold pedantry, and sluggish pertinacity of Theobald.

Pope was ignorant enough of his own interest to make another change, and introduced Osborne contending for the prize among the booksellers.[36] Osborne was a man entirely destitute of shame, without sense of any disgrace but that of poverty. He told me, when he was doing that which raised Pope's resentment, that he should be put into *The Dunciad,* but he had the fate of Cassandra.[37] I gave no credit to his prediction till in time I saw it accomplished. The shafts of satire were directed equally in vain against Cibber and Osborne; being repelled by the impenetrable impudence of one, and deadened by the impassive dullness of the other. Pope confessed his own pain by his anger; but he gave no pain to those who had provoked him. He was able to hurt none but himself: by transferring the same ridicule from one to another he destroyed its efficacy; for, by showing that what he had said of one he

35. At a whorehouse, according to Cibber. "Idle" means frivolous or trifling.
36. Thomas Osburne (d. 1767) appears in *The Dunciad,* ii. 167–190.
37. The Trojan princess, whose true prophecies were fated never to be believed.

was ready to say of another, he reduced himself to the insignificance of his own magpie, who from his cage calls cuckold at a venture.[38]

Cibber, according to his engagement, repaid *The Dunciad* with another pamphlet,[39] which, Pope said, "would be as good as a dose of hartshorn to him;[40] but his tongue and his heart were at variance. I have heard Mr. Richardson[41] relate that he attended his father the painter on a visit, when one of Cibber's pamphlets came into the hands of Pope, who said, "These things are my diversion." They sat by him while he perused it, and saw his features writhen with anguish; and young Richardson said to his father, when they returned, that he hoped to be preserved from such diversion as had been that day the lot of Pope.

From this time, finding his diseases more oppressive, and his vital powers gradually declining, he no longer strained his faculties with any original composition, nor proposed any other employment for his remaining life than the revisal and correction of his former works, in which he received advice and assistance from Warburton, whom he appears to have trusted and honored in the highest degree.

He laid aside his epic poem, perhaps without much loss to mankind; for his hero was Brutus the Trojan, who, according to a ridiculous fiction, established a colony in Britain. The subject, therefore, was of the fabulous age; the actors were a race upon whom imagination has been exhausted and attention wearied, and to whom the mind will not easily be recalled when it is invited in blank verse, which Pope had adopted with great imprudence, and, I think, without due consideration of the nature of our language. The sketch is, at least in part, preserved by Ruffhead; by which it appears that Pope was thoughtless enough to model the names of his heroes with terminations not consistent with the time or country in which he places them.

He lingered through the next year; but perceived himself, as he expresses it, "going down the hill."[42] He had for at least five years been afflicted with an asthma and other disorders, which his physicians were unable to relieve. Towards the end of his life he consulted Dr. Thomson, a man who had, by large promises and free censures of the common practice of physic,[43] forced himself up into sudden reputation. Thomson declared his distemper to be a dropsy, and evacuated part of the water by tincture of jalap,[44] but confessed that his belly did not

38. At random (*Of the Characters of Men*, ll. 5–6).

39. *Another Occasional Letter to Mr. Pope* (1744).

40. Pope to Warburton, January 12, 1744. Hartshorn (ammonia) is a stimulant.

41. Jonathan Richardson, the younger (1694–1771), writer on art and collector. His father was a well-known painter and theorist.

42. Pope to Warburton, February 21, 1744.

43. Medicine.

44. A purgative drug.

subside. Thomson had many enemies, and Pope was persuaded to dismiss him.

While he was yet capable of amusement and conversation, as he was one day sitting in the air with Lord Bolingbroke and Lord Marchmont, he saw his favorite Martha Blount at the bottom of the terrace, and asked Lord Bolingbroke to go and hand her up. Bolingbroke, not liking his errand, crossed his legs and sat still; but Lord Marchmont,[45] who was younger and less captious, waited on the lady, who, when he came to her, asked, "What, is he not dead yet?" She is said to have neglected him with shameful unkindness in the latter time of his decay; yet, of the little which he had to leave, she had a very great part. Their acquaintance began early: the life of each was pictured on the other's mind; their conversation, therefore, was endearing, for when they met there was an immediate coalition of congenial notions. Perhaps he considered her unwillingness to approach the chamber of sickness as female weakness or human frailty; perhaps he was conscious to himself of peevishness and impatience, or, though he was offended by her inattention, might yet consider her merit as overbalancing her fault; and, if he had suffered his heart to be alienated from her, he could have found nothing that might fill her place: he could have only shrunk within himself; it was too late to transfer his confidence or fondness.

In May, 1744, his death was approaching; on the sixth he was all day delirious, which he mentioned four days afterwards as a sufficient humiliation of the vanity of man; he afterwards complained of seeing things as through a curtain and in false colors, and one day, in the presence of Dodsley, asked what arm it was that came out from the wall. He said that his greatest inconvenience was inability to think.

Bolingbroke sometimes wept over him in this state of helpless decay, and being told by Spence that Pope, at the intermission of his deliriousness, was always saying something kind either of his present or absent friends, and that his humanity seemed to have survived his understanding, answered, "It has so." And added, "I never in my life knew a man that had so tender a heart for his particular friends, or a more general friendship for mankind." At another time he said, "I have known Pope these thirty years, and value myself more in his friendship than—"[46] his grief then suppressed his voice.

Pope expressed undoubting confidence of a future state. Being asked by his friend Mr. Hooke, a Papist, whether he would not die like his father and mother, and whether a priest should not be called, he answered, "I do not think it essential, but it will be very right; and I thank you for putting me in mind of it."

45. Hugh Hume, third Earl of Marchmont (1708–94), a close friend.

46. Spence, *Observations*, #652–53.

In the morning, after the priest had given him the last sacraments, he said, "There is nothing that is meritorious but virtue and friendship, and indeed friendship itself is only a part of virtue."

He died in the evening of the thirtieth day of May, 1744, so placidly that the attendants did not discern the exact time of his expiration. He was buried at Twickenham, near his father and mother, where a monument has been erected to him by his commentator, the Bishop of Gloucester.[47]

He left the care of his papers to his executors, first to Lord Bolingbroke, and if he should not be living to the Earl of Marchmont, undoubtedly expecting them to be proud of the trust and eager to extend his fame. But let no man dream of influence beyond his life. After a decent time Dodsley the bookseller went to solicit preference as the publisher, and was told that the parcel had not been yet inspected; and whatever was the reason the world has been disappointed of what was "reserved for the next age."[48]

He lost, indeed, the favor of Bolingbroke by a kind of posthumous offense. The political pamphlet called *The Patriot King*[49] had been put into his hands that he might procure the impression of the very few copies to be distributed according to the author's direction among his friends, and Pope assured him that no more had been printed than were allowed; but soon after his death the printer brought and resigned a complete edition of fifteen hundred copies which Pope had ordered him to print and to retain in secret. He kept, as was observed, his engagement to Pope better than Pope had kept it to his friend; and nothing was known of the transaction till, upon the death of his employer, he thought himself obliged to deliver the books to the right owner, who, with great indignation, made a fire in his yard and delivered the whole impression to the flames.

Hitherto nothing had been done which was not naturally dictated by resentment of violated faith: resentment more acrimonious as the violator had been more loved or more trusted. But here the anger might have stopped; the injury was private, and there was little danger from the example.

Bolingbroke, however, was not yet satisfied; his thirst of vengeance excited him to blast the memory of the man over whom he had wept in his last struggles, and he employed Mallet, another friend of Pope, to tell the tale to the public with all its aggravations.[50] Warburton, whose heart was warm with his legacy and tender by the recent separation, thought it proper for him to interpose, and undertook, not indeed to

47. Warburton became Bishop of Gloucester in 1759.

48. *Imitations of Horace, Satires,* II. i. 59–60.

49. Written by Bolingbroke.

50. David Mallet (?1705–65), minor poet and dramatist, attacked Pope in the Advertisement to an edition of *The Patriot King* published in 1749.

vindicate the action, for breach of trust has always something criminal, but to extenuate it by an apology.[51] Having advanced, what cannot be denied, that moral obliquity is made more or less excusable by the motives that produce it, he inquires what evil purpose could have induced Pope to break his promise. He could not delight his vanity by usurping the work, which, though not sold in shops, had been shown to a number more than sufficient to preserve the author's claim; he could not gratify his avarice, for he could not sell his plunder till Bolingbroke was dead; and even then, if the copy was left to another, his fraud would be defeated, and if left to himself would be useless.

Warburton therefore supposes, with great appearance of reason, that the irregularity of his conduct proceeded wholly from his zeal for Bolingbroke, who might perhaps have destroyed the pamphlet, which Pope thought it his duty to preserve, even without its author's approbation. To this apology an answer was written in a *Letter to the Most Impudent Man Living.*[52]

He brought some reproach upon his own memory by the petulant and contemptuous mention made in his will of Mr. Allen, and an affected repayment of his benefactions. Mrs. Blount, as the known friend and favorite of Pope, had been invited to the house of Allen, where she comported herself with such indecent arrogance that she parted from Mrs. Allen in a state of irreconcilable dislike, and the door was forever barred against her. This exclusion she resented with so much bitterness as to refuse any legacy from Pope, unless he left the world with a disavowal of obligation to Allen. Having been long under her dominion, now tottering in the decline of life and unable to resist the violence of her temper, or, perhaps with the prejudice of a lover, persuaded that she had suffered improper treatment, he complied with her demand and polluted his will with female resentment.[53] Allen accepted the legacy, which he gave to the Hospital at Bath, observing that Pope was always a bad accomptant, and that if to 150£ he had put a cipher more he had come nearer to the truth.

The person of Pope is well known not to have been formed by the nicest model. He has, in his account of the "Little Club."[54] compared himself to a spider, and by another is described as protuberant behind and before. He is said to have been beautiful in his infancy; but he was of a constitution originally feeble and weak, and as bodies of a tender frame are easily distorted his deformity was probably in part the effect of his application. His stature was so low that, to bring him to a level

51. *A Letter to the Editor of the Letters on the Spirit of Patriotism* (1749).
52. By Bolingbroke (1749).
53. Pope also left Allen and Warburton most of his books.
54. *Guardian,* no. 92.

with common tables, it was necessary to raise his seat. But his face was not displeasing, and his eyes were animated and vivid.

By natural deformity or accidental distortion his vital functions were so much disordered that his life was a "long disease."[55] His most frequent assailant was the headache, which he used to relieve by inhaling the steam of coffee, which he very frequently required.

Most of what can be told concerning his petty peculiarities was communicated by a female domestic of the Earl of Oxford, who knew him perhaps after the middle of his life. He was then so weak as to stand in perpetual need of female attendance; extremely sensible of cold, so that he wore a kind of fur doublet under a shirt of very coarse warm linen with fine sleeves. When he rose he was invested in bodice made of stiff canvas, being scarce able to hold himself erect till they were laced, and he then put on a flannel waistcoat. One side was contracted. His legs were so slender that he englarged their bulk with three pair of stockings, which were drawn on and off by the maid; for he was not able to dress or undress himself, and neither went to bed nor rose without help. His weakness made it very difficult for him to be clean.

His hair had fallen almost all away, and he used to dine some times with Lord Oxford, privately, in a velvet cap. His dress of ceremony was black, with a tie-wig and a little sword.

The indulgence and accommodation which his sickness required had taught him all the unpleasing and unsocial qualities of a valetudinary man. He expected that everything should give way to his ease or humor, as a child whose parents will not hear her cry has an unresisted dominion in the nursery.

C'est que l'enfant toujours est homme,
C'est que l'homme est toujours enfant.[56]

When he wanted to sleep he "nodded in company";[57] and once slumbered at his own table while the Prince of Wales was talking of poetry.

The reputation which his friendship gave procured him many invitations; but he was a very troublesome inmate. He brought no servant, and had so many wants that a numerous attendance was scarcely able to supply them. Wherever he was he left no room for another, because he exacted the attention and employed the activity of the whole family. His errands were so frequent and frivolous that the footmen in time avoided and neglected him, and the Earl of Oxford discharged some of the servants for their resolute refusal of his messages. The maids, when they had neglected their business, alleged that they had been employed by Mr. Pope. One of his constant demands was of coffee in the night, and to the woman that waited on him in his chamber he was very

55. *Epistle to Dr. Arbuthnot,* l. 132.
56. "The child is always a man, the man always a child."
57. See *Imitations of Horace, Satires,* II. i. 13.

burthensome; but he was careful to recompense her want of sleep, and Lord Oxford's servant declared that in a house where her business was to answer his call she would not ask for wages.

He had another fault, easily incident to those who suffering much pain think themselves entitled to whatever pleasures they can snatch. He was too indulgent to his appetite: he loved meat highly seasoned and of strong taste, and, at the intervals of the table, amused himself with biscuits and dry conserves. If he sat down to a variety of dishes he would oppress his stomach with repletion, and though he seemed angry when a dram was offered him, did not forbear to drink it. His friends, who knew the avenues to his heart, pampered him with presents of luxury, which he did not suffer to stand neglected. The death of great men is not always proportioned to the luster of their lives. Hannibal, says Juvenal, did not perish by a javelin or a sword; the slaughters of Cannae were revenged by a ring.[58] The death of Pope was imputed by some of his friends to a silver saucepan, in which it was his delight to heat potted lampreys.

That he loved too well to eat is certain; but that his sensuality shortened his life will not be hastily concluded when it is remembered that a conformation so irregular lasted six and fifty years, notwithstanding such pertinacious diligence of study and meditation.

In all his intercourse with mankind he had great delight in artifice, and endeavored to attain all his purposes by indirect and unsuspected methods. "He hardly drank tea without a stratagem."[59] If at the house of his friends he wanted any accommodation he was not willing to ask for it in plain terms, but would mention it remotely as something convenient; though, when it was procured, he soon made it appear for whose sake it had been recommended. Thus he teased Lord Orrery till he obtained a screen. He practiced his arts on such small occasions that Lady Bolingbroke used to say, in a French phrase, that "he played the politician about cabbages and turnips." His unjustifiable impression of *The Patriot King*, as it can be imputed to no particular motive, must have proceeded from his general habit of secrecy and cunning: he caught an opportunity of a sly trick, and pleased himself with the thought of outwitting Bolingbroke.

In familiar or convivial conversation it does not appear that he excelled. He may be said to have resembled Dryden, as being not one that was distinguished by vivacity in company. It is remarkable that, so near his time, so much should be known of what he has written, and so little of what he said: traditional memory retains no sallies of raillery nor

58. Juvenal, *Satires*, x. 163–66. The greatest of Hannibal's victories over the Romans occurred at Cannae (216 B.C.) in southern Italy. Eventually he committed suicide by taking poison which he kept in a ring.

59. Johnson echoes a phrase in the poet Edward Young's satires: *Love of Fame, The Universal Passion: Satire VI, On Women* (1728), l. 188.

sentences of observation; nothing either pointed or solid, either wise or merry. One apophthegm only stands upon record. When an objection raised against his inscription for Shakespeare was defended by the authority of Patrick,[60] he replied,—*horresco referens*[61]—that "he would allow the publisher[62] of a dictionary to know the meaning of a single word, but not of two words put together."

He was fretful and easily displeased, and allowed himself to be capriciously resentful. He would sometimes leave Lord Oxford silently, no one could tell why, and was to be courted back by more letters and messages than the footmen were willing to carry. The table was indeed infested by Lady Mary Wortley,[63] who was the friend of Lady Oxford, and who, knowing his peevishness, could by no entreaties be restrained from contradicting him, till their disputes were sharpened to such asperity that one or the other quitted the house.

He sometimes condescended to be jocular with servants or inferiors; but by no merriment, either of others or his own, was he ever seen excited to laughter.

Of his domestic character frugality was a part eminently remarkable. Having determined not to be dependent he determined not to be in want, and therefore wisely and magnanimously rejected all temptations to expense unsuitable to his fortune. This general care must be universally approved; but it sometimes appeared in petty artifices of parsimony, such as the practice of writing his compositions on the back of letters, as may be seen in the remaining copy of the *Iliad,* by which perhaps in five years five shillings were saved; or in a niggardly reception of his friends and scantiness of entertainment, as when he had two guests in his house he would set at supper a single pint upon the table, and having himself taken two small glasses would retire and say, "Gentlemen, I leave you to your wine." Yet he tells his friends that "he has a heart for all, a house for all, and, whatever they may think, a fortune for all."[64]

He sometimes, however, made a splendid dinner, and is said to have wanted no part of the skill or elegance which such performances require. That this magnificence should be often displayed, that obstinate prudence with which he conducted his affairs would not permit; for his revenue, certain and casual, amounted only to about eight hundred pounds a year, of which, however, he declares himself able to assign one hundred to charity.

60. Samuel Patrick (1684–1748), classical scholar and lexicographer.

61. "I shudder in speaking of it" (*Aeneid,* ii. 204). Johnson was, of course, himself a lexicographer.

62. Editor.

63. Lady Mary Wortley Montagu (1689–1762), whom Pope perhaps loved at one time; in later life they became satirical enemies.

64. To Swift, March 23, 1737.

Of this fortune, which as it arose from public approbation was very honorably obtained, his imagination seems to have been too full: it would be hard to find a man, so well entitled to notice by his wit that ever delighted so much in talking of his money. In his letters and in his poems, his garden and his grotto, his quincunx and his vines, or some hints of his opulence, are always to be found. The great topic of his ridicule is poverty: the crimes with which he reproaches his antagonists are their debts, their habitation in the Mint,[65] and their want of a dinner. He seems to be of an opinion, not very uncommon in the world, that to want money is to want everything.

Next to the pleasure of contemplating his possessions seems to be that of enumerating the men of high rank with whom he was acquainted, and whose notice he loudly proclaims not to have been obtained by any practices of meanness or servility; a boast which was never denied to be true, and to which very few poets have ever aspired. Pope never set genius to sale: he never flattered those whom he did not love, or praised those whom he did not esteem. Savage, however, remarked that he began a little to relax his dignity when he wrote a distich for "his Highness's dog."[66]

His admiration of the great seems to have increased in the advance of life. He passed over peers and statemen to inscribe his *Iliad* to Congreve, with a magnanimity of which the praise had been complete, had his friend's virtue been equal to his wit. Why he was chosen for so great an honor it is not now possible to know; there is no trace in literary history of any particular intimacy between them. The name of Congreve appears in the letters among those of his other friends, but without any observable distinction or consequence.

To his latter works, however, he took care to annex names dignified with titles, but was not very happy in his choice; for, except Lord Bathurst, none of his noble friends were such as that a good man would wish to have his intimacy with them known to posterity: he can derive little honor from the notice of Cobham, Burlington, or Bolingbroke.[67]

Of his social qualities, if an estimate be made from his letters, an opinion too favorable cannot easily be formed; they exhibit a perpetual and unclouded effulgence of general benevolence and particular fondness. There is nothing but liberality, gratitude, constancy, and tenderness.[68] It has been so long said as to be commonly believed that

65. A district in Southwark, in which debtors were immune to arrest.

66. For the dog's collar: "I am his Highness' dog at Kew;/Pray tell me, Sir, whose dog are you?" His Highness was Frederick, Prince of Wales.

67. Bolingbroke was a deistic philosopher and rake. Burlington was an extravagant architect and patron of the arts; perhaps Johnson thought he lessened his dignity by the practice of architecture. Sir Richard Temple, Viscount Cobham (1675–1749) was a general; Stowe, his estate, was noted for its gardens. What Johnson held against him is unknown.

68. Pope tampered with his letters before publishing them. The practice was common at the time.

the true characters of men may be found in their letters, and that he who writes to his friend lays his heart open before him. But the truth is that such were the simple friendships of the Golden Age, and are now the friendships only of children. Very few can boast of hearts which they dare lay open to themselves, and of which, by whatever accident exposed, they do not shun a distinct and continued view; and certainly what we hide from ourselves we do not show to our friends. There is, indeed, no transaction which offers stronger temptations to fallacy and sophistication than epistolary intercourse. In the eagerness of conversation the first emotions of the mind often burst out before they have considered; in the tumult of business interest and passion have their genuine effect; but a friendly letter is a calm and deliberate performance in the cool of leisure, in the stillness of solitude, and surely no man sits down to depreciate by design his own character.

Friendship has no tendency to secure veracity, for by whom can a man so much wish to be thought better than he is as by him whose kindness he desires to gain or keep? Even in writing to the world there is less constraint: the author is not confronted with his reader, and takes his chance of approbation among the different dispositions of mankind; but a letter is addressed to a single mind of which the prejudices and partialities are known, and must therefore please, if not by favoring them, by forbearing to oppose them.

To charge those favorable representations, which men give of their own minds, with the guilt of hypocritical falsehood, would show more severity than knowledge. The writer commonly believes himself. Almost every man's thoughts, while they are general, are right; and most hearts are pure while temptation is away. It is easy to awaken generous sentiments in privacy; to despise death when there is no danger; to glow with benevolence when there is nothing to be given. While such ideas are formed they are felt, and self-love does not suspect the gleam of virtue to be the meteor of fancy.

If the letters of Pope are considered merely as compositions, they seem to be premeditated and artificial. It is one thing to write because there is something which the mind wishes to discharge, and another to solicit the imagination because ceremony or vanity requires something to be written. Pope confesses his early letters to be vitiated with "affectation and ambition";[69] to know whether he disentangled himself from these perverters of epistolary integrity his book and his life must be set in comparison.

One of his favorite topics is contempt of his own poetry. For this, if it had been real, he would deserve no commendation, and in this he was certainly not sincere; for his high value of himself was sufficiently observed, and of what could he be proud but of his poetry? He writes,

69. Pope's Preface to his *Letters* (1737).

he says, when "he has just nothing else to do";[70] yet Swift complains that he was never at leisure for conversation because he "had always some poetical scheme in his head."[71] It was punctually required that his writing box should be set upon his bed before he rose; and Lord Oxford's domestic related that, in the dreadful winter of '40, she was called from her bed by him four times in one night to supply him with paper, lest he should lose a thought.

He pretends insensibility to censure and criticism, though it was observed by all who knew him that every pamphlet disturbed his quiet, and that his extreme irritability laid him open to perpetual vexation; but he wished to despise his critics, and therefore hoped that he did despise them.

As he happened to live in two reigns when the Court paid little attention to poetry he nursed in his mind a foolish disesteem of kings, and proclaims that "he never sees courts."[72] Yet a little regard shown him by the Prince of Wales melted his obduracy, and he had not much to say when he was asked by his Royal Highness "how he could love a Prince while he disliked Kings?"[73]

He very frequently professes contempt of the world, and represents himself as looking on mankind, sometimes with gay indifference, as on emmets[74] of a hillock below his serious attention, and sometimes with gloomy indignation, as on monsters more worthy of hatred than of pity. These were dispositions apparently counterfeited. How could he despise those whom he lived by pleasing, and on whose approbation his esteem of himself was superstructed? Why should he hate those to whose favor he owed his honor and his ease? Of things that terminate in human life the world is the proper judge: to despise its sentence, if it were possible, is not just; and if it were just is not possible. Pope was far enough from this unreasonable temper; he was sufficiently "a fool to fame,"[75] and his fault was that he pretended to neglect it. His levity and his sullenness were only in his letters; he passed through common life, sometimes vexed and sometimes pleased, with the natural emotions of common men.

His scorn of the great is repeated too often to be real: no man thinks much of that which he despises; and as falsehood is always in danger of inconsistency he makes it his boast at another time that he lives among them.

It is evident that his own importance swells often in his mind. He is afraid of writing lest the clerks of the post office should know his secrets; he has many enemies; he considers himself as surrounded by

70. Preface to his *Works* (1717).
71. Swift to Mary Caesar, July 30, 1733.
72. Pope to Swift, ?January 1728.
73. Ruffhead, *Life of Pope*, p. 535.
74. Ants.
75. *Epistle to Dr. Arbuthnot*, l. 127.

universal jealousy; "after many deaths, and many dispersions, two or three of us," says he, "may still be brought together, not to plot, but to divert ourselves, and the world too, if it pleases"; and they can live together, and "show what friends wits may be, in spite of all the fools in the world."[76] All this while it was likely that the clerks did not know his hand: he certainly had no more enemies than a public character like his inevitably excites, and with what degree of friendship the wits might live very few were so much fools as ever to inquire.

Some part of this pretended discontent he learned from Swift, and expresses it, I think, most frequently in his correspondence with him. Swift's resentment was unreasonable, but it was sincere; Pope's was the mere mimicry of his friend, a fictitious part which he began to play before it became him. When he was only twenty-five years old he related that "a glut of study and retirement had thrown him on the world," and that there was danger lest "a glut of the world should throw him back upon study and retirement."[77] To this Swift answered with great propriety that Pope had not yet either acted or suffered enough in the world to have become weary of it. And, indeed, it must be some very powerful reason that can drive back to solitude him who has once enjoyed the pleasures of society.

In the letters both of Swift and Pope there appears such narrowness of mind as makes them insensible of any excellence that has not some affinity with their own, and confines their esteem and approbation to so small a number, that whoever should form his opinion of the age from their representation, would suppose them to have lived amidst ignorance and barbarity, unable to find among their contemporaries either virtue or intelligence, and persecuted by those that could not understand them.

When Pope murmurs at the world, when he professes contempt of fame, when he speaks of riches and poverty, of success and disappointment, with negligent indifference, he certainly does not express his habitual and settled sentiments, but either willfully disguises his own character, or, what is more likely, invests himself with temporary qualities, and sallies out in the colors of the present moment. His hopes and fears, his joys and sorrows, acted strongly upon his mind, and if he differed from others it was not by carelessness. He was irritable and resentful: his malignity to Philips, whom he had first made ridiculous, and then hated for being angry, continued too long. Of his vain desire to make Bentley contemptible, I never heard any adequate reason.[78]

76. To Swift, September 14, 1725, and March 23, 1737.

77. To Swift, ?August 1723.

78. Richard Bentley (1662–1742), the greatest classical scholar of the age. Pope attacked him in *The Dunciad,* iv. 189–274, and elsewhere. Bentley is supposed to have remarked about Pope's translation of the *Iliad,* "It is a pretty poem, Mr. Pope, but you must not call it Homer."

He was sometimes wanton in his attacks, and before Chandos, Lady [Mary] Wortley, and Hill, was mean in his retreat.

The virtues which seem to have had most of his affection were liberality and fidelity of friendship, in which it does not appear that he was other than he describes himself. His fortune did not suffer his charity to be splendid and conspicuous, but he assisted Dodsley with a hundred pounds that he might open a shop; and of the subscription of forty pounds a year that he raised for Savage twenty were paid by himself. He was accused of loving money, but his love was eagerness to gain, not solicitude to keep it.

In the duties of friendship he was zealous and constant: his early maturity of mind commonly united him with men older than himself, and therefore, without attaining any considerable length of life, he saw many companions of his youth sink into the grave; but it does not appear that he lost a single friend by coldness or by injury: those who loved him once continued their kindness. His ungrateful mention of Allen in his will was the effect of his adherence to one whom he had known much longer, and whom he naturally loved with greater fondness. His violation of the trust reposed in him by Bolingbroke could have no motive inconsistent with the warmest affection; he either thought the action so near to indifferent that he forgot it, or so laudable that he expected his friend to approve it.

It was reported, with such confidence as almost to enforce belief, that in the papers entrusted to his executors was found a defamatory Life of Swift, which he had prepared as an instrument of vengeance to be used, if any provocation should be ever given. About this I inquired of the Earl of Marchmont, who assured me that no such piece was among his remains.[79]

The religion in which he lived and died was that of the Church of Rome, to which in his correspondence with Racine he professes himself a sincere adherent.[80] That he was not scrupulously pious in some part of his life is known by many idle and indecent applications of sentences taken from the Scriptures; a mode of merriment which a good man dreads for its profaneness, and a witty man disdains for its easiness and vulgarity. But to whatever levities he has been betrayed, it does not appear that his principles were ever corrupted, or that he ever lost his belief of revelation. The positions which he transmitted from Bolingbroke he seems not to have understood, and was pleased with an interpretation that made them orthodox.

A man of such exalted superiority and so little moderation would naturally have all his delinquences observed and aggravated: those who could not deny that he was excellent would rejoice to find that he was not perfect.

79. No evidence that Pope wrote a Life of Swift has ever appeared.
80. Pope to Louis Racine, September 1, 1742.

Perhaps it may be imputed to the unwillingness with which the same man is allowed to possess many advantages that his learning has been depreciated. He certainly was in his early life a man of great literary curiosity, and when he wrote his *Essay on Criticism* had for his age a very wide acquaintance with books. When he entered into the living world it seems to have happened to him as to many others that he was less attentive to dead masters: he studied in the academy of Paracelsus,[81] and made the universe his favorite volume. He gathered his notions fresh from reality, not from the copies of authors, but the originals of nature. Yet there is no reason to believe that literature ever lost his esteem; he always professed to love reading, and Dobson, who spent some time at his house translating his *Essay on Man,* when I asked him what learning he found him to possess, answered, "More than I expected." His frequent references to history, his allusions to various kinds of knowledge, and his images selected from art and nature, with his observations on the operations of the mind and the modes of life, show an intelligence perpetually on the wing, excursive, vigorous, and diligent, eager to pursue knowledge, and attentive to retain it.

From this curiosity arose the desire of traveling, to which he alludes in his verses to Jervas,[82] and which, though he never found an opportunity to gratify it, did not leave him till his life declined.

Of his intellectual character the constituent and fundamental principle was good sense, a prompt and intuitive perception of consonance and propriety. He saw immediately, of his own conceptions, what was to be chosen, and what to be rejected; and, in the works of others, what was to be shunned, and what was to be copied.

But good sense alone is a sedate and quiescent quality, which manages its possessions well, but does not increase them; it collects few materials for its own operations, and preserves safety, but never gains supremacy. Pope had likewise genius; a mind active, ambitious, and adventurous, always investigating, always aspiring; in its widest searches still longing to go forward, in its highest flights still wishing to be higher; always imagining something greater than it knows, always endeavoring more than it can do.

To assist these powers he is said to have had great strength and exactness of memory. That which he had heard or read was not easily lost; and he had before him not only what his own meditation suggested, but what he had found in other writers that might be accommodated to his present purpose.

These benefits of nature he improved by incessant and unwearied diligence; he had recourse to every source of intelligence, and lost no opportunity of information; he consulted the living as well as the dead; he read his compositions to his friends, and was never content with

81. (?1493–1541), physician and alchemist.
82. "Epistle to Mr. Jervas," ll. 23–40.

mediocrity when excellence could be attained. He considered poetry as the business of his life, and, however he might seem to lament his occupation, he followed it with constancy: to make verses was his first labor, and to mend them was his last.

From his attention to poetry he was never diverted. If conversation offered anything that could be improved he committed it to paper; if a thought, or perhaps an expression more happy than was common, rose to his mind, he was careful to write it; an independent distich was preserved for an opportunity of insertion, and some little fragments have been found containing lines, or parts of lines, to be wrought upon at some other time.

He was one of those few whose labor is their pleasure; he was never elevated to negligence, nor wearied to impatience; he never passed a fault unamended by indifference, nor quitted it by despair. He labored his works first to gain reputation, and afterwards to keep it.

Of composition there are different methods. Some employ at once memory and invention, and, with little intermediate use of the pen, form and polish large masses by continued meditation, and write their productions only when, in their own opinion, they have completed them. It is related of Virgil that his custom was to pour out a great number of verses in the morning, and pass the day in retrenching exuberances and correcting inaccuracies. The method of Pope, as may be collected from his translation, was to write his first thoughts in his first words, and gradually to amplify, decorate, rectify, and refine them.

With such faculties and such dispositions he excelled every other writer in *poetical prudence;* he wrote in such a manner as might expose him to few hazards. He used almost always the same fabric of verse; and, indeed, by those few essays which he made of any other, he did not enlarge his reputation. Of this uniformity the certain consequence was readiness and dexterity. By perpetual practice language had in his mind a systematical arrangement; having always the same use for words, he had words so selected and combined as to be ready at his call. This increase of facility he confessed himself to have perceived in the progress of his translation.

But what was yet of more importance, his effusions were always voluntary and his subjects chosen by himself. His independence secured him from drudging at a task, and laboring upon a barren topic: he never exchanged praise for money, nor opened a shop of condolence or congratulation. His poems, therefore, were scarce ever temporary.[83] He suffered coronations and royal marriages to pass without a song, and derived no opportunities from recent events, nor any popularity from the accidental disposition of his readers. He was never

83. Written for some immediate occasion, topical.

reduced to the necessity of soliciting the sun to shine upon a birthday, of calling the Graces and Virtues to a wedding, or of saying what multitudes have said before him. When he could produce nothing new, he was at liberty to be silent.

His publications were for the same reason never hasty. He is said to have sent nothing to the press till it had lain two years under his inspection: it is at least certain that he ventured nothing without nice examination. He suffered the tumult of imagination to subside, and the novelties of invention to grow familiar. He knew that the mind is always enamored of its own productions, and did not trust his first fondness. He consulted his friends, and listened with great willingness to criticism; and, what was of more importance, he consulted himself, and let nothing pass against his own judgment.

He professed to have learned his poetry from Dryden, whom, whenever an opportunity was presented, he praised through his whole life with unvaried liberality; and perhaps his character may receive some illustration if he be compared with his master.

Integrity of understanding and nicety of discernment were not allotted in a less proportion to Dryden than to Pope. The rectitude of Dryden's mind was sufficiently shown by the dismission of his poetical prejudices,[84] and the rejection of unnatural thoughts and rugged numbers. But Dryden never desired to apply all the judgment that he had. He wrote, and professed to write, merely for the people; and when he pleased others, he contented himself. He spent no time in struggles to rouse latent powers; he never attempted to make that better which was already good, nor often to mend what he must have known to be faulty. He wrote, as he tells us, with very little consideration; when occasion or necessity called upon him, he poured out what the present moment happened to supply, and, when once it had passed the press, ejected it from his mind; for when he had no pecuniary interest, he had no further solicitude.

Pope was not content to satisfy; he desired to excel, and therefore always endeavored to do his best: he did not court the candor, but dared the judgment of his reader, and, expecting no indulgence from others, he showed none to himself. He examined lines and words with minute and punctilious observation, and retouched every part with indefatigable diligence, till he had left nothing to be forgiven.

For this reason he kept his pieces very long in his hands, while he considered and reconsidered them. The only poems which can be supposed to have been written with such regard to the times as might hasten their publication were the two satires of *Thirty-eight;*[85] of which Dodsley told me that they were brought to him by the author, that they might be fairly copied. "Almost every line," he said, "was then written

84. Prepossessions, such as the farfetched conceits of his early poem *Astrea Redux.*
85. Of *1738;* the two Dialogues now known as the *Epilogue to the Satires.*

twice over; I gave him a clean transcript, which he sent some time afterwards to me for the press, with almost every line written twice over a second time."

His declaration that his care for his works ceased at their publication[86] was not strictly true. His parental attention never abandoned them; what he found amiss in the first edition, he silently corrected in those that followed. He appears to have revised the *Iliad,* and freed it from some of its imperfections; and the *Essay on Criticism* received many improvements after its first appearance. It will seldom be found that he altered without adding clearness, elegance, or vigor. Pope had perhaps the judgment of Dryden; but Dryden certainly wanted the diligence of Pope.

In acquired knowledge the superiority must be allowed to Dryden, whose education was more scholastic,[87] and who before he became an author had been allowed more time for study, with better means of information. His mind has a larger range, and he collects his images and illustrations from a more extensive circumference of science. Dryden knew more of man in his general nature, and Pope in his local manners.[88] The notions of Dryden were formed by comprehensive speculation, and those of Pope by minute attention. There is more dignity in the knowledge of Dryden, and more certainty in that of Pope.

Poetry was not the sole praise of either, for both excelled likewise in prose; but Pope did not borrow his prose from his predecessor. The style of Dryden is capricious and varied, that of Pope is cautious and uniform; Dryden obeys the motions of his own mind, Pope constrains his mind to his own rules of composition. Dryden is sometimes vehement and rapid; Pope is always smooth, uniform, and gentle. Dryden's page is a natural field, rising into inequalities, and diversified by the varied exuberance of abundant vegetation; Pope's is a velvet lawn, shaven by the scythe, and leveled by the roller.

Of genius, that power which constitutes a poet; that quality without which judgment is cold and knowledge is inert; that energy which collects, combines, amplifies, and animates—the superiority must, with some hesitation, be allowed to Dryden. It is not to be inferred that of this poetical vigor Pope had only a little, because Dryden had more, for every other writer since Milton must give place to Pope; and even of Dryden it must be said that if he has brighter paragraphs, he has not better poems. Dryden's perfomances were always hasty, either excited by some external occasion, or extorted by domestic necessity; he composed without consideration, and published without correction. What

86. *Guardian,* no. 40.

87. Better grounded in the medieval philosophy of the "schools," which still largely prevailed at Oxford and Cambridge.

88. Immediate social behavior.

his mind could supply at call, or gather in one excursion, was all that he sought, and all that he gave. The dilatory caution of Pope enabled him to condense his sentiments, to multiply his images, and to accumulate all that study might produce, or chance might supply. If the flights of Dryden therefore are higher, Pope continues longer on the wing. If of Dryden's fire the blaze is brighter, of Pope's the heat is more regular and constant. Dryden often surpasses expectation, and Pope never falls below it. Dryden is read with frequent astonishment, and Pope with perpetual delight.

This parallel will, I hope, when it is well considered, be found just; and if the reader should suspect me, as I suspect myself, of some partial fondness for the memory of Dryden, let him not too hastily condemn me; for meditation and inquiry may, perhaps, show him the reasonableness of my determination.

The works of Pope are now to be distinctly examined, not so much with attention to slight faults or petty beauties, as to the general character and effect of each performance.

It seems natural for a young poet to initiate himself by pastorals, which, not professing to imitate real life, require no experience, and, exhibiting only the simple operation of unmingled passions, admit no subtle reasoning or deep inquiry. Pope's *Pastorals* are not however composed but with close thought; they have reference to the times of the day, the seasons of the year, and the periods of human life. The last, that which turns the attention upon age and death, was the author's favorite. To tell of disappointment and misery, to thicken the darkness of futurity, and perplex the labyrinth of uncertainty, has been always a delicious employment of the poets. His preference was probably just. I wish, however, that his fondness had not overlooked a line in which the "zephyrs" are made "to lament in silence."[89]

To charge these *Pastorals* with want of invention is to require what never was intended. The imitations are so ambitiously frequent that the writer evidently means rather to show his literature than his wit. It is surely sufficient for an author of sixteen not only to be able to copy the poems of antiquity with judicious selection, but to have obtained sufficient power of language and skill in meter to exhibit a series of versification[90] which had in English poetry no precedent, nor has since had an imitation.

The design of *Windsor Forest* is evidently derived from *Cooper's Hill*, with some attention to Waller's poem on "The Park";[91] but Pope cannot be denied to excel his masters in variety and elegance, and the art of

89. *Pastorals*, iv. 49–50 ("Winter").

90. A sequence of versified compositions.

91. Sir John Denham, *Cooper's Hill* (1643); Edmund Waller, "On St. James's Park" (1661).

interchanging description, narrative, and morality. The objection made by Dennis is the want of plan, of a regular subordination of parts terminating in the principal and original design.[92] There is this want in most descriptive poems, because as the scenes, which they must exhibit successively, are all subsisting at the same time, the order in which they are shown must by necessity be arbitrary, and more is not to be expected from the last part than from the first. The attention, therefore, which cannot be detained by suspense, must be excited by diversity, such as his poem offers to its readers.

But the desire of diversity may be too much indulged: the parts of *Windsor Forest* which deserve least praise are those which were added to enliven the stillness of the scene, the appearance of Father Thames, and the transformation of Lodona. Addison had in his *Campaign* derided the "rivers" that "rise from their oozy beds" to tell stories of heroes,[93] and it is therefore strange that Pope should adopt a fiction not only unnatural but lately censured. The story of Lodona is told with sweetness; but a new metamorphosis is a ready and puerile expedient: nothing is easier than to tell how a flower was once a blooming virgin, or a rock an obdurate tyrant.[94]

The Temple of Fame has, as Steele warmly declared, "a thousand beauties."[95] Every part is splendid; there is great luxuriance of ornaments; the original vision of Chaucer was never denied to be much improved; the allegory is very skillfully continued, the imagery is properly selected and learnedly displayed: yet, with all this comprehension of excellence, as its scene is laid in remote ages, and its sentiments, if the concluding paragraph be excepted, have little relation to general manners or common life, it never obtained much notice, but is turned silently over, and seldom quoted or mentioned with either praise or blame.

That the "Messiah" excels the "Pollio"[96] is no great praise, if it be considered from what original[97] the improvements are derived.

The "Verses on the Unfortunate Lady" have drawn much attention by the illaudable singularity of treating suicide with respect, and they must be allowed to be written in some parts with vigorous animation, and in others with gentle tenderness; nor has Pope produced any poem in which the sense predominates more over the diction. But the tale is not skillfully told: it is not easy to discover the character of either the lady or her guardian. History relates that she was about to disparage herself by a marriage with an inferior; Pope praises her for the dignity

92. *Remarks on Pope's Homer* (1717).

93. *The Campaign*, 1. 470; see *Windsor Forest*, l. 329.

94. *Windsor Forest*, ll. 171–210. The nymph Lodona, when pursued by Pan, was turned into a river.

95. Steele to Pope, November 12, 1712.

96. Virgil, *Eclogue* IV.

97. The book of Isaiah.

of ambition, and yet condemns the uncle to detestation for his pride: the ambitious love of a niece may be opposed by the interest, malice, or envy of an uncle, but never by his pride. On such an occasion a poet may be allowed to be obscure, but inconsistency never can be right.

The "Ode for St. Cecelia's Day" was undertaken at the desire of Steele: in this the author is generally confessed to have miscarried, yet he has miscarried only as compared with Dryden;[98] for he has far outgone other competitors. Dryden's plan is better chosen; history will always take stronger hold of the attention than fable: the passions excited by Dryden are the pleasures and pains of real life, the scene of Pope is laid in imaginary existence. Pope is read with calm acquiescence, Dryden with turbulent delight; Pope hangs upon the ear, and Dryden finds the passes of the mind.

Both the odes want the essential constituent of metrical compositions, the stated recurrence of settled numbers. It may be alleged that Pindar is said by Horace to have written *numeris lege solutis,*[99] but as no such lax performances have been transmitted to us, the meaning of that expression cannot be fixed; and perhaps the like return might properly be made to a modern Pindarist, as Mr. Cobb received from Bentley, who, when he found his criticisms upon a Greek exercise which Cobb had presented, refuted one after another by Pindar's authority, cried out at last, "Pindar was a bold fellow, but thou art an impudent one."[1]

If Pope's "Ode" be particularly inspected it will be found that the first stanza consists of sounds well chosen indeed, but only sounds.

The second consists of hyperbolical commonplaces, easily to be found, and perhaps without much difficulty to be as well expressed.

In the third, however, there are numbers, images, harmony, and vigor, not unworthy the antagonist[2] of Dryden. Had all been like this—but every part cannot be the best.

The next stanzas place and detain us in the dark and dismal regions of mythology, where neither hope nor fear, neither joy nor sorrow can be found: the poet however faithfully attends us; we have all that can be performed by elegance of diction or sweetness of versification; but what can form avail without better matter?

The last stanza recurs again to commonplaces. The conclusion is too evidently modeled by that of Dryden; and it may be remarked that both end with the same fault, the comparison of each is literal on one side, and metaphorical on the other.

Poets do not always express their own thoughts; Pope, with all this

98. Dryden's "Alexander's Feast" (1697).

99. "In verses not fixed by rule" (*Odes,* IV. ii. 11–12).

1. Samuel Cobb (1675–1713), poet. His *Ode Attempted in the Style of Pindar* appeared in *The Gentleman's Magazine* for 1753.

2. Rival.

labor in the praise of music, was ignorant of its principles, and insensible of its effects.

One of his greatest though of his earliest works is the *Essay on Criticism,* which if he had written nothing else would have placed him among the first critics and the first poets, as it exhibits every mode of excellence that can embellish or dignify didactic composition: selection of matter, novelty of arrangement, justness of precept, splendor of illustration, and propriety of digression. I know not whether it be pleasing to consider that he produced this piece at twenty, and never afterwards excelled it: he that delights himself with observing that such powers may be so soon attained, cannot but grieve to think that life was ever after at a stand.

To mention the particular beauties of the *Essay* would be unprofitably tedious; but I cannot forbear to observe that the comparison of a student's progress in the sciences with the journey of a traveler in the Alps[3] is perhaps the best that English poetry can show. A simile, to be perfect, must both illustrate and ennoble the subject; must show it to the understanding in a clearer view, and display it to the fancy with greater dignity: but either of these qualities may be sufficient to recommend it. In didactic poetry, of which the great purpose is instruction, a simile may be praised which illustrates, though it does not ennoble; in heroics, that may be admitted which ennobles, though it does not illustrate. That it may be complete it is required to exhibit, independently of its references, a pleasing image; for a simile is said to be a short episode. To this antiquity was so attentive that circumstances were sometimes added, which, having no parallels, served only to fill the imagination, and produced what Perrault ludicrously called "comparisons with a long tail."[4] In their similes the greatest writers have sometimes failed: the ship race, compared with the chariot race, is neither illustrated nor aggrandized;[5] land and water make all the difference: when Apollo running after Daphne is likened to a greyhound chasing a hare,[6] there is nothing gained; the ideas of pursuit and flight are too plain to be made plainer, and a god and the daughter of a god are not represented much to their advantage by a hare and dog. The simile of the Alps has no useless parts, yet affords a striking picture by itself: it makes the foregoing position better understood, and enables it to take faster hold on the attention; it assists the apprehension, and elevates the fancy.

Let me likewise dwell a little on the celebrated paragraph in which it is directed that "the sound should seem an echo to the sense";[7] a pre-

3. *An Essay on Criticism,* ll. 219–32.

4. Charles Perrault (1628–1703), French poet and spokesman for the age of Louis XIV, in his *Parallel of the Ancients and the Moderns* (1688–98).

5. *Aeneid,* v. 144–47.

6. Ovid, *Metamorphoses,* i. 533–39.

7. *Essay on Criticism,* ll. 337–83.

cept which Pope is allowed to have observed beyond any other English poet.

This notion of representative meter, and the desire of discovering frequent adaptations of the sound to the sense, have produced, in my opinion, many wild conceits[8] and imaginary beauties. All that can furnish this representation are the sounds of the words considered singly, and the time in which they are pronounced. Every language has some words framed to exhibit the noises which they express, as *thump, rattle, growl, hiss.* These, however, are but few, and the poet cannot make them more, nor can they be of any use but when sound is to be mentioned. The time of pronunciation was in the dactylic measures of the learned languages[9] capable of considerable variety; but that variety could be accommodated only to motion or duration, and different degrees of motion were perhaps expressed by verses rapid or slow, without much attention of the writer, when the image had full possession of his fancy: but our language having little flexibility our verses can differ very little in their cadence.[10] The fancied resemblances, I fear, arise sometimes merely from the ambiguity of words; there is supposed to be some relation between a *soft* line and a *soft* couch, or between *hard* syllables and *hard* fortune.

Motion, however, may be in some sort exemplified; and yet it may be suspected that even in such resemblances the mind often governs the ear, and the sounds are estimated by their meaning. One of the most successful attempts has been to describe the labor of Sisyphus:

> With many a weary step, and many a groan,
> Up a high hill he heaves a huge round stone;
> The huge round stone, resulting[11] with a bound,
> Thunders impetuous down, and smokes along the ground.[12]

Who does not perceive the stone to move slowly upward, and roll violently back? But set the same numbers to another sense;

> While many a merry tale, and many a song,
> Cheered the rough road, we wished the rough road long.
> The rough road then, returning in a round,
> Mocked our impatient steps, for all was fairy ground.

We have now surely lost much of the delay, and much of the rapidity.

But to show how little the greatest master of numbers can fix the principles of representative harmony, it will be sufficient to remark that the poet, who tells us that

8. Conceptions, fancies.
9. Greek and Latin.
10. Flow of versification.
11. Moving back quickly.
12. Pope, *Odyssey,* xi. 735–38. The punishment of Sisyphus in Hades is to roll a stone perpetually up a hill.

When Ajax strives [some rock's vast weight to throw,
The line too labors and] the words move slow:
Not so when swift Camilla scours the plain,
Flies o'er th' unbending corn, and skims along the main;[13]

when he had enjoyed for about thirty years the praise of Camilla's lightness of foot, tried another experiment upon *sound* and *time*, and produced this memorable triplet:

Waller was smooth; but Dryden taught to join
The varying verse, the full resounding line,
The long majestic march, and energy divine.[14]

Here are the swiftness of the rapid race and the march of slow-paced majesty exhibited by the same poet in the same sequence of syllables, except that the exact prosodist will find the line of *swiftness* by one time[15] longer than that of *tardiness.*

Beauties of this kind are commonly fancied; and when real are technical and nugatory,[16] not to be rejected and not to be solicited.

To the praises which have been accumulated on *The Rape of the Lock* by readers of every class, from the critic to the waiting-maid, it is difficult to make any addition. Of that which is universally allowed to be the most attractive of all ludicrous compositions, let it rather be now inquired from what sources the power of pleasing is derived.

Dr. Warburton, who excelled in critical perspicacity, has remarked that the preternatural agents are very happily adapted to the purposes of the poem. The heathen deities can no longer gain attention: we should have turned away from a contest between Venus and Diana. The employment of allegorical persons always excites conviction of its own absurdity: they may produce effects, but cannot conduct actions; when the phantom is put in motion, it dissolves; thus Discord may raise a mutiny, but Discord cannot conduct a march, nor besiege a town. Pope brought into view a new race of beings, with powers and passions proportionate to their operation. The sylphs and gnomes act at the toilet and the tea table what more terrific and more powerful phantoms perform on the stormy ocean or the field of battle; they give their proper help, and do their proper mischief.

Pope is said by an objector not to have been the inventor of this petty

13. *Essay on Criticism,* ll. 370–73. Johnson does not quote the words in square brackets. Ajax was the strongest of the Greeks; Camilla was a swift maiden-warrior, who fought against Aeneas.

14. *Imitations of Horace, Epistles,* II. i. 267–69.

15. Prosodic unit equal to one syllable. Apparently Johnson counts "th'un" (*Essay,* l. 373) as two syllables. This elision and the immediately preceding "o'er" may, however, be felt as giving a kind of speed to the line. See *Rambler* no. 94, where Johnson ponders the same problem of "representative meter."

16. Trifling.

nation;[17] a charge which might with more justice have been brought against the author of the *Iliad,* who doubtless adopted the religious system of his country; for what is there but the names of his agents which Pope has not invented? Has he not assigned them characters and operations never heard of before? Has he not, at least, given them their first poetical existence? If this is not sufficient to denominate his work original, nothing original ever can be written.

In this work are exhibited in a very high degree the two most engaging powers of an author: new things are made familiar, and familiar things are made new. A race of aerial people never heard of before is presented to us in a manner so clear and easy that the reader seeks for no further information, but immediately mingles with his new acquaintance, adopts their interests, and attends their pursuits, loves a sylph and detests a gnome.

That familiar things are made new every paragraph will prove. The subject of the poem is an event below the common incidents of common life; nothing real is introduced that is not seen so often as to be no longer regarded, yet the whole detail of a female day is here brought before us invested with so much art of decoration that, though nothing is disguised, every thing is striking, and we feel all the appetite of curiosity for that from which we have a thousand times turned fastidiously away.

The purpose of the poet is, as he tells us, to laugh at "the little unguarded follies of the female sex."[18] It is therefore without justice that Dennis charges *The Rape of the Lock* with the want of a moral, and for that reason sets it below *The Lutrin,* which exposes the pride and discord of the clergy.[19] Perhaps neither Pope nor Boileau has made the world much better than he found it; but if they had both succeeded, it were easy to tell who would have deserved most from public gratitude. The freaks, and humors, and spleen, and vanity of women, as they embroil families in discord and fill houses with disquiet, do more to obstruct the happiness of life in a year than the ambition of the clergy in many centuries. It has been well observed that the misery of man proceeds not from any single crush of overwhelming evil, but from small vexations continually repeated.

It is remarked by Dennis likewise that the machinery is superfluous; that by all the bustle of preternatural operation the main event is neither hastened nor retarded. To this charge an efficacious answer is not easily made. The sylphs cannot be said to help or to oppose, and it must be allowed to imply some want of art that their power has not been

17. By Joseph Warton in his *Essay on the Writings and Genius of Pope,* vol. I (1756). Many of the criticisms of Pope's poetry answered by Johnson in this section of the "Life" were made by Warton.

18. Dedication of *The Rape of the Lock,* "To Mrs. Arabella Fermor" (1714).

19. Dennis makes this charge in his *Remarks on Mr. Pope's "Rape of the Lock"* (1728). *Le Lutrin (The Lectern)* is a mock-epic poem (1684) by Boileau.

sufficiently intermingled with the action. Other parts may likewise be charged with want of connection; the game at ombre might be spared, but if the lady had lost her hair while she was intent upon her cards, it might have been inferred that those who are too fond of play will be in danger of neglecting more important interests. Those perhaps are faults; but what are such faults to so much excellence!

The Epistle of *Eloise to Abelard* is one of the most happy productions of human wit: the subject is so judiciously chosen that it would be difficult, in turning over the annals of the world, to find another which so many circumstances concur to recommend. We regularly interest ourselves most in the fortune of those who most deserve our notice. Abelard and Eloise were conspicuous in their days for eminence of merit. The heart naturally loves truth. The adventures and misfortunes of this illustrious pair are known from undisputed history. Their fate does not leave the mind in hopeless dejection; for they both found quiet and consolation in retirement and piety. So new and so affecting is their story that it supersedes invention, and imagination ranges at full liberty without straggling into scenes of fable.

The story thus skillfully adopted has been diligently improved. Pope has left nothing behind him which seems more the effect of studious perseverance and laborious revisal. Here is particularly observable the *curiosa felicitas,*[20] a fruitful soil, and careful cultivation. Here is no crudeness of sense nor asperity of language.

The sources from which sentiments which have so much vigor and efficacy have been drawn are shown to be the mystic writers by the learned author of the *Essay on the Life and Writings of Pope;*[21] a book which teaches how the brow of criticism may be smoothed, and how she may be enabled, with all her severity, to attract and to delight.

The train of my disquisition has now conducted me to that poetical wonder, the translation of the *Iliad:* a performance which no age or nation can pretend to equal. To the Greeks translation was almost unknown; it was totally unknown to the inhabitants of Greece.[22] They had no recourse to the Barbarians for poetical beauties, but sought for everything in Homer, where, indeed, there is but little which they might not find.

The Italians have been very diligent translators; but I can hear of no version, unless perhaps Anguillara's Ovid[23] may be excepted, which is read with eagerness. The *Iliad* of Salvini[24] every reader may discover to be punctiliously exact; but it seems to be the work of a linguist skillfully

20. "Careful felicity" (Petronius, *Satyricon,* section 118).

21. Joseph Warton's *Essay.*

22. Presumably, as distinct from the Greeks of Asia Minor, Sicily and other outlying parts of the Greek world.

23. Giovanni Andrea dell' Anguillara's poetic translation of the *Metamorphoses* appeared in 1561.

24. Antonio Maria Salvini, *Iliad* (1723).

pedantic, and his countrymen, the proper judges of its power to please, reject it with disgust.[25]

Their predecessors, the Romans, have left some specimens of translation behind them, and that employment must have had some credit in which Tully and Germanicus[26] engaged; but unless we suppose what is perhaps true, that the plays of Terence were versions of Menander,[27] nothing translated seems ever to have risen to high reputation. The French, in the meridian hour of their learning, were very laudably industrious to enrich their own language with the wisdom of the ancients; but found themselves reduced, by whatever necessity, to turn the Greek and Roman poetry into prose. Whoever could read an author could translate him. From such rivals little can be feared.

The chief help of Pope in this arduous undertaking was drawn from the versions of Dryden. Virgil had borrowed much of his imagery from Homer, and part of the debt was now paid by his translator. Pope searched the pages of Dryden for happy combinations of heroic diction, but it will not be denied that he added much to what he found. He cultivated our language with so much diligence and art that he has left in his Homer a treasure of poetical elegances to posterity. His version may be said to have tuned the English tongue, for since its appearance no writer, however deficient in other powers, has wanted melody. Such a series of lines so elaborately corrected and so sweetly modulated took possession of the public ear; the vulgar was enamored of the poem, and the learned wondered at the translation.

But in the most general applause discordant voices will always be heard. It has been objected by some, who wish to be numbered among the sons of learning, that Pope's version of Homer is not Homerical; that it exhibits no resemblance of the original and characteristic manner of the father of poetry, as it wants his awful simplicity, his artless grandeur, his unaffected majesty. This cannot be totally denied, but it must be remembered that *necessitas quod cogit defendit,*[28] that may be lawfully done which cannot be forborne. Time and place will always enforce regard. In estimating this translation consideration must be had of the nature of our language, the form of our meter, and, above all, of the change which two thousand years have made in the modes of life and the habits of thought. Virgil wrote in a language of the same general fabric with that of Homer, in verses of the same measure, and in an age nearer to Homer's time by eighteen hundred years; yet he found even then the state of the world so much altered, and the de-

25. Distaste.

26. Germanicus (15 B.C.–A.D. 19), general, translated Aratus's *Phaenomena,* a Greek astronomical work.

27. Menander was a famous Greek comic dramatist (c.342 - c.290 B.C.), whose plots were borrowed by the Roman dramatist Terence (c.195–159 B.C.).

28. The Latin is translated in the next phrase. Its source is untraced.

mand for elegance so much increased, that mere nature would be endured no longer; and perhaps, in the multitude of borrowed passages, very few can be shown which he has not embellished.

There is a time when nations emerging from barbarity, and falling into regular subordination, gain leisure to grow wise, and feel the shame of ignorance and the craving pain of unsatisfied curiosity. To this hunger of the mind plain sense is grateful;[29] that which fills the void removes uneasiness, and to be free from pain for a while is pleasure; but repletion generates fastidiousness, a saturated intellect soon becomes luxurious,[30] and knowledge finds no willing reception till it is recommended by artificial diction. Thus it will be found in the progress of learning that in all nations the first writers are simple, and that every age improves in elegance. One refinement always makes way for another, and what was expedient to Virgil was necessary to Pope.

I suppose many readers of the English *Iliad,* when they have been touched with some unexpected beauty of the lighter kind, have tried to enjoy it in the original, where, alas! it was not to be found. Homer doubtless owes to his translator many Ovidian graces not exactly suitable to his character; but to have added can be no great crime if nothing be taken away. Elegance is surely to be desired if it be not gained at the expense of dignity. A hero would wish to be loved as well as to be reverenced.

To a thousand cavils one answer is sufficient; the purpose of a writer is to be read, and the criticism which would destroy the power of pleasing must be blown aside. Pope wrote for his own age and his own nation: he knew that it was necessary to color the images and point the sentiments of his author; he therefore made him graceful, but lost him some of his sublimity.

The copious notes with which the version is accompanied and by which it is recommended to many readers, though they were undoubtedly written to swell the volumes, ought not to pass without praise: commentaries which attract the reader by the pleasure of perusal have not often appeared; the notes of others are read to clear difficulties, those of Pope to vary entertainment.

It has, however, been objected with sufficient reason that there is in the commentary too much of unseasonable levity and affected gaiety; that too many appeals are made to the ladies, and the ease which is so carefully preserved is sometimes the ease of a trifler. Every art has its terms[31] and every kind of instruction its proper style; the gravity of common critics may be tedious, but is less despicable than childish merriment.

29. Pleasing.
30. Refined, exquisite in its pleasures.
31. Every branch of knowledge has its technical vocabulary.

Of the *Odyssey* nothing remains to be observed; the same general praise may be given to both translations, and a particular examination of either would require a large volume. The notes were written by Broome, who endeavored not unsuccessfully to imitate his master.

Of *The Dunciad* the hint is confessedly taken from Dryden's *MacFlecknoe*, but the plan is so enlarged and diversified as justly to claim the praise of an original, and affords perhaps the best specimen that has yet appeared of personal satire ludicrously pompous.

That the design was moral, whatever the author might tell either his readers or himself, I am not convinced. The first motive was the desire of revenging the contempt with which Theobald had treated his Shakespeare, and regaining the honor which he had lost, by crushing his opponent. Theobald was not of bulk enough to fill a poem, and therefore it was necessary to find other enemies with other names, at whose expense he might divert the public.

In this design there was petulance and malignity enough; but I cannot think it very criminal. An author places himself uncalled before the tribunal of criticism, and solicits fame at the hazard of disgrace. Dullness or deformity are not culpable in themselves, but may be very justly reproached when they pretend to the honor of wit or the influence of beauty. If bad writers were to pass without reprehension, what should restrain them? *impune diem consumpserit ingens "Telephus";*[32] and upon bad writers only will censure have much effect. The satire which brought Theobald and Moore[33] into contempt, dropped impotent from Bentley, like the javelin of Priam thrown at Neoptolemus.[34]

All truth is valuable, and satirical criticism may be considered as useful when it rectifies error and improves judgment: he that refines the public taste is a public benefactor.

The beauties of this poem are well known; its chief fault is the grossness of its images. Pope and Swift had an unnatural delight in ideas physically impure, such as every other tongue utters with unwillingness, and of which every ear shrinks from the mention.

But even this fault, offensive as it is, may be forgiven for the excellence of other passages; such as the formation and dissolution of Moore, the account of the Traveler, the misfortune of the Florist,[35] and the crowded thoughts and stately numbers which dignify the concluding paragraph.

The alterations which have been made in *The Dunciad*, not always for

32. "Shall an interminable *Telephus* occupy an entire day without censure?" (Juvenal, *Satires*, i. 4–5). *Telephus* was the title of a realistic play by Euripides, not extant.

33. *Dunciad*, ii. 35–50. James Moore Smythe was a minor writer, accused of plagiarizing Pope. Pope's rival, the Shakespearian scholar Lewis Theobald, was the hero of the original *Dunciad* (1728), celebrated in Books i, ii, and iii.

34. A Greek warrior (see *Aeneid*, ii. 544–46).

35. *The Dunciad*, ii. 31–120, iv. 293–336, 403–18.

the better, require that it should be published, as in the last collection,[36] with all its variations.

The *Essay on Man* was a work of great labor and long consideration, but certainly not the happiest of Pope's performances. The subject is perhaps not very proper for poetry, and the poet was not sufficiently master of his subject; metaphysical morality was to him a new study, he was proud of his acquisitions, and, supposing himself master of great secrets, was in haste to teach what he had not learned. Thus he tells us, in the first Epistle, that from the nature of the Supreme Being may be deduced an order of beings such as mankind, because infinite excellence can do only what is best. He finds out that these beings must be "somewhere," and that "all the question is whether man be in a wrong place."[37] Surely if, according to the poet's Leibnitian reasoning,[38] we may infer that man ought to be only because he is, we may allow that his place is the right place, because he has it. Supreme Wisdom is not less infallible in disposing than in creating. But what is meant by "somewhere" and "place" and "wrong place" it had been vain to ask Pope, who probably had never asked himself.

Having exalted himself into the chair of wisdom he tells us much that every man knows, and much that he does not know himself; that we see but little, and that the order of the universe is beyond our comprehension, an opinion not very uncommon; and that there is a chain of subordinate beings "from infinite to nothing," of which himself and his readers are equally ignorant. But he gives us one comfort which, without his help, he supposes unattainable, in the position "that though we are fools, yet God is wise."[39]

This *Essay* affords an egregious instance of the predominance of genius, the dazzling splendor of imagery, and the seductive powers of eloquence. Never were penury of knowledge and vulgarity of sentiment[40] so happily disguised. The reader feels his mind full, though he learns nothing; and when he meets it in its new array no longer knows the talk of his mother and his nurse. When these wonder-working sounds sink into sense and the doctrine of the *Essay,* disrobed of its ornaments, is left to the powers of its naked excellence, what shall we discover? That we are, in comparison with our Creator, very weak and ignorant; that we do not uphold the chain of existence; and that we could not make one another with more skill than we are made. We may learn yet more: that the arts of human life were copied from the instinctive operations of other animals; that if the world be made for man, it may be said that man was made for geese. To these profound principles

36. Of Warburton, 1751.
37. *Essay of Man,* i. 47–50.
38. The reasoning of Gottfried Wilhelm Leibnitz (1646–1716), German philosopher.
39. See *Essay on Man,* i. 240–41, ii. 293–94.
40. Commonplace ideas.

of natural[41] knowledge are added some moral instructions equally new: that self-interest well understood will produce social concord; that men are mutual gainers by mutual benefits; that evil is sometimes balanced by good; that human advantages are unstable and fallacious, of uncertain duration and doubtful effect; that our true honor is not to have a great part, but to act it well; that virtue only is our own; and that happiness is always in our power.

Surely a man of no very comprehensive search may venture to say that he has heard all this before, but it was never till now recommended by such a blaze of embellishment or such sweetness of melody. The vigorous contraction of some thoughts, the luxuriant amplification of others, the incidental illustrations, and sometimes the dignity, sometimes the softness of the verses, enchain philosophy, suspend criticism, and oppress judgment by overpowering pleasure.

This is true of many paragraphs; yet if I had undertaken to exemplify Pope's felicity of composition before a rigid critic I should not select the *Essay on Man,* for it contains more lines unsuccessfully labored, more harshness of diction, more thoughts imperfectly expressed, more levity without elegance, and more heaviness without strength, than will easily be found in all his other works.

The *Characters of Men and Women* are the product of diligent speculation upon human life; much labor has been bestowed upon them, and Pope very seldom labored in vain. That his excellence may be properly estimated I recommend a comparison of his *Characters of Women* with Boileau's *Satire;*[42] it will then be seen with how much more perspicacity female nature is investigated and female excellence selected; and he surely is no mean writer to whom Boileau shall be found inferior. The *Characters of Men,* however, are written with more, if not with deeper, thought, and exhibit many passages exquisitely beautiful. "The Gem and the Flower" will not easily be equalled.[43] In the women's part are some defects: the character of Atossa is not so neatly finished as that of Clodio,[44] and some of the female characters may be found, perhaps more frequently among men; what is said of Philomedé[45] was true of Prior.

In the *Epistles to Lord Bathurst* and *Lord Burlington* Dr. Warburton has endeavored to find a train of thought which was never in the writer's

41. Philosophic; scientific. See *Essay on Man,* i. 17–42, iii. 169–200 and 45–46. "While Man exclaims, 'See all things for my use!'/ 'See man for mine!' replies a pampered goose.' " The "moral instructions equally new" which Johnson next enumerates occur at various places in Epistles ii, iii, and iv of Pope's *Essay.*

42. *Satire X.*

43. *Of the Characters of Men,* ll. 141–48.

44. *Of the Characters of Women,* ll. 115–50 (Atossa); *Of the Characters of Men,* ll. 180–207 (Clodio). Pope later drops the pseudonym of Clodio and calls this character Wharton, alluding to Philip, Duke of Wharton, who went over to the Jacobite cause in 1726 and died in exile in 1731.

45. *Of the Characters of Women,* ll. 69–86.

head, and, to support his hypothesis, has printed that first which was published last.[46] In one the most valuable passage is perhaps the elogy on good sense, and the other the end of the Duke of Buckingham.[47]

The *Epistle to Arbuthnot,* now arbitrarily called the *Prologue to the Satires,* is a performance consisting, as it seems, of many fragments wrought into one design, which by this union of scattered beauties contains more striking paragraphs than could probably have been brought together into an occasional work. As there is no stronger motive to exertion than self-defense, no part has more elegance, spirit, or dignity than the poet's vindication of his own character. The meanest[48] passage is the satire upon Sporus.[49]

Of the two poems which derived their names from the year,[50] and which are called the *Epilogue to the Satires,* it was very justly remarked by Savage that the second was in the whole more strongly conceived and more equally supported, but that it had no single passages equal to the contention in the first for the dignity of Vice and the celebration of the triumph of Corruption.[51]

The *Imitations of Horace* seem to have been written as relaxations of his genius. This employment became his favorite by its facility; the plan was ready to his hand, and nothing was required but to accommodate as he could the sentiments of an old author to recent facts or familiar images; but what is easy is seldom excellent: such imitations cannot give pleasure to common readers. The man of learning may be sometimes surprised and delighted by an unexpected parallel; but the comparison requires knowledge of the original, which will likewise often detect strained applications. Between Roman images and English manners there will be an irreconcilable dissimilitude, and the work will be generally uncouth and parti-colored; neither original nor translated, neither ancient nor modern.

Pope had, in proportions very nicely adjusted to each other, all the qualities that constitute genius. He had invention, by which new trains of events are formed and new scenes of imagery displayed, as in *The Rape of the Lock,* and by which extrinsic and adventitious embellishments and illustrations are connected with a known subject, as in the *Essay on Criticism;* he had imagination, which strongly impresses on the writer's mind and enables him to convey to the reader the various forms of nature, incidents of life, and energies of passion, as in his

46. *To Burlington* was published originally in 1731 and *To Bathurst* in 1733.

47. *To Burlington,* ll. 39–46 (good sense); *To Bathurst,* ll. 299–314 (Buckingham). An "elogy" is a discourse of praise.

48. Lowest; most lacking in dignity.

49. Ll. 305–33.

50. These two poems originally were called *One Thousand Seven Hundred and Thirty Eight* (Dialogues I and II).

51. *Epilogue to the Satires,* i. 105–70.

Eloisa, Windsor Forest, and the *Ethic Epistles.*[52] He had judgment, which selects from life or nature what the present purpose requires, and, by separating the essence of things from its concomitants, often makes the representation more powerful than the reality; and he had colors of language always before him ready to decorate his matter with every grace of elegant expression, as when he accommodates his diction to the wonderful multiplicity of Homer's sentiments and descriptions.

Poetical expression includes sound as well as meaning. "Music," says Dryden, "is inarticulate poetry";[53] among the excellences of Pope, therefore, must be mentioned the melody of his meter. By perusing the works of Dryden he discovered the most perfect fabric of English verse, and habituated himself to that only which he found the best; in consequence of which restraint his poetry has been censured as too uniformly musical, and as glutting the ear with unvaried sweetness. I suspect this objection to be the cant of those who judge by principles rather than perception; and who would even themselves have less pleasure in his works if he had tried to relieve attention by studied discords, or affected to break his lines and vary his pauses.

But though he was thus careful of his versification he did not oppress his powers with superfluous rigor. He seems to have thought with Boileau that the practice of writing might be refined till the difficulty should overbalance the advantage. The construction of his language is not always strictly grammatical; with those rhymes which prescription had conjoined he contented himself, without regard to Swift's remonstrances,[54] though there was no striking consonance; nor was he very careful to vary his terminations or to refuse admission at a small distance to the same rhymes.

To Swift's edict for the exclusion of alexandrines and triplets he paid little regard;[55] he admitted them, but, in the opinion of Fenton, too rarely: he uses them more liberally in his translation than his poems.

He has a few double rhymes, and always, I think, unsuccessfully, except once in *The Rape of the Lock.*[56]

Expletives[57] he very early ejected from his verses; but he now and then admits an epithet rather commodious than important. Each of the six first lines of the *Iliad* might lose two syllables with very little diminution of the meaning; and sometimes, after all his art and labor, one verse seems to be made for the sake of another. In his latter produc-

52. This name was applied both to the *Essay on Man* and to the four poems which Warburton called the *Moral Essays (Of the Characters of Men and Women,* and the *Epistles to Bathurst and Burlington).* Apparently Johnson refers to the *Moral Essays.*

53. Preface to *Tyrannic Love* (1670).

54. Swift to Pope, June 28, 1715.

55. An alexandrine is an iambic hexameter line; triplets are three rhyming lines in succession, usually iambic pentameter. For Swift's "edict," see his letter to Thomas Beach, April 12, 1735.

56. *Rape of the Lock,* iii. 153–54.

57. Words used to fill out a line, such as "do."

tions the diction is sometimes vitiated by French idioms, with which Bolingbroke had perhaps infected him.

I have been told that the couplet by which he declared his own ear to be most gratified was this:

> Lo, where Maeotis sleeps, and hardly flows
> The freezing Tanais thro' a waste of snows.[58]

But the reason of this preference I cannot discover.

It is remarked by Watts[59] that there is scarcely a happy combination of words or a phrase poetically elegant in the English language which Pope has not inserted into his version of Homer. How he obtained possession of so many beauties of speech it were desirable to know. That he gleaned from authors, obscure as well as eminent, what he thought brilliant or useful, and preserved it all in a regular collection, is not unlikely. When, in his last years, Hall's *Satires*[60] were shown him he wished that he had seen them sooner.

New sentiments and new images others may produce, but to attempt any further improvement of versification will be dangerous. Art and diligence have now done their best, and what shall be added will be the effort of tedious toil and needless curiosity.

After all this it is surely superfluous to answer the question that has once been asked, whether Pope was a poet?[61] otherwise than by asking in return, if Pope be not a poet, where is poetry to be found? To circumscribe poetry by a definition will only show the narrowness of the definer, though a definition which shall exclude Pope will not easily be made. Let us look round upon the present time, and back upon the past; let us inquire to whom the voice of mankind has decreed the wreath of poetry; let their productions be examined and their claims stated, and the pretensions of Pope will be no more disputed. Had he given the world only his version the name of poet must have been allowed him; if the writer of the *Iliad* were to class his successors he would assign a very high place to his translator, without requiring any other evidence of genius.[62]

58. *The Dunciad,* iii. 87–88.

59. Isaac Watts, *Improvement of the Mind* (1741), I. xx. 36.

60. Joseph Hall, *Virgidemiarum* (1597–98).

61. In his *Essay on Pope,* Joseph Warton had classed Pope as a poet of the second rank, an "ethical" poet, falling short of the "sublime" and the "pathetic."

62. At the end of this "Life," Johnson prints one of Pope's letters, and an essay of his own on Pope's Epitaphs which had originally been published in 1756.

Richard Savage
?1697–1742

It has been observed in all ages that the advantages of nature or of fortune have contributed very little to the promotion of happiness; and that those whom the splendor of their rank, or the extent of their capacity, have placed upon the summits of human life have not often given any just occasion to envy in those who look up to them from a lower station. Whether it be that apparent superiority incites great designs, and great designs are naturally liable to fatal miscarriages, or that the general lot of mankind is misery, and the misfortunes of those whose eminence drew upon them an universal attention have been more carefully recorded because they were more generally observed, and have in reality been only more conspicuous than those of others, not more frequent or more severe.

That affluence and power, advantages extrinsic and adventitious and therefore easily separable from those by whom they are possessed, should very often flatter the mind with expectation of felicity which they cannot give, raises no astonishment; but it seems rational to hope that intellectual greatness should produce better effects, that minds qualified for great attainments should first endeavor their own benefit, and that they who are most able to teach others the way to happiness should with most certainty follow it themselves.

But this expectation, however plausible, has been very frequently disappointed. The heroes of literary as well as civil history have been very often no less remarkable for what they have suffered than for what they have achieved; and volumes have been written only to enumerate the miseries of the learned and relate their unhappy lives and untimely deaths.

To these mournful narratives I am about to add the Life of Richard Savage, a man whose writings entitle him to an eminent rank in the classes of learning, and whose misfortunes claim a degree of compassion not always due to the unhappy, as they were often the consequences of the crimes of others rather than his own.

In the year 1697, Anne Countess of Macclesfield, having lived for some time upon very uneasy terms with her husband, thought a public confession of adultery the most obvious and expeditious method of obtaining her liberty, and therefore declared that the child with which she was then great was begotten by the Earl Rivers. Her husband, as may be easily imagined, being thus made no less desirous of a separation than herself, prosecuted his design in the most effectual manner; for he applied not to the ecclesiastical courts for a divorce, but to the parliament for an act by which his marriage might be dissolved, the nuptial contract totally annulled, and the child of his wife illegitimated.[1] This act, after the usual deliberation, he obtained, though without the approbation of some, who considered marriage as an affair only cognizable by ecclesiastical judges; and on March 3rd, was separated from his wife, whose fortune, which was very great, was repaid her, and who having as well as her husband the liberty of making another choice, was in a short time married to Colonel Brett.

While the Earl of Macclesfield was prosecuting this affair, his wife was, on the 10th of January, 1697–8, delivered of a son; and the Earl Rivers, by appearing to consider him as his own, left none any reason to doubt of the sincerity of her declaration, for he was his godfather and gave him his own name, which was by his direction inserted in the register of St. Andrew's parish in Holborn; but unfortunately left him to the care of his mother, whom, as she was now set free from her husband, he probably imagined likely to treat with great tenderness the child that had contributed to so pleasing an event. It is not indeed easy to discover what motives could be found to overbalance that natural affection of a parent, or what interest could be promoted by neglect or cruelty. The dread of shame or of poverty, by which some wretches have been incited to abandon or to murder their children, cannot be supposed to have affected a woman who had proclaimed her crimes and solicited reproach, and on whom the clemency of the legislature had undeservedly bestowed a fortune that would have been very little diminished by the expenses which the care of her child could have brought upon her. It was therefore not likely that she would be wicked without temptation; that she would look upon her son from his birth with a kind of resentment and abhorrence; and, instead of supporting, assisting, and defending him, delight to see him struggling with misery; that she would take every opportunity of aggravating his misfortunes and obstructing his resources, and with an implacable and restless

1. Actually Lady Macclesfield denied the charge of adultery and fought the divorce action. Johnson's "facts" throughout, largely based on an anonymous *Life of Savage* (1727) and Savage's own version of events, are frequently mistaken.

cruelty continue her persecution from the first hour of his life to the last.

But, whatever were her motives, no sooner was her son born than she discovered a resolution of disowning him; and in a very short time removed him from her sight by committing him to the care of a poor woman, whom she directed to educate him as her own, and enjoined never to inform him of his true parents.

Such was the beginning of the life of Richard Savage: born with a legal claim to honor and to riches, he was in two months illegitimated by the parliament, and disowned by his mother, doomed to poverty and obscurity, and launched upon the ocean of life only that he might be swallowed by its quicksands or dashed upon its rocks.

His mother could not indeed infect others with the same cruelty. As it was impossible to avoid the inquiries which the curiosity or tenderness of her relations made after her child, she was obliged to give some account of the measures that she had taken, and her mother, the Lady Mason, whether in approbation of her design or to prevent more criminal contrivances, engaged to transact with his nurse, pay her for her care, and superintend his education.

In this charitable office she was assisted by his godmother, Mrs. Lloyd, who while she lived always looked upon him with that tenderness which the barbarity of his mother made peculiarly necessary; but her death, which happened in his tenth year, was another of the misfortunes of his childhood; for though she kindly endeavored to alleviate his loss by a legacy of three hundred pounds, yet, as he had none to prosecute his claim, to shelter him from oppression, or call in law to the assistance of justice, her will was eluded[2] by the executors, and no part of the money was ever paid.

He was, however, not yet wholly abandoned. The Lady Mason still continued her care, and directed him to be placed at a small grammar school near St. Albans, where he was called by the name of his nurse, without the least intimation that he had a claim to any other.

Here he was initiated in literature and passed through several of the classes, with what rapidity or what applause cannot now be known. As he always spoke with respect of his master, it is probable that the mean[3] rank in which he then appeared did not hinder his genius[4] from being distinguished or his industry from being rewarded; and if in so low a state he obtained distinction and rewards, it is not likely that they were gained but by genius and industry.

It is very reasonable to conjecture that his application was equal to his abilities, because his improvement was more than proportioned to the opportunities which he enjoyed; nor can it be doubted that if his ear-

2. Evaded.
3. Low.
4. Natural ability.

liest productions had been preserved like those of happier students, we might in some have found vigorous sallies of that sprightly humor which distinguishes *The Author to be Let,* and in others strong touches of that ardent imagination which painted the solemn scenes of *The Wanderer.*[5]

While he was thus cultivating his genius, his father the Earl Rivers was seized with a distemper which in a short time put an end to his life. He had frequently inquired after his son, and had always been amused[6] with fallacious and evasive answers; but being now in his own opinion on his deathbed, he thought it his duty to provide for him among his other natural children, and therefore demanded a positive account of him with an importunity not to be diverted or denied. His mother, who could no longer refuse an answer, determined at least to give such as should cut him off forever from that happiness which competence[7] affords, and therefore declared that he was dead; which is perhaps the first instance of a lie invented by a mother to deprive her son of a provision which was designed him by another, and which she could not expect herself though he should lose it.

This was therefore an act of wickedness which could not be defeated, because it could not be suspected; the Earl did not imagine there could exist in a human form a mother that would ruin her son without enriching herself, and therefore bestowed upon some other person six thousand pounds which he had in his will bequeathed to Savage.

The same cruelty which incited his mother to intercept this provision which had been intended him prompted her in a short time to another project, a project worthy of such a disposition. She endeavored to rid herself from the danger of being at any time made known to him, by sending him secretly to the American plantations.[8]

By whose kindness this scheme was counteracted, or by what interposition she was induced to lay aside her design, I know not; it is not improbable that the Lady Mason might persuade or compel her to desist, or perhaps she could not easily find accomplices wicked enough to concur in so cruel an action; for it may be conceived that even those who had by a long gradation of guilt hardened their hearts against the sense of common wickedness would yet be shocked at the design of a mother to expose her son to slavery and want, to expose him without interest and without provocation; and Savage might on this occasion find protectors and advocates among those who had long traded in crimes, and whom compassion had never touched before.

Being hindered, by whatever means, from banishing him into

5. *The Author to be Let* is a prose satire similar in theme to Pope's *Dunciad. The Wanderer* is a long, romantically meditative poem in heroic couplets.

6. Distracted, deceived.

7. A sufficient income.

8. Colonies.

another country, she formed soon after a scheme for burying him in poverty and obscurity in his own; and that his station of life, if not the place of his residence, might keep him forever at a distance from her, she ordered him to be placed with a shoemaker in Holborn, that, after the usual time of trial, he might become his apprentice.

It is generally reported that this project was for some time successful, and that Savage was employed at the awl longer than he was willing to confess; nor was it perhaps any great advantage to him that an unexpected discovery determined him to quit his occupation.

About this time his nurse, who had always treated him as her own son, died; and it was natural for him to take care of those effects which by her death were, as he imagined, become his own; he therefore went to her house, opened her boxes, and examined her papers, among which he found some letters written to her by the Lady Mason, which informed him of his birth and the reasons for which it was concealed.

He was now no longer satisfied with the employment which had been allotted him, but thought he had a right to share the affluence of his mother; and therefore without scruple applied to her as her son, and made use of every art to awaken her tenderness and attract her regard. But neither his letters nor the interposition of those friends which his merit or his distress procured him made any impression upon her: she still resolved to neglect, though she could no longer disown him.

It was to no purpose that he frequently solicited her to admit him to see her; she avoided him with the most vigilant precaution and ordered him to be excluded from her house, by whomsoever he might be introduced, and what reason soever he might give for entering it.

Savage was at the same time so touched with the discovery of his real mother that it was his frequent practice to walk in the dark evenings for several hours before her door, in hopes of seeing her as she might come by accident to the window or cross her apartment with a candle in her hand.

But all his assiduity and tenderness were without effect, for he could neither soften her heart nor open her hand, and was reduced to the utmost miseries of want while he was endeavoring to awaken the affection of a mother: he was therefore obliged to seek some other means of support and, having no profession, became by necessity an author.

At this time the attention of all the literary world was engrossed by the Bangorian controversy, which filled the press with pamphlets and the coffee-houses with disputants.[9] Of this subject, as most popular, he made choice for his first attempt, and, without any other knowledge of the question than he had casually collected from conversation, published a poem against the Bishop.

9. Benjamin Hoadly, Bishop of Bangor, was the center of a complicated quarrel between the "high" and "low" clergy of the Church of England.

What was the success or merit of this performance I know not; it was probably lost among the innumerable pamphlets to which that dispute gave occasion. Mr. Savage was himself in a little time ashamed of it and endeavored to suppress it by destroying all the copies that he could collect.

He then attempted a more gainful kind of writing, and in his eighteenth year offered to the stage a comedy borrowed from a Spanish plot, which was refused by the players, and was therefore given by him to Mr. Bullock,[10] who, having more interest,[11] made some slight alterations and brought it upon the stage under the title of *Woman's a Riddle,* but allowed the unhappy author no part of the profit.

Not discouraged, however, at this repulse, he wrote two years afterwards *Love in a Veil,* another comedy, borrowed likewise from the Spanish, but with little better success than before; for though it was received and acted, yet it appeared so late in the year that the author obtained no other advantage from it than the acquaintance of Sir Richard Steele[12] and Mr. Wilks,[13] by whom he was pitied, caressed,[14] and relieved.

Sir Richard Steele, having declared in his favor with all the ardor of benevolence which constituted his character, promoted his interest with the utmost zeal, related his misfortunes, applauded his merit, took all opportunities of recommending him, and asserted that "the inhumanity of his mother had given him a right to find every good man his father."

Nor was Mr. Savage admitted to his acquaintance only, but to his confidence, of which he sometimes related an instance too extraordinary to be omitted, as it affords a very just idea of his partron's character.

He was once desired by Sir Richard, with an air of the utmost importance, to come very early to his house the next morning. Mr. Savage came as he had promised, found the chariot at the door, and Sir Richard waiting for him and ready to go out. What was intended, and whither they were to go, Savage could not conjecture and was not willing to inquire, but immediately seated himself with his friend; the coachman was ordered to drive, and they hurried with the utmost expedition to Hyde Park Corner, where they stopped at a petty tavern and retired to a private room. Sir Richard then informed him that he intended to publish a pamphlet, and that he had desired him to come thither that he might write for him. They soon sat down to the work, Sir

10. An actor who became manager of Lincoln's Inn Theater.

11. Influence.

12. Sir Richard Steele (1672–1729), joint editor with Addison of *The Spectator.* Savage made little from the play because the author received only the profit of every third night's performance, and the play, being acted so late in the season, had few performances.

13. Robert Wilks (1665–1720) made his name as an actor in Colley Cibber's plays.

14. Made much of.

Richard dictated, and Savage wrote, till the dinner that had been ordered was put upon the table. Savage was surprised at the meanness of the entertainment, and after some hesitation ventured to ask for wine, which Sir Richard, not without reluctance, ordered to be brought. They then finished their dinner and proceeded in their pamphlet, which they concluded in the afternoon.

Mr. Savage then imagined his task over, and expected that Sir Richard would call for the reckoning and return home; but his expectations deceived him, for Sir Richard told him that he was without money, and that the pamphlet must be sold before the dinner could be paid for; and Savage was therefore obliged to go and offer their new production to sale for two guineas, which with some difficulty he obtained. Sir Richard then returned home, having retired that day only to avoid his creditors, and composed the pamphlet only to discharge his reckoning.

Mr. Savage related another fact equally uncommon, which, though it has no relation to his life, ought to be preserved. Sir Richard Steele having one day invited to his house a great number of persons of the first quality, they were surprised at the number of liveries which surrounded the table; and after dinner, when wine and mirth had set them free from the observation of rigid ceremony, one of them inquired of Sir Richard how such an expensive train of domestics could be consistent with his fortune. He with great frankness confessed that they were fellows of whom he would very willingly be rid. And being then asked why he did not discharge them, declared that they were bailiffs, who had introduced themselves with an execution,[15] and whom, since he could not send them away, he had thought it convenient to embellish with liveries that they might do him credit while they stayed.

His friends were diverted with the expedient, and by paying the debt discharged their attendance, having obliged Sir Richard to promise that they should never again find him graced with a retinue of the same kind.

Under such a tutor, Mr. Savage was not likely to learn prudence or frugality, and perhaps many of the misfortunes which the want of those virtues brought upon him in the following parts of his life might be justly imputed to so unimproving an example.

Nor did the kindness of Sir Richard end in common favors. He proposed to have established him in some settled scheme of life, and to have contracted a kind of alliance with him by marrying him to a natural daughter, on whom he intended to bestow a thousand pounds. But though he was always lavish of future bounties, he conducted his affairs in such a manner that he was very seldom able to keep his promises or execute his own intentions; and as he was never able to

15. An order to seize a debtor's goods.

raise the sum which he had offered, the marriage was delayed. In the meantime he was officiously informed that Mr. Savage had ridiculed him; by which he was so much exasperated that he withdrew the allowance which he had paid him, and never afterwards admitted him to his house.

It is not indeed unlikely that Savage might by his imprudence expose himself to the malice of a talebearer; for his patron had many follies, which, as his discernment easily discovered, his imagination might sometimes incite him to mention too ludicrously. A little knowledge of the world is sufficient to discover that such weakness is very common, and that there are few who do not sometimes, in the wantonness of thoughtless mirth, or the heat of transient resentment, speak of their friends and benefactors with levity and contempt, though in their cooler moments they want neither sense of their kindness nor reverence for their virtue. The fault therefore of Mr. Savage was rather negligence than ingratitude; but Sir Richard must likewise be acquitted of severity, for who is there that can patiently bear contempt from one whom he has relieved and supported, whose establishment he has labored and whose interest he has promoted?

He was now again abandoned to fortune without any other friend than Mr. Wilks, a man who, whatever were his abilities or skill as an actor, deserves at least to be remembered for his virtues, which are not often to be found in the world, and perhaps less often in his profession than in others. To be humane, generous, and candid,[16] is a very high degree of merit in any state; but those qualities deserve still greater praise when they are found in that condition which makes almost every other man, for whatever reason, contemptuous, insolent, petulant, selfish, and brutal.

As Mr. Wilks was one of those to whom calamity seldom complained without relief, he naturally took an unfortunate wit[17] into his protection, and not only assisted him in any casual distresses, but continued an equal and steady kindness to the time of his death.

By his interposition Mr. Savage once obtained from his mother fifty pounds, and a promise of one hundred and fifty more; but it was the fate of this unhappy man that few promises of any advantage to him were performed. His mother was infected, among others, with the general madness of the South Sea traffic;[18] and, having been disappointed in her expectations, refused to pay what perhaps nothing but the prospect of sudden affluence prompted her to promise.

Being thus obliged to depend upon the friendship of Mr. Wilks, he

16. Charitably inclined.
17. Man of letters.
18. Speculation in the shares of the South Sea Company ruined many investors in 1720–21.

was consequently an assiduous frequenter of the theaters; and in a short time the amusements of the stage took such possession of his mind that he never was absent from a play in several years.

This constant attendance naturally procured him the acquaintance of the players and, among others, of Mrs. Oldfield,[19] who was so much pleased with his conversation and touched with his misfortunes that she allowed him a settled pension of fifty pounds a year, which was during her life regularly paid.

That this act of generosity may receive its due praise, and that the good actions of Mrs. Oldfield may not be sullied by her general character, it is proper to mention that Mr. Savage often declared in the strongest terms that he never saw her alone, or in any other place than behind the scenes.

At her death he endeavored to show his gratitude in the most decent manner, by wearing mourning as for a mother but did not celebrate her in elegies, because he knew that too great profusion of praise would only have revived those faults which his natural equity did not allow him to think less because they were committed by one who favored him; but of which, though his virtue would not endeavor to palliate them, his gratitude would not suffer him to prolong the memory or diffuse the censure.

In his *Wanderer* he has indeed taken an opportunity of mentioning her; but celebrates her not for her virtue, but her beauty, an excellence which none ever denied her: this is the only encomium with which he has rewarded her liberality, and perhaps he has even in this been too lavish of his praise. He seems to have thought that never to mention his benefactress would have an appearance of ingratitude, though to have dedicated any particular performance to her memory would have only betrayed an officious partiality that, without exalting her character, would have depressed his own.

He had sometimes, by the kindness of Mr. Wilks, the advantage of a benefit, on which occasions he often received uncommon marks of regard and compassion; and was once told by the Duke of Dorset that it was just to consider him as an injured nobleman, and that in his opinion the nobility ought to think themselves obliged, without solicitation, to take every opportunity of supporting him by their countenance and patronage. But he had generally the mortification to hear that the whole interest of his mother was employed to frustrate his applications, and that she never left any expedient untried by which he might be cut off from the possibility of supporting life. The same disposition she endeavored to diffuse among all those over whom nature or fortune gave her any influence, and indeed succeeded too well in her design but could not always propagate her effrontery with her cruelty, for some

19. A celebrated actress (1683–1730).

of those whom she incited against him were ashamed of their own conduct, and boasted of that relief which they never gave him.

In this censure I do not indiscriminately involve all his relations; for he has mentioned with gratitude the humanity of one lady whose name I am now unable to recollect, and to whom therefore I cannot pay the praises which she deserves for having acted well in opposition to influence, precept, and example.

The punishment which our laws inflict upon those parents who murder their infants is well known, nor has its justice ever been contested; but if they deserve death who destroy a child in its birth, what pains can be severe enough for her who forbears to destroy him only to inflict sharper miseries upon him; who prolongs his life only to make it miserable; and who exposes him, without care and without pity, to the malice of oppression, the caprices of chance, and the temptations of poverty; who rejoices to see him overwhelmed with calamities; and when his own industry, or the charity of others, has enabled him to rise for a short time above his miseries, plunges him again into his former distress?

The kindness of his friends not affording him any constant supply, and the prospect of improving his fortune by enlarging his acquaintance necessarily leading him to places of expense, he found it necessary to endeavor once more at dramatic poetry, for which he was now better qualified by a more extensive knowledge and longer observation. But having been unsuccessful in comedy, though rather for want of opportunities than genius, he resolved now to try whether he should not be more fortunate in exhibiting a tragedy.

The story which he chose for the subject was that of Sir Thomas Overbury, a story well adapted to the stage, though perhaps not far enough removed from the present age to admit properly the fictions necessary to complete the plan:[20] for the mind, which naturally loves truth, is always most offended with the violation of those truths of which we are most certain; and we of course conceive those facts most certain which approach nearest to our own time.

Out of this story he formed a tragedy, which, if the circumstances in which he wrote it be considered, will afford at once an uncommon proof of strength of genius and evenness of mind, of a serenity not to be ruffled and an imagination not to be suppressed.

During a considerable part of the time in which he was employed upon this performance he was without lodging and often without meat;[21] nor had he any other conveniences for study than the fields or the streets allowed him; there he used to walk and form his speeches,

20. The death of Sir Thomas Overbury was a scandal of the reign of James I (1603–25); it was commonly thought he had been poisoned by Lady Essex for opposing her marriage to the King's favorite, Robert Carr.

21. Food, in general.

and afterwards step into a shop, beg for a few moments the use of the pen and ink, and write down what he had composed upon paper which he had picked up by accident.

If the performance of a writer thus distressed is not perfect, its faults ought surely to be imputed to a cause very different from want of genius, and must rather excite pity than provoke censure.

But when under these discouragements the tragedy was finished, there yet remained the labor of introducing it on the stage, an undertaking which to an ingenuous mind was in a very high degree vexatious and disgusting; for, having little interest or reputation, he was obliged to submit himself wholly to the players, and admit, with whatever reluctance, the emendations of Mr. Cibber,[22] which he always considered as the disgrace of his performance.

He had indeed in Mr. Hill[23] another critic of a very different class, from whose friendship he received great assistance on many occasions, and whom he never mentioned but with the utmost tenderness and regard. He had been for some time distinguished by him with very particular kindness, and on this occasion it was natural to apply to him as an author of an established character. He therefore sent this tragedy to him, with a short copy of verses in which he desired his correction. Mr. Hill, whose humanity and politeness are generally known, readily complied with his request; but as he is remarkable for singularity of sentiment and bold experiments in language, Mr. Savage did not think his play much improved by his innovation, and had even at that time the courage to reject several passages which he could not approve; and, what is still more laudable, Mr. Hill had the generosity not to resent the neglect of his alterations, but wrote the Prologue and Epilogue, in which he touches on the circumstances of the author with great tenderness.

After all these obstructions and compliances he was only able to bring his play upon the stage in the summer, when the chief actors had retired and the rest were in possession of the House for their own advantage. Among these Mr. Savage was admitted to play the part of Sir Thomas Overbury, by which he gained no great reputation, the theater being a province for which nature seemed not to have designed him; for neither his voice, look, nor gesture were such as are expected on the stage; and he was himself so much ashamed of having been reduced to appear as a player that he always blotted out his name from the list when a copy of his tragedy was to be shown to his friends.

In the publication of his performance he was more successful, for the rays of genius that glimmered in it, that glimmered through all the

22. Colley Cibber (1671–1757), dramatist, actor, and theater manager; Poet Laureate in 1730. But Savage actually acknowledged the help of his son, Theophilus Cibber, in the play's dedication.

23. Aaron Hill (1685–1750), minor poet and dramatist.

mists which poverty had been able to spread over it, procured him the notice and esteem of many persons eminent for their rank, their virtue, and their wit.

Of this play, acted, printed, and dedicated, the accumulated profits arose to an hundred pounds, which he thought at that time a very large sum, having been never master of so much before.

In the Dedication, for which he received ten guineas, there is nothing remarkable. The Preface contains a very liberal encomium on the blooming excellencies of Mr. Theophilus Cibber, which Mr. Savage could not in the latter part of his life see his friends about to read without snatching the play out of their hands.

The generosity of Mr. Hill did not end on this occasion; for afterwards, when Mr. Savage's necessities returned, he encouraged a subscription to a *Miscellany of Poems* in a very extraordinary manner, by publishing his story in *The Plain Dealer,* with some affecting lines, which he asserts to have been written by Mr. Savage upon the treatment received by him from his mother, but of which he was himself the author, as Mr. Savage afterwards declared. These lines, and the paper in which they were inserted, had a very powerful effect upon all but his mother, whom, by making her cruelty more public, they only hardened in her aversion.

Mr. Hill not only promoted the subscription to the *Miscellany,* but furnished likewise the greatest part of the poems of which it is composed, and particularly "The Happy Man," which he published as a specimen.

The subscriptions of those whom these papers should influence to patronize merit in distress, without any other solicitation, were directed to be left at Button's Coffee-house; and Mr. Savage going thither a few days afterwards, without expectation of any effect from his proposal, found to his surprise seventy guineas, which had been sent him in consequence of the compassion excited by Mr. Hill's pathetic representation.

To this *Miscellany* he published a Preface, in which he gives an account of his mother's cruelty in a very uncommon strain of humor, and with a gaiety of imagination which the success of his subscription probably produced.

The Dedication is addressed to the Lady Mary Wortley Montagu[24] whom he flatters without reserve, and to confess the truth with very little art. The same observation may be extended to all his dedications: his compliments are constrained and violent, heaped together without the grace of order, or the decency of introduction: he seems to have written his panegyrics for the perusal only of his patrons, and to have imagined that he had no other task than to pamper them with praises

24. Then known as a poetess and later famous as a letter writer (1689–1762).

however gross, and that flattery would make its way to the heart without the assistance of elegance or invention.

Soon afterwards the death of the King[25] furnished a general subject for a poetical contest, in which Mr. Savage engaged, and is allowed to have carried the prize of honor from his competitors: but I know not whether he gained by his performance any other advantage than the increase of his reputation; though it must certainly have been with farther views that he prevailed upon himself to attempt a species of writing of which all the topics had been long before exhausted, and which was made at once difficult by the multitudes that had failed in it, and those that had succeeded.

He was now advancing in reputation, and, though frequently involved in very distressful perplexities, appeared however to be gaining upon mankind, when both his fame and his life were endangered by an event, of which it is not yet determined whether it ought to be mentioned as a crime or a calamity.

On the 20th of November 1727, Mr. Savage came from Richmond, where he then lodged that he might pursue his studies with less interruption, with an intent to discharge another lodging which he had in Westminster; and accidentally meeting two gentlemen, his acquaintances, whose names were Merchant and Gregory, he went in with them to a neighboring coffee-house, and sat drinking till it was late, it being in no time of Mr. Savage's life any part of his character to be the first of the company that desired to separate. He would willingly have gone to bed in the same house; but there was not room for the whole company, and therefore they agreed to ramble about the streets, and divert themselves with such amusements as should offer themselves till morning.

In their walk they happened unluckily to discover light in Robinson's Coffee-house near Charing Cross, and therefore went in. Merchant with some rudeness demanded a room, and was told that there was a good fire in the next parlor, which the company were about to leave, being then paying their reckoning. Merchant, not satisfied with this answer, rushed into the room, and was followed by his companions. He then petulantly placed himself between the company and the fire, and soon after kicked down the table. This produced a quarrel, swords were drawn on both sides, and one Mr. James Sinclair was killed. Savage, having wounded likewise a maid that held him, forced his way with Merchant out of the house, but being intimidated and confused, without resolution either to fly or stay, they were taken in a back court by one of the company and some soldiers whom he had called to his assistance.

Being secured and guarded that night, they were in the morning

25. George I died in June, 1727.

carried before three justices, who committed them to the Gatehouse,[26] from whence, upon the death of Mr. Sinclair, which happened the same day, they were removed in the night to Newgate, where they were however treated with some distinction, exempted from the ignominy of chains, and confined, not among the common criminals, but in the press-yard.[27]

When the day of trial came the court was crowded in a very unusual manner, and the public appeared to interest itself as in a cause of general concern. The witnesses against Mr. Savage and his friends were the woman who kept the house, which was a house of ill fame, and her maid, the men who were in the room with Mr. Sinclair, and a woman of the town, who had been drinking with them, and with whom one of them had been seen in bed. They swore in general that Merchant gave the provocation, which Savage and Gregory drew their swords to justify; that Savage drew first, and that he stabbed Sinclair when he was not in a posture of defense, or while Gregory commanded his sword; that after he had given the thrust he turned pale, and would have retired, but the maid clung round him, and one of the company endeavored to detain him, from whom he broke, by cutting the maid on the head, but was afterwards taken in a court.

There was some difference in their depositions; one did not see Savage give the wound, another saw it given when Sinclair held his point towards the ground, and the woman of the town asserted that she did not see Sinclair's sword at all: this difference however was very far from amounting to inconsistency, but it was sufficient to show that the hurry of the quarrel was such that it was not easy to discover the truth with relation to particular circumstances, and that therefore some deductions were to be made from the credibility of the testimonies.

Sinclair had declared several times before his death that he received his wound from Savage, nor did Savage at his trial deny the fact but endeavored partly to extenuate it, by urging the suddenness of the whole action and the impossibility of any ill design or premeditated malice; and partly to justify it by the necessity of self-defense and the hazard of his own life, if he had lost that opportunity of giving the thrust: he observed that neither reason nor law obliged a man to wait for the blow which was threatened, and which, if he should suffer it, he might never be able to return; that it was always allowable to prevent an assault, and to preserve life by taking away that of the adversary by whom it was endangered.

With regard to the violence with which he endeavored his escape, he declared that it was not his design to fly from justice, or decline a trial,

26. An apartment at Westminster Palace used as a temporary prison.
27. The courtyard of Newgate prison.

but to avoid the expenses and severities of a prison; and that he intended to have appeared at the bar without compulsion.

This defense, which took up more than an hour, was heard by the multitude that thronged the court with the most attentive and respectful silence: those who thought he ought not to be acquitted owned that applause could not be refused him, and those who before pitied his misfortunes now reverenced his abilities.

The witnesses which appeared against him were proved to be persons of characters which did not entitle them to much credit: a common strumpet, a woman by whom strumpets were entertained, and a man by whom they were supported; and the character of Savage was by several persons of distinction asserted to be that of a modest, inoffensive man, not inclined to broils or to insolence, and who had, to that time, been only known for his misfortunes and his wit.

Had his audience been his judges, he had undoubtedly been acquitted; but Mr. Page, who was then upon the bench, treated him with his usual insolence and severity, and when he had summed up the evidence, endeavored to exasperate the jury as Mr. Savage used to relate it, with this eloquent harangue:

> Gentlemen of the jury, you are to consider that Mr. Savage is a very great man, a much greater man than you or I, gentlemen of the jury; that he wears very fine clothes, much finer clothes than you or I, gentlemen of the jury; that he has abundance of money in his pocket, much more money than you or I, gentlemen of the jury; but, gentlemen of the jury, is it not a very hard case, gentlemen of the jury, that Mr. Savage should therefore kill you or me, gentlemen of the jury?

Mr. Savage hearing his defense thus misrepresented, and the men who were to decide his fate incited against him by invidious comparisons, resolutely asserted that his cause was not candidly explained, and began to recapitulate what he had before said with regard to his condition and the necessity of endeavoring to escape the expenses of imprisonment; but the judge having ordered him to be silent, and repeated his orders without effect, commanded that he should be taken from the bar by force.

The jury then heard the opinion of the judge that good characters were of no weight against positive evidence, though they might turn the scale where it was doubtful; and that though, when two men attack each other, the death of either is only manslaughter, but where one is the aggressor, as in the case before them, and, in pursuance of his first attack, kills the other, the law supposes the action, however sudden, to be malicious. They then deliberated upon their verdict and determined that Mr. Savage and Mr. Gregory were guilty of murder, and Mr. Merchant, who had no sword, only of manslaughter.

Thus ended this memorable trial, which lasted eight hours. Mr. Savage and Mr. Gregory were conducted back to prison, where they were more closely confined and loaded with irons of fifty-pounds weight: four days afterwards they were sent back to the court to receive sentence, on which occasion Mr. Savage made, as far as it could be retained in memory, the following speech:

> It is now, my Lord, too late to offer anything by way of defense or vindication; nor can we expect aught from your Lordships in this court but the sentence which the law requires you, as judges, to pronounce against men of our calamitous condition.—But we are also persuaded, that as mere men, and out of this seat of rigorous justice, you are susceptive of the tender passions, and too humane not to commiserate the unhappy situation of those whom the law sometimes perhaps—exacts—from you to pronounce upon. No doubt you distinguish between offenses which arise out of premeditation and a disposition habituated to vice or immorality, and transgressions which are the unhappy and unforeseen effects of a casual[28] absence of reason and sudden impulse of passion: we therefore hope you will contribute all you can to an extension of that mercy which the gentlemen of the jury have been pleased to show Mr. Merchant, who (allowing facts as sworn against us by the evidence) has led us into this our calamity. I hope this will not be construed as if we meant to reflect upon that gentleman, or remove anything from us upon him, or that we repine the more at our fate because he has no participation of it: no, my Lord! For my part I declare nothing could more soften my grief than to be without any companion in so great a misfortune.

Mr. Savage had now no hopes of life but from the mercy of the Crown, which was very earnestly solicited by his friends, and which, with whatever difficulty the story may obtain belief, was obstructed only by his mother.

To prejudice the Queen[29] against him, she made use of an incident which was omitted in the order of time that it might be mentioned together with the purpose which it was made to serve. Mr. Savage, when he had discovered his birth, had an incessant desire to speak to his mother, who always avoided him in public and refused him admission into her house. One evening walking, as it was his custom, in the street that she inhabited, he saw the door of her house by accident open; he entered it, and, finding none in the passage to hinder him, went up stairs to salute[30] her. She discovered him before he could enter her chamber, alarmed the family[31] with the most distressful outcries,

28. Chance, accidental.
29. Caroline, wife of George II.
30. Greet, embrace.
31. Household.

and when she had by her screams gathered them about her, ordered them to drive out of the house that villain who had forced himself in upon her and endeavored to murder her. Savage, who had attempted with the most submissive tenderness to soften her rage, hearing her utter so detestable an accusation, thought it prudent to retire and, I believe, never attempted afterwards to speak to her.

But, shocked as he was with her falsehood and her cruelty, he imagined that she intended no other use of her lie than to set herself free from his embraces and solicitations, and was very far from suspecting that she would treasure it in her memory as an instrument of future wickedness, or that she would endeavor for this fictitious assault to deprive him of his life.

But when the Queen was solicited for his pardon, and informed of the severe treatment which he had suffered from his judge, she answered, that however unjustifiable might be the manner of his trial, or whatever extenuation the action for which he was condemned might admit, she could not think that man a proper object of the King's mercy who had been capable of entering his mother's house in the night with an intent to murder her.

By whom this atrocious calumny had been transmitted to the Queen, whether she that invented had the front[32] to relate it, whether she found anyone weak enough to credit it, or corrupt enough to concur with her in her hateful design, I know not; but methods had been taken to persuade the Queen so strongly of the truth of it that she for a long time refused to hear any of those who petitioned for his life.

Thus had Savage perished by the evidence of a bawd, a strumpet, and his mother, had not justice and compassion procured him an advocate of rank too great to be rejected unheard, and of virtue too eminent to be heard without being believed. His merit and his calamities happened to reach the ear of the Countess of Hertford, who engaged in his support with all the tenderness that is excited by pity, and all the zeal which is kindled by generosity; and, demanding an audience of the Queen, laid before her the whole series of his mother's cruelty, exposed the improbability of an accusation by which he was charged with an intent to commit a murder that could produce no advantage, and soon convinced her how little his former conduct could deserve to be mentioned as a reason for extraordinary severity.

The interposition of this lady was so successful that he was soon after admitted to bail, and, on the 9th of March 1728, pleaded the King's pardon.

It is natural to inquire upon what motives his mother could prosecute him in a manner so outrageous and implacable; for what reason she could employ all the arts of malice and all the snares of calumny to take

32. Effrontery.

away the life of her own son, of a son who never injured her, who was never supported by her expense, nor obstructed any prospect of pleasure or advantage; why she should endeavor to destroy him by a lie—a lie which could not gain credit but must vanish of itself at the first moment of examination, and of which only this can be said to make it probable, that it may be observed from her conduct that the most execrable crimes are sometimes committed without apparent temptation.

This mother is still alive[33] and may perhaps even yet, though her malice was so often defeated, enjoy the pleasure of reflecting that the life which she often endeavored to destroy was at least shortened by her maternal offices; that though she could not transport her son to the plantations,[34] bury him in the shop of a mechanic, or hasten the hand of the public executioner, she has yet had the satisfaction of embittering all his hours and forcing him into exigencies that hurried on his death.

It is by no means necessary to aggravate the enormity of this woman's conduct by placing it in opposition to that of the Countess of Hertford; no one can fail to observe how much more amiable it is to relieve than to oppress, and to rescue innocence from destruction than to destroy without an injury.

Mr. Savage, during his imprisonment, his trial, and the time in which he lay under sentence of death, behaved with great firmness and equality of mind, and confirmed by his fortitude the esteem of those who before admired him for his abilities. The peculiar circumstances of his life were made more generally known by a short account, which was then published, and of which several thousands were in a few weeks dispersed over the nation: and the compassion of mankind operated so powerfully in his favor, that he was enabled by frequent presents not only to support himself but to assist Mr. Gregory in prison; and when he was pardoned and released, he found the number of his friends not lessened.

The nature of the act for which he had been tried was in itself doubtful; of the evidences which appeared against him, the character of the man was not unexceptionable, that of the women notoriously infamous; she whose testimony chiefly influenced the jury to condemn him afterwards retracted her assertions. He always himself denied that he was drunk, as had been generally reported. Mr. Gregory, who is now Collector[35] of Antigua, is said to declare him far less criminal than he was imagined even by some who favored him; and Page himself afterwards confessed that he had treated him with uncommon rigor. When

33. In the year 1743 (Johnson's footnote in the first edition of 1744).
34. See p. 564. Transportation was a punishment for criminals.
35. Chief revenue or tax officer.

all these particulars are rated together, perhaps the memory of Savage may not be much sullied by his trial.

Some time after he obtained his liberty, he met in the street the woman that had sworn with so much malignity against him. She informed him that she was in distress, and, with a degree of confidence not easily attainable, desired him to relieve her. He, instead of insulting her misery and taking pleasure in the calamities of one who had brought his life into danger, reproved her gently for her perjury, and changing the only guinea that he had, divided it equally between her and himself.

This is an action which in some ages would have made a saint, and perhaps in others a hero, and which, without any hyperbolical encomiums, must be allowed to be an instance of uncommon generosity, an act of complicated virtue: by which he at once relieved the poor, corrected the vicious, and forgave an enemy; by which he at once remitted the strongest provocations and exercised the most ardent charity.

Compassion was indeed the distinguishing quality of Savage; he never appeared inclined to take advantage of weakness, to attack the defenseless, or to press upon the falling; whoever was distressed was certain at least of his good wishes; and when he could give no assistance to extricate them from misfortunes, he endeavored to soothe them by sympathy and tenderness.

But when his heart was not softened by the sight of misery, he was sometimes obstinate in his resentment and did not quickly lose the remembrance of an injury. He always continued to speak with anger of the insolence and partiality of Page, and a short time before his death revenged it by a satire.

It is natural to inquire in what terms Mr. Savage spoke of this fatal action when the danger was over and he was under no necessity of using any art to set his conduct in the fairest light. He was not willing to dwell upon it, and, if he transiently mentioned it, appeared neither to consider himself as a murderer nor as a man wholly free from the guilt of blood. How much and how long he regretted it appeared in a poem which he published many years afterwards. On occasion of a copy of verses in which the failings of good men were recounted, and in which the author had endeavored to illustrate his position, that "the best may sometimes deviate from virtue," by an instance of murder committed by Savage in the heat of wine, Savage remarked that it was no very just representation of a good man to suppose him liable to drunkenness, and disposed in his riots to cut throats.

He was now indeed at liberty, but was, as before, without any other support than accidental favors and uncertain patronage afforded him: sources by which he was sometimes very liberally supplied, and which at other times were suddenly stopped; so that he spent his life between want and plenty, or, what was yet worse, between beggary and extravagance; for, as whatever he received was the gift of chance, which might as well favor him at one time as another, he was tempted to squander what he had, because he always hoped to be immediately supplied.

Another cause of his profusion was the absurd kindness of his friends, who at once rewarded and enjoyed his abilities by treating him at taverns, and habituated him to pleasures which he could not afford to enjoy, and which he was not able to deny himself, though he purchased the luxury of a single night by the anguish of cold and hunger for a week.

The experience of these inconveniences determined him to endeavor after some settled income, which, having long found submission and entreaties fruitless, he attempted to extort from his mother by rougher methods. He had now, as he acknowledged, lost that tenderness for her which the whole series of her cruelty had not been able wholly to repress, till he found, by the efforts which she made for his destruction, that she was not content with refusing to assist him and being neutral in his struggles with poverty, but was as ready to snatch every opportunity of adding to his misfortunes; and that she was to be considered as an enemy implacably malicious, whom nothing but his blood could satisfy. He therefore threatened to harass her with lampoons and to publish a copious narrative of her conduct, unless she consented to purchase an exemption from infamy by allowing him a pension.

This expedient proved successful. Whether shame still survived though virtue was extinct, or whether her relations had more delicacy than herself and imagined that some of the darts which satire might point at her would glance upon them, Lord Tyrconnel whatever were his motives, upon his promise to lay aside his design of exposing the cruelty of his mother, received him into his family, treated him as his equal, and engaged to allow him a pension of two hundred pounds a year.[36]

This was the golden part of Mr. Savage's life, and for some time he had no reason to complain of fortune; his appearance was splendid, his expenses large, and his acquaintance extensive. He was courted by all who endeavored to be thought men of genius, and caressed by all who valued themselves upon a refined taste. To admire Mr. Savage was a proof of discernment, and to be acquainted with him was a title to poetical reputation. His presence was sufficient to make any place of public entertainment popular, and his approbation and example constituted the fashion. So powerful is genius when it is invested with the

36. Tyrconnel was Lady Macclesfield's nephew. Johnson's account of events here is extremely unreliable. Tyrconnel had taken Savage under his protection before the killing of Sinclair (1727), and Savage wrote some of his harshest attacks on his supposed mother while living with Tyrconnel. He and Tyrconnel did not quarrel until 1735.

glitter of affluence; men willingly pay to fortune that regard which they owe to merit, and are pleased when they have an opportunity at once of gratifying their vanity and practicing their duty.

This interval of prosperity furnished him with opportunities of enlarging his knowledge of human nature by contemplating life from its highest gradations to its lowest; and, had he afterwards applied to dramatic poetry, he would perhaps not have had many superiors; for as he never suffered any scene to pass before his eyes without notice, he had treasured in his mind all the different combinations of passions and the innumerable mixtures of vice and virtue which distingush one character from another; and, as his conception was strong, his expressions were clear, he easily received impressions from objects and very forcibly transmitted them to others.

Of his exact observations on human life he has left a proof, which would do honor to the greatest names, in a small pamphlet called *The Author to be Let,* where he introduces Iscariot Hackney, a prostitute scribbler, giving an account of his birth, his education, his disposition and morals, habits of life, and maxims of conduct. In the Introduction are related many secret histories of the petty writers of that time, but sometimes mixed with ungenerous reflections on their birth, their circumstances, or those of their relations; nor can it be denied that some passages are such as Iscariot Hackney might himself have produced.

He was accused likewise of living in an appearance of friendship with some whom he satirized, and of making use of the confidence which he gained by a seeming kindness to discover failings and expose them; it must be confessed that Mr. Savage's esteem was no very certain possession and that he would lampoon at one time those whom he had praised at another.

It may be alleged that the same man may change his principles, and that he who was once deservedly commended may be afterwards satirized with equal justice; or that the poet was dazzled with the appearance of virtue and found the man whom he had celebrated, when he had an opportunity of examining him more nearly, unworthy of the panegyric which he had too hastily bestowed; and that, as a false satire ought to be recanted for the sake of him whose reputation may be injured, false praise ought likewise to be obviated, lest the distinction between vice and virtue should be lost, lest a bad man should be trusted upon the credit of his encomiast, or lest others should endeavor to obtain the like praises by the same means.

But though these excuses may be often plausible and sometimes just, they are very seldom satisfactory to mankind; and the writer who is not constant to his subject quickly sinks into contempt, his satire loses its force and his panegyric its value, and he is only considered at one time as a flatterer and as a calumniator at another.

To avoid these imputations, it is only necessary to follow the rules of virtue and to preserve an unvaried regard to truth. For though it is undoubtedly possible that a man, however cautious, may be sometimes deceived by an artful appearance of virtue or by false evidences of guilt, such errors will not be frequent; and it will be allowed that the name of an author would never have been made contemptible had no man ever said what he did not think, or misled others but when he was himself deceived.

The Author to be Let was first published in a single pamphlet and afterwards inserted in a collection of pieces relating to *The Dunciad*[37] which were addressed by Mr. Savage to the Earl of Middlesex, in a Dedication which he was prevailed upon to sign though he did not write it, and in which there are some positions that the true author[38] would perhaps not have published under his own name, and on which Mr. Savage afterwards reflected with no great satisfaction.

The enumeration of the bad effects of the "uncontrolled freedom of the press," and the assertion that the "liberties taken by the writers of journals with their superiors were exorbitant and unjustifiable" very ill became men who have themselves not always shown the exactest regard to the laws of subordination in their writings, and who have often satirized those that at least thought themselves their superiors, as they were eminent for their hereditary rank, and employed in the highest offices of the kingdom. But this is only an instance of that partiality which almost every man indulges with regard to himself; the liberty of the press is a blessing when we are inclined to write against others, and a calamity when we find ourselves overborne by the multitude of our assailants; as the power of the Crown is always thought too great by those who suffer by its influence and too little by those in whose favor it is exerted; and a standing army is generally accounted necessary by those who command, and dangerous and oppressive by those who support it.

Mr. Savage was likewise very far from believing that the letters annexed to each species of bad poets in the *Bathos*[39] were, as he was directed to assert, "set down at random"; for when he was charged by one of his friends with putting his name to such an improbability, he had no other answer to make than that "he did not think of it"; and his friend had too much tenderness to reply that next to the crime of writing contrary to what he thought was that of writing without thinking.

After having remarked what is false in this Dedication, it is proper that I observe the impartiality which I recommend by declaring, what Savage asserted, that the account of the circumstances which attended

37. The first version of Pope's satire was published in 1728.

38. Presumably Pope.

39. In Pope's *Treatise of the Bathos, or of the Art of Sinking in Poetry,* bad poets were designated by initials.

the publication of the *Dunciad,* however strange and improbable, was exactly true.

The publication of this piece at this time raised Mr. Savage a great number of enemies among those that were attacked by Mr. Pope, with whom he was considered as a kind of confederate and whom he was suspected of supplying with private intelligence and secret incidents: so that the ignominy of an informer was added to the terror of a satirist.

That he was not altogether free from literary hypocrisy, and that he sometimes spoke one thing and wrote another, cannot be denied; because he himself confessed that when he lived in great familiarity with Dennis,[40] he wrote an epigram against him.

Mr. Savage, however, set all the malice of all the pigmy writers at defiance, and thought the friendship of Mr. Pope cheaply purchased by being exposed to their censure and their hatred; nor had he any reason to repent of the preference, for he found Mr. Pope a steady and unalienable friend almost to the end of his life.

About this time, notwithstanding his avowed neutrality with regard to party, he published a panegyric on Sir Robert Walpole,[41] for which he was rewarded by him with twenty guineas, a sum not very large, if either the excellence of the performance or the wealth of the patron be considered; but greater than he afterwards obtained from a person of yet higher rank,[42] and more desirous in appearance of being distinguished as a patron of literature.

As he was very far from approving the conduct of Sir Robert Walpole, and in conversation mentioned him sometimes with acrimony and generally with contempt; as he was one of those who were always zealous in their assertions of the justice of the late Opposition,[43] jealous of the rights of the people, and alarmed by the long-continued triumph of the Court, it was natural to ask him what could induce him to employ his poetry in praise of that man who was, in his opinion, an enemy to liberty and an oppressor of his country? He alleged that he was then dependent upon the Lord Tyrconnel, who was an implicit[44] follower of the ministry; and that being enjoined by him, not without menaces, to write in praise of his leader, he had not resolution sufficient to sacrifice the pleasure of affluence to that of integrity.

On this and on many other occasions, he was ready to lament the misery of living at the tables of other men, which was his fate from the beginning to the end of his life; for I know not whether he ever had, for

40. John Dennis (1657–1734), critic and enemy of Pope.

41. Chief minister to George I and George II, and leader of the Whigs.

42. Frederick, Prince of Wales (see pp. 601–04).

43. The self-styled "patriot" Opposition, with which Pope was associated. Johnson calls it the "late" Opposition, because by 1744 Walpole had been forced out of office and the Opposition had been largely absorbed into the Ministry.

44. Unquestioning.

three months together, a settled habitation in which he could claim a right of residence.

To this unhappy state it is just to impute much of the inconstancy of his conduct; for though a readiness to comply with the inclination of others was no part of his natural character, yet he was sometimes obliged to relax his obstinacy and submit his own judgment, and even his virtue, to the government of those by whom he was supported: so that if his miseries were sometimes the consequence of his faults, he ought not yet to be wholly excluded from compassion, because his faults were very often the effects of his misfortunes.

In this gay period of his life, while he was supported by affluence and pleasure, he published *The Wanderer,* a moral poem, of which the design is comprised in these lines:

> I fly all public care, all venal strife,
> To try the still, compared with active, life;
> To prove by these, the sons of men may owe
> The fruits of bliss to bursting clouds of woe;
> That even calamity, by thought refined,
> Inspirits and adorns the thinking mind.

And more distinctly in the following passage:

> By woe, the soul to daring action swells,
> By woe, in plaintless patience it excels;
> From patience prudent, clear experience springs,
> And traces knowledge through the course of things.
> Thence hope is formed, thence fortitude, success,
> Renown—whate'er men covet and caress.

This performance was always considered by himself as his masterpiece; and Mr. Pope, when he asked his opinion of it, told him that he read it once over, and was not displeased with it, that it gave him more pleasure at the second perusal, and delighted him still more at the third.

It has been generally objected to *The Wanderer* that the disposition of the parts is irregular, that the design is obscure, and the plan perplexed; that the images, however beautiful, succeed each other without order; and that the whole performance is not so much a regular fabric as a heap of shining materials thrown together by accident, which strikes rather with the solemn magnificence of a stupendous ruin than the elegant grandeur of a finished pile.

This criticism is universal, and therefore it is reasonable to believe it at least in a great degree just; but Mr. Savage was always of a contrary opinion; he thought his drift could only be missed by negligence or stupidity, and that the whole plan was regular and the parts distinct.

It was never denied to abound with strong representations of nature and just observations upon life, and it may easily be observed that most of his pictures have an evident tendency to illustrate his first great position, "that good is the consequence of evil." The sun that burns up the mountains fructifies the vales; the deluge that rushes down the broken rocks with dreadful impetuosity is separated into purling brooks; and the rage of the hurricane purifies the air.

Even in this poem he has not been able to forbear one touch upon the cruelty of his mother, which, though remarkably delicate and tender, is a proof how deep an impression it had made upon his mind.

This must be at least acknowledged, which ought to be thought equivalent to many other excellencies that this poem can promote no other purposes than those of virtue and that it is written with a very strong sense of the efficacy of religion.

But my province is rather to give the history of Mr. Savage's performances than to display their beauties[45] or to obviate the criticisms which they have occasioned; and therefore I shall not dwell upon the particular passages which deserve applause: I shall neither show the excellence of his descriptions, nor expatiate on the terrific[46] portrait of suicide, nor point out the artful touches by which he has distinguished the intellectual features of the rebels, who suffer death in his last canto. It is, however, proper to observe that Savage always declared the characters wholly fictitious and without the least allusion to any real persons or actions.

From a poem so diligently labored and so successfully finished, it might be reasonably expected that he should have gained considerable advantage; nor can it without some degree of indignation and concern be told that he sold the copy for ten guineas, of which he afterwards returned two, that the two last sheets of the work might be reprinted, of which he had in his absence entrusted the correction to a friend, who was too indolent to perform it with accuracy.

A superstitious regard to the correction of his sheets was one of Mr. Savage's peculiarities: he often altered, revised, recurred to his first reading or punctuation, and again adopted the alteration; he was dubious and irresolute without end, as on a question of the last importance, and at last was seldom satisfied; the intrusion or omission of a comma was sufficient to discompose him, and he would lament an error of a single letter as a heavy calamity. In one of his letters relating to an impression of some verses, he remarks that he had with regard to the correction of the proof "a spell upon him"; and indeed the anxiety with which he dwelt upon the minutest and most trifling niceties deserved no other name than that of fascination.[47]

That he sold so valuable a performance for so small a price was not to be imputed either to necessity, by which the learned and ingenious are

45. Nevertheless, Johnson includes here in footnotes long extracts from *The Wanderer*.

46. Terrifying.

47. From Latin, *fascinare*, to bewitch.

often obliged to submit to very hard conditions, or to avarice, by which the booksellers are frequently incited to oppress that genius by which they are supported; but to that intemperate desire of pleasure and habitual slavery to his passions which involved him in many perplexities; he happened at that time to be engaged in the pursuit of some trifling gratification, and, being without money for the present occasion, sold his poem to the first bidder, perhaps for the first price that was proposed, and would probably have been content with less if less had been offered him.

This poem was addressed to the Lord Tyrconnel, not only in the first lines, but in a formal Dedication filled with the highest strains of panegyric and the warmest professions of gratitude, but by no means remarkable for delicacy of connection or elegance of style.

These praises in a short time he found himself inclined to retract, being discarded by the man on whom he had bestowed them and whom he then immediately discovered not to have deserved them. Of this quarrel, which every day made more bitter, Lord Tyrconnel and Mr. Savage assigned very different reasons, which might perhaps all in reality concur, though they were not all convenient[48] to be alleged by either party. Lord Tyrconnel affirmed that it was the constant practice of Mr. Savage to enter a tavern with any company that proposed it, drink the most expensive wines with great profusion, and when the reckoning was demanded, to be without money: if, as it often happened, his companions were willing to defray his part, the affair ended without any ill consequences; but if they were refractory and expected that the wine should be paid for by him that drank it, his method of composition was to take them with him to his own apartment, assume the government of the house, and order the butler in an imperious manner to set the best wine in the cellar before his company, who often drank till they forgot the respect due to the house in which they were entertained, indulged themselves in the utmost extravagance of merriment, practiced the most licentious frolics, and committed all the outrages of drunkenness.

Nor was this the only charge which Lord Tyrconnel brought against him: having given him a collection of valuable books stamped with his own arms, he had the mortification to see them in a short time exposed to sale upon the stalls, it being usual with Mr. Savage when he wanted a small sum to take his books to the pawnbroker.

Whoever was acquainted with Mr. Savage easily credited both these accusations; for having been obliged from his first entrance into the world to subsist upon expedients, affluence was not able to exalt him above them; and so much was he delighted with wine and conversation,

48. Appropriate, proper.

and so long had he been accustomed to live by chance, that he would at any time go to the tavern without scruple and trust for his reckoning to the liberality of his company, and frequently of company to whom he was very little known. This conduct indeed very seldom drew upon him those inconveniences that might be feared by any other person; for his conversation was so entertaining, and his address so pleasing that few thought the pleasure which they received from him dearly purchased by paying for his wine. It was his peculiar happiness that he scarcely ever found a stranger whom he did not leave a friend; but it must likewise be added that he had not often a friend long without obliging him to become a stranger.

Mr. Savage, on the other hand, declared that Lord Tyrconnel quarreled with him because he would not subtract from his own luxury and extravagance what he had promised to allow him, and that his resentment was only a plea for the violation of his promise. He asserted that he had done nothing that ought to exclude him from that subsistence which he thought not so much a favor as a debt, since it was offered him upon conditions which he had never broken; and that his only fault was that he could not be supported with nothing.

He acknowledged that Lord Tyrconnel often exhorted him to regulate his method of life and not to spend all his nights in taverns, and that he appeared very desirous that he would pass those hours with him which he so freely bestowed upon others. This demand Mr. Savage considered as a censure of his conduct, which he could never patiently bear; and which, even in the latter and cooler part of his life, was so offensive to him that he declared it as his resolution "to spurn that friend who should presume to dictate to him"; and it is not likely that in his earlier years he received admonitions with more calmness.

He was likewise inclined to resent such expectations as tending to infringe his liberty, of which he was very jealous when it was necessary to the gratification of his passions; and declared that the request was still more unreasonable, as the company to which he was to have been confined was insupportably disagreeable. This assertion affords another instance of that inconsistency of his writings with his conversation which was so often to be observed. He forgot how lavishly he had, in his Dedication to *The Wanderer,* extolled the delicacy and penetration, the humanity and generosity, the candor and politeness of the man whom, when he no longer loved him, he declared to be a wretch without understanding, without good nature, and without justice, of whose name he thought himself obliged to leave no trace in any future edition of his writings, and accordingly blotted it out of that copy of *The Wanderer* which was in his hands.

During his continuance with the Lord Tyrconnel, he wrote "The Triumph of Health and Mirth" on the recovery of Lady Tyrconnel from a languishing illness. This performance is remarkable not only for the gaiety of the ideas[49] and the melody of the numbers,[50] but for the agreeable fiction upon which it is formed. Mirth, overwhelmed with sorrow for the sickness of her favorite, takes a flight in quest of her sister Health, whom she finds reclined upon the brow of a lofty mountain amidst the fragrance of perpetual spring, with the breezes of the morning sporting about her. Being solicited by her sister Mirth, she readily promises her assistance, flies away in a cloud, and impregnates the waters of Bath[51] with new virtues, by which the sickness of Belinda is relieved.

As the reputation of his abilities, the particular circumstances of his birth and life, the splendor of his appearance, and the distinction which was for some time paid him by Lord Tyrconnel, entitled him to familiarity with persons of higher rank than those to whose conversation he had been before admitted, he did not fail to gratify that curiosity which induced him to take a nearer view of those whom their birth, their employments, or their fortunes necessarily place at a distance from the greatest part of mankind, and to examine whether their merit was magnified or diminished by the medium through which it was contemplated; whether the splendor with which they dazzled their admirers was inherent in themselves or only reflected on them by the objects that surrounded them; and whether great men were selected for high stations, or high stations made great men.

For this purpose he took all opportunities of conversing familiarly with those who were most conspicuous at that time for their power or their influence; he watched their looser moments and examined their domestic behavior with that acuteness which nature had given him, and which the uncommon variety of his life had contributed to increase, and that inquisitiveness which must always be produced in a vigorous mind by an absolute freedom from all pressing or domestic engagements. His discernment was quick, and therefore he soon found in every person, and in every affair, something that deserved attention; he was supported by others without any care for himself, and was therefore at leisure to pursue his observations.

More circumstances to constitute a critic on human life could not easily concur; nor indeed could any man who assumed from accidental advantages more praise than he could justly claim from his real merit admit any acquaintance more dangerous than that of Savage; of whom likewise it must be confessed, that abilities really exalted above the common level, or virtue refined from passion or proof against corruption, could not easily find an abler judge or a warmer advocate.

What was the result of Mr. Savage's inquiry, though he was not much

49. Images.
50. Verses.
51. A celebrated health resort.

accustomed to conceal his discoveries, it may not be entirely safe to relate, because the persons whose characters he criticized are powerful, and power and resentment are seldom strangers; nor would it perhaps be wholly just, because what he asserted in conversation might, though true in general, be heightened by some momentary ardor of imagination, and, as it can be delivered only from memory, may be imperfectly represented; so that the picture, at first aggravated, and then unskillfully copied, may be justly suspected to retain no great resemblance of the original.

It may, however, be observed that he did not appear to have formed very elevated ideas of those to whom the administration of affairs or the conduct of parties has been entrusted; who have been considered as the advocates of the Crown or the guardians of the people, and who have obtained the most implicit confidence and the loudest applauses. Of one particular person who has been at one time so popular as to be generally esteemed, and at another so formidable as to be universally detested, he observed that his acquisitions had been small, or that his capacity was narrow, and that the whole range of his mind was from obscenity to politics and from politics to obscenity.[52]

But the opportunity of indulging his speculations on great characters was now at an end. He was banished from the table of Lord Tyrconnel and turned again adrift upon the world, without prospect of finding quickly any other harbor. As prudence was not one of the virtues by which he was distinguished, he had made no provision against a misfortune like this. And though it is not to be imagined but that the separation must for some time have been preceded by coldness, peevishness, or neglect, though it was undoubtedly the consequence of accumulated provocations on both sides, yet everyone that knew Savage will readily believe that to him it was sudden as a stroke of thunder; that though he might have transiently suspected it, he had never suffered any thought so unpleasing to sink into his mind, but that he had driven it away by amusements or dreams of future felicity and affluence, and had never taken any measures by which he might prevent a precipitation from plenty to indigence.

This quarrel and separation, and the difficulties to which Mr. Savage was exposed by them, were soon known both to his friends and enemies; nor was it long before he perceived, from the behavior of both, how much is added to the luster of genius by the ornaments of wealth.

His condition did not appear to excite much compassion; for he had not always been careful to use the advantages which he enjoyed with that moderation which ought to have been with more than usual caution preserved by him, who knew, if he had reflected, that he was only a

52. Probably Johnson refers to Walpole.

dependent on the bounty of another whom he could expect to support him no longer than he endeavored to preserve his favor by complying with his inclinations, and whom he nevertheless set at defiance and was continually irritating by negligence or encroachments.

Examples need not be sought at any great distance to prove that superiority of fortune has a natural tendency to kindle pride, and that pride seldom fails to exert itself in contempt and insult; and if this is often the effect of hereditary wealth and of honors enjoyed only by the merit of others, it is some extenuation of any indecent[53] triumphs to which this unhappy man may have been betrayed that his prosperity was heightened by the force of novelty and made more intoxicating by a sense of the misery in which he had so long languished and perhaps of the insults which he had formerly borne, and which he might now think himself entitled to revenge. It is too common for those who have unjustly suffered pain to inflict it likewise in their turn with the same injustice, and to imagine that they have a right to treat others as they have themselves been treated.

That Mr. Savage was too much elevated by any good fortune is generally known; and some passages of his Introduction to *The Author to be Let* sufficiently show that he did not wholly refrain from such satire as he afterwards thought very unjust when he was exposed to it himself; for, when he was afterwards ridiculed in the character of a distressed poet, he very easily discovered that distress was not a proper subject for merriment or topic of invective. He was then able to discern that if misery be the effect of virtue it ought to be reverenced; if of ill fortune, to be pitied; and if of vice, not to be insulted, because it is perhaps itself a punishment adequate to the crime by which it was produced. And the humanity of that man can deserve no panegyric who is capable of reproaching a criminal in the hands of the executioner.

But these reflections, though they readily occurred to him in the first and last parts of his life, were, I am afraid, for a long time forgotten; at least they were, like many other maxims, treasured up in his mind rather for show than use, and operated very little upon his conduct, however elegantly he might sometimes explain, or however forcibly he might inculcate them.

His degradation, therefore, from the condition which he had enjoyed with such wanton thoughtlessness was considered by many as an occasion of triumph. Those who had before paid their court to him without success soon returned the contempt which they had suffered; and they who had received favors from him—for of such favors as he could bestow he was very liberal—did not always remember them. So

53. Offensive.

much more certain are the effects of resentment than of gratitude: it is not only to many more pleasing to recollect those faults which place others below them than those virtues by which they are themselves comparatively depressed, but it is likewise more easy to neglect than to recompense; and though there are few who will practice a laborious virtue, there will never be wanting multitudes that will indulge an easy vice.

Savage, however, was very little disturbed at the marks of contempt which his ill fortune brought upon him from those whom he never esteemed and with whom he never considered himself as leveled by any calamities; and though it was not without some uneasiness that he saw some whose friendship he valued change their behavior, he yet observed their coldness without much emotion, considered them as the slaves of fortune and the worshipers of prosperity, and was more inclined to despise them than to lament himself.

It does not appear that, after this return of his wants, he found mankind equally favorable to him as at his first appearance in the world. His story, though in reality not less melancholy, was less affecting because it was no longer new; it therefore procured him no new friends, and those that had formerly relieved him thought they might now consign him to others. He was now likewise considered by many rather as criminal than as unhappy; for the friends of Lord Tyrconnel and of his mother were sufficiently industrious to publish his weaknesses, which were indeed very numerous, and nothing was forgotten that might make him either hateful or ridiculous.

It cannot but be imagined that such representations of his faults must make great numbers less sensible of his distress; many who had only an opportunity to hear one part made no scruple to propagate the account which they received; many assisted their circulation from malice or revenge; and perhaps many pretended to credit them that they might with a better grace withdraw their regard or withhold their assistance.

Savage, however, was not one of those who suffer themselves to be injured without resistance, nor was less diligent in exposing the faults of Lord Tyrconnel, over whom he obtained at least this advantage, that he drove him first to the practice of outrage and violence; for he was so much provoked by the wit and virulence of Savage that he came with a number of attendants, that did no honor to his courage, to beat him at a coffee-house. But it happened that he had left the place a few minutes, and his Lordship had without danger the pleasure of boasting how he would have treated him. Mr. Savage went next day to repay his visit at his own house but was prevailed on by his domestics to retire without insisting upon seeing him.

Lord Tyrconnel was accused by Mr. Savage of some actions which scarcely any provocations will be thought sufficient to justify, such as seizing what he had in his lodgings and other instances of wanton cruelty, by which he increased the distress of Savage without any advantage to himself.

These mutual accusations were retorted on both sides for many years with the utmost degree of virulence and rage, and time seemed rather to augment than diminish their resentment; that the anger of Mr. Savage should be kept alive is not strange, because he felt every day the consequences of the quarrel; but it might reasonably have been hoped that Lord Tyrconnel might have relented and at length have forgot those provocations which, however they might have once inflamed him, had not in reality much hurt him.

The spirit of Mr. Savage indeed never suffered him to solicit a reconciliation; he returned reproach for reproach and insult for insult; his superiority of wit supplied the disadvantages of his fortune, and enabled him to form a party and prejudice great numbers in his favor.

But though this might be some gratification of his vanity, it afforded very little relief to his necessities; and he was very frequently reduced to uncommon hardships, of which, however, he never made any mean or importunate complaints, being formed rather to bear misery with fortitude than enjoy prosperity with moderation.

He now thought himself again at liberty to expose the cruelty of his mother; and therefore, I believe, about this time published "The Bastard," a poem remarkable for the vivacious sallies of thought in the beginning, where he makes a pompous enumeration of the imaginary advantages of base birth, and the pathetic sentiments at the end, where he recounts the real calamities which he suffered by the crime of his parents.[54]

The vigor and spirit of the verses, the peculiar circumstances of the author, the novelty of the subject, and the notoriety of the story to which the allusions are made, procured this performance a very favorable reception; great numbers were immediately dispersed, and editions were multiplied with unusual rapidity.

One circumstance attended the publication which Savage used to relate with great satisfaction. His mother, to whom the poem was "with due reverence" inscribed, happened then to be at Bath, where she could not conveniently retire from censure, or conceal herself from observation; and no sooner did the reputation of the poem begin to spread than she heard it repeated in all places of concourse, nor could she enter the assembly rooms, or cross the walks, without being saluted with some lines from "The Bastard."

This was perhaps the first time that ever she discovered a sense of shame, and on this occasion the power of wit was very conspicuous: the wretch who had, without scruple, proclaimed herself an adulteress,

54. Actually "The Bastard" was published in 1728, much earlier than Johnson implies. In a note Johnson quotes thirty-four lines from the beginning of the poem.

and who had first endeavored to starve her son, then to transport him, and afterwards to hang him, was not able to bear the representation of her own conduct; but fled from reproach, though she felt no pain from guilt, and left Bath with the utmost haste to shelter herself among the crowds of London.

Thus Savage had the satisfaction of finding that, though he could not reform his mother, he could punish her, and that he did not always suffer alone.

The pleasure which he received from this increase of his poetical reputation was sufficient for some time to overbalance the miseries of want, which this performance did not much alleviate; for it was sold for a very trivial sum to a bookseller who, though the success was so uncommon that five impressions were sold, of which many were undoubtedly very numerous, had not generosity sufficient to admit the unhappy writer to any part of the profit.

But though he did not lose the opportunity which success gave him of setting a high rate on his abilities, but paid due deference to the suffrages[55] of mankind when they were given in his favor, he did not suffer his esteem of himself to depend upon others, nor found anything sacred in the voice of the people when they were inclined to censure him; he then readily showed the folly of expecting that the public should judge right, observed how slowly poetical merit had often forced its way into the world; he contented himself with the applause of men of judgment, and was somewhat disposed to exclude all those from the character of men of judgment who did not applaud him.

But he was at other times more favorable to mankind than to think them blind to the beauties of his works and imputed the slowness of their sale to other causes: either they were published at a time when the town was empty, or when the attention of the public was engrossed by some struggle in the parliament, or some other object of general concern; or they were by the neglect of the publisher not diligently dispersed, or by his avarice not advertised with sufficient frequency. Address, or industry, or liberality was always wanting; and the blame was laid rather on any other person than the author.

By arts like these, arts which every man practices in some degree and to which too much of the little tranquillity of life is to be ascribed, Savage was always able to live at peace with himself. Had he indeed only made use of these expedients to alleviate the loss or want of fortune or reputation, or any other advantage which it is not in man's power to bestow upon himself, they might have been justly mentioned as instances of a philosophical mind and very properly proposed to the imitation of multitudes, who, for want of diverting their imaginations

55. Opinions.

with the same dexterity, languish under afflictions which might be easily removed.

It were doubtless to be wished that truth and reason were universally prevalent; that everything were esteemed according to its real value, and that men would secure themselves from being disappointed in their endeavors after happiness by placing it only in virtue, which is always to be obtained; but if adventitious and foreign pleasures must be pursued, it would be perhaps of some benefit, since that pursuit must frequently be fruitless, if the practice of Savage could be taught, that folly might be an antidote to folly, and one fallacy be obviated by another.

But the danger of this pleasing intoxication must not be concealed; nor indeed can anyone, after having observed the life of Savage, need to be cautioned against it. By imputing none of his miseries to himself, he continued to act upon the same principles and follow the same path; was never made wiser by his sufferings, nor preserved by one misfortune from falling into another. He proceeded throughout his life to tread the same steps on the same circle; always applauding his past conduct, or at least forgetting it, to amuse himself with phantoms of happiness which were dancing before him; and willingly turned his eyes from the light of reason, when it would have discovered the illusion and shown him what he never wished to see, his real state.

He is even accused, after having lulled his imagination with those ideal opiates, of having tried the same experiment upon his conscience; and, having accustomed himself to impute all deviations from the right to foreign causes, it is certain that he was upon every occasion too easily reconciled to himself; and that he appeared very little to regret those practices which had impaired his reputation. The reigning error of his life was that he mistook the love for the practice of virtue, and was indeed not so much a good man as the friend of goodness.

This at least must be allowed him, that he always preserved a strong sense of the dignity, the beauty, and the necessity of virtue; and that he never contributed deliberately to spread corruption amongst mankind; his actions, which were generally precipitate, were often blamable, but his writings, being the productions of study, uniformly tended to the exaltation[56] of the mind and the propagation of morality and piety.

These writings may improve mankind when his failings shall be forgotten, and therefore he must be considered upon the whole as a benefactor to the world; nor can his personal example do any hurt, since whoever hears of his faults will hear of the miseries which they brought upon him, and which would deserve less pity had not his condition been such as made his faults pardonable. He may be consid-

56. Refinement.

ered as a child *exposed* to all the temptations of indigence, at an age when resolution was not yet strengthened by conviction, nor virtue confirmed by habit; a circumstance which, in his "Bastard," he laments in a very affecting manner:

> No mother's care
> Shielded my infant innocence with prayer;
> No father's guardian-hand my youth maintained,
> Called forth my virtues, or from vice restrained.

"The Bastard," however it might provoke or mortify his mother, could not be expected to melt her to compassion, so that he was still under the same want of the necessaries of life; and he therefore exerted all the interest which his wit, or his birth, or his misfortunes could procure, to obtain, upon the death of Eusden,[57] the place of Poet Laureate, and prosecuted his application with so much diligence that the King publicly declared it his intention to bestow it upon him; but such was the fate of Savage that even the King, when he intended his advantage, was disappointed in his schemes; for the Lord Chamberlain, who has the disposal of the laurel as one of the appendages of his office, either did not know the King's design or did not approve it, or thought the nomination of the Laureate an encroachment upon his rights, and therefore bestowed the laurel upon Colley Cibber.

Mr. Savage, thus disappointed, took a resolution of applying to the Queen that, having once given him life, she would enable him to support it, and therefore published a short poem on her birthday, to which he gave the odd title of "Volunteer Laureate."The event of this essay he has himself related in the following letter, which he prefixed to the poem, when he afterwards reprinted it in *The Gentleman's Magazine*, from whence I have copied it entire, as this was one of the few attempts in which Mr. Savage succeeded.

> Mr. Urban,—In your *Magazine* for February you published the last "Volunteer Laureate," written on a very melancholy occasion, viz. the death of the royal patroness of arts and literature in general, and of the author of that poem in particular; I now send you the first that Mr. Savage wrote under that title.—This gentleman, notwithstanding a very considerable interest, being, on the death of Mr. Eusden, disappointed of the Laureate's place, wrote the following verses; which were no sooner published but the late Queen sent to a bookseller for them. The author had not at the time a friend either to get him introduced, or his poem presented at Court; yet such was the unspeakable goodness of that Princess that, notwithstanding this act of ceremony was wanting, in a few days after publication Mr. Savage received a bank bill of fifty pounds and a gracious message from her Majesty, by the

57. Laurence Eusden died in 1730.

> Lord North and Guilford, to this effect: "That her Majesty was highly pleased with the verses; that she took particularly kind his lines there relating to the King; that he had permission to write annually on the same subject; and that he should yearly receive the like present till something better (which was her Majesty's intention) could be done for him." After this, he was permitted to present one of his annual poems to her Majesty, had the honor of kissing her hand, and met with the most gracious reception.
>
> Yours, etc. . . .[58]

Such was the performance, and such its reception; a reception which, though by no means unkind, was yet not in the highest degree generous: to chain down the genius of a writer to an annual panegyric showed in the Queen too much a desire of hearing her own praises, and a greater regard to herself than to him on whom her bounty was conferred. It was a kind of avaricious generosity, by which flattery was rather purchased than genius rewarded.

Mrs. Oldfield had formerly given him the same allowance with much more heroic intention; she had no other view than to enable him to prosecute his studies and to set himself above the want of assistance, and was contented with doing good without stipulating for encomiums.

Mr. Savage, however, was not at liberty to make exceptions, but was ravished with the favors which he had received, and probably yet more with those which he was promised; he considered himself now as a favorite of the Queen, and did not doubt but a few annual poems would establish him in some profitable employment.

He therefore assumed the title of "Volunteer Laureate," not without some reprehensions from Cibber, who informed him that the title of "Laureate" was a mark of honor conferred by the King, from whom all honor is derived, and which therefore no man has a right to bestow upon himself; and added that he might with equal propriety style himself a Volunteer Lord, or Volunteer Baronet. It cannot be denied that the remark was just, but Savage did not think any title which was conferred upon Mr. Cibber so honorable as that the usurpation of it could be imputed to him as an instance of very exorbitant vanity, and therefore continued to write under the same title and received every year the same reward.

He did not appear to consider these encomiums as tests of his abilities, or as anything more than annual hints to the Queen of her promise, or acts of ceremony, by the performance of which he was entitled to his pension, and therefore did not labor them with great diligence, or print more than fifty each year, except that for some of the last years he regularly inserted them in *The Gentleman's Magazine*, by which they were dispersed over the kingdom.

58. Johnson here included Savage's first poem as Volunteer Laureate in early editions of the *Life of Savage*.

Of some of them he had himself so low an opinion that he intended to omit them in the collection of poems for which he printed proposals, and solicited subscriptions; nor can it seem strange that, being confined to the same subject, he should be at some times indolent, and at others unsuccessful; that he should sometimes delay a disagreeable task till it was too late to perform it well; or that he should sometimes repeat the same sentiment on the same occasion, or at others be misled by an attempt after novelty to forced conceptions and far-fetched images.

He wrote indeed with a double intention which supplied him with some variety; for his business was to praise the Queen for the favors which he had received, and to complain to her of the delay of those which she had promised: in some of his pieces, therefore, gratitude is predominant, and in some discontent; in some, he represents himself as happy in her patronage, and in others as disconsolate to find himself neglected.

Her promise, like other promises made to this unfortunate man, was never performed, though he took sufficient care that it should not be forgotten. The publication of his "Volunteer Laureate" procured him no other reward than a regular remittance of fifty pounds.

He was not so depressed by his disappointments as to neglect any opportunity that was offered of advancing his interest. When the Princess Anne was married, he wrote a poem upon her departure, only, as he declared, "because it was expected from him," and he was not willing to bar his own prospects by any appearance of neglect.

He never mentioned any advantage gained by this poem or any regard that was paid to it; and therefore it is likely that it was considered at Court as an act of duty, to which he was obliged by his dependence, and which it was therefore not necessary to reward by any new favor: or perhaps the Queen really intended his advancement, and therefore thought it superfluous to lavish presents upon a man whom she intended to establish for life.

About this time not only his hopes were in danger of being frustrated, but his pension likewise of being obstructed, by an accidental calumny. The writer of *The Daily Courant,* a paper then published under the direction of the ministry, charged him with a crime which, though not very great in itself, would have been remarkably invidious in him and might very justly have incensed the Queen against him. He was accused by name of influencing elections against the Court by appearing at the head of a Tory mob; nor did the accuser fail to aggravate his crime by representing it as the effect of the most atrocious ingratitude and a kind of rebellion against the Queen, who had first preserved him from an infamous death, and afterwards distinguished him by her favor, and supported him by her charity. The charge, as it was open and confident, was likewise by good fortune very particular. The place of the transaction was mentioned, and the whole series of the rioter's conduct related. This exactness made Mr. Savage's vindication easy; for he never had in his life seen the place which was declared to be the scene of his wickedness, nor ever had been present in any town when its representatives were chosen. This answer he therefore made haste to publish, with all the circumstances necessary to make it credible; and very reasonably demanded that the accusation should be retracted in the same paper that he might no longer suffer the imputation of sedition and ingratitude. This demand was likewise pressed by him in a private letter to the author of the paper, who, either trusting to the protection of those whose defense he had undertaken, or having entertained some personal malice against Mr. Savage, or fearing lest by retracting so confident an assertion, he should impair the credit of his paper, refused to give him that satisfaction.

Mr. Savage therefore thought it necessary, to his own vindication, to prosecute him in the King's Bench;[59] but as he did not find any ill effects from the accusation, having sufficiently cleared his innocence, he thought any further procedure would have the appearance of revenge, and therefore willingly dropped it.

He saw soon afterwards a process commenced in the same court against himself on an information in which he was accused of writing and publishing an obscene pamphlet.

It was always Mr. Savage's desire to be distinguished and, when any controversy became popular, he never wanted some reason for engaging in it with great ardor and appearing at the head of the party which he had chosen. As he was never celebrated for his prudence, he had no sooner taken his side and informed himself of the chief topics of the dispute, than he took all opportunities of asserting and propagating his principles, without much regard to his own interest, or any other visible design than that of drawing upon himself the attention of mankind.

The dispute between the Bishop of London and the Chancellor is well known to have been for some time the chief topic of political conversation; and therefore Mr. Savage, in pursuance of his character, endeavored to become conspicuous among the controvertists with which every coffee-house was filled on that occasion.[60] He was an indefatigable opposer of all the claims of ecclesiastical power, though he did not know on what they were founded; and was therefore no friend to the Bishop of London. But he had another reason for appearing as a warm advocate for Dr. Rundle; for he was the friend of Mr. Foster and Mr. Thomson, who were the friends of Mr. Savage.

Thus remote was his interest in the question, which, however, as he imagined, concerned him so nearly that it was not sufficient to harangue and dispute but necessary likewise to write upon it.

59. The Court of the King's Bench.

60. The dispute was over whether Thomas Rundle, a "low" Churchman, was to be made Bishop of Gloucester.

He therefore engaged with great ardor in a new poem, called by him *The Progress of a Divine;* in which he conducts a profligate priest by all the gradations of wickedness from a poor curacy in the country to the highest preferments of the Church, and describes with that humor which was natural to him, and that knowledge which was extended to all the diversities of human life, his behavior in every station; and insinuates that this priest, thus accomplished, found at last a patron in the Bishop of London.

When he was asked by one of his friends, on what pretense he could charge the Bishop with such an action, he had no more to say than that he had only inverted the accusation, and that he thought it reasonable to believe that he who obstructed the rise of a good man without reason would for bad reasons promote the exaltation of a villain.

The clergy were universally provoked by this satire, and Savage who, as was his constant practice, had set his name to his performance, was censured in *The Weekly Miscellany* with a severity which he did not seem inclined to forget.

But a return of invective was not thought a sufficient punishment. The Court of King's Bench was therefore moved against him, and he was obliged to return an answer to a charge of obscenity. It was urged in his defense that obscenity was criminal when it was intended to promote the practice of vice, but that Mr. Savage had only introduced obscene ideas with the view of exposing them to detestation, and of amending the age by showing the deformity of wickedness. This plea was admitted, and Sir Philip Yorke, who then presided in that court, dismissed the information with encomiums upon the purity and excellence of Mr. Savage's writings.

The prosecution, however, answered in some measure the purpose of those by whom it was set on foot, for Mr. Savage was so far intimidated by it that, when the edition of his poem was sold, he did not venture to reprint it; so that it was in a short time forgotten, or forgotten by all but those whom it offended.

It is said that some endeavors were used to incense the Queen against him, but he found advocates to obviate at least part of their effect; for though he was never advanced, he still continued to receive his pension.

This poem drew more infamy upon him than any incident of his life; and, as his conduct cannot be vindicated, it is proper to secure his memory from reproach by informing those whom he made his enemies that he never intended to repeat the provocation; and that, though whenever he thought he had any reason to complain of the clergy, he used to threaten them with a new edition of *The Progress of a Divine,* it was his calm and settled resolution to suppress it forever.

He once intended to have made a better reparation for the folly or injustice with which he might be charged by writing another poem, called *The Progress of a Freethinker,* whom he intended to lead through all the stages of vice and folly, to convert him from virtue to wickedness, and from religion to infidelity, by all the modish sophistry used for that purpose; and at last to dismiss him by his own hand into the other world.

That he did not execute this design is a real loss to mankind, for he was too well acquainted with all the scenes of debauchery to have failed in his representations of them, and too zealous for virtue not to have represented them in such a manner as should expose them either to ridicule or detestation.

But this plan was, like others, formed and laid aside, till the vigor of his imagination was spent and the effervescence of invention had subsided; but soon gave way to some other design, which pleased by its novelty for a while and then was neglected like the former.

He was still in his usual exigencies, having no certain support but the pension allowed him by the Queen which, though it might have kept an exact economist[61] from want, was very far from being sufficient for Mr. Savage, who had never been accustomed to dismiss any of his appetites without the gratification which they solicited, and whom nothing but want of money withheld from partaking of every pleasure that fell within his view.

His conduct with regard to his pension was very particular.[62] No sooner had he changed the bill than he vanished from the sight of all his acquaintances, and lay for some time out of the reach of all the inquiries that friendship or curiosity could make after him; at length he appeared again penniless as before but never informed even those whom he seemed to regard most where he had been; nor was his retreat ever discovered.

This was his constant practice during the whole time that he received the pension from the Queen: he regularly disappeared and returned. He indeed affirmed that he retired to study, and that the money supported him in solitude for many months; but his friends declared that the short time in which it was spent sufficiently confuted his own account of his conduct.

His politeness and his wit still raised him friends, who were desirous of setting him at length free from that indigence by which he had been hitherto oppressed, and therefore solicited Sir Robert Walpole in his favor with so much earnestness that they obtained a promise of the next place that should become vacant, not exceeding two hundred pounds a year. This promise was made with an uncommon declaration "that it was not the promise of a minister to a petitioner, but of a friend to his friend."

Mr. Savage now concluded himself set at ease forever and, as he

61. One who accounts exactly for his income and expenses.
62. Odd.

observes in a poem written on that incident of his life, *trusted* and *was trusted;* but soon found that his confidence was ill-grounded, and this *friendly* promise was not inviolable. He spent a long time in solicitations, and at last despaired and desisted.

He did not indeed deny that he had given the minister some reason to believe that he should not strengthen his own interest by advancing him, for he had taken care to distinguish himself in coffee-houses as an advocate for the ministry of the last years of Queen Anne and was always ready to justify the conduct and exalt the character of Lord Bolingbroke, whom he mentions with great regard in an "Epistle upon Authors," which he wrote abut that time but was too wise to publish, and of which only some fragments have appeared, inserted by him in the *Magazine* after his retirement.[63]

To despair was not, however, the character of Savage; when one patronage failed, he had recourse to another. The Prince[64] was now extremely popular and had very liberally rewarded the merit of some writers whom Mr. Savage did not think superior to himself, and therefore he resolved to address a poem to him.

For this purpose he made choice of a subject which could regard only persons of the highest rank and greatest affluence, and which was therefore proper for a poem intended to procure the patronage of a prince; and having retired for some time to Richmond that he might prosecute his design in full tranquillity, without the temptations of pleasure or the solicitations of creditors, by which his meditations were in equal danger of being disconcerted, he produced a poem *On Public Spirit, with Regard to Public Works.*[65]

The plan of this poem is very extensive and comprises a multitude of topics, each of which might furnish matter sufficient for a long performance and of which some have already employed more eminent writers; but as he was perhaps not fully acquainted with the whole extent of his own design, and was writing to obtain a supply of wants too pressing to admit of long or accurate inquiries, he passes negligently over many public works which, even in his own opinion, deserved to be more elaborately treated.

But though he may sometimes disappoint his reader by transient touches upon these subjects, which have often been considered, and therefore naturally raise expectations, he must be allowed amply to compensate his omissions, by expatiating in the conclusion of his work, upon a kind of beneficence not yet celebrated by any eminent poet,

63. *The Gentleman's Magazine.* Walpole had opposed the Tory ministry which ruled during the last years of Queen Anne's reign. Bolingbroke had been one of its leaders, and Walpole thought him still a dangerous opponent.

64. Frederick Louis (1701–51), Prince of Wales, on notoriously bad terms with his parents, became the center of the Opposition to Walpole's Ministry.

65. Many "public works" of this period were undertaken by individuals or private companies rather than by the government.

though it now appears more susceptible of embellishments, more adapted to exalt the ideas and affect the passions than many of those which have hitherto been thought most worthy of the ornaments of verse. The settlement of colonies in uninhabited countries, the establishment of those in security whose misfortunes have made their own country no longer pleasing or safe, the acquisition of property without injury to any, the appropriation of the waste and luxuriant bounties of nature, and the enjoyment of those gifts which Heaven has scattered upon regions uncultivated and unoccupied, cannot be considered without giving rise to a great number of pleasing ideas and bewildering the imagination in delightful prospects; and, therefore, whatever speculations[66] they may produce in those who have confined themselves to political studies, naturally fixed the attention, and excited the applause of a poet. The politician, when he considers men driven into other countries for shelter, and obliged to retire to forests and deserts, and pass their lives and fix their posterity in the remotest corners of the world, to avoid those hardships which they suffer or fear in their native place, may very properly inquire why the legislature does not provide a remedy for these miseries, rather than encourage an escape from them. He may conclude that the flight of every honest man is a loss to the community, that those who are unhappy without guilt ought to be relieved, and the life which is overburthened by accidental calamities set at ease by the care of the public; and that those who have by misconduct forfeited their claim to favor ought rather to be made useful to the society which they have injured than be driven from it. But the poet is employed in a more pleasing undertaking than that of proposing laws which, however just or expedient, will never be made, or endeavoring to reduce to rational schemes of government societies which were formed by chance, and are conducted by the private passions of those who preside in them. He guides the unhappy fugitive from want and persecution to plenty, quiet, and security, and seats him in scenes of peaceful solitude and undisturbed repose.

Savage has not forgotten, amidst the pleasing sentiments which this prospect of retirement suggested to him, to censure those crimes which have been generally committed by the discoverers of new regions, and to expose the enormous wickedness of making war upon barbarous nations because they cannot resist, and of invading countries because they are fruitful; of extending navigation only to propagate vice and of visiting distant lands only to lay them waste. He has asserted the natural equality of mankind and endeavored to suppress that pride which inclines men to imagine that right is the consequence of power.

His description of the various miseries which force men to seek for refuge in distant countries affords another instance of his proficiency

66. Theoretical views.

in the important and extensive study of human life; and the tenderness with which he recounts them, another proof of his humanity and benevolence.

It is observable that the close of this poem discovers a change which experience has made in Mr. Savage's opinions. In a poem written by him in his youth and published in his *Miscellanies*, he declares his contempt of the contracted views and narrow prospects of the middle state of life,[67] and declares his resolution either to tower like the cedar or be trampled like the shrub; but in this poem, though addressed to a prince, he mentions this state of life as comprising those who ought most to attract reward, those who merit most the confidence of power, and the familiarity of greatness; and, accidentally mentioning this passage to one of his friends, declared that in his opinion all the virtue of mankind was comprehended in that state.

In describing villas and gardens, he did not omit to condemn that absurd custom which prevails among the English of permitting servants to receive money from strangers for the entertainment that they receive, and therefore inserted in his poem these lines:

But what the flowering pride of gardens rare,
However royal or however fair,
If gates, which to access should still give way,
Ope but, like Peter's paradise, for pay?
If perquisited varlets frequent stand,
And each new walk must a new tax demand?
What foreign eye but with contempt surveys?
What Muse shall from oblivion snatch their praise?

But before the publication of his performance he recollected that the Queen allowed her garden and cave at Richmond to be shown for money, and that she so openly countenanced the practice that she had bestowed the privilege of showing them as a place of profit on a man whose merit she valued herself upon rewarding, though she gave him only the liberty of disgracing his country.[68]

He therefore thought, with more prudence than was often exerted by him, that the publication of these lines might be officiously represented as an insult upon the Queen, to whom he owed his life and his subsistence, and that the propriety of his observation would be no security against the censures which the unseasonableness of it might draw upon him; he therefore suppressed the passage in the first edition, but after the Queen's death thought the same caution no longer necessary, and restored it to the proper place.

The poem was therefore published without any political faults, and

67. Of the middle class.

68. Merlin's Cave was a small building on the royal estate at Richmond, ornamented with figures of Merlin and others, and containing a small library. Its librarian was Stephen Duck, a peasant poet.

inscribed to the Prince; but Mr. Savage, having no friend upon whom he could prevail to present it to him, had no other method of attracting his observation than the publication of frequent advertisements, and therefore received no reward from his patron, however generous on other occasions.

This disappointment he never mentioned without indignation, being by some means or other confident that the Prince was not ignorant of his address to him; and insinuated that if any advances in popularity could have been made by distinguishing him, he had not written without notice or without reward.

He was once inclined to have presented his poem in person and sent to the printer for a copy with that design; but either his opinion changed or his resolution deserted him, and he continued to resent neglect without attempting to force himself into regard.

Nor was the public much more favorable than his patron, for only seventy-two were sold, though the performance was much commended by some whose judgment in that kind of writing is generally allowed. But Savage easily reconciled himself to mankind without imputing any defect to his work, by observing that his poem was unluckily published two days after the prorogation of the Parliament, and by consequence at a time when all those who could be expected to regard it were in the hurry of preparing for their departure or engaged in taking leave of others upon their dismission from public affairs.

It must be however allowed, in justification of the public, that this performance is not the most excellent of Mr. Savage's works; and that though it cannot be denied to contain many striking sentiments, majestic lines, and just observations, it is in general not sufficiently polished in the language, or enlivened in the imagery, or digested in the plan.

Thus his poem contributed nothing to the alleviation of his poverty, which was such as very few could have supported with equal patience; but to which, it must likewise be confessed, that few would have been exposed who receive punctually fifty pounds a year: a salary which, though by no means equal to the demands of vanity and luxury, is yet found sufficient to support families above want and was undoubtedly more than the necessities of life require.

But no sooner had he received his pension than he withdrew to his darling privacy, from which he returned in a short time to his former distress and for some part of the year generally lived by chance, eating only when he was invited to the tables of his acquaintances, from which the meanness of his dress often excluded him, when the politeness and variety of his conversation would have been thought a sufficient recompense for his entertainment.

He lodged as much by accident as he dined, and passed the night sometimes in mean houses which are set open at night to any casual wanderers, sometimes in cellars among the riot and filth of the meanest and most profligate of the rabble; and sometimes, when he had no money to support even the expenses of these receptacles, walked about the streets till he was weary, and lay down in the summer upon a bulk,[69] or in the winter with his associates in poverty among the ashes of a glass-house.[70]

In this manner were passed those days and those nights which nature had enabled him to have employed in elevated speculations, useful studies, or pleasing conversations. On a bulk, in a cellar, or in a glass-house among thieves and beggars, was to be found the author of *The Wanderer,* the man of exalted sentiments, extensive views, and curious[71] observations; the man whose remarks on life might have assisted the statesman, whose ideas of virtue might have enlightened the moralist, whose eloquence might have influenced senates, and whose delicacy might have polished courts.

It cannot be imagined but that such necessities might sometimes force him upon disreputable practices, and it is probable that these lines in *The Wanderer* were occasioned by his reflections on his own conduct:

> Though misery leads to fortitude and truth,
> Unequal to the load, this languid youth . . . .
> (O, let none censure, if, untried by grief,
> Or, amidst woes, untempted by relief),
> He stooped reluctant to mean acts of shame,
> Which then, even then, he scorned, and blushed to name.

Whoever was acquainted with him was certain to be solicited for small sums, which the frequency of the request made in time considerable, and he was therefore quickly shunned by those who were become familiar enough to be trusted with his necessities; but his rambling manner of life and constant appearance at houses of public resort always procured him a new succession of friends, whose kindness had not been exhausted by repeated requests, so that he was seldom absolutely without resources but had in his utmost exigences this comfort, that he always imagined himself sure of speedy relief.

It was observed that he always asked favors of this kind without the least submission or apparent consciousness of dependence, and that he did not seem to look upon a compliance with his request as an obligation that deserved any extraordinary acknowledgments; but a refusal was resented by him as an affront, or complained of as an injury; nor did he readily reconcile himself to those who either denied to lend or gave him afterwards any intimation that they expected to be repaid.

He was sometimes so far compassionated by those who knew both his

69. Framework in front of a store, a stall.
70. Glass factory.
71. Discriminating, noteworthy.

merit and his distresses that they received him into their families, but they soon discovered him to be a very incommodious inmate; for, being always accustomed to an irregular manner of life, he could not confine himself to any stated hours or pay any regard to the rules of a family, but would prolong his conversation till midnight without considering that business might require his friend's application in the morning; nor when he had persuaded himself to retire to bed was he, without equal difficulty, called up to dinner; it was therefore impossible to pay him any distinction without the entire subversion of all economy,[72] a kind of establishment which, wherever he went, he always appeared ambitious to overthrow.

It must therefore be acknowledged, in justification of mankind, that it was not always by the negligence or coldness of his friends that Savage was distressed, but because it was in reality very difficult to preserve him long in a state of ease. To supply him with money was a hopeless attempt, for no sooner did he see himself master of a sum sufficient to set him free from care for a day than he became profuse and luxurious. When once he had entered a tavern or engaged in a scheme of pleasure, he never retired till want of money obliged him to some new expedient. If he was entertained in a family, nothing was any longer to be regarded there but amusements and jollity; wherever Savage entered he immediately expected that order and business should fly before him, that all should thenceforward be left to hazard, and that no dull principle of domestic management should be opposed to his inclination or intrude upon his gaiety.

His distresses, however afflictive, never dejected him; in his lowest state he wanted not spirit to assert the natural dignity of wit, and was always ready to repress that insolence which superiority of fortune incited and to trample the reputation which rose upon any other basis than that of merit: he never admitted any gross familiarities or submitted to be treated otherwise than as an equal. Once when he was without lodging, meat, or clothes, one of his friends, a man indeed not remarkable for moderation in his prosperity, left a message that he desired to see him about nine in the morning. Savage knew that his intention was to assist him, but was very much disgusted that he should presume to prescribe the hour of his attendance and, I believe, refused to visit him, and rejected his kindness.

The same invincible temper, whether firmness or obstinacy, appeared in his conduct to the Lord Tyrconnel, from whom he very frequently demanded that the allowance which was once paid him should be restored; but with whom he never appeared to entertain for a moment the thought of soliciting a reconciliation, and whom he treated at once with all the haughtiness of superiority and all the bitter-

72. Domestic order.

ness of resentment. He wrote to him not in a style of supplication or respect, but of reproach, menace, and contempt; and appeared determined, if he ever regained his allowance, to hold it only by the right of conquest.

As many more can discover that a man is richer than that he is wiser than themselves, superiority of understanding is not so readily acknowledged as that of condition; nor is that haughtiness which the consciousness of great abilities incites borne with the same submission as the tyranny of wealth; and therefore Savage, by asserting his claim to deference and regard, and by treating those with contempt whom better fortune animated to rebel against him, did not fail to raise a great number of enemies in the different classes of mankind. Those who thought themselves raised above him by the advantages of riches hated him because they found no protection from the petulance of his wit. Those who were esteemed for their writings feared him as a critic and maligned him as a rival; and almost all the smaller wits were his professed enemies.

Among these Mr. Miller[73] so far indulged his resentment as to introduce him in a farce and direct him to be personated on the stage in a dress like that which he then wore, a mean insult, which only insinuated that Savage had but one coat, and which was therefore despised by him rather than resented; for though he wrote a lampoon against Miller, he never printed it: and as no other person ought to prosecute that revenge from which the person who was injured desisted, I shall not preserve what Mr. Savage suppressed, of which the publication would indeed have been a punishment too severe for so impotent an assault.

The great hardships of poverty were to Savage not the want of lodging or of food, but the neglect and contempt which it drew upon him. He complained that as his affairs grew desperate, he found his reputation for capacity visibly decline; that his opinion in questions of criticism was no longer regarded when his coat was out of fashion; and that those who in the interval of his prosperity were always encouraging him to great undertakings by encomiums on his genius and assurances of success, now received any mention of his designs with coldness, thought that the subjects on which he proposed to write were very difficult, and were ready to inform him that the event of a poem was uncertain; that an author ought to employ much time in the consideration of his plan, and not presume to sit down to write in consequence of a few cursory ideas and a superficial knowledge; difficulties were started on all sides, and he was no longer qualified for any performance but the "Volunteer Laureate."

Yet even this kind of contempt never depressed him, for he always preserved a steady confidence in his own capacity and believed nothing

73. James Miller (1706–44), minor poet and dramatist.

above his reach which he should at any time earnestly endeavor to attain. He formed schemes of the same kind with regard to knowledge and to fortune, and flattered himself with advances to be made in science, as with riches to be enjoyed in some distant period of his life. For the acquisition of knowledge he was indeed far better qualified than for that of riches; for he was naturally inquisitive and desirous of the conversation of those from whom any information was to be obtained, but by no means solicitous to improve those opportunities that were sometimes offered of raising his fortune; and was remarkably retentive of his ideas, which, when once he was in possession of them, rarely forsook him, a quality which could never be communicated to his money.

While he was thus wearing out his life in expectation that the Queen would some time recollect her promise, he had recourse to the usual practice of writers and published proposals for printing his works by subscription, to which he was encouraged by the success of many who had not a better right to the favor of the public; but, whatever was the reason, he did not find the world equally inclined to favor him, and he observed, with some discontent that though he offered his works at half a guinea, he was able to procure but a small number in comparison with those who subscribed twice as much to Duck.

Nor was it without indignation that he saw his proposals neglected by the Queen, who patronized Mr. Duck's with uncommon ardor, and incited a competition among those who attended the court who should most promote his interest and who should first offer a subscription. This was a distinction to which Mr. Savage made no scruple of asserting that his birth, his misfortunes, and his genius gave a fairer title than could be pleaded by him on whom it was conferred.

Savage's applications were, however, not universally unsuccessful; for some of the nobility countenanced his design, encouraged his proposals, and subscribed with great liberality. He related of the Duke of Chandos particularly that upon receiving his proposals he sent him ten guineas.

But the money which his subscriptions afforded him was not less volatile than that which he received from his other schemes; whenever a subscription was paid him he went to a tavern; and as money so collected is necessarily received in small sums, he never was able to send his poems to the press but for many years continued his solicitation and squandered whatever he obtained.

This project of printing his works was frequently revived and, as his proposals grew obsolete, new ones were printed with fresher dates. To form schemes for the publication was one of his favorite amusements; nor was he ever more at ease than when, with any friend who readily fell in with his schemes, he was adjusting the print, forming the advertisements, and regulating the dispersion of his new edition, which he really intended some time to publish, and which, as long experience had shown him the impossibility of printing the volume together, he at last determined to divide into weekly or monthly numbers, that the profits of the first might supply the expenses of the next.

Thus he spent his time in mean expedients and tormenting suspense, living for the greatest part in fear of prosecutions from his creditors, and consequently skulking in obscure parts of the town, of which he was no stranger to the remotest corners. But wherever he came his address secured him friends whom his necessities soon alienated, so that he had, perhaps, a more numerous acquaintance than any man ever before attained, there being scarcely any person eminent on any account to whom he was not known or whose character he was not in some degree able to delineate.

To the acquisition of this extensive acquaintance every circumstance of his life contributed. He excelled in the arts of conversation, and therefore willingly practiced them. He had seldom any home or even a lodging in which he could be private; and therefore was driven into public-houses for the common conveniences of life and supports of nature. He was always ready to comply with every invitation, having no employment to withhold him and often no money to provide for himself; and by dining with one company he never failed of obtaining an introduction into another.

Thus dissipated was his life, and thus casual his subsistence; yet did not the distraction of his views hinder him from reflection, nor the uncertainty of his condition depress his gaiety. When he had wandered about without any fortunate adventure by which he was led into a tavern, he sometimes retired into the fields and was able to employ his mind in study, to amuse it with pleasing imaginations; and seldom appeared to be melancholy but when some sudden misfortune had just fallen upon him, and even then in a few moments he would disentangle himself from his perplexity, adopt the subject of conversation, and apply his mind wholly to the objects that others presented to it.

This life, unhappy as it may be already imagined, was yet embittered in 1738 with new calamities. The death of the Queen[74] deprived him of all the prospects of preferment[75] with which he had so long entertained his imagination; and as Sir Robert Walpole had before given him reason to believe that he never intended the performance of his promise, he was now abandoned again to fortune.

He was, however, at that time supported by a friend; and as it was not his custom to look out for distant calamities or to feel any other pain than that which forced itself upon his senses, he was not much afflicted at his loss, and perhaps comforted himself that his pension would be now continued without the annual tribute of a panegyric.

74. In November 1737.
75. Official position or financial support.

Another expectation contributed likewise to support him; he had taken a resolution to write a second tragedy upon the story of Sir Thomas Overbury, in which he preserved a few lines of his former play but made a total alteration of the plan, added new incidents, and introduced new characters; so that it was a new tragedy, not a revival of the former.

Many of his friends blamed him for not making choice of another subject; but, in vindication of himself, he asserted that it was not easy to find a better and that he thought it his interest to extinguish the memory of the first tragedy, which he could only do by writing one less defective upon the same story; by which he should entirely defeat the artifice of the booksellers, who, after the death of any author of reputation, are always industrious to swell his works by uniting his worst productions with his best.

In the execution of this scheme, however, he proceeded but slowly, and probably only employed himself upon it when he could find no other amusement; but he pleased himself with counting the profits and perhaps imagined that the theatrical reputation which he was about to acquire would be equivalent to all that he had lost by the death of his patroness.

He did not in confidence of his approaching riches neglect the measures proper to secure the continuance of his pension, though some of his favorers thought him culpable for omitting to write on her death; but on her birthday next year he gave a proof of the solidity of his judgment and the power of his genius.

He knew that the track of elegy had been so long beaten that it was impossible to travel in it without treading in the footsteps of those who had gone before him; and that therefore it was necessary, that he might distinguish himself from the herd of encomiasts, to find out some new walk of funeral panegyric.

This difficult task he performed in such a manner that his poem may be justly ranked among the best pieces that the death of princes has produced. By transferring the mention of her death to her birthday he has formed a happy combination of topics which any other man would have thought it very difficult to connect in one view, but which he has united in such a manner that the relation between them appears natural; and it may be justly said that what no other man would have thought on, it now appears scarcely possible for any man to miss.

The beauty of this peculiar combination of images is so masterly that it is sufficient to set this poem above censure; and therefore it is not necessary to mention many other delicate touches which may be found in it, and which would deservedly be admired in any other performance.

To these proofs of his genius may be added, from the same poem, an instance of his prudence, an excellence for which he was not so often distinguished; he does not forget to remind the King, in the most delicate and artful manner, of continuing his pension.

With regard to the success of this address he was for some time in suspense but was in no great degree solicitous about it, and continued his labor upon his new tragedy with great tranquillity, till the friend who had for a considerable time supported him, removing his family to another place, took occasion to dismiss him. It then became necessary to inquire more diligently what was determined in his affair, having reason to suspect that no great favor was intended him because he had not received his pension at the usual time.

It is said that he did not take those methods of retrieving his interest which were most likely to succeed; and some of those who were employed in the Exchequer cautioned him against too much violence in his proceedings; but Mr. Savage, who seldom regulated his conduct by the advice of others, gave way to his passion and demanded of Sir Robert Walpole, at his levee,[76] the reason of the distinction that was made between him and the other pensioners of the Queen, with a degree of roughness which perhaps determined him to withdraw what had been only delayed.

Whatever was the crime of which he was accused or suspected, and whatever influence was employed against him, he received soon after an account that took from him all hopes of regaining his pension; and he had now no prospect of subsistence but from his play, and he knew no way of living for the time required to finish it.

So peculiar were the misfortunes of this man, deprived of an estate and title by a particular law, exposed and abandoned by a mother, defrauded by a mother of a fortune which his father had allotted him, he entered the world without a friend; and though his abilities forced themselves into esteem and reputation, he was never able to obtain any real advantage, and whatever prospects arose were always intercepted as he began to approach them. The King's intentions in his favor were frustrated; his Dedication to the Prince, whose generosity on every other occasion was eminent, procured him no reward; Sir Robert Walpole, who valued himself upon keeping his promise to others, broke it to him without regret; and the bounty of the Queen was after her death withdrawn from him, and from him only.

Such were his misfortunes, which yet he bore not only with decency but with cheerfulness; nor was his gaiety clouded even by his last disappointment, though he was in a short time reduced to the lowest degree of distress and often wanted both lodging and food. At this time he gave another instance of the insurmountable obstinacy of his spirit; his clothes were worn out, and he received notice that at a coffee-house some clothes and linen were left for him; the person who sent them did

76. A general reception, usually held once or twice a week.

not, I believe, inform him to whom he was to be obliged, that he might spare the perplexity of acknowledging the benefit; but though the offer was so far generous, it was made with some neglect of ceremonies, which Mr. Savage so much resented that he refused the present and declined to enter the house till the clothes that had been designed for him were taken away.

His distress was now publicly known, and his friends therefore thought it proper to concert some measures for his relief; and one of them[77] wrote a letter to him in which he expressed his concern "for the miserable withdrawing of his pension," and gave him hopes that in a short time he should find himself supplied with a competence, "without any dependence on those little creatures which we are pleased to call the great."

The scheme proposed for this happy and independent subsistence was that he should retire into Wales and receive an allowance of fifty pounds a year, to be raised by a subscription, on which he was to live privately in a cheap place, without aspiring any more to affluence or having any farther care of reputation.

This offer Mr. Savage gladly accepted, though with intentions very different from those of his friends; for they proposed that he should continue an exile from London forever, and spend all the remaining part of his life at Swansea; but he designed only to take the opportunity which their scheme offered him of retreating for a short time that he might prepare his play for the stage and his other works for the press, and then to return to London to exhibit his tragedy and live upon the profits of his own labor.

With regard to his works, he proposed very great improvements, which would have required much time or great application; and when he had finished them, he designed to do justice to his subscribers by publishing them according to his proposals.

As he was ready to entertain himself with future pleasures, he had planned out a scheme of life for the country, of which he had no knowledge but from pastorals and songs. He imagined that he should be transported to scenes of flowery felicity, like those which one poet has reflected to another; and had projected a perpetual round of innocent pleasures, of which he suspected no interruption from pride, or ignorance, or brutality.

With these expectations he was so enchanted that when he was once gently reproached by a friend for submitting to live upon a subscription, and advised rather by a resolute exertion of his abilities to support himself, he could not bear to debar himself from the happiness which was to be found in the calm of a cottage, or lose the opportunity of listening without intermission to the melody of the nightingale, which

77. Alexander Pope.

he believed was to be heard from every bramble, and which he did not fail to mention as a very important part of the happiness of a country life.

While this scheme was ripening, his friends directed him to take a lodging in the liberties of the Fleet[78] that he might be secure from his creditors, and sent him every Monday a guinea, which he commonly spent before the next morning and trusted, after his usual manner, the remaining part of the week to the bounty of fortune.

He now began very sensibly to feel the miseries of dependence: those by whom he was to be supported began to prescribe to him with an air of authority, which he knew not how decently to resent nor patiently to bear; and he soon discovered from the conduct of most of his subscribers that he was yet in the hands of "little creatures."

Of the insolence that he was obliged to suffer he gave many instances, of which none appeared to raise his indignation to a greater height than the method which was taken of furnishing him with clothes. Instead of consulting him and allowing him to send to a tailor his order for what they thought proper to allow him, they proposed to send for a tailor to take his measure and then to consult how they should equip him.

This treatment was not very delicate, nor was it such as Savage's humanity would have suggested to him on a like occasion; but it had scarcely deserved mention had it not, by affecting him in an uncommon degree, shown the peculiarity of his character. Upon hearing the design that was formed, he came to the lodging of a friend with the most violent agonies of rage; and being asked what it could be that gave him such disturbance, he replied with the utmost vehemence of indignation, "That they had sent for a tailor to measure him."

How the affair ended was never inquired for fear of renewing his uneasiness. It is probable that upon recollection he submitted with a good grace to what he could not avoid and that he discovered no resentment where he had no power.

He was, however, not humbled to implicit and universal compliance; for when the gentleman who had first informed him of the design to support him by a subscription attempted to procure a reconciliation with the Lord Tyrconnel, he could by no means be prevailed upon to comply with the measures that were proposed.

A letter was written for him to Sir William Leman[79] to prevail upon him to interpose his good offices with Lord Tyrconnel, in which he solicited Sir William's assistance "for a man who really needed it as much as any man could well do"; and informed him that he was retiring "forever to a place where he should no more trouble his relations,

78. Section next to the Fleet prison, where debtors were immune from arrest.

79. Husband of Lady Macclesfield's daughter by her second marriage. Pope wrote the letter.

friends, or enemies"; he confessed that his passion had "betrayed" him to some conduct with regard to Lord Tyrconnel "for which he could not but heartily ask his pardon"; and as he imagined Lord Tyrconnel's passion might be yet so high that he would not "receive a letter from him," begged that Sir William would endeavor to soften him; and expressed his hopes that he would comply with his request and that "so small a relation[80] would not harden his heart against him."

That any man should presume to dictate a letter to him was not very agreeable to Mr. Savage; and therefore he was, before he had opened it, not much inclined to approve it. But when he read it, he found it contained sentiments entirely opposite to his own and, as he asserted, to the truth; and therefore instead of copying it wrote his friend a letter full of masculine resentment and warm expostulations. He very justly observed that the style was too supplicatory and the representation too abject, and that he ought at least to have made him complain with "the dignity of a gentleman in distress." He declared that he would not write the paragraph in which he was to ask Lord Tyrconnel's pardon, for "he despised his pardon, and therefore could not heartily, and would not hypocritically, ask it." He remarked that his friend made a very unreasonable distinction between himself and him; for, says he, when you mention men of high rank "in your own character," they are "those little creatures whom we are pleased to call the great"; but when you address them "in mine," no servility is sufficiently humble. He then with great propriety explained the ill consequences that might be expected from such a letter, which his relations would print in their own defense and which would forever be produced as a full answer to all that he should allege against them; for he always intended to publish a minute account of the treatment which he had received. It is to be remembered to the honor of the gentleman by whom this letter was drawn up that he yielded to Mr. Savage's reasons and agreed that it ought to be suppressed.

After many alterations and delays a subscription was at length raised, which did not amount to fifty pounds a year, though twenty were paid by one gentleman:[81] such was the generosity of mankind that what had been done by a player without solicitation could not now be effected by application and interest; and Savage had a great number to court and to obey for a pension less than that which Mrs. Oldfield paid him without exacting any servilities.

Mr. Savage, however, was satisfied and willing to retire, and was convinced that the allowance, though scanty, would be more than sufficient for him, being now determined to commence a rigid economist and to live according to the exactest rules of frugality; for

80. So short or plain a narrative (?).
81. Presumably Pope.

nothing was in his opinion more contemptible than a man who, when he knew his income, exceeded it, and yet he confessed that instances of such folly were too common and lamented that some men were not to be trusted with their own money.

Full of these salutary resolutions, he left London in July 1739, having taken leave with great tenderness of his friends, and parted from the author of this narrative with tears in his eyes. He was furnished with fifteen guineas and informed that they would be sufficient not only for the expense of his journey but for his support in Wales for some time; and that there remained but little more of the first collection. He promised a strict adherence to his maxims of parsimony and went away in the stagecoach; nor did his friends expect to hear from him till he informed them of his arrival at Swansea.

But when they least expected, arrived a letter dated the fourteenth day after his departure, in which he sent them word that he was yet upon the road and without money, and that he therefore could not proceed without a remittance. They then sent him all the money that was in their hands, with which he was enabled to reach Bristol, from whence he was to go to Swansea by water.

At Bristol he found an embargo laid upon the shipping, so that he could not immediately obtain a passage; and being therefore obliged to stay there some time, he with his usual felicity ingratiated himself with many of the principal inhabitants, was invited to their houses, distinguished at their public feasts, and treated with a regard that gratified his vanity and therefore easily engaged his affection.

He began very early after his retirement to complain of the conduct of his friends in London and irritated many of them so much by his letters that they withdrew, however honorably, their contributions; and it is believed that little more was paid him than the twenty pounds a year which were allowed him by the gentleman who proposed the subscription.

After some stay at Bristol he retired to Swansea, the place originally proposed for his residence, where he lived about a year very much dissatisfied with the diminution of his salary; but contracted, as in other places, acquaintance with those who were most distinguished in that country, among whom he has celebrated Mr. Powell and Mrs. Jones, by some verses which he inserted in *The Gentleman's Magazine*.

Here he completed his tragedy, of which two acts were wanting when he left London, and was desirous of coming to town to bring it upon the stage. This design was very warmly opposed, and he was advised by his chief benefactor[82] to put it into the hands of Mr. Thomson and Mr. Mallet[83] that it might be fitted for the stage, and to allow his friends to

82. Pope.

83. James Thomson (1700–48) and David Mallet (?1705–65) had recently collaborated in writing a successful masque, *Alfred*.

receive the profits, out of which an annual pension should be paid him.

This proposal he rejected with the utmost contempt. He was by no means convinced that the judgment of those to whom he was required to submit was superior to his own. He was now determined, as he expressed it, to be "no longer kept in leading strings," and had no elevated idea of "his bounty" who proposed to "pension him out of the profits of his own labors."

He attempted in Wales to promote a subscription for his works and had once hopes of success; but in a short time afterwards formed a resolution of leaving that part of the country, to which he thought it not reasonable to be confined for the gratification of those who, having promised him a liberal income, had no sooner banished him to a remote corner than they reduced his allowance to a salary scarcely equal to the necessities of life.

His resentment of this treatment which, in his own opinion at least, he had not deserved, was such that he broke off all correspondence with most of his contributors and appeared to consider them as persecutors and oppressors; and in the latter part of his life declared that their conduct toward him since his departure from London "had been perfidiousness improving on perfidiousness, and inhumanity on inhumanity."

It is not to be supposed that the necessities of Mr. Savage did not sometimes incite him to satirical exaggerations of the behavior of those by whom he thought himself reduced to them. But it must be granted that the diminution of his allowance was a great hardship, and that those who withdrew their subscription from a man who, upon the faith of their promise, had gone into a kind of banishment and abandoned all those by whom he had been before relieved in his distresses, will find it no easy task to vindicate their conduct.

It may be alleged, and perhaps justly, that he was petulant and contemptuous, that he more frequently reproached his subscribers for not giving him more than thanked them for what he had received; but it is to be remembered that his conduct, and this is the worst charge that can be drawn up against him, did them no real injury; and that it therefore ought rather to have been pitied than resented; at least the resentment that it might provoke ought to have been generous and manly, epithets which his conduct will hardly deserve that starves the man whom he has persuaded to put himself into his power.

It might have been reasonably demanded by Savage that they should, before they had taken away what they promised, have replaced him in his former state, that they should have taken no advantages from the situation to which the appearance of their kindness had reduced him, and that he should have been recalled to London before he was abandoned. He might justly represent that he ought to have been considered as a lion in the toils and demand to be released before the dogs should be loosed upon him.

He endeavored, indeed, to release himself and, with an intent to return to London, went to Bristol, where a repetition of the kindness which he had formerly found invited him to stay. He was not only caressed and treated, but had a collection made for him of about thirty pounds with which it had been happy if he had immediately departed for London; but his negligence did not suffer him to consider that such proofs of kindness were not often to be expected and that this ardor of benevolence was in a great degree the effect of novelty, and might probably be every day less; and therefore he took no care to improve the happy time but was encouraged by one favor to hope for another, till at length generosity was exhausted and officiousness[84] wearied.

Another part of his misconduct was the practice of prolonging his visits to unseasonable hours and disconcerting all the families into which he was admitted. This was an error in a place of commerce which all the charms of his conversation could not compensate; for what trader would purchase such airy satisfaction by the loss of solid gain, which must be the consequence of midnight merriment, as those hours which were gained at night were generally lost in the morning?

Thus Mr. Savage, after the curiosity of the inhabitants was gratified, found the number of his friends daily decreasing, perhaps without suspecting for what reason their conduct was altered; for he still continued to harass with his nocturnal intrusions those that yet countenanced him and admitted him to their houses.

But he did not spend all the time of his residence at Bristol in visits or at taverns, for he sometimes returned to his studies and began several considerable designs. When he felt an inclination to write, he always retired from the knowledge of his friends and lay hid in an obscure part of the suburbs, till he found himself again desirous of company, to which it is likely that intervals of absence made him more welcome.

He was always full of his design of returning to London to bring his tragedy upon the stage; but having neglected to depart with the money that was raised for him, he could not afterwards procure a sum sufficient to defray the expenses of his journey; nor perhaps would a fresh supply have had any other effect than, by putting immediate pleasures into his power, to have driven the thoughts of his journey out of his mind.

While he was thus spending the day in contriving a scheme for the morrow, distress stole upon him by imperceptible degrees. His conduct had already wearied some of those who were at first enamored of his conversation; but he might, perhaps, still have devolved[85] to others whom he might have entertained with equal success, had not the decay

84. Helpfulness.
85. Passed on.

of his clothes made it no longer consistent with their vanity to admit him to their tables or to associate with him in public places. He now began to find every man from home at whose house he called and was therefore no longer able to procure the necessaries of life, but wandered about the town slighted and neglected in quest of a dinner, which he did not always obtain.

To complete his misery he was pursued by the officers for small debts which he had contracted, and was therefore obliged to withdraw from the small number of friends from whom he had still reason to hope for favors. His custom was to lie in bed the greatest part of the day and to go out in the dark with the utmost privacy and, after having paid his visit, return again before morning to his lodging, which was in the garret of an obscure inn.

Being thus excluded on one hand and confined on the other, he suffered the utmost extremities of poverty and often fasted so long that he was seized with faintness, and had lost his appetite, not being able to bear the smell of meat till the action of his stomach was restored by a cordial.

In this distress he received a remittance of five pounds from London, with which he provided himself a decent coat and determined to go to London, but unhappily spent his money at a favorite tavern. Thus was he again confined to Bristol, where he was every day hunted by bailiffs. In this exigence he once more found a friend who sheltered him in his house, though at the usual inconveniences with which his company was attended; for he could neither be persuaded to go to bed in the night nor to rise in the day.

It is observable that in these various scenes of misery he was always disengaged and cheerful; he at some times pursued his studies and at others continued or enlarged his epistolary correspondence; nor was he ever so far dejected as to endeavor to procure an increase of his allowance by any other methods than accusations and reproaches.

He had now no longer any hopes of assistance from his friends at Bristol, who as merchants and by consequence sufficiently studious of[86] profit, cannot be supposed to have looked with much compassion upon negligence and extravagance, or to think any excellence equivalent to a fault of such consequence as neglect of economy. It is natural to imagine that many of those who would have relieved his real wants were discouraged from the exertion of their benevolence by observation of the use which was made of their favors and conviction that relief would only be momentary, and that the same necessity would quickly return.

At last he quitted the house of his friend, and returned to his lodging at the inn, still intending to set out in a few days for London; but on the 10th of January 1742–3, having been at supper with two of his friends,

86. Concerned with.

he was at his return to his lodgings arrested for a debt of about eight pounds, which he owed at a coffee-house, and conducted to the house of a sheriff's officer. The account which he gives of his misfortune, in a letter to one of the gentlemen with whom he had supped, is too remarkable to be omitted:

> It was not a little unfortunate for me that I spent yesterday's evening with you, because the hour hindered me from entering on my new lodging; however, I have now got one, but such an one as I believe nobody would choose.
>
> I was arrested at the suit of Mrs. Read, just as I was going upstairs to bed at Mr. Bowyer's, but taken in so private a manner that I believe nobody at the White Lion is apprised of it. Though I let the officers know the strength (or rather weakness) of my pocket, yet they treated me with the utmost civility; and even when they conducted me to confinement, 'twas in such a manner that I verily believe I could have escaped, which I would rather be ruined than have done, notwithstanding the whole amount of my finances was but threepence halfpenny.
>
> In the first place I must insist that you will industriously conceal this from Mrs. S——s, because I would not have her good nature suffer that pain which I know she would be apt to feel on this occasion.
>
> Next I conjure you, dear Sir, by all the ties of friendship, by no means to have one uneasy thought on my account, but to have the same pleasantry of countenance and unruffled serenity of mind which (God be praised!) I have in this and have had in a much severer calamity. Furthermore, I charge you, if you value my friendship as truly as I do yours, *not* to utter or even harbor the least resentment against Mrs. Read. I believe she has ruined me, but I freely forgive her; and (though I will never more have any intimacy with her) would, at a due distance, rather do her an act of good, than ill will. Lastly (pardon the expression), I *absolutely command* you not to offer me any pecuniary assistance, nor to attempt getting me any from any one of your friends. At another time, or on any other occasion, you may, dear friend, be well assured, I would rather write to you in the submissive style of a request than that of a peremptory command.
>
> However, that my truly valuable friend may not think I am too proud to ask a favor, let me entreat you to let me have your boy to attend me for this day, not only for the sake of saving me the expense of porters, but for the delivery of some letters to people whose names I would not have known to strangers.
>
> The civil treatment I have thus far met from those whose prisoner I am makes me thankful to the Almighty that, though he has thought fit to visit me (on my birthnight) with affliction, yet (such is His great goodness!) my affliction is not without alleviating circumstances. I murmur not, but am all resignation to the *Divine Will.* As to the world, I hope that I shall be endued by Heaven with

> that presence of mind, that serene dignity in misfortune, that constitutes the character of a true nobleman; a dignity far beyond that of coronets; a nobility arising from the just principles of philosophy, refined and exalted by those of Christianity.

He continued five days at the officer's in hopes that he should be able to procure bail and avoid the necessity of going to prison. The state in which he passed his time and the treatment which he received are very justly expressed by him in a letter which he wrote to a friend: "The whole day," says he, "has been employed in various people's filling my head with their foolish, chimerical systems, which has obliged me coolly (as far as nature will admit) to digest and accommodate myself to every different person's way of thinking; hurried from one wild system to another till it has quite made a chaos of my imagination, and nothing done—promised—disappointed—ordered to send every hour from one part of the town to the other."

When his friends, who had hitherto caressed and applauded, found that to give bail and pay the debt was the same, they all refused to preserve him from a prison at the expense of eight pounds; and therefore, after having been for some time at the officer's house "at an immense expense," as he observes in his letter, he was at length removed to Newgate.

This expense he was enabled to support by the generosity of Mr. Nash[87] at Bath who, upon receiving from him an account of his condition, immediately sent him five guineas and promised to promote his subscription at Bath with all his interest.

By his removal to Newgate he obtained at least a freedom from suspense and rest from the disturbing vicissitudes[88] of hope and disappointment; he now found that his friends were only companions who were willing to share his gaiety but not to partake of his misfortunes; and therefore he no longer expected any assistance from them.

It must however be observed of one gentleman that he offered to release him by paying the debt, but that Mr. Savage would not consent, I suppose, because he thought he had been before too burthensome to him.

He was offered by some of his friends that a collection should be made for his enlargement, but he "treated the proposal" and declared "that he should again treat it, with disdain. As to writing any mendicant letters, he had too high a spirit and determined only to write to some ministers of state to try to regain his pension."

He continued to complain of those that had sent him into the country and objected to them that he had "lost the profits of his play, which had been finished three years"; and in another letter declares his resolution

87. The famous Beau Nash (1674–1761), whose "rule" over Bath transformed it into a fashionable spa.

88. Alternations.

to publish a pamphlet, that the world might know how "he had been used."

This pamphlet was never written, for he in a very short time recovered his usual tranquillity and cheerfully applied himself to more inoffensive studies. He indeed steadily declared that he was promised a yearly allowance of fifty pounds and never received half the sum; but he seemed to resign himself to that as well as to other misfortunes, and lose the remembrance of it in his amusements and employments.

The cheerfulness with which he bore his confinement appears from the following letter which he wrote January 30th[89] to one of his friends in London:

> I now write to you from my confinement in Newgate, where I have been ever since Monday last was seven-night[90], and where I enjoy myself with much more tranquillity than I have known for upwards of a twelvemonth past; having a room entirely to myself and pursuing the amusement of my poetical studies uninterrupted and agreeable to my mind. I thank the Almighty I am now all collected in myself,[91] and though my person is in confinement, my mind can expatiate on ample and useful subjects with all the freedom imaginable. I am now more conversant with the Nine[92] than ever, and if instead of a Newgate bird I may be allowed to be a bird of the Muses, I assure you, Sir, I sing very freely in my cage; sometimes indeed in the plaintive notes of the nightingale; but, at others, in the cheerful strains of the lark.

In another letter he observes that he ranges from one subject to another without confining himself to any particular task, and that he was employed one week upon one attempt, and the next upon another.

Surely the fortitude of this man deserves at least to be mentioned with applause, and whatever faults may be imputed to him, the virtue of *suffering well* cannot be denied him. The two powers which, in the opinion of Epictetus,[93] constitute a wise man, are those of *bearing* and *forbearing,* which cannot indeed be affirmed to have been equally possessed by Savage, but it was too manifest that the want of one obliged him very *frequently* to practice the other.

He was treated by Mr. Dagge, the keeper of the prison, with great humanity; was supported by him at his own table without any certainty of recompense, had a room to himself to which he could at any time retire from all disturbance, was allowed to stand at the door of the prison, and sometimes taken out into the fields; so that he suffered fewer hardships in the prison than he had been accustomed to undergo in the greatest part of his life.

89. 1743 New Style.
90. A week ago Monday. January 30th was a Sunday.
91. Self-composed.
92. The nine Muses.
93. Stoic philosopher of the first century A.D.

The keeper did not confine his benevolence to a gentle execution of his office but made some overtures to the creditor for his release, though without effect; and continued, during the whole time of his imprisonment, to treat him with the utmost tenderness and civility.

Virtue is undoubtedly most laudable in that state which makes it most difficult, and therefore the humanity of a gaoler certainly deserves this public attestation; and the man whose heart has not been hardened by such an employment may be justly proposed as a pattern of benevolence. If an inscription was once engraved to "the honest toll gatherer," less honors ought not to be paid to the "tender jailer."

Mr. Savage very frequently received visits and sometimes presents from his acquaintances, but they did not amount to a subsistence, for the greater part of which he was indebted to the generosity of this keeper; but these favors, however, they might endear to him the particular persons from whom he received them, were very far from impressing upon his mind any advantageous ideas of the people of Bristol, and therefore he thought he could not more properly employ himself in prison than in writing the following poem.[94]

When he had brought this poem to its present state which, without considering the chasm,[95] is not perfect, he wrote to London an account of his design, and informed his friend[96] that he was determined to print it with his name, but enjoined him not to communicate his intention to his Bristol acquaintance. The gentleman, surprised at his resolution, endeavored to dissuade him from publishing it, at least from prefixing his name, and declared that he could not reconcile the injunction of secrecy with his resolution to own it at its first appearance. To this Mr. Savage returned an answer agreeable to his character in the following terms:

> I received yours this morning, and not without a little surprise at the contents. To answer a question with a question, you ask me concerning "London and Bristol," "why will I add 'Delineated'?" Why did Mr. Wollaston add the same word to his *Religion of Nature?*[97] I suppose that it was his will and pleasure to add it in his case, and it is mine to do so in my own. You are pleased to tell me that you understand not why secrecy is enjoined, and yet I intend to set my name to it. My answer is—I have my private reasons, which I am not obliged to explain to anyone. You doubt my friend Mr. S——— would not approve of it. And what is it to me whether he does or not? Do you imagine that Mr. S——— is to dictate to me? If any man who calls himself my friend should assume such

94. Johnson includes in early editions this poetic fragment called "London and Bristol Delineated." Delineated means "contrasted."

95. Break in the poem.

96. Edward Cave, publisher of *The Gentleman's Magazine.*

97. William Wollaston's *Religion of Nature Delineated* (1724) was a popular moral treatise.

> an air, I would spurn at his friendship with contempt. You say I seem to think so by not letting him know it. And suppose I do, what then? Perhaps I can give reasons for that disapprobation, very foreign from what you would imagine. You go on in saying, suppose, I should not put my name to it. My answer is that I will not suppose any such thing, being determined to the contrary; neither, Sir, would I have you suppose that I applied to you for want of another press; nor would I have you imagine that I owe Mr. S——— obligations which I do not.

Such was his imprudence, and such his obstinate adherence to his own resolutions, however absurd. A prisoner! supported by charity! and, whatever insults he might have received during the latter part of his stay at Bristol, once caressed, esteemed, and presented with a liberal collection, he could forget on a sudden his danger and his obligations to gratify the petulance of his wit or the eagerness of his resentment, and publish a satire by which he might reasonably expect that he should alienate those who then supported him and provoke those whom he could neither resist nor escape.

This resolution, from the execution of which it is probable that only his death could have hindered him, is sufficient to show how much he disregarded all considerations that opposed his present passions and how readily he hazarded all future advantages for any immediate gratifications. Whatever was his predominant inclination, neither hope nor fear hindered him from complying with it; nor had opposition any other effect than to heighten his ardor and irritate his vehemence.

This performance was however laid aside while he was employed in soliciting assistances from several great persons; and one interruption succeeding another hindered him from supplying the chasm, and perhaps from retouching the other parts which he can hardly be imagined to have finished in his own opinion, for it is very unequal, and some of the lines are rather inserted to rhyme to others than to support or improve the sense; but the first and last parts are worked up with great spirit and elegance.

His time was spent in the prison for the most part in study, or in receiving visits; but sometimes he descended to lower amusements and diverted himself in the kitchen with the conversation of the criminals; for it was not pleasing to him to be much without company, and though he was very capable of a judicious choice, he was often contented with the first that offered; for this he was sometimes reproved by his friends who found him surrounded with felons; but the reproof was on that, as on other occasions, thrown away; he continued to gratify himself and to set very little value on the opinion of others.

But here, as in every other scene of his life, he made use of such opportunities as occurred of benefiting those who were more miserable than himself, and was always ready to perform any offices of humanity to his fellow prisoners.

He had now ceased from corresponding with any of his subscribers except one,[98] who yet continued to remit him the twenty pounds a year which he had promised him and by whom it was expected that he would have been in a very short time enlarged;[99] because he had directed the keeper to inquire after the state of his debts.

However, he took care to enter his name according to the forms of the court, that the creditor might be obliged to make him some allowance if he was continued a prisoner, and when on that occasion he appeared in the hall was treated with very unusual respect.

But the resentment of the city was afterwards raised by some accounts that had been spread of the satire, and he was informed that some of the merchants intended to pay the allowance which the law required and to detain him prisoner at their own expense. This he treated as an empty menace and perhaps might have hastened the publication, only to show how much he was superior to their insults, had not all his schemes been suddenly destroyed.

When he had been six months in prison he received from one of his friends,[1] in whose kindness he had the greatest confidence and on whose assistance he chiefly depended, a letter that contained a charge of very atrocious ingratitude, drawn up in such terms as sudden resentment dictated. Henley, in one of his advertisements, had mentioned "Pope's treatment of Savage." This was supposed by Pope to be the consequence of a complaint made by Savage to Henley, and was therefore mentioned by him with much resentment.[2] Mr. Savage returned a very solemn protestation of his innocence, but however appeared much disturbed at the accusation. Some days afterwards he was seized with a pain in his back and side which, as it was not violent, was not suspected to be dangerous; but growing daily more languid and dejected, on the 25th of July he confined himself to his room and a fever seized his spirits. The symptoms grew every day more formidable, but his condition did not enable him to procure any assistance. The last time that the keeper saw him was on July the 31st, when Savage, seeing him at his bedside, said with an uncommon earnestness, "I have something to say to you, Sir," but after a pause moved his hand in a melancholy manner, and finding himself unable to recollect what he was going to communicate, said, "'Tis gone!" The keeper soon after left

98. Pope.
99. Freed.
1. Pope.
2. Henley was a fanatical preacher who used to advertise the subjects of his sermons in the newspapers. Pope included him in *The Dunciad.* The two preceding sentences were first printed in the 1783 edition of this *Life.*

him, and the next morning he died. He was buried in the churchyard of St. Peter[3] at the expense of the keeper.

Such were the life and death of Richard Savage, a man equally distinguished by his virtues and vices, and at once remarkable for his weaknesses and abilities.

He was of a middle stature, of a thin habit of body, a long visage, coarse features, and melancholy aspect; of a grave and manly deportment, a solemn dignity of mien, but which upon a nearer acquaintance softened into an engaging easiness of manners. His walk was slow and his voice tremulous and mournful. He was easily excited to smiles but very seldom provoked to laughter.

His mind was in an uncommon degree vigorous and active. His judgment was accurate, his apprehension quick, and his memory so tenacious that he was frequently observed to know what he had learned from others in a short time better than those by whom he was informed, and could frequently recollect incidents, with all their combination of circumstances, which few would have regarded at the present time, but which the quickness of his apprehension impressed upon him. He had the peculiar felicity that his attention never deserted him; he was present to every object and regardful of the most trifling occurrences. He had the art of escaping from his own reflections and accommodating himself to every new scene.

To this quality is to be imputed the extent of his knowledge, compared with the small time which he spent in visible endeavors to acquire it. He mingled in cursory conversation with the same steadiness of attention as others apply to a lecture, and amidst the appearance of thoughtless gaiety lost no new idea that was started nor any hint that could be improved. He had therefore made in coffee-houses the same proficiency as others in studies, and it is remarkable that the writings of a man of little education and little reading have an air of learning scarcely to be found in any other performances, but which perhaps as often obscures as embellishes them.

His judgment was eminently exact both with regard to writings and to men. The knowledge of life was indeed his chief attainment; and it is not without some satisfaction that I can produce the suffrage of Savage in favor of human nature, of which he never appeared to entertain such odious ideas as some, who perhaps had neither his judgment nor experience, have published either in ostentation of their sagacity, vindication of their crimes, or gratification of their malice.

His method of life particularly qualified him for conversation, of which he knew how to practice all the graces. He was never vehement or loud, but at once modest and easy, open and respectful; his language

3. In Bristol.

was vivacious or elegant, and equally happy upon grave or humorous subjects. He was generally censured for not knowing when to retire, but that was not the defect of his judgment but of his fortune; when he left his company he was frequently to spend the remaining part of the night in the street, or at least was abandoned to gloomy reflections, which it is not strange that he delayed as long as he could, and sometimes forgot that he gave others pain to avoid it himself.

It cannot be said that he made use of his abilities for the direction of his own conduct; an irregular and dissipated manner of life had made him the slave of every passion that happened to be excited by the presence of its object, and that slavery to his passions reciprocally produced a life irregular and dissipated. He was not master of his own motions[4] nor could promise anything for the next day.

With regard to his economy, nothing can be added to the relation of his life: he appeared to think himself born to be supported by others and dispensed from all necessity of providing for himself; he therefore never prosecuted any scheme of advantage nor endeavored even to secure the profits which his writings might have afforded him.

His temper was, in consequence of the dominion of his passions, uncertain and capricious; he was easily engaged and easily disgusted; but he is accused of retaining his hatred more tenaciously than his benevolence.

He was compassionate both by nature and principle and always ready to perform offices of humanity; but when he was provoked, and very small offenses were sufficient to provoke him, he would prosecute his revenge with the utmost acrimony till his passion had subsided.

His friendship was therefore of little value; for though he was zealous in the support or vindication of those whom he loved, yet it was always dangerous to trust him, because he considered himself discharged by the first quarrel from all ties of honor or gratitude, and would betray those secrets which in the warmth of confidence had been imparted to him. This practice drew upon him an universal accusation of ingratitude; nor can it be denied that he was very ready to set himself free from the load of an obligation; for he could not bear to conceive himself in a state of dependence, his pride being equally powerful with his other passions, and appearing in the form of insolence at one time and of vanity at another. Vanity, the most innocent species of pride, was most frequently predominant: he could not easily leave off when he had once begun to mention himself or his works, nor ever read his verses without stealing his eyes from the page to discover in the faces of his audience how they were affected with any favorite passage.

A kinder name than that of vanity ought to be given to the delicacy with which he was always careful to separate his own merit from every

4. Impulses; actions.

other man's, and to reject that praise to which he had no claim. He did not forget, in mentioning his performances, to mark every line that had been suggested or amended; and was so accurate as to relate that he owed *three words* in *The Wanderer* to the advice of his friends.

His veracity was questioned, but with little reason; his accounts, though not indeed always the same, were generally consistent. When he loved any man, he suppressed all his faults, and when he had been offended by him, concealed all his virtues: but his characters were generally true, so far as he proceeded; though it cannot be denied that his partiality might have sometimes the effect of falsehood.

In cases indifferent, he was zealous for virtue, truth, and justice; he knew very well the necessity of goodness to the present and future happiness of mankind; nor is there perhaps any writer who has less endeavored to please by flattering the appetites or perverting the judgment.

As an author therefore, and he now ceases to influence mankind in any other character, if one piece which he had resolved to suppress be excepted, he has very little to fear from the strictest moral or religious censure. And though he may not be altogether secure against the objections of the critic, it must however be acknowledged that his works are the productions of a genius truly poetical; and, what many writers who have been more lavishly applauded cannot boast, that they have an original air which has no resemblance of any foregoing writer; that the versification and sentiments have a cast peculiar to themselves which no man can imitate with success, because what was nature in Savage would in another be affectation. It must be confessed that his descriptions are striking, his images animated, his fictions justly imagined, and his allegories artfully pursued; that his diction is elevated, though sometimes forced, and his numbers sonorous and majestic, though frequently sluggish and encumbered. Of his style, the general fault is harshness, and the general excellence is dignity; of his sentiments, the prevailing beauty is simplicity, and uniformity the prevailing defect.

For his life or for his writings, none who candidly consider his fortune will think an apology[5] either necessary or difficult. If he was not always sufficiently instructed in his subject, his knowledge was at least greater than could have been attained by others in the same state. If his works were sometimes unfinished, accuracy cannot reasonably be exacted from a man oppressed with want which he has no hope of relieving but by a speedy publication. The insolence and resentment of which he is accused were not easily to be avoided by a great mind irritated by perpetual hardships and constrained hourly to return the spurns of contempt and repress the insolence of prosperity; and vanity surely may be readily pardoned in him to whom life afforded no other

5. Justification.

comforts than barren praises, and the consciousness of deserving them.

Those are no proper judges of his conduct who have slumbered away their time on the down of plenty; nor will a wise man easily presume to say, "Had I been in Savage's condition, I should have lived or written better than Savage."

This relation will not be wholly without its use if those who languish under any part of his sufferings shall be enabled to fortify their patience by reflecting that they feel only those afflictions from which the abilities of Savage did not exempt him; or if those who, in confidence of superior capacities or attainments, disregard the common maxims of life, shall be reminded that nothing will supply the want of prudence; and that negligence and irregularity long continued will make knowledge useless, wit ridiculous, and genius contemptible.

William Collins
1721–1759

William Collins was born at Chichester on the twenty-fifth of December, about 1720.[1] His father was a hatter of good reputation. He was in 1733, as Dr. Warton has kindly informed me, admitted scholar of Winchester College,[2] where he was educated by Dr. Burton. His English exercises were better than his Latin.

He first courted the notice of the public by some verses "To a Lady Weeping," published in *The Gentleman's Magazine.*[3]

In 1740 he stood first in the list of the scholars to be received in succession at New College, but unhappily there was no vacancy. This was the original misfortune of his life. He became a commoner of Queen's College,[4] probably with a scanty maintenance; but was, in about half a year, elected a demy of Magdalen College,[5] where he continued till he had taken a Bachelor's degree, and then suddenly left the University, for what reason I know not that he told.

He now (about 1744) came to London a literary adventurer, with many projects in his head, and very little money in his pocket. He designed many works; but his great fault was irresolution, or the frequent calls of immediate necessity broke his schemes, and suffered him to pursue no settled purpose. A man doubtful of his dinner, or trembling at a creditor, is not much disposed to abstracted meditation, or remote inquiries. He published proposals for a History of the Revival of Learning; and I have heard him speak with great kindness of Leo the

1. 1721.
2. One who has his tuition and living expenses paid. Joseph Warton, critic and poet, was headmaster of Winchester school (1766–93).
3. In October 1739 under the title "Sonnet."
4. An undergraduate not supported by a scholarship from his college. The colleges named are at Oxford.
5. A scholar of Magdalen College, so called because the allowance or "commons" was originally half that of a Fellow.

Tenth, and with keen resentment of his tasteless successor.[6] But probably not a page of the history was ever written. He planned several tragedies, but he only planned them. He wrote now and then odes and other poems, and did something, however little.

About this time I fell into his company. His appearance was decent and manly; his knowledge considerable, his views extensive, his conversation elegant, and his disposition cheerful. By degrees I gained his confidence; and one day was admitted to him when he was immured by a bailiff that was prowling in the street. On this occasion recourse was had to the booksellers, who, on the credit of a translation of Aristotle's *Poetics,* which he engaged to write with a large commentary, advanced as much money as enabled him to escape into the country. He showed me the guineas safe in his hand. Soon afterwards his uncle, Mr. Martin, a lieutenant-colonel, left him about two thousand pounds,[7] a sum which Collins could scarcely think exhaustible, and which he did not live to exhaust. The guineas were then repaid, and the translation neglected.

But man is not born for happiness. Collins, who, while he "studied to live," felt no evil but poverty, no sooner "lived to study" than his life was assailed by more dreadful calamities: disease and insanity.

Having formerly written his character,[8] while perhaps it was yet more distinctly impressed upon my memory, I shall insert it here.

> Mr. Collins was a man of extensive literature, and of vigorous faculties. He was acquainted not only with the learned tongues,[9] but with the Italian, French, and Spanish languages. He had employed his mind chiefly upon works of fiction, and subjects of fancy; and, by indulging some peculiar habits of thought, was eminently delighted with those flights of imagination which pass the bounds of nature, and to which the mind is reconciled only by a passive acquiescence in popular traditions. He loved fairies, genii, giants, and monsters; he delighted to rove through the meanders of enchantment, to gaze on the magnificence of golden palaces, to repose by the waterfalls of Elysian gardens.
>
> This was, however, the character rather of his inclination than his genius; the grandeur of wildness, and the novelty of extravagance, were always desired by him, but were not always attained. Yet, as diligence is never wholly lost, if his efforts sometimes caused harshness and obscurity, they likewise produced in happier moments sublimity and splendor. This idea which he had formed of excellence led him to Oriental fictions and allegorical imagery; and perhaps, while he was intent upon description, he did not sufficiently cultivate sentiment. His poems are the pro-

6. Adrian VI (pope, 1522–23).
7. Col. Edmund Martin died in April 1749.
8. In *The Poetical Calendar,* ed. Francis Fawkes and William Woty, 12 (1763).
9. Greek and Latin.

ductions of a mind not deficient in fire, nor unfurnished with knowledge either of books or life, but somewhat obstructed in its progress by deviation in quest of mistaken beauties.

His morals were pure, and his opinions pious; in a long continuance of poverty, and long habits of dissipation,[10] it cannot be expected that any character should be exactly uniform. There is a degree of want by which the freedom of agency[11] is almost destroyed; and long association with fortuitous companions will at last relax the strictness of truth, and abate the fervor of sincerity. That this man, wise and virtuous as he was, passed always unentangled through the snares of life, it would be prejudice and temerity to affirm; but it may be said that at least he preserved the source of action unpolluted, that his principles were never shaken, that his distinctions of right and wrong were never confounded, and that his faults had nothing of malignity or design, but proceeded from some unexpected pressure or casual temptation.

The latter part of his life cannot be remembered but with pity and sadness. He languished some years under that depression of mind which enchains the faculties without destroying them, and leaves reason the knowledge of right without the power of pursuing it. These clouds which he perceived gathering on his intellects, he endeavored to disperse by travel, and passed into France; but found himself constrained to yield to his malady, and returned. He was for some time confined in a house of lunatics, and afterwards retired to the care of his sister in Chichester, where death, in 1756,[12] came to his relief.

After his return from France, the writer of this character paid him a visit at Islington, where he was waiting for his sister, whom he had directed to meet him: there was then nothing of disorder discernible in his mind by any but himself; but he had withdrawn from study, and traveled with no other book than an English Testament, such as children carry to the school: when his friend took it into his hand out of curiosity to see what companion a man of letters had chosen, "I have but one book," said Collins, "but that is the best."

Such was the fate of Collins, with whom I once delighted to converse, and whom I yet remember with tenderness.

He was visited at Chichester in his last illness by his learned friends Dr. Warton and his brother,[13] to whom he spoke with disapprobation of his *Oriental Eclogues,* as not sufficiently expressive of Asiatic manners,[14] and called them his Irish Eclogues. He showed them, at the same time, an ode inscribed to Mr. John Hume, on the superstitions of

10. "A scattered habit of attention" (Johnson's *Dictionary*).
11. Ability to act on one's own, or to accomplish a purpose.
12. Actually 1759.
13. Thomas Warton, professor at Oxford, poet and literary historian.
14. Customary modes of behavior.

the Highlands; which they thought superior to his other works, but which no search has yet found.[15]

His disorder was not alienation of mind, but general laxity and feebleness, a deficiency rather of his vital than intellectual powers. What he spoke wanted neither judgment nor spirit; but a few minutes exhausted him, so that he was forced to rest upon the couch, till a short cessation restored his powers, and he was again able to talk with his former vigor.

The approaches of this dreadful malady he began to feel soon after his uncle's death; and, with the usual weakness of men so diseased, eagerly snatched that temporary relief with which the table and the bottle flatter and seduce. But his health continually declined, and he grew more and more burthensome[16] to himself.

To what I have formerly said of his writings may be added, that his diction was often harsh, unskillfully labored, and injudiciously selected. He affected the obsolete when it was not worthy of revival; and he puts his words out of the common order, seeming to think, with some later candidates for fame, that not to write prose is certainly to write poetry. His lines commonly are of slow motion, clogged and impeded with clusters of consonants. As men are often esteemed who cannot be loved, so the poetry of Collins may sometimes extort praise when it gives little pleasure.[17]

15. John Hume (usually spelled Home), Presbyterian minister and dramatist. Home's imperfect copy of the *Ode on the Popular Superstitions of the Highlands of Scotland* was discovered and printed in 1788.

16. Burdensome.

17. The "Life of Collins" concludes with a short poem wrongly attributed to Collins, here omitted.

Thomas Gray
1716–1771

Thomas Gray, the son of Mr. Philip Gray, a scrivener[1] of London, was born in Cornhill, November 26, 1716. His grammatical education he received at Eton under the care of Mr. Antrobus, his mother's brother, then assistant to Dr. George; and when he left school, in 1734, entered a pensioner at Peterhouse in Cambridge.[2]

The transition from the school to the college is, to most young scholars, the time from which they date their years of manhood, liberty, and happiness; but Gray seems to have been very little delighted with academical gratifications; he liked at Cambridge neither the mode of life nor the fashion of study, and lived sullenly on to the time when his attendance on lectures was no longer required. As he intended to profess the Common Law, he took no degree.

When he had been at Cambridge about five years, Mr. Horace Walpole,[3] whose friendship he had gained at Eton, invited him to travel with him as his companion. They wandered through France into Italy; and Gray's letters contain a very pleasing account of many parts of their journey. But unequal friendships are easily dissolved: at Florence they quarreled, and parted; and Mr. Walpole is now content to have it told that it was by his fault. If we look, however, without prejudice on the world, we shall find that men whose consciousness of their own merit sets them above the compliances of servility are apt enough in their association with superiors to watch their own dignity with troublesome and punctilious jealousy, and in the fervor of independence to exact that attention which they refuse to pay. Part they did, whatever was the quarrel, and the rest of their travels was doubtless more unpleasant to

1. Notary, money lender, and professional copyist; he was also an "exchange broker."
2. Peterhouse College, where "pensioners" were students who paid their own expenses.
3. Son of Sir Robert Walpole, Prime Minister of England; author of the first English Gothic novel, *The Castle of Otranto* (1765), and a famous letter-writer.

them both. Gray continued his journey in a manner suitable to his own little fortune, with only an occasional servant.

He returned to England in September 1741, and in about two months afterwards buried his father; who had, by an injudicious waste of money upon a new house, so much lessened his fortune, that Gray thought himself too poor to study the law. He therefore retired to Cambridge, where he soon after became Bachelor of Civil Law; and where, without liking the place or its inhabitants, or professing to like them, he passed, except a short residence at London, the rest of his life.

About this time he was deprived of Mr. West, the son of a chancellor of Ireland, a friend on whom he appears to have set a high value, and who deserved his esteem by the powers which he shows in his letters and in the "Ode to May" which Mr. Mason[4] has preserved, as well as by the sincerity with which, when Gray sent him part of "Agrippina,"[5] a tragedy that he had just begun, he gave an opinion which probably intercepted the progress of the work, and which the judgment of every reader will confirm. It was certainly no loss to the English stage that "Agrippina" was never finished.

In this year (1742) Gray seems first to have applied himself seriously to poetry; for in this year were produced the "Ode to Spring," his "Prospect of Eton," and his "Ode to Adversity." He began likewise a Latin poem, *De Principiis Cogitandi.*[6]

It may be collected[7] from the narrative of Mr. Mason that his first ambition was to have excelled in Latin poetry: perhaps it were reasonable to wish that he had prosecuted his design; for though there is at present some embarrassment in his phrase, and some harshness in his lyric numbers,[8] his copiousness of language is such as very few possess; and his lines, even when imperfect, discover a writer whom practice would quickly have made skillful.

He now lived on at Peterhouse, very little solicitous what others did or thought, and cultivated his mind and enlarged his views without any other purpose than of improving and amusing himself; when Mr. Mason, being elected Fellow of Pembroke Hall, brought him a companion who was afterwards to be his editor, and whose fondness and fidelity has kindled in him a zeal of admiration which cannot be reasonably expected from the neutrality of a stranger, and the coldness of a critic.

In this retirement he wrote (1747) an ode on the "Death of Mr. Walpole's Cat"; and the year afterwards attempted a poem of more importance, on "Government and Education," of which the fragments which remain have many excellent lines.

4. William Mason (1724–97), who published *Memoirs and Poems* of Gray in 1775.
5. Agrippina was murdered by her son, the Emperor Nero.
6. *On the Principles of Thinking.*
7. Gathered.
8. Verses.

His next production (1750) was his far-famed "Elegy in the Churchyard," which, finding its way into a magazine, first, I believe, made him known to the public.

An invitation from Lady Cobham about this time gave occasion to an odd composition called "A Long Story," which adds little to Gray's character.

Several of his pieces (1753) were published with designs by Mr. Bentley,[9] and, that they might in some form or other make a book, only one side of each leaf was printed. I believe the poems and the plates recommended each other so well, that the whole impression was soon bought. This year he lost his mother.

Some time afterwards (1756) some young men of the college, whose chambers were near his, diverted themselves with disturbing him by frequent and troublesome noises, and, as is said, by pranks yet more offensive and contemptuous. This insolence, having endured it a while, he represented to the governors of the society, among whom perhaps he had no friends; and finding his complaint little regarded, removed himself to Pembroke Hall.

In 1757 he published "The Progress of Poetry" and "The Bard," two compositions at which the readers of poetry were at first content to gaze in mute amazement. Some that tried them confessed their inability to understand them, though Warburton[10] said that they were understood as well as the works of Milton and Shakespeare, which it is the fashion to admire. Garrick[11] wrote a few lines in their praise. Some hardy champions undertook to rescue them from neglect, and in a short time many were content to be shown beauties which they could not see.

Gray's reputation was now so high, that, after the death of Cibber,[12] he had the honor of refusing the laurel, which was then bestowed on Mr. Whitehead.

His curiosity, not long after, drew him away from Cambridge to a lodging near the Museum,[13] where he resided near three years, reading and transcribing; and, so far as can be discovered, very little affected by two odes on "Oblivion" and "Obscurity,"[14] in which his lyric performances were ridiculed with much contempt and much ingenuity.

When the Professor of Modern History at Cambridge died, he was, as he says, "cockered and spirited up" till he asked it of Lord Bute, who

9. Son of the famous scholar Richard Bentley. This edition was published in 1753.

10. William Warburton (1698–1779), editor of Pope and Shakespeare.

11. David Garrick (1717–79), the most famous of English actors; friend of Johnson.

12. Colley Cibber (1671–1757), actor-manager and Poet Laureate.

13. The great public library at the British Museum, in London, had been founded in 1753.

14. These two odes were parodies of Gray's poems; the first, by George Colman, especially pleased Johnson.

sent him a civil refusal; and the place was given to Mr. Brocket, the tutor of Sir James Lowther.[15]

His constitution was weak, and believing that his health was promoted by exercise and change of place, he undertook (1765) a journey into Scotland, of which his account, so far as it extends, is very curious[16] and elegant: for, as his comprehension was ample, his curiosity extended to all the works of art, all the appearances of nature, and all the monuments of past events. He naturally contracted a friendship with Dr. Beattie, whom he found a poet, a philosopher, and a good man.[17] The Marischal College at Aberdeen offered him the degree of Doctor of Laws, which, having omitted to take it at Cambridge, he thought it decent to refuse.

What he had formerly solicited in vain was at last given him without solicitation. The Professorship of History became again vacant, and he received (1768) an offer of it from the Duke of Grafton.[18] He accepted, and retained it to his death; always designing lectures, but never reading them; uneasy at his neglect of duty, and appeasing his uneasiness with designs of reformation, and with a resolution which he believed himself to have made of resigning the office, if he found himself unable to discharge it.

Ill health made another journey necessary, and he visited (1769) Westmorland and Cumberland. He that reads his epistolary narration wishes that to travel, and to tell his travels, had been more of his employment; but it is by studying at home that we must obtain the ability of traveling with intelligence and improvement.

His travels and his studies were now near their end. The gout, of which he had sustained many weak attacks, fell upon his stomach, and, yielding to no medicines, produced strong convulsions, which (July 30, 1771) terminated in death.

His character I am willing to adopt, as Mr. Mason has done, from a letter written to my friend Mr. Boswell by the Rev. Mr. Temple,[19] rector of St. Gluvias in Cornwall; and am as willing as his warmest well-wisher to believe it true.

> Perhaps he was the most learned man in Europe. He was equally acquainted with the elegant and profound parts of science,[20] and that not superficially, but thoroughly. He knew every branch of history, both natural and civil; had read all the original historians of England, France, and Italy; and was a great anti-

15. Lord Bute was Prime Minister at this time (1762). Lowther, Bute's son-in-law, was an influential politician.

16. Discriminating.

17. James Beattie, Professor of Moral Philosophy and Logic at Marischal College.

18. The Chair of Modern History carried a salary of £400 a year. The Duke of Grafton was then Prime Minister.

19. William Johnson Temple (1739–96) had know Gray at Cambridge.

20. Learning, knowledge.

quarian. Criticism, metaphysics, morals, politics, made a principal part of his study; voyages and travels of all sorts were his favorite amusements; and he had a fine taste in painting, prints, architecture, and gardening. With such a fund of knowledge, his conversation must have been equally instructing and entertaining; but he was also a good man, a man of virtue and humanity. There is no character without some speck, some imperfection; and I think the greatest defect in his was an affectation in delicacy, or rather effeminacy, and a visible fastidiousness, or contempt and disdain of his inferiors in science. He also had, in some degree, that weakness which disgusted Voltaire so much in Mr. Congreve:[21] though he seemed to value others chiefly according to the progress they had made in knowledge, yet he could not bear to be considered himself merely as a man of letters; and though without birth, or fortune, or station, his desire was to be looked upon as a private independent gentleman, who read for his amusement. Perhaps it may be said, What signifies so much knowledge, when it produced so little? Is it worth taking so much pains to leave no memorial but a few poems? But let it be considered that Mr. Gray was to others at least innocently employed; to himself, certainly beneficially. His time passed agreeably; he was every day making some new acquisition in science; his mind was enlarged, his heart softened, his virtue strengthened; the world and mankind were shown to him without a mask; and he was taught to consider everything as trifling and unworthy of the attention of a wise man, except the pursuit of knowledge and practice of virtue in that state wherein God hath placed us.

To this character Mr. Mason has added a more particular account of Gray's skill in zoology. He has remarked that Gray's effeminacy was affected most "before those whom he did not wish to please"; and that he is unjustly charged with making knowledge his sole reason of preference, as he paid his esteem to none whom he did not likewise believe to be good.

What has occurred to me from the slight inspection of his letters in which my undertaking has engaged me is that his mind had a large grasp; that his curiosity was unlimited, and his judgment cultivated; that he was a man likely to love much where he loved at all, but that he was fastidious and hard to please. His contempt, however, is often employed, where I hope it will be approved, upon skepticism and infidelity. His short account of Shaftesbury[22] I will insert.

You say you cannot conceive how Lord Shaftesbury came to be a philosopher in vogue; I will tell you: first, he was a lord; secondly, he was as vain as any of his readers; thirdly, men are very

21. Voltaire was scornful when he learned that William Congreve (1670–1729) preferred to be considered a gentleman of leisure rather than a writer.

22. Lord Shaftesbury (1671–1713) was a deist, a believer in the religion of nature and reason as opposed to the Christian revelation.

prone to believe what they do not understand; fourthly, they will believe anything at all, provided they are under no obligation to believe it; fifthly, they love to take a new road, even when that road leads nowhere; sixthly, he was reckoned a fine writer, and seems always to mean more than he said. Would you have any more reasons? An interval of above forty years has pretty well destroyed the charm. A dead lord ranks with commoners; vanity is no longer interested in the matter, for a new road is become an old one.

Mr. Mason has added, from his own knowledge, that though Gray was poor, he was not eager of money; and that out of the little that he had he was very willing to help the necessitous.

As a writer he had this peculiarity, that he did not write his pieces first rudely[23] and then correct them, but labored every line as it arose in the train of composition; and he had a notion not very peculiar, that he could not write but at certain times, or at happy moments; a fantastic foppery, to which my kindness for a man of learning and of virtue wishes him to have been superior.

Gray's poetry is now to be considered; and I hope not to be looked on as an enemy to his name, if I confess that I contemplate it with less pleasure than his life.

His "Ode on Spring" has something poetical, both in the language and the thought; but the language is too luxuriant, and the thoughts have nothing new. There has of late arisen a practice of giving to adjectives derived from substantives the termination of participles; such as the *cultured* plain, the *daisied* bank; but I was sorry to see, in the lines of a scholar like Gray, the *honied* Spring. The morality is natural, but too stale; the conclusion is pretty.

The poem "On the Cat" was doubtless by its author considered as a trifle, but it is not a happy trifle. In the first stanza "the azure flowers *that* blow"[24] show [how] resolutely a rhyme is sometimes made when it cannot easily be found. Selima, the cat, is called a nymph, with some violence both to language and sense; but there is [no] good use made of it when it is done; for of the two lines,

> What female heart can gold despise?
> What cat's averse to fish?

the first relates merely to the nymph, and the second only to the cat. The sixth stanza contains a melancholy truth, that "a favorite has no friend"; but the last ends in a pointed sentence[25] of no relation to the purpose: if *what glistered* had been *gold*, the cat would not have gone into the water; and if she had, would not less have been drowned.

23. Roughly.
24. Bloom.
25. Maxim. The last line of this poem reads, "Nor all, that glisters, gold."

The "Prospect of Eton College" suggests nothing to Gray which every beholder does not equally think and feel. His supplication to Father Thames, to tell him who drives the hoop or tosses the ball, is useless and puerile. Father Thames has no better means of knowing than himself. His epithet "buxom health" is not elegant; he seems not to understand the word.[26] Gray thought his language more poetical as it was more remote from common use: finding in Dryden "honey redolent of spring," an expression that reaches the utmost limits of our language, Gray drove it a little more beyond common apprehension by making "gales" to be "redolent of joy and youth."

Of the "Ode to Adversity," the hint was at first taken from *O Diva, gratum quæ regis Antium,*[27] but Gray has excelled his original by the variety of his sentiments, and by their moral application. Of this piece, at once poetical and rational, I will not by slight objections violate the dignity.

My process has now brought me to the "wonderful wonder of wonders," the two sister odes;[28] by which, though either vulgar ignorance or common sense at first universally rejected them, many have been since persuaded to think themselves delighted. I am one of those that are willing to be pleased, and therefore would gladly find the meaning of the first stanza of the "Progress of Poetry."

Gray seems in his rapture to confound the images of "spreading sound" and "running water." A "stream of music" may be allowed; but where does music, however "smooth and strong," after having visited the "verdant vales," "rowl down the steep amain," so as that "rocks and nodding groves rebellow to the roar"? If this be said of music, it is nonsense; if it be said of water, it is nothing to the purpose.

The second stanza, exhibiting Mars's car and Jove's eagle, is unworthy of further notice. Criticism disdains to chase a schoolboy to his commonplaces.

To the third it may likewise be objected that it is drawn from mythology, though such as may be more easily assimilated to real life. Idalia's "velvet-green" has something of cant.[29] An epithet or metaphor drawn from nature ennobles art: an epithet or metaphor drawn from art degrades nature. Gray is too fond of words arbitrarily compounded. "Many-twinkling" was formerly censured as not analogical;[30] we may say "many-spotted," but scarcely "many-spotting." This stanza, however, has something pleasing.

26. In his *Dictionary* Johnson gives a number of different meanings for *buxom*: obedient; gay, lively; wanton, jolly.

27. "O Goddess, who rulest over pleasant Antium," the first line of Horace's *Odes*, I. xxxv.

28. "The Progress of Poesy" and "The Bard."

29. *Idalia* is Mount Ida, in Crete. Johnson defines *cant* as "barbarous language." The next sentence explains his objection to "velvet-green."

30. Comparable to recognized grammatical forms.

Of the second ternary of stanzas, the first endeavors to tell something, and would have told it had it not been crossed by Hyperion;[31] the second describes well enough the universal prevalence of poetry; but I am afraid that the conclusion will not rise from the premises. The caverns of the North and the plains of Chile are not the residences of "glory" and "generous shame." But that poetry and virtue go always together is an opinion so pleasing that I can forgive him who resolves to think it true.

The third stanza sounds big with "Delphi," and "Aegean," and "Ilissus," and "Meander,"[32] and "hallowed fountain," and "solemn sound"; but in all Gray's odes there is a kind of cumbrous splendor which we wish away. His position is at last false: in the time of Dante and Petrarch, from whom he derives our first school of poetry, Italy was overrun by "tyrant power" and "coward vice"; nor was our state much better when we first borrowed the Italian arts.

Of the third ternary, the first gives a mythological birth of Shakespeare. What is said of that mighty genius is true; but it is not said happily: the real effects of his poetical power are put out of sight by the pomp of machinery. Where truth is sufficient to fill the mind, fiction is worse than useless; the counterfeit debases the genuine.

His account of Milton's blindness, if we suppose it caused by study in the formation of his poem—a supposition surely allowable—is poetically true, and happily imagined. But the "car" of Dryden, with his "two coursers," has nothing in it peculiar; it is a car in which any other rider may be placed.

"The Bard" appears at the first view to be, as Algarotti[33] and others have remarked, an imitation of the prophecy of Nereus.[34] Algarotti thinks it superior to its original, and if preference depends only on the imagery and animation of the two poems, his judgment is right. There is in "The Bard" more force, more thought, and more variety. But to copy is less than to invent, and the copy has been unhappily produced at a wrong time. The fiction of Horace was to the Romans credible; but its revival disgusts us with apparent and unconquerable falsehood. *Incredulus odi.*[35]

To select a singular event, and swell it to a giant's bulk by fabulous appendages of specters and predictions, has little difficulty, for he that forsakes the probable may always find the marvelous. And it has little

31. The sun god in Greek mythology. He appears, perhaps intrusively, at the end of the stanza in question.

32. Greek names of an ancient oracular shrine of Apollo, of the sea, of a river near Athens, and of a river in Asia Minor.

33. Count Francesco Algarotti, a rich Italian dilettante of the arts and sciences, author of *Newtonism for the Ladies.*

34. Theme of an ode by Horace (*Odes* I. xv). Nereus, a sea-god, halted the ship of Paris abducting Helen and prophesied the Trojan war.

35. "I abhor it because I do not believe it" (Horace, *Art of Poetry,* l. 188).

use: we are affected only as we believe; we are improved only as we find something to be imitated or declined. I do not see that "The Bard" promotes any truth, moral or political.

His stanzas are too long, especially his epodes; the ode is finished before the ear has learned its measures, and consequently before it can receive pleasure from their consonance and recurrence.

Of the first stanza the abrupt beginning has been celebrated; but technical beauties can give praise only to the inventor. It is in the power of any man to rush abruptly upon his subject that has read the ballad of "Johnny Armstrong":

Is there ever a man in all Scotland. . . .

The initial resemblances, or alliterations, "ruin," "ruthless," "helm or hauberk,"[36] are below the grandeur of a poem that endeavors at sublimity.

In the second stanza the Bard is well described; but in the third we have the puerilities of obsolete mythology. When we are told that "Cadwallo hushed the stormy main," and that "Modred" made "huge Plinlimmon bow his cloud-topped head,"[37] attention recoils from the repetition of a tale that, even when it was first heard, was heard with scorn.

The "weaving" of the "winding sheet" he borrowed, as he owns, from the Northern bards,[38] but their texture, however, was very properly the work of female powers, as the act of spinning the thread of life in another mythology. Theft is always dangerous; Gray has made weavers of his slaughtered bards, by a fiction outrageous and incongruous. They are then called upon to "weave the warp, and weave the woof," perhaps with no great propriety; for it is by crossing the *woof* with the *warp* that men *weave* the *web* or piece; and the first line was dearly bought by the admission of its wretched correspondent, "Give ample room and verge enough." He has, however, no other line as bad.

The third stanza of the second ternary is commended, I think, beyond its merit. The personification is indistinct. Thirst and Hunger are not alike; and their features, to make the imagery perfect, should have been discriminated. We are told in the same stanza how "towers" are "fed." But I will no longer look for particular faults; yet let it be observed that the ode might have been concluded with an action of better example; but suicide is always to be had without expense of thought.

These odes are marked by glittering accumulations of ungraceful ornaments; they strike, rather than please; the images are magnified by affectation; the language is labored into harshness. The mind of the

36. Helmet; coat of mail.

37. Cadwallo and Modred are the names of legendary Welsh bards; Plinlimmon is a mountain in Wales.

38. Gray was much interested in Old Norse poetry, which he read in Latin translations.

writer seems to work with unnatural violence. "Double, double, toil and trouble."[39] He has a kind of strutting dignity, and is tall by walking on tiptoe. His art and his struggle are too visible, and there is too little appearance of ease and nature.

To say that he has no beauties would be unjust: a man like him, of great learning and great industry, could not but produce something valuable. When he pleases least, it can only be said that a good design was ill directed.

His translations of Northern and Welsh poetry deserve praise; the imagery is preserved, perhaps often improved; but the language is unlike the language of other poets.

In the character of his "Elegy" I rejoice to concur with the common reader; for by the common sense of readers uncorrupted with literary prejudices, after all the refinements of subtilty and the dogmatism of learning, must be finally decided all claim to poetical honors. The "Churchyard" abounds with images which find a mirror in every mind, and with sentiments to which every bosom returns an echo. The four stanzas beginning "Yet even these bones" are to me original: I have never seen the notions in any other place; yet he that reads them here persuades himself that he has always felt them. Had Gray written often thus, it had been vain to blame, and useless to praise him.

39. *Macbeth,* IV. i. 10.